THE BOARDMAN
TASKER OMNIBUS

THE BOARDMAN TASKER OMNIBUS

SAVAGE ARENA
by Joe Tasker

THE SHINING MOUNTAIN
by Peter Boardman

SACRED SUMMITS
by Peter Boardman

EVEREST THE CRUEL WAY
by Joe Tasker

**THE
MOUNTAINEERS**

ISBN 0–89886–436–4

First published in Great Britain by
Hodder and Stoughton
a division of Hodder Headline PLC
338 Euston Road, London NW1 3BH

Published in the United States of America by
The Mountaineers, 1011 SW. Klickitat Way, Seattle WA 98134
Published simultaneously in Canada by Douglas & McIntyre Ltd.,
1615 Venables St., Vancouver B.C. V5L 2H1

Printed and bound in Great Britain by
Mackays of Chatham PLC, Chatham, Kent

Illustrations

Photographic credits

JB = John Barry
PB = Peter Boardman
PN = Paul Nunn

DR = Dick Renshaw
DS = Doug Scott
JT = Joe Tasker

The publishers are grateful to John Barry, Paul Nunn, Dick Renshaw and Doug Scott for the loan of their photographs.

A GREAT PARTNERSHIP
A Foreword by Chris Bonington

It was 15th May 1982 at Advance Base on the north side of Everest. It's a bleak place. The tents were pitched on a moraine of dark shale, the debris of an expedition in its end stage scattered over the rocks and dirty snow. Pete and Joe fussed around with final preparations, packing their rucksacks and putting in a few last minute luxuries. Then suddenly they were ready, crampons on, rope tied, set to go. I think we were all trying to underplay the moment.

'See you in a few days.'

'We'll call you tonight at six.'

'Good luck.'

At last they were off, plodding up the little ice slope beyond the camp through flurries of wind-driven snow. Two days later, in the fading light of a cold dusk, Adrian Gordon and I were watching their progress high on the North-East Ridge through our telescope. Two tiny figures on the crest outlined against the golden sky of the late evening. They were moving painfully slowly, one at a time. Was it because of the difficulty of the ground or the extreme altitude, for they must have been at approximately 27,000 feet (8230 metres)?

Gradually they disappeared from sight behind the jagged tooth we had named the Second Pinnacle. They never appeared again, although Peter's body was discovered by members of a Russian/Japanese expedition in the spring of 1992 just beyond where we had last seen them. It was as if he had lain down in the snow, gone to sleep and never woken. We shall probably never know just what happened in those days around 17th May, but in that final push to complete the unclimbed section of the North-East Ridge of Everest, we lost two very special friends and a unique climbing partnership whose breadth of talent went far beyond mountaineering. Their ability as writers is amply demonstrated in this collection of their works.

My initial encounter with Peter was in 1975 when I was recruiting for the South-West Face of Everest expedition. I was impressed by his maturity at the age of twenty-three, yet this was combined with a real sense of fun and a touch of 'the little boy lost' manner, which he could use with devastating effect to get his own way. In addition, he was both physically and intellectually talented. He was a very strong natural climber and behind that diffident, easy-going manner had a personal drive and unwavering sense of purpose. He also had a romantic love of the mountains and the ability to express it in writing. He was the youngest member of the Everest team and went to the top with our Sherpa sirdar, Pertemba, making the second complete ascent of the previously unclimbed South-West Face.

As National Officer of the British Mountaineering Council Pete proved to be a patient diplomat and a good committee man. After Dougal Haston's death in an avalanche in Switzerland, he took over Dougal's International School of Mountaineering in Leysin. He went on to climb the sheer West Face of Changabang with Joe Tasker, which was the start of their climbing partnership. It was a remarkable achievement, in stark contrast to the huge expedition we had had on Everest. On Changabang there had just been Pete and Joe. They had planned to climb it alpine-style, bivouacking in hammocks on the face, but it had been too cold, too great a strain at altitude, and they had resorted to siege tactics. Yet even this demanded huge reserves of determination and endurance. The climb, in 1976, was probably technically the hardest that had been completed in the Himalaya at that time, and Pete describes their struggles in his first book, *The Shining Mountain*, which won the John Llewelyn Rhys Prize in 1979.

Pete packed a wealth of varied mountaineering into a very few years. In 1978 both Pete and Joe joined me on K2. We attempted the West Ridge but abandoned it comparatively low down after Nick Estcourt was killed in an avalanche. In early 1979 Pete reached the summit of the Carstensz Pyramid, the highest peak of New Guinea, with his future wife, Hilary, just before going to Kangchenjunga, the third highest mountain in the world, with Joe and Doug Scott. That same autumn he led a small and comparatively inexperienced team on a very bold ascent of the South Summit of Gauri Sankar.

The following year he returned to K2 with Joe, Doug and Dick Renshaw. They first attempted the West Ridge, the route that we had tried in 1978, but abandoned this a couple of hundred metres higher than our previous high point. Doug Scott returned home but the remaining three made two very determined assaults on the Abruzzi Spur, getting to within 600 metres of the summit before being avalanched off on their first effort, and beaten by bad weather on a subsequent foray. Two years later Pete and Joe, with Alan Rouse, joined me on Kongur, at the time the third highest unclimbed peak in the world. It proved a long drawn out, exacting expedition.

Joe Tasker was very different to Peter, both in appearance and personality. This perhaps contributed to the strength of their partnership. While Pete gave an impression of being easy going and relaxed, Joe was very much more intense, even abrasive. He came from a large Roman Catholic family on Tees-side and went to a seminary at the age of thirteen to train for the priesthood, but by the age of eighteen he had begun to have serious doubts about his vocation and went to Manchester University to study sociology. Inevitably, his period at the seminary left its mark. Joe had a built-in reserve which was difficult to penetrate but, at the same time, he had an analytical, questioning mind. He was not prepared to accept an easy answer and kept going at a point until he was satisfied that it had been answered in full.

In their climbing relationship there was a jokey yet very real competitive tension in which neither of them ever wanted to be the first to admit weakness or to suggest retreat. It was a trait that not only contributed to their drive but could also cause them to push themselves to the limit.

Joe served an impressive alpine apprenticeship in the early 'seventies when, with his climbing partner Dick Renshaw, they worked through some of the hardest climbs in the Alps, both in summer and winter. These included the first British ascent (one of the very few ever ascents) of the formidable and very remote East Face of the Grandes Jorasses. In addition they made the first British winter ascent of the North Wall of the Eiger. With Renshaw, he went on to climb in alpine-style, the South Ridge of Dunagiri in the Garhwal Himalaya. It was a bold ascent by any standards, outstandingly so for a first Himalayan expedition. Dick was badly frost-bitten and this led to Joe inviting Pete to join him on Changabang and the start of their climbing partnership.

On our K2 expedition in 1978, I had barely had the chance to get to know Joe well, but I remember bring exasperated by his constant questioning of decisions, particularly while we were organising the expedition. At the time I felt he was a real barrack-room lawyer but, on reflection, realised that he probably found my approach equally exasperating. We climbed together throughout the 1981 Kongur expedition and I came to know him much better, to find that under that tough outer shell there was a very warm heart. Prior to that, in the winter of 1980–1, he went to Everest with a strong British expedition to attempt the West Ridge in winter. He told the story in his first book, *Everest the Cruel Way*.

Our 1982 expedition to the North-East Ridge of Everest represented a huge challenge but our team was one of the happiest and most closely united of any trip I have been on. There were only six in the party and just four of us, Joe, Pete, Dick Renshaw and I, were planning to tackle the route. Charlie Clarke and Adrian Gordon were there in support and were to go no further than Advance Base. However, there was a sense of shared values, affection and respect, that grew stronger through adversity, as we came to realise just how vast was the undertaking our small team was committed to. It remained through those harsh anxious days of growing awareness of disaster, after Pete and Joe went out of sight behind the Second Pinnacle, to our final acceptance that there was no longer any hope.

Yet when Pete and Joe set out for that final push on 17th May I had every confidence that they would cross the Pinnacles and reach the upper part of the North Ridge of Everest, even if they were unable to continue to the top. Their deaths, quite apart from the deep feeling of bereavement at the loss of good friends, also gives that sense of frustration because they still had so much to offer in their development, both in mountaineering and creative terms. This compendium of their work is a tribute to that ability and a fascinating cross reference of shared experience, collected together under a single cover.

Chris Bonington
Caldbeck, September 1994

SAVAGE ARENA

Joe Tasker

Contents

MAPS

DIAGRAMS

The maps and diagrams were drawn from the author's
roughs by Neil Hyslop.

Publisher's Note

Joe Tasker delivered the typescript of this book on the eve of his departure with the British Everest Expedition 1982. The aim of the expedition was to tackle the unclimbed North-East Face by the East-North-East Ridge of Mount Everest. On 17 May Joe and his close friend and long-time climbing companion, Peter Boardman, were last seen at a height of over 27,000 feet, making a push for the summit.

In mourning the death of two such young and gifted men, we hope that the publication of *Savage Arena* will act as a fitting memorial to Joe Tasker – climber, writer and photographer.

ONE

Or Men Will Come For You

The mountains of the Alps formed a difficult school in which to learn but, for whatever unfathomable reason, I found it hard to avoid going back time and again. And although I tried to find partners who would allow themselves a little luxury and who were similarly bemused by their own involvement with climbing mountains as I was by mine, each time I found myself teaming up with one person more often than with any other, a person whose single-mindedness and asceticism were the opposite of my own nature.

It is easy to understand the attraction of rock-climbing, which is an exercise of physical skill, gymnastic ability and intense concentration to scale increasingly smoother walls of rock, larger overhangs and fiercesome cracks. The physical and mental effort is in itself rewarding, but the greater pleasure is attempting to climb a rock face, which seems hardly possible, and succeeding against all odds with those skills being tested to the limit.

At some point there is a transition from an interest in solving the problems of climbing a rock face, and the idyllic days in the sun which one always hopes for, to an interest in solving the problem of climbing bigger mountains, and the acceptance of a more gruelling way of life. The bigger mountains take more physical effort, more total commitment, and escape from them is not easy if the weather should take a turn for the worse.

The mountains of the Alps have a stark beauty, but this alone is not enough to elicit the extreme exertion which is needed to climb there. It is possible to go up in some places on a mountain railway or in a cable car which will open up vast panoramas for the price of a ticket, and if it were only the view that was sought, no one would ever climb. For a climber there is more, though it may be little understood. The mountains are a testing ground where he is confronted by challenges which not only demand all his skill in meeting them but make him face up to his own motivation, perseverance and resilience when danger, hardship and fatigue all conspire to turn him back from his chosen objective.

Given the chance, few can explain the compulsive fascination which draws them back year after year to this difficult school and makes them want to look further and higher, to push themselves all the harder.

I was no exception but found in a companion from university days, Dick Renshaw, someone who accepted without question the hardship entailed and who seemed motivated by a blind drive to climb and climb, without stopping to wonder about the purpose of it all.

Unlike me, he could switch his mind off to the tedium and effort which are inevitable in the mountains and, though opposites, we climbed together and learned together: how to negotiate crevasses, deep snow, loose rock and altitude; how to cope with hunger, fear and exhaustion. We climbed on small peaks carrying too much and taking too long; we graduated to climbing the Matterhorn and the Eiger, to classic routes from the past and to bold new routes. We began to prefer the shadowy north faces of the mountains, thinking we should climb these precipices of ice-coated rocks while we were young and save the more pleasant walls of sun-warmed granite and limestone for later years.

We accumulated a shared store of experiences; the midnight starts from alpine huts, hurrying to reach safety while the rocks were frozen into immobility; the many sleepless, anxious hours of waiting for and wanting to escape the moment of departure into the dark night, and those dreadful and unavoidable moments when we left the safe eyrie of the hut and climbed away, ill-tempered from nerves, picking a way on crampon points by dim torchlight into a dark no man's land.

It is necessary to start in the middle of the night or very early hours of the morning to reach a chosen climb because often the route to its start is menaced by other parts of the mountain from which ice or rocks may fall, or avalanches come sweeping down. In the night, when the temperature drops below zero, the blocks of ice and loose rocks are frozen into place, and snow slopes become firm, and passage through these hazards is safest, but there is a surreal quality about the midnight fumblings and preparations to leave at an hour when most people are sound asleep.

Again and again Dick and I were companions in the night across glaciers, over crevasses and under avalanche zones to reach the mountain of our choice. On one occasion we huddled together, afraid, under blocks of ice as pitiful shelter against an unexpected avalanche which we heard roaring down out of the darkness; on another we clung together for warmth as we stood all night on a wall of ice waiting for a storm to abate and dawn to arrive.

We saw many sunrises and saw mountains turning pink at sunset; we shared the satisfaction of overcoming difficulties, of succeeding on climbs we had hardly dared dream of, and in our minds we stopped looking for those climbs which we knew we could do and started looking for those which were more difficult.

Arguments and misunderstandings became fewer, we recognised the strains imposed by the harsh discipline of the mountains; there was less and less need for talk between us, our aims and evaluations were the same.

We felt at home in the mountains, but we still had much to learn. When three British climbers disappeared in a blizzard on Mont Blanc we, in the valley below, did not know what we should do to institute a search or where to turn to summon help. When the search had taken place and all possibility that the three climbers should still be alive was ruled out, we asked a mountain guide who had helped organise the search what we should do in any similar event in the future to get things under way more quickly. He had smiled, flattered by such a request from two whom he saw as apprentices looking to a master for advice, but his reply was unhelpful. 'Look for an old hand like myself,' he had said, 'one who has been around a long time, and ask him.' I took him to be saying that if you lived long enough in the mountains you accumulated the necessary experience to deal with most things, but that was not of much use for the present, and we were made aware that there is no tidy answer to accidents.

The mountains filled our dreams and permeated our subconsciousness. We were so conditioned by the sounds experienced during a climb that we found ourselves ducking for shelter if a plane droned overhead, thinking that it was the sound of an avalanche starting. On one climb, sleeping on a ledge under the shelter of a prow of rock, I believed that I could hear the purr of a paraffin stove heating some tea, but woke to find that the sound was the hum of stones falling from above.

There were odd coincidences which we could not explain, such as the time in 1972 when Dick dreamt one night, as we slept in a hut, that he was falling from the side of a mountain and that I was not holding the rope to which he was attached. He woke me with his shouts, telling me to catch him. Two days later he did fall – on the North Face of the Dent d'Hérens in Switzerland – eighty feet down a wall of ice and landed head first in a bank of snow above a 2,000-foot drop, and at the time, thinking him safe, I was not holding the rope.

There were faint superstitions too. We went in wintertime to Wengen, a mountain village near Interlaken. Wengen is close to the famous ski resort of Mürren, high up above the cliffs of the Lauterbrunnen valley. The valley is encircled by steep-sided mountains, the most impressive of which are the Eiger, Mönch and Jungfrau, forming a solid rampart with the ridges which link them together into the Lauterbrunnen wall. We were intending to climb the North Face of the Gspaltenhorn, one of the biggest walls in the Alps, hidden away up a secluded side valley. The old lady who ran the hostel where we stayed heard of our plans and warned us, 'You should come here to ski in winter, not to climb. It is too dangerous. If you go to climb the Gspaltenhorn you will not do it and come back, or men will come for you and you will be dead.' We did not do it.

Across the valley from Wengen the sombre wall of the North Face of the Eiger seemed to hold an air of brooding menace. We had climbed it in the summer of 1973, taking two nights and two days. We knew how hard, intricate and long the route was up the North Face and I could not conceive of climbing it in winter. We knew that only two or three parties had done so and that each time it had taken almost a week on that forbidding wall before they had reached the top. As we watched, we would see, even at the distance we were, avalanches sweeping constantly down the face, and I shuddered at the long nights, the cold and the storms which would have to be endured to climb it in winter. I looked with respect on that mountain and with awe for the parties who had dared to climb it in winter, but for myself felt that such an ascent was outside my ambitions. I had no wish to take on such difficulty and danger for the many days that an ascent would entail. Our knowledge of the mountain made us no less daunted; if anything we had more to be afraid of, since we knew how much harder the North Face would be in the deep snow and hard ice of winter.

We parted after that winter and went our separate ways, odd-jobbing, climbing and mixing with new friends. But we were as hand to glove and the next winter we met and, probing with words for a hint of the other's thoughts, we sounded each other out:

'Yes, a winter route in the Alps.'

'What were you thinking of?'

'I wondered about the Eiger.'

'Yes, I've come round to thinking of that too.'

'It will be hard. Need a lot of preparation.'

So we worked as temporary teachers to raise the money, having to impose a discipline, which I did not feel myself, onto the rebellious youth of Moss Side in Manchester. We accumulated the equipment needed and made some of the clothing such as climbing salopettes and specialised pieces of gear such as over-boots ourselves when we could not obtain the right item for our purpose in the shops. We made calculations on how many days it would take us, how much food and fuel we would need, how much weight we could carry. We told no one of our plans except Ellis Brigham, a climbing shop owner, who lent a fatherly ear to the young aspirants who came to him for advice. He made us a gift of one-piece suits of fleecy pile material as an under-garment into which we inserted zips, all the way round to the small of the back, so that we would be able to relieve ourselves without undressing.

Neither of us felt at home in the classroom and were relieved to leave in the February of 1975 for Switzerland, driving there in my old Ford Anglia.

Dick and I had been climbing together in the Alps for four years by this time, but journeying now towards the greatest test we had yet faced I knew him little more than at the start. He still had the same quiet, relentless dedication to climbing that he had when I first met him. When the rest of us were lying in our sleeping bags on a summer's morning in the Lake District, Dick would be outside the tent cooking breakfast, making more tea and waiting, eager to be off climbing, without a word of complaint, for us to stir ourselves. I never knew what drove him; he seemed unaffected by discomfort, undaunted by the folly of what we were doing. When we stood, clinging to each other all night through snow-storm and avalanche on the north face of the Dent Blanche, passing the long, chill night with idle chatter, all he could think to say was, 'What climb do you fancy doing next?'

I felt he looked askance at my self-indulgence if I bought a glass of beer, as if I was recklessly squandering valuable resources, but never a word passed.

In smoking, as in all things, he was completely controlled. He would take along one cigarette for each bivouac, so friends could estimate how long we thought a climb might take us by the number of cigarettes Dick took. Three cigarettes meant a serious route.

Physically, Dick was the opposite to me, 'Little Richard' we used to call him, but he was broad in the chest. He looked more suited to weight-lifting or body-building than climbing.

It always puzzled me whether he did not feel cold and discomfort as much as me or whether he just put up with it more stoically. Tall and thin as I was, I always felt the cold and could not sleep if I was not comfortable. I passed many nights shuffling myself about on uneven ledges trying to find the optimum position while Dick snored gently, sleeping where he had first settled down. I suspected that, as with everything else, he had long since disciplined himself not to pay attention to physical discomfort and had he done so would have regarded it as a weakness, a flaw in the overall plan he had for himself. It was as if he was training his body for something, toning it into shape, with no place in the design for feelings such as comfort. There was something of a religious asceticism in him. I could recognise it but I had chosen a different path.

Dick was a creature of nature, he had seen no need as yet to learn to drive. I even felt self-conscious that I actually possessed a car.

The Eiger, or more accurately, its North Face had permeated my first years of climbing. In the seminary where I spent seven years training to be a Catholic priest, two mealtimes of the day were made more formal by the reading out of a book. Originally the books read out were probably intended to be of a spiritually edifying nature but by the time I was there the criteria seemed to be simply that the book should be 'good'. Any books were, of course, carefully vetted before being read out.

In 1965 I was in the fourth year when a book called *The Climb up to Hell* by Jack Olsen was chosen for the supper-time reading. The book described how the North Face of the Eiger, a mountain which I had hardly heard of, was the most difficult and dangerous of all the mountain faces in the Alps. The mountain, in the Bernese Oberland of Switzerland, is part of the northern bulwark of the Alps and is thus particularly subject to violent changes in weather. Air movement and air pressures are sharply altered when the air comes up against this first obstacle of the main Alpine mass. Sudden and prolonged storms can occur, and the concave wall of the Eiger can seem to be holding its own furious storm when the meadows below are clear. The wall is so big and the route up it so intricate, long and difficult that several tragic accidents took place as climbers attempted to be the first to solve the problems of climbing that face. So many accidents occurred that the Swiss government at one stage banned all attempts on the North Face; but still men came. In 1938 an Austro/German party of four succeeded in being the first to reach the top via the North Face, but the accidents did not lessen and the Eiger became notorious for the dramas enacted in full view, when the clouds permitted, of the binoculars and telescopes on the verandah of the hotel at Kleine Scheidegg, only an hour from the foot of the wall and reachable by rock and pinion railway from Grindelwald or Lauterbrunnen.

The Climb up to Hell recounted the struggles and tragedies of the attempts to climb the Eiger's North Face, culminating in the disappearance in 1957 of two German climbers and the death of an Italian, stranded high on the face. He died within shouting distance of the rescue party who were trying to reach him, when the snow-storm had closed in on him for the last time. The book is full with the drama of the attempts on the mountain and for the only time I ever knew the whole dining hall of three hundred people subsided into absolute quiet. Not a knife rattled, not a cup clattered as another tragedy was described, that of a party of four in 1937, making one of the earliest attempts on the face. Toni Kurz, sole survivor of the four young Germans, was trying to reach the guides who had come to rescue him. One of his arms was frozen and he was very weak, but after two days of rescue efforts he was at last sliding down a rope to the waiting guides. Then a knot in the rope jammed in the karabiner attaching the rope to his waist and he had no strength left to free himself. Only an arm's length away from the waiting rescuers he keeled over and died. None of us students understood the terminology of climbing, none of us knew what abseiling was, nor what karabiners were, but every one of us was enthralled by the account of this moving tragedy.

During the days when that book was being read out, days when we looked forward as never before to supper time for the next rivetting chapter, I was unexpectedly asked by one of the teaching priests in the college if I would like to try a bit of climbing myself. Although I had never remotely considered the possibility of climbing before I was asked, it suddenly seemed the most enthralling prospect. Rather than being deterred by the dangers as described in *The Climb up to Hell*, the book provided an inspiration for my own first steps and those of another friend on the small sandstone walls of the quarry from which the college had been built. The quarry, though only twenty feet high with two walls only thirty feet across, was the focal point of my days. My every thought was taken up by the sport, though for months at a time our activities were confined to that tiny quarry. It was as if a wondrous new world had been opened up to me. I read avidly every book on the subject that I could get hold of. I borrowed Heinrich Harrer's book, *The White Spider*, which documented all the attempts and successes to date on the Eiger's North Face and devoured it by torchlight at night. I read it at every spare moment and for long after 'lights out', until my eyes grew weary and the words seemed to dance on the page.

Shortly after I first started climbing, early in 1966, the siege was on to make the first winter ascent of a direct line on the North Face. In order to climb as directly as possible to the summit, avoiding the zig-zags entailed by following natural fault lines as on the 1938 route, the climbers would leave themselves exposed to the rockfall in many sections. Two teams had had the same idea of attempting such a line in winter when, though conditions would be more rigorous, the rocks would be frozen in place day and night.

The siege lasted a month. They used the tactics developed on Himalayan expeditions of climbing a certain distance, fixing rope on that section, then descending to a well-established camp at the bottom of the face or a snow hole on the face itself. Once most of the wall had the rope fixed up it they would make a bid to reach the summit.

As a young climber I swallowed greedily the regular news reports and television bulletins. I was awestruck by the bleak lives of the climbers in their snow holes or battling upwards in blizzards. The death in an accident on the wall of John Harlin, the driving force behind one of the teams, came as a great shock. He was an American who had settled in Switzerland, and though at first his team were in competition with the team of Germans whom he found to have the same designs, he died in trying to assist them. Both teams were pinned down on the mountain by storms and he was carrying up to the Germans some much-needed supplies when a damaged rope snapped and he fell to his death.

In 1966 I had no thoughts of going to the Eiger, even though I called myself a climber, any more than when flying in an aeroplane I think of going to the moon. I considered such climbers to be of a different order of people and though I was fascinated by every aspect of the sport I was content to climb rock and my aspirations only stretched as far as acquiring sufficient skill to do some winter climbing in Scotland.

TWO

It is Forbidden
to Walk on the Track

THE EIGER

I

Ten years later I was on my way to climb the Eiger a second time. Our ascent in summer had been a traditional one. Though we had known more about that mountain by reputation and accounts than any other, we still had to go and climb it, and having climbed it we were coming back because it was the longest and most complex route we could think of and, if we dared admit it to ourselves, the most difficult. We wanted something substantial, something we could get our teeth into. We did not want to overcome a mountain with ease, we needed to struggle, needed to be at the edge of what was possible for us, needed an outcome that was uncertain. Sometimes I wondered if the climbing had become an addiction, if the pleasure of this drug had gone and only the compulsion to take it in ever stronger doses remained.

The brakes on the Anglia were terrible. We called in to see André in Switzerland, an engineering contractor for whom Dick and I had both worked instead of returning to Britain after the summer's climbing in 1973. His foreman gave us a hand to mend the brakes and a tongue-lashing for driving such a suicidal machine. We did not have to tell them our plans, the name of the group of mountains was enough – the Bernese Oberland. Their concern was matched by their pride. I borrowed a crash helmet from Danielle, André's cousin; my own had somehow been left behind.

In the Lauterbrunnen valley we found lodgings in the Naturfreundhaus, a hotel run by a kindly Frau Gertsch. She was surprised and pleased to find she had climbers staying rather than the periodic groups of skiers. We had the place to ourselves – long communal platforms of foam mattresses to stretch out on for beds, but none of the summer crowds to share them with.

When we returned from a five-day outing making an ascent of the North Face of the Breithorn, Frau Gertsch took us as sons. She assigned the second dining-room completely to us for sorting out and drying our gear.

The North Face of the Breithorn was a preparatory climb for us, some-thing on which we could try ourselves out and get the feel of climbing in winter. There was deep snow all the way to the foot of the mountain and it took eight hours of agonising toil before the climbing started. Then for three days we steadily made our way up gullies of snow, turning to ice, and of loose rock held in place by ice. As a climb it was interesting, well within our capabilities. We did not want an epic, did not want to stretch ourselves so much that we would lose the drive for our real purpose. Winter climbing is solitary; we had the mountains to ourselves. A lone plane one day was the only sign of life we saw the whole time we were away in that frozen wilderness.

We had a few days' rest after that, rest from climbing, not rest from activity. Dick went off on a nature trek on cross-country skis, shunning the contrived sport of skiing on a piste with cable cars, chair lifts and tows. He had worked in the resort of Montana one winter as a dish-washer. During the afternoon break he would hoist his skis onto his shoulder and walk up the piste rather than indulge in taking the *téléphérique*. In this way he became very fit but did not improve his skiing much as it took him all his time to walk up for a single run down. I did not find Dick much company. I took the train up to Kleine Scheidegg, the station at the foot of the Eiger, and skied below the dark wall of limestone, ice and snow, trying to absorb

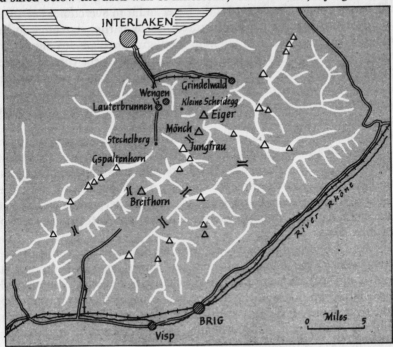

1. The Eiger and surrounding area.

some impression from it, trying to attune myself to it, trying to penetrate its inscrutable aspect. At sunset I slid away, down to the cosy warmth of the Naturfreundhaus. It was time for us to make ready and go.

Twenty rock pitons, thirty-two aluminium karabiners, eleven ice pitons, ice axes, ice hammers, crash helmets, we laid all the gear and food and clothing out on the tables in the dining-room. There was a lot of weight, but it was a huge wall and if we had to retreat we would need many pitons to drive into rock or ice to safeguard our descent. There was much snow low down, I had noticed, but the ice fields in the middle of the face seemed to be nothing but dark, hard ice. We expected our progress to be slow and we were consequently taking food for a week.

On 14 February, early in the morning, we joined the skiers who were boarding the train to Scheidegg to make best use of the morning snow. There were curious glances at our untidy appearance amidst the sleekly clad throng. There were hostile glances at the ice axes protruding from our bulging rucksacks; we did not fit into the normal pattern.

It was strange to think that the railway track continued up inside the mountain we were intending to climb. In order to reach the Jungfraujoch, a vantage point on a ridge between two valleys, a tunnel has been carved through two mountains. The ventilation holes from the tunnel open onto the lower part of the North Face of the Eiger and have sometimes been used to avoid descending the last few hundred feet by parties retreating in bad weather. I had not been able to locate through binoculars any sign of the entrance to these air shafts, and assumed that they were concealed deep beneath the snow. The idea of a train trundling up inside the mountains we would be living on for days was bizarre but it did not detract from the seriousness of the mountain, since the air vents are located low down where there are few difficulties.

When the train disgorged its load, the skiers busied themselves clipping on skis and Dick and I trudged off away from the crowds, into the shadow cast by the wall. There were hundreds of people around us but I felt quite alone. Our tracks led away from the ski pistes in a rising contour until, after an hour of wading through deep snow, we reached steepening ice, the start of the climbing. The crevasses along the foot of the face were covered by the winter snows.

Always I feel nagging doubts and uncertainties before a climb, always I wonder what I am doing launching out, away from more immediate pleasures and certain comforts. Now, faced with the long, unpredictable voyage ahead, up this wall, the feeling was stronger than ever, reinforced by the stray shouts of the tiny skiers in the distance. Dick, as ever, seemed unaffected by any such self-questioning and I wondered to what extent I rode on the wave of this determination.

The sky was clear, the air chill, but there was no wind. I felt I was lingering over the ritual of strapping crampons to boots, of uncoiling ropes and tying on, one of us to each end. We needed the points of the crampons to dig in to the steep ice in front of us, but there was much snow too. We sandwiched a layer of polythene between the crampon framework and the sole of each boot so that the snow would not stick, forming a heavy, unstable ball beneath each foot. Then Dick was off, no reasons for delay left, sack on his back, karabiners and pitons jangling from his seat harness, ice axe and hammer driven alternately into smooth ice and himself moving with increasing certainty upwards on the front points of his crampons.

In summer the lower part of the North Face is not difficult, the first 1,500 feet can be climbed in a few hours, up terraces littered with loose rocks, avoiding steep walls by taking a zig-zag course along ledges. Now we were confronted by a largely featureless area of snow, broken only by infrequent outcrops of rock. Had the snow been firm, had it supported our weight, it would have made our task much easier, but we sank into it, knee deep, thigh deep, and beneath there was sometimes steep rock, sometimes ice. We could not see or feel the ledges up which we had zig-zagged in summer, it was as if we were runners on a race track we knew but with a ball and chain on each foot.

Our ropes were 150 feet long. We had two, and each of us attached one end of both ropes with a karabiner to the harness round our waists. Like this, whichever of us was leading a pitch could climb for the full length of the ropes, clipping them one at a time, with karabiners, onto pitons or nylon loops on rock spikes, to safeguard movement upwards. With two lengths of rope there is more safety, but using the two alternately also prevents the friction of the ropes, as they run through karabiners, placed unavoidably in a zig-zag manner, from becoming too great. In retreat, too, having two ropes of 150 feet enables long sections to be descended with ease, provided a sound anchor point is found. A rope longer than 150 feet becomes unmanageable, or the friction through the snap-links usually becomes too great after a certain distance.

By mid-afternoon, taking it in turns, we had run out the rope only nine times. Not much more than 1,000 feet, given that some of the rope was taken up with the knots tying the rope to our waists and to the pitons or other anchor points used to fasten one of us to the side of the mountain whilst the other was leading. There is 10,000 feet of climbing on this wall – 6,000 feet – more than a mile – in height. The route follows the lines of weakness, avoiding overhanging sections where possible, thus almost doubling the distance to be covered. Nearly two miles upwards on hands and knees. In one day we had barely done one-tenth, and the major difficulties were still to come. It was dark by 4.30 p.m. so we had to have chosen our bivouac site for the night before then. There were no natural ledges, all was concealed by the blanket of snow. Dick traversed to the left, towards a feature called the Shattered Pillar, but there was nowhere there to rest. We set to digging out a ledge in the snow and ice beneath a small wall of rock. It felt safer to have a solid wall beside us and some pitons driven into the rock to secure ourselves to during the night.

Night overcame us before we were settled down, facing each other, warm in sleeping bags and down jackets, insulated from the cold ledge of snow by a light foam mat each. We had a plastic bag containing the food for each day, six of these bags in all, and a litre of petrol for the stove. We were disappointed at ourselves and at the mountain, alarmed at all that lay ahead, but for the moment we had the consolation of food and sleep. Little whispers of icy wind troubled my face as I settled down, so I pulled the sleeping bag tight over my head, leaving only a small hole through which to breathe.

My sleep was disturbed by the wind penetrating even that small hole and blowing snow onto my face. I turned and pulled the hood closer round my face but still the snow stung me. I thought, through the mental inertia of only half-wakefulness, that the wind must have grown very strong. I tried to regain sleep, having exerted myself to the minimum to escape the plaguing winds. I could not bear the thought of making a radical effort to solve the problem, such as getting into our bivouac tent. But Dick woke me with his shout: 'Joe, it's snowing, let's put the tent up.'

I roused myself, fought clear of the constrictions of the hoods of the sleeping bag and by torchlight saw the thickly falling, swirling flakes coating everything on the ledge. We had intended to use the bivouac tent as little as possible because it was not much more than a nylon envelope and the condensation from breathing and cooking would cause our sleeping bags and down jackets to get damp and, in a couple of nights, useless. On a still, clear night we could sleep outside, with our sleeping bags tucked into our rucksacks as protection against the windblown snow, but we needed the tent in snowfall such as this. It was of course Dick, unhampered by any sense of lethargy or inertia, who had made the move which was most sensible, chill as it was at first to leave the warmth of the sleeping bag.

We gathered up food, stove and gear before they should disappear in the snow and struggled one by one into the tent, shuffling about to find a tolerable position. The tent was designed for two people lying side by side, but our ledge was long and narrow. We strained against opposite ends, both of us trying to lie full length without one of us sliding off the edge of the ledge. There were no poles in this tent. We attached the two corners at the top to the pitons driven into the rock and the loose fabric of the tent sagged down onto us with the weight of the falling snow. We each had a rope tied to our waists and fastened to the pitons too, just in case a heavy slide of snow from above should knock us off the ledge. A fitful sleep returned.

I think I was glad next morning when it was still snowing and the mountain was covered in cloud. I did not feel rested at all after the disturbed night and though it would not be good in the long run to consume a day's rations if we should run short of food higher up, I did welcome the prospect of a day's rest, waiting for the weather to improve. It was too wild outside the tent to contemplate moving and we passed the day, pressed close against each other, with little conversation, dozing and nibbling at morsels of food.

It was airless inside the tent. We had to choose between ventilation and the chill wind streaming in with flurries of snow, or stale air and near suffocation, but we were snug.

The grey day of silent mist and hissing snow-slides passed into night. Tiny avalanches of snow had slid between the tent and the wall so that the tent fabric inside bulged between Dick and me. It only happened at dark so we did not want to move. We settled down to sleep with even less space than the night before, and growing doubts about the point of staying on the mountain in this spell of bad weather.

I woke to the sound of rushing snow, a senseless, brutal pounding down onto the tent, onto my head, between the tent and the wall, prising the tent irresistibly from the mountain. Dick was awake too and we struggled together in darkness, breathless, pressing as hard as we could against the side of the tent nearest the wall, trying to halt the slow advance away from it, trying to make the falling snow slide over us before the tent was wrenched from the pitons holding it in place and we should tumble down the mountain.

It only lasted seconds, not a word had passed between us; when the snow stopped pouring down we were encased in snow, but able to work ourselves free. Snow had entered the tent and our cosy cocoon was contaminated by an alien whiteness which penetrated every gap in clothing and sleeping bags. But we were alive.

Dick wormed his way outside to dig clear the snow from between the tent and rock before the taut nylon should tear. I found my head torch but before I could join him another remorseless battering started up. The light from my head torch danced to the rhythm of the falling snow as I was struck again and again. This time I could see by the shaking light the dark blue tent shrinking before my helpless eyes as I was crushed and I thought of Dick outside, catching the full force of the avalanche and wondered if he was gone. It stopped. I was held fast as if in concrete. I started to move.

'Joe, are you all right?' It was Dick still there. 'I couldn't see the tent at all when that stopped – I thought you were a goner.'

'I thought the same about you.'

We shifted enough snow for us to breathe and move. 'What can we do?' It was snowing steadily, thick heavy flakes, more avalanches were certain to come. We had survived two small ones but we could not hope to last the night in this spot.

'The rock bulges out just over here. If we can dig a hollow out beneath it we should at least be out of the way if any more do come.'

We dug by the light of our torches into the bank of snow with a little protective roof of rock jutting out above us. It was not at all comfortable or convenient but we thought that if it would help us survive the next few hours until dawn it would suffice.

Some of our gear we could not find in the snow which covered the ledge we had vacated, but most things we recovered and packed crudely into our sacks. We thrust the sacks into the snow in the protected hollow and crouched on top of them. The tent we draped over ourselves and sat for the rest of the night, weary, stamping our feet to keep the blood flowing in them, shivering and waiting. More avalanches slid past. They came frequently so they had not accumulated the devastating force which some avalanches possess. We were just protected by the roof above us. We contrived to make a warm drink. I held the stove on my knee and Dick held the pan on the stove, melting some of the snow gathered from round our feet.

Cold cramps shook my body but the heat from the stove helped in spite of the clammy condensation.

'How long do you think it will take us to get down?' I asked Dick.

'Down? What if the weather clears up?'

We were thoroughly damp and weary. Sometimes I used to think we were on the same wavelength and at other times I realised we were poles apart.

'We've got to go down, we're soaking, we've lost half the food and we've hardly started the climb.'

'I suppose you're right.'

The admission was wrung from him with such reluctance that I felt as if I was chickening out, but I could not see how we could possibly continue without dying of exposure.

It was still snowing at daybreak and even Dick could not offer a good case for staying on the mountain longer.

'We'll have a hard enough time getting down as it is,' I said, to reaffirm and justify my point of view.

Dick went first down the two ropes held in the snap-link attached to a piton. He disappeared, snow coating his dark clothes, and camouflaging him in the mist. He was only 150 feet away but I could see nothing, and I waited for his shouts to tell me he had hammered in another piton, he was attached and it was safe for me to slide down the ropes and join him. As I arrived, Dick was already busy preparing the next abseil. The doubled rope passed through the karabiner above, I pulled one end of the rope, the other end disappeared up the slope to pass through the karabiner and back down to us. At each anchor point we had to abandon the piton and karabiner, but this was the most rapid way to descend. We did not want to waste time in case we were caught in the open by another avalanche.

Dick set off again. This time the piton was only half embedded in a crack. It was a thin blade of a piton, only 3 inches long. The $1\frac{1}{2}$ inches protruding from the crack flexed and bent as Dick's weight came on it. I took his weight on the rope in my hands, relieving the strain on the piton as he carefully edged downwards. It was a long time before he shouted up to me to come and I nervously put my weight on the rope, watching the piton bend before my eyes, trusting that Dick had found a really good anchor point this time and that he would have tied the other ends of the ropes to it. If the piton above me did come out I thought I might have some chance if at least the bottom ends of the rope were securely attached.

When I came alongside him I saw nothing.

'Where's the anchor?'

He looked sheepish. 'I couldn't find anywhere, it's hopeless with all this snow.' Anger was pointless since I had arrived safely.

Nine times we had to rig up the ropes and abseil down. Nine times my heart was in my mouth until the last leap, clear of the vertical step of ice at the bottom of the wall, and we hurried, as best we could, away from any avalanche zone, before stopping to catch our breaths and pack away harness and ropes.

It was a little warmer down out of the wind and I felt overdressed. We made for the black line of the railway track cutting through the white hillside. We were floundering thigh deep, sometimes waist deep in the snow, and the railway line, kept open for the trains bringing the skiers, was the only clear track. We could relax mentally, there was no danger, just tedium and effort as we sank helplessly into the snow at every step.

At last we staggered clear, out of the wilds, back to civilisation and communication with the real world.

We walked tiredly up the track towards a small hut near a siding. A round, florid rail guard appeared from the hut. He spoke in German.

'Where have you come from? The Wall?'

'Yes.'

'How many days?'

'Two or three.'

He looked wonderingly at us.

'It is forbidden to walk on the track.'

'Where do you want us to walk?'

He gestured at the snow we had just left.

'Which is the nearest station, Alpiglen or Scheidegg?'

'It is forbidden to walk on the railway.'

We set off downhill, along the line, away from him. We reached the station at Alpiglen and climbed onto the platform. The station master came rushing out.

'Can we buy tickets for Lauterbrunnen please?'

'It is forbidden to walk on the railway line.'

He would not sell us tickets. We boarded the train when it came and paid a fine for not having tickets when we got on.

II

Frau Gertsch fussed over us, beaming her pride. Mountaineering is in the blood of the Swiss. There was a meter on the shower, half a franc for ten minutes. I put six coins in and stood letting the hot jets of water stroke away the discomforts, the memories, the anxieties of the last few days. The huge sleeping platforms were wonderful to stretch out on full length and sleep on in complete security.

We skied and waited. I could not relax in this period. It was as if a very difficult exam was hanging over us, one whose starting date we did not know. I did not look forward with excitement to getting back on the mountain, the experience would be too cold, too painful to be enjoyed, but neither could I walk away from the objective we had set ourselves. We did not have to do it. All those skiers were quite happy to ski below the mountain, they did not feel the need to go up and spend days and days trying to climb it. I could not answer to myself why I should want to.

After a day's rest I went up to ski again at Scheidegg and was surprised to see that much of the snow had come off the face. Instead of the white wall we had last seen, the rock stood out bare and the dark expanses of the ice fields were just ice. It shook me a little. We had expected to wait a week for the snow to clear or consolidate so that there was less risk of avalanche, but the cold of winter caused the snow to stay light and mobile instead of fusing together as in the warmer temperatures of summer. It had all slid off immediately or been blown off by the winds. Now we would have to face up to going back on the mountain immediately.

When I got back I persuaded Dick that we should postpone departure for a day. The forecast was not too certain but inwardly I was not prepared for so sudden a return. I needed time to adjust to it, time to be quiet, to savour normal life, without the distraction of conversation and activity before committing myself to the wild forces of the mountain.

We journeyed up again on the train on 25 February, managing to find a seat this time so I was able to stare dumbly out at the passing woods, heavy with snow, the chalets sending up blue tendrils of smoke from roofs which almost merged with the snowy hillside. It was beautiful but it meant nothing. I was a prisoner, stunned by a sentence just received, on my way back to serve out my time, and my senses only observed, they did not appreciate.

We needed some more pitons to replace the ones lost on our retreat. The little sports shop at Scheidegg sells only ski gear in winter and the shop-keeper had to search in his storeroom for pitons. He had given me a lift two years before when I was hitchhiking to the Eiger for the first time. We told him our intentions. It felt a little better that someone knew. We did not expect a rescue if we were in difficulty, but last time it had felt very lonely on that mountain, with all this life going on down below and ourselves completely anonymous, not in anyone's mind high up on that awful wall.

'Good luck. Come in for a drink when you get back.'

'Thanks, we'll need it,' and we plodded once more through the snow towards the bottom of the wall where the ice steepened.

We climbed further than on our first attempt, sixteen rope-lengths, nearly 2,000 feet, before we started looking for some place to spend the night. We were both more optimistic. Our knowledge of the mountain helped us to avoid the false lines we had tried the first time.

We were at the top of a bank of snow, at the foot of a vertical step of rock over 100 feet high. There did not seem to be any possibilities of a safe place to stop where we were and Dick started testing the rock wall inquisitively, feeling for hand-holds and foot-holds, looking for a line up it in case we should need to climb it before nightfall to see if there was a better chance of a place above in which to spend the night. He was making exploratory moves when his feet gave way beneath him and his legs disappeared from sight. He pulled himself out of the soft snow, glanced into the hole he had left and looked at me, grinning with pleasure: 'Guess what I've found – a cave.'

To us it had looked as if the wall of rock rose straight out of the snow, but the bottom of the wall was undercut and the bank of snow had concealed a hollow beneath the overhang at the foot of the wall. We crawled in through the hole, hollowed out the cave further and made ourselves at home. When we had finished we had a level floor, large enough for us both to lie down on comfortably, there was a place for the stove, a crack in the roof to drive pitons into from which we hung our gear – it was palatial. We were safe from any avalanche and secure against the worst storm. Had we found this on the first attempt we might have been able to stay on the mountain.

We could have been anywhere. Warm in our sleeping bags, there was none of the discomfort of a big mountain. So cosy were we that we overslept. Dick, relying on an innate sense of the time, was equally fooled by the peacefulness of our eyrie. Outside the day was clear.

The wall above was not easy. Both of us searched along the bottom for a point of departure upwards. I tried one line, climbed up fifteen feet and then there were no holds for hands nor cracks for pitons. A coating of snow concealed much of the rock and baffled further progress. I retreated, hands numb from scraping holds clear of snow.

Dick tried to the left. A few feet up he drove a piton into a crack. An hour later he was not much further. He had fingerless gloves on beneath his mitts. On this sort of climbing we needed our fingers clear, but he could only move for a few minutes without stopping to blow warm breath onto his senseless fingers. He edged slowly leftwards; my feet froze; two hours had passed; eight thousand more feet to climb; the third hour and my body was screaming with the cold. I could not let my tongue say anything; at times I thought Dick was going to come back and ask me to try, but I would have been as slow; the whole situation was impossible, it was midday and we had not climbed even a hundred feet. The tempo of Dick's movement quickened; he was still slow and deliberate, each step was controlled, he let the displaced snow or ice stop falling from the holds each time he settled his crampon points onto a lip of rock. It is better climbing rock without crampons, but there is no better way if the rock is iced over. The deliberate movements were more constant by the end of the third hour and then he shouted that the worst was over. There was still a lot of rope left; he could have gone further but I knew he would be exhausted. As Dick hammered in pitons and secured himself I tried to shake some life back into my stiff limbs. At no time did the futility of our efforts seem as great as when battling with this wall so low down on the whole climb.

I had the security of the rope above me and I needed it. I could hardly feel anything in my fingers, and lacked the confidence to move when I could not be sure of my strength to hold on. It was typical of Dick's persistence, his utter refusal to admit to discomfort, to give in to what he saw as weakness, that he should have pressed on for three hours, painstakingly warming his fingers before every move. It had been too difficult for him to climb wearing his sack. In the middle of the pitch he had taken it off, hung it on a peg and now I untied one of the ropes from my waist, tied the sack to it and while I warmed my fingers, Dick pulled in the rope. With help from Dick pulling gently on the other rope it took me half an hour to reach him.

By evening we had gained the bottom of the Difficult Crack. This pitch, eighty feet in length, is a key link in the route up the lower part of the climb. It is not exceedingly difficult, but in summer it was wet and unpleasant. This time we found it dry, with little ice in it, but by the time we were ready to start up, the night had come.

There was no place to spend the night below the crack; from summer we remembered that above there were some broad ledges. We needed to reach those so I dumped my sack and led off by torchlight. The crack is in the back of a corner; I groped over the walls of the corner for any little knob of rock, or flake on which to pull myself up. I hammered in a piton and felt more reassured. Dick, anxious in the dark below, called up from time to time to ask how it was going. I was slow, but I was progressing.

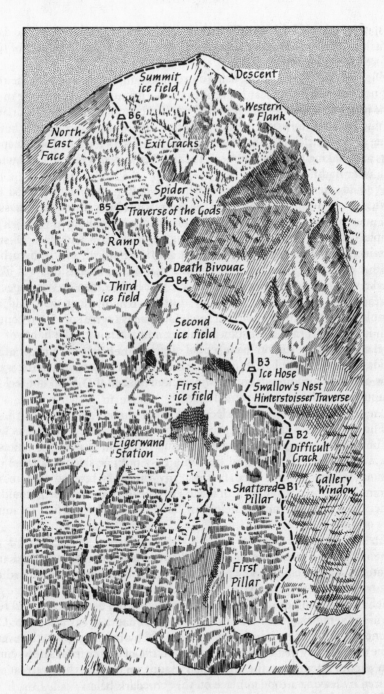

1. The line of our ascent on the North Face of the Eiger.

In spite of myself I felt a thrill at the performance of climbing in the dark. At half height the difficulties eased and I knew it was only a matter of time before I would be able to relax.

Dick climbed up the rope, using a prusik clamp, which slides up the rope but not down, I could hear his scufflings, his grunting and groaning in the dark and the beam of his torch sometimes flicked upwards. When he arrived we dug into the snow and ice, cutting out a platform for three hours before being able to settle down. It was nine o'clock before we were in our sleeping bags and making the evening meal. We thanked our luck that it was another still, clear night.

We had climbed seven rope-lengths this day, only a few hundred feet vertically. Above us the dark bulk of the rest of the wall towered massive and uncompromising. I wondered at our chances. I wondered what sort of people we would be at the end of this; if after days and days of such sustained, punishing effort we would be a little deranged, a little disturbed. Neither of us had gone through anything that was as long as this was likely to take whether we succeeded or not. We just had to keep on, we expected to reach the ice-fields the next day, but for the moment we could not complain, we were warm, we had food. Our fingers were sore from contact with icy rock, from the constant numbing and warming. The lights of the hotel at Scheidegg station made a pool of green far below. I thought of the holiday-makers in the bar, or just finishing their evening meals, in the warm glow of Swiss accommodation in winter, and wished that I did not feel the compulsion to do what we were doing.

I stared into the night until sleep took me.

The third day. A quarter of the way up the wall. Some of the links with life below had snapped; no longer were my thoughts escaping to fantasies of a warm shower, or a pint of beer in a cosy pub, or sleep in a large bed without wearing boots. The furthest my thoughts strayed was to the evening's halt on a ledge, in a bivouac I always promised myself would be better than the last, and the height of luxury would be the first steaming mug of soup.

An old rope was in place on the 120-foot stretch of rock called the Hinterstoisser Traverse after the brilliant young climber who had first found the way across this key pitch but who had not been able to lead the way back during the enforced retreat of his team. The ensuing tragedy in which they had all perished was that described in the book I had heard read out in the seminary which had first brought the Eiger to my attention. One by one the climbers had died, leaving Toni Kurz alone to explain the events to the rescue party before he too died only a few feet away from safety. Since then parties attempting the climb had made certain that their retreat was assured by leaving a rope in place on that crucial section.

Dick led off, climbing horizontally leftwards. The old rope was frayed, its central core was exposed in places due to the erosion of the winds. Huge icicles and, in parts, sheets of ice hung from it. I could see Dick trying to climb relying solely on the rock, but the rope, rotten as it was, hung temptingly close. As the climbing became harder and harder, his hands more and more numb, he nervously tested his weight on the rope. I had him safeguarded on our own ropes and would hold him if he fell but he was a hundred feet away from me in a horizontal line and he would fall in a long bruising arc.

'Watch me here, Joe.'

I watched; he meant me to take extra care that I had the ropes held tight, and then he had done it. He crossed the last twenty feet in a frantic scuttle, looking as if he was willing himself to float.

We bypassed the Swallow's Nest, a niche, secure from all stonefall, on the edge of the first ice field. Now it was blanked out with snow, but we did not want to stop there. That had been our first bivouac when we had climbed the face in summer; this time we had taken two and a half days to reach it.

The first ice field was silent, though in summer as we slept in the Swallow's Nest stones had droned past most of the night. Without the apprehension of being smashed by rocks falling from above, we tiptoed up the right-hand edge of the ice-field to the steepening runnel of ice snaking its way up through rock.

It was too long and steep to climb carrying my rucksack; I left it with Dick. As I wound myself up to face the difficulties of climbing the column of pure ice, testing the hold of my axe in the ice, testing the purchase of the front points of my crampons and massaging the stiffness out of my calf muscles, an alien drone broke the stillness. A distant speck, small as a fly, came towards us growing larger and larger – a helicopter. It hovered a few hundred feet away from us. We could see the occupants, cameras or binoculars masking their faces, and I could not move. From stage fright at realising I was a performer in a gigantic vertical arena my feelings turned to resentment that our very private world should become the focus for the curiosity and pastime of others. I could not concentrate until it was gone, could not rid myself of the thought that those visitors, anonymous and safe in their plastic bubble, would have had the most perfect outing if they could only have seen one of us fall.

Somehow I regained the concentration that had been dented after three days by that bizarre visitation and worked my way up the wall of ice. We used to lead out four rope-lengths each, between four and six hundred feet of climbing. In this way the mental and physical strain of leading is concentrated into one section, and as second on the ropes one can then enjoy a spell of mental relaxation and less physical strain. So it came about that I had all this uncompromising ground to lead between the First and Second

Ice Fields. In summer there had been no ice, just water-worn slabs, on which we had felt insecure, though the climbing was not difficult. It was different in winter. Though the angle of the rock became easier, bands of hard ice stretched across the slabs of rock. My crampon points scarcely bit into the brittle ice, and they grated off when they touched rock. I hammered in a piton and felt safer with my rope passing through the karabiner attached to it. I attempted to climb without my crampons, trying to step on the rock clear of ice with the rubber of my boots, but there was too much ice, and the rubber skated treacherously at its touch.

I moved further left, beginning to feel thwarted; it was no better. I had been trying for an hour. Crampons back on. Still no good. Insignificant in the midst of that huge wall, I was defeated.

'Dick, I can't do it.' It was hopeless and depressing.

'Try without your sack,' he shouted back.

I fastened my sack to the peg and tried again. It did help not having that weight pulling me out of balance. I was able to climb six feet higher.

At chest height there was a sloping ledge of rock with a band of ice an inch thick across it. I drove the points of my ice axe and hammer into the ice. I felt them jar against the rock beneath the ice but they held. I pulled up on them, contorting myself to raise my leg and stick my crampon points into the ice as well. The crampons slipped on the rock before they reached the ice, my foot fell and I was holding on only by the points of axe and hammer. I placed the crampon on another lip of rock and again it slipped and this time I saw the pick of the ice hammer levering itself out of the ice. I lunged, pressing my shoulder onto the hammer to keep its pick in the ice, I twisted my body, fear removed the pain from my aching, weary muscles and I flung my foot upwards beside the axe. The crampon points bit into the ice and I pushed myself upright and into balance. The moment was over, exhaustion overtook me, I shook nervously and waited a while before moving to the easier ground now within reach. The far eastern wing of the mountain was catching the rosy glow of the evening – I had no idea how long I had taken on that pitch.

Our ledge that night was only a foot wide. We slept with nylon slings attaching our chests and legs to pitons in the rock against which we pressed. We hardly spoke to each other by this time. There was no outside stimulus for conversation; we each performed the role we had to; we were working steadily if slowly; after all these years together Dick was still an enigma to me. I had ceased to worry about it. I struggled momentarily with sleep to stare at the constellations of stars and wish I had more knowledge about them and the energy to figure out which was which.

Normally we tried to wake before dawn. We slept fully clothed, only crampons, boots and sunglasses did we take off, but the morning ritual of re-fastening boots, attaching crampons, sealing clothing against the wind and blowing snow took half an hour. We had both somehow disciplined ourselves to excreting only once a day and the most convenient time for that was in the morning. There was no need to undress, only zips and velcro flaps to undo and layers of clothing to be parted. To have undressed would have been to expose ourselves to the heat-stealing wind.

The fourth day was all ice and Dick started the day. The Second Ice Field is not steep and on ice each movement is similar and repetitive, but I was glad it was Dick to lead. This was the ice of winter, dark, hard, repulsive, a thousand feet before the next bit of rock, a thousand steps, kicking crampon points with toe-bruising force at the ice trying to make them stick there, hammering at the ice with the picks of axe and hammer to make them bite in as hand-holds. When I followed Dick my hands became numb and insensible as I hit them against the ice inadvertently in trying to get the axe to bite deeper. The shaft of the hammer was shorter and my left hand suffered more.

We were creatures of the mountain now, lost to our former lives, remote from the tourists far away, remote even from any more visitors that might come to stare. The starting for me is always the hardest; once under way I could almost forget the passing of the days.

We switched round leads four times on this everlasting day. Fourteen rope-lengths of climbing in all, with the last two hundred feet up, escaping from the ice field, too difficult to climb with the weight of my sack. I left it behind to haul up later and clawed at the rock with senseless, bleeding fingers. It was so cold that each piton, each karabiner stuck to my hand and took away a little more skin.

Our sacks were still heavy and we had begun to consider a change of plan. We were two-thirds of the way up the wall and to speed progress we planned to consume as much of our food as we could and make a dash next day for the summit. We stopped earlier than usual to prepare a good platform for the night – if we intended to rush to the finish we needed to be well rested. It took three hours to complete the platform and only then, so engrossed had we been with the work, did we notice the grey streamers of cloud sliding across the sky with the dusk.

If bad weather came we could not risk scoffing all the food at once. We reverted to our former plans.

We used the tent for the first time. A small wall of rock leaned gently over the platform, protecting us from any stones falling from above and holding the tent upright. This was the infamous Death Bivouac where the first two men to attempt to climb the face, Sedlmayer and Mehringer, had arrived in 1935 and died in blizzards to stand, frozen sentinels, for long after their attempt had halted in the storm. I felt no foreboding, unhaunted by any ghosts; my mind was preoccupied with our own practical problems. We needed to hurry now. For once I was impatient for morning, keen to start moving, to get as close as possible to the top before we were engulfed in the storm which was threatening.

I noticed Dick stealing secret glances outside, checking the weather. It preyed on both our minds. We did not need discussion. If the storm came we would have to decide whether to go up or down; this Death Bivouac was the last place from which it would be sensible to attempt a retreat, and once we left here the only rational way off the mountain was upwards. My hands smarted all night from the slowly suppurating cuts they had now acquired and sleep eluded me.

In the morning there was a grey expectancy in the sky but no snow was falling. I was slow from lack of sleep but we could move upwards through the Third Ice Field, more dark, splintering ice and the diagonal slash of the Ramp, scything leftwards towards the complex exit pitches. The Ramp was so long, so huge we were in it all day. We had expected ice in a chimney that had been pouring with water in summer but there was none and we felt favoured. The steep rib above the chimney was clean of snow; Dick tried to talk me into leading it in a sudden loss of confidence but I was as worried as he and I bullied him on.

There was some tension between us. Dick led another pitch and was perched out of the way on a ledge as I climbed up the gully of ice at the top of the Ramp.

'Joe, could you carry on, it will be too awkward to change over here?'

I really did not want to and grudgingly felt out-manoeuvred.

'Joe, could you take that ice piton out as well, so I don't have to go down for it?'

'Bloody hell, Dick, you ask me to take your turn leading, you ask me to take pegs out for you, do you want me to climb the bloody mountain for you?'

I felt self-righteous and I hated Dick's stupidity. I climbed off upwards. It mattered only for a moment. Five days on a knife edge, everything was close to the surface.

That fifth night was the worst up to then. All we had was a seat smashed from the ice and loose rock. We sat with legs in our sleeping bags hanging over the edge, and a sling of nylon round our chests to stop ourselves lolling forward as we dozed off. For the second night the sky was grey with a pregnant expectancy. I remembered that my first climbing partner, Stefan, was getting married on this day. I had had to write to say that I probably could not make it.

My rucksack hung from a piton beside me. I wedged my head behind it to stop it falling forward as drowsiness began to take hold of me. I dreamt there was a policeman with his notebook out taking down my particulars:

'Hello officer, what's this for?'

'I'm booking you for driving a piton too fast down this groove.'

'But, officer, I didn't know anyone else knew about this groove.'

'I often drive down this way myself.'

I woke to find that Dick had continued to lie down. His head was resting in my lap and his feet were wedged somehow behind a rock projection.

'You don't mind do you, Joe?'

'No, it's O.K.'

We moved on, in the semi-darkness before the dawn, feeling the pressure now to use every moment of light. There was no snowfall but the heavy greyness was still in the sky. I was shaky and unnerved as I climbed rightwards along the Traverse of the Gods. I knew from summer that it was sensational rather than hard but I was still apprehensive. Ice coated every hold. I had memories of my struggles on the icy rock below; beneath my feet the face curved inwards, revealing the whole of the rest of the climb.

This horizontal section took us back into the heart of the mountain to the last of the ice fields, the White Spider, the catchment area for all the rockfall from above, though now silent. The ice was the worst yet, more black glass and steeper than any of the other ice fields. It fell to me to scrape and claw my way up it for five hundred feet. The ice was so hard that no technique helped; only brute strength made any impression. I kicked with my feet and smashed with my axe, never feeling secure as the brittle ice splintered away from my crampon points or axe pick.

An old rope hung down to my right, remnant from some previous epic. I climbed out of my way across to it and unashamedly used it as a handline for fifty feet. When it ran out I had to return to the blank, dark glass and regretted ever sampling the security of that rope. I longed for some excuse to hand over the lead to Dick, to stand by whilst he felt some of the terrible insecurity. But we had reached the start of the Exit Cracks, the final obstacle on the wall, before it was his turn to go first for four lengths of the rope. My fingers, cracked and bruised with the hammering, raw with the cold, were bleeding profusely.

The most difficult pitch remaining, the Quartz Crack, was concealed by a huge bulge of ice. Stubbornly Dick butted away at it. Watching him I could see no way that he could get past, then the mass of snow collapsed, brushing him to one side, but he clung on and the rock above him was clear. He climbed up and leftwards out of the difficulty and into sunlight. For the first time in days we were leaving the shadow of the face and it was as if we were being welcomed and congratulated for the climb. Feeble though the rays of the sinking sun were, some warmth soaked through my clothes and suddenly I had had enough. There were only hundreds of feet left to the summit, not thousands, but I had no time for the painstaking precautions we needed. The rock was loose, treacherous beneath a thin covering of snow, not difficult but insecure. I grew impatient and careless, then the sun was gone, clouds swirled round the summit, a wind caught us when we reached the exposed upper slopes and snow began to fall. Dark was upon us before we were near the summit and all we could do was push a few loose rocks to one side and squat down with the bivouac tent pulled over our heads.

The threatening storm had broken, the wind tore at the tent, snow soon covered over bits of equipment we had strewn on the ledge.

We huddled together for warmth, battered by the wind through the tent. At first we crouched over the stove, slowly suffocating from its fumes until we had eaten and drunk. Then we wriggled one at a time into our sleeping bags, boots and all while the air without the stove quickly chilled. Ice formed on our beards and on the inside of the tent only to shake off and fall like snow as the nylon flapped furiously in the relentless winds. The cracked and festering sores on my fingers hurt all the more in the warmth of my sleeping bag as the salt of perspiration aggravated each cut. Dick confessed that he was suffering too.

A little voice in my mind kept whispering 'You've done it, you've done it,' but I did not want to listen until I was down off the mountain, down on flat ground. I held the fabric of the tent in my teeth to stop it flapping against my face and disturbing me with showers of ice.

It was a fitful night. We were two lost souls in a bleak, forlorn limbo, shuffling about to ease the cramps and aches of our constricted quarters.

At dawn we left, without reluctance, without food, racing now before the storm strengthened and we were stranded and lost in ever-deepening snow. I felt humbled and undeservedly favoured to look down and see the snow covering those last loose pitches we had scrambled up the night before. Only a few easy pitches on comforting soft, blue ice were left for us, and then we were on the sharp crest of the ridge leading to the rounded summit.

We were pushed and tugged by the wind, there was no view of distant peaks over the ridge, only heavy swirling cloud. Dick was there first; he flopped down in the snow at the highest point and pulled in the rope with which he was joined to me. It was 8.00 a.m. on Monday 3 March, six days after leaving the station at the foot of the mountain.

There was no time for congratulation, no time for the indulgence of regret at achieving a goal, the blasts of wind and stinging snow drove us on and down, sliding, scrabbling, gasping in pouring streams of avalanching snow. We had anticipated bivouacking but we were being allowed to escape. I held my breath, stayed tense and watchful. We kept checking with each other, trying to recall the devious way down, disguised now by winter, and then we were clear, free from the steep ground, free from the slipping and sliding, entering a gully which eased out onto level ground and from there it was only wading through deep snow, sometimes crawling, but we were safe.

It was the middle of the afternoon when we reached the small hotel on the railway line. There seemed to be something happening; a small group of people were outside, and then they clapped – it was for us. They helped us off with our rucksacks. Dick winced with pain as he tried to peel his inner gloves from his damaged hands and a girl took charge and cut the gloves away.

Inside, heads turned and stared, we were wild in appearance and with long icicles hanging from our beards. We sat down and the manager sent over beer and soup. An Englishman was sitting across from us reading a newspaper – '41 killed in Moorgate Tube Disaster' – on the juke box someone was singing 'I've got two strong arms, I can help'.

I left Dick at the table to go and buy the train tickets for our descent to the valley. As I walked away I heard the incredulous Englishman asking: 'You mean you only bought one way tickets?' and Dick, with his enigmatic smile that spoke of hidden strengths, not knowing what to answer.

THREE

It Could Be Worse

DUNAGIRI

I

We called in to see Frau Gertsch to pick up the key to the hostel.

'*Tous les gens parlent de vous,*' she said, knowing we understood some French.

'*Quels gens?*'

'*Les gens de la région; vous êtes merveilleux.*'

She was homely and reassuring. In the hostel she bustled about making the place as warm as she could. Dick and I shambled around aimlessly. Too late to obtain anything from the shops; no celebratory meal; the same rations we had been eating for the last month; we went out to the only bar in the village and sat silently over a drink, nothing to converse about. I lay awake most of the night, feeling lost on the spacious bed, still highly strung, physically weary but mentally alert.

'Joe, would you fasten my buttons please, my fingers hurt too much.'

Next day we left, back to England, to Manchester, to school and class-rooms full of children most of whom, like myself, wanted to be anywhere but behind a desk.

At the same time as we had been planning to climb the Eiger in winter we had begun thinking of going further afield. Initially those people who went on expeditions to the Himalayas or the Andes had seemed a select group, eligible for a place on an expedition team by virtue of their great experience, proven ability and stamina. We could not see how people became eligible without having already been on an expedition and it seemed a double-bind situation. So without really knowing what we were taking on, we resolved to form our own 'expedition', and before leaving for the Eiger we had sent applications in to the government of India for permission to climb one of their mountains.

We had applied for permission to climb a beautiful mountain called Shivling in northern India, launching ourselves into our first skirmishes with the complex formalities of going on what inevitably we had to call an expedition. 'Expedition' was a grandiose title for what was no more than the climbing of mountains higher than the ones we had so far climbed but the remoteness, the greater degree of organisation needed, and the official approvals required, seemed to impose an identity which transcended our simple intentions. We wanted to climb bigger mountains than in the Alps, we wanted to climb a difficult route on a big mountain; we did not know about the time it would take to deal with the bureaucracies of the East; we did not know that to climb a mountain in any of the Himalayan countries wewouldhavetopayabookingfee.Thepeoplewhowentonexpeditionsseemeda small, tightly-knit group, and we did not feel qualified enough to expect admission into that closed circle which from the outside seemed to hold all the knowledge we needed. We could not understand what was different about going to the Himalayas, except that it was further; we did not know anything about the logistics of large groups and it seemed that the best way to climb would be as a pair, but since the mountains were so remote we decided to invite another pair to come along. It would not be much different from sharing a vehicle to go out to France and it would mean there were other people to lend a hand to us or us to them if an accident should happen.

Ideally, as a team of four people, a compact group, we could travel overland in a transit van, and climb a new and difficult route on the mountain we chose. Our ambitions were limited to peaks of around 20,000 to 23,000 feet, since we did not have the confidence to plan for anything higher, and at this height we hoped to be able to do what we knew best, routes of technical difficulty but without the need for fixed camps and massive organisation.

So we planned ahead, further than I had ever planned before. Always I had a certain reserve about planning beyond the next climb when so much depended on fate, but to go to the Himalayas, to go forward for us, meant making arrangements almost a year in advance. It meant also broadcasting our intentions, again something we were unaccustomed to. Not that we worried about competition, we just felt reservations about making claims that we were going to do a climb about which we felt not the least bit of confidence. In order to obtain permission, however, we had to present a confident manner and a positive approach in our application to the Indian government, and we had to present the same confidence to win the approval of the official mountaineering bodies in Britain.

But even organising a group as small as four had its problems.

One of the other pair we asked, a friend of Dick's, was doing a college course. He could only go during holidays, which would restrict us to climbing in the monsoon period, a most undesirable time of the year with constant heavy rains and snow, or to climbing in an area outside the Himalayan chain. Neither prospect held any appeal. We arranged to meet in Wales one weekend to talk it over. As the evening wore on with no sign of the other pair, Dick and I rationalised the situation.

'If they can't even turn up to discuss the expedition how reliable are they going to be on the trip itself?'

'Well, what shall we do? Just go as the two of us?'

'At least we would know where we stood. We probably won't need to buy a transit van if there's just two of us.'

'Would your car make it?'

Dick, who could not drive and was delightfully innocent of many of the practicalities of life, saw one vehicle as much the same as another.

'My old heap probably wouldn't get us to the Alps again. We'll have to buy an Escort van or something like that. Should be able to get one for about £150. You'll have to learn to drive, though. I'm not doing all the driving myself.'

So it was decided.

We could not have Shivling since it was in a restricted area close to the border; we could not have Changabang for some other reason. As beginners we were faced with the whole chain of the Himalayas to choose from and

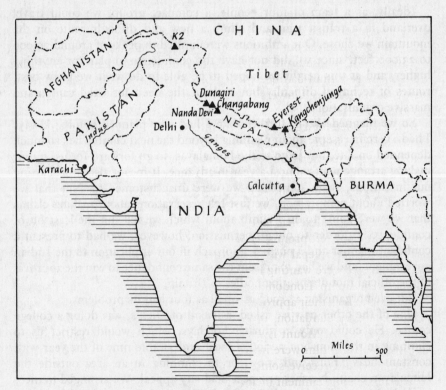

2. General location of mountains climbed by the author and other notable peaks in the Karakoram and Himalayas.

it was all academic, choosing a mountain out of a book, trying to piece together all that would be needed to reach that mountain and to climb it, and then pouring all energies into obtaining permission. At first I did not know where Kathmandu was in relation to Everest, which mountains were in India, which were in Pakistan or Nepal. Gradually patterns emerged and we began to know which mountains were where and what we were interested in.

Then more refusals came back. Two was considered an insufficient number from a safety point of view, all the mountains we were choosing were close to the border and for that reason out of bounds to expeditions.

It was discouraging carrying on with arrangements to go, buying the van, accumulating a few more items of equipment, when all the likelihood of ever going seemed minimal. Dick took up a teaching job in Manchester and started learning to drive.

It was a marvellous summer for rock-climbing, rushing away from school to climb in the long evenings on the crags around the city, sunny days in Wales and the Lake District. I met a girl called Muriel, full of vitality and dynamism, who caused me to wonder at how much I could lose by going off for so long on such an unpredictable venture.

To all but ourselves our 'expedition' was very definite. Then we met a Mrs Beaumont, whose brother had disappeared exploring a lake in Africa. In his memory a fund had been set up which disbursed small amounts of money to Manchester University students or graduates going on exploratory trips.

We had applied for a grant and were interviewed by Mrs Beaumont, now a trustee of the fund, a lively, grey-haired lady, driving a sports car and quizzing us in a motherly but encouraging manner.

'Did you say you were having difficulties with the Nepalese government? My husband has some friends out there. We might be able to help.'

She was kind, but it was with the Indian government we were having problems; the Nepalese had not even replied. We gave her details of our proposals and she left promising to chivvy them up in Nepal. I wondered if she knew where Nepal was, but expected little from it anyway since it was in India we were wanting to climb.

Dick went up to London for an interview with the Mount Everest Foundation to seek their approval and a grant towards the 'expedition'. The Mount Everest Foundation, or MEF, was set up as a result of the first successful ascent of Mount Everest in 1953, and all monies accruing from lectures, book and film were invested to provide a fund from which other expeditions could receive some financial support. The committee of the MEF is made up of eminent members of the mountaineering and scientific fraternity and approval by this august body carries some weight with foreign governments.

The interviews take place in the council room of the distinguished premises of the Royal Geographical Society on Kensington Gore. A huge polished table runs the length of the room and on one side are ranged the mostly grey- or white-haired dignitaries who conduct the interview with the applicant who sits alone across the table.

Dick had never learnt how to present an appearance of being anything else but himself.

'Why are there only two of you for this proposed expedition?'

'What if one of you sprains an ankle and needs helping down off the mountain?'

'Who have you consulted about your plans?'

'What are your plans? What mountain do you intend to climb?'

At the time we intended to try a steep and difficult ridge on Changabang. A frail-looking, white-haired gentleman at the far end of the table, who seemed to have been asleep, opened his eyes and asked: 'Why don't you try Kalanka?'

'It looks too easy,' replied Dick without hesitation or embarrassment. Later he discovered that the white-haired gentleman was Eric Shipton who had explored and climbed in the area since long before either of us had been born, and still knew it better than anyone.

Then Mrs Beaumont rang us. 'The Indians aren't happy about there only being the two of you but we've twisted their arms and they are sending you a letter to say you can choose one of three peaks. So don't go and fall off otherwise there'll be hell to pay.'

And it was all definite. Expeditions are one hurdle after another, this major one was over. We were given the choice of Devisthan, Mrigthuni and Dunagiri, all three in the same region. We chose Dunagiri, the highest of the three at over 23,000 feet, and climbed only once before, in 1939, by an expedition led by André Roche. We wanted to do a new route on it, and from pictures decided that a steep buttress, the south-east ridge, looked excellent for our purposes. The other two mountains were lower and not as interesting.

Then came more problems, and more costs. We had to have a Liaison Officer, whom we had to equip and feed. In the letter of information we were told that he was to assist us with the selection of porters, purchasing provisions and advise us on the climate and acclimatisation, snow conditions, risks and the feasibility of climbing the mountain.

It was nonsensical. We were going to the Himalayas because we felt capable of climbing there, not on a course at a climbing school; we did not want someone imposed on us who almost certainly would not know as much about mountaineering as we did ourselves, and on top of that we were being asked to feed and equip him.

One hurdle after another.

The days of summer sped by; I was climbing better than ever before – never with Dick, somehow we knew each other too well, needed a relief from each other in Britain – was also very much in love, and I could not help but feel that I was committed to something which could take away all this happiness. The pleasure of climbing rock is the pleasure of the gymnast, whilst the mountaineer is more like a marathon runner. The life of a lover of necessity is one of togetherness and voluntarily, I hardly knew if I wanted to or not, I was abandoning that for a solitary life on a mountain. Naive as I was, I did not know if it was normal to worry that we might not come back.

We bought an 1100cc Ford Escort van for £170 and had it checked over by the A.A. The engineer's report was discouraging:

> Considering vehicle's age, recorded mileage, faults evident, a below-average example of the model. Urgent attention required to engine, suspension, brakes and corroded bodywork. This work will prove expensive and its economic justification should be thought out initially.

> In its present condition, in my opinion, the vehicle is not roadworthy for the journey I am informed was proposed for the vehicle. The best way of using this van to reach the Himalayas is to drive down in it to Heathrow and fly.

We had some work done on it but could not afford to do all that he suggested. We could only trust to luck.

We were going for a post-monsoon attempt on the mountain, the season after the end of the summer rains and before the start of the winter snows. School ended and we packed ready to leave.

There was something of the boredom as before an exam. I had been involved in the preparations for too long and, ready or not, I just wanted to start. I used to wake up to immediate consciousness – no more the slow, lazy surfacing to see what a new day had to offer – it was as if I had just turned away for a moment, everything was there waiting to be attended to. Letters, phone calls, equipment, medicine, insurance, vaccinations, maps, itineraries, food and on and on.

I lived with my two friends Don and Jenny, who never murmured about the constant phone calls, mounds of equipment and food, early morning calls from the postman with yet another parcel.

On Monday 4 August 1975 Dick passed his driving test and on Tuesday the 5th we left for India.

At 8.00 a.m. Dick was sitting at Jenny's sewing machine finishing his cagoule for the mountain as I packed the van. We had never made any estimate of how much would have to go into the van; it was the biggest vehicle either of us had had anything to do with and we had not thought to question its capacity. We had even been considering selling a place in the van to someone for the overland journey. The van sank lower and lower on the suspension as we loaded everything in. There was not a bit of space spare when we had finished. The leaf springs bent back over on themselves in an inverted ⋂.

We discarded one or two bits of gear, closed the door on the house, started the van and lurched forward out of the driveway. The exhaust grated on the ramp of the drive as we entered the road at the start of the 6,000-mile journey.

We called in to see Ken Wilson, editor of *Mountain* magazine, and an authoritative spokesman on world mountaineering. Not known for being indifferent about any subject on earth, he favoured us with his enthusiastic approval: 'I like it, I really like it. You guys just going off, chucking your gear into the back of a van and going to the Himalayas. It's got to be the shape of things to come. Great. Go for it.'

He gave us the news he had just received that Messner and Habeler had climbed one of the highest mountains in the world, Hidden Peak in the Karakoram, as a twosome. As always in comparison to people who seemed more proficient we felt self-conscious at pitting ourselves against a similar objective.

The drive became a job like any other. Up at dawn, breakfast; driving by 8.00. Lunch. Finish at 5.00 p.m. The smooth tarmac and order of Europe changed to ruts and chaos as we drove further east. No one seemed to obey rules; it was all observation and luck.

Dick had recorded some classical music to play on the car's cassette player during the drive. Mine was mostly rock music. By the time we reached Turkey, the hot air streaming in through the wide open windows, the classical music lost out. The noise of car, wind and road drowned the subtleties of Dvorak, Beethoven and Mahler. It was Dylan above all who, with his nasal, insistent drone, won the day.

Dick had organised the food. Frugal to the last, our diet for the journey was to be sandwich-spread on bread for as long as we could obtain bread, home-made muesli with powdered milk, an omelette made from egg powder, and at night sometimes a tin of meat with whatever vegetables we could find. We were passing through countries each with their own particular cuisine but in the interests of thrift, if it served a final goal, Dick could discipline himself to put up with anything. We differed radically on this. Always I felt the spendthrift, the wastrel, the hedonist in his company. Always, without expressing a word, he managed to instil in me an uncomfortable sense of guilt and self-consciousness about any deviation from the spartan diet he had calculated as meeting all our calorific needs even if it did not meet the needs of the soul.

I tried to explain my point of view by telling him how much regret I would feel if I was to die in the mountains, to die whilst doing something so arduous, uncomfortable and painful as mountaineering and knowing that all the time I had been off the mountain I had led a spartan life as well.

I never knew whether the enigmatic smile concealed puzzlement or philosophical acquiescence. Dick continued contentedly munching chupattis covered in sandwich-spread when we could no longer get bread.

The wild, amiable disorder of Istanbul gave way to deserts and a breakdown. It seemed to be the coil that was at fault. We were unable to speak the language and met with incomprehension at every garage. The van limped on for two days until we met a Turk who had worked in Germany and arranged a replacement for the faulty part.

Then we met the savage, unsmiling rush of Tehran. Dick still had a studied air of concentration when at the wheel, betraying that he was not so familiar with driving that it was second nature yet. Not long after entering Iran on the open road in front of us a goat strayed from a herd and wandered across the road. A second goat began to follow and Dick, at the wheel, not calculating that the goat had only to walk a few steps before being full in the path of the van whilst the van had to travel twenty yards to get past, put his foot down to try to squeeze through the gap between the two goats. He hit the second goat square on and it was flung backwards into the ditch.

We stopped the van. The goat-herd rushed up, shouting and gesticulating at us and the injured goat, making chopping motions at its neck with the hoe he held. We had heard that it was better to knock down a man than an animal in some of the eastern countries; we had visions of languishing in gaol, trying to pay off an impossible fine. The van was not damaged.

We could not communicate at all, and being in the middle of a desert had the blessing that we were not immediately surrounded by a curious mob.

'What shall we do, Joe?' Dick looked bewildered.

The goat-herd turned his attention from us and saw more of his herd wandering across the road into the path of an oncoming lorry. He ran at them, shouting and shooing them out of the way.

'Let's go.'

We jumped into the van and drove for two hundred miles before stopping.

'I thought he was going to chop its head off at first,' said Dick.

A few days later, leaving Mashad, the last town before the eastern border of Iran, at the busiest time of the morning Dick seemed to be trying to imitate the apparently effortless weaving in and out of the traffic that some of the cars were doing. Not realising that it was a deft play between accelerator, clutch and brake, he seemed to be trying to achieve the flowing movement simply by turning the steering wheel from side to side. He hit a car a glancing blow and stopped.

'What shall we do?'

The car was caught up in the stream of traffic going in the opposite direction.

'Keep going.'

We left behind the cunning, plausible con-men of Iran and met the wild-looking, amiable rogues of Afghanistan, fierce with their ancient rifles and huge knives tucked into their waist-bands. Each rest-house we stayed at was like a miniature fortress, with an enclosed courtyard where we could sleep beside the van which contained more than a life's fortune to any of the local bandits.

We met people of all nationalities journeying east: a couple in a little Citroën 2CV, with wire mesh across the screen as protection against flying stones; a French-Canadian who smoked a lot of hashish and became very argumentative about independence for Quebec; a Belgian and a Frenchman, partners of the road, and Willie from Dundee, a dustman until he was fifty-five and his mother had died. With no more responsibilities he had set out for India, something he had wanted to do all his life, and he was heading for Varanesi where he had heard you could stay in the temples and get fed. He was worried that he did not have enough money to get across some of the borders, having heard that everyone had to have a minimum amount.

To all of these travellers we seemed to have a more tangible purpose in travelling east; to some the van was a wondrous machine when parked in their midst, with stereophonic music drumming out of it. To me these people seemed to have an enviable, carefree existence, wandering at will, with no burning ambitions eating away at their insides.

We crossed into India, out of the deserts into the lush greenery of the end of the monsoon, along roads that were forever lined with people walking, walking, from no definable source and towards no obvious destination.

After three weeks on the road we reached Delhi and telephoned the office of 'the friends' who had pleaded our case and obtained permission from the Indian government.

The office of J. D. Kapoor was an oasis of cool out of the enervating heat. He sat filling his armchair, holding court, with meek servants being summoned and dismissed at the touch of a concealed buzzer.

'Well, it was very lucky you see, it turned out that this fellow Chakravarty works for a firm on the floor above this. I just went up to see him and told him you were excellent climbers. The best in Britain and so we got permission.'

'But you have never met us.'

'Ah, I was given my orders. Mrs Beaumont instructed me.'

He beamed hugely as at a joke.

We stayed in a guest-house, costing 7 rupees per night, approximately 30p. There were three rooms, each holding about eight people. We intended to stay only one or two nights but we were there two weeks.

There was some problem over the Liaison Officer. He was not available when we arrived. We made a daily visit to the Indian Mountaineering Foundation headquarters in the Ministry of Defence. Munshi Ram, Assistant Secretary, laboured there over another expedition application, surrounded by unstable stacks of yellowing records whose tattered edges waved in the draught from the endlessly creaking fan on the ceiling.

We would sit sweating in the heat for a couple of hours, clearly being expected to understand by our being allowed to wait there that they too were as nonplussed as us and by sharing the waiting they were somehow trying to show us they were trying their hardest. Still nothing happened.

'Mr Tasker,' in a sing-song voice, 'I think he will not come today now. He will be here tomorrow. Please come back tomorrow.'

The bureaucracy could not cope with an expedition without a leader. There were only two of us but they wanted one of us to be 'Leader'. Dick asked me to do it. He did not feel comfortable adhering to what he saw as a pointless formality.

We suspected that the delays we were experiencing were due to the tacit disapproval of our two-man expedition; on top of this we had come overland on the 'hippy-trail', we wore jeans like hippies and stayed in the cheap sort of doss-house where hippies generally stayed. In Britain there is no class difference amongst climbers, a homogeneous group which does not make judgements on the basis of dress or financial standing. In the east, in the countries where worn and dishevelled clothing is not a sign of disregard for the importance of superficial or material symbols of merit but an indication of material poverty, the westerner who through choice abandons his potential wealth and voyages like one from the lower classes is looked down upon and is not taken seriously. The well-dressed in India are at pains to demonstrate their distinction from the lower classes and it was almost an insult to them that they had to have anything to do with us who did not act as visibly worthy ambassadors of our highly privileged country.

The days slipped by; we sat in the guest-house watching Mr Sony, the morose but friendly proprietor, de-lousing the beds, and we could do nothing. We suggested that we be allowed to go up into the mountains ourselves and the Liaison Officer could join us when he arrived in Delhi, but that was vetoed. Dunagiri, the mountain we had come to climb, was only a few miles from the border and the area was militarily very sensitive.

One day an English lad, Peter Roberts, came to see us. He wanted to go trekking in the mountains and Munshi Ram had suggested he join us. One way or another the authorities were determined to increase the size of our team. Peter was not a climber. He was on holiday in India with his girlfriend, in a Volkswagen minibus, packed with tins of food and goodies from Britain. He was a down-to-earth, humorous chap and we had no objections to his coming to Base Camp with us. He would be welcome company, though his intention to leave his girlfriend to fend for herself for six weeks or so seemed strange.

J.D. and his company came to our rescue again. With many muttered imprecations he shouted questions down the phone and within two days things were moving. Six weeks after leaving Britain, the van was toiling up the steep, winding road along the Rishi Ganga, up the pilgrim route, with Inder Kapoor, an athletics teacher, as our Liaison Officer.

We parked the van in Joshimath, at the Neelkanth 'Motel', run by Bhupal Singh, an amiable man of Tibetan appearance. He had been a trader until the border with Tibet had closed and he had opened this rest-house for the pilgrims on their way to the sacred shrines of Badrinath, a further day's journey by bus. Neelkanth was a mountain visible from Badrinath, but I asked him what had made him call the rest-house a 'motel'. He explained with amusement, in imperfect English, that his brother had been to Europe once and the name had taken his fancy as being more impressive than a plain 'hotel'.

He seemed a most honest and reliable man, so we left the van in his charge when we set off for the mountain, climbing up from the road, a few hours by bus from Joshimath, on the six-day trek towards our Base Camp.

II

On the second day of the walk to Base Camp I developed toothache. Dick and I had hired from the villages of Lata and Reni, where we had left the road, ten porters to carry food and gear for ourselves and Inder. Peter hired another three to carry all the tins of delicious foodstuffs he was bringing along out of his supply. We made the long, steep climb up from the side of the road over two days to a camp-site at 11,000 feet, and then I was almost incapacitated with toothache. I pressed on with the rest of the party next day up to Dharansi Pass and along the high plateau at 13,000 feet but the throbbing pain in my gums made me feel sick. The porters were sympathetic; one gave me a piece of root produced from a dirty rag secreted about his person. I pressed the root against my gum; Dick, with implicit faith in things of the earth which he did not have in man-made medicines, felt sure it would work. Neither root, nor aspirin, nor anything else made any difference.

That night, after a long descent down three thousand feet from the plateau, I consumed antibiotics and extra-strong painkillers. By morning I was delirious, my lower jaw numb and swollen.

I was asked questions, asked to make decisions, but I was in a daze; through a blur of nausea and searing frustration I could not think and Dick took charge. He told me to take a porter and go back to Joshimath where there was a Military Camp and possibly a doctor. He would continue to Base

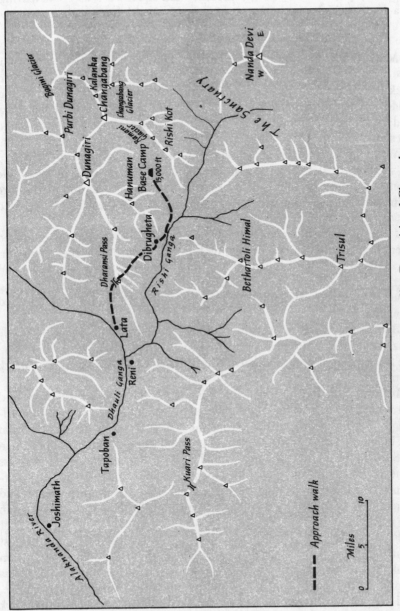

3. The approach and area surrounding Dunagiri and Changabang.

Camp with the rest of the porters, and he and Peter would wait for me there. He put his hand on my shoulder and squeezed it as I was leaving, in a gesture which spoke volumes of sympathy he felt but was unaccustomed to expressing.

'Take care, Joe, you'll be all right. Good luck. See you soon.'

More ill than I could ever remember I climbed back up the 3,000-foot rise to the plateau we had crossed the previous day. Bijay Singh, the porter, took my rucksack. I carried nothing but still could hardly move. It was midday when we reached the top, but I could go no further; I felt dizzy and at each rest I fell into a doze. I could not imagine how I had ever dared presume to climb in the Himalayas. I impressed on Bijay the need to halt.

With the long-suffering patience of people accustomed to hardship he set about making a shelter as best he could. There were no trees. He stretched a piece of polythene over a wall built from rocks and made a fire from some roots he collected during a long search over the plateau. I crawled inside to sleep with a miserable apology.

I woke periodically to know it was raining and Bijay was sitting crouched over a fire, another square protecting him and the fire from the downpour. A couple of times he handed me tea, then I woke to find it was night and there was a bundle of sackcloth beside me; that was Bijay; it was still pouring down. I writhed all night, dreams mingled with bodies and tattered thoughts.

By morning the fever was over, and the sky clear. Bijay shepherded my dizzy steps across the plateau, over the ridges and down, after glimpsing the frozen, magnificent sentinel of Nanda Devi, which only seemed to mock from afar.

In Joshimath I visited the army compound. The dentist was away and I was partially glad when I saw the pedal-operated drill and rusty instruments. To the doctor, a man from the plains, I was a distraction from the boredom of this posting in the mountains, where alcohol was forbidden due to the proximity of some sacred shrines. He diagnosed an abscess beneath the tooth and prescribed penicillin injections. An orderly performed the injection, fishing the syringe out of a glass of murky water and squeezing it hard into my arm before realising that there was a blockage in the needle.

From the damp, bug-infested room of the Neelkanth Motel in the utmost depths of depression I looked out onto a beautiful valley. There was warm sunlight, and cool shade, the comical proprietor of the Motel clucked his sympathy; the tough, hard life of a mountain village went its busy course, and everywhere I looked there were the elusive hills. I calculated that Dick and Peter would have reached Base Camp by this time but for me the nine months of planning, preparations, frustrations, setbacks and advances had ended in a dark room whose walls sweated and were stained with the damp oozing from the toilet and wash room above. I asked myself over and over if I could ever rise from this bed of pain to reach 23,000 feet. I felt as if nothing, not anything, could touch me, nothing could ever affect me again, after coming so far to be turned back at the last moment. I was completely numb, a wound cauterised. I had never realised that climbing meant so much to me. Twice daily I trailed up to the compound for more injections and more discouragement from the doctor.

In front of myself I could never again maintain that I was caught up in this game unwillingly. I knew now what I wanted to do. Willingly would I accept the hardship and fear, the discipline and the sacrifices, if only I could be given back the chance to climb that mountain.

Then the course of treatment was completed. My jaw was still painful and swollen but the sickness was over. I was admonished to return to Britain but my excuse was that Dick was at Base Camp and I would have to let him know.

I raced back up the hillsides on my own, sleeping out with a polythene sheet against the rain. I was driven like a man possessed. I continued to take the antibiotics we had in our medical kit as advised by the doctor, the pain had become a dull ache and I nurtured a quiet hope that by taking the tablets for as long as they lasted I might be able to climb the mountain.

I looked with new eyes and new pleasure at Nanda Devi, 25,645 feet high, the biggest mountain in India. It no longer seemed to mock, but was the beautiful 'Seat of the goddess Nanda' which had attracted so many of the famous pioneers to attempt to climb her and which had finally succumbed in 1936 to Bill Tilman and Noel Odell. The route to Dunagiri lay partly along the Rishi gorge, which comes down from the so-called sanctuary of Nanda Devi, but branches off up a side valley towards the Ramani glacier and the cirque of peaks comprising Rishi Kot, Changabang, Dunagiri and Hanuman.

On the second day, in a clearing, I came across a ribbon of coloured plastic tied to a bush and a note pinned to a tree.

> Joe,
>   Hope you're in good shape. From here the track winds up the steep grassy slope to the right of the crag facing the clearing. I can't make it out from here but Hart Singh assures me it will go. We will leave markers.
>   There are 2 tins of pilchards under the flat stone next to the cliff 3 ft from this tree.
>
> Dick

Towards mid-afternoon, feeling satisfyingly fit now, I crested a ridge and caught sight of two figures coming my way. I was dumbfounded. It was Dick and Peter.

Dick reached me first. He was mightily pleased to see me in much better form than the ailing figure he had said goodbye to some days before.

'Peter has decided to go back. Couldn't stand it at Base Camp. Found it too lonely. I don't think I'm very good company for him. I think he missed you making fun of him and chatting.'

Peter was apologetic and disillusioned, feeling that he had set himself a goal and found himself inadequate. I knew, however, that the mountains themselves, though beautiful, are barren, and that Dick, who is so self-contained that he seems not to need other people, would have daunted the gregarious Peter with his self-sufficiency and silence. I was daunted myself by Dick's reserve but I knew what to expect.

We camped together for the night telling stories, laughing and joking around a fire. This was what Peter had expected to find in the mountains with his two friends, not solitude and not the single-minded, self-abnegation and devotion to one sole aim to the exclusion of all else. I could see twinges of regret in him that he had decided to leave, but if he had stayed he would have been lonely. He could not understand what was wrong. He had longed to see Nanda Devi, to camp near its base and wander about in the mountains, but it had all been different when it happened. The mountains were perfect but he felt isolated; there was no enjoyment or sharing of the experience.

Next day I carried his rucksack for him back along the track, up steep slopes. I was bursting with energy now. Random flickers of pain in my jaw kept my enthusiasm in check but I was more and more sure that I could go on the mountain. Peter told me of the loneliness he had felt at the Base Camp, in a bleak, misty plain, with only the taciturn Dick for company. How they had spent two days in their separate tents in the rain, suffering a little from the altitude, and how they had hardly spoken in that time.

We parted in good humour, each of us with a clearer understanding of our goals and of ourselves, and I hurried back to join Dick, who was clearing up the camp.

Together we reached Base Camp the following day, Dick showing me the way and pointing out features with a proprietorial air as if he was taking me round his country estate. We could see little, a heavy mist filled the small valley where nestled the tent which was our Base Camp, and we were completely alone.

III

Dick had already walked up from Base Camp to the vantage point from where Dunagiri could be seen. Our tent was on a level grassy plain, enclosed by long hills of loose rock and earth. These were moraines, the residue heaps from the passage of glaciers over bedrock in millennia past.

To the east the 20,000-foot mountain Rishi Kot formed an outlying buttress to the rim wall of peaks surrounding the so-called sanctuary of the revered mountain of Nanda Devi, home of the goddess Nanda, and the highest mountain in India. To the north a steep mound of rubble concealed more peaks, and to the west was the rounded summit of the peak of Hanuman, the monkey god.

I climbed for an hour up the narrow valley of the water course running down into our camp, feeling the excitement mount as the bullet-shaped tip of Changabang started rising into view. At the same time as I reached a position to see the full length of the peak, Dunagiri came into view at the head of the valley to my left. We had first aspired to climb Changabang – it was a magnificent spectacle, symmetrical and sheer. Secretly Dick and I cherished the hope of climbing Dunagiri and then, if we coped well enough with that, climbing a long ridge which offered the only possible way up Changabang from the west.

Dunagiri did not look as fearsome. It resembled mountains we had looked at in the Alps, and having looked at decided on the line to follow and then climbed. At the west end of the mountain an ice-fall and buttress led up to a long, low-angled ridge which culminated in the summit. This was the way by which the mountain had been climbed once before and was a possible means of descent for us if we reached the top by a more difficult route.

Across a wasteland of moraines and ice, immediately in front of me and leading directly up towards the summit, was a steeper buttress and ridge, which, forming the south-east spur, seemed to offer a direct and more difficult line, with a steep barrier of rock 800 feet high some 1,000 feet below the summit. We had come to find difficulty, we did not want the low-angled ridges by which we knew a mountain could be climbed; we wanted the uncertainty of a difficult route. Further right than the south-east spur were big walls of rock which looked featureless and improbable. The obvious line for us to attempt seemed to me to be the south-east spur.

I returned to Base happy, now that the mountain had resolved into definite shapes and features. Dick had also picked out a line and we seemed to be in agreement until, discussing it in more detail, it transpired that he was thinking of the huge walls of rock to the right of the south-east ridge. The lurid reds and orange of that rock indicated that it might be loose and in the end Dick agreed that for our level of knowledge about the Himalayas and limited experience at altitude we would be better on the south-east ridge which looked more probable. Sometimes Dick annoyed me by what I regarded as unrealistic suggestions, and we finished the discussion with my feeling somewhat uncomfortable at having yet again advocated a more cautious plan than Dick had been pressing for. The same question perennially bothered me whether I was more realistic, more balanced in my

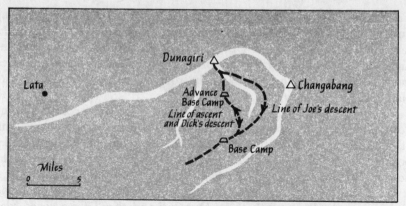

4. The ascent and separate descent routes of Dunagiri.

judgement than Dick or whether I was more timid, lazy and cowardly than he would ever allow himself to be.

We built a wall of stones in an arc against a huge boulder, made a roof over this with our remaining sheet of polythene and stored all our food inside. This was our Base Camp shelter, for we dismantled the tent and carried it up to a spot only two hours from the foot of the mountain with all the food and gear we would need on the climb.

We were concerned at the amount of time we had lost in reaching this point. It was the last week of September and lest we got caught in the first snows of winter we did not dare spend time acclimatising and getting fit on smaller mountains. We moved up and occupied the tent with the intention of starting out early next morning on the climb.

We wrote a note giving the date of our departure for the mountain and expected arrival back, and placed it in the shelter. It was not that we anticipated any visitors coming this way, for the valley we were in was a dead end, surrounded by mountains and high ridges. There would be no villagers passing through on their way to market, nor any chance passers-by. We left the note out of knowledge that if we disappeared on the mountain, the definite date of our departure would clarify once and for all the likelihood of our being found alive or not if in months to come a search party should be mounted as relatives and friends in England grew anxious.

It snowed in the night and I welcomed the reprieve. During the day Dick sat inexpertly practising tunes on a flute which I had known him attempt to play for several years. Driven off by boredom and the irritation of the repetitive practising of scales and nursery-rhyme tunes I went back down to Base Camp for a book to read. There I discovered that in our brief absence some creature had invaded our shelter, gnawed into various packets of food and scattered outside innumerable of our boiled sweets. I blocked up the entrance as best I could and returned with a tin of meat and some tinned fruit for the evening meal from the store which Peter had abandoned when he left Base Camp.

Next day it was clear. We hoisted heavy rucksacks onto our backs, sealed up the tent and left for the gullies of snow and ice leading up onto the southeast spur. In spite of the understanding of myself and my true intentions which I had come to when my illness seemed likely to rob me of the mountain, all the usual doubts and hesitations still niggled away inside. Dick, as ever, seemed untroubled by such thoughts and was eager in his preparations.

There were several of these gullies over one thousand feet long all terminating near where the spur became a rock ridge. We chose the most difficult and the most direct because we were new to this game and did not think about conserving our energies for higher up.

We climbed together, each of us with a rope coiled over a shoulder. There was no need to use rope at first until unexpectedly the rays of the sun touched the top of the gully, and rocks, loosened from the ice by the sun's warmth, bounced down towards us. We escaped out of the line of fire onto the steep side walls, tying onto the ropes and moving one at a time.

I did not feel attuned to the rhythm of the climb at first; I was too aware of myself, aware that we were treading new ground in a practical sense and strange ground in terms of what we were accustomed to. Already we were above the height of the highest mountain in Europe, higher than either of us had been, with more than another 5,000 feet of climbing before the summit. It was silly but we kept checking with each other to see how we both felt. There was a slight breathlessness and our sacks were heavy but that was little different from what we had already experienced.

I was leading at one point when I saw a bulge in the ice above. I intended to stop when I reached it to let Dick go ahead as he was carrying most of the pitons for hammering into ice. When I reached the bulge the ice was running with water and would not hold any pitons. I had to lead on. Dick would have known that my stopping was only an excuse, and we came onto the crest of the ridge in the late afternoon at 19,200 feet; only 4,000 feet to go.

We made room for ourselves for the night on some shattered ledges, settling into our sleeping bags without using the bivouac tent. The petrol stove would not work properly; it spluttered and flared constantly, taking long hours to melt snow and heat water. We witnessed a breathtaking transformation of the milky white walls of Changabang's granite through deepening shades of gold and orange to red as the beams of the setting sun played on that mountain, then finally lifted away to leave a colourless twilight. The night was spoilt for us by the malfunctioning stove.

Our progress was satisfactory. The vertical interval of the route we had chosen was the same as the North Face of the Eiger. It did not look as difficult so we had estimated we would take four days to reach the summit and allowed ourselves two days to descend. Our food and fuel was calculated accordingly. Six days' rations and a litre of fuel, the same as for the Eiger in winter.

The shallow ridge of rock above had appeared, from a distance, discoloured, indicating poor rock, though not too steep. We pulled onto ledges covered in loose blocks, sometimes skirted difficulties and at times had to climb steep towers of granite that reared up out of the camouflage of the surrounding rock. Sometimes whoever led had to leave his sack behind and haul it up afterwards, sometimes difficulties disappeared once we were at grips with an apparently problematical wall. The weather stayed fine, the strangeness vanished and I felt at home solving the vertical problem we had taken on.

We took photographs because it had become an ingrained habit, though sometimes I wondered for whose benefit I took them – as a record, for a magazine or because I liked photography. I no longer knew, it had become more natural to use a camera than to leave it hanging as superfluous weight.

Though I felt more at home I was not relaxed; the climbing seemed just like the hard work of the Alps only more tiring. We passed 20,000 feet, ticking off the altitude mentally by checking with the altimeter. There was no problem with the climbing except the effort needed. It was not that I did not want to do it, my brain was active and alert, racing ahead, but my body had trouble putting thoughts into action. I felt well but it was as if lead weights were in my legs; it was fine at each halt. I would not relax, no matter how well we were going, until the whole thing was over.

I do not know how many rope-lengths we climbed each day, sometimes we made 1,000 feet in height. Dick had an idea that this was pretty good; he had read that on Annapurna Mick Burke and Tom Frost were very pleased to have fixed 1,000 feet of rope.

Some time in the afternoon, without words, there was a consensus that we should stop and prepare the bivouac for the night. It was dark by 6.00 p.m. and we had to be ready by then. At the least we had to find a ledge on which we could, ideally, lie down, though more often we spent the night in a semi-reclining position. Sometimes we had to clear a ledge of loose rocks or dig one out of the snow.

The second bivouac was on top of a prow jutting out from the ridge. It was windy and flakes of snow were in the air so we used the small tent, without poles, which we had with us. Dick woke to find he was hanging half outside the tent and off the edge of the ledge. He was ill pleased and blamed me for having secured the best place on the ledge for myself.

The summit was still a long way off. I had ceased to think about it, ceased to think far ahead at all. I had learnt on the Eiger not to look to the end of the punishing effort, otherwise I would go out of my mind with impatience.

I was looking to the comforts and consolations at hand; making sure the bivouac was as comfortable as possible; relishing the piece of fruit cake saved for the end of the evening meal; lingering over the mugful of hot cocoa and savouring its warmth as it slipped down seemingly to the tingling ends of my toes as I sat ensconced in my sleeping bag.

But like this, one loses sense of time and somewhere we lost a day, somewhere we spent a night that we cannot account for. More rock and ice and a granite wall. I thought we had bypassed the 800-foot barrier below the summit but we had not. That great cliff was still waiting for us when we climbed out onto a corniced ridge which ran directly into it.

Though there was some daylight left, and Dick wanted to press on, there were only steep slopes ahead and the snowy shoulder on which we stood was flat and would provide by far the most comfortable bed. Dick capitulated and we dug a square hole a foot deep into the snow, in which to lie with some shelter from the wind. We settled down with muttered comments from him about not sleeping near the edge of the ledge that night though we were on the flat top of the rounded shoulder and we could hardly fall off it.

We had a tin of sardines or pilchards for each night as part of the meal, but to cut down on weight Dick had disposed of the cardboard box and thrown away the little opener which makes opening the tin so easy. I tried to open the square tin with his Swiss Army knife and had trouble at the corners. The tin bent in my hands, tomato juice and morsels of fish squirted out as I mangled the tin using brute force to tear into it and cursed Dick for his counter-productive scheme for lightening our loads. He cursed me in return for the mess I had made of the tin, and my lack of dexterity with a knife, which I took as a comment on my life which relied more on gadgets than his.

We had been on the mountain for three or four days. Mostly the weather had been fine. The snowfall, cloud and winds had not lasted long. The rock barrier was the only real obstacle remaining, once up that the summit slopes fell back in an easier angle and, though our food might be running low we expected to be able to descend rapidly. We relied upon the south-west ridge to provide an easy descent.

A ramp of snow ran diagonally leftwards into the centre of the wall. There was an area of bare rock, then above that snow and ice on the rock indicated that the barrier was no longer vertical.

Dick led for four rope-lengths up to and along the ramp. It was my turn to lead when we reached the bare rock.

The ramp of snow faded to a thin sliver of ice which squeezed itself vertically upwards into a bay in the rock wall, and then the bay closed to form a narrow chimney split by several cracks and clefts.

I left my rucksack behind and climbed upon crampon points in the ice until the ice was no more. Crampons were now useless, the rubber sole of my boots would have held better on the granite, but I did not dare take the crampons off. I could see the fingers of more ice reaching down from above the block which closed the chimney and up there I would need the crampons to be still on my boots.

I hooked crampon points onto the edges of cracks, hammered pitons into the cracks and wedged chock-stones of aluminium into wider cracks; I used anything I could to pull myself any bit further upwards. A huge flake of rock frightened me with its hollow sound, it seemed only to be stuck in place by the ice behind it, but I needed to pull up on it; I was high in the chimney, sweating, thrown out of balance by the steepness and beginning to feel the surge of panic as I tried to move on without obvious means of reaching safety. I could stand with my legs straddled across the chimney, feet braced against opposite walls, crampons scraping on the rock as my muscles began to ache with fatigue. To go on I needed to launch myself over the block which jutted out above me, launch out with no security, with little possibility of reversing any move I made, in the hope that out of sight above me there would be holds to grasp once I committed myself to moving.

Eighty feet below, Dick peered questioningly upwards asking what it was like. I did not want to break my concentration to answer.

I hauled myself on my arms out of the chimney, out round the great block, my crampons scraped and sparked on the granite walls. The lead weights seemed to be fastened to my back now, and I did not have long before my hands would uncurl their grip and I would fall. I thrust one cramponed foot at the cleft where the block met the wall and pushed upwards. Everything suddenly flowed smoothly, I was in balance, there was a small ledge to step onto, the much prayed-for stroke of luck. I was safe.

'What's it like?' came up from below.

'O.K.', and I smashed my fist with a sob of relief and pent-up feeling against the rock.

We had to sit all night on an uncomfortable promontory of ice in the upper part of the rock barrier; most of the day had disappeared into that difficult pitch. It was a relief to stop anyway, physically I was drained, and the next day we expected to reach the summit.

It was not to be so. On anything but an easy snow slope time just slips away. We dug another bivouac site the next night a few hundred feet below the summit; this time there were definitely no more obstacles.

We were slow with the altitude, stopping every few steps to gasp for air, we were tired mentally and physically. The sunsets and sunrises had become empty spectacles; it was a cold, uninviting beauty. Somewhere deep inside there must have remained the spark of determination, when it

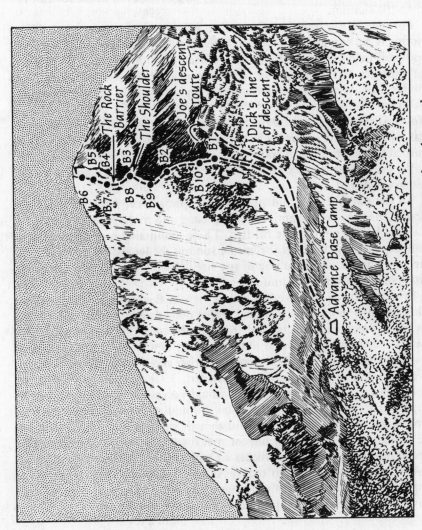

2. Our ascent up Dunagiri, showing where we separated on the way down.

was all suffering, all lung punishing effort, all mental and physical fatigue, to keep on; not to question the sense, not to have considered retreat.

We climbed out of the rosy glow of sunrise to a small cliff of ice beneath which we left our rucksacks. To descend the south-west ridge we would have to come back to this point. An easy slope to the left of the ice cliff ran up to the summit.

For once I was ahead of Dick when it was only a matter of plodding. Normally he can drive himself on when I give in to the need to rest. We both still held our axes, using them to lean on, but they had short shafts for steep ice and the slope we were on was at a very shallow angle. Bent double, like old men, we advanced to the highest point of the summit dome.

When the mountain sloped down away from me in every direction I crouched down and turned round. Dick had stopped fifty yards away, he was lying prostrate on his back staring vacantly into the sky. Eventually he pushed himself to his feet and made his way up the last slight incline.

We grinned as best we could. Dick was apologetic and alarmed that he felt so exhausted.

To the east the splendid pyramid of Nanda Devi poked through the clouds, the rounded summit of Changabang and more pointed summit of Kalanka barely pierced the blanket. These mountains had been our constant companions for days. From the summit we looked for mountains to the west but there was nothing of any size. The cloud layer beneath us ran disappointingly clear to a uniform horizon.

From where we were we had a clear view of the south-west ridge down which we had intended to descend. From our vantage point it now looked complex, precarious and formed from insubstantial flutings of snow. We were so tired that if we tried to climb down it we would run the risk of making mistakes from lapses of concentration and falling through a deceptive cornice of snow. And so it was decided. After a good night's sleep we would descend the way we came; it would necessitate abseiling down the upper barrier of rock but from then on it would go more easily. At the very most it would take us two days and though we only had a little food left we thought we could spin it out for that time, since we would be gaining strength as we descended to thicker air with more oxygen to help us along.

We turned to go back to our rucksacks. I felt only the tiniest bit of satisfaction that was anything other than relief at not having to step upwards again, and no compulsion at all to linger on the top.

IV

We slept comfortably in a hollow beneath the cliff of ice where we had dumped our rucksacks on the way to the top. We had had time left to go some way down but we reasoned that the slopes as far as the top of the rock barrier were uniform and would take very little time to descend. We would best utilise the time by resting in readiness for making a big effort next day to get down as far as possible.

We used up the last of the fuel. It had lasted about the length of time we had calculated it should. The food we apportioned out, keeping a little fruit cake, a tin of sardines, a few boiled sweets and some squares of chocolate for the next night.

The ascent had taken longer by two days than we had planned for and now we had to descend with no fuel and a minimum of food. I wondered what had happened to my usual caution and aversion to effort which would normally have made me seize on the unexpected difficulty and time it was taking as a short-term excuse to go down and rest, postponing the final effort until a later date when we could return refreshed and with more supplies.

I mentioned this to Dick, in self-mocking pride that for once he had not had to sustain my flagging enthusiasm with his own relentless drive.

'I can't understand why it didn't occur to me to suggest going down before we came into the rock barrier. It should have been obvious then that we would be cutting things fine. Not like me, is it?'

And Dick replied: 'No, but it occurred to me that it would be more sensible for us to go down then, and come back later, but I thought you would be suggesting it at any moment so I just carried on and you never said anything!'

Without fuel for the stove we could melt no snow for water and without liquid we would deteriorate rapidly. We needed a minimum of eight pints of liquid each day to avoid rapid physical deterioration, and though we were surrounded by snow we had no means of melting it. The total food we had left amounted to no more than a snack, hardly enough to sustain us, but even if we had had more we could not have swallowed anything without liquid to wash it down.

Our situation was serious but we pinned our hopes on being able to descend more rapidly than we had climbed up. We regarded the rock barrier as being the most difficult stretch, but knew that we could abseil down that and any other awkward places below. Without the constant struggle upwards in thin air, against the force of gravity, with heavy loads on our backs, we calculated that it should not take us more than two days to reach the bottom, where we would find water and food at our tent. We would be very weak by then, but we were confident that we could do it, and we left at morning to overcome the worst obstacle, the rock barrier.

Great gaps in time exist from those days. We only reached part way down the rock barrier next day and nothing remains in my mind of all that we did before evening came and we had to chop out a precarious ledge in some ice. The ledge was a foot wide. It was a struggle to work ourselves into the bivouac tent as shelter against the gusts of wind and showers of snow. With my head swathed in the folds of nylon I heard the clatter of the pan lid falling as Dick shuffled into position. I thought that it didn't matter as there was no fuel for the stove and we could not use the pan anyway. Dick told me that the pan and the stove had gone too and still it did not seem to matter. On the contrary, they had all become surplus weight once the fuel ran out and we had not had the wit to discard them anyway.

We ate nothing, not having the wit either to realise how weak we were becoming and that in a short while our throats would become too parched to swallow even the morsels of food which did remain. We were too cramped on the tiny ledge and too exhausted to scrape about in the bottom of our sacks amongst the wrappers and empty food bags on the chance of finding something edible. Sleep was a merciful oblivion when it came.

We left that bivouac and continued to abseil down. I can remember only that it was difficult to find somewhere to drive the pitons from which to hang the ropes. As we slowly descended the weather deteriorated, clouds covered the sky and the bitter wind brought more snow. We spoke little. Any word was a curt passing only of essential information, talking took energy. We needed no words to perform manoeuvres which we had rehearsed on every climb we came down from. We were mute collaborators in a performance for surviving, Siamese twins and yet strangers, muffled in now ragged garb smattered with snow.

We came out of the rock barrier some distance to one side of the snow ramp by which we had entered it some days ago. An expanse of hard, blue ice separated us from the shoulder on the ridge where we had spent a night on the way up.

We pulled the ropes down from the anchor point lost now in the mist. Dick coiled one rope and placed it over his shoulder. He fastened himself to two barbed pegs driven into the ice and stood on a tiny step he had scraped out for his feet. I had made ready the other rope and having tied one end to my waist harness started across the hard, brittle surface of the ice slope with Dick paying out the rope as I moved across in a horizontal line.

There was an initial area where snow covered the ice and my crampon points bit in quite well, then I was on the bare, uncompromising ice itself. After days of use, the points of my crampons had become blunted. I kicked at the ice with all the force I could muster, trying to embed the metal spikes in far enough to hold my weight, but my legs had no strength and my movements were listless, like those of someone in a nightmare trying to move faster.

My arms struck powerlessly at the surface with axe and hammer but the ice flew off in tiny fragments and the picks skated wildly away from where they had struck. Somehow I had to cross another seventy feet of this ice before I was safe.

Dick seemed unaware of my predicament. I felt the rope tighten on my waist, pulling me off balance, as something prevented him from paying it out, then he spoke:

'Joe, can you hold on while...'

My patience snapped and I shouted at him in desperation: 'Can I, hell? This ice is terrible,' so that he would know I was in trouble.

I was weakening fast. My calves ached unendurably. I cut a small step out of the ice with my axe and stood on it while I hammered in an ice peg. I passed the rope attached to my waist through a snap-link in the peg and moved on with a little more reassurance. The dreamlike state persisted. Dick became a vague silhouette eighty feet away through the mist and driving snow. I kept making the motions of driving in axe, hammer and crampon points, moving imperceptibly further, but my adhesion was only tenuous. Wearily and inevitably, but with surprise, I fell, banging down the ice to be stopped twenty feet below the ice peg, dangling from the end of the rope.

I had stopped, and I had no thought for the danger of the situation. Four thousand feet of mountain stretched away beneath me, and one six-inch spike of metal had held in the ice, taking my weight on the rope which I had attached to it. My brain filtered out all but the essential. I needed no concern for myself, I knew I was safe, but I called out to my partner, 'Are you all right, Dick?', concerned at the shock he must have had in stopping my fall and the strain he would be feeling in holding my weight still.

'Yes, I'm all right,' he shouted back in a tone which said, 'It's you that's fallen off, are *you* all right?'

I was more surprised that I had actually been held on an ice peg than frightened and unnerved by the experience.

'Dick, I can't climb across this, I'll tension across from the peg to where the ice is better.'

I had fallen to an area of even harder, steeper ice and with even less strength than before I could not kick my crampon points far enough into it. Dick held my weight on the rope which ran through the karabiner on the peg. In delicate balance, not thinking that the peg might have been loosened by my fall, I edged across, leaning against the pull of the rope, clawed with the points of my axe and hammer and pushed with the tips of my crampons. Fifteen feet, ten feet remaining and then I reached the white, snow-covered, softer ice.

'How much rope, Dick?'

'Forty feet.'

I advanced to where a rock buttress came down into the ice and drove some pitons into a crack. They were really secure. I knew that Dick, as fatigued as I was, would have an equally hard time crossing the ice.

The wind was hurling the snow into my face, inside the hood of my anorak and around my neck. After an age Dick still had not moved.

'Dick,' I screamed into the mist, 'what's the matter?'

My throat was dry and sore from thirst.

'Just getting the pegs out. Coming now.'

I drew the rope in, feeling him moving, though only vaguely seeing. I wondered what it would be like to hold onto the rope like this if Dick fell. My hands were in thick mitts, matted with ice, I was shaking with cold and hardly able to stand upright. Without warning Dick swung off, tumbled down the ice and came to a halt dangling from the end of the rope, much as I had been some time before. It was not anything terrible to hold his weight. The rope still ran through the karabiner on the peg that had held my fall. I just felt the uncomfortable strain of holding a weight I must not let go.

'Are you all right?'

'Yes.'

From the position he was now in, the rope would not be long enough for Dick to reach me. If he climbed up to release the rope from where it ran through the ice peg he would still be stranded in the middle of the dreadfully hard ice. Without the safeguard of the ice peg to take some of the strain, if he fell, all his falling weight would come onto me. I was no longer strong enough to be sure of being able to hold a fall which came directly onto me.

'Dick, you'll have to take the rope you're carrying and join it to the one you're tied to. That will give you extra length so that you can have a back-rope from the ice peg to reach here. Put another ice peg in where you are while you tie the two ropes together.' The effort of shouting all this exhausted me further.

He hammered in an ice peg and fiddled about uncoiling the rope he had been carrying over his shoulder. I could not quite see through the wind-driven snow and cloud but I could sense that something was not right.

'How am I going to get this other rope to you?' he asked.

'There's no need to; just tie it to the rope you were first tied to, I'll take it in till the knot comes to the top peg, then tie yourself into that second rope; that should give you enough free rope to reach me here using it as a back-rope on the higher ice peg.'

'Well what's this ice peg for here?'

Somehow Dick was not thinking straight.

'That's so you don't fall off whilst you're doing all this.'

I was not annoyed or even impatient, it was simply essential that all this be done in the shortest possible time. There was no sarcasm in the way I spelt out all these basic manoeuvres as if to a novice. It was urgent that there be no misunderstanding and that we reach the bivouac spot, on the shoulder only minutes away from me, and get into our sleeping bags out of the cold. This time he was doing it right. After those minutes of waiting which stretch into hours, Dick started to move. Then he stopped.

'What's the matter?'

'I haven't got the ice peg out.'

'Stuff the ice peg.'

'I'll get it tomorrow.'

'All right, tomorrow.' Anything to keep him moving. 'But please hurry,' I pleaded. I was freezing and beginning to panic at the desperation of our situation. Carefully he arrived.

'Good lad.'

'That's what comes of being hassled,' he spat at me as he came alongside, waving a foot. The crampon dangled loose from the boot and I gathered that somehow he blamed me for it.

We were both suffering from an advanced state of exposure and we did not know it. Dick's lack of comprehension of the simplest instructions, slowness of reaction and irrational behaviour were classic symptoms of sustained exposure to extreme cold which not only dulls fatally the central core of the body but affects the functioning of the brain as well. I should have recognised these tell-tale signs and taken control but I too was so affected that I could not think beyond my own misery and felt he was only being abnormally perverse.

After twenty feet the angle of the snow slope eased off into the almost horizontal shoulder on the ridge where we had dug a shallow hole against the wind on the way up. I vacated the stance I had been in for some unconscionable time and hurried down the easy ground towards the hole. The rope came taut before I reached the chosen stopping place and I waited for Dick to free himself from the pegs and follow me. He started hammering the pegs loose. I waited and froze. He hammered and hammered. He was only dimly discernible. The cold was terrible.

'Joe, one of the pegs won't come out.'

'Stuff the peg. Leave it.'

'I'll get it tomorrow.'

'All right, tomorrow.'

At last he moved. He sat down for a rest. We moved on again at opposite ends of the taut rope.

'Another fifteen feet . . . I'm almost there . . . I'm at the bivouac, Dick.'

Another step into the slight hollow remaining of our previous hole. I flung my sack to the ground, sat on it and started to pull in the rope. Dick stopped again. After the normal interval for a rest he was still there. All I craved for was sleep. Not food, nor drink, only sleep; but there still seemed to be so many things to do before we could settle down. I sat holding the rope.

'Joe, you look after yourself...'

I could not catch the next words, they were garbled in the wind and mist. Then I heard: 'I'm strangling myself. Got to sort the rope out.'

I realised he must have got his legs caught up in the rope, but he was nearly with me, only thirty feet away. He had reached the rounded crest of the shoulder, whose broad, almost flat top was nearly fifteen feet wide. He was safe now, so I left him to untangle himself while I made ready the hollow for us to spend the night.

I pulled out the bivouac tent, put my piece of foam mat inside, sleeping bag on top of that; duvet jacket on, crampons off, boots off, inner boots slackened, a quick photograph of Dick through the airhole of the tent, and I snuggled down into my sleeping bag. In seconds I was asleep.

'Joe, do you want something to eat?' Dick's voice came from outside through the blue folds of the tent. I had no idea how much time had passed, but there was a dimness, as of twilight, outside.

'Is there a piece of cake left?' It was the only thing with any moisture in it, and I hoped that the moisture would help the food slide down the dry and inflamed tube of my throat.

A small morsel of cake appeared through the entrance. I bit into it and a filling fell out from one of my teeth. It was too much effort to eat. I put the cake to one side and fell asleep again.

'Joe, do you want any of those sardines you've got?'

'No,' and in the unspoken language of the intimate rapport we had developed this meant that the sardines did not get opened. We had to do things together. If I did not eat my half of the sardines at the same time as Dick we would have the problems of carrying round the half-empty tin. It did not occur to me that I could eat them in the morning, or that they would be frozen anyway and could be easily carried.

After another unmeasured period of time, I woke again; it was dark and Dick was still not in the tent beside me.

'Dick?'

'What?'

'What are you doing?'

'Nothing. It's clear out here now. It's a three-quarter moon too. Really beautiful.'

The thought never came to me that he needed help, that his mind was waning with his strength. I thought it was only his everlasting toughness and resilience which enabled him to sit out and look at the stars when all that I could think of was the oblivion of sleep. I did not know that he sat out there possessed of a strange excitement and intoxicated by a silvery landscape illuminated by the rising sliver of moon.

I simply thought that I was with a person who was tougher and who had more mental reserves than I would ever have, and I fell back to sleep.

It was morning, but the sun was not yet out, when next Dick woke me.

'Joe, what do you think of these?'

I struggled to find him through the folds of the bivouac bag. He was sitting up, half outside, and he held out his hands. At any time Dick's fingers look fat or plump, now as he thrust them towards me, they emerged from his fingerless gloves swollen and BLUE; solid, hard BLUE.

'Jesus Christ, do they hurt?'

'They're . . . I'm not sure'.

'Can you use them?'

'I think so.'

I was lost. It was up to him to express pain and disquiet, or to complain; he just seemed to be commenting on an extraordinary phenomenon.

There was another four thousand feet of mountain to descend before we were back on the glacier, back on level ground, and able to walk or crawl in relative safety back to Base Camp. We had by this time been without water for two days, what little food remained was virtually impossible to swallow without any liquids. It was in trying to chew some chocolate the previous night that Dick had realised that there was something wrong with his hands. He had discovered a couple of squares of chocolate when he had finally settled into his sleeping bag and sat up while eating them. Suddenly he became aware that he had finished the chocolate and was nibbling at his own fingers, which were dark, hard and unyielding as the chocolate had been. The ends of his fingers were senseless and frozen.

He told me how the discovery that his fingers were frostbitten had not worried him at the time and he had woken to think that it had all been part of a bad dream, until he had pulled his hands out of his sleeping bag to check.

Both hands were the same. It must have happened when he took his gloves off to hammer in the ice peg and tie the ropes together, but he had said nothing about the cold then, and after a while his hands had probably gone numb so that he stopped feeling any pain.

We usually waited until the sun rose from behind Changabang and warmed us a little before we started to move. There was no longer the ritual of melting snow, making some tea, having breakfast, which had been the normal introduction to the day, not for the two days past. With so little intake of liquid and food we also had had no cause to delay over the intricate process of relieving ourselves, for there were no solids or fluids passing through our bodies at all.

I led most of the abseils that day. We had thought we would be able to scramble down easily but the mountain was steeper than we remembered it. All day I prepared anchor points, hung the ropes in position, pulled them down to us when we had both slid to the end and looked for the next anchor point to repeat the procedure. Dick seemed to be ill as well as afflicted by his frostbitten hands, but he was nonetheless apologetic.

'I'm sorry you're having to do everything for me, Joe.'

'That's all right, I want to get myself off this mountain as well.'

I went down the ropes to the end of a rock rib and on further down a slope of snow to within sight of some more rocks. Dick came on down and stopped at the top of the snow slope.

'What time is it, Joe? Is it too early to stop?' he shouted down.

In the unspoken language which held most of our communication now, I knew Dick was really telling me he had to stop for the night. I was surprised; it was only 3.00 p.m. and it was unlike him to give in to himself.

'Is there a good place up beside you?' It was understood that he would not have suggested stopping without having spotted a convenient site.

'There's the start of one; one and a half places here to sit down, and one there. We'll have to dig them out.'

'It had better be really good for me to climb back up there.'

It was only fifty feet back up an easy snow slope but I had to rest many times, I had to stop and pant hard for breath before I reached Dick, and experienced a wordless disappointment when I saw the two tiny, inadequate hollows on either side of a prow of rock. Futile to criticise; the decision had been made.

I hacked at the snow and ice, disloging a rock which gave a little more space. Dick, round a corner from me, was similarly preparing his place for the night.

'This is going to be a hanging bivouac,' I complained out loud.

'Sounds grim,' said Dick, and I presumed he was better off round that corner.

'What's your place like?'

'All right.' I could visualise him sitting in comfort.

Into the rock I hammered a couple of pegs. In a horizontal line with them I drove in an ice peg and further along thrust my ice axe into the snow. From the rock pegs I hung my rucksack into which I slipped my foam mat and sleeping bag, and with great exertion I inserted my legs into the sleeping bag, attached my waist to the ice peg and my chest to the ice axe. Though the ledge was only a few inches wide, the rucksack held my legs in place, and the nylon loops attached to the ice peg and ice axe held the rest of my body against the side of the mountain. I was ready for sleep.

Dick was fiddling about with something round the corner. I asked what he was doing and he said that he had found a candle in his bag and was melting some snow. Drink was the one thing we craved above all but I thought he had dropped the pan days ago, and of course we had long since run out of petrol even if the stove had not been dropped too. He said he was using his mug. The mug was made of plastic, and from the other life, before this climb, I was sure that I had a memory that plastic melted in flame, but I thought that maybe I had been mistaken and that perhaps plastic did not melt after all. We had been on the go a long time; I could easily be wrong. No water appeared and I dozed off.

From the lethargic sleep of exhaustion I became aware that it was snowing. I pulled my hood further down over my face so as not to be disturbed by the cold flakes, and hoped that the snow would be sufficiently dry due to the extreme cold that it would not make my sleeping bag any damper.

Dick disturbed himself from whatever his arrangements were to reach round for the bivouac tent which was hanging unused by my feet. It did not surprise me that he did not allow himself to be affected by the lethargy which had prevented me from rigging up the tent.

I dreamt of various things, but mostly of food; hot steaming pans of vegetables and casseroles of meat.

Dick was up first, before the rays of the sun had reached us. He thrust the opened tin of sardines at me. There were three left in it, a good tin, some only had four. The volume was probably the same but it seemed as if you were getting more.

Forced into movement, I grumbled accusatorily as I packed things away: 'This was a lousy bivouac. What was yours like?'

'All right.'

He was away well before me, hands in pain or not, prospecting the rocks below for the first anchor point. I glanced round the corner enviously to examine the spacious platform I had visualised him sleeping on. There was a minute ledge six inches wide and at most two feet long. The ledge was marked with indentations of crampon points and I realized now why he had stirred himself to open up the bivouac tent. He had not been able to get into his sleeping bag at all but had spent all night crouched on the ledge, had not even taken his crampons off. He had needed the tent as a cover all the more when the snow started. I knew now why he was up so early; he needed to get moving to restore his circulation. 'All right,' he had said it was, 'all right'!

Neither of us had any idea of how many days we had been descending. Dick had recovered from the state of illness of the previous day and now it was only his hands which hindered him apart from the gradual wasting away which was common to us both. But I lapsed into a state of weakness from which I was losing the will to emerge. I felt that I could so easily sit down and rest forever. I felt no regret for the life that was slipping away, no regret for the way of life back home and people I would be leaving behind; I only wanted the suffering to come to an end. I now, in my turn, relied on Dick. If there was one person I had ever known who would go on until he dropped in his tracks it was Dick. I did not think I had the strength any more to get down off this mountain but I felt I had just a little strength left with which I could follow Dick's example. I forced myself to imitate his movements and resolved to do so until the end took me.

At midday I asked him to stop for a breather; putting one foot in front of another even downhill was wearying. He scrambled about in the bottom of his rucksack and produced a polythene bag which had the remains of a portion of muesli in it and a boiled sweet. In spite of the dire straits in which we were, we still carried with us all the rubbish of food wrappers and empty bags from the time when we had had food. We had kept the rubbish deliberately, not wanting to litter this barren wilderness, but now our reward was finding once-overlooked or spurned remnants of things to eat from when we had had plenty. Dick's mug was blackened and misshapen but it had not been destroyed by his attempts to melt snow the previous night. He mixed the sprinkling of oats with snow and ground up the sweet into the mug. The result was a slightly flavoured, slightly more moist slush than the snow from which it originated, and it momentarily relieved our dry and burning throats. We were surrounded by tons of snow, but it was no use to us without the means to melt it. Sucking snow or ice only very briefly alleviated our parched mouths. It took too much body heat to melt even a trickle of water in the mouth and the cold caused our mouths to crack and chap worse than before. We needed a minimum of several pints of liquid each day to avoid physical deterioration and for some days now we had had only a few mouthfuls of snow.

Both of us remembered the lower third of the spur, the region of the lurid, discoloured rock, to be loose, but fairly easy. It was for this reason we had decided to descend this way, expecting to get down it speedily. It all took so much more time than we could ever have imagined in a nightmare. Huge, loose blocks lined the way, threatening our every step. In our fatigue we were a danger to ourselves. We were both stumbling, trailing our legs and arms along, stopping to sit down at every opportunity.

'How many more abseils do you think it is, Dick, to the Col?' The Col at the top of the snow gully was the end of all our ambitions. From there we reckoned we could descend without using the rope.

'About three or four.'

'Do you fancy stopping for the night?'

He looked at me strangely: 'I thought you were serious for a moment.'

'I was, but it doesn't matter.'

We did another abseil, so long and steep and devious that I could not see Dick as I slid down the ropes, hanging free away from the rock. I wondered if he had fallen off the end of the ropes. He was sitting behind a rock. It was quarter to four.

'How many abseils now, Dick?'

'Not more than two.'

'You know we won't make it to the Col before dark and we can't descend that gully with the torch broken. Do you fancy stopping here and finishing the descent tomorrow? I'm knackered.'

'What's the matter with you?'

'I dunno, all the spit's been knocked out of me.'

We were on a shelf of shale and loose rock. We each levelled out a ledge and collected snow in polythene bags. These we were going to take into our sleeping bags to try to melt some of the snow by our own body heat in the night. I was in my sleeping bag first as Dick was still working away at preparing his ledge. We would both be able to stretch out full length here.

'Could have chosen a better place,' he was muttering, and then, as I was sinking into the torpor of rest, he spoke up.

'Joe, do you want to see a crystal vein?'

'What's a crystal vein?'

'One of the wonders of nature,' he said in the tone of reverence he used for mountains and things of the earth.

I was cosily established in my sleeping bag, my leg muscles were slowly relaxing for the first time that day, crystal veins were unnecessary to me and I had no energy for rising to look at one.

'No, it's all right.'

It seemed as if we might survive after all. We were a little more relaxed with each other that night and chatted briefly.

'What do you fancy doing next, Joe?'

I knew he was thinking about that ridge on Changabang. I did not know whether to believe his persistence and again I questioned myself as to whether I was more realistic and logical or whether I was inadequate and cowardly beside his undaunted determination.

'For me Dunagiri has given me everything I hope to get out of climbing for this year, and apart from that your hands are in a bad way. You'll have to get to hospital as soon as possible with them.' This last was absolutely true, but saying it to Dick, it somehow seemed like a lame and invalid excuse.

'I suppose you're right,' he said, as if it were a new thought.

I vowed never again to get far away from the basic essentials of life. Comfort was what I promised myself forever, total self-indulgence, never far from warmth and liquid and food. A life of ease, a life of luxury, was what I wanted and I would never put it at risk again.

In the night we woke several times to press moist snow from the polythene bags into our mouths to alleviate the dreadful sensation of burning. I dreamt of food again, dreamt that I was skivvying in the kitchens of a big hotel and could help myself to all kinds of choice morsels.

Dick dreamt that there had been an accident round the corner and that a helicopter was coming in to pick up the injured. He woke me to ask if I had heard the voices.

'No, but if you do see anyone, ask them to give us a hand as well.'

We were sleeping on the east side of the ridge so that we caught the first rays of sun. Some of the snow in my polythene bag had melted and I had resisted the temptation to swallow it all at one gulp. We found more bits of oats among the dirt in the bottom of our rucksacks and a few boiled sweets, overlooked in a pocket. We shared another of the snow mushes Dick had invented, and this one was quite moist.

I felt fortified enough at the knowledge that we were almost certainly going to live now, and that by the end of the day we should be in safety with food and drink, so that I found myself able to consider someone other than myself. Dick handled everything tentatively, and I knew that he was in constant pain from those black finger-ends. They were a strange sight, incongruously dark where normally there was white flesh, and it was not the surface blackness of a bruise or blister but blackness deep as the bone. It was as if alien growths had come out of him which he needed to be rid of but which were part of his own flesh.

I tried to convey some sympathy by a question:

'Are your hands painful, Dick?'

'It could be worse.' And that was all he said. There was no complaint, no looking for sympathy, and I did not ask again.

Dick was away again first. We had got into a routine in which he would put in a peg or arrange a loop of nylon round a rock spike and put the rope into it, then I would tie the knots and afterwards would pull the rope down to save more suffering from those terrible hands. He had started taking some Ronicol tablets which improve circulation and help prevent frostbite, though it was perhaps too late. He was taking Fortral too to kill the pain.

Pulling the ropes down after an abseil was exhausting; sometimes the rope caught on every little projection and flake. Somehow I had lapsed into letting Dick do all the thinking and leaned more and more heavily upon him psychologically; I did the physical tasks and he did the brain work. I was the hands to his mind. I felt as if all my climbing life had been a preparation for this; a constant rehearsal so that when this need arose every movement came automatically.

Descending on the ropes had become such an unrelenting chore that we could scarcely believe it when the last one was completed and we could scramble down over large terraces to the shaly slope and new snow leading to the top of the gully we had chosen to descend. This was a different gully from the one we had used to gain the ridge. It was just as long but looked much easier. Only another thousand feet down to level ground and back to the camp.

For all that it looked very easy I did not feel that I had the strength to hold myself upright, flexing my knees over and over again for a thousand feet downwards. The other side of the Col looked to be an easy slope and much shorter, leading down to an upper branch of the Ramani glacier. The glacier appeared flat and free from crevasses. To descend to that glacier would mean a longer walk back to Base Camp but it would be a quicker way to reach level ground on which to walk upright.

I mentioned my thoughts to Dick but he was not interested. Suddenly he was anxious for his hands and he preferred to descend the gully, on his backside if necessary, to reach the tent at our Advance Camp where there was food and a stream.

So we parted. In the back of my mind, as I stepped off downhill, I could see the pundits muttering about the folly of separating like this in the mountains, and I could see the wise, grey heads of the Mount Everest Foundation Committee wagging their disapproval in an attitude of 'We told you so; it was too much for the two of you'. If anything should happen to either of us there would be never-ending recriminations about our splitting up and dividing our forces. I was talking to myself; they would just have to understand; I was pleading that there was not enough elastic left in my legs to bend them and straighten them up after each step so many times descending that couloir.

I called after Dick.

'Will you be all right on your own?', a pang of doubt surfacing in me.

'Yes, will you?'

A sense of cheerfulness grew inside me as I moved rapidly down the gentle angle of the snow, and imagined myself only a few minutes away from being able to walk erect like a human being and from finding a rivulet of water on the surface of the glacier. Still five hundred feet above the glacier I noticed a rocky band cutting across the snow slope below me. I reached it and looked over the edge to discover that it was a cliff fifty feet high with no way of avoiding it. Numb with shock and horror I collapsed, defeated.

On the crest of the ridge there was now no sign of Dick. It would take me days to climb back up to where I had last seen him, I felt so weak. I had no pitons, or lengths of nylon, no gear at all save the rope, my axe and hammer. I took off my sack and scrambled backwards and forwards searching for a projection of rock, anything to which to fasten the rope. The rock was all broken, shattered and insecure.

I discovered a crack in which was lodged a small rock. I picked it out and wedged it back into the crack more securely. From my hammer I detached the thin line by which it was fastened to my waist, and made a loop with the nylon round the rock. Through the loop I threaded the rope and was gratified to see both ends reach the ground below the cliff.

I slid down the rope and retrieved it. After that I made no further pretence at walking. On my backside I slid down the remaining slopes of snow and shale to the edge of the glacier.

The crevasse, where the more level ice of the glacier met the steeper slope I was on, was covered in snow, its existence marked by a shadowed depression. I could not judge whether the snow covering the hole would hold my weight when I stepped onto it. I hesitated, staring at the concealed crevasse, wondering whether it had a benign or hostile personality, whether it was going to swallow me up or allow me to pass safely over it.

I advanced at a crouch, waving uselessly in front of me my short-shafted ice axe; it was too short to probe the snow. I crossed the crevasse at a run and felt elated on reaching the other side, as if I had won a great victory. I took off my rucksack and sat on it to celebrate the achievement on the edge of the great white desert stretching out ahead which I had to cross.

This desert was flat, absolutely flat and glaring white. The snow was crisp under foot and firm; I took it for granted until I sank into a soft patch and the surface broke at every step. Then it was firm again. I walked towards a bend in the glacier where it swept round a small peak towards Changabang and the valley down to Base Camp. Changabang looked nearer; much time seemed to have elapsed. I stopped, sat on my rucksack and glanced back to the slope I had left. It appeared to be only a hundred yards away. I never looked back again.

Every so often I stopped and sat. It became as much of an effort to raise my rucksack from the ground and put it back on my shoulders as it was to walk. I needed to rest frequently, so after a while I just flopped down into the snow without taking the rucksack off. A brilliant sun burst down out of a clear blue sky. It was all so silent.

At one point there swam into my vision, insidiously and suddenly like a shark, a sharp undulation in the snow which marked a hidden crevasse. I trod warily lest it came any closer, but it swam by harmlessly.

It was folly, utter folly to wander about alone as I was on this glacier with the danger of falling into a deep crevasse, concealed beneath the surface snow, and of dying there, lost without trace. The decision to come this way, to separate from Dick, had been the decision of a mind deranged from thirst, hunger, cold and physical deprivation. Had there been the two of us, we could have stayed roped together and proceeded cautiously, well separated in our tracks, so that if one of us fell into a crevasse the other could hold him on the rope and effect a rescue. But now was no time for regrets. I was committed and there was no way back.

My only remaining sunglasses were a very cheap pair and had become hopelessly scratched, so my clear vision was limited to only ten yards. I strained my eyes frequently, peering ahead to check my course; the glare on the snow from the sun was too painful to allow me to leave aside the sunglasses.

I was nearing the bend where the glacier turned sharp right into the main valley back towards Base Camp when I remembered spotting from on the mountain, some crevasse shapes in this region. Two of them drifted into view. I skirted them on the left and was congratulating myself on my escape when dimly, and so bizarre that I was startled, there appeared, down to my right, at the centre of a concave bowl, a circular crevasse hole. I had never come across a circular crevasse before and could not judge its size, whether it was large or small, or how far away it was. I circled uneasily round it, watching lest it did something unpredictable; I was drawn, mesmerised, irresistibly, into its vortex. I continued circling until out of the corner of my vision I glimpsed some rocks on the glacier far away. My brain registered that rocks on glaciers can mean water and the trance was broken, my gaze snatched away by the distant rocks.

A great flat table of rock sat on a column of ice. The water formed by the rock absorbing the heat of the sun and melting the ice around it had run into a pool at the bottom of the column. A crust of ice covered it, untouched as yet by the day's heat.

My axe, short-shafted and useless as a walking stick, had dangled on its strap at my side or caught between my legs, not really knowing its purpose on the glacier. Now it asserted itself and in a few blows had broken through the crust of ice.

From my pockets and the bottom of my rucksack I scooped up a dirty palmful of oats, from when we had had muesli, two squares of chocolate and two boiled sweets. I had nothing else. I mixed half the oats into a mugful of water, ground up the sweets and chocolate and settled back against a rock to savour this heavenly mixture.

Liquid, cold, wet and liberal spilled into my mouth and out of the sides. I spooned up from the bottom of the mug the thicker sludge and then several spoonfuls of the thinner liquid from the top to spin out the delicious concoction for as long as possible.

I was aware that there seemed to be an American family standing a few paces away staring at me. A young boy said to his father, with a note of distaste: 'Why is he making such a scene about that mixture as if it was something great?' The whole family wittered on in silly chatter. I rose to refill my mug; it came as no surprise to find there was no family there at all; they were only in my mind.

Changabang loomed above me; the south-west ridge which Dick and I had contemplated climbing looked magnificent, and fearfully hard; far too difficult for us, I thought, and the incredible, ice-smattered precipice of its west wall was so smooth it made me think of a cinema screen on which there would never be any actors. I took a photograph, thinking that someone might want to attempt to climb the mountain from the west some day. The photograph was not for me. Dunagiri had done for me. I had had to drive myself to limits I never wanted to reach again and I was certain that I would never be going to any mountains again, let alone the Himalayas and something as awe-inspiring as that great wave of rock with ice dripping from its crest that was Changabang. I drank more mugfuls of water and settled back for a rest, sheltering myself from the sun with my down jacket.

After the second mugful of liquid and the last of the 'mixture', I knew I was saved. All that remained was graft, sheer hard work for several hours. I knew I could do it, knew that much as I disliked hard work I was capable of doing it. The long years of self-discipline in the seminary had left me with the knowledge that I could put up with things I did not like for a long time. There were no more major obstacles. I would make it eventually.

At 1.00 p.m. I left, reckoning that five hours of daylight should be enough for me to reach Base Camp. Various other people, apart from the American family, were with me now, all wandering along near me and watching with interest.

When I reached the long, low ridge of rocks along the edge of the glacier I recalled Dick mentioning that he had seen a rough track along the rocks. I left the glacier, stumbling over the boulders, into holes and against mounds. I did not usually decide to rest, it just happened. I could not force myself to keep going for ten minutes, nor even five minutes with the promise of a rest for an equal length of time as I had been walking. I would just find myself reclining after perhaps fifty yards with my rucksack resting on a rock, appalled at the thought of settling it onto my back again.

It occurred to me several times to stop where I was for the night, but the mountain wall near which I was walking was continually spilling off rocks and although I felt in harmony with nature, with the mountains, with the world, with those falling rocks, I knew as an instinct that I could not stay near where they were coming down.

I could hear the American family complaining about my being slow and wondered why they did not offer to carry my rucksack for me, for it was that which was slowing me down. They never offered and for some reason there was a barrier of silence between us.

I could hear the down-to-earth comments of Maurice about this escapade. He was a worldly-wise transport driver we had met in Iran. He had advised us to set fire to our van if it broke down and collect the insurance.

Old Willie was with me too, the dustman from Dundee. 'Be careful lads, but you'll be all right,' he was saying.

Then the comments of the Americans made me think again of my sack and like the resting there was no decision. I left my sack and the rope by a rock, building a cairn of stones to mark the spot. There was nothing in the sack I needed, since there was a sleeping bag at Base Camp. It was 4.00 p.m. and I set off anew, trailing thoughts and fantasies like streamers in my wake.

Vaguely I knew where I was, I could see Dunagiri now, that old adversary appearing from behind the small peak I had been skirting round. I could not quite locate the exact spot which I was searching for to give me my bearings until I tumbled down a rocky slope and into a grassy bay. It was the head of the narrow valley running straight down to Base Camp.

It was only another half hour to Base Camp, all downhill to home, and Dick too, if he had not stopped off at the tent of Advance Camp. I wondered what his purgatory had been and hoped that he was all right.

When I reached Base Camp there was no sign of Dick, so I presumed he had stopped off at the tent where there was also food and running water. It got dark before I could find matches. I gorged myself on cold tins of fruit and rice pudding, relics from Peter's brief sojourn. I ate indiscriminately, discarding part-eaten tins as my teeth hurt with the cold of the contents. I settled down into the shelter we had made from rocks with a roof of clear plastic.

I could not sleep. Beside me I kept a pan of water and by touch alone I found other foods and sweetmeats to nibble at. I glowed with the ecstasy of life. Thoughts fizzled round my mind, ricocheting and bursting with sparkling trails. I stirred myself to leave the bliss of the sleeping bag, feeling an insistent nagging in my bowels. And suddenly I was running out of the shelter, tearing at straps and zips but too late. Embarrassed, I found I was coated in faeces; my body had not known how to cope with food after so long without. I had no energy left to undress. I closed the zips and returned to bed.

I lay on the grass soaking up the morning sunlight expecting to see Dick arriving at any moment. He was never one to stay in bed. I knew he would have been up at dawn. Lazily I made drink after drink, ate wantonly and scoured the narrow cleft of the valley down which I anticipated his arrival at any time.

Doubts began to gnaw at me. It was a couple of hours at most from Advance Camp. If he had stayed there the night, had food and water, he would have been fit enough to get down by 9.00 a.m. It was impossible to imagine Dick lying in bed enjoying a rest and a long lie-in. By 11.00 a.m. I was very worried. I began to visualise him lying at the bottom of that gully with a broken leg – I could not bear to let myself think of him as dead.

I resolved to leave by noon with a rucksack of food, fuel, stove, clothing, everything he would need to survive lying at the foot of the mountain until I had had time to race out to the nearest village and bring help to carry him down. Mentally I was reconstructing a scene of what I feared to have happened.

I glanced up every time I packed another item into the rucksack, hoping and hoping, gripped round the heart by a black foreboding. Then I saw him, or saw movement which had to be him, and I tried to run, but it was a breathless hobble and I met him part-way up the valley. I pulled his sack off his shoulders and put my arm round him.

'What's the rush, Joe, what are you so excited about?'

'I thought you might have had an accident, I was really worried. You've been so late coming down.'

He looked as if the thought of anything untoward happening had not occurred to him. Then I noticed he was carrying a stick I had taken up to Advance Camp. I had picked it up on my way in to Base Camp and had become attached to it.

'I see you've brought my stick down.'

'Yes, well, I slipped in the bottom of the gully and I seem to have sprained my ankle. I've been using it as a walking stick.' Then I realised he was limping.

We sat on the grass outside the stone-built shelter and I plied him with drinks. He told me how he had been up at daybreak but his boots were frozen. Once out of the boot his ankle had swollen up, and he could not get the boot back on until the sun came and thawed the boots out. Then it took him an hour with his frostbitten fingers to get the boots fastened, and he had been slow once he got moving as his ankle was painful.

'What was it like getting from the gully to the tent?'

'Horrible. I couldn't decide which way to cross a really bad area. Then I heard your voice telling me which way to go and it was the right way.'

He was very anxious about his hands. The fingers were black at the ends now and I could sense some of the dismay he felt at the thought that the thing he held most dear, climbing, would be curtailed if some of the fingers had to be amputated.

I cut away the tattered remnants of gloves which still clung to his hand, cut away loose, dead skin from around the blackened ends and cleaned up each finger, sprinkling them with antibiotic powder before dressing them with light lint and finger bandage. On top of the dressed fingers on each hand I eased a large silk glove.

We had some antibiotic tablets remaining and Dick started to take a course of these to discourage infection. We were not sure if it was the right thing to do but it was all we could think of.

He wanted to leave next day to get to hospital as soon as he could. I knew now he was in pain. The keys to the car and our money were up at Advance Camp. Late in the afternoon, I left to go back to the tent. I had little strength left for such an effort but also I was reluctant to break the relief of being together again, and the spell of being considerate to each other in a way we had not been before. We were like lovers after a quarrel, seeing depths of feeling in the other person previously unsuspected.

It was night before I returned. I brought back with me the tent and everything else I could carry to save my going back up again. I still did not have full control over my movements and my mind roamed free as I picked my way back across the outlandish badlands, apprehensive and unnerved under a full moon, until I came upon the familiar grassy valley down to home.

Dick chose to sleep away from me that night so that he would not disturb me with his restlessness and groans of pain. He left next morning after I had changed his dressings, hobbling off with a long ice axe which we had brought for the Liaison Officer as a walking stick, and promising to organise and send three porters in to carry out all the gear. I was to gather it up and pack it all ready for their arrival.

I had no way of checking the passage of days. Each day I tried to write a sentence in my pocket diary just to note that a day had passed, but I had no notion what the date was. Sometimes I was not sure if I had noted a day's passage or not.

The fastest I expected the porters to arrive was in four days. On what I thought to be the fourth day I noted: 'Porters didn't arrive.'

Fifth day: 'Porters still not here.'

I finished reading the few books we had brought with us to pass the time. I set off one day to walk back up towards Changabang and take some photos, but my feet were very painful and my throat still extremely sore. I did not go as far as I had intended. I bivouacked out and took some photographs by moonlight, and returned next day after collecting the rucksack I had dumped several days before.

I sat outside the shelter.

Sixth day: 'Still no porters.'

I had no sense of loneliness during this period. I was not alone because I had been rejected by other people. There was a purpose in my being where I was, and if that entailed being on my own too, it was tedious but did not arouse any anxiety or self-questioning.

I spent hours trying to trap some unseen creature which had raided my food store in the night. It had eaten into an opened tin of delicious pork I was saving for the next day, and carried off the remaining piece of fruit cake which I had apportioned out as a luxury to enjoy at the end of each evening meal. My dealings with the creature lasted several days. Fragile as my mental balance was, I began to feel in a state of siege. My toothbrush also disappeared.

I was lying on the grass, staring into the sky, when I thought I heard a

voice. I jumped up and scanned the lower entrance to the valley, imagining
the arrival of a loveable trio of hillsmen come to my rescue. There was no
one. Out loud I abused myself for hearing things.

I jumped up again when I thought I heard voices a second time and still
saw nothing. Six days of solitude, I thought, and I was talking to myself
and hearing things. I ignored the chattering which I thought I could still
hear. Then I saw some figures descending the rocky hillside from a different direction to where I had been looking.

There were only two of them. They were expecting a third. I made them
welcome and offered them food to eat. There were several tins which it was
pointless to carry all the way back. They opened them all and gorged
themselves, wasting a good deal.

The third porter did not arrive. I had to abandon some of the gear and
re-pack the loads, promising extra money by sign language.

The two porters seemed related. One was strong and capable, the other
was thin, more elegantly dressed and started asking for things straight
away. When we set off the next day, the thin one could not carry very much.
I was very weak myself and had all that I could take in my sack. The strong
one shouldered more from his partner, but whined demands for gifts of
clothing.

It was a demoralising progress. We lost time with constant complaints
from the thin one; he indicated that he felt dizzy on the track along steep
hillsides and could not carry a load. I began to build up a resentment for
these two. I softened when the thin one hurried up from behind and handed
me the crash helmet which had fallen from my sack and tumbled down the
slope.

They stopped frequently to smoke and inevitably we did not get far. We
had to stop in poor camping places beside the track. Next day it was the
same halting progress. They started the day smoking hashish and did not
seem to want to move at all. I hassled them on but we had to camp at the
foot of the steep slope I had had to climb when ill with toothache.

In the night it snowed. Six inches of snow fell on the tent and was thigh
deep on the slope up to the pass before we reached the top. The two porters
insisted on abandoning their loads; they could hardly keep their footing
under the heavy weight. They buried them under a rock somewhere in the
middle of that vast, uneven hillside.

At the top of the slope, on the plateau, conditions were worse. It was no
longer steep but the cloud was thick and the falling snow flakes were dense.
I tried to go ahead to break the trail, since I had better footwear, but I had
no idea what to make for. The plateau steepened and became a series of
ridges. The strong porter shouted unintelligibly and pointed at an indistinct rock feature. I tried to follow his directions. He grunted again but did
not wait this time, going off ahead himself. Sometimes I saw him pause and

peer into the swirling mist. A darkening in the mist denoted some rock on the mountainside, and taking his bearing somehow from what he saw, he would surge forward again. I hated this tedious, exhausting battle, in a direction I was unsure of and for a length of time I had no way of guessing. The direction he was following went across a more and more precipitous series of ridges. I could only guess that he had herded sheep or goats this way and was familiar with every contour and every rock, even when covered in snow. We came over a final ridge and started to descend. I could not guess how he had found this point, and it was dark by the time we started on the descent.

We stopped by some huge boulders and dug out two hollows in the snow beneath them. We had no tent, but I was still carrying my sleeping bag. I was passably warm, but could hear the two porters chattering all night, wrapped only in a blanket which caught the falling snow in its folds. I shared with them a tin of meat I was carrying and some sweets.

At first light we started down. His mountain sense deserted the porter and by following his directions about how best to reach the village he lived in we became entangled in dense thickets and caught up in thorn bushes. My clothes were in shreds by the time we came into the village in early afternoon.

The two porters disappeared. Someone gave me some tea and chupatti. The headman came over with a villager who could speak some English. I had almost written off the chances of retrieving the gear, now that the first falls of winter snow had arrived, but the villager announced with grand gestures that he would lead men to recover it. I agreed a fee and the headman suggested that a goat be sacrificed to offer up thanks for our safe deliverance from the mountains. I was touched by the gesture but checked first who would pay for the goat. A bony finger pointed unwaveringly in my direction. The headman, by gestures and cast-down looks, showed his sympathy for my partner, Dick, whom he had obviously met. He made sorrowful gestures of chopping at the ends of his fingers, indicating his view of what would happen.

I visited the doctor at the army camp who had treated my tooth.

'Poor fellow,' he said. 'I told him he would have to have them chopped off. They are quite gone.'

I could imagine how traumatic such comments would have been to Dick and how he must be questioning still the chances of his ever climbing again if his finger-ends had to be amputated. I did not know where he would be by this time, but I journeyed on to Delhi when the abandoned gear was eventually retrieved.

I became ill in Joshimath with severe stomach pains which kept me prostrate and helpless in that same room in which I had nursed my toothache so many weeks ago. When I drove down the Ganges valley, and across the plains of northern India, I could not stop to eat, as food only made me more ill.

In Delhi I rang J.D. and he told me that Dick was in the military hospital. I met him there, lying in bed in a spacious and clean ward. Thankfully he had as yet had nothing amputated.

He looked grubby, and he explained that the nurses seemed reluctant to give him a bed bath as would be normal in Britain. We guessed that it was a taboo of the Hindu religion for a nurse to wash a man's body. He could not wash himself for fear of getting contamination into his fingers.

They put him on a drip feed of a glucose solution. It was designed to promote recovery of his tissues. He had lain for some hours after the needle had been inserted, feeling his arm growing heavier and fatter as the solution fed into it. The arm became so heavy that he could not raise it. He called a nurse. The needle had been wrongly inserted and the fluid was building up in his arm rather than being absorbed into his system.

Painful as it was to his sense of thrift, he resolved to take a plane back to Britain to get treatment there. For me the prospect of spending another three weeks driving before I got back seemed like entering a long and endless tunnel.

V

I advertised in the Tea Rooms of Connaught Circus, in the centre of Delhi, a place much frequented by travellers, a place in the van back to Britain for $150 or £70. I had very little money left and on my own had not enough for the petrol. The van was discovered to have a fractured piston when I was having it serviced ready for the return journey. There was no piston available to replace it and even had there been it would have cost far too much. The mechanics welded up the piston and I left with my passenger, a New Zealander called Donald, on his way to Cardiff to play the violin in an orchestra and taking the overland route in order to see something of the countries on the way.

It was November, cool at night but pleasantly hot in the day. Donald appreciated the amenities of the van, the books he could read while I was driving, Dick's classical music and a tent at night.

I was wise to many of the ruses and pitfalls of the road after having travelled along it once. To drive up to the Khyber Pass we were asked to pay a toll. We had no Pakistan currency left. I offered dollars, the officials refused, there was no foreign exchange counter. I promised to pay at the border where I could change money, we were allowed to pass and not troubled again.In Afghanistan I had learnt the Urdu numerals from one to ten. It helped to keep check on the petrol pumps and of how much we were charged. A favourite trick was for the pump attendant to say how much was owed and once the money was handed over, by very deft sleight of hand, the notes somehow were changed to ones of lower denomination though of a similar colour. Being strangers to the currency it was usual to suspect oneself of making a mistake and to pay the extra demanded. It was the eagle eye of Dick that had spotted this trick and thereafter I enjoyed the predictable confrontation each time we had filled up in Afghanistan and paid the exact amount only to be confronted by a so-plausible request for more, from an innocent and hurt-looking attendant, appealing to the policeman who gazed on the scene impassively. Donald came to think I was very shrewd and cavalier to stand up to all these tricks, but it was simply a matter of experience.

We reached Kabul at evening and drove down a street towards the rest-house which Dick and I had stayed in. As I pulled onto the main street I was flagged down by a policeman. He pointed to a sign and someone from the crowd that soon gathered explained that we had driven down a one-way street in the wrong direction and were being fined $20. Donald said he did not remember any such sign at the other end of the street. I protested that I could not be expected to read Urdu. I was told that $10 would do. I insisted on seeing his superior officer. The policeman squeezed into the van with us and we drove down dark alleyways to the walled enclosure of the police station. I refused to drive inside and left Donald in the van with instructions about going to the British Embassy if I did not appear in an hour's time.

The superior officer looked as if he had been summoned out of bed. An interpreter came in too and they both sat on the opposite side of a dusty table in the dimly lit room. The traffic policeman explained his case in Afghan. My 'offence' was explained to me by the interpreter.

My cash was concealed in a money belt under my shirt. I asked if they would take traveller's cheques, knowing they would not. I could not pay the fine until I went to the bank next day and changed some money. They demanded my passport. I needed it for changing the traveller's cheques in the bank. It was like a game of chess. I offered my International Driving Permit as guarantee that I would come back next day. They knew as well as I that it was worthless as such a security. Stalemate.

'Have you got no cash?'

With a dramatic gesture I flung my loose change of mixed currencies onto the table. It was worth only a few pence, and I pulled my pockets inside out to illustrate my lack of any more.

With a wave I was dismissed. The officer had grown bored with the game. I left and drove back into town with Donald. Later we checked that street-traffic was flowing both ways and there was no sign of any kind at the other end.

We had trouble with the van in trying to leave Kabul. I had to buy a new dynamo costing £40. It would not start in the bitter cold mornings. I had to hire a taxi to give us a tow. One demanded an extortionate $20 in payment. I disagreed. He drove off with the climbing rope which I was using for the tow. Three times we tried to get on our way, each time we came limping back. Ominous screeching sounds came from the engine before it started and for a while afterwards. Gradually I came to terms with the idea that the van was not going to make it back to Britain. Donald was very decent about it. I returned his money and he lent me £90 as now I was flat broke.

It is difficult to leave some countries if it is stamped in your passport that you entered the country with a vehicle. This is to prevent a black market in motor cars. In Afghanistan it is possible to make a gift of a vehicle, if it is in working order, to the government. This I resolved to do. Providing the engine was warm, no unhealthy sounds emanated from it. I reckoned I could pass it off as in working order.

A Turk in the rest-house I was staying in was appalled that I should be so generous to the government. He had some involvement with a bus company, Akel Tours, which ran coaches all the way from Kabul to London, and he promised that in return for the van he would give me a seat on the bus and fix all the formalities about transferring the vehicle onto his passport.

It took two days of bribes and official fees to complete the arrangement, but it was done. I only hoped he did not want to start the van before I left. I went to the main hospital in Kabul and sold a pint of my blood for £5. It felt like manna from heaven. The easiest money I had ever made. Things were beginning to go right at last.

There were fourteen items of baggage when I packed up everything out of the van. All my gear, Dick's gear, the tents, a huge and heavy kitbag of gear from an English climber who had asked me to take it in the van since he was returning by public transport and did not want to carry that weight about. I was charged the equivalent of an extra seat for all the baggage I wanted to bring with me.

The coach was only half full when we left Kabul. There was plenty of room to stretch out and relax, the gear all packed beneath the floor and someone else to do the driving. A bus all the way to London was the answer to all my prayers. I had parked the van in a courtyard. The Turk was mightily pleased with his acquisition, but I never saw him try to get it started. I felt a criminal thrill of relief at my escape when the bus pulled away.

The journey has become a blend of sunsets across deserts, long hours gazing into space day-dreaming and tragi-comic interactions between the random companions of the bus. It was some time during that journey that

I started thinking of that impossible wall on Changabang. It was far away now, distance and time softened its features and inclined its precipices to an easier angle. It certainly seemed an interesting wall to examine. I found I was trying to guess at how it would be in the middle of the wall; whether it was as smooth as it appeared or whether its size dwarfed every feature and that in reality it was a huge staircase. On the other hand, I had been told that the meaning of the name 'Changabang' was 'slippery' or 'smooth'.

Somewhere along the road I met some friends from my home town of Teesside. They told me that some mutual friends were going to Changabang the next year. The news made me suddenly eager to get back to Britain to see what they were planning. I presumed that they were aiming to try that wall on Changabang.

I chatted to Donald on the bus, trying to reassure him that he had not seen the last of his money, and that I would pay him back as soon as I reached Britain. I had none at home either but from somewhere I would borrow it.

At first we were sitting just in front of the back seat. Behind us I could hear a conversation going on in a harsh, strange language. I glanced round to catch sight of the people talking and to guess at their nationality. There was only one person visible. I presumed the other was lying full length on the seat.

The bus journeyed on through the night. We had been assured that there were always two and sometimes three drivers to relieve each other so that there was no need to halt. The bus was empty enough to have a seat each to lie on. The guttural chattering continued. A broad-shouldered, blond-haired youth appeared to be having an endless conversation with himself. I lay full length on the floor of the coach sleeping soundly. Objects fell to the floor around me and I presumed they had rolled off seats. I was woken by someone protesting: 'Sven, stop throwing things about.' Sven was the lad who had been talking to himself, and we began to realise that he was affected by something more than a heavy intake of hashish or opium.

At the border we had to empty the bus of everything. I was preoccupied with my fourteen pieces of luggage, having them checked by the customs official. The Afghan border post is a clay-daubed brick building in a dusty compound surrounded by desert. Without any hitch it can take two hours to complete the formalities. There was a commotion beside the bus. Two Americans were asked to help. Sven was lying inside the bus, stark naked, and refusing to leave. The American couple dressed him and carried him from the coach. He was limp and they supported his sagging body. He straightened up, his arms outstretched, and in clear English pronounced: 'I am the light, the light who has come to save the world.' He turned to his two helpers and told them he was all right now and they could leave hold of him. They let go and he crashed face down, arms still outstretched, into the dust. The ragamuffin soldiers of the Afghan army stood linking hands with each other, completely bemused. The Americans took complete control of Sven then and shepherded him round the numerous offices, getting his baggage checked for him.

When we left that border post we were all united on the coach by a common concern – Sven. The Iranian border post was five miles distant across no man's land. There are exhibit cases there of some of the means by which people have tried to smuggle drugs through Iran with a photograph of each individual involved and the heavy sentence each one received on being caught. It is an effective and alarming deterrent. We were all convinced that Sven's behaviour would immediately rouse their suspicions and that all our belongings would be gone through meticulously and the coach would become one of the vehicles we could see behind a wire fence with holes drilled through panels and the roof cut open.

By a miracle it did not happen. The police accepted the story of Sven being sick and the promise that he would be taken to his Embassy in Tehran to be repatriated. There was even little problem with all my baggage. I had to carry it all through the inspection room piece by piece and on my own because few travellers in the east will take the risk of holding any luggage which might contain drugs.

In Tehran there was no Icelandic Embassy. It was a holiday and the Danish Embassy would do nothing. Sven continued with us.

The coach filled up. We could no longer stretch out and sleep. We journeyed day and night in the same position. It became clear that we only had one driver. The American girl stood over him insisting that he stop after he had been driving almost continually for four days with only brief rests in Mashad and Tehran. This time he had driven thirty hours without stopping and was swaying over the wheel, causing the bus to swerve on the road. The scene became ugly when he produced a knife but some hours later we stopped by a small hotel and slept in beds for the only time on the whole journey.

Sven seemed to be losing more and more control of himself as the journey went on. It became clear that he had soiled himself and the stench from his clothing wafted down the bus. A Swedish couple took charge of him and washed him down at one food halt. Thereafter they took him away at every opportunity to oversee his toilet.

A couple from the Channel Isles told me their tale of woe about how this was the final blow to a holiday which had been their lifetime ambition. For years they had planned to visit Kathmandu and had paid their money for the coach all the way from Istanbul. In Herat, in Afghanistan, the driver had refused to go any further, thrown everyone off the bus and told them to get to Kabul to see about getting their money back. In Kabul they were told they would have to go back to Istanbul to sort it out and it was only as a favour that they were allowed to travel on this coach as their tickets had been bought from a different company, Viper Tours. The incidents with Sven were the last straw. They confided in me as someone of their own nationality who could understand their point of view. The only consolation they could find was that Sven was not violent.

The days and nights filed past the windows. At one period, in the dark there were commotions up towards the front round where Sven was sitting. The interior lights came on and I could see Sven erect, turned towards the passenger behind him, one of the Swedes. Sven was hitting him hard. A couple of other passengers jumped up and dragged Sven off. I noticed the arm of his seat had gone. The lights went off and we carried on.

The commotions immediately prompted the lights to come on. This time they caught Sven upright, his fist raised, drawn back ready to strike. The Swede was stating plainly, pleadingly: 'No, Sven, you must not beat me, this is the last time.'

Before he could be held, Sven lunged towards the Swede, who cringed back, but the driving fist opened into a spread of fingers and stopped short. Sven smiled, the tension snapped and the whole coach applauded with relief. He did not use violence any more.

In Turkey he had to be rescued from irate tea-stall owners whose rows of waiting glasses full of the black Turkish tea Sven had gleefully upended.

I last saw him being shepherded about Istanbul by the Swedes as I tried to sort out getting back to Britain. The coach was not going any further than Istanbul. Sammy, an oily Levantine, protested he had been trying to inform the Kabul office by phone for the past fortnight that he had not been sending buses to London for a month. It was a struggle to extract part of the money back; he maintained that the van must have been a private arrangement with the Turk in Kabul since I had no receipt. In the end I prevailed and shunned his offer of a coach to Munich. The Channel Isles couple tried to extract money for their aborted journey. They had bought their ticket from him but since at the time he was working for a different company he maintained he was no longer responsible for the actions of that company.

In the Pudding Shop near the Blue Mosque, which Sammy also seemed to own, I met a friend from university days. He was flying back next day to London. How I envied such mobility! I booked a seat on the Orient Express and the American girl said she would accompany me; she had had enough of buses. She was on her way back to America to marry a fiancé she had not seen for nine months.

In the railway station I was having problems getting all my baggage onto the train. Suddenly a white-haired lady waded into the confrontation spouting Turkish and the problems disappeared.

'They try it on, you know,' she said to me in English.

'Where are you going? We can travel together.'

So we made a trio: Vera, at sixty, returning from one of her solo excursions round Turkey, the American girl, going home to get married and myself, with hardly any memory of how I came to have so much baggage, nor where I had been.

We crossed a frozen eastern Europe with a compartment to ourselves. Vera vetted all who tried to come in. She let a ruddy-faced Yugoslav join us. He was seventy, he said, and pointed out of the window at his farm as we passed it. He plied us liberally with slivovic from an earthenware bottle he carried.

'I thought that's what it was,' whispered Vera, 'that's why I let him in.'

We had to vacate the train at Ljubljana when it broke down. When we boarded another six hours later we had no seats and the three of us reclined on top of my luggage spread down the length of a coach. Each border meant a passport check and baggage inspection. Dick's flute, shiny tubes of metal in a black case, roused most suspicion.

In Paris there is no connection between the two stations on opposite sides of the city. I persuaded a taxi driver to take me and all the baggage. He charged a franc for each item and tried to convince me that I had sixteen pieces.

At Dover I had to have porters to get the gear through customs on a trolley.

'How much do you want?'

'Treat us like a gentleman should, sir.'

In London Ken Wilson collected me from the station and all I could talk about was the journey. I phoned my parents to say hello, Don and Jenny to see if they could put up with me as a lodger again, and Muriel to see if she still wanted me. Ken scowled his displeasure at having his phone taken up for so long. It was not the cost – I was paying for the calls – he just felt out of touch with world mountaineering for as long as his phone was occupied.

FOUR

Figures on a Screen

CHANGABANG

I

Changabang had wormed its way into my subconscious; the days on Dunagiri were days of continual exposure to the subliminal presence of that stupendous mountain. It had been a thing of beauty beyond our reach, a wall of difficulty beyond our capabilities, it had been the obstacle which blocked the sun's warming rays in the early morning and the silent witness to my delirious wanderings. For days it had hovered on the edge of my vision and when I returned home it re-emerged on the periphery of my imagination.

I had candidly dismissed as impossible the chances of climbing the mountain from the west, certainly with a small team. The calculations and evaluations which I took to doing on the journey back were simply mental exercises; the team which had permission for Changabang were not after all going for the west side, which I had taken to be the most compelling objective. I do not know at what point my mentality changed from working out ways and means of climbing something like the west wall of Changabang as an academic exercise to the positive frame of mind of asking myself how I was going to do it and with whom. There was a period when it was a lonely dream whose substance I was unsure of. I projected a picture of that west face onto the sitting-room wall to a friend looking for a mountain to climb. I showed him the mountain and pointed out the wall without expressing any intentions, hoping for some critical appraisal to give me guidance by which to judge how much grounding in reality my dreams had.

The mountain had been in my mind and in my life for too long by this time for me to make a detached judgement on it. I did not know whether the idea of climbing it was a perfectly reasonable one or a fanciful dream with no basis in fact. I could not put a proposal to Dick. He was receiving treatment for his frostbitten fingers and it was uncertain as yet how much he would have to have amputated. It was too early to plan with him for another major climb.

From being a plaything of my imagination, returning to Changabang had become not only a positive wish but also an ambition to be fulfilled urgently, and my thoughts turned to the practical necessities. I needed a partner and we needed permission.

My days were free at this time. I had found work for the Christmas period in a cold store, working nights to load up wagons with frozen food for distribution during the daytime to freezer centres. It was a convenient occupation. I earned enough money to pay off the debts accumulated over the Dunagiri expedition and had had to make no long-term promises to obtain the job.

One day I called in to see Pete Boardman in the office of the British Mountaineering Council where he worked. During this visit to Pete, who was sitting with the attitude of a wild animal, caged by his desk, I mentioned Changabang and its impressive western facet. I was sounding him out for a sign of interest in it as a desirable objective.

I had first met Pete on a climb in the French Alps. The meeting was implanted in my memory by the circumstances of the encounter. He and his partner, Martin, had slipped past Dick and myself in the early hours of the morning as we stirred ourselves from a chilly bivouac. All that day we climbed as separate pairs a few hundred feet apart. We spent similarly unpleasant nights on inadequate ledges sitting out a prolonged storm and retreated together next day to escape the snow. We shared the work of rigging up abseils and pulling the ropes down to use again. We were almost down from the steepest part of the mountain. I was standing on a tiny foot-hold a few feet below the other three; there was no room for me beside them. Martin was pulling the ropes down when I saw the three above me duck. Instinctively I pressed myself close to the mountain, heard the rush and sensed the mass of an enormous block falling past, brushing my rucksack and tearing my axe free. The rope had caught on and dislodged the block. By a miracle we were all safe.

That was in 1971, apprentice days in the Alps. Subsequently I had bumped into Pete a number of times and saw him more often when he moved down to Manchester from his post as an Outdoor Pursuits Instructor at Glenmore Lodge in Scotland. I knew he had done good things in the Alps and wanted to do more; I knew he loved rock-climbing; I knew of a trip to the Hindu Kush he had gone on from university in 1972; I knew of course that he had reached the top of Everest whilst I was away on Dunagiri. But it was not these things which made Pete in my eyes the right person to ask about Changabang. It was not the record of achievements that I saw in him but the attitude of mind that I sensed. With some people it is not necessary to have climbed in their company to know that they are of the same inclination and share the same spirit as oneself.

When, in the December of 1975, I talked to Pete of Changabang, I could see that there was a conflict within him caused by his role in the massive machine of the Everest expedition, which, after the successful ascent, was still at the focus of attention. With lecture tours and frequent public appearances taking up all his time, he felt that he was living a life far removed from his basic wish simply to climb.

He was interested, as a climber, in the fantastic mountain I had described to him, but he was doubtful if he would be able to escape from the office for a second year running on something which would not court and carry with it the publicity which inevitably surrounds an ascent of Everest, thereby lending prestige to an expedition which climbs it.

Most importantly, however, he was keen on the idea of climbing the west face of Changabang, and the dream began to take form in reality.

Unexpectedly he received the blessing of his superiors and without further reservation took to his heart the whole project. He came to see the few pictures I had of the mountain, and I was conscious of my failure to take more. His questions were specific and practical: where was the line I thought possible? What height was the wall?

I had been enthusiastic in my effort to inspire him with the idea of the climb but I had never been so detailed in my analysis of what line we could take. It was the concept of climbing a seemingly impossible wall that attracted me, but faced with Pete's practical questions I felt vague and unconvincing and the project sounded implausible.

I pointed feebly to patches of ice and shadowy lines, indicating that it was not a completely featureless face we were looking at. But Pete was not sceptical, his questions did not express doubts but real interest and a growing fascination with the idea. He was not convinced of the likelihood of us climbing it but he too was interested to give it a try, to go and see what would be possible. It was the reassurance that I needed, the affirmation that I was not out of touch with the real world, unless Pete was equally mad.

We sought the comments of others whose opinions we respected and when they told us it was a preposterous idea and that we did not stand a chance we were suitably awed and said we would like to take a look anyway and see what the best way to climb it would be. But our dedication must have been equally awesome and inspiring as Doug Scott rang me and asked to come. He had seen the west face himself and told me that it was beyond the bounds of possibility, but he wanted to give it a try.

I had never thought of going with more than two and given the chance I realised that I was lacking in the confidence to perform alongside someone whose high reputation in the climbing world made me feel distant and dwarfed. Succeed or fail, I preferred to do so unobserved. In Pete I sensed a kindred spirit. The expedition was to be our own very private folly.

The expedition to Dunagiri had cost £1,600. One-third of that we had received in grants and the rest we had raised ourselves by working as teachers. The van had proved more expensive than anticipated and this time we decided to fly, the cost of travel being cheaper if the extra time available for working was taken into account. The overall cost we estimated as being slightly higher, approximately £1,800 due to air freight charges and the extra heavy equipment which we were taking. To raise money we had to speak about our plans with a conviction I did not feel. To counter the arguments about the impossible difficulty we were taking on, we said that we had to rub noses against it before we could give it up. To justify the risks we were said to be taking by going as a twosome, we evolved the theory of being contained in our own self-sufficient cosmos in which we had everything we needed for survival and without the errors and misunderstandings possible in relying upon others.

From the Mount Everest Foundation and British Mountaineering Council combined we received a total grant of £650. From the Greater Manchester Council we received £200, since we were both based in Manchester and the expedition was seen to be a credit to the city. We made up the remaining £1,000 or so from our own pockets.

I worked the unsociable hours of night shift in the cold store, and climbed badly at the weekends. I divided the days between sleeping and preparing for the expedition. To make it possible to go off on another expedition I seemed stuck in a dull routine which neither exercised my mind nor encouraged the forming of any satisfying relationships. I was alone. My relationship with Muriel had not survived the long absence of Dunagiri. I lived only for myself. Sometimes the life I was leading seemed empty and pointless without anyone to share it; it had all the trappings of adventure and variety but I wondered what purpose it all served if it was only for myself. Sometimes I wondered if it was only because I thought I would lose face amongst my peers that I kept on riding the merry-go-round I had stepped onto. Sometimes, in the deepest recesses of my consciousness, I wondered if there lurked the secret hope that permission would be refused and we would be given an honourable reprieve from our self-imposed trial. But the doubts and self-questioning did not take a form active enough to hinder my efforts to overcome the objections raised on all sides against our plans and to bring into being the expedition. Our friends in India once more pleaded our case to the Indian government, which at first expressed complete opposition to an expedition of only two people going to attempt a route as difficult as the West Face of Changabang. Finally they relented in their opposition and I felt anew the onus of responsibility and of the trust which those friends of Mrs Beaumont had in us.

Gradually the chaos of preparations was channelled towards a departure date; the team from Cumbria which intended to attempt the south face of the mountain agreed to take two heavy boxes of food overland in the truck they had bought, thus saving us the cost of some of the air freight. They were friends and would be on the mountain at the same time as us but completely out of touch. Our approach to the mountain would be the same for two days, and from there they would take a divergent path to swing round in a long arc to the other side of the mountain from us. Our two base camps would be only a few miles apart but separated by a huge and difficult ridge linking Changabang to other mountains. To reach one base camp from another would necessitate a major climb or a trek of two or three days.

I came to know Pete more and inevitably to compare him with Dick. There was a rivalry between us in our climbing, there was a mutual weighing up and assessment of each other. Pete's progress in life seemed to have followed a straighter course than mine. From obtaining a degree in English, he had gone on to take a teaching certificate in Outdoor Pursuits, and then to intruct at Glenmore Lodge in Scotland, one of the most prestigious instruction centres in Britain. His current job as National Officer for the British Mountaineering Council involved him in countless meetings about safety standards, access rights to climbing areas and a host of other topics related to mountaineering. He conducted himself in this job with a calmness and diplomacy which I believed I could never have found the patience for. I did not even understand the issues involved. As an active climber he had perhaps the most respectable occupation related to the sport that any of his peers would contemplate holding. As such he seemed to feel a certain self-consciousness about his role when in the more anarchic milieu of the everyday world of climbers. He constantly expressed amazement at the more outrageous escapades of those around him and, with an ingenuousness which disarmed everyone, sought tuition in the fantastical world in which he believed all but he were at home.

We all live with preconceptions of those around us and Pete saw me as belonging to the indefinable community of 'the lads', who seemed to be more at home with worldly affairs than he felt. He looked to me to introduce him to girls, amongst whom he always professed to be shy and with whom he sought only to make gentle conversation. But beneath the gentlemanly politeness and urbane diplomacy there was unsuspected forcefulness and determination when it came to mountains. He might be diffident about asking for a lift or borrowing a book but he had no hesitation in taking the lead on a difficult climb. As with many people, he showed more self-confidence when contending against himself than when meeting the challenge of interacting with people on a daily basis.

His girlfriend had returned to Australia when she had overheard him by chance discussing with a friend the possibilities of climbing Changabang, before ever he had mentioned his plans to her. She took as callous lack of consideration what was in reality the forgetfulness of an over-full schedule of meetings and travel and endless debates and repetitions associated with his work.

I was the demon who was drawing him away and I was under appraisal by his own close circle of friends who were concerned at what he was taking on. I sensed the unease of Pete's parents too when I called in with Dick to visit him at home and look at more pictures of the mountain. Pete pleaded ignorance of the workings of his new slide projector and with a confident assumption of my mastery of things practical I rapidly proceeded to set it to work. A fuse blew and molten plastic dropped from the projector onto the table. Having shown myself to be impetuous and clumsy within minutes of arrival, I felt more strongly the scepticism of Pete's mother and father whom I was meeting for the first time, and I was aware of their frequent, wordless glances towards Dick, who had developed the habit of keeping his still blackened finger-ends out of sight under his arms. I could imagine as if it was written up clearly that they were asking themselves what I would do to *their* son on this trip we were planning. The irrational guilt feelings I had over Dick's injuries and my own lack of damage surfaced easily.

Pete and I persevered with our preparations. From all that we could judge, there were no ledges large enough for a tent on the central steep area of the mountain. We planned to use hammocks to sleep in. Neither of us knew how seriously to take ourselves. We knew of no one who had tried to use hammocks on so high a mountain and in cold such as we expected. The question arose constantly – if the mountain was so hard, what chance did we have? It was like the game of 'chicken' – each person runs as close to a chosen danger as he dare and loses points by the extent to which he bales out before reaching the danger. Neither of us ever let himself express doubts in front of the other.

We tried out hammocks in the cold store where I was working, spending three particularly miserable nights in temperatures akin to those we expected to experience on the mountain. The hammocks were altered and improved in accordance with the lessons we learnt in the cold store, but to what extent we believed in what we were doing or were taken in by our own hyperbole is hard to say.

There was a certain credit attached to going ahead with plans to attempt 'the preposterous'; there was a seductive temptation to believe in the pre-expedition proclamations and pronouncements put out by journalists hungry for copy and based on our own brief prepared to explain and justify our intentions. I would rather have slipped away quietly to succeed or fail in private but we needed to explain ourselves in order to obtain permission and receive the blessings of the official bodies and we needed to justify ourselves to show we were worth supporting and had made a careful assessment of what we were doing. However it seemed to anyone else, I was too much aware that ahead of us was a test greater than any that either of us had ever undertaken to be able to obtain the slightest satisfaction from the approval of anyone. Rather, I was daunted by the faith which was shown in us.

I called home to visit my parents, who had come to accept my departures to the mountains as being more important to me than a mere whim. I knew that they had received a certain amount of satisfaction when for a brief spell they were able to describe me as a teacher in the months before I went to Dunagiri. However many doubts and anxieties they felt, they had never expressed any dismay that I should graduate from university only to spend my time odd-jobbing in order to pursue more fully the urge to climb mountains. Initially, climbing had been incomprehensible to them and they had expressed their anxieties in advising me to take up a more normal sport, but they became accustomed to my coming back and saw this bizarre pursuit taking me to many places, making me many friends, and giving me a rich store of experiences. I came to rely upon the moral support and the confidence I felt in knowing that they were interested in what I was doing and would help in any way they could.

They were never deluded, however, over the dangers which we ran in the mountains and I tried always to ease the pain of worry. One incident revealed to me the apprehension with which they listened to the news whilst I was away. When Dick and I had set off to climb the Matterhorn we heard that two Englishmen had been killed on it the day before. I rang home as soon as we got down to Zermatt under the pretence of saying hello and lightheartedly telling them we had climbed the mountain. I was not over-reacting and my mother probably guessed why I called. 'That's where two people were killed, isn't it?' and I tried to pass it off as if it was as remote from us and as unsensational as a road accident hundreds of miles away.

Always I tried to call home just before leaving to say a last goodbye which none of us admitted to being a possible final goodbye. Always I like to call home as soon after I return as feasible to take them some gifts from the places I have visited, to share with them some of the tales and experiences, to let them know that it was not all danger and to try to give to them something of the quality of my life which I believe to be enriched by visiting such distant places and climbing such difficult mountains. I want also to give them proof by my physical presence that I am really alive.

II

We left for India on 22 August and it was the first time I had been in an aeroplane. I could not help but think of the weeks I had spent on the road the year before and how effortless this was by contrast, and no more expensive, boarding a plane to arrive in a few hours back in the steamy heat of India at the tail end of the monsoon. I had not thought I would ever be back and yet, less than twelve months later, as normal as if it were a weekend outing, I was returning to Delhi, where nothing seemed to have changed. The streets still thronged with teeming crowds of people, the vendors in the bazaars still tugged insistently at our sleeves as we walked past, and Mr Sony still sat outside his guest-house where Dick and I had stayed. His guest-house was full so we booked into another one nearby. This was just as cheap as Mr Sony's and was frequented by impecunious travellers on the hippy-trail. I felt as if I was introducing Pete to a side of India he had been cushioned from when he had passed through Delhi on the way back from Everest and stayed at the luxurious Inter-continental Hotel.

Nothing seemed to have changed at the GKW offices either. The staff greeted me with recognition and J. D. was holding court, as ever, behind his enormous desk with several attendants on hand making notes and running off to carry out his instructions.

Perhaps the single attribute of J. D. for which I most respected him was that he took us as we were. In a country where big means beautiful and wealthy and where small and casual means poor, J. D. did not register any reservation or diffidence to us. He made us feel that he had all the time in the world for us and that no obstacle was too great for him to sort out if we needed his help. He was a jovial Hindu who joked that he should come with us as a way to lose weight and alleviate his blood pressure. He had no conception of why we wanted to climb mountains, nor of what it entailed, but it was he more than anyone who, for a second time, had ensured that we were granted permission and given the opportunity to bring our dreams to reality. He wanted no thanks, and was embarrassed at a gift. 'It is my duty,' he protested. 'I was asked by my colleagues in England to do this for you.'

He ushered us on our way by train and ramshackle but sturdy bus up out of the heat of the plains to the Swiss climate of Joshimath. It was pleasing to meet again the acquaintances of the year before, Bhupal Singh of the Neelkanth Motel and Yasu, a sturdy youth of the hills. We delayed there with some of the friends who would be on the opposite side of the mountain, waiting as they were for their truck, with our two boxes of food. It was amusing to note the formation of a sub-group even out of their small team of six. Their leader was of the same age and background as they, but leadership had endowed him with a charisma which went beyond any rational explanation. The group of three who had come on ahead by bus had the definite air of charges who had escaped supervision, having been given an unexpected holiday through the delay caused by landslip some distance back along the road.

We retrieved our boxes when their truck arrived and slipped off ahead with fifteen porters and our Liaison Officer, Flight Lieutenant Palta.

We reached Base Camp in four days, a journey which for me was

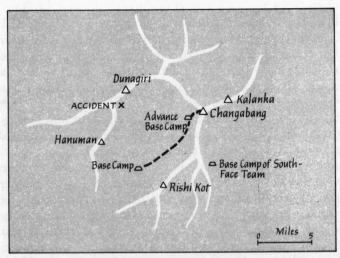

5. The route up Chàngabang.

nostalgic with memories of struggling out through deep snow less than twelve months before. Pete found it a delight, having read much about Garhwal, the Garden of the Himalayas. He showed an interest in flowers which set me to photographing them as well. He also expressed a patience and interest in our Liaison Officer which I did not feel. When I declaimed vociferously against the ignorant bureaucracy which imposed upon us an extra person who increased our costs, did nothing we could not have done ourselves and, having had a month of training in a climbing school, expected to be asked to climb the mountain with us, Pete deflated my arguments with an irritating placidity and spent time discussing with Flight Lieutenant Palta his views on life, religion and politics.

Our trip did not coincide with the image he had held of expeditions when he had volunteered his services; his attitudes appeared structured by notions of class or caste and his judgement of our expedition was influenced by his preconceptions about what was a fitting manner in which to live in the mountains for people of his and our standing.

I did not have any inclination to justify the manner in which we were doing things, and did not have any time for the diplomacy which enabled Pete to go along tolerantly with Palta's misguided notions that a month's tuition would fit him to climb a mountain we dreaded to confront after years of experience.

I felt a trace of reproach from Pete when Palta announced to us that he was so disgusted with the food we had brought, so disillusioned with the duties which we expected of him in sitting at Camp whilst we were on the mountain, that he wanted us to send him back to Delhi as soon as the march-in to Base was over. I was cold-humoured enough to think that it would be nothing but a relief to have only problems with the mountain to contend with rather than the extra problems of keeping a superfluous attendant happy and I resented all the formalities which we had had to go along with, all the façades we had to put on in order to achieve our simple ends.

Palta left with our band of porters and I walked up with Pete to look at Changabang from the vantage point at the head of the small valley, showing him the mountain as if it were a cherished possession.

The totem from my dreams of the year past confronted us, every bit as difficult, as impossible as when I had first seen it. A year thinking about it had done nothing to soften its severity, nothing to prepare me for facing up to it again in actuality. My resolve was very fragile at the moment when we stood gazing at the smooth monolith of granite, over five thousand feet high, smeared with ice. If it had been Pete who had brought me to this place, I would have shrunk less from the prospect of taking on the mountain; I would have assumed that he was either out of his mind ever to have contemplated such a thing or that he knew something I did not – either way he would be the fall guy. But Pete had come relying upon my judgement, trusting to my mountain sense, and faced with the climb I had enthused about I could not betray that inwardly I was horrified at what was before us.

He may have been shy in his personal relationships, diplomatic in committees and amenable in behaviour, but faced with a mountain to climb, when it was mainly himself he had to contend with, he showed no compromise. Whatever doubts he felt inwardly, none were expressed. Perhaps we both kept up the façades we had developed over the past year, even now when there was no other party to convince. We did not decide on a line we would try to follow all the way to the summit; we did not consider how to reach the summit at all. We discussed a way of reaching the crest of a small ridge which ran into the steepest part of the mountain one thousand feet above the glacier. From there we would be able to examine more closely the difficulties. We did not look too far ahead, lest the scale of the whole should dwarf and frighten us so much that we would hesitate to make the first step.

A lone Austrian, Hans, had trekked up to our Base Camp at the same time as us, upsetting all our Liaison Officer's credence in his role as a guardian of his country's border security. Hans enjoyed walking amongst and photographing mountains, apparently content with his own company, and wandered on when he had observed enough of one place. He left our camp after a couple of days and we were completely alone for the trial ahead.

III

We spent a week carrying food and equipment up to a camp close to the foot of the mountain. It was a four-hour walk from 15,000 feet to 17,000 feet, back along the route I had staggered down in my delirium from Dunagiri. The loads we carried weighed between thirty and forty pounds, requiring quite an effort at that altitude but providing a useful chance to adjust to the more rarified air, and accustom ourselves to rigorous physical exercise. It allowed us also to grow familiar with the mountain, and to scrutinise at different times of the day each little feature.

We came to accept the idea of being alone with each other. Dick and I had gone onto Dunagiri almost straight away, so I had not noticed the isolation so much. I knew Pete less and there were many idiosyncrasies we each had for which we both had to make allowances. I noticed how Pete used to make copious entries into a diary, so many that I could not visualise how he could do or say anything without the awareness that he was going to record that action or word. I had found after Dunagiri the value of recording the days as they passed, in order to keep track of time and I made one-line notes in the form of a diary. Pete was sceptical of the value of this at all as an aid to remembering events. I countered this by his own tactic of quoting, for greater authority, from other authors, saying that Graham Greene had written that as an author it was not trying to remember things that was difficult but trying to forget them. I could only just remember this saying and Pete was dubious about its authenticity.

We dug a ledge for a tent on the crest of the ridge where it ran into the steepest part of the west face. Above was the inscrutable wall, the first few hundred feet of which was not vertical and looked feasible to climb. Reaching the crest of the ridge had opened up a panorama of peaks, diluting to some extent the sense of confinement we both felt on the glacier, surrounded by steep slopes of ice or rock. I did not mind so much as Pete, who verbalised his frustration at having such a restricted horizon. Perhaps it was that I had surveyed the mountains for so long on Dunagiri and now I could see them in my mind's eye. Pete had read about the mountains, knew more about them than I did even though he had not visited them previously, and felt cheated that he had not even glimpsed Nanda Devi, which was shrouded in cloud when we were walking within sight of it. Partly I was defensive over his complaints, as if he was comparing 'my' mountains with 'his' mountains, the mountains he had been to before; partly I was apprehensive that his complaints were the beginnings of disillusionment.

We worked from the tent for days, learning more about the climb and about each other. We made progress sufficient to postpone any basic questioning about our overall chances of success. As the wall steepened, we made slower but still steady progress, fixing a line of ropes up from the tent, adding more ropes each day as we pressed on further, and slipping back down those ropes each evening to the haven of the tent. The days were hard but, dressed up in a routine, acceptable because we only had to think a little at a time.

The rock was sound granite, not loose and unreliable as on Dunagiri. Runnels of ice clung firmly to the grooves in the rock. Deciding which way to go was complex, and solving the problems of each section was both mentally and physically taxing. At first I felt conscious of Pete's critical observation when I led a pitch. I noticed an assumption of superiority in his performance and an authoritarian attitude in his climbing techniques and manoeuvres which I put down to his days of instructing. When I paused, working out a move, or summoning up the nerve to commit myself to an unpredictable position, I imagined him champing at the bit and thinking he could have led the pitch so much better or faster than me.

It was when not actually climbing that I noticed his inadequacies. He always took longer to arrange things to make himself comfortable, always found I had something or contrived something that he had not, such as a pillow from coils of rope, or my boots pushed together, and he gave off an air of being badly done by. He was nervous of situations where I relaxed, knowing that we had done all possible to make ourselves safe and dismissing as pointless any further worrying. Pete ended up sleeping on the side of the tent nearest the edge of the ledge and he often voiced his uneasiness at the thousand-foot precipice inches away from him.

We fell into a pattern of defined roles. Pete stirred himself first in the morning and made breakfast; I lingered in sleep, hiding from another day, for as long as possible. At evening I busied myself with the main meal, while Pete flopped into the back of the tent, glad to rest immediately from the day's exertions.

The climbing was mostly a delight, exhausting but enough inside our capabilities to encourage our optimism. We shared the leads, each of us leading four rope-lengths at a time. The difficulties, however, were time-consuming, so we only managed more than four rope-lengths on the first day, and Pete had been in the lead all day. After that it became normal for one of us to spend the whole day out in front whilst the other spent the whole day paying out the rope and following more rapidly the sections once the rope was in place.

I spent an afternoon on a ledge six inches wide and two feet long, while Pete moved upwards, ever so slowly towards a barrier of overhangs. The mist came in and he was lost to sight, though no more than a hundred feet away. Hours went by and I had no thoughts left to fill the time. The wind was too strong to let words be heard. I tried to shout information into the

Bivouac

Ramp

Kalanka

Hammock
bivouacs
2 and 3

C 2

Ice field

Overhangs

Hammock
bivouac 1

C1

Advance Base Camp

3. The line of our ascent up Changabang.

mist but heard no reply. There was little rope left to pay out and if he did not halt soon he would be stopped from moving further by the restriction of the rope. I could faintly hear scraping sounds of metal on rock and snatches of words shredded by the wind. I thought I could see a figure near the overhangs when the mist thinned momentarily. I untied the parts of the rope I was using to tie myself to pitons and spikes of rock, freeing a few feet more. Again the rope came tight but I heard the positive sound of a hammer firmly striking a piton and knew he was safe. It was late in the day, Pete arrived out of the mist, having anchored the rope to the piton at his highest point. He told me how hard and worrying it had all been up there in the mist, about the rock becoming increasingly steeper, the cracks getting fainter and how far he had had to go without any assurance of reaching a place to rest, tiring all the time, knowing that he was coming to the end of the rope. That was a worry and fear he was up to, that was when he came into his own, when facing difficulties he could solve by superlative skill and dangers he could ignore in the concentration needed to solve the problem, or put up with in the knowledge that he was committed to a test of skill which he welcomed. He was a different person when climbing from the one who slept uneasily by the side of a steep drop, no matter how securely he was tied in place.

It came about that the two most difficult pitches up to that point were in Pete's rota of leading. I spent three hours next day under the shadow of the overhangs, watching and freezing while Pete struggled, only feet away in the sunlight, to find a solution to the biggest problem we had yet met. The barrier of overhangs spanned the whole area above us. If we could not find a way through then we would have to start all over again. The previous day Pete had moved rightwards towards where the overhangs formed a notch at the top of the rounded corner where the wall curved out of sight. He had not seen round the corner, but had been forced in that direction by the impossibility of climbing leftwards or straight up.

Now he was exploring the unknown. I could see only the lower half of his body and hear his grunts and imprecations. He could not tell me more than that he could see the next few feet were all right, though difficult. The rest was out of sight round more steps of overhangs. I watched his legs twitch upwards out of my range of vision and heard him hammering more pitons in to aid his progress. I dabbled my own foot in the sunlight which touched the slab on which I was standing, a captive tied to the shadows, hoping some of the warmth would creep up my leg into my frozen body. I was disgruntled that it was my turn again to be second on the rope with none of the thrill of breaking new ground and not even warmth from physical exertion, but each of us had to accept a turn in this secondary role every other day. It had been absorbed into my subconscious many years before that physical discomfort was a valuable penance and I sometimes wondered whether our penances and frequent deprival of physical pleasure did indeed benefit our souls and make us better people.

I was frustratingly out of touch with what Pete was doing. No longer able to see any part of him, I became dissatisfied with his uninformative replies to questions with which I could not help pestering him. I longed to have a go myself, unable to comprehend why he was taking so long if it was, as he said, possible.

When at last I could move I was stiff with cold: I was clumsy and awkward in the contortions needed to follow the tortuous line of the rope through the overhangs and up to join Pete at the top of an icy ramp. Justifiably he was proud of breaking through that barrier, finding the vital link to bring us within reach of the vast ice field at mid-height on the mountain. Justifiably he expected praise and pragmatically I thought he had only done his job, much as he made breakfast and I cooked tea; another time it would be my turn and all I could manage was: 'Good lead, mate.' It was an enormous psychological boost to reach that ice field. We were halfway to achieving what we had thought might be impossible, and by the time we had skirted up its left edge and anchored the ropes to its top rim, our thoughts had changed to knowing that we could do it. The wall above the ice field looked equally hard and a huge tower looked more difficult still, but we had found confidence in the progress we had made and no longer had such doubts as we had started with.

It took almost a week of climbing every day to reach the top of the ice field at half-height on the wall. We had brought along a thousand feet of rope at Pete's suggestion to fix on the mountain. This was one of the results of his applying his mind to the problems of the mountain and based on his experiences of the value of fixed rope on Everest.

At the top rim of the ice field I stood drawing in the rope as Pete came up towards me. I had skirted the left edge of ice, which was green and hard, contriving a way up the little ripples in the smooth rock slabs at the side. It was a delicate tip-toe all the time on the verge of insecurity which I revelled in as each gamble of a move paid off. It was nothing like as strenuous as the pitches Pete had led earlier, but every few movements upwards had left me panting from the exertion. I watched Pete as he followed up the rope, retrieving all the intermediate anchor points, leaving only the main one at the bottom, since we needed to re-use the pitons and karabiners time and again. I held my camera ready with my eye to the view finder, composing the shot in the frame, waiting for Pete to move into a dynamic pose. The pose was not right but I took a shot in case something should prevent me taking a better one, and readied the camera again. He moved up, into a better position this time, I squeezed the shutter, but his head had sunk to his arm as he panted for breath, still not the pose I looked for, but it was real, showing the agony of climbing at altitude. Pete looked up, hearing the click of the shutter, and shouted: 'If you take another shot of me like this I'll come up there and thump you,' and the day turned black for me. I was sickened at what I regarded as a childish fit of temper; I wondered whether he only wanted photographs to be taken showing him in his best light; he already had pictures of me in similar pose. The fragile, often begrudging rapport which had held us together was for me destroyed; a sense of aimlessness and futility overwhelmed me; we were both far apart however well we had done so far with the climb. What little joy I had felt on reaching the upper edge of the ice field, our halfway stage, the confirmation that we could probably climb this mountain, all vanished. I felt empty and rebuffed. I looked forward no more to the upper part of the mountain, I simply wanted it to be over with.

Pete was repentant and I held back from catalysing the incident further, noting in my diary, 'This is no place for an argument'. I had had a glimpse of a Pete I had not suspected before, in whom there was anger so close to the surface, and knew that he too, despite the diplomacy and urbanity, was as subject to the stresses and strains of the mountain situation as anyone.

An element of non-cooperative, mute hostility arose in things which did not matter such as whose turn it was to make an extra cup of tea, but we were both aware of the strange circumstances in which we were living and of the inevitable tensions which were arising. It became a practice to defuse situations by putting a perspective onto confrontations by a comment relating back to normal life. 'Don't worry, it will be all right and won't matter when we get back down to the valley,' was a catch-phrase we both took to using.

Our days consisted by this time of several hours of tiring, anxious ascent up the hundreds of feet of the single line of rope we had fastened in place. Then hours of taxing climbing, with long, fraught abseils back down the rope, down more hundreds of feet, to the tent, at the end of the day. Under these circumstances we could not escape from strain; the high tension which sparked off arguments came from the same highly strung frame of mind which enabled us to keep up the concentration to solve the problems of the climb we had started on with such doubts. The magnificence of our situation, the beauty of the sun setting behind the cloud-wreathed Dunagiri, my old adversary, the deep blue of the sky on a cloudless day and the descent in the rosy glow of evening were all phenomena only partially observed, scarcely appreciated, in a corner of my mind and recorded by photograph for a time when I could view them in comfort.

We had not intended to make a line of rope all the way up the mountain, but thought we might have to prepare difficult sections first, fasten rope in place and then return for a mobile assault with the hammocks. All the mountain was difficult and we wished we had had more rope to leave in place. We added up all the lengths of extra climbing ropes we had brought with us and found we had nearly two thousand feet. We just managed to stretch this out to reach from Camp 1 on the ridge to the top of the ice field. From there we descended to rest and return with more food and the hammocks.

IV

Our stay at Base Camp was only overnight and we returned to the mountain next day. There had been a rumour in Joshimath that an American expedition was coming to attempt Dunagiri and would have a Base Camp near us. We had descended in anticipation of meeting them but there was no sign of anyone. The note we had left outside our solitary tent addressed to any passers-by was untouched. I re-wrote the note, changing the date of departure and expected date of return; I entered details of the point we had reached on the mountain. Of course there were no 'passers-by', our valley was a cul-de-sac ending at Changabang, but if we should disappear forever, without intending any melodrama, we were leaving details of our last location to avoid as many as possible of those uncertainties which make death in the mountains even more fraught for those one leaves behind.

For three weeks now Pete and I had known no other company. A little note from anyone who had trekked up to our camp would have delighted us; the discovery that we had new neighbours in the shape of another expedition would have let me feel that our partnership, though it seemed to us intense and jaded, had achieved much and was working well. Meeting more people would have brought more normality into our closed world.

We took hammocks back with us having, as we had suspected, spied no trace of a ledge wide enough to take a tent. On the way back we disagreed about the weather prospects. Pete had a similar drive to Dick, and seemed untroubled by any tendency to welcome an enforced delay in returning, so when we paused to contemplate the heavy cloud and snow flurries, he won the day as I knew that at least half of my proposal to defer departure was due to laziness. But bad weather did come in force. We were caught, late in the afternoon, hopelessly ambitious to regain the top of the ice field.

We had by-passed Camp 1, with loads much too heavy, and reached only halfway up the fixed ropes, before dusk and storm overtook us. It took three hours to produce one mug each of warm water with the stove perched exposed to the wind. Conversation was terse and to the point. We abandoned further wretched attempts at cooking in the wind and snow. It was time for the hammocks to be tried in earnest. We each attached a hammock by its single suspension point to the line of rope we had fixed in place over the previous week, and which we were now following back up the mountainside. Pete was suspended a few feet below me and I was pleased to notice that a large flake of rock protruded beneath me; I cherished the notion that if a falling lump of ice should cut through the rope whilst I was sleeping I might be caught on the flake or rock rather than fall all the way down.

The hammocks were the full length of our bodies. Three straps from each side were designed to hold a person securely in the hammock in a horizontal position. The straps converged on one point so that in such places as mountainsides where it is rare to find two convenient points to which to attach a conventional hammock, we could suspend the hammock from that single point. The material was nylon with a thin layer of insulating foam. We had brought synthetic sleeping bags to use in the hammocks, as down compresses too much under pressure and is then less effective against the cold. To cover the hammock we had a cape of nylon which draped over the straps and could be clipped in place with elasticated straps beneath the main part of the hammock. In the cold store we had found that we were crushed by the effect of our own body weights which tended to pull the straps together, so we had made some light alloy rods to hold the straps apart, but for our first night of using the hammocks in earnest we did not have the essential rods as they were up at our high point.

It was an awkward and uncoordinated night. Real mountain cold and discomfort made a mockery of using the hammocks. Inserting myself into mine was exhausting. I lay panting on my back, and struggled further to take my boots off. Any time my movements caused the canopy and the base of the hammock to part, gusts of snow-filled wind jetted in from the night. I tied my boots onto the hammock so as not to lose them and, still on my back, pulled my sleeping bag over my feet and along my body. I took a sleeping pill to deaden the discomfort and woke some hours later to find the foot of my sleeping bag hanging outside in the cold and my feet numb. The night stretched endlessly to that point in time when dawn would bring movement and the hope of warmth. Any change seemed desirable. Our situation could not have been worse. Snow squirted in through the slightest parting; I felt crushed by the hammock, and found breathing difficult.

I peeped out when a subtle lightening of the darkness signified dawn. The long journey through the night was over, but the world outside the red cocoon of my hammock and canopy was a world of wind, spirals of snow and heavy cloud. I shrank from the thought of moving into even worse cold.

It was not until 10.00 a.m. that Pete shouted from below: 'Are you getting up, Joe?'

'All right,' and I started the complex procedure of removing my sleeping bag and donning my boots whilst still lying on my back, in order to emerge fully dressed to face the day. Pete and I had conversed little during the last eighteen hours. His silence in the night I took to indicate his greater comfort over mine. He was calling again, so impatient I assumed he was ready and criticising my slothfulness.

I was closing the last zips and pulling back on my gloves when he shouted with real anger in his voice to ask why I was not up yet. I replied placatingly and pulled apart the canopy and hammock to step out onto the flake below. Pete was ten feet lower, still not completely clothed. He was bent double, his hands thrust into his groin, mutterings of pain escaping from his bowed hood.

'What's the matter, Pete, I thought you were ready?'

'I've been doing my boots up outside and my fingers have gone numb.'

He showed me his blanched fingers, holding up a hand as a palsied man might reach in supplication. He could not move his fingers easily, his face was taut with pain.

Immediately I forgave him his harsh words, my sympathy wiped away any trace of hostility lingering from earlier confrontations. I felt concern with no reservations, no embarrassment.

'How do they feel?'

He misread my concern for him as concern at the loss of a partner to climb the mountain.

'They're coming round now, but they're sore. Don't worry, it's not going to stop me.'

In doing up his boots outside in the wind he had lost sensation in his fingers, only realising that they were frozen when they failed to obey his thoughts. He winced in pain as the circulation returned and blood filled the damaged cells. His fingers took on a discoloured appearance. They were giving him pain each time he used them.

The incident served to focus our basic intentions in being on the mountain; whatever antagonisms might flare up, when it came to a real test of resolve there was no question but that we wanted to go on. I did not hesitate to let him see my concern, checking to make sure he could cope with each manoeuvre, packing down his hammock to save him bruising further his hands. It had needed an incident such as this to crack the shell of mute hostility which I had felt building up over the last weeks.

We made no attempt at melting snow for a drink, pressing on in the hope of finding a better place for the next night. We knew well that without a plentiful intake of liquid and food we would rapidly lose strength and would feel the cold all the more, but we were deceived by our memories of ascending these fixed ropes in a few hours and preferred to put off the task of melting snow until we had reached the top of the ice field where we promised to ourselves a spacious ledge with room to sit and a place to shelter the stove. But we had not reckoned with the slow pace imposed by our heavy sacks.

The morning cleared and encouraged us on, but it took all the rest of the day for us to reach the top of the ice field and by that time the storm had returned. There was no ledge to be found. I tried to climb further but showers of hail obliterated every foot-hold and hand-hold and we resigned ourselves to a repetition of the previous night's miserable performance. We managed again only one mug each of warm liquid and then struggled abjectly once more into our hammocks and sleeping bags. Then there were the tedious hours of waiting, marginally more comfortable, until dawn.

This was the end of a second day with little to eat and drink. Unavoidably we were slipping into a dangerous state of dehydration and starvation, but without a place where we could sit, and shelter the stove from the wind, we were helpless. Inside the hammocks we could not use the stove for fear of burning the fabric or spilling the contents of the pan over ourselves. Pete complained little about his hands.

Our values had become so debased that we only longed for a ledge to sit on, with room enough for the stove as well, not for a bed or our tent below. We only wanted hot drinks, not a feast. The next day we climbed 150 feet beyond the end of the fixed ropes and hacked some foot-holds from the ice. It was all we had time for before the day was gone and we entered the third night of misery.

It was a blessing next day to wake to the storm; it left no doubt in the decision. In three days we had made 150 feet of progress beyond what we had already done, we had scarcely drunk a pint of liquid a day and had eaten virtually nothing. We were both suffering from exposure and the chances of climbing the remaining 2,500 feet to the summit seemed minimal.

Retreat was welcoming; defeat was sweetened by the relief of escape from such physical distress. I did not think of it as a tactical withdrawal, I just wanted to get out of that misery, descend to warmth, drink and food.

On reaching the tent of Camp 1, I lay down inside, sheltered from the gusts of wind and lulled by the warmth of the sun which was beginning to make an appearance through the cloud. I was dozing when Pete arrived and he was furious to discover that I had fallen asleep without lighting the stove and melting snow for a drink. There was an implicit understanding that the first one back would always prepare a drink, which was the thing we most looked forward to all day. I knew I was in the wrong but made some feeble excuse about not having a pan and Pete indicated an empty tin I should have thought to use.

The ordeal of the night in the hammocks and days with no shelter from the storms endowed the mountain with a ferocity we had not noticed previously. Glancing back, as we hastened on down to Base Camp, we were as children looking incomprehendingly and nervously at a fire which has inflicted unaccountable pain. The confidence which had grown during the days of steady progress up to the ice field was now shattered; no longer did success seem to depend solely on perseverance. Above the ice field were areas of rock, steeper than below, and with no camp to work from we could not see how we would be able to guard strength enough to climb them.

We spent two full days at Base Camp and it seemed like a week. After three weeks of constant effort, these were our first rest days. We relaxed and ate, losing the furtive mannerisms of those who have come in from the cold. We chatted about home life, about the girls we knew, untouchable idols about whom we dreamed from our self-imposed monasticism. I photographed the ice crystals in the stream at dawn and sparkling droplets on the petals of tiny flowers. We talked about the mountain when the fear had mellowed and Pete suggested taking the inner part of a tent so that we could sit together on the mountain if we could dig out a ledge large enough. I dressed his fingers, now cracked and inflamed at the ends.

They were nothing like as bad as Dick's fingers had been the year before, but Pete was more prepared to admit to the pain he felt than Dick had ever let himself. This I found more comprehensible. His fingers did look painful and I could relate to someone who expressed his feelings of pain rather than subdued them in a stoic acceptance of misfortune. Dick had had no choice but to keep on moving if he wanted to survive. Pete and I were in a situation where we could decide not to go back on the mountain if we thought it too hard or if his fingers were too much of an affliction. At no time, however, did I hear him waver in his intentions of climbing the mountain.

It was implicit that we would try again. Inevitably we would miss our flights home and Pete would be so far overdue on his return to the office that he resigned himself to losing his job. We had come so far and we felt so close to knowing whether the climb was possible or not that we could not bring ourselves to walk away in order to keep to a timetable. Parents and friends would be worried too but we had no contact with everyday life, no external stimuli to alter a decision. The mountain was our main stimulus and it prevailed.

We packed to leave, altering once again the wording of the note 'to passers-by'. Then movement in the little valley out from Base Camp signified life, but it was not an animal, it was a person, and then two more. We were dumbstruck, more humans had reached our planet. They were two members and the Liaison Officer of the American expedition which we had heard about. Pete and I poured out a medley of questions, hardly waiting for their answers in the excitement of communicating with people other than ourselves. We did, however, gather something from their replies: Yes, they were attempting Dunagiri, by the original route of 1939. There were ten of them altogether. The Liaison Officer was sick and was being accompanied back by one of the expedition who had to return home. The other member was going back onto the mountain to rejoin the rest of the team. Yes, they had seen our note and when did we expect to go home now? Perhaps we could work together in summoning porters. Yes, their camp was nearby, about ten minutes away but out of sight in a hollow. They told us also the sad news of the death on Nanda Devi of a twenty-one-year-old girl, also named Nanda Devi. She was the daughter of an American climber who had been on the first ascent of the mountain many years before, and who had returned with her for what was intended to be a momentous ascent of a beautiful mountain by a beautiful girl with the same name. But she had taken ill on the mountain and had forced herself on until she had died. It was a disturbing story. We said our 'good lucks' and went our separate ways.

It had been an odd encounter, so casual when it could have been so significant. Certainly, had we been aware of their presence it would have given us some feeling of contact with the rest of the world, reassured us that we still had a place amongst humans. Both Pete and I had found the pair we had met puzzling. They were quite elderly, we thought, to be active climbers on a mountain in the Himalayas and their equipment was all new, as if bought for the occasion, with none of the individuality of tools that are familiar and well used. It was odd to walk down from an Advance Camp anyway to Base Camp carrying an ice axe and crampons, when most of the way was on slopes of rubble or earth. They struck us as people who like the mountains and buy the equipment recommended without a proper appreciation of when to use it. If their whole team was the same as the two members we had met, it emphasised the criteria that the Indian government used to judge expeditions. Age equated with experience and numbers with safety. They had had no trouble obtaining permission.

Pete voiced his puzzlement as we were on the way back up to our own Advance Camp, thus giving shape to an uneasiness we both shared:

'If anyone is going to have an accident it will be them, don't you think?' We knew, however, that these visitors in their turn probably shared the same view of our efforts on Changabang.

Our own unfinished task menaced every moment we were not on the mountain. We stayed a day at Advance Camp to prospect a possible route of descent. The strain of what still lay ahead imbued me with a depression which made me blame Pete for everything that went wrong. We both overslept and I blamed Pete for not doing his breakfast chores. I blamed him for the late start and late return, resenting the lack of time before I had to busy myself with the evening meal. I felt cheated of the moments I value in which to relax and savour the remaining life before the headlong momentum towards a confrontation with a mountain of which the outcome is uncertain.

Much of the anxiety was due to the apprehension inspired by our experiences with the hammocks. We tried to rationalise our fears, re-examined the progress we had made and the time taken, referred back to the previous year when Dick and I had spent ten consecutive nights on a mountain with much inferior preparation, as proof that we could do at least the same again.

We were delayed at Camp 1 on the ridge by a thunderstorm and the strain was more intense. It seemed as if we were aware of every movement, every action and even every thought of each other. There were no arguments, few words, a mute passivity, clipped and curt, non-volunteering responses. For a month we had had to push ourselves to maximum effort and support entirely ourselves the full burden of the physical and mental strain. At no time could we take a day off to let someone else do the work and bear the strain, always the problem was waiting exactly as we had left it. We knew this was our last attempt. We had not food enough for another return. The heavy snow and relentless wind eroded our expectations.

The sky, however, cleared, the wind swept the snow from the mountain and we regained the scene of our ordeal in the hammocks, taking up with us the line of ropes from the lower part of the mountain. We laboured for hours, hacking at the ice, and formed a ledge just wide enough to lie on side by side. Here, at 20,000 feet, we made our Camp 2. We suspended the thin nylon of the inner tent by two corners, attaching them to pitons driven into ice and rock. It was a tight squeeze for us both to fit into the tent and stay on the ledge and one side of the tent hung off the edge. It was my turn to take the outside position. Only one of us could move at a time, every shift in position required consultation with the other person and it was a constant worry that we might drop or dislodge some essential item such as boots or stove.

The climbing above was more difficult and very much more sustained. We had disappointments at our slow rate of progress but we were solving a tangible problem. We spent days climbing up steep walls and icy runnels and hours zig-zagging round corners. We came to blank spots and strained blindly on the rope to reach other fault lines; we had moments of terror such as when a sharp edge part cut through the rope as I was climbing, and moments of joy at the end of the day as we swung down the ropes fixed as a life-line back to our cramped and tiny tent on the side of a mountain flaming red with the sunset.

The slowness was frustrating, but each advance added to a state of satisfaction. Each day we were exhausted and at no time were we far from the borderline with danger. Late one night, caught out by the dark, I detached myself in error from the rope and almost fell. If I had fallen, Pete would never have known what had happened. The days became almost routine. I was back first, Pete had lost his descending device and had to use a slower method on the long line of ropes. Back at the tent I would chop lumps from the ice, place them at the front of the tent, then slip inside to have them already melting for when I heard the clatter of Pete arriving and swinging across from the line of the rope.

It took four hard days to climb 1,200 feet above Camp 2, to a point from which we were certain we could reach a broad ramp of snow cutting across the face above and leading to easier ground and the summit. We rested for a day with bated breath lest the mountain should notice we were confident again of reaching the summit. We lay cosy in the sun-warmed confines of the tent, eating, sleeping, relishing the magnificent panorama through the entrance and the splendour of our airy perch 3,000 feet above the glacier. Without a hint of the strains from the previous days, I noted briefly on a piece of paper:

Wednesday 13 October. Today we are both knackered and having a rest day. Can see smoke from the Americans' camp direction. They must be packing up. This expedition seems to have gone on for ages. Be glad to get it over with. Hell of a situation up here. Hope the weather lasts. People must be worried at home now.

Action and confrontation with the problem that had menaced us for so long was more acceptable than the ordeal of waiting. There was neither the constant whittling away of confidence nor the psychological demoralisation of being dominated by the whole problem. We had tackled it in parts and restored our confidence as we found the solution, no matter how difficult, to each one. There remained one stretch of a hundred feet before we reached the ramp and from all that we could judge there were no more obstacles between the ramp and the summit.

In the cold of the morning, before the sun reached round to the West Face, Pete led the way up that last pitch towards the ramp. He paused often to warm his hands, nursing fingers that were still painful. He reached the ramp as the sun pushed a halo of colours over the summit ridge. It was a sign of a change in the weather.

We did not follow the ramp, but climbed straight up, miscalculating the difficulty. It took until evening to gain the bottom of the slope leading uniformly up to the summit.

Bliss was the cessation of movement, shelter from the wind, food and sleep. We were deadly tired.

I ignored the strict demarcation of tasks in the morning and produced a warm drink before we left for the summit. We trailed upwards, moving together, linked by the rope. I was in front and never looked back. If the rope tugged at my waist I never knew whether Pete was moving more slowly or if the rope had caught on a fluting of snow. We crawled closer to the summit, the fatigue and exertion of altitude familiar and not disconcerting; dimly I was aware that at long last we were clawing our way to the top of the slope awesomely poised 5,000 feet above the precipice of the West Face. A few points of metal on our boots and metal tools in our hands were all that kept us there.

I tried to do the last twenty steps to the summit in one go but stopped short, panting for breath. I approached cautiously. The summit was a sharp crest dropping steeply away on the opposite side. Pete joined me and moved along to a spot which looked slightly higher fifty feet away.

The top was simply an end to the struggle upwards. Nanda Devi was clear for a moment long enough for Pete to satisfy his wish to see it. An advancing bank of cloud was bringing the bad weather heralded by the rainbow around the sun the previous day. No anthems played in my head; I only wanted to get down. The summit was just one stage in the process of climbing the mountain. I felt no ecstasy at our achievement nor pleasure at the panoramas on every side. The practical problems of descent and the further days of exertion needed before we would truly be safe prevented me feeling anything more than a relief that we had no more upward movement. For me the exultation and satisfaction could wait until we were back on firm ground. We looked for any remnants left by our friends in case they had reached the top but the snow was deep and we saw none. We were on the summit for less than half an hour, sharing some chocolate and taking photographs, then we started down as the first flurries of snow came and the valleys merged with the grey clouds.

I felt again the superiority in Pete's comments when he saw the piton I had driven in at the start of the long, steep abseil down to the ramp. It protruded for half its length and flexed as I settled my weight on it.

'You're not going down on that are you?'

I was curt in my reply, resenting the implied criticism that he could have arranged something different.

'Can you find anything better?'

He could not, and I sensed he was glad that I was going first. Foolishly light-headed, or with the trust that, having investigated every alternative, faith would add strength to the anchor point, I slid apprehensively down. Having done all possible, we needed now a little luck. The piton held.

It was twilight when we regained the fixed rope at the bottom of the ramp. The rope was our life-line and I felt reassured when I clipped into it and started the more mechanical manoeuvres to slide back down to the tent. In the thirty-six hours since last using this life-line, the wind had tossed it about in parts. It had been blown loose from one anchor point and I had to haul myself back onto course and refix the rope securely in place to make it easier for Pete. In the dark everything had to be done by touch and memory. My hands were stiffening with cramp by the time I was making the pendulum towards our tent. I hacked out lumps of ice as usual before tumbling into the tent and lying there, allowing myself to feel more exultation than I had ever permitted on the summit. Halfway down, halfway to safety, I waited for Pete to come jangling in.

Warm inside my sleeping bag, I revelled in the sensual ache of relaxation and started melting ice for a drink. The ice had melted, the water was hot and Pete had still not arrived. I turned the stove down, delaying drinking myself until I could share the pleasure.

I shook myself out of a doze to realise that the pan was still bubbling away and there was no sound of Pete. I peered out into the blackness. Nothing. I shouted. No reply.

I lay back, dredging up from my subconscious any sound from the last hour or two which might have been Pete falling, thus allowing the thought of accident to crystallise. Hopeless despair invaded me as the pan simmered pointlessly for the drink I had hoped to share and now, in spite of a great thirst, I had no taste for it. My mind chased up and down the alleyways of action, ruling out all possibilities of arresting a calamity if it had already happened. I longed to hear the familiar jangle of Pete's arrival which would make foolish all my worries, but I had been back over two hours by this time.

And then it came, the rattle of gear, the scrape of crampons on rock, no sudden rush of catastrophe but the slowness of control. My fears vanished but I could not find again the exultation with which I had wanted to greet him.

'Joe, can you see those lights?'

I looked out and saw nothing.

'Oh, they're gone. Can you hear voices?'

I could hear nothing, and wondered if he were delirious.

'You've been a long time. I thought you had an accident.'

'I did. A peg came out and I almost fell off. I ended up upside down, holding on by one hand.'

We were accustomed to recovering quickly from shocks; together again we lingered over eating and making hot drinks, without the discipline of another day of upward progress hanging over us. We indulged ourselves a little early in self-congratulations. Even if we died now we had proved that it was not impossible to climb such a route as the West Face of Changabang.

I was unquestionably pleased to be passing down the mountain for the last time. It was true that we had mastered it but all the time I had felt on edge, at every moment the forbidding nature of this colossal wall made itself felt. We were late leaving Camp 2 and it was night once more when we were still five hundred feet from the tent of Camp 1.

I stared and strained with my eyes into the darkness, trying to pick out details below. We were on the mixed ground of snow and rock, groping about from memory to find the rocks in which we had left pitons and marker ribbons. If we were only fifty feet off course in the dark we could miss the tent completely.

It became another bitter ordeal of cold, wind and fatigue, with my body screaming 'no more'. It was hard to think clearly. We could not find one marker and piton and we had differing memories about which direction we should aim. Pete had better vision in the dark and went down on a rope which I paid out, hoping to take his weight if he fell. After 150 feet he had found nothing. I tied on another rope and paid that out. We had to find the final marker point through the last stretch of icy rock otherwise we would never find the tent. He had gone 300 feet down into the blackness when his muffled shouts drifted up with the welcome news that he was on course. My feet were frozen and my legs shook with cold.

I descended, climbing down the snow slope, with the rope hanging loosely from my waist. I kept shouting to Pete for directions. I was thoroughly scared, able to see nothing and relying on my feet to tell of the changes in the texture of snow and ice.

The whole descent had become a fiasco, but I marvelled at Pete's psychic powers in finding the anchor points and markers and bringing us within striking distance of the tent. I slid down the rope, recognising the contours of the slope; my legs folded beneath me as the angle eased. A few steps more and I was home, collapsing on the platform we had levelled out and feeling a suffused elation welling up as I realised we were safe. We had been three hours groping down in the dark.

The urgency had gone from our actions. We did not reach the tent of Advance Camp till late in the afternoon of the next day. There was barely anything to eat there but we stayed overnight in order to retrieve from the glacier the bundles of equipment we had been unable to carry and had thrown down from Camp 1. It was 18 October, we had seats booked on a plane for this day and, with no hope of meeting this deadline, we had no more cause to hurry. We went about everything now in the leisurely manner that our weary bodies and spirits demanded.

Later that day we trudged with heavy loads back towards Base Camp. There were only the ties from home to hurry us on but they could influence little our pace. Base Camp itself held little attraction; the Americans had said they would be leaving around 10 or 12 October, so there was no welcome congratulation or celebration to look forward to. We stopped often, relaxed with each other as never before, resting our sacks on convenient boulders to save the effort of taking them off. I thought I heard voices but Pete heard nothing. When I heard them again I was not alarmed that hunger and exhaustion might be inducing more hallucinations on this same track that I had walked in delirium the year before from Dunagiri.

We paused at the vantage point from which we had a last view of Changabang before dropping down into the little valley leading to Base Camp. Streamers of cloud drifted past the mountain, revealing periodically the summit cone glowing red in the rays of the setting sun.

We photographed the sight until the colour left it and we stumbled in the rapid dark down the narrow valley, slipping in the dust and tripping over stones.

There was a smell of woodsmoke, and voices, this time we both agreed. We saw lights, a campfire. We hurried then, delighted to know there were people to meet. We shouted but had no reply; we approached our tent cautiously; it was dark, undisturbed, and the note unmoved. We dropped our sacks and hurried uncertainly and awkwardly in the dark across to the fire. A large tent loomed up, voices chattered away inside in a strange tongue oblivious of our presence outside.

We poked our heads inside. It was a huge tent full of people, warmth, colour, food, noise. They seemed to know who we were and to be half expecting us.

'Changabang West Face? Boardman, Tasker?'

'Yes.'

Mugs of lemon tea were pressed into our hands and chunks of parmesan cheese; we were made welcome and indulged ourselves in the glory of their admiration; the inevitable pride we felt in our accomplishment, drinking thirstily of their praise.

They were a group of Italians who had come to climb Kalanka, but having followed mistaken directions had arrived in the wrong valley for tackling that mountain. It did not seem to affect their joyous spirits; they had climbed a small peak, had even gone onto the lower slopes of Changabang, though one had broken his fingers in some stone fall. It was cosy in the tent, there were too many things and too many faces to absorb at first; it did not matter, we were accepted into the comradeship of fellow climbers and swept along in a lively exchange of experiences and climbs.

Pete was closer in to the main group than I, speaking for both of us, and he knew many people in Italy through his work at the British Mountaineering Council. I was light-headed from elation, fatigue and the return to safety. The warmth of the tent induced a drowsiness. I was content to let Pete do the talking.

I became aware that I was sitting next to the only woman of the group, a tired, drawn-looking woman who, I realised with surprise, spoke English very well. Without having to make the effort of conversing in pidgin English, I started to talk with her.

She told me she was a member of the American expedition and I wondered at the reasons for her staying on alone when the rest of the expedition had arranged porters for their departure several days ago. Then she told me that there had been an accident and I presumed this had caused a delay, imagining someone with a broken arm being helped slowly down the mountain, and that she would be leaving soon with the rest of the equipment.

I grew conscious of the selfish indulgence of Pete and myself revelling in our own success when others had not been so lucky. I tried to show some consideration for an event which had thwarted their ambitions.

'I'm sorry. Was anyone hurt?'

'Yes. Four were killed.'

And there it was, a stark non sequitur to my train of thought. A reply as outlandish and different to that anticipated as one would experience in a conversation with someone who was crazy. And it was over to me to adapt to this terrible fact, to assimilate and comprehend. Killed? How could she say killed? Why wasn't such an awful fact apparent on everyone's face, apparent in everything around me? Why wasn't it the topic of all our talk? How could something so awful be said so quietly, so casually? I looked to her for rescue from thoughts I could not contain.

'Was anyone related to you?'

'Yes, my husband.'

She said it so unobtrusively, in such a matter-of-fact way, her drawn face registered no change of emotion. For over a month Pete and I had run the gauntlet with death and escaped, to return shouting our triumph. But now I was meeting another side of such encounters. This woman was telling me that her husband had played the same game and lost, as had his three friends. My words, coming from someone who continually played such a game, seemed facile. I fled out of the tent, away from the warmth and chatter, to look at the stars and feel the cool night air.

She had told me that Yasu, my friend from Joshimath, was in a tent outside. I went to find him and he embraced me warmly.

He explained in shocked, subdued tones that Ruth, the woman, had been on the mountain when the accident had happened. Five of the members of the team had already gone home, the remaining five had gone onto the mountain. Ruth went as far as a tent on a shoulder of the mountain and waited there for her husband and the three other men while they made an attempt to reach the summit. The four had reached the crest of the ridge and spent a night out. Next day she had seen them coming down. She did not know if they had reached the summit or not. She was observing them from the tent doorway when she saw two of them fall and plunge three thousand feet to the foot of the mountain. When next she brought herself to look out, the second pair had fallen too and were lying near the two bodies a long way below her. She had tried to descend herself but had been too shaken to get down on her own. She spent a night in the tent watching the Advance Camp for any sign of Yasu, who had been asked to come up to help with clearing the camp on a certain date. When she saw his tiny figure approaching the lower camp she had shouted and waved. He had realised immediately what had happened, being able to see the shapes of the bodies at the foot of the mountain. By that time the Italian Kalanka expedition had arrived at Base Camp and he went back to obtain their help in rescuing the woman. Ruth did not know about the Italians and presumed that Yasu had understood her to be indicating that he should not clear the camp and had gone back to Base to wait until he was summoned. The next day, which was only this morning, Yasu had returned with some of the Italians and brought the woman down from the camp where she was stranded. Theirs had been the voices I had heard as Pete and I walked down the glacier from another direction. Yasu was going back to the mountain next day with his companion, Balu, to examine the bodies.

Pete and I had left gear up at our Advance Camp which we intended to retrieve next day, and I offered to Yasu that we would come over to Dunagiri on our way back. The whole story was shocking and incomprehensible, my reactions were those of someone stunned; this drama had come upon us totally unexpectedly and I was unprepared for the role I should play. The darkness hid any need to worry about what my facial expressions showed or failed to show.

I was starving with hunger; Pete and I had eaten virtually nothing all day. Yasu prepared a huge meal over his fire and Pete came stumbling out into the dark, rightly suspecting that I would have discovered some food.

Pete had learnt of the tragedy and that night in our tent we discussed the matter. It was not at all clear whether our help was needed; unquestionably the four would be dead after such a long fall, so it was not a matter of rescue. It did not seem right that the bodies should be left exposed on the mountainside. On the other hand, the Italians were probably fitter than we were for going up to the bodies, but they were not making any plans to do so. Pete and I both knew of the complications caused through deaths in the mountains, the endless problems for relatives when no evidence of death is produced, the long wrangles with insurance companies and government offices. We resolved to go up there ourselves next day with Yasu and Balu if the Italians made no move.

We both woke before dawn, restless from weeks of conditioning to hyperactivity, still highly charged from the weeks of tension. As Pete went off in the dawn twilight to find water, I went over to Ruth's tent.

She emerged, a tear revealing the pain of her night alone, and was quietly grateful as I explained our intentions. We were going to identify the bodies, and I felt clinically callous as I asked for any means of identifying them. I had to tell her that it was possible after having fallen so far that the bones which gave shape to a person's face would be damaged and the faces unrecognisable. Identification from their passport photographs might not be possible. She said her husband had a gold ring and that so far as she was concerned it was more appropriate that his body be left to rest on the mountain.

We left with empty sacks and long ice axes borrowed from the Italians. Pete and I trailed far behind Yasu and Balu, pushing on limbs which protested their need for rest.

Yasu indicated details of the Americans' route on the way to their camp on the glacier and when we reached it he pointed out the dots which were the bodies high up on a shelf above an ice cliff. We inspected them through binoculars and hoped that the many objects scattered round them were not their dismembered limbs.

We climbed up a steepening slope of the glacier. I could see the ridge, not very far away, on which Dick and I had spent so long the year before. It was impossible now for me to conceive of what had gone on. Now I felt strong and capable, with enough in reserve to go to the assistance of people less fortunate.

The bodies lay on an ice shelf, in a direct line 3,000 feet below the ice slope from which they had fallen. From what I could judge at a distance, that ice slope was very similar to the one on which Dick and I had both fallen the year before and, though the two places were thousands of feet apart, I suspected that both incidents were due to the same cause – fatigue and hard ice.

As we climbed up, Yasu and Balu, who had been so fit at the start, dropped back, Balu complaining that he was feeling ill. They were out of sight when we arrived on the sloping shelf at 20,000 feet close to the foot of the mountain. Fortunately the bodies were intact, the objects scattered around being items from their burst rucksacks. Some objects clung to a rock buttress above us, showing where they must have struck in their headlong fall.

We examined all four. They were joined together by ropes in two pairs. A fractured ice axe near to one body indicated a possible reason why they had not been able to stop each other from falling. We cut open their frozen pockets and searched inside, looking for a means of positive identification. But no one carries his passport or wallet on a mountain. We looked for cameras to retrieve the film so that we would know if they had reached the summit, but found none. We found Ruth's husband with his gold ring. I forced myself to photograph each body, aware of the morbid misinterpretation that this action was open to. To obtain a death certificate a body needs to be identified by a relative and certified as dead by a doctor. We were neither, but there was no way we could take the bodies back for identification, and our only sort of 'proof' that they were indeed dead, apart from our word, was a photograph.

Pete told me he felt sick. I was as if anaesthetised, I let myself feel nothing in order to cope with the job in hand. Pete was uncertain about burying the bodies, concerned that we were acting beyond our responsibilities. I had no time for the bureaucratic formalities which would leave the bodies exposed as food for the crows for weeks before anyone could return here if anyone ever should. I insisted that we bury them and we took a rope each, drawing the bodies in pairs to the edge of a crevasse. They were frozen and awkward in shape. I sensed Pete's wordless sorrow and saw the tears in his eyes. I slid two of the bodies into the depths, resting them on a bridge some distance below the surface. I took over from Pete, who seemed in a daze.

'Watch out, Joe, on the edge of that crevasse.'

I slid the second pair in to join the others and scrambled away from the brink to sink down beside Pete.

'Do you believe in God?'

'I don't know, do you?'

'If the prayers are for anyone, they're for those left behind.'

'Prayers don't need words. Let's just stay here silent for a while.'

In a few days the winter snows would start and cover the bodies completely. In time the crevasse would close and the bodies would become part of the mountain glacier forever.

We gathered up all the equipment we could squash into our rucksacks, responding to an unformulated notion of tidying up any loose ends. Descending, we could see the summit of Changabang poking over a small peak in the foreground – that dome we had been privileged to walk on and return from.

Back at the camp on the glacier we found Yasu and Balu warming water over a stove and we drank gratefully. They were visibly relieved to see us back and we understood now that they had been terrified of going any further and glimpsed something of the awe with which they regarded us now for having gone up to have dealings with the dead.

They loaded themselves up with all that they could carry – Yasu wickedly asked if we had found any watches or cameras – and we plodded down together.

It was night as we reached Base Camp, noisy hordes of people making movements round a campfire. Porters for the Italians had arrived and a sing-song was taking place. Ruth was in the circle and Pete and I pushed in to give her a report, feeling the unwanted bearers of bad tidings in the midst of a happy throng.

We both felt too estranged from such merriment to partake in it and we left to find our own tent and make a meal. I borrowed a large tin can from the Italians and went off to fetch water. It was much colder now than it had been all those weeks ago when we had first arrived. The stream near our tent was dried up. I went off up the hillside in the dark, tracking down the sound of trickling water. It was a long way before I found a flow substantial enough to scoop up into my bucket. I tripped and staggered all the way back, spilling water down my legs, longing for the rest I felt we so much deserved. Implicitly I imagined Pete getting the stove going and waiting impatiently for my return.

I heard no sound as I regained the tent. Pete was inside warmly clad and settling down into his sleeping bag. I presumed he had had trouble starting the stove.

'What's the matter with the stove?'

'Nothing. I've just been getting myself settled in.'

'Settled in? And I've been running about in the dark for the last half hour to find water!'

I was really angry that I had postponed relaxing until all was ready, assuming that Pete would be similarly motivated without need to discuss what we each should do. It was a jolt to realise that my impression of us complementing each other and working as a unity was an illusion. The paring away over the last few weeks of all superfluous niceties made me blunt and forthright in my indignation.

'I suppose you were waiting for me to cook you a meal as well?'

He grabbed the stove and worked furiously at it. In a while he had some water heating in a pan and the evening meal was in progress.

Yasu and Balu had come over and sat in front of our tent round a small fire. I sat with them. It was a simple life. Time passed; a little warmth was thrown up by the flames and we were three shadowy figures sharing it.

Yasu looked up: 'You know the monkey god, Hanuman? They say he has servants who are also monkeys and who rush about doing everything for him.'

He looked over at our tent.

'Just like Pete does for you,' and his eyes twinkled.

There were not porters enough for Pete and myself, so we agreed between us that I would leave with the Italian party and Ruth in order to send back five porters. Meanwhile Pete would go back up to our Advance Camp and bring down the rest of our gear. I was glad to be the one to leave. I had spent too long the year before on my own waiting for porters to want to go through that experience again. Pete for his part was glad to stay on because his feet were sore and he could have a couple of days' rest before having to do anything.

I packed a few essentials into a rucksack for my journey and raced after the main party who had left an hour before. The day was beautiful, I felt fit and strong, confident and satisfied. I crossed a plateau of grass browning with the arrival of autumn, and delighted in my effortless progress. I wanted the sensation of strength and capability to go on and on. I crested a hill and came upon Yasu and Balu, waiting for me. The spell was broken, I was amongst men again.

I fell into step with Ruth, the Italians chattered in their own little groups and I sensed that they felt inadequate at communicating in their imperfect English with someone whose sorrow was so deep. She was unsteady on some awkward steps where the track led over precipitous ridges. I slowed my pace and stayed with her. She never asked for help but I felt I needed to stay with her and I talked about anything to bring her away from that solitary vigil she had endured for two days and nights looking down on her husband's body and not knowing whether she herself would die too. I could not keep repeating how sorry I was at her loss, I just talked about anything, to give her a person, out of a crowd of strangers, to whom she could relate. I talked about my past and my ambitions, I told her about my training to be a priest and what a different life I now had. She told me something of how she had passed the time alone in the tent, reading a book until help should come and how she had despaired when she saw Yasu turn back. She told me of the things she had done with her husband and the plans they had had to travel round India after the trip, how she needed to return before it was in all the papers and burglars would raid their home because they would know she was absent. I wondered at her calm and control and told her how important it was to inform immediately the relatives of the other three dead before the merciless press should seize the news and broadcast it without thought for the hurt it might cause.

We stumbled together late at night through the woods into the clearing at Dibrugheta and I climbed with her next day up to Dharansi Pass and across the plateau. I told her the story of Dick and myself on Dunagiri the year before but felt guilty at the end of my tale as I realised that we had survived where her husband and friends had not.

I left her when we reached a broad path and it was all downhill. I met Jim Duff from the expedition to the south side of Changabang and his girlfriend, Sue. They had stayed on after the expedition to trek around the hills. His team had reached the top of the mountain a week before we had, by a route which had taken them two days, and clearly the snow had covered all trace of them before we had arrived on the summit. I asked Jim and Sue to take care of Ruth and rushed down to reach the road for the bus which I knew went past at 4.00 p.m.

I saw the bus, the only one of the day, when I was still some minutes from the road. I did not reach Joshimath until the next day and sent the telegrams which I hoped would appease the anxieties of all at home. 'Changabang West Face climbed. Both of us safe and well. Joe.'

I sent one to each of our parents. I knew that Pete's parents would wonder why my name was at the end of the telegram, but I decided against making it seem as if Pete had sent it. He still had to reach here from Base Camp and until he did I could not bring myself to pretend that he had.

Two days later the first snows of winter whitened the tops of the hills and my anxieties grew with the knowledge of the stuggle I had had to escape from Base Camp at the same time twelve months before in deep snow. I was thankful that I had not telegrammed any pretence. But Pete was safe and came striding into the rest-house late in the afternoon some days later, still carrying with him the wildness of mountain life and the aura of one newly returned amongst people.

We had by this time run out of money. Anticipating this possibility we had cabled home for more but it had not arrived. Bhupal Singh, proprietor of the Motel, loaned us Rs 1,000 on the promise that we would send it to him as soon as we reached Delhi. But his trust in us was so great that he said it could wait till we reached England. Rs 1,000 was approximately £50 but in that small hill town it was the equivalent of £1,000 and he lent on trust alone. In my two encounters with him I had come to regard him as a close friend whom I admired and respected.

We used the money to purchase bus tickets back to Delhi and returned there in a twenty-four-hour cramped and bone-jarring journey which was made unpleasant by the onset of the usual stomach pains and diarrhoea on coming out of the sterile hills.

In Delhi we made statements about burying the bodies and saw the stress on Ruth's face as round after round of questions from officials and press and acquaintances wore down the control and calmness she had managed to achieve for herself.

We made our goodbyes and boarded a plane. Pete, forgiven his long absence, to return to his office and myself, with no other ambition to fulfil, to look for employment. The adventure was over.

For nearly two years I had been totally absorbed with climbing three mountains. Each one had represented something different, each one had been at that moment, in its own way, the greatest test I could conceive of. Each test had been passed and I was left bewildered. I was alarmed to have succeeded; in a way it would have been more reassuring to have failed. Instead success left me with an uneasy, unsettling questioning about where to go next; something harder, something bigger? Where would it all lead? What had I gained from the last two years if all that was left to me was an indefinable dissatisfaction? Was I destined to be forever striving, questing, unable to find peace of mind and contentment?

We had met death and lent a hand in coping with the accident practically, as if it were an everyday occurrence in our sport, and I blocked out the questions those bodies had raised. As I had shut off all emotion in order to complete the task of burying them, I shut out all the doubts and uncertainties about my own involvement in a game which courted death in order to continue playing that game. I was certain that I did not want to die but I knew that the risk in climbing gave it its value. The sensation of being stretched to the limit mentally and physically was what gave me satisfaction and if there was danger it was another problem to solve, it made me more careful, made me perform at my best, and added a special uniqueness to the experience. If there was courage needed it was only the same courage required to meet all the everyday problems of life, to go for an interview, to bring children into the world, to propose to a girl, to take any new step. If we had shown courage in going up to bury four fellow climbers, the only difference was that our everyday problems were located on the side of a mountain and we were on the spot and suited to the task.

If I had died, I would have wanted no sorrow, I would have been achieving my ambitions, would have been exercising the drive and vitality which made me friends or enemies in ordinary life. If I did not do something to the limit, if I had not channelled my energies into climbing, I would not be a person liked or disliked, but someone mediocre. When a friend was killed in the mountains I could only regret that he had not fulfilled his dreams; when a friend was killed drunk and driving as usual too fast, my sorrow was selfish, I wished I had seen more of him. He lived fast, he lived at the limit, and his absence made the world a little less fun for those who knew him, but he died in the way he lived and in a way which he had escaped from only by a hair's breadth many times.

Four people had died and we knew how painful this loss would be for their relatives and friends. For them we had buried the dead and to them we wrote to let them know it was not all loss, that they had our sympathy, that they had contact with us who had last seen their loved ones.

Pete and I were united as one person, if need be one spoke for both; we had emerged from the trial of six weeks of confinement together with a friendship which needed no words. The animosities and estrangements of that period sank into insignificance, seen for what they were, products of particularly trying circumstances. Through it all the unity had prevailed, and the cooperation which had been needed to succeed had always outweighed any differences.

No longer strangers, there was now no need for the 'small talk' which Pete had felt at first; we knew each other so well there was also less need for more serious discussion. I could guess Pete's views and reactions so closely I was sometimes unsure whether we had actually talked about a matter or whether I had mentally resolved what would be his opinion. A girl complained to me once resentfully about Pete: 'The thing about you two is you don't need to talk to each other.'

He offered me a place in his house until I found a new direction in life, and I set about looking for a job.

FIVE

'Let's Draw Matchsticks'

K2

I

The invitation to join an expedition to K2, the second highest mountain in the world, marked the end of a naive attitude to climbing mountains. It was an introduction to an expedition, monolithic by contrast with anything I had known before, and to the massive organisational capabilities of Chris Bonington. It entailed the search for sponsorship on a scale undreamt of on the expeditions to Dunagiri and Changabang, and a courting of publicity in order to establish the importance and prestige of the venture.

Suddenly the business of climbing a mountain had become very much more complicated, surrounded with responsibilities to more than ourselves and subject to pressures from the attention of so many people.

It was autumn of 1977, a year since the sojourn on Changabang. I had more money and a more comfortable life-style than I had known before. I worked for a company which manufactured mountain boots, hoping to link my interests with my job. I went to the Alps and returned to get back to work. I felt empty and unfulfilled. The mountains of the Alps, which had absorbed me totally at one time, now seemed too civilised, too accessible. They were as difficult and dangerous as ever, but the adventure was lessened when it came home to me that no mountain there was more than a few hours away from a cable car or railway line. I did some climbs, had some narrow escapes and returned to work. Back in England, driving my car, meeting and making small talk with people, it was as if I had never been away. Six weeks in the European Alps and it had been almost a package-tour climbing holiday. There was none of the catharsis of total involvement with a foreign culture, of responsibility for the basic decisions and organisation of everyday existence, of planning survival in a barren land and of being removed by many days and much effort from any outside help.

There had been no compelling objective in my mind when we returned from Changabang. Pete had his job to go back to and a place on a team to attempt K2. I had drifted into finding work without any clearly defined intentions. I started discussions with friends about mountains to climb in the Himalayas and had already decided on one scheme when I was asked to join the team planning to climb K2 in 1978. I felt responsibilities to my earlier plans but was overwhelmed by the prospect of an attempt on one of the highest, most beautiful mountains in the world.

At 28,253 feet, K2 is second only in height to Mount Everest, but is considered to be a more difficult mountain. It has a history of tragedies associated with the attempts to climb it and by 1977 had been successfully climbed only twice. So far is the mountain from any habitation that no local name could be found for it and when this peak, denoted by the code K2 (K standing for Karakoram), was measured to be the second highest mountain in the world, the code stuck as a name and has become accepted worldwide.

The Karakoram range stretches across the north of Pakistan, forming a border with China, and K2 straddles that border. The mountains are more rugged, more barren, more remote than most other areas of the Himalayas, the approach to K2 taking fourteen days on foot from the nearest jeep track. The cost of mounting an expedition to any of the mountains in the Karakoram is much higher than an equivalent expedition in India or Nepal. Rates for the porters are higher, more porters are needed as the distances are greater and more supplies have to be carried. For the British expedition of 1978, Chris was working on a budget somewhere between £50,000 and £60,000.

The team was to have eight members, one of whom, Jim Duff, was specifically asked due to his experience as a doctor on expeditions and one, Tony Riley, for his expertise in film-making. The other six members were on the team solely on the strength of their climbing experience, with Chris having acknowledged supremacy in organising and raising money for expeditions.

I attended a meeting at Nick Estcourt's house with the whole team present. After the two previous trips, when any matter could be resolved by a phone call or quick chat with the other person, it took some adjusting to the need for organised meetings coordinating the whereabouts of eight people, to the steady stream of expedition circulars which poured through the letter box, the minuting of discussions and decisions in the meetings, and the endless talk of the money needed and the means of obtaining it.

I knew Pete, of course, more than I did any of the others. There were six new people to relate to, six people some of whom were already well-established figures in the climbing world when I was only starting. Chris was more organised and mechanised than I would ever have believed. His office was a den packed with typewriter, slide copier, ansaphone, intercom, computer, memory typewriter, racks of meticulously documented slides, bookshelves spilling out their contents and seats for himself and his secretary Louise, without whom he admitted he would be lost. He is a self-confessed addict of gadgets and with the enthusiasm of a kid with a new toy he used to encourage us all to visit him and try to work out for ourselves the logistics of climbing K2 and to estimate our chances of success on the computer he had borrowed from IBM for the purpose.

Chris's role in the past few years had been seen to be that of an expedition leader who organised and coordinated the younger members of a team. His more than any had become a household name associated with climbing. It was true he was older than all of us, being in his early forties, and if he had been climbing longer than any of us his record of achievement was also longer. If he himself had not reached the summit himself of the two biggest mountains to which he had led expeditions – Annapurna and Everest – it was not from lack of experience or drive, but more from the need to coordinate the movements of everyone else and make sure that the expedition machine was functioning successfully before allowing himself up to the front line.

He lived in the north of the Lake District with his wife Wendy and two children. More than anyone I knew who had moved to live in the mountains, he had maintained a boundless enthusiasm for climbing at its simplest. When I called in to go over some more details of the expedition, he insisted that we find time to fit in a climb in order to keep a freshness and perspective for the mass of paperwork and calculations that filled the rest of his time.

There was a separateness about him, living as he did out of the way of the main group of us, out of the main circles of social interaction which promotes an easy familiarity. He was self-contained in his family unit, his wife Wendy complementing his bursts of feverish activity. But there was also a remoteness which was noticeably accentuated if someone asked for his autograph and he was made to realise that he was no longer private but public and observed. His voice would become firmer and lose any uncertainty, and he would speak as if pronouncing to an audience.

As leader of the expedition he was the one who bore most responsibility, was the focal point for sponsors and media, and somehow had to relate to the disparate group of ambitious individualists whom he had selected as offering the best chance of climbing K2.

Nick Estcourt was the closest to Chris, having climbed with him in Britain for many years and provided unselfish and reliable support for the interests of expeditions as a whole on many occasions. Nick was unlikely as a climber. The wildness of his enthusiasms and vehemence of his expression were the opposite of what one would expect in a sport where calmness and control are essential. He was noisy and forthright in his opinions, but if he erred himself he was equally forceful in his own self-criticism. His appearance was unruly, a shaggy black mop of hair and an expressive face with piercing eyes would not help one to guess at his occupation as a computer analyst. Nick was a pillar for Chris, and, as a lively participant in the climbing scene, a contact for him with a world he lived away from.

Nick lived in Altrincham with his wife Carolyn, and their house as a halfway point was the usual place for us all to congregate for the periodic meetings.

Doug Scott I only knew very slightly as a powerful and determined individual. His relaxed manner belied the strength of his personality and weight of his opinions. Physically he dominated us all; he was built like a boxer. The drive which had taken him to the top of Everest and enabled him to crawl down another mountain, the Ogre, with two broken legs carried with it a charisma which it was difficult to ignore.

Paul Braithwaite, or 'Tut' as he was universally known, was a firm friend of Doug's. They had been on several expeditions together and seemed to have developed a cooperative rapport. Tut had become known for his superlative skill in climbing rock and ice in Britain and in recent years had turned his attention to mountains further afield. He lived to the north of Manchester and had a down-to-earth attitude to the extravagance of such a big expedition and the pomposity of some of Chris's pronouncements. In the course of the preparations for the expedition he became engaged to a girl who occupied his thoughts more than he cared to admit to us. Tut was given the task of organising all the equipment for the expedition and I was asked to help.

Tony Riley had taken part in making a couple of mountaineering films and was invited along as climbing cameraman. Making a film and sending back news reports was one of the means we had for raising money. I had climbed with him in Wales and found him agreeable company, perhaps feeling he was a kindred spirit amongst all the other well-known people on the expedition. He had a tendency to look on the worst side of life; his songs of preference were some by the band Dr Hook and the Medicine Show, expressing a morbid disenchantment with life. He would turn up the volume on the cassette player when they came to the words in a song, 'a coldness like something dying' or 'This is the last time I'll stay in this dirty, rat-infested apartment', and he would let out a harsh, cackling laugh, as if he knew well the sentiments the songs expressed. He was generous and cooperative but presented himself with such an air of disillusionment that this was easy to miss. In Wales we did a route in very cold weather and he excused himself for not getting his camera out by saying it was too cold. I wondered if he would find it warmer on K2. Next day we both stood shivering together on another climb, both wishing we were at home in front of a warm fire, reading the Sunday papers. When I learnt to take less seriously his moroseness I found him fun to be with.

Jimmy Duff, climber and doctor, I had known over a number of years. His leisured manner of talking and air of deep consideration gave him a reassuring bedside manner, much as his suave good looks and gracious politeness endeared him to all women. He had taken part in the expedition to Mount Everest in 1975 and reached the top of Changabang from the opposite side of the mountain to Pete and myself in 1976. Of any climber I knew, Jim carried such an aura of hedonistic indulgence that I could not comprehend him choosing to subject himself to the trials and discomforts that he had undergone in his mountain climbs.

I had never thought of having a doctor on a trip before but in Pakistan the rules stipulate that a party larger than four has to have a doctor along. With a doctor on the team there was a tendency to anticipate and worry about every possible contingency and add more and more suggestions to Jim's list of medicines, pills and medicaments.

With Pete, the rapport established during the long trial of Changabang persisted. He had abandoned his job at the British Mountaineering Council in the meantime to take up a role in Switzerland running courses in mountaineering. This suited him well as it enabled him to be near his girlfriend, who was also working in Switzerland not far from him. Currently he was at work writing an account of our exploits on Changabang and he volunteered to take on the work of estimating and accumulating all the food we would need for the three months of the expedition.

There were mixed views about the likelihood of our success. We had decided to make an attempt on the unclimbed West Ridge of the mountain. This looked to be a much more difficult route than the way K2 had been climbed previously. The first ascent, by an Italian expedition in 1954, had been conducted like a military campaign. The second, in 1976 by a Japanese team, had been the first million-dollar expedition. Both of these expeditions had been on the South-East Spur, or Abruzzi Ridge as it was called. Both expeditions had had many climbers and had used much oxygen.

The difficulties on our chosen route seemed to be high up on the mountain and we only planned to take sixteen bottles of oxygen for the whole expedition. There was beginning to be strong debate in climbing circles about the need for the use of supplementary oxygen on even the biggest mountains. The discussion rested on whether man was capable of functioning in any way at very high altitude and whether, if he did, he would receive permanent brain damage. There were reports of a Chinese expedition which had climbed Everest without the use of oxygen, but practically no information was available about this and the event tended to be ignored. Certainly no one had tackled difficulties as great as those high up on the West Ridge of K2 without oxygen and it seemed likely that anyone trying to do so would be moving so slowly that he would be physically deteriorating too rapidly to make any useful progress.

These were the doubts that assailed us and which fed the scepticism of the critics. We decided to take a limited amount of oxygen to give ourselves some margin for success without making the expedition so unwieldy that we would be hampered by the problems of the greater numbers of people needed to ferry vast quantities of oxygen cylinders up the mountain.

The editor of *Mountain* magazine, Ken Wilson, had, as always, his own strongly held opinion. He thought that we did not stand any chance of getting to more than two-thirds height, and felt that we should not be going given that we could not possibly climb the mountain. He maintained that no one succeeds unless he is totally convinced that a thing is possible. This viewpoint was radically opposed to my own, which was one of going to see how far we could climb. There was too much likelihood with the whole game of climbing that if one sat down rationally and analysed what one was doing or planned to do it could be proved to be not only beyond the bounds of possibility but pointless as well.

I could remember Ken's damning condemnations of some very big expeditions, so I was puzzled now to hear him criticising us because our expedition was too small to have a chance of success. As an authoritative spokesman on the sport, he surprised me in not seeming to understand the basic attraction of leaving an element of uncertainty in a project.

Chris had obtained sponsorship from a large firm, London Rubber Company. The money which they put up, together with the sale of the rights to news reports, a contract for a book subsequent to the expedition, a payment by the burgeoning film company Chameleon for film rights and a contribution of £800 by each member of the team, meant that all the money for the expedition had been found.

It was more important than ever to cooperate with the publicising of the expedition. Having accepted all the financial commitments from these various parties, it was no longer possible to engage in a private struggle with the mountain as we had done on Dunagiri and Changabang. Now, whatever reservations and anxieties I felt, I found myself making statements about hopes I would rather have hidden, presenting rationalisations for an activity which at root I believed to be irrational.

Having to justify ourselves in this way was uncomfortable but it seemed to affect Doug worse than the rest of us. He struck me as being in a dilemma in that publicity had made it possible for him to go on the expeditions and subsequently to earn a living lecturing and writing, yet he fought shy of the media, suspicious of the seductive lure of fame. He was ever dubious of the motives of anyone from the media, fearing lest they twist some statement round to mean something different from what was intended.

I had had less cause for such suspicions, and felt that if we chose to do something which put us in the public eye we stood the best chance of controlling the interpretations which people might put upon actions and statements. What I feared was that I might begin to believe the oft-repeated superlatives which reporters like to use, and begin to be taken in by their hyperbole. So long as I could keep a check on my real values, so long as I knew that we were not the best, we were only some out of many, and lucky at that, so long as I knew we were not invincible, so long as I knew how transient all this attention was anyway, it did not seem to matter what other people might mistakenly think. For better or worse, it would all matter little tomorrow.

In contrast with the other arrangements for the other expeditions I had been on, I discovered an element of alienation in my attitude to any problems which loomed up in the course of getting everything ready. Various people were doing different jobs and it was as if any shortcomings related only to the individual. If the oxygen sets did not turn up, that was Jim's problem; if cases of food did not arrive, that was up to Pete to sort out; if there seemed likely to be difficulties taking walkie-talkies overland, Chris would solve it; when the two van loads of gear had gone and were in Afghanistan at the moment of a military coup, what did it matter if the vans were hi-jacked, Chris would get things straightened out.

Many people had assumed that the expedition to Everest in 1975 would be Chris's last big expedition but now that he was in the full swing of organising this trip everyone was saying that he obviously wanted to make a success of it because this would be his swan-song. Chris undoubtedly had authority, his leadership of the expedition had attracted the sponsorship, and he himself aroused the interest of the public and media. Chris was the opposite to Doug; he knew how to use publicity to its maximum advantage and it was this calculating element, this ever-present ingredient of control which made him seem less relaxed, less of a 'giggle' than some of the others. I felt the sting in his comments and force of his authority when he rang to ask why I had not sent him the expedition contract with my signature. I had no experience of contracts and had wanted to read through it to see what was implied by abrogating the rights to use diary notes for one's own writing until after publication of the expedition book, of agreeing not to give lectures on one's own behalf until the official expedition lectures had taken place and all the other stipulations in the contract. With countless other things to do I had not looked again at the contract and when I brought out my questions to Chris he reacted angrily as if I was questioning his leadership or style of leadership. He seemed so hurt by my questions that I signed the contract without looking at it again and sent it off.

So much of the time associated with expeditioning is taken up with not being on expedition. Time spent preparing, meeting, discussing, anticipating. At another meeting there were still many loose ends to tie up. Tut was pressing for us to take some lighter 7 mm rope for high on the mountain; Pete, after the anxieties about ropes on Changabang and his ingrained concern for safety, was worried that the slightest abrasion would seriously weaken the rope.

On Changabang we had spent days at a time trusting to rope only 8 mm thick. In itself it would hold a ton, but we had had to rely on that rope when it had been fixed in place on the mountain, exposed to storms, rock-fall and the wearing action of the wind rubbing it against coarse granite. We had been so uneasy about the risk of the rope snapping or coming loose that we had taken it in turns to go first up the fixed ropes each day.

Chris resolved this argument with his comment: 'We'll be taking so many risks on that upper part of the wall that abrasion of the ropes will be the least of our worries.' And the meeting evolved into random discussions. Chris would be incommunicado for a month as he was booked up every day with lectures. Pete aired his problems about making a prior commitment to a publisher over a book. Tony was feeling left out because now that most of the money for the expedition was assured he saw his role of film cameraman as being less important. It was all far removed from what was going to be an inconceivably big test of every bit of our abilities. Tut's job with the gear was complete, Pete was going back to Switzerland, Doug was going off to Canada climbing. As 'new boy' on the big expedition I had the job of finishing off all the tasks which were minor in themselves but time-consuming when amassed together. I asked Chris what he did to keep fit. Did he go running? 'Yes, well my secretary is very good at that.' I was baffled at how he managed to deputise even his physical exercise.

I read the book about the 1975 expedition to the South-West Face of Everest. All of the rest of our K2 team except for Tony had been on that expedition. It was a relief to read of all the 'ups and downs' of the climbers in a physical and psychological sense. Even being as close to them as I was, I still tended to think they were superhumanly different. I was concerned at how I would perform alongside these others, whether the expedition would dissolve into a competitive scramble to grab what oxygen we had to go for the summit. I always doubted my own ability, tending to withdraw from competitive situations and being more confident, when unobserved, with total responsibility on my shoulders.

I seemed to be less physically active than the rest. Pete was ski-touring in Switzerland, Tut was packing in lots of ice climbs in Scotland, Doug was away climbing, Nick was 'being a good boy' as he put it, working hard and trying to establish a good impression of himself with his company. He was planning to become freelance after the expedition and he wanted good recommendations. I had grave doubts about how I could hope to perform alongside them when all that I was doing was driving up and down the country as a salesman and attending sales conferences. Before we left in the May of 1978 I had resolved to embark on a new venture, opening a shop selling equipment for camping, climbing and the outdoors generally. Being my own boss would, I hoped, give me more freedom to be absent for the frequent spells I needed.

Though the months of preparation for the expedition were not ideal as a way of passing the time, if the expedition was going to take place they were necessary. I had started going out with a girl, Louise, whom I presumed as a matter of course would be interested in the expedition. She helped with the packing of gear, spending many hours of her spare time loading boxes with the equipment and food. So sure was I that I wanted to go on this expedition that it did not occur to me to question what would be her attitude to it. Neither did she put any objections in the way. The single-mindedness and sense of purpose was what attracted her at the start, but the exclusiveness of my interests was hardly fair. A question I was beginning to ask was to what extent I could expect a girl to wait for me for perhaps three long, anxious months whilst I took part in such a dangerous pursuit. Chris had managed to maintain a happy marriage in spite of years of frequent absences but many other marriages had foundered under the strain. Had roles been reversed, had it been the women who were absent, the men may not have been so tolerant. I was interested to hear Maggie Boysen, married to a well-known climber, telling of how worried the men had been when Pete, whom they knew well, and myself were overdue from Changabang, of the days of fretting and phone calls to the Foreign Office to see if any accident had been reported. She had been amazed at how these other climbers reacted under circumstances she had known only too well many times over.

When we finally left for K2, my parents came down to Heathrow to see us off and my mother pressed on me a religious medal for each member of the team, a symbol of the concern she implicitly felt at such absences, whatever reward she received from seeing her son fulfilling himself.

II

We were met off the plane in the sweltering heat of pre-monsoon Islamabad by one of our vans. Most of the gear and food had been driven overland in two Sherpa vans, by Tony Riley of the expedition and Allen Jewhurst and Chris Lister from Chameleon Films. Allen was to accompany us for the early part of the long approach to K2 in order to get the feel of the film which Chameleon would put together from Tony's camera-work.

Being in the entourage of a Bonington expedition brought with it certain advantages. We were welcomed at the British Embassy and obliging members of the staff put their air-conditioned homes at our disposal. We no longer seemed in control of events: sumptuous banquets were laid on for us by the Ministry of Tourism in Pakistan, at the embassy we had available the open-air swimming pool and a liberal supply of drinks. Having left Britain, it was as if we had surrendered individual volition. Only Chris seemed in total control, coordinating events and channelling arrangements towards getting all of us and our equipment flown to Skardu, a town an hour away by plane, unreachable then by road, from where a jeep would take us to the start of the fourteen-day march-in to our mountain.

The white-painted buildings of the embassy residential enclosure were a haven for us from the debilitating heat. As mountaineers we were favoured guests, and the trust that our hosts had in our ability to climb K2 was touching. The embassy is the largest of the British embassies abroad, in order to service the close ties of the two countries. There was something of the old colonial air about the attitudes in the place, though the buildings were modern. Attendants sat in the shade of trees at the entrances to the enclosure, keeping out unwelcome intruders. Drinks from the embassy club were handed to us in the swimming pool by ever-present servants. Our only justification in being there was that we were a welcome distraction and breath from home for these exiles serving out their assignments in this posting.

Pete went off with the army captain, Shafiq ur Rahman, our Liaison Officer, to purchase the requisite local produce in the bazaar; Nick and I escorted each other to the banks where we changed £15,000 into local currency in notes of small denomination for paying our porters. The quantity of notes was voluminous and filled a small trunk which we carted around with us in the boot of a taxi. Nick, with a meticulous mind for figures, was treasurer of the expedition. We both fantasised on the vistas open to us by this quantity of money, formulating in fun a scheme for abandoning the expedition and running off to South America. Our progress through Islamabad, counting out the wads of money under the watchful eye of an armed guard, scouting up and down the street before rushing to a waiting taxi, flinging the trunk into the boot and ordering the driver to move, encouraged such gangsterish daydreams. Nick was ideal as a treasurer. If anything would stop him running off to South America with money it would be his fanatical desire for exactitude and the discomfort he would feel at not being able to balance the books by such an untidy method of disbursing the funds.

My memories of our departure are coloured by my feelings of being extremely ill with dysentery, lying on the floor of the lounge, rising periodically to vomit into a nearby receptacle. Chris, attending to last-minute arrangements, was at work on his typewriter, oblivious of anything around him, changing plans, rearranging ideas. Somehow a decision had been made to retain ten porters to ferry loads up to Camp 1, three or four to carry loads to Camps 2 and 3. The number of porters needed overall was creeping up astonishingly and at present count we looked to need three hundred all told.

Chris noticed my presence as I rose to be sick once again. 'Joe, could you tidy this place up? Could you start loading the van? Could you find out what the others are doing?' It was typical of his total concentration that he could be quite insensitive to anything peripheral.

The flight to Skardu is only an hour in length, but reputed to be amongst the most dangerous in the world. The planes are small and the mountains high. The wing-tips sometimes seem to be only a few feet away from jagged hillsides. It is not unusual to be held up in Islamabad or stranded for days in Skardu if the weather is not clear enough for flights. For me the flight passed in torment, as each jerk in the progress of the plane brought waves of nausea.

Skardu was an earthenware-coloured town, littered with oasis greenery where irrigation channels made fertile patches in the desert. Here we selected the majorty of our porters, trying to impose some sort of order on an unruly mob of eager, insistent Baltis. They had trekked in from miles around, some walking for two days, at news of the work on the expedition.

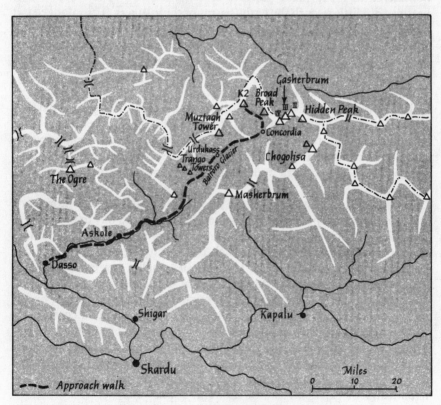

6. The location of, and walk-in route to, K2.

In the daytime the arid land burned under a powerful sun, but they congregated, all wearing their layers of homespun wool, the same colour as the earth. Our expedition meant good employment, and money for the local economy, so the local police were on hand to lend authority to the proceedings.

Doug took charge of selecting the porters. He had been to the area twice before and could remember some faces. In theory he inspected each one for any obvious signs of illness; in practice he selected the ones whom he thought looked interesting characters. And they were interesting. Though dressed in the same drab, camouflage attire, each face had an expressive distinctiveness, and most of them could brandish letters from previous expeditions testifying to their efficiency and worth. The police were liberal in their use of the sticks they carried, beating back the crowds as they pressed forward in their keenness to be hired. Doug was appalled; such violence offended against his philosophy of gentleness and peace. He remonstrated with a policeman who understood not a word and looked bewildered as Doug made gestures of using his own stick on him. The beatings did little to curb the enthusiasms of the villagers. They dodged out of the way till the blows had stopped, laughed at their comrades who had not escaped and returned to press forward again at the first opportunity. Jim Duff, also checking for illness, waxed eloquent about 'these beautiful people'.

The Karakoram region is much more arid than the mountain areas of India and Nepal, and the scenery is harsh and rugged. For several days we walked as if through a desert, with only infrequent oases where huts clustered round a stream. Here villagers eked out an existence, enduring the extremes of climate to live in the mountain valleys, separated from the next village by huge gorges with walls of mud which are dangerous to pass under in the rains.

We had with us Tony Robinson, a director of London Rubber Company, who had chosen to spend his holidays coming part of the way to Base Camp, and Allen Jewhurst of Chameleon Films. The approach to K2 is as hard as anything I have come across which is not actually climbing. Each day we had obstacles to face, rivers to cross, steep-sided gorges to negotiate, hills to climb, and all under the blazing heat of the sun with no streams of water to rely on. The Braldu river, a mighty torrent of water fed by the meltwater from glaciers high in the mountains, was a frequent companion. But its waters were dark with mud and silt carried along under its frantic momentum. The rumbling of boulders could be heard as they too were swept along the bed of the river. It contained the effluent of all the villages along its banks and thus, though water was near us for much of the time in our thirsty trek, it was as little desirable as sea water.

Tony Robinson and Allen Jewhurst were the least at home in this environment, but they coped well with the brutal contrast to their accustomed ways of life in boardroom and TV centre. Tony put his administrative skills to work in assisting with payment of the porters and Allen jumped to help with the worst chore of the day, doling out the vast quantities of rations to our porters. In city life Allen had been a flamboyant, quick-witted playboy whose company I greatly enjoyed. As one day gave way to yet another of toil and sweat with never enough to drink during the most exhausting part of the day, his chirpy conversation came to a complete halt. The further we drew from civilisation, the more withdrawn he became. In spite of knowing him well I found I preferred the company of the members of the expedition. I felt uneasy about what we had before us and was more at home with those who shared the burden. Inevitably it was as though our discussions and behaviour were being observed by these two who could not share the hopes, anxieties and uncertainties of the rest of us.

We travelled on through that ochre-brown land of dust and over the hills of mud with our ragged army of porters. They were a cheerful bunch but, without language, we had little interaction with them. At dawn we would wake to see them emerging from the ground as silent shadows, facing Mecca in prayer; then they would leave, governed by an indiscernible order, each with his numbered load tied to his shoulders by the rope of his trade.

We made our own pace, carrying little, guarding our energies for our big undertaking. It varied from day to day, from hour to hour just who one walked with. The track was long enough and the number of people large enough to spend time with someone, then to slip off to walk with another as if going to call in at someone else's house for a chat. I walked with Tut and listened to his unsettled and uncertain dreams. I chanced upon Jim and Nick, overcome by the heat, sheltering under a solitary tree and risking a drink of the murky Braldu water. Nick, with his adamant views and forthright opinions, was always good for a laugh. We congregated at the hot springs, lounging in the warm pools in view of snowy peaks, listening to the stories of those who had been there before on other trips. Until we had walked for a week we would always have to live the places we were in through the eyes of those who would reveal what was round the next corner before we reached it, or predict the length of time to the next camp-site and describe the mountains that would be in view.

On the way to Paiju camp we caught our first glimpse of K2, a hazy pyramid poking above the intervening mountains. It was only for a moment, as our course altered and it disappeared from view.

That night the camp-site was on the lower slopes of the beautiful peak of Paiju, in a small wood, out of place in so barren a land. From here we were to go onto the Baltoro glacier, the great untidy serpent of ice snaking down from the mountains many miles distant, carrying with it and pushing before it mounds of rubble scoured from the sides of the hills it passed. At Paiju camp we paid off twenty of our porters. Between ourselves and our three hundred porters we ate so much each day that we now had twenty fewer loads. With the porters, Tony Robinson and Allen Jewhurst were to return too. We had had to cross a wide, deep river two days previously and if they were to continue any further with us they ran the risk of finding it had become too deep to cross as the meltwater increased with the heat of the summer. We had a rest day at that camp. Some tensions came to a head in a violent confrontation between Captain Shafiq and a porter. Tut, who had organised and packed most of the gear, was seriously alarmed that a strike by the porters might make all his work useless if the gear never reached Base Camp. He castigated my theorising about the amount of bluff and counter-bluff in the behaviour of the two sides as being unreal and irresponsible. Chris pushed himself to the centre of the row and through the barriers of a four-stage translation of statements and proposals managed to exert some of the authority he presumed would have influence even with these Baltis.

That night, tensions defused, no trace of resentment was left, the darkness was noisy with singing and bright with fires. Allen took an active part in the dancing instigated by the porters, winning approving applause and gaining much popularity with the audience. I was sad to have him leave next day but the dangers for him and Tony on their own, with little experience of the mountains, were too real to ignore.

Chris produced a new plan for two people to go ahead of the main party to break trail up to Base Camp. The weather had deteriorated and we envisaged deep snow for the last few days before reaching the mountain. It would avoid delay and forestall any objections from the porters if a trail was already made through the snow. Doug and I were the only ones who did not have a specific task which would prevent us going ahead. Jim, as doctor, had to stay with the main party; Tut, as the one who knew most intimately all the different loads, of necessity had to be with the bulk of the baggage; Nick as treasurer, had to make regular payments as a few more porters were paid off each day according to the diminution of the loads of food. Everyone apart from Doug and myself had an indispensable role. The prospect of going ahead was exciting but the thought of breaking trail through deep snow was unwelcome. Tut seemed to fret at being tied to the main party. I did not know if he was keen to get ahead himself or felt that I was encroaching on his friendship with Doug. Most people work well in the mountains as partnerships and it was inevitable that we should all be getting to know each other with this in mind. On this trip, with Chris in overall command, there was a tendency to analyse his every statement or action, to sift out his train of thought and underlying intentions. On other expeditions he had engineered the pairing of people and subsequently the ordering of the movements on the mountain which would dictate the role of anyone in an attempt on the summit.

Chris was changeable in his opinion and his great failing or strength was that he usually thought aloud. This gave the impression of uncertainty but was simply a process which most people conduct within themselves and then produce a considered, final decision. An interpretation of Chris's overt mental process as uncertainty, and any subsequent attempts to impose a decision on him, was a mistake. No one succeeded in changing Chris's mind by any outright statement and each of us guarded the conceit that we had worked out the way to get Chris to adopt our own point of view, whatever premise he had started from, as if it were his own.

In the camp-site at Urdukass, the night before Doug and I were to leave to go ahead, we all conspired to see whether we could each manage to win Chris over to doing what we wanted him to do given that we knew that his initial reaction had been negative. Tut set out to overcome Chris's inexplicable objection to us sending off the mail runners before reaching Base Camp. It was going to be nearly six weeks after leaving Britain before we got any mail at this rate, but Chris felt it preserved the value of news reports if they were not diluted by the leaking out of titbits beforehand. Doug and I set out to convince Chris that Quamajan, our Hunza high-altitude porter, would be better off coming with us than staying with the main party. Quamajan was excellent company, intelligent, good-humoured and capable. He was to assist us on the mountain but before we reached there part of his duties were to assist Shere Khan, our cook. Quamajan was proving to be much more effective and reliable than Shere Khan, always ready to help and resourceful at sorting out problems. Doug and I thought he would be very useful coming ahead with us, but the rest of the team were equally keen that he should stay with them.

In the night it snowed. Our tents sagged under the weight, but by morning the sky was clear. The camp at Urdukass was on a grassy promontory above the glacier. Here the porters insisted on another day of rest in order to prepare their chupattis and dahl for the next few days when each night the halt would be in the middle of the ice. Doug and I left with a handful of porters and Quamajan, who had been assigned to us as our only means of communicating with other porters.

It was a relief to escape from the chores of the main group and head off towards the massive snowy peaks at the head of the valley. I was glad of the opportunity of getting to know Doug better. As a powerful personality it was not easy to pick out the real person in him from the role imposed

by the dynamics of the group we were in. Alone together, the very business
of basic interaction with each other would reveal much more of our real
persons to each other. On either side we were enclosed by great mountain
walls of untamed rock. The Trango Towers, the Baltoro Cathedrals, the
shapely summits of Masherbrum and the Muztagh Tower. They were all
names to conjure with; names I had only read of for years were now taking
form. For three days we travelled towards Concordia, junction point of
three glaciers, dominated by the stupendous wedge of Gasherbrum IV with
Broad Peak as a neighbour, gentle-shaped but huge.

On the first day the sun was bright on the new snow, so we issued
sunglasses to all the porters. They regarded them as ornaments or charms
and try as we could to keep check they wore them anywhere but over their
eyes. That night they complained of headaches and came for medication for
their eyes which had become inflamed from the rays of the sun, un-
weakened by its passage through the rarified air. At 13,000 feet the atmosphere absorbs much less of the damaging ultraviolet light than it does at
sea level. By morning three of the eight were completely snow-blind and
all but two were in extreme pain.

We were late starting anyway as when we made camp for the night I
opened the box which I had selected as containing fourteen days' worth of
food to discover it was box 14E, not box 14, and contained only gas
cartridges. Without food we were helpless and despatched the two still-
healthy porters back to Urdukass to bring, in double-quick time for extra
pay, the box we needed.

They arrived back with the box by 10.00 a.m. next day but our group
made a sorry sight as the snow-blinded porters held onto those who could
see in order to make a halting progress. Doug took the load from one and
carried it himself to hasten movement, but it was a waste of effort. We went
less than a mile before having to halt completely with the sick and woeful
porters.

Our camp on the rubble covering the ice was at 14,500 feet. When the
sun left the sky the cold immediately made itself felt. Doug and I stayed
up on a mound in the ice photographing the sunset till we were thoroughly
chilled and rushed back to our tent, sleeping bags and down jackets. The
porters settled themselves down inside a circular wall of stones which they
had rapidly constructed. They had little as insulation against the cold rocks
they lay on and for covering had only a blanket each. For warmth some of
them doubled up, sharing body heat and blankets with a partner. How they
slept in that cold I could not imagine.

By morning their eyes had recovered and we hurried on to keep ahead
of the main party, but there was no deep snow, and no trail to make. At
Concordia we caught the first full view of our mountain, K2. It was
colossal, a symmetrical pyramid, so vast that we could only gaze on it with

faith that somewhere in all that mass were the lines of weakness which would enable us to reach the top. Clouds came in and saved us from looking at it more until we were too close beneath it and the upper reaches were obscured by the lower buttresses.

We were half a day behind schedule when we reached a camp-site at the foot of the South-West Ridge of K2, a site overlooked by the snowy pinnacle of Angel Peak, a 20,000-foot adjunct to the main mountain. Our objective, the West Ridge, lay out of sight up the Savoia glacier, which curved down round the flanks of Angel Peak. Doug and I planned to survey the route up the Savoia glacier to where we wanted our main Base Camp. The weather was unsettled and we planned to wait but we were made to look foolish as the 'spearhead' of the team by the arrival of the main party only an hour or two after ourselves. There were complaints from them at Chris's insistence on doing a double stage to Concordia which had irritated the porters at the extra-long day and annoyed the team since it was dark before the baggage arrived and they were chilled and hungry in a spot exposed to wind from every direction.

Pete told me of how he had felt enthralled at the sight of the glacial valleys radiating from Concordia, and the breathtaking mountains which enclosed them. He said that he wanted to play some Bach or Beethoven on the tape deck and had been horrified when Nick, with characteristic irreverence, had played 'Bat out of Hell' by a modern band called Meatloaf, at full blast.

The presence of more than two hundred porters introduced an urgency which Doug and I had escaped from for a few days. With a large wage bill for every extra day the porters were with us, there was no longer any option about waiting till the weather cleared to find the way up to Base Camp. We left in deteriorating weather with a couple of porters from our advance group and skirted the flanks of Angel Peak to gain the upper plateau of the glacier.

Visibility was poor and we had to return after three hours, sure we had found the approximate region for the camp but unable to see more than a few yards in the thick mist.

There was old avalanche debris where we came onto the glacier but the mist hid the area of mountain it had come from. Doug was insistent that the trail we should take ought to be much further out on the glacier, but there were many crevasses and the deep snow concealing them made me favour risking the quicker route close to the mountain. Doug stressed his point of view in an opinionated way which seemed to have a self-importance I had not suspected in him. I offered the view that it might be more dangerous to take two hundred porters across an area riddled with innumerable hidden and deep crevasses when the alternative was an exposure of short duration to risk of avalanche. Neither option was ideal and neither of us conceded the point. The porters with us indicated that their preference was to stay close to the mountain, on firm ground for as long as possible.

Back with the rest of the team our efforts seemed futile anyway as another of those decisions had been made which reinforced the sense of being detached from the ordering of events. All except twenty-five of the porters were being paid off, and Base Camp was not going to be established in one day with one carry of all the equipment. Instead, the twenty-five porters selected would be issued with extra clothing and paid extra money to ferry the loads up over the next week.

When eventually Base Camp was habitable and we occupied it as our duties lower down permitted, Pete was overdue in arriving one afternoon and the fears about the dangers of the route along the flanks of Angel Peak were revived. He had stayed down at what we came to call the 'dump camp', to supervise the despatch upwards of the food loads, as Tut was doing with the gear. We knew he was due to arrive but by mid-afternoon there was no sign. Nick and Quamajan went back, keeping contact by radio, to ascertain the reasons for the non-appearance. They reappeared not long after with Pete, who was looking shaken and was coughing fitfully.

He had been later leaving the dump camp than he had intended. Tut was staying down there longer to continue his supervision of the movement of the loads but had opened a bottle of Pernod to celebrate his birthday. Pete was drunk by the time he left and had just stepped onto the glacier, an hour above the dump camp, when an avalanche broke loose from the mountain-side above him. He dropped his sack and ran back, collapsing in exhaustion when he reached the safety of the rocks he had not long left as the outlying flurries of powder snow from the avalanche dusted over him and entered his lungs. He had had to lie there for an hour before he felt recovered enough to retrieve his sack and carry on upwards.

Early on in my climbing career, before I had experienced their force, I had not understood how powerful and deadly an avalanche could be. I could not understand why people were killed and whole villages swept away by snow which I only knew as soft and insubstantial. But I had come to know how snow, even only a few inches deep, can slide down a slope gathering more snow on its way to form a colossal falling mass weighing thousands of tons which will obliterate or sweep away all in its path. In the mountains we had to be wary of every open expanse of snow. Firm, consolidated snow is the safest, and usually only moves if the warmth of the sun increases the moisture content and alters the equilibrium of the mass. Fresh snow on a firm base is the worst, as the firm base provides a smooth, frozen surface to which the new snow will not adhere and that new snow has no cohesion when it first falls. Ideally, one should avoid all potential avalanche zones, but it is not always possible.

I felt responsible for having urged this route in the first place; and of course my reasoning that a once-and-only passage across it would be safer than an intricate course through the crevasses had been lost in the process of altering the manner of establishing Base Camp.

III

Gradually we came together as a group and the chaos was channelled upwards into an agreed route through another frightening zone of crevasses and narrow clefts between ice and rock. We fixed ropes when we started up the mountainside as a hand-line for the ten porters who were ferrying loads up to Camp 1 for us. With eight of us expecting to be on the mountain at the same time, and the need to establish the six camps we were calculating on, much had to be carried up. Using the porters to carry the loads up the easier lower slopes liberated us to get on with making the route higher up.

We sat long and often staring at the mountain, trying to make sense of its features, trying to visualise whether a shadow indicated a gully, whether the rock step between two slopes of snow could be climbed, whether there were ledges high up wide enough for a tent. We discussed the possible lines we could take, discussed the likelihood of succeeding; we were all ambitious and without jostling for place we all wanted to reach the top. Nick stood out in one discussion, and I saw why he was so valuable when a group effort is needed. We were all agonising about whether individually we could make it to the top when Nick outclassed us all by saying, 'I don't care if I don't get to the top, so long as someone else does. It'll be bloody marvellous if any of us get up this,' and the vain soul-searching of the rest of us was made to look selfish.

Camp 1 was made beneath a buttress of rock, at the top of a smooth slope of snow. Always we liked the security of solid rock near which to camp, and, tucked in as we were on a platform dug by ourselves, we could sleep without fear of being overwhelmed in the night.

We occupied the camp on the mountain as we were liberated from the tasks below. Pete had completed his work with the food, Doug and I had been 'assistants' with no main responsibility for anything, so the three of us were first to take up residence in the camp.

It was snowing steadily as we erected the tents. I was slower arriving than the other two, any load seeming inordinately heavy, and I realised I was not yet sufficiently acclimatised. I did not feel ill, my mind was alive and willing, my body just would not move any faster. Doug was pouring abuse on the tent he had unpacked as I arrived. It was a model he had used before and found needlessly complicated to erect and, once erected, too confined for comfort. The wily old hand used this as a basis for suggesting, without waiting for demur, that Pete and I should have that tent whilst he chose another which he preferred for himself and in which, as compensation, he offered to do the cooking for all three of us.

We had radio contact with Base and thus had a chance to rectify omissions which had occurred through being out of practice with the business of making ourselves totally self-sufficient. At 4.00 p.m. there was no response but at the fall-back time half an hour later we were able to ask for mugs, spoons and plates, for my toothbrush and pens for Doug to keep his diary, and some down boots for use inside our sleeping bags. We wrote letters and cards to be taken down next day ready for despatch with the mail runners who were finally being sent off.

We led out more rope and fixed it in place up steeper snow. Camp 1 was at 19,500 feet and though we were slow from the altitude it was pleasing to be free of the tasks below to concentrate on the climbing.

It was a paradox of the expedition that those of us who had had least responsibility in organising the essentials should be first to be in the prime position, lead-climbing, breaking new ground and savouring the excitement of discovery – the very reason we had come.

Pete was going well. He had made an effort to stay fit by running as often as he could on the hills near the village where he lived in Switzerland. It seemed to be paying dividends; he and Doug were resolute in pressing on up in snow I thought too soft. I carried ropes in support and left them to finish the day when there was no more I could do. Doug had energy to spare for philosophical discussion, analysis of the people around him and of the progress of the trip. I talked with him a while before descending to Camp 1 as Pete was leading above. He told me how he did not find me easy company and wondered if there was any antagonism; he canvassed strongly his interest in trying to climb the mountain without using the oxygen equipment at all, since we had heard shortly before leaving about the ascent of Everest without oxygen by Messner and Habeler. He was always the same, always pushing forward plans to do more, go further that I had the confidence to promise.

Chris closed down on his administrative calculations and came up to join us at Camp 1. Tut still had work to do sorting out the gear into a logical sequence for sending it up the mountain, but he welcomed the stay below since he was feeling weak from a chill and a harsh cough contracted during the cold hours at Concordia waiting for the tents to arrive. Tony was filming some news reports but he too was not well. Jim stayed below to be on hand with the sick and to tend the ailments of the porters. Nick still had duties as a paymaster to the porters bringing gear up to Base from the dump camp.

Chris and I shared the lead next day from the high point Doug and Pete had reached. Chris was becoming a different person now that he was on the mountain. He seemed to relax from his assertive role once free of his paperwork, calculations and the onerous duty of presenting reports on progress for TV news, radio and newspaper. It was only the second time I had climbed with him, and he was eager to do as much as anyone. He took pleasure in the progress so far and enthused simply and directly about how well everything was going.

We climbed up a narrow, snowy gully and onto a rock rib leading directly up to the ridge. Above us the ridge, in profile, was horizontal running into the main mass of the mountain. I had favoured going onto the ridge but the profile was broken by towers of rock and it was impossible to tell from this distance whether our progress would be frustrated if not halted altogether by the many fruitless ups and downs on those towers. From the rib of rock we dropped down onto a steep slope of snow and gained a niche below a bulge of ice fifty feet away. From there the angle of the slope was much more gentle. We no longer fixed ropes in place because we were

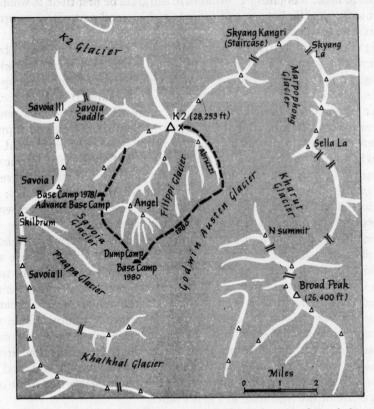

7. K2, showing the attempted lines of ascent for 1978 and 1980 and the second attempt in 1980 up the Abruzzi Ridge.

moving horizontally – it was little more than walking – and a rope would not have speeded up or made any easier passage across this section.

Chris went first for a while, breaking the trail. That was the hard work, tramping down the soft snow to make it easier for everyone else. He stopped frequently, as anyone would, tired by the effort, but pushed himself on and on, as if proving that he was not only good as an organiser. Every one of us had a similar struggle through the pain barrier of acclimatisation, every one of us had that struggle on his own, with only private reasons to drive him on. And everyone assumed, in the absence of complaint, that everyone else was better suited to the struggle. Chris stopped and asked if I wanted to go ahead in a tone which told me he had been waiting for me to offer. So I went further than he had, stung by the implication that I was not pulling my weight, and in six hundred feet we reached a cleft in the slope, twenty feet below some rock, which we thought would be safe for a camp. Doug and Pete arrived and dumped their loads of rope and tents. It was agreed to make this Camp 2. From here the ground steepened; it would be more difficult, take longer and offer less chance of a site for a camp. At 21,400 feet it was high enough.

No one was to occupy the camp that night, tomorrow we would bring more gear up from Camp 1 and two of us would then install ourselves, taking the first place in a rota of people climbing and fixing rope up the ground above.

We expected to place six camps on the route. Camp 1 would have to be able to accommodate us all, but thereafter the number of tents and supplies at each camp would diminish according to the number of climbers it was thought useful to occupy a particular camp. Ultimately the final camp needed to be only one tent for the summit pair. Even if we did all reach the summit, it was highly unlikely that it would be on the same day, and one tent would suffice, since anyone who had reached the summit would immediately be trying to descend lower than the top camp.

Nick had arrived at Camp 1 while we were away, bringing a liveliness and no-nonsense good humour to the company. We had to decide who would take up the choice position occupying and pushing on with the route from Camp 2. The lead pair would have all the excitement whilst the rest ferried supplies up to keep them moving. On the mountain, in a situation where we were all on an equal footing in terms of ability, Chris was reluctant to impose the authority he had exerted when there had been organisational and logistical problems earlier on in the expedition. It was Nick who resolved the question. 'Let's draw matchsticks,' he said, and the contrast could not have been more acute with the computerised print-outs of logistics for the mountain in Chris's office.

'Changabang rules,' said Nick, as the shortest matchsticks were drawn by Pete and myself. Out of five people it was not wildly unlikely that Pete and I should be selected by chance, but I did feel that it was something more than coincidental that we, who had grown to complement each other so well, should be thrown together again.

On 8 June, barely a week after reaching Base Camp, Pete and I moved up to occupy Camp 2. The other three carried loads up and scurried off down as we dug a platform out of the snow on the lip of the crevasse below the rock buttress we were relying on to prevent any slides of snow coming onto the tent. Clouds had moved in and squalls of snow forestalled any plans to do more than make ourselves comfortable in the tent. By the afternoon only radio contact at 3.30 p.m. kept us from feeling totally isolated in the swirling maelstrom of wind and snow that raged outside. I appreciated now Doug's fury over the tent below. Pete and I were again in a similar model only worse weather forced us to keep the entrances zipped tightly closed. We had no other tent to cook in and we had to choose between suffering constant flurries of snow if we ventilated the tent or suffocating in the fumes from the stove. Thickly falling snow weighed heavily against the tent and constricted the space inside. Lying full length we could feel with head and feet and side the walls pressing in under the weight.

I woke with a headache and when Pete tried to look outside we realised that the tent was almost buried under new snow. We cleared the air hole and resigned ourselves to another long wait. The storm was still strong and we could not move from the tent.

We were quite relaxed and passed the time eating, sleeping and reading. Pete had not lost his assiduous habit of keeping copious diary notes. I read Evelyn Waugh's *Scoop*, finding it light relief, but it was soon over and I too resorted to scribbling to pass the time. Pete persevered with a book called *Meetings With Remarkable Men* by Gurdjieff, exclaiming in amazement every so often.

On the second morning we were all but suffocated again by the depth of snow over the tent. Only a corner poked clear. Pete spent a long time braving the furious wind to dig free the tent. Most of the time we did not need to stir outside. Doctor Jim had even issued us with hospital 'pee-bottles'. I contributed to the communal well-being by erecting a makeshift canopy over one entrance in an attempt to create a ventilated but wind-free area for cooking. Time had begun to drag. With the lack of exercise and poor ventilation I seemed to have a headache most of the time. On the radio we learnt that the others at Camp 1 were only better off in that they had more tent space and more people. News from Base Camp was discouraging. Pete and I had no cause to speak to Base but we listened in at the separate time arranged for communication between Camp 1 and Base. This was another break in the monotony, another milestone round which the time could hinge. Tut was very disillusioned by the jobs which had kept him below, by sickness and now by the relentless storm which imbued the expedition with an air of hopelessness. Tony too was still unwell. Certainly the quantities of snow which had fallen would not help us once the storm did abate. A radio call full of such pessimism was worse than the isolation we had known on Changabang. Here we were with other people, but from them, whom we imagined walking about freely, we felt not a morsel of optimism or encouragement.

By the third morning we accepted the continued howling of the wind and swirling snow with the resignation of lethargy. Then Pete went outside at 10.00 a.m. to relieve himself and shouted in that he could see figures leaving Camp 1 and moving upwards. Snow had stopped falling and only the wind blowing snow from the surface gave the impression of a storm. We hastened to depart, fearing their wrath should they arrive to find us in bed.

We need not have worried. Pete and I led out and fixed six hundred feet of rope, watching the ant-like progress of the three figures from below. We could not distinguish who was who, tiny specks as they were from our height. They were slower than any of us had been on the stretch above Camp 1. We could not say why, whether they too were feeling the effects of two days of inactivity, whether the snow was too deep and soft or their loads were very heavy. There was no deep snow on the slope Pete and I climbed. It was steep ice, too steep to hold new snow, and then we reached stretches of rock also steep. From there we turned back – it was well on in the afternoon – and as we did we noticed that the three from below had not reached our tent but were turning back, having dumped their loads.

On the radio Chris said the snow was terribly deep and they had had to dig clear all the ropes fixed in place. Tomorrow they would start earlier and really try to reach Camp 2 because we were almost out of gear and food.

At Camp 2 we had grown accustomed to the discomfort of our cramped quarters and had agreed on the routine from Changabang days of Pete cooking breakfast and me the evening meal. Pete read his book, announcing his growing conviction that *Meetings With Remarkable Men* was not the light sort of reading he would choose in future for the mountain. I unwrapped the evening ration packed all those months ago in a Salford warehouse and wrapped for fun in a centre-spread from *Playboy* or *Mayfair*. The pictures, contrived at the best of times, now were as meaningless as arcane hieroglyphs. It had been a secret joke to amuse the other members, not ourselves.

We lay content after breakfast till the sun warmed us and eased the start to the day. At last the weather was fine. The night had been a cold, inky blue. At dawn it changed to pale and still it was fine. We left the tent, pulling ourselves along the ropes from yesterday. The headaches and lethargy of days of confinement in the tent evaporated with the clear air and satisfaction of movement.

High point 1980 23,000 ft

High point 1978 22,500 ft

C 2 1978

C 1 1980 21,000 ft

C 1 1978

*Site of
avalanche, 1978*

Base Camp 1978
Advance Base Camp 1980

4. The route up K2, showing the high points reached in 1978 and the first
attempt in 1980.

It was Pete's turn in the lead. I stood paying out the ropes, watching the three little dots leaving Camp 1 at the start of their long haul upwards, bringing supplies so that we could keep going without any break in progress. The three anonymous specks were still moving slowly as on their previous sortie, but there would be plenty of time for them to reach our camp with their loads.

It was wonderful to be out in front. I looked forward to the time when I would take over from Pete, even though that would be harder work. Meanwhile I stood gazing at countless mountains that had come into view now that we were so high. The day was completely calm, I was content to be there. There was something unreal about the situation, something of the atmosphere of a bank holiday in sunny weather, a day quite different from an ordinary work day. I had to bring myself back to reality, remind myself that this was just another day in the life of the Karakoram, that on just such a day Herman Buhl had died on Chogolisa, Bride Peak, which I could see in the distance.

Two of the matchstick men from below had started across the slope to our camp when it was time for me to follow up the ropes and take over the leading. I carried coils of more rope, adjusted the zig-zag course that Pete had laid as he sought the best way up. This was the toil without interest. Mechanical actions one after the other and a pause for breath. Always we subjected ourselves to this mindless effort; there was no inadequacy, one could only do so much at a time.

I heard vaguely the roar of an avalanche. There were so many in this cirque of mountains that one hardly glanced up any more. We could often hear the roar echoing from mountains miles away. I heard Pete shout and caught the note of awe in his voice as if this avalanche was particularly spectacular. I glanced round and looked at the distant peaks. Seeing nothing, I turned to move upwards again.

'No, look!' It was urgency, not awe, and below me I saw the slope beyond our tent sliding away in a billowing column of cloud. Where I had last seen two figures there was now only one.

The foreground hid the tent itself from view and I prayed that the impossible had happened and that the missing figure was also concealed there.

I shouted. There was no response. Pete was not certain if anyone had been on that part of the slope. I dumped my load and slid off down towards the tent a thousand feet away. I could see nothing for a time as a rise in the slope still hid the tent and figure. Tears of anticipation sparked my eyes as I rose over the hump seconds away from knowing. Only one figure was there. It was Doug, drinking from a water bottle. I was relieved that he was safe. I could see another figure six hundred feet away across the other side of the avalanche-swept slope. Still I hoped.

'Was anyone in that avalanche?'

'Nick.'

I sank down and cried.

Pete arrived and Doug told us how he had escaped. He had been crossing the slope first. It was deep in snow and he was taking a thin line across to fix as a hand-rail lest the surface of the slope should slide away and someone lose their footing. Nick had set off after him, following in his tracks, with a karabiner clipped to his waist, running freely along the rope. Doug said he felt a tremor in the snow and then another. Looking back, he saw the slope above Nick breaking away and then Nick was engulfed in huge blocks and carried off down towards the glacier thousands of feet below. Doug himself, though clear of the avalanching area, was dragged down too because tied to his waist was the rope to which Nick was clipped. He had tumbled in the air helplessly, landed heavily in the deep snow and stopped. The rope had snapped. He was still clear of the avalanche but Nick had been taken with it. He showed us the frayed, uneven end of the thin line where it had parted and threw it down in disgust. A friend was dead.

We could not say if anyone else knew. Across the slope was Quamajan, our Hunza helper. Chris had felt unwell and stayed behind. Doug suggested trying to make radio contact. Pete made a few attempts at raising Camp 1 or Base but there was no response. We left the radio open as we talked over what to do. We had to go down, go and meet the others, and then . . . ? A friend, a husband, a father, a son was dead and it had happened so quickly. I could not take it in. I had always associated death with a struggle, the inevitable end to suffering or deprivation. But this did not seem right. Nick had gone so unexpectedly, with so little fuss, that I half-imagined we were enacting a scenario, that we would go down and find he was at Camp 1, chortling mischievously at our foolish fancies.

The radio crackled with a voice.

'Camp 1 to Camp 2, anyone listening? Over.'

Doug, big hands, capable and in control, took it up and spoke.

'Hello, Camp 1, Doug here. Nick has been killed in an avalanche. Repeat Nick has been killed in an avalanche. Over.'

There was no response for a while. Then we heard words and sobbing and Doug told them we were coming down.

We had not decided to end the expedition at that but we took down with us anything of personal value lest we did not return. The slope from which Nick had been lost was now swept clear of snow. Firm ice was the foundation left. There was no danger as we made our way across it. Doug went first, running out a rope from the tent back across to where Quamajan was waiting and trembling. I saw the hollow in the snow where Doug had landed in his somersault downwards and the tracks he had made to climb back to the tent. Inexplicably the snow he had been on had not moved, though there had been nothing visible to distinguish it from where Nick had been. The frayed end of the other half of the line was still lying in the area where Nick had last been seen.

At Camp 1 Chris was waiting, unashamed tears streaking his face, as if he too was hoping desperately that there had been some error, that his best friend was not really dead, that somehow we could discuss it, go over it and solve the problem and that all would not be as hopeless as it now seemed. Quamajan's face too showed sadness, regret and dismay. He opened his hands for me to see the burn marks where he had tried to hold the rope as Nick was being dragged down until the snapping of the rope had eased the strain. He had shared a cigarette with Nick and had got up to carry on but Nick had stopped him and said he would go next.

Jim Duff was at Camp 1. It was he who had been apprehensive when he saw the avalanche. Chris had thought it was well away from where any of us would be and had been taking photographs of the monstrous column of snow as it fell. Jim's uneasiness prevailed and he had switched on the radio on the chance that anyone from Camp 2 might be listening or trying to call and that was when we had picked up his reply.

We were lost and aimless. The day was too late for us to descend to Base Camp, and we settled into the tents to pass a bleak night. Quamajan shared a tent with Shere Khan, who had also come up to Camp 1. As cook, Shere Khan had been leisurely and uninspired. On the mountain now he looked quite out of place, staring about, weakly smiling for reassurance. Pete appeared composed, seeming to have come to terms already with the accident with the resigned fatalism of a doctor on a casualty ward. He pushed himself into the tent with Chris, seeming to sense that he needed someone near to share his grief. Doug and Jim shared a tent and I lay alone as darkness came and tried not to think of Nick in the frozen chaos of those thousands of tons of ice and snow below.

I could hear Doug voicing aloud his heart-searching questions about the point of what we were doing, the point of coming to the mountains, the damage it does to ourselves, our friends, our families. For those moments when he too was being dragged down by the rope he had thought the end had come for him. He had not been afraid, he said, just interested to see what there was on the other side of that thing called death.

I felt the need for some company and I edged precariously over to the tent where Chris and Pete were also talking. Chris welcomed me with an unnecessary look of apology for his obvious display of emotion. He was heartbroken. We shared memories of Nick and talked of what to do. I had no intuitive feeling about it. Whatever we decided I knew Nick would not mind. He had always been eminently practical and in a similar situation I believed he would have come up with a rational rather than emotive decision.

At first light we went down. Doug was away first to scour the avalanche debris on the glacier below. There was no trace. The mountain was heavy with cloud, the tents of Base Camp were hardly visible until we were on them. Thick snow had started to fall.

As soon as he was back, Chris initiated the discussion about the future of the expedition. We all sat in the huge box tent, a leftover from the 1975 Everest expedition. There was an awkwardness about the gathering, an attempt to talk about other things, talk heartily about any petty detail rather than the real issue. Experience did not help to decide how to behave after a death.

This expedition, the product of two years of preparation, the hopes of many of us, the object in which other people had invested money and their aspirations, an entity in itself fashioned by press and television, had been in the end the means by which someone was killed.

We had each to decide what we wanted to do; in this no order could be issued, only personal volition carried each individual upwards. There were always a multitude of reasons on a big mountain for not going on, and every reason a valid one, but the most powerful, the one which decides above all others, is the lack of will. Without the will to go on, no amount of authority could force anyone upwards.

Chris's mind was made up. In the long, restless night he had come to the conclusion that we would achieve nothing by abandoning the expedition, that we had put too much into the preparations for this climb to call a halt now. If we could find a safer route up the mountain there was every justification in having another attempt.

Doug was adamant against going on. He had experienced Nick's death in a way none of us had, and was deeply affected. It threw into question the reasons for climbing at all, it showed how dangerous our route was and he felt our progress had been slow anyway, showing our route to be impractical. His heart was no longer in it and he would not be able to settle down to spending more weeks on the mountain when his wife, Jan, and his family and all our families and friends would be living through agonies for the next weeks when they heard the news, unless we all returned at once.

Jim Duff was of the same mind. The prospect of climbing K2 had ceased to promise any enjoyment.

Pete was as strong as Chris for continuing with the climb. To him it was illogical to abandon the climb when that was the reason he had come. He said he felt more at home in the mountains and that to come to them, with all that they had to offer, was a decision he had made long ago.

Tut had given up hope of achieving much himself on the mountain; the illness which had bedevilled him for the last two weeks was still with him. He thought we should give up the climb, but if it was decided to carry on he would go along with that and do what he could in a supporting role.

Tony wanted to continue but he felt ambivalent about voting for that because he too had not acclimatised well and felt that he had not contributed much to the climbing so far.

I tried to sort out in my own mind, as everyone else was talking, what I wanted to do. Chris had said on his arrival back that there was no point in delaying the discussion about the future of the trip and I thought I must be alone in not knowing my own mind. Either decision would be justified, I thought. There was no shame in abandoning the climb because a colleague had been killed; it emphasised the risks of this route, risks which had been with us since the dump camp, up through the narrows, across the crevassed areas, up and across avalanche-strewn slopes. It was understandable to call a halt and draw back for breath. Returning now would be a demonstration to Nick's wife, Carolyn, of the sincerity of our sympathy and regrets. On the other hand, nothing we could do would bring him back, and only that would be a satisfactory solution to the awful catastrophe. We had all climbed for years, we all knew and accepted the risks. We had come to climb K2 because implicitly we had decided the risk was worthwhile, to attempt to climb something so difficult and improbable. We had taken on commitments, accepted sponsorship, had responsibilities to more than ourselves, because we had chosen to sell our project to make it possible. If we returned now we would be £20,000 in debt.

The team was now substantially weakened. Of the seven of us remaining, two were not confident of recovering sufficiently to make any positive contribution. It did not seem at all fair to expect assistance from our two Hunzas or any of the ten high-altitude porters who were still with us. We were here because we chose to be; if it was dangerous, we had made up our minds to court that danger against the chance of obtaining the satisfaction of climbing a mountain. Our porters were with us because the pay was good and they would go further and run risks if we asked them because they needed the money for their families, but it was wrong for us to rely upon such pressures purely for our own gratification.

Chris, with his mind made up, argued forcefully and Pete gave him strong support. But Doug and Jim were at a polar extreme in their attitudes. The debate was concluded with a decision to call off the expedition. Enthusiasm is not something that can be engendered by a majority vote; it had to be all of us or nothing. No one would make any progress if only half-hearted about continuing.

Once the basic question was resolved, events had to move fast. We had to decide how best to get the news back to Carolyn and avoid any leak before she had been personally told. We did not dare risk using the radio transmitter, for once on the air we would have no control over the distribution of the information. Someone would have to go back immediately and only break the news publicly once Carolyn had been informed. Chris, whose influence would gain him a seat on a plane and access to communication which we would not have, was the best person and Doug was to accompany him.

In the afternoon, having mulled over the decision and obviously dissatisfied with it, Chris brought everything up again. He was anxious that we were being too hasty in the decision. Even now it was barely twenty-four hours since the accident and there was still time to reconsider. But the decision of the morning had crystallised everyone's views and if there had been little chance of convincing anyone by argument then, there was less chance now that the decision had banished one possibility and directed thoughts along a separate path.

We began the heart-rending process of dismembering the expedition, jettisoning the unnecessary food and equipment to rationalise the amount of gear we would take back, once Chris and Doug had sent back sufficient porters. They left; Pete and I returned to Camp 1 to clear that of all valuable gear and all of us ferried loads down to the dump camp ready for the arrival of the porters some two weeks hence.

We waited in a limbo, reluctant sharers of a knowledge which would shatter some lives still continuing their daily routine. We learnt to live with the knowledge, came to terms with it in our own ways, though I still had the feeling that it was all a mistake, and that Nick was still there, lying in the tent next door, listening to some music. As the days went on and I accepted the fact that he was no longer with us, I grew apprehensive of the arrival of the porters and the return to another life where we would meet people, Nick's family and friends, and where the horror would revive, kindled by their reactions.

I saw more clearly now the reasons for some of the reluctance I had sensed in Ruth, the American woman, when I had accompanied her back from Dunagiri – a reluctance to face a reawakening of grief which she had begun to bring under control.

Shafiq spent his time hammering out a memorial plaque to Nick from a large disc of aluminium, one of the covers from a big cooking pot. Pete and I took the plaque up to our Camp 1 when we returned to retrieve sleeping bags and clothing.

The walk-out was joyless exertion. Long, hard days trying to cover as much ground as possible, but even so it still took eight days of walking from Base Camp before we arrived at the pick-up point for the jeep. The rivers were much more swollen and we spent the latter days alternately sweltering under the heat of the sun and being numbed by the cold of the rushing torrents across which we had to wade.

We arrived in Skardu on 29 June and a week later we were still there. There were supposed to be one or more flights per day to Islamabad but none came. We were only an hour away by plane but the planes used on that sector are not strong enough to outfly the bad weather which builds up over the intervening mountains. The planes would set off from Islamabad each day but turn back from halfway, and each day we would journey down to the airstrip to sit in the dust and wait with new hope and eventual disappointment. When the first plane did arrive, Tut and Jim talked their way on board, but officially we were down for the third plane and it was another three days before the rest of us reached Islamabad. After all the forced marching to reach Skardu, we had had to wait a frustrating ten days, able to do nothing because a substantial part of each day was taken up with the waiting for the possible arrival of another plane.

During this period of waiting Pete and I began to discuss returning to K2, returning to climb it by any route, as Pete had never wanted to abandon the attempt and I was coming to feel a growing resolve to complete our unfinished business with the mountain.

SIX

In the Treasure House of the Great Snow

KANGCHENJUNGA

I

Shortly before we had all left for K2, Doug had asked me if I wanted to join him and his American friend, Mike Covington, on an expedition to Nepal, to a mountain called Nuptse in the Everest region. Nuptse, 25,850 feet high, is one of the three peaks of the horseshoe of mountains which includes Everest and Lhotse. Doug had planned to go there the year before but had been prevented by the accident on the Ogre in which both his legs were broken. His interest in Nuptse was undiminished and, having booked the mountain, he wanted a third member for his team.

Without a thought I agreed, although the climb was planned for the autumn of 1978 and that would leave me only three months in England between the two expeditions.

We were not at all successful on the mountain. Hampered by frequent storms and constant heavy falls of snow we gave up before long. This second failure in a matter of months left me disillusioned and dissatisfied. I wondered if we did not have sufficient motivation after being so recently away, wondered if we had really tried hard enough and whether other things were drawing us back. After K2 I had regretted agreeing to embark so soon on another expedition, though, after a week back in England, I was yearning to be away again. I had not thought to consult my girlfriend, Louise, taking it for granted that the decision to go concerned me alone, but when the time came I was sorry to leave. Doug was to be a father again around the time of the expedition and I did not know what strains this might impose.

During the expedition, Mike Covington became critically ill and never recovered enough to come onto the mountain, which left just Doug and myself. We spent days in the Western Cwm encircled by the horseshoe of mountains – Everest, Lhotse and Nuptse – as the snow piled deeper and deeper over the tents. When we did get onto the mountain we floundered to a halt, having taken many hours to climb up only a few hundred feet of normally easy ground. Conditions on the mountain seemed unanswerable and we turned back, but afterwards I could never be sure if I had pushed hard enough. Afterwards there was always the niggling doubt that I was not strong enough in resolve for when the going was rough, and the doubts undermined my intentions for the future.

The expedition to Kangchenjunga was planned for the spring of 1979, a few months hence, but that held no consolation. I was beginning to see that my whole way of life was dependent upon the pursuit of a most difficult and unlikely goal – the climbing of mountains by their hardest routes. All my hopes and aspirations seemed to have become linked with that objective, and I no longer knew if I wanted that sort of life.

Nepal had been fun; after the rigorous atmosphere of Islam, there was a relaxed good humour about this little country imbued with Hindu and Buddhist tradition. As a trio we had worked together well, Doug showing an energetic commitment that had not seemed to be there when he was swamped by the size of the K2 expedition. I only met Mike Covington for the first time the evening before we left for Nepal. He was easy to get along with and seemed to look with wry amusement on Doug's philosophising and soul-searching which I found wearing. In the end it was Mike who surprised us all by announcing he was not coming back with us but was staying on in the mountains for a while to marry the Sherpa girl who had nursed him while he was sick. Later she joined him in America, leaving her village which had neither water nor electricity, more than a week on foot from a road, for a future in Colorado.

The winter of 1978/79 back in England was one of deep snow and frustration. Louise had had enough of a boyfriend who was away for half the year and when not away was preoccupied with preparing to go. The Kangchenjunga departure date in March drew near and every spare moment was taken up with the arrangements to go away. The snowfalls which kept the country disrupted and the village where I lived frequently cut off emphasised the illogicality of this chosen way of life, preparing in the depths of winter for an expedition into more cold and snow, and setting off at the approach of spring.

Doug and Pete had been talking about this expedition to Kangchenjunga for some time. They had first asked me to go in the autumn of 1977, making up a team of four. Doug, with his typical presumption, put the question:

'Do you want to come to Kanch in 1979?'

'Yes, of course.'

'Good. We've already got you on the notepaper.'

Tut Braithwaite had also been coming but he had not sufficiently recovered from the chest infection he contracted on the K2 expedition. We needed a fourth. In the autumn of 1978 I suggested that Doug ring Georges Bettembourg, a French climber living in America. I had met him for ten minutes in a bank in Islamabad and Doug had met him on a couple of other occasions. None of us could say we knew him, but we had all been impressed at the very rapid ascent he had made of Broad Peak in the Karakoram with Yannick Seigneur. Only nine days after establishing their Base Camp they had climbed this mountain of over 26,000 feet. Subsequently he had been phoning Doug, dropping very large hints that he was available for an expedition if the opportunity should occur. Oddly enough there were few people who did have the experience for a mountain as big as Kangchenjunga who were available.

Doug phoned Georges and he accepted immediately.

For long thought to be the highest mountain in the world, Kangchenjunga was finally recognised during the precise tabulation of heights undertaken by the survey of India in the nineteenth century as ranking third in height. The two higher peaks, Everest and K2, lurk scarcely visible from places of habitation. Kangchenjunga, on the other hand, lying at the eastern end of the Himalayan chain, is readily visible from Darjeeling. To the colonials, escaping to that hill station from the heat of the plains of India, the ethereal mass of Kangchenjunga, sprawling above the clouds, came to represent the Himalayas.

The mountain sits astride the border between Nepal and Sikkim, and is regarded by the people of Sikkim as the home of a deity, and therefore sacred. The name Kangchenjunga means 'The Five Treasure Houses of the Great Snow'. The 'Great Snow' refers to the eternal snow which rests on the mountain, contrasting sharply with the heat of pre-monsoon India. The 'Five Treasure Houses' refers to the five distinct summits which stand up from the main mass of the mountain.

By the time we were coming to climb the mountain the main summit of 28,208 feet had been reached by only six people – four British, one Indian and one Sherpa. All had promised not to set foot on the summit itself out of deference to the belief of the Sikkim. They feared that if anyone did set foot in the home of the gods then avalanches, floods, landslides and pestilence would be unleashed in retribution.

Attempts on the mountain had been made as early as 1905 when a motley assortment of individuals under the leadership of Alistair Crowley arrived in Nepal. They set up camp at the head of the Yalung glacier and reached an estimated 21,325 feet when tragedy struck. Three European members of the expedition and three porters were on their way up to Camp 7, situated at 20,500 feet, when one of the porters fell and pulled the others off balance one by one. Their efforts to arrest their fall came to nought when the snow broke away beneath their feet and they were swept down in an avalanche. One of the Europeans, Pache, and the three porters were buried deeply in the snow. The two survivors, Guillarmod and de Righi, extracted themselves but had an impossible task trying to dig free their buried companions with their bare hands. On hearing of the accident, Crowley refused to descend to help. He stayed in his tent drinking tea and declaimed: 'A mountain accident of this sort is one of the things for which I have no sympathy whatever ... Tomorrow I hope to go down and find out how things stand ... the doctor is old enough to rescue himself, and nobody would want to rescue de Righi.' The four buried in the snow died and their bodies were not recovered till three days later.

The sentiments expressed by Crowley during that incident indicate an attitude to events quite different from the ethos which normally governs behaviour on a mountain.

Kangchenjunga is a massive mountain, with long ridges and subsidiary peaks sprawling over many miles on axes north-south, east-west. To go from one part of the mountain to another – from the south-west to the north-west or south-west to south-east – requires an arduous journey of several days or a difficult ascent over one of the ridges. These practical difficulties prevented ready exploration of all the possible ways of climbing the mountain but they were political reasons which usually dictated the way the mountain was tackled.

A German expedition under Paul Bauer made two attempts in 1929 and 1931 on the North-East Ridge, starting from Sikkim. They were driven back by storms on both occasions but their efforts met with the highest praise and Kangchenjunga came to be regarded as a 'German' mountain, much as Everest was long considered a 'British' mountain as most of the attempts to climb it originated from Britain.

The only expedition to make an attempt from the north-west, which was where our intentions lay, was an international expedition in 1930 led by George Dyhrenfurth. He had managed to obtain permission to enter through Nepalese territory to reach the mountain, but called off the expedition when an avalanche from the route killed one of the Sherpas.

The mountain was not climbed until 1955 when a British team led by Charles Evans put four people on top – Joe Brown, George Band, Norman Hardie and Tony Streather. They found a way up the South-West Face, using oxygen equipment from their top camp.

The only other expedition which was successful in climbing the mountain was from India in 1977 led by Colonel N. Kumar. Major Prem Chand and Naik Nima Dorje Sherpa reached the top, thus completing the route attempted by the German expeditions. They also used oxygen, and described the route from the north-east as being particularly long and difficult.

In recent years no expeditions have been allowed to attempt Kang-chenjunga from Sikkim, apart from the one from India. In Nepal the mountain is in an area not easily accessible to foreigners and relatively few expeditions are allowed there either. We regarded it as a great coup when, in October of 1977, we learnt from our expedition agent Mike Cheney, in Kathmandu, that permission to attempt the mountain from the north-west had been granted to us.

II

For Kangchenjunga we worked on a budget of £9,000. We each paid in £1,700 and the rest was found in the grants from the Mount Everest Foundation and British Mountaineering Council. This expedition swallowed up the rest of the money I had saved over the last couple of years, but it was more important to me and to the other members of the team to go on the expedition than relish the security of money in the bank or anything it could buy. Georges had an extensive collection of rare crystals, some of which he sold to find his share of the money.

Returning to Nepal in March of 1979 was like coming home; it was as if I had just slipped away briefly for a holiday and had returned to a mountain country where I most belonged. I emerged from the storerooms of Sherpa Cooperative, our expedition agency, after a day spent packing gear, sorting supplies and making arrangements for insurance and mail despatch. Kathmandu was busy with movement, the sky above was blue and the youthful Nepalese flowed past the gates. I realised that all day I had not given a thought to where I was, to the different culture we had come into, to the wonder of arriving in a place which excited the imagination of my brothers and sisters and all my friends. That evening, having a meal in one of the convivial restaurants of the city, I found I was looking about expectantly as if I was in a pub at home and people I knew might drop in at any time.

Georges impressed us all with his dynamism. He bubbled with energy and darted about forever active with the preparations for departure. Beside him, we three who had been together several times on expeditions appeared to be leisured old-timers who had learnt the tricks of the trade and had absorbed some of the unhurried pace of life in the East.

Pete flew out two days later than Georges, Doug and myself. He had had some commitments in England which had prevented him leaving with us. We chastised him for the delay, since it threw more work onto us, but it enabled him to bring out my cameras, which I had forgotten, and some new plastic boots we wanted to test on the mountain. Always feet and hands are most at risk from the cold and we had heard that these plastic boots were much more effective than conventional leather boots, so we intended to try them. When we opened the boxes we were disappointed to discover that they looked little different from normal ski-mountaineering boots.

Doug too was quite at home in Kathmandu, having visited it so many times that he now had a small cache of equipment there and friends among the Sherpas who had come to settle in the city in order the more easily to be on hand for work with expeditions.

Because we were uncertain of the scale of our objective, and because we wanted a replacement on hand lest any of us became sick, we asked the agency for the services of two Sherpas who were known to be competent climbers. Doug knew Ang Phurba from Khumjung to be an excellent Sherpa, having climbed with him on Everest in 1975, and subsequently regarded him with high esteem. Ang Phurba selected Nima Tensing from Pangboche as a partner and though Nima seemed to be older than someone we would have chosen, we were intrigued to learn that, as a youngster, he had been a Sherpa on the first successful expedition to Kangchenjunga in 1955.

We believed four to be the best number to tackle the mountain but were aware of the risk of illness weakening the team. The alternative would have been to have more climbers from Britain, but the expedition would have been much bigger and more unwieldy, and any climber would expect to have more than a secondary role if he was in fact capable of climbing the mountain.

Since we were planning to climb the mountain, if possible, without oxygen equipment, there was no need for the logistical build-up necessary when many weighty oxygen bottles have to be carried up a mountain to a position in which they will be useful for a summit assault. Once the lower part of the route was assessed and climbed, our intention was to go for the summit, carrying all that was necessary on our backs, in one go. At this time, however, we knew of no mountain as big as Kangchenjunga that had been climbed by a new and difficult route for the first time without oxygen and by a team as small as four. There were many unknowns and, unlike the detailed planning that had gone into the K2 expedition, there were many things we could not plan for until we were confronted by the mountain itself.

Ang Phurba was quiet and reflective. He listened to a question with his head tilted to one side, his cheeks sucked in, as he considered all the implications and then he would answer in a serious and assured manner. He knew the mountains, he knew the people and he was totally reliable. We entrusted him with money and he made the necessary purchases of food, hired and paid off porters as was needed and when he came to the end of the money he presented us with meticulously detailed accounts on scraps of paper of how it had been spent. Nima was ever present as his dependable colleague. His English was not fluent, so he transmitted his good-will and readiness to do anything with a huge smile and alacrity of response.

The first time I went to the Himalayas I was worried about everything; I stayed with the porters to keep check on the loads, I could not discern any order in their behaviour and felt that the success of the expedition was subject to their whims. Kangchenjunga was the fifth expedition I had been on and now I had learnt to relax, to leave the ordering of events to our trusted men of the hills. They arranged more efficiently than we could the porters to hire, the food to buy, the places to stop each night.

It suited us to be relieved of these everyday duties and when we started walking we could use the time to relax after the frantic months preceding the expedition and begin to re-focus on the mountain ahead.

From the previous autumn I carried a memory of the approach to the mountains in Nepal as being one long, leech-filled tunnel through jungle greenery and I dreaded the walk-in to Kangchenjunga. The route starts in the plains of the Terai region and passes for days through humid, leech-infested terrain, up along forested hillsides and down into sweltering valleys. We had been told that this region was worse than most but we were lucky that it was March, for we learnt that the leeches do not appear till the monsoon rains of the summer.

We started from a Gurkha camp in Dharan Bazaar in a long toil upwards. It was a punishing climb in the heat of the day, dripping with sweat, the aches from a sedentary life making themselves felt as our bodies were introduced to the new regimen. It was unclear for how long we would have to walk before reaching Base Camp; so few expeditions had been this way that there was no defined routine of stopping places, length of a day's march, nor exact route that we could ascertain. The closest estimate was that it would take us between two and three weeks of walking to reach the northern side of the mountain.

Doug tended to make his own pace, shouldering his sack soon after breakfast and disappearing along the track, preferring to walk alone with his own thoughts, reading and writing at every stop, as if not a moment was to be wasted in his search for insights into the mystery of life. Sometimes we would come upon him having already soaked up all he wanted to see and photograph of an interesting village or temple, profferring for us to sample some delicious oranges, another of his discoveries.

Georges, Pete and I often walked together. It was fun to have someone as boisterous and volatile as Georges to discover as a person. Perhaps because we knew so little of him or perhaps because, being French, there was a cultural difference in his attitude, Georges had a viewpoint on many topics quite different from any I had known. He spoke English very well but he still retained the directness of language of someone speaking a foreign tongue and was not inhibited in his words and expression. He had not learnt to cloak his meaning with nuance and metaphor.

Georges fulfilled in many ways the stereotype of the eligible Frenchman. He was married and talked often of his wife, so we felt that we knew her, but he could not resist playing the Gallic charmer. He was dark-haired, bronzed and wore a neat head-band which gave him a cavalier attractiveness. On the flight from London we had touched down in Moscow and, seeing two Russian air stewardesses sitting alone, Georges sat himself beside them. He embarked on a rapid chat, of which they understood not a word, looking at him in confusion until an armed guard inspired them to move off.

Georges talked freely of many things. He spoke of his love life and his attitude to relations with his wife and other women with a frankness which Pete, with all his reserve and delicacy of expression, found astonishing. Pete talked more frequently than I had noticed before of sex and marriage, questioning Georges, as if he were an expert, about the whole business. Georges was glad to expand on his ideas about 'chicks' or 'birds', as he put it, using the words consciously, proud of their acquisition into his vocabulary as marking a step forward in his grasp of the language. He believed in open relationships and felt that if two people were living together or married this need not preclude relationship of a temporary nature with other people, given that one understood who one really loved. If two people were separated for a long spell, such as we ourselves going off on this expedition would be separated from wife or girlfriend, he thought it perfectly acceptable that either partner should form a relationships with someone if the need was felt during the separation. Pete would listen in open-mouthed amazement to these opinions which were radically opposed to his own concepts of love and marriage. But he was fascinated by Georges's openness and quizzed him again and again about subjects he himself was normally too reticent to discuss except in most general terms.

We were all aware that we were imposing a strange mode of living on ourselves by cutting ourselves off for many weeks from our loved ones. Doug believed that having any female company on a trip would exercise a civilising influence on behaviour and introduce a more balanced element into the little, isolated society of the expedition. For some reason Pete thought I was opposed to the idea, giving me a glimpse of the impression he had formed of me as a single-minded fanatic, who wanted no distraction from the chosen objective. In principle everyone agreed that a mixed expedition or female company on an expedition would be desirable, but we suspected that many people held an idealised view of expedition life and did not see it for the hard work and deprivation it was.

We were some days along the way before I really turned my attention to the mountain we had come to climb. For two days I was ill with severe stomach cramps, nausea and diarrhoea, wanting to do nothing but rest and forcing myself along the track oblivious of the surroundings. Doug was all solicitous and caring, seeking out medicines and preparing herbal teas which he thought would cure me. He gave me a bottle of Kaolo Morphine and I walked with it in my hand, taking swigs to quell the nausea and hoping the morphine would drug me enough to blank out the physical distress.

Pete voiced his concern that we were being too casual in our approach to the mountain, that we would all have to be at the peak of form to have a hope of reaching the top and that we were perhaps taking too much for granted. He had taken to following Doug's example in taking milk drinks in Kathmandu instead of beer; he followed Georges in what he ate and the exercise he took. Georges had climbed a very high mountain without oxygen in a rapid time and Pete wanted to find and use the formula for success which he believed Georges must have had. Lest the secret lay in his diet or training schedule, he imitated Georges's every move. If Georges went for a run, so did Pete; in the evening when the restless Georges scrambled about on boulders, practising climbing moves, so did Pete.

When I thought about it seriously I knew he was right, I knew I too should be pursuing a rigorous training programme, and wondered if I had left it too late to achieve the fitness necessary to climb this mountain. Always I intended to join them but always the next chapter of the book I was reading drew me on and they would be back from their exercise before I was ready to go.

For two days we walked along the crest of the rounded ridge dividing the Arun and Tamur valleys. We passed through the villages of well-built houses and forests of rhododendrons. The track was the main highway for the villages of the region and streams of porters dwarfed by their colossal loads passed in both directions, carrying vegetables and fruit one way, returning days later with boxes of footwear and products bought in the bazaar. The climate was ideal for those two days, for we had climbed out of the sticky heat to 8,000 feet and a cooling breeze made life pleasant.

We reached a village at the end of the ridge and from there we had to descend to the valley, to the jungle and heat once again. Above the village, in the sky hovering white and unobtrusive in the distance so I thought it was a cloud, was the mountain. We were not yet halfway there and it stood up big and massive. From the warmth of the track amidst this greenery I could not imagine how cold it would be twenty thousand feet higher, amongst those snows, and I could not imagine how we four could climb a mountain so big. Suddenly I was aware of how small we were.

We passed above a cluster of huts from where the metallic reverberation of transistorised music made itself heard. It seemed grotesquely out of place in these surroundings, many miles from the roads and pylons which symbolise modern life, to hear the strains of an English song, the words and music distorted by too much volume, but just discernible as 'Goodbye my friends it's hard to die . . .'. We had to laugh at the irony of the coincidence of our passing at that moment. Georges was full of equally macabre comments about what might happen to us on the mountain and preyed on Pete's nerves in his artless manner.

There were none of the tensions which might have been expected under the pressure of the difficulties and prolonged effort ahead. Most of the everyday chores were attended to by our cook, Kami, and the cook boy whom we had not asked for but had known better than to object to when Kami brought him along. There was some dispute with the porters when we reached a halfway point in the approach about a week after starting. Ang Phurba and Nima sorted out the problem while we lay in the sunshine and swam in a clear, pleasantly warm river. The Liaison Officer, Mohan Bahadur Thapa, who had been assigned to us, turned out to be a comic character. He always wore a little woollen hat, shy of revealing the bald patch on his head, and blaming that for his failure to marry. He spoke English well, with the quaintness of tongue of someone reared on Dickens and Shakespeare, using words which were appropriate but had long passed out of common usage. He liked to talk with us, gaining practice in the use of English and recounting tales from his life in the police force. Some of his anecdotes were very amusing and he recited them, rolling words round with his tongue and repeating a word if he liked its sound, so that it was as much a pleasure to listen to his manner of speech as to his story of some narrow escape. In theory he was with us to make sure that we did not contravene any of his country's laws; in practice he knew that we had no intention of doing this and he was settling into the expedition to enjoy a break from his routine duties, to enjoy the company of visitors from abroad and the prospect of valuable clothing and equipment at the end of the expedition.

On the ninth day of the walk-in we had reached the camp-site for the night by early afternoon. I lay in the shade of a rock reading *The Seven Pillars of Wisdom* by T. E. Lawrence, intending to finish a chapter before joining the other three who were a short distance away, scrambling up and down steep walls on the huge boulders littering the clearing in the forest. Pete appeared from behind the rock in whose shade I was lying and I saw that he was limping.

'What have you done?'

'I don't know. Georges bloody well pushed me. I heard something crack. He was really stupid. It might be broken.'

Georges had climbed a smooth slab of rock, tilted at an angle of 70°, relying upon the friction of his footwear on the rough rock to inch his way up the fifteen feet to the top. It was a game, Pete, Georges and Doug each trying to find something to climb which the other two could not follow. Pete did follow up this problem and Georges, boisterous as ever, had played

'King of the Castle', pushing playfully at Pete as he made to stand on the top. Knocked out of balance, Pete had nothing positive to grasp for, and he fell to the ground, landing awkwardly on a tuft of grass. His foot twisted under him and he both felt and heard a crack somewhere in his left ankle.

At first he had thought it was a bad wrench, but the pain was so intense that he could hardly stand on his foot. Georges, looking very contrite and crestfallen, hovered about, regretting the outcome of his restless energy. Doug took Pete's foot in his large hands, squeezing gently but firmly, searching for the source of pain and trying to decide whether a bone was broken or some ligaments sprained.

The full implications of the situation only gradually emerged as Pete's ankle became more and more swollen, the pain grew no less and any attempt to walk on it was unbearable.

We were nine days along the trail. Three days away in another direction was an airstrip with one flight each week. For us all to go back could mean the end of the expedition and for Pete to go back for treatment in a hospital would mean he would have a difficult task, if his foot did recover in time, to get back into sequence with us and reach the level of acclimatisation which we would have achieved after a couple of weeks on the mountain. Whatever he was to do there was the problem of how to do it in this mountainous country, where narrow paths wound up and down precipitous hillsides and the only means of movement was by foot. Suddenly Pete's chances of climbing Kangchenjunga were thrown into doubt, a heavy depression emanated from him and influenced the whole camp.

He controlled his appearance of anger, but let fly occasional biting comments which revealed his inner turmoil. Georges flinched at every word, mortified now, like a child who had meant no harm, at the consequences of a thoughtless action.

I tried to reassure Pete that he would be all right, that break or sprain there was still a week before we would even reach the mountain; a break would have time to knit together by then, a sprain would linger on but, supported in a boot, should be better.

We ordered bowls of hot water from the cook and bathed his foot to ease the pain, then someone said cold water was better for sprains so we ordered cold water and he bathed his foot in that. If the worst happened and he could not walk by morning we toyed with the idea of hiring a yak, though whether he would be able to ride such a beast of uncertain temper along these narrow tracks we did not know.

The spirit had left the boisterous Georges, he took on a lack-lustre appearance and his innocent spontaneity seemed to be gone forever. From that one incident he had become wise. Nothing would revive his former playfulness and sense of fun; he tried to apologise with that anguish of regret for a thing done that cannot be undone, and lay sombre and silent in a black mood of guilt and paranoia. Pete shuffled restlessly, unable to settle comfortably. In whatever position he lay or sat he seemed to feel the stones from the ground, the rock behind dug into his back. He did not know what to do with himself. Everything depended on his being able to walk again in time to climb the mountain. I could only guess at the disappointment he was feeling, because he appeared so normal. I thought back to the time when I too had faced the prospect of failing even to reach a mountain through a simple toothache. I told him that story as a parable of hopes shattered and then restored to show him how all might not be lost however bad things looked for the moment. He stopped making notes in his diary – there seemed little point in keeping a diary of a non-expedition.

At evening a cluster of hill people formed round the cook's fire. Among them was a young girl, the prettiest we had seen among the mountain people. To distract Pete from his woes I asked the cook to persuade the girl to carry the evening meal over to him, but even her good looks failed to lighten the misery which had settled on him.

At daybreak it was clear that Pete's foot had not improved. He had resolved to carry on with the expedition in the hope that the injury would heal and give him back the chance of climbing the mountain, but even on makeshift crutches he could not get more than a few yards on the rough ground.

Ang Phurba, resourceful as ever, produced the answer. A yak would be too unpredictable on the mountain paths but he had found a porter who was prepared to carry Pete on his back for the same price as we had intended paying for the hire of the yak. The porter stood behind Ang Phurba, barely five foot in height. He had on short cotton trousers and a well-used jacket. He wore nothing on his feet and his bare legs were thin, all sinew and muscle, with no surplus flesh. Tucked under his arm was the hemp rope, blackened from much use, the symbol of his trade. He could hardly have weighed eight stone and he was proposing to carry Pete, who weighed thirteen stone.

A conical basket, normally used to carry fruit or vegetables to market, was cut into and fashioned to make a seat. Pete was helped into it and the porter cradled the basket in his loop of rope, settling the other end of the loop over his forehead. Carefully he eased himself upright, taking the strain on his forehead, and a slow, halting progress was achieved, with Pete facing back along the track, swaying uncertainly as he accustomed himself to this odd means of transportation.

The porter could only walk for a few minutes before having to stop, resting his heavy burden on the T-shaped stick he carried for this purpose, to avoid the laborious procedure of having the basket lifted down and back up. Pete would sit, helpless and immobile, as the rest of the porters plodded by, as if symbolising the expedition drawing away from its wounded member. There was an invisible and unmentioned barrier between the injured Pete and us who were fit. We hovered near his litter, reining in on our natural pace to keep him company so that he would not feel an outcast. But walking more slowly than usual, and halting more frequently than needed, was fatiguing. There was also hesitation in that Pete might feel we were pitying him, so gradually but inevitably he was left behind, and we would see him after hours apart when we halted for a tea break.

After two days of extremely slow progress two porters were hired to carry Pete in relays. The narrow track wound up ever-steeper hillsides, zig-zagging upwards above dizzying heights. Looking back at the tiny figures on the track which was barely two feet wide, I wondered at the likelihood of the porter stumbling and sending Pete flying over the edge, down the thousands of feet to the torrent whose noise was faint by the time it reached us.

The porters who shared the enormous burden seemed resigned; when they hoisted the load upwards, their faces set into the grim expression of someone under the utmost strain, sinews on neck and legs stood out like cords and they strode purposefully, unable to linger long under the load. The task represented a way of earning more money. They showed neither pleasure nor displeasure, as if resigned to an existence which was always hard work.

For the first two days Pete had a problem with sunburn, since he had to sit motionless in the fierce heat of the sun, but the weather changed to days of mist and rain. What had been at the start alarming and extra-ordinary became everyday and matter of fact. A routine was established in which Nima took charge of the attendants who carried Pete and it seemed that they could carry him almost anywhere. It was certain now that he would physically reach Base Camp but his morale was low.

The pretty girl whom we first saw on the day of Pete's accident had joined our convoy. She was with her mother, a sister and a brother. They too were going in the same direction, making for their summer home in the village of Ghunza. We learnt that the pretty girl's name was Dawa and when the mother saw us photographing the girl and enquiring of Ang Phurba about her marital status she replied that the girl was married to a very big man who had an equally big gun and was very jealous. But it was all light-hearted. They shared our campfires at night and when it rained we lent them tents. The mother sought help from Doug for her hard cough and fractured ribs. I felt that we belonged more to the country travelling as we were. Only the four of us were foreigners. Our fifty porters were all from the region, Ang Phurba and Nima knew the area and spoke the language, though it was a different dialect from their own. We were not so big a foreign group that we swamped the villages we entered. We needed local produce and the local people came to us for medicine. Walking was the normal mode of travel and it seemed a sign that we were accepted when the family tagged on to our party and later policemen and their wives, on the way to the police post at Ghunza, joined us too.

I dreamt one night that one of us was killed in an avalanche on the mountain, but in the dream there were five in the team. There was panic because the news had leaked out before we had time to inform all concerned; then I woke with a restless sense of disquiet. I did not like to admit to any superstition in myself which would give credence to the content of a dream and I did not tell the others for fear of arousing thoughts which might undermine confidence. Later in the day I wrote down the dream, wanting to face up squarely to the thoughts and fears in my subconscious and hoping thus to exorcise any morbidity from my mind.

On another night I dreamt that Pete and I were going for the summit. I did not think that this was prophetic either but I told Pete about the dream to let him see that I was not simply encouraging his hopes out of charity but even subconsciously I still saw him as capable of getting up the mountain. He was visibly cheered as if I had passed him a compliment.

At Ghunza we had to wait for a while. The village was at 11,480 feet and here we paid off the lowland porters and arranged to hire yaks for the remaining days up to Base Camp. After four days of being carried, Pete began to make his first faltering steps. We waited an extra day as we all felt breathless from the altitude and Pete's mobility was increasing daily.

Georges, who had been subdued ever since the accident, was further adversely affected by a heavy cold which made him fret and sample every sort of tablet and medicine he could find.

We had each brought a selection of cassette tapes, but Georges, as with books, showed least interest in listening to music and he found punk rock completely intolerable. Doug played mostly Bob Dylan on a small cassette deck which he never let far from himself, as if he could not bear to be without the solace of music. Pete and I played mostly rock music, though in more reflective moments Pete liked to listen to something classical or some jazz. We had only one other cassette deck so Pete and I usually camped close to each other so that we could each hear the music no matter who actually had the machine. One night I had the tape deck on low close to my ear and had fallen asleep to the sound of Pink Floyd, wondering if it was loud enough for Pete nearby to hear. I was startled awake by Georges shouting to me to turn the volume down as he couldn't sleep, and by the time the message had got through to my sleepy brain I was aware by the sounds from the other tents that everyone else had been woken up too.

Next morning the camp was woken again by Georges announcing that he was feeling much better, and his cold seemed to be gone. A few minutes later he announced that it was snowing heavily outside and that we should go back to sleep for a while till the sun should be up. Georges's extrovert spontaneity was quite different from the more silent and deliberated behaviour I sought myself. I did not like being woken needlessly but in many other ways Georges's manner contributed a freshness and vitality to the reserve and restraint which had come to be the mode of interaction between Pete, Doug and myself.

When we left the village Pete was able to make the distance to the hamlet of Kangbachen, our next stopping place, in good time. He limped along, leaning heavily on ski-sticks, to ease the pressure on his foot. In the determination which he showed in overcoming the seemingly hopeless restrictions imposed by a broken foot, and not to let himself be beaten in his resolve to climb Kangchenjunga, it was possible to glimpse something of the relentless sense of purpose which drove the man. Beneath an exterior which sometimes seemed helpless and awkward there was an iron-hard will which was only applied when the need arose. With the improvement in Pete's performance, some of the old restlessness returned to Georges. He shot off up the hillside as soon as we made camp and finished the afternoon scrambling about on another boulder.

The distance to Base Camp was nothing like as far as the wily villagers of Ghunza had described it to be. It was three days, not five, and each day we were only walking for three or four hours. The camp was on a level grassy shelf, half a mile long, a quarter of a mile wide. It appeared suspended part way up the slopes of the mountain. Above were rock-strewn slopes rising to snow and below a steeper slope of crumbling mud and boulders dropped clear for five hundred feet to the glacier. Base Camp was at 16,000 feet, rather low for such a high mountain, but this was the last stretch of grass before we had to start onto the icy wastes of the glacier. As a place to rest and recuperate when not on the mountain a camp on grass was more preferable to a bleak existence in tents on the ice. Certainly our Sherpas, cook and Liaison Officer preferred to stay on the grassy camp-site. The shelf of Pang Perma was also the site of the camp of the 1930 expedition which made an attempt from the north, and the remains of the rough wall they had constructed as a windbreak were still evident. Our Sherpas made a large cooking-cum-dining shelter using the existing wall of stones and a light tarpaulin for a roof. We paid off the porters and yak herders and settled in for the long siege on the mountain which dominated the valley opposite the camp.

III

We spent a week exploring the approaches to the north ridge, carrying tents and supplies onto the glaciers and making Camps 1 and 2. Camp 1 was quite low, only 17,500 feet, but the site of Camp 2 at 19,000 feet was too long a day for us from Base Camp at first; we were not sufficiently fit nor acclimatised for such a long day's walk.

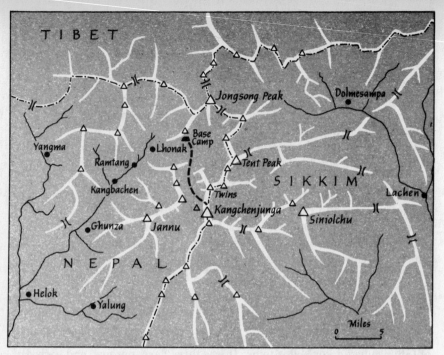

8. The location of Kangchenjunga, showing the route from Base Camp to the
mountain.

The week was useful to help us all adjust mentally and physically to our
surroundings. It allowed time, before we were committed to the mountain,
for Pete to gain confidence and strength in his foot for the work ahead, and
it allowed time for bouts of sickness and dysentery to pass which affected
Georges and Pete in turn.

By all accounts Kangchenjunga had a fearsome reputation for danger.
Being the highest mountain mass at the eastern extremity of the Himalayas,
it is subject to ferocious winds and heavy deposits of snow. All the earlier
expeditions had warned of the constant avalanches from its slopes and
during the days when we placed and stocked the lower camps our ears and
responses grew accustomed to the roar of yet another ice cliff breaking away
and crashing thousands of feet down, or another mass of snow breaking
loose and falling to drum with menacing force against the slopes below.
Georges had only been on the one expedition to the Himalayas and that had
been so quick that he had not witnessed many avalanches. The frequent
thunderous roars which ruptured the silence of the days were new and
worrying for him. They worried us all but we tried to find a way across the
glacier least threatened by slopes above, and to place the tents far enough
away from danger zones so that we could sleep in peace.

The first night at Base Camp was disturbed by the noise of a wind which
seemed likely to ruin our tents and confirmed us in our fear for what lay
in store high on the mountain.

Camp 1 was below Twins Peak, a small neighbour to Kangchenjunga, on whose flanks was perched a huge cliff of ice. We were wary of its threat but thought that the crevasses and ridges of the glacier between our tents and the side of the mountain would swallow up anything breaking loose from the cliff. The night we occupied Camp 1 Pete started up at the sound of an avalanche, but it was far away, and he settled back into his sleeping bag, confessing that he believed himself more timid than the rest of us, and rationalising out loud that he would have to accept that we would hear those roars every day, and even every hour, for the whole northern face of our mountain seemed to send down avalanches at any time of the day or night. Our chosen route was designed to avoid these dangers, climbing up to reach a ridge which stood clear above any avalanche slopes. I was sharing the tent with Pete and felt nervous too, without the reassurance that we had got the feel or the measure of the opponent we had come to face. I expressed my fears less readily than Pete, knowing how easily he could be influenced and made more nervous. I preferred to face my fears alone first, to come to terms with them in the process of making a decision before voicing my thoughts aloud. I could look at our situation in a way which let me laugh at our anxieties if there was nothing we could do or nothing we were going to do to resolve it or make it more safe. Pete told me that I was heartless and lacked imagination and we both drifted off to sleep listening to the ice of the glacier creaking and groaning beneath us.

On Friday 13 April, the Good Friday of Easter, all four of us were at Camp 1, Doug and Georges in one tent, Pete and I in another. Ang Phurba and Nima were with us too, occupying a third tent, ready to help us with the move up to Camp 2 the next day. Not long after dark the sound of an avalanche, louder than usual, grew outside. I could hear Georges's muffled, frantic exclamations and Pete leapt to the tent door.

'Oh, my God, look at this!'

Reluctantly I left the warmth of my sleeping bag to peer through the door of the tent. Out of the darkness of the night a white wall of billowing snow was advancing towards us, colossal and implacable. We could not tell how substantial it was, whether it was a dust-cloud of snow which would pass over with little damage or a solid mass which would bury us or sweep us for a mile across the glacier.

'Zip your tent closed,' I yelled to the others, and seconds before it reached us we zipped ours closed too, to keep out the choking powder of the snow. There was nowhere to run to, the advancing wall would reach us and toss us out of the way, or pass harmlessly over, far more quickly than we could move. We held onto the tent as the first winds of the avalanche tugged at its fabric. In that moment it was impossible to know if we would be there when the avalanche stopped, but I felt no fear for there was nothing I could do, as if my emotions were frozen until I knew that there was a future for them.

The wind grew stronger and shook the tent furiously; snow battered at the outside and forced its way in through tiny openings; then the commotion subsided, all of a sudden, and all we could hear was the murmur of Nima chanting his prayers and Georges swearing in disbelief.

The main force of the avalanche had been broken and swallowed by the small valley along the edge of the glacier and by the mounds and ridges in between. We had been hit by the wind of the displaced air and settling debris from the ice which had disintegrated in the fall. Minutes later the same thing was repeated and we resolved to move the camp to a different place at daybreak. I felt uneasy for the rest of the night but Pete was visibly shaken by the occurrence and complained bitterly about the folly of siting the camp in such a place.

Camp 2 was notably quieter than Camp 1 had been, in a snowy basin encircled on three sides by the wall of Kangchenjunga's North Face, the wall up to the North Ridge and another facet of Twins Peak. We pitched the tents to one side of a chute on Twins Peak which seemed to present the only danger, and were able to observe with more equanimity the puffs of white cloud on the mountainsides which marked the distant falls of ice before the sound reached us.

We worked in pairs on the steep wall up to the lowest point on the ridge between Kangchenjunga and Twins Peak. The wall was almost 3,000 feet high, and it was the most difficult part of the route we had chosen. None of the photographs we had seen before we arrived showed this wall, and we had come in faith that there would be a way. The way was hard, up steep ice and ice-covered rock which took us days to climb. The only alternative was the line chosen by the expedition in 1930, further to our right, but there a Sherpa had been killed by a fall of ice, and though we saw no avalanche from that area, blocks littering the glacier pointed to the need for continued caution.

The wall was two hours from the camp, across a gentle slope of snow-covered ice. A few crevasses made us worry and we marked the way with bamboo sticks so that we could always retrace our steps in mist or after new snow. Georges and I were standing together so we started the rota. Pete and Doug dumped their loads and went back to camp. Only one could climb at a time, so rather than waste time awaiting a turn in the lead, it was a more efficient arrangement for two of us to climb and fix rope for a day, then to let the other pair take over the lead for another day. The days could thus be alternated between resting and working, the resting pair being able to have food cooking ready for the return of the workers.

At the end of the first day Georges and I returned, weary after our efforts, to a lavish meal inspired by Doug's vegetarian preferences: cabbage, red beans, tofu and a tin of lamb slices for those who liked meat. It was delicious, and we all congratulated Doug. But in the night we all woke with sickness and diarrhoea, and the next day no one was well enough to move. Ang Phurba chortled with amusement when he arrived with a load of rope from Camp 1 and nodded with understanding when he saw the red beans in the snow.

'Ha ha, beans not properly cooked.'

The rest was welcome. The day slipped by in the lazy completion of the many little tasks outstanding; the heat of the sun was trapped and concentrated in the windless basin of glaring snow. Until the sun sank below the horizon we crept about listlessly, all energy sapped by the heat, and nibbled cautiously at food lest we be struck down again.

Doug and Pete spent a day fixing rope on the wall, and we could see that that section was hard by the way they moved so slowly. They returned towards evening, Doug shambling along weakly, ill from over-exertion and pausing intermittently to retch green bile onto the snow.

One day as Georges and I were high on the wall a thundering crash caused us to look around and see leaping down from Twins Peak and hurtling across our tracks far below the column of a colossal avalanche. We were safe above its path and Camp 2 was far enough away on the other side, but the avalanche covered our tracks for a quarter of a mile and travelled for two miles before subsiding. Returning that evening, we crossed the solid mound of ice debris and blocks which had fallen from the mountain, thankful that we had been safe above. We heard the rumble of another avalanche far away and Georges told me, with pride in his voice, that he had not even looked up to see where it was.

In four days of climbing between 15 and 20 April, we had overcome most of the difficulties on the wall. On what had been a huge, uncharted obstacle we had mapped out a route and fixed in place the ropes which would facilitate more rapid movement upwards and retreat when the time came.

On the 21 April all four of us left together, carrying sleeping bags, tents, stoves and food, intending to reach the top of the wall and make a camp at the North Col on the crest of the ridge. At the foot of the wall we stood in a group, adjusting harness and making ready prusik clamps with which to haul ourselves up on the ropes. Doug was apprehensive about the possibility of one of us dislodging loose rock onto those below.

'Have you got your crash helmet, youth?' he asked Pete.

'Yes.'

'Well you can go at the back. I've forgotten mine.'

'Hold on. Why didn't you bring yours?'

'I don't like climbing with it on. Gets in the way.'

And Doug's persuasiveness won the day.

With heavy sacks we toiled upwards for hours, but a blizzard was blowing by mid-afternoon when we reached the high point, there was no

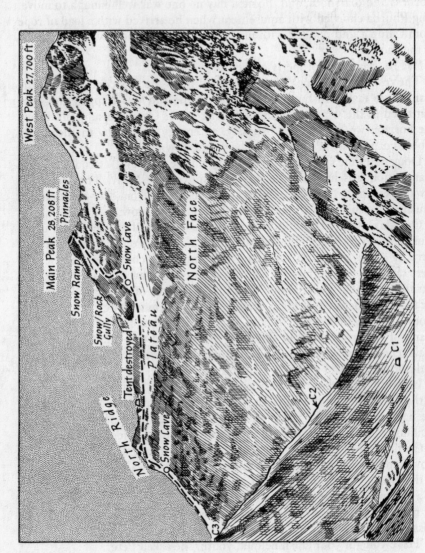

5. The line of ascent up the North Ridge of Kangchenjunga.

time left to climb the remaining unprepared sections and we slid off down, first dumping our loads, and went back down to Base Camp next day when we woke to a sky heavy with snow.

We had worked hard for a week and the sudden return to grass and the comfort of a fire made me realise how weary I was. Kami, the cook, prepared chips, eggs and tinned fish for us, and we let ourselves be spoilt by his constant concern that we had enough to eat and drink. Mohan, the Liaison Officer, beamed his pleasure at our return, proud of what we were doing but happy to have our company again.

We stayed down for four days. Heavy snowfalls covered the grass but it was still more reassuring than snow-covered ice with all the hidden pitfalls and inherent inhospitality. Ang Phurba went off for us with a message to a Czechoslovak expedition, camped three days away for an attempt on Jannu. They had sent up their good wishes with our mail runner whom they had met on the trail. The wall up to the North Col had taken up most of our ropes and in the note we asked if they had any rope to spare.

When not on the mountain I liked to relax completely. I could not find the energy to go off and explore the valleys and smaller peaks nearby, preferring to read and linger over meals. I felt a great sense of freedom from the threat and fear; any rumblings I knew were no sort of danger to us. Our grassy plateau was safe from any avalanche and no crevasses lay hidden to catch us unawares. Only now did I realise the strain we had been living under up on the glacier, menaced constantly by the avalanches, whose sound waged a campaign of fear even if most of them fell safely far away.

But I was keen to return. The lack of fitness and reluctance to face physical effort had gone; the subconscious, panicky fear of the unknown had disappeared; we knew the mountain now for what it was. The dangers were still there but we had had a chance to take their measure, we had tested ourselves on the difficulties and found we could master them. I was still anxious about the altitude, about how I would feel higher up when, without oxygen, we would try to reach the summit. We knew that there were difficulties close to the summit, we knew that we would have long distances to travel from our last bivouac, but whether it would be possible without the support from oxygen equipment we knew not at all. We had read of the dangers of damage to the brain from going high into rarefied air, we had read Messner's account of his double vision and distorted perception on the summit of Everest when he reached it without oxygen support. We knew from the descriptions of others who had tried to go high how slowly they moved and how difficult the simplest task was when the oxygen content of the air was less than half that of normal. Kangchenjunga is a bare 800 feet lower than Everest and on its summit there is only a quarter of the amount of oxygen in the air that there is at sea level. Apart from the difficulty of performing any action with such a low oxygen intake, there is also an unquantifiable risk of contracting pulmonary or cerebral oedema, the sickness of high altitude which fills the lungs or brain with fluids. This, at best, is incapacitating and at worst is fatal. The slow acclimatisation of climbing gradually higher over days and weeks is the best way to avoid this illness, and optimum acclimatisation is only reached after a month or six weeks of such preparation, in which time the blood alters in composition to absorb more oxygen from the thin air. We had spent nearly three weeks walking in to our Base Camp and another three weeks since then working on the mountain and felt that we should be fit enough and well enough adjusted, but there was no guarantee that any one or all of us would not be adversely affected by this altitude.

The only cure for severe high-altitude sickness is descent to a lower altitude or an increase in the supply of oxygen by artificial means. We had brought with us one bottle of oxygen and one set of breathing apparatus in case any of us became critically ill. It was not enough to climb the mountain – the bottle would last perhaps eight hours – and if anyone was to carry it to near the top he would not be able to carry anything else. It did, however, offer the chance of saving a life, for cerebral oedema can be fatal in a matter of hours, and we discussed frequently the merits of taking the bottle up to the North Col at 22,500 feet where it would be most needed to help someone down who might have contracted high-altitude sickness.

Doug and Pete had climbed Everest using oxygen equipment, and Doug had survived a bivouac on the descent at 28,700 feet without oxygen. Georges had climbed Broad Peak, a mountain 26,402 feet high, without oxygen. All three had more experience at high altitude than I had and I presumed that they shared a confidence in their ability to perform high up which I did not have. To make the first ascent of Kangchenjunga without oxygen and to do so by a new and difficult route would be a major achievement for us all but, with the insecurity of one who always expects the worst, I felt as if it was more of a step into the unknown in terms of whether my body would function high up in the way that the others had already proved theirs would. We all had the greatest respect for the handful of people who had forced themselves to the top of the highest mountains without oxygen equipment and we discussed often what it was that made them different from us. We could not believe they were supermen but somehow they seemed to possess a confidence which we did not have when we looked at the mountain we had come to climb. Everest and K2, the two highest mountains in the world, had been climbed without oxygen equipment. Kangchenjunga, the third highest, had not. Now that we were close to the mountain, the final 2,000 feet appeared more difficult than the final part of the other two, and our team was certainly very much smaller than usual for so high a mountain. Those who had reached the top of Everest and K2 had done so as members of large teams, many of whom had contributed to the effort of ferrying loads up the mountain and fixing ropes, and most of whom had used oxygen equipment. It puzzled me sometimes how we had presumed to come here at all, and why there were so few of us.

The snow-storm which had chased us off the mountain deposited a layer of snow at Base Camp too. Six inches of snow fell but it soon cleared in the heat of the sun. I lay outside my tent on the grass in view of the mountain, feeling in a state of suspended mental animation. I had grown accustomed to Doug spending his time on expeditions in abstract reflection, often absorbed in books of a philosophical nature, the *Tibetan Book of the Dead*, the *I Ching*, the Carlos Castaneda series on the teachings of Don Juan, or any of many others which he kept by him for constant reference. I preferred the escapist reading of racy novels but these were soon finished so I borrowed a Carlos Castaneda book and devoured that rapidly, which Doug thought did not do justice to the content.

I did not like to spend too much time in reflection since on expedition we were cut off from contact with the real world and could have no influence over events there. In the years in the seminary I used to spend the weeks of term-time planning all the wonderful things I would do in the holidays which I visualised as being the ideal. The reality was always less wonderful than the dream and I grew wary of the habit of living in the mind. Our situation here was similar and I hesitated to try to resolve problems with relationships, and make plans for when I returned, or resolutions for a mode of living, when I knew that so many things would interfere and alter the most careful plans.

I did think in general terms about why we were here, why I was here. I had once nurtured the thought that you could not be a climber if you were a 'bad person', a thought springing from the religious conviction that 'sin' brings its own retribution and that in climbing there are too many situations of risk, of which the 'almighty powers that be' could take advantage, to discourage any climber from 'bad behaviour'. I could no longer separate my thoughts from the religion instilled from early on and I could not answer my own questions of whether I was here because I really wanted to be or whether I felt I had to drive myself on no matter the suffering involved. Certainly climbing Kangchenjunga was a long way from the fun of climbing a small rock cliff, vying with a school mate to see who could do the hardest things. I wondered if climbing one of the world's highest mountains made one a better person, if it would give courage and strength in other aspects of life. Only reaching the top would answer that and I no longer knew what the motivation was which would enable me to put one foot in front of the other when there was only pain, and shortage of air and no fun or enjoyment.

I was glad that on the return from this trip I had nothing planned for almost a year. Doug had asked me to go on a trip to Everest in the autumn but I had decided not to go. In the last eighteen months I had been away three times, so that I had had no time to do anything satisfactorily. I was either away or preparing to go away, and work and friendships suffered. After this trip I wanted time to pause and take stock of what I was doing and where I was going.

Ang Phurba returned with 500 feet of rope and a tin of Czechoslovak alcohol. He had made the round trip in only two days. We needed the rope to fasten in place on a buttress at 25,000 feet forming a step in the ridge. That buttress looked to be the last difficult section before the final 2,000 feet of the summit pyramid. We had not rope enough to fix a safety line all the way up that, but even if we had we could not have carried its weight. We could only trust that the difficulties would not be so great that we could not descend them quickly enough without a line in place.

We could see how well we had adjusted to the altitude and how fit we had become by the speed with which we returned to Camp 2. The distance we had covered in two days we could now do in a few hours, suffering more from the furnace heat of the sun concentrated on us by the snowy bowl than from the stress of altitude.

After a night at Camp 2 we returned to the wall. Georges and Doug went up first carrying lighter loads, to climb and make secure with rope the last few hundred feet from which we had retreated in the blizzard. Ang Phurba and Nima were with us too, carrying rucksacks of gear and food so that we would have a good stock in the camp on the ridge.

Such steep climbing, even with ropes in place, was new to the two Sherpas, so Pete took care that Nima was coping all right and I looked after Ang Phurba. They were competent enough once they started, but they needed some initiation in techniques where the rock was vertical and ice on the ledges prevented secure purchase. At half height Nima turned back, saying he was tired, to wait at the foot of the wall for Ang Phurba's return.

It took hours and hours of tedious effort, pushing the clamp upwards on the rope, stepping upwards in the nylon loop attached to the clamp, pushing up the other clamp which attached my chest to the rope. Slow and boring, with none of the satisfaction that Georges and Doug would have, knowing that they were going to solve the last problems of climbing this wall and be first to stand on the crest of the ridge on which all our attentions had been focused for two weeks now.

The ropes up which we were climbing were 150 feet long, anchored in place at each end of their lengths by a piton driven into rock or ice. We kept an anchor point between each of us so that none of them would have to take the weight of more than one person. Georges and Doug were far ahead, out of sight. Ang Phurba was above me and Pete below, each a hundred feet away. I had started up a rope which hung free for part of its length, coming over a bulge of rock which Georges had climbed most skilfully one day that I was with him. As I came over the bulge I looked upwards to see how Ang Phurba was progressing and at that moment saw a mass of black objects falling through the air towards me. I ducked under the bulge instinctively, the rocks crashing above, below and to one side of me, but I was safely sheltered, hearing the rising crescendo of noise as the rocks rushed past. When the murderous crashes quietened, I looked up to see Ang Phurba crouching in fear but unscathed. Below, Pete was doubled up and I realised he had been hit.

'Are you all right, Pete?'

'I've been hit on the wrist,' he shouted in pain and frustration.

I took off my sack and slid back towards him. He had taken off his mitt and showed me the rapidly swelling lump where the rock had struck him. Already the swelling seemed as large as an egg. He could not use his hand, could not grip or take any weight on it. He seemed close to tears at the injustice of it all, this new injury, after he had recovered from the injury to his foot, seeming as if it might rob him yet again of his chance of reaching the top of the mountain. This was a hurt greater than physical pain. The angry red swelling mocked any attempt I made at showing sympathy.

Pete said that he felt able enough to descend to the foot of the wall where Nima would be waiting and he set off down, fumbling awkwardly with his injured hand. I could not assist him, only one could descend at a time on the rope, and I continued upwards to let Georges and Doug know what had happened.

The afternoon was well advanced by this time and Ang Phurba turned to go back in order to return to Camp 2 before darkness came. I took from him the sleeping bag he was carrying for Georges and crossed the ice slope to the bottom of the dark cleft of a chimney. The chimney was eighty feet high, narrow and difficult. Doug's sack hung near the bottom, obviously left there to ease his passage upwards. He appeared some distance above me, lowering a rope with an empty sack for me to fill with his gear so that he could haul it up. I argued with him when he asked me to go back to his sack for his books and it was almost dark when I hauled myself up the chimney and over the ledges above covered in loose rock. Doug showed me the way into the shallow-angled gully of snow at the top of which was Georges busy making ready the tent.

A keen wind knifed through my clothes as I waited in the dark outside while Doug settled himself into the tent. It was a two-man tent with little room for a third person, but it was too dark for me to erect my own tent so I had to make do with the space that was left in the porch of the tent and along the side of a wall where the other two squeezed together to make some room.

The wind howled all night, buffeting the tent and spraying the taut fabric
with hail and snow. Each of us shuffled and moved constantly through the
night, trying to find more comfort in the cramped space. By morning I had
slumped to the end of the tent in a ball, and woke feeling ill and listless.
The wind was furious outside, cloud enveloped us and regular volleys of
snow showered the tent.

The previous day had been long and hard for all three of us and the night
barely tolerable. With the wind as fierce as it was and with such poor
visibility we put off any thought of trying to get further up the ridge. Then
Doug braved the elements to relieve himself and came back shouting some
good news.

He had climbed over the crest of the ridge looking for a corner less
exposed to the wind where he could open up his clothing without it filling
with spindrift. He found the crest of the ridge to be a rounded hump and
the slope only twenty or thirty feet down below the ridge on the other side
was almost calm. The relentless wind coming from the west streamed
across the ridge running north and south but the east side, looking down
into Sikkim, was protected. We packed up and dragged the tent, which
bucked like a kite in the wind, to the calmer slopes and dug a platform large
enough to take a second tent.

At last we had space to stretch out in and peace to rest by. Georges and
I shared a tent which linked up to the second tent, occupied by Doug, with
a nylon sleeve through which we could communicate and pass drinks. The
wind still hurled itself at the ridge above us, but was only a dull roar from
where we were and the snow did not fly with such force in the lee of the
slope. We made drinks and ate to make up for the nourishment we had
missed when we had had hardly space to stand the stove upright, and
looked forward to resting for the remainder of the day.

I needed the rest. A headache lingered on from the discomfort of the
previous night and a nauseous feeling periodically brought me to my knees
in fits of retching. The col on the ridge where we were camped was 22,500
feet high, high enough to make every step an effort. As I felt at the moment,
I could not hope to climb any higher along the ridge and I dosed myself
with pain-killers and sleeping tablets to rid myself of the headache. But
headaches at altitude can be the warning signs of high-altitude sickness and
they do not disappear easily.

Next day I was no better and the sleeping tablets had not helped me pass
any better a night. I did not feel capable of joining Doug and Georges when
they went down to retrieve the rest of the loads dumped below that difficult
chimney.

I lay in the tent when they had gone, feeling sorry for myself, wondering
if this was my limit, if after all I could only reach altitudes of 22,000 to
23,000 feet. Doug and Georges seemed unaffected by any headaches, able

to put in the extra effort to descend the five hundred feet to the gear and ferry it back up.

I must have dozed off because they seemed to be back in no time at all with the news that Pete and the two Sherpas were on the way up. This was a complete surprise as the weather was still wild outside and we had not expected any movement at all from Camp 2. With this in mind, Georges and Doug had been clearing loose rock from the chimney area which had been the source of the rock-fall which had injured Pete. Their good intentions had been embarrassed by the sight of figures below, but they returned pleased with the sacks of gear they had retrieved.

Pete and Ang Phurba flopped down outside some time later. It was marvellous to see Pete again and to hear that he thought he could now use his hand sufficiently to carry on with the climb. He had strapped it up with bandages and, though swollen and painful in use, it was bearable. I could not help admiring his utter determination to let nothing stop him. Nima had gone back down from halfway again and was waiting at the foot of the wall for Ang Phurba. After a drink and an appraising examination of our camp-site, Ang Phurba set off down with instructions to wait for our return at Camp 2.

Pete settled in with Doug, chatting chirpily in his relief to be back in the front once again. He threw questions at me through the connecting sleeve but I could only respond feebly and apologetically that I was not on such good form as he seemed to be.

After a third wretched night I had to accept that I was not going to improve if I stayed up longer, I was extremely tired but unable to sleep and my head ached constantly. I told the other three I would have to descend if I was going to recover, and they made their sympathetic farewells.

I was dejected and lonely as I plodded the short distance over the ridge to the top of the line of ropes leading down the wall. I paused before starting down, wondering if I was making a great mistake. If I went down I would be completely out of sequence with the other three. They had enough food and equipment to reach the top from the col and if it were possible they would have to press on making use of whatever spells of fine weather there might be. We had reckoned that another two camps would be necessary, so there was a chance that it would be some days yet before they would be in a position to reach the summit, but if they were too far ahead I would never catch up with them. Today anyway there would be no movement, the weather was still too wild. I dithered, unresolved whilst there was still time to change my mind, but I knew it was hopeless; even if I stayed I would never be able to keep up with them.

With the greatest sense of regret I slid off down the ropes, seeing now, with a sense of resentment, our handiwork which had traced a masterly route up that huge wall only to find that I was almost certainly excluded from reaping the rewards of all that effort.

At Camp 2 Ang Phurba and Nima welcomed me with a touch of sympathy. There was little solace in plunging into the comparative luxury of the largest tent and letting them bring me meals and drinks. I fell into a deep sleep. Three thousand feet lower in altitude, with slightly more substantial air, was enough to banish the headaches and nausea. I slept more soundly than at any time on the expedition so far and woke feeling refreshed and restored. The damage of three sleepless nights had begun to be repaired. Another night's sleep and I believed I would be able to go back up onto the ridge.

Down at Camp 2 the weather was calm but the clouds still churned about the ridge and hung off the mountain in long streamers. In the middle of the morning Ang Phurba's acute eyesight picked out three figures moving upwards along the ridge and through the binoculars I could see them leaning against the wind but making rapid progress.

I felt sickened at the inadequacy that had let me down and jealous of the prowess which enabled the other three to move so steadily upwards. I envied them the success which seemed within their grasp. At the rate they were going they seemed certain to reach the summit in another day or two. My jealousy and envy were irrational. I knew well that they could not afford to delay if conditions were favourable, that the weather was all too unpredictable, and delay when it was fine might cost them the summit. Still I fretted and longed to get back up onto the mountain.

I asked Ang Phurba if he wanted to accompany me onto the mountain to make an attempt on the summit as my partner. He laughed in his non-committal way and said he would wait and see how the others found it. He told me that Nima was not well and needed to descend to Base Camp. For the first time I realised that Nima's usual smile and willingness to help had been lacking. I had been so wrapped up in my own woes that I had not been aware that Nima was injured and in pain.

He explained that a rock had hit him in the back and he showed me the bruise. I could not tell if a rib was broken and though there was little that could be done to treat it he would be better off at Base Camp. He appeared feverish and moved about in obvious discomfort.

My own ambitions seemed selfish beside the distress of one who had been injured whilst working so hard for us. I prepared to go down to Base Camp next morning with Nima when the snow was frozen hard, to safeguard him across the crevasses which had begun to open as the season advanced towards full summer, and to ensure that all possible was done to alleviate his pain.

I loved the greenery of Base Camp, the luxurious cushioning of grass underfoot, but the pleasure and comfort felt fraudulent and transitory, much as the pleasures of freedom seem to a prisoner who has briefly escaped. I was over-sensitive to the sympathy I suspected behind the warm welcome from Kami and Mohan, feeling diminished in their eyes by my failure.

The air was wholesome at Base Camp, richer in oxygen than higher up, and I felt strong and fit once more, capable of anything. As we walked down from Camp 2 I had scrutinised the mountain often through the binoculars and saw the distinctive shape of a tiny figure reaching the vast terrace which spanned the whole of the North Face. From there only one more camp would be needed before the summit. It seemed certain that they would be on their way there next day whilst I was stuck at Base Camp.

Mohan was overjoyed that I was there. He bubbled with enthusiasm and cheerfulness, telling me how he missed our company. He had sat in his tent most of the time we had been gone, bored and lonely; he described himself as behaving like a young bird in a nest, sitting there, mouth wide open to have food dropped into it, with no other thing in the day to look forward to but the arrival of more food. Mohan's main distraction was the radio which we had given him and to which he listened most of the time. In the evening there was a weather bulletin in English for the benefit of the foreign expeditions in Nepal and Mohan paid assiduous attention to it, fulfilling, as he saw it, a duty to the expedition. We were never punctual enough to remember to tune in on time. On the day that we came down with Nima, Mohan told me that for the past few days very strong winds had been forecast at high altitude. This confirmed the experience we had had on the North Ridge of the mountain. That evening the forecast predicted winds of 120 mph at 23,000 feet, and I feared for the safety of the three on the mountain.

I could not settle at Base Camp. Nima was visibly reassured to be back on solid ground and had regained something of his former spirit. The following day I returned with Ang Phurba to Camp 2, revelling in our ability to reach the camp in three and a half hours instead of the two days it had initially taken us. Ang Phurba was prepared to come back up onto the mountain but was not keen on committing himself to going for the summit. I was in a quandary. There had been no more sightings of the other three and I went over all the possible variations of their movements on the mountain. If they had gone across the great terrace we should have been able to see them; if they had found a better way on the east side of the ridge they would not be visible. There was a possibility that they had dug a snow hole and in the back of my mind there was the knowledge that they could have had an accident. We could have brought walkie-talkies but, as a small team, we had imagined ourselves being together all the time and had decided against them. If we had had radio contact, much of the uncertainty about movements and intentions would have been taken out of the occasions when we were separated.

It was like solving a complex puzzle with people, food and equipment as the variables. If there was no tent or stove left at the North Col, Ang Phurba and I would not be able to stay there; if there was no pan we would be equally frustrated. Whether there was any chance at all of my reaching the summit I no longer knew. I thought we would have to go up to the camp on the Col at the least with supplies of food and possibly the bottle of oxygen, about which we were still undecided. If they had reached the top and were retreating, or if they had had an accident or someone was ill, they might have been depending on the supplies I had said I would try to bring up with me.

We had reached Camp 2 before the sun had come onto the tents, and consequently had all day to wait. There was plenty of time but it would have been an exhausting day to go from Base Camp to 22,500 feet in one day. The long day only gave me time to worry and fret more. My enjoyment of the expedition was completely gone; I was heartily sick of the whole enterprise and wanted it over. The worst of it all was being totally out of touch with the other three, not knowing what was going on. I appreciated the agony of frustration which Pete must have felt first with the injury to his foot, then to his wrist, but he had come through all of that to be up at the front again.

Clouds filled the sky to the west and raced across the mountains, catching in trailing streamers on the ridges of Kangchenjunga which thrust up far above any other peak. The noise of the wind built up into a roar over the North Col and could be heard above the sound of the wind which was battering at the tents of Camp 2.

By late afternoon the volume of sound from the wind on the mountain was indescribable. It had that massive power which makes one duck instinctively outside airports as jets take off. I read Eric Newby's book, *Love and War in the Apennines*, to fill the time. His pastoral descriptions made me homesick for England as outside gusts of snow hurtled against the tents and reaffirmed my fears for the other three. I kept listening for footsteps and voices. If they were exposed on the mountains in this weather they could not hope to survive. Their only chance would be if they were in a snow cave, protected from the wind; no tent would stand up to such force.

I asked Ang Phurba to wake me at 4.00 a.m. so that we could start early for the Col, but we were both up all night with the noise of the wind, tying down and retying the tents which were being ripped and flattened. By morning the wind had eased off around Camp 2, though it was still roaring on the ridge above. I felt that we should be taking more food and gaz to the Col in case it was needed but we were both exhausted and fell deeply asleep.

My night had been troubled with thoughts about the fate of the other three. I tried to come up with something positive that we could do from Camp 2. If they had had an accident, would we be able to get up to help them in the present wind; could they all have perished; how could I tell their wives and families; how could I explain that I alone had survived; would there forever be doubts about whether I was being completely honest about the accident?

After a rest it was imperative that Ang Phurba and I returned to the mountain as soon as the wind eased off to go as far as we could in looking for any trace of Pete, Georges and Doug, but it would not be possible to search the whole mountain.

Then late in the morning Ang Phurba woke me, shouting to say that he could see three figures on the ridge, and the tension lifted away.

They were out of sight for a long time at the camp on the Col; so long that I began to doubt that they were coming down. But by mid-afternoon they appeared over the crest of the ridge one by one and made their way down the ropes on the wall and slowly back to camp. My earlier gloom had turned to joy at seeing them safe and the loathing with which I had come to regard the mountain reverted to respect. My hopes soared of joining with them once again for an attempt on the summit when I saw they carried nothing. Had they reached the top they would have been heavily laden, but now I knew everything had been left on the mountain for the return.

Doug arrived first, his movements giving off an aura of weariness. Snow goggles shielded his eyes, which he said were smarting from wind and sun. He held out fingers for me to see the cracked and inflamed tips, symbols of the ordeal he had survived, and he started to tell what had happened as Pete and Georges, similarly battle-scarred, trailed into camp. I noticed that for the first time since he had hurt his foot, Pete was no longer limping. The events he had just come through had been so traumatic that all other aches and pains had become insignificant.

On the days when I had observed them on the ridge they had dug out a snow cave at 24,500 feet and carried up to it supplies from the tents at the North Col. Unable to know that I had gone down to Base Camp with the ailing Nima, they had kept watch for any movements from Camp 2 which might indicate that I was coming back up to join them. The weather had seemed fine and all three were fit so, rather than delay, they left with a tent in an attempt to reach the summit.

The previous day they had climbed onto the plateau, five hundred feet above the snow cave, and reached the crest of the ridge at 26,000 feet by the afternoon. A fierce wind was blowing from the west so they had pitched their tent on the east side of the ridge, below the crest, where they were sheltered from the wind. All three of them were squashed in the tiny tent which began to be buffeted by gusts of wind in the middle of the night. The wind had seemed to change direction, and from being sheltered they began to receive the full force of that wind which was keeping Ang Phurba and me awake far below with its noise and the damage it was doing to the tents.

The wind they felt bludgeoning their tent was unbelievable in its force. Their situation, perched high on the ridge, was precarious and when they felt the tent begin to lurch free of its anchorage under the wind's onslaught they started to pack ready to leave. The fabric of the tent was ripped by the wind, the centre pole snapped and gradually their shelter disintegrated before their eyes. Doug held onto the poles, trying vainly to hold the tent together till sleeping bags and all other essentials were packed into rucksacks. They evacuated the tent and when all were clear they let it go. The wind snatched it away into the night.

Safety lay in descent. A gentle slope led to the ridge and down the other side onto the plateau. They could hardly move against the wind. Even downhill, to reach the plateau, they crawled on hands and knees, pulling themselves forward with their ice axes clawing into the snow ahead. Georges had lost his rucksack. Before he had time to put it on, the wind had whipped it away to follow the tent down into Sikkim.

Georges was as awestricken by the power of the wind as he had been by avalanches earlier in the expedition: 'You should 'ave seen them, the rocks, they were 'alf a metre across, and the wind it just picked them up and blew them off the mountain. It was terrible.' He pronounced the word as 'terreeble', lending colour with his French accent to what was a horrifying memory. Georges kept shaking his head and muttering exclamations as if he could not believe he had been through the events they were now recalling.

Paradoxically I envied their experience, though I knew it must have all been hell. They had gone through the worst that the mountain could offer and, having survived it, were all the stronger. They had the togetherness of having shared hardship and a weary expectation of rest well deserved.

Doug's fingertips had been damaged by the cold as he held the poles of the tent together, Pete's fingers and nose were frost-nipped too. Georges was quite shocked by the savage fury of the elements to which they had been subjected and he was slightly snow-blind.

They drank gratefully the liquid which we had ready for them but did not want to stay long at Camp 2. They had been on the mountain, above 20,000 feet, for nine days and they longed to see the greenery of Base Camp and rest for a while. Together we all hurried downwards before nightfall to meet Mohan and our Sherpas, who showed their happiness at seeing all safe and relief that their mountains had not claimed more victims.

Rather than being a deterrent or cause for further doubts about the feasibility of climbing the mountain, the ordeal at 26,000 feet gave renewed confidence and a finer appraisal of the objective. Doug reassured me that 'wandering' about at 26,000 feet without oxygen equipment had been all right, not the crippling effort we had feared it might be, and said how he had regretted the lack of radio communication so that they had had to set off for the summit in the absence of any information about whether I was feeling well enough to rejoin them. They were all encouraging that I should have no more trouble than they with the altitude. Most reassuring of all was their achievement in descending all the way from 26,000 feet back to Base Camp at 16,000 feet, covering many miles, in one day. They had done this in appalling weather conditions and that gave us cause to believe that we could survive such storms again should they arrive when we were high up.

We plotted the next moves, scouring the upper reaches of the mountain through binoculars. Another snow cave was needed rather than tents and we pinned our hopes on finding deep enough snow into which to burrow in a gully beside a crescent-shaped buttress of rock 2,000 feet below the summit. Georges propounded a different idea. He suggested that we should abandon thoughts of digging a cave at 26,000 feet and use all our energy in making a push for the summit from the existing cave at 24,500 feet.

'We should go for 'eet,' he would say forcefully, backing up his idea by reasoning that if we carried nothing we could move faster and if we left at midnight we would be in position on the difficult lower part of the summit pyramid by dawn, with all day to climb the final 2,000 feet.

The idea was a radical departure from the methodical approach of digging out another snow cave at the start of the difficulties, and going from there to the summit. Whether we could climb those 2,000 feet in one day was questionable, but Georges was suggesting we try to do nearly 4,000 feet, covering two or three miles horizontally, in one stretch. Whatever plan was decided upon, everything depended on being able to climb that gully through the rocks at the base of the summit pyramid.

The gully was in shadow and no matter how much we scrutinised it through binoculars we could not determine if there was a continuous line of snow forming a link with the snowy ramp above the rocks or whether a step of rock blocked the way. If the gully was passable, the way to the summit seemed assured. The ramp above, being snow, we expected to be at an easier angle than the rocks. Only on reaching the gully would we know for sure if we could climb it.

We stayed at Base Camp for a while. It took three days for the weariness to leave the limbs of Pete, Doug and Georges, and we waited an extra day because the mail runner was expected, and we thought it would be nice to receive letters before going off once more. Time seemed to drag once everyone was rested, there was no purpose to the day and, though many uncertainties remained, only returning to the mountain would restore a sense of purpose. It was early May and we had been at Base Camp for over a month, almost two months since we had left England. There was an air of tedium about the camp as if the expedition had gone on long enough. Mohan was dropping hints that he would have to be back in Kathmandu soon to attend training camp, the implication being that we too should be on our way back soon. Kami had discovered that a large part of our milk powder was unusable and we were running short of other supplies; the stream near the camp had all but dried up. It was as if a subtle conspiracy of hints was being made to us to end the expedition.

By evening the mail runner had still not arrived. It was the fifteenth day since he had left and he was well overdue. We congregated for the evening meal, disconsolate that we would have to leave for the mountain next day without the satisfaction afforded by letters from home. I had grown accustomed to many things since my first couple of times in the Himalayas and hiring a mail runner had come to be almost an essential expense. The seclusion of expedition life endows the receipt of letters with an importance beyond measure and the failure of the mail to arrive was a great disappointment. Home was prominent in all our minds, and the often-expressed, fervent wish was that one more attempt would see us on the summit.

Then, when we had given up hope, he appeared out of the night and was welcomed with a warmth inspired by the treasure he carried. The package was opened and we all waited expectant but anxious lest this time there be letters for all but oneself. There were letters for all but the light in the dining shelter was too dim and soon after eating we retired to our tents to read by candle-light.

I played the romantic hits of Motown on the cassette deck, angling the speaker so that Pete could hear the music too. It was 8.00 p.m. At 4.00 a.m. we planned to be up and on our way to Camp 2 before the heat of the sun made uncomfortable the walk up the glacier.

I heard Georges shouting: 'Hey, Pete, Pete,' but Pete could not hear him. I suspected that Georges thought Pete had the music machine and wanted it turning low, but I said nothing; it was very low anyway. If he failed to make Pete hear him I thought that Georges might give up shouting, but he called me the next time: 'Hey, Joe, can you ask Pete to turn the music down. I want to sleep.'

I turned the sound lower. Then Pete was shouting to ask why he could not hear the music any more.

IV

Back at Camp 2 we rested with the restrained enthusiasm of anyone who faces a major contest. We shared a confidence about reaching the summit this time, but ever-present doubts and anxieties kept the atmosphere highly charged. Georges snapped in response to the taunts about him, a mountain guide, losing his rucksack on the mountain. He was restless and erratic in considering our chances and his own ability. At one moment he was advocating his plan for a daring rush to the summit, at another he was worrying over the slightest trace of a headache and searching out every sort of pill with which to treat himself. Pete and Doug had long since attained a mode of living on expeditions which enabled them to cope more readily with these spells of unsettling anticipation. They both read and made notes while I read and dozed.

Ang Phurba was going to carry a load up to the Col and we debated still the pros and cons of taking the oxygen cylinder and mask up in preference to extra food. Pete often showed more caution than the rest of us and he was firmly for taking it to the Col, where it would most be needed if any of us was taken ill. On the other hand, more food taken to the Col would be an asset if we should have to spend a long time on the mountain. A compromise was reached by which Ang Phurba would carry the oxygen halfway up the wall to where Nima had left a sack full of food. There he would leave the oxygen and carry on up with the food, thus bringing the food stocks up to a high level but also making the oxygen more accessible.

Nima was not going to attempt to come up the wall but he was to come to its foot in order to wait there for Ang Phurba's return, as a partner on the return journey across the glacier.

We started out early on the morning of 10 May, just two days before my birthday, and I could hardly remember whether I would be thirty or thirty-one years old. At the foot of the wall we learnt that Ang Phurba had not brought his prusik clamps with which to climb up the rope. As with much of the equipment issued to him, he was keeping these in good condition for the return to Kathmandu where he could sell them for a high price. We were angry at this acquisitiveness when the prusik clamps were essential for climbing the mountain. There was no question of returning to Base Camp for them and we had to divide up the eight clamps we did have between the five of us. Doug needed two as his fingers were very sore and he would make progress up the ropes more easily with two of the clamps. We gave Ang Phurba two because we felt obliged to ensure his safety, and for the four clamps that were left Pete, Georges and I drew lots. Georges won, leaving Pete and I to make the best we could of hauling ourselves up with one clamp and one bare hand.

Doug mentioned crash helmets, impenitent that he had left his yet again at Base Camp and insistent that he should go first lest he be hit on the head by a rock dislodged by any of us going first. He won his point but agreed to wait at the final chimney, where the rock was loosest, until all below were safely to one side. Then we started upwards one at a time.

For over five hours each of us was alone in that vertical journey. I found my mind going over problems, re-examining mentally what lay ahead. Climbing up ropes fixed in place is uninteresting and exhausting, but the mind is free to wander. With only one prusik clamp, the effort was twice as great. Instead of being able to move up, alternately supporting my weight on one clamp or the other, for half the time I had to grasp the rope in my hand and pull myself upwards. It consumed much more energy. Pete was having a similar struggle.

In the chimney, high up and not far from the camp, a sharp-edged block of rock came loose as I brushed past. Before it could fall I pressed my body against it, holding it in place lest it fall and hit Pete or Ang Phurba below. The block was two feet high, several inches thick and very heavy. It was all I could do to keep it from falling. I waited until they were clear from below me before trying to move, but still did not want to let the block fall for fear it should damage the ropes below. I took its weight in my hands and edged it up to a deep cleft in the chimney, fighting for balance and straining to lever it upwards before my arms gave out. I could feel its sharp edge cutting into my hands and when I finally heaved the block into the cleft, patting it to make sure it was stable, I saw blood oozing through my torn glove and could see a deep gash in the flesh of my fingers before I clenched my fist tight to staunch the flow. I was thankful that the main difficulties were almost over and the camp on the Col was only half an hour away.

Ang Phurba arrived last, bringing with him the oxygen bottle after all through some misunderstanding or perhaps, because in his own inscrutable reasoning, he thought we had more need for the oxygen than for the food. He slipped away down to join Nima and to return to Camp 2. We asked him to keep watch and to come to meet us at the foot of the wall if he saw that we had reached the summit and needed helping back with our heavy loads.

At last all four of us were together, unhampered by injury or illness, on our way upwards. Pete's wrist still hurt and Doug's fingertips were painful but both of them had achieved a working relationship with their disabilities. From the camp on the Col every step further was new to me. We left after a night's rest, Doug and myself paired off, Pete and Georges coming up behind. A steady wind streamed across the ridge, every upward step was tiring. I assumed that I felt the effort more because it was my first time higher than the Col, but Doug told me that he found it more taxing than the other times he had been up. Pete and Georges were weary too so, on reaching the cave, we decided to stay for a day. We had come up from Base Camp at 16,000 feet to 24,500 feet in three days, taking in some hard climbing on the way. No matter how fit we were, it was little wonder that we felt fatigued.

Doug woke me the morning after our arrival at the cave with a 'Happy birthday, youth,' and I realised it was 12 May. We idled away the day, savouring the view of the mountains of Sikkim bordering with Tibet and the sight of Everest and Makalu far away to the west. I tried to compose a speech I would have to make as best man at the wedding of Don and Jenny, the two friends who had put up with all the disruption of my earlier preparations for expeditions. In a way, having to give the speech gave me more cause for worry than the rest of the mountain ahead. The anxieties of climbing a mountain were the sort which were familiar, but standing up in public, making a speech, having to be witty, was a disquieting prospect. The other three all chipped in with their suggestions about what I could say.

The cave was palatial. I was told how it had taken hours of excavation to achieve a chamber large enough for four people to lie in side by side and to sit in without banging against the ceiling. They had started digging from opposite sides of a wide rib of snow. The snow rib was formed by the wind in a bay at the base of the rampart of rock, 'the castle' as we referred to it, barring access to the vast plateau above. It had been for this rampart that we had asked the Czechoslovaks for the rope. The plateau was 500 feet above the snow cave and the intervening barrier of rock and steep ice was difficult enough to warrant fixing with rope to assure safe progress up or down, whatever the weather. This had been done during the previous attempt by Pete, Doug and Georges. The way to the summit was now largely prepared.

Georges had persisted with his proposal that we should try to reach the summit in one long push from the snow cave and gradually we had come round to his way of thinking. Vertically we had almost 4,000 feet of ascent to reach the 28,200-foot summit, and we would have to cover nearly two miles to get there. It was a lot to do in one stretch, so high up, and we knew of no precedents. The attraction of this plan lay in not carrying much weight. A rucksack of twenty pounds is a wearisome burden at altitude, but with no necessity to carry more than a little chocolate and sweets, with no need for sleeping bags if we were not going to spend the night out, we hoped that the lightness of our loads would compensate for the distance we had to travel. Another factor influencing our decision was the brightness of the moon. The moon was almost full and not only would this light our way, but the deprivation of altitude made us impressionable and receptive to Doug's contention that we would all be at our greatest strength as the moon waxed larger.

All day too of 13 May we lay in the cave, or outside on a platform in the snow when the wind dropped. The waiting preyed on our minds and we began to regret the passage of fine weather whilst we were inactive. We had planned to leave at 1.00 a.m., using the hours of darkness to climb the 500 feet of rope above and to cross the plateau to the base of the final pyramid. However, the waiting aggravated our impatience and we knew we would not sleep if we were to leave at 1.00 a.m. so we prepared to leave earlier. Activity appeared more desirable than the constant checking of watches in anticipation of departure and without any firm suggestion it seemed logical to start before dark to have done with the roped section by nightfall. So we left in the afternoon, in spite of an approaching bank of cloud, climbed up the ropes through the rampart of rock and congregated in darkness on the edge of the plateau. The wind had freshened, so we huddled together for warmth and to make ourselves heard. Stinging flurries of snow were blown up from the ground, but the plateau was set at a gentle angle, the surface was mostly small stones, and progress was only a matter of walking, bowed against the wind.

We stayed roped together in pairs to keep in contact, for all we could see of each other was a head-torch beam, or a dark shape outlined by the light. The heavy cloud of the afternoon obscured the moon and, though roped together, we were each alone in this journey through the night. The wind increased in strength and the driving snow was more persistent; time crept by in hours.

Though we were moving steadily, the movement was monotonous and I felt drowsy. My thoughts floated freely and it was as if the landscape around me, glimpsed by torchlight, and the figures moving in it were not real. The hood of my down suit, drawn protectively round my face, became the frame of a television screen from inside which I was observing the outside world. Instead of watching images on the screen, I was an image, detached from the discoloured rocks, the moving shapes, the wind, the cold, the snow.

I would snap out of this delusion to realise that I had to keep control of my imagination, that tiredness combined with the altitude and hunger were inducing hallucinations, then I would be caught up in them again, an observer, not a participant, my mind roaming independently of the automaton movements of my limbs.

Anything positive pulled me back to reality. We all crouched down in the shelter of a large rock discussing which way to go, whether to go on, whether attempting to reach the summit now was too ambitious. We pressed on, hoping that the weather might improve by morning.

At midnight we were in the region of the crescent-shaped buttress beside which was the gully we had to climb. All our plans had depended on being able to see our way at this point either by the arrival of dawn or by the light of the moon. Dense cloud blocked the beams of our torches and vicious streams of snow kept our faces turned to the ground.

Doug and I favoured digging in to the snow where we were, and forming a cave in which to shelter until dawn, but Pete suggested going further to where the base of the buttress above could just be seen. There he believed the snow would be better for a cave. Georges set off to follow Pete; I untied and stayed with Doug to burrow into the snow where we stood.

The snow was hard, it was not such a good place to burrow into, but in a while we had a passable shelter. By this time we simply wanted to escape from the harrowing wind and snow. We tried to communicate with Pete and Georges but the words were lost in the wind. We saw a flash of torch as the cloud thinned momentarily and set off towards it. But we saw nothing more and lost our direction in the swirling whiteness. We retreated to the hollow we had dug in the snow only finding it with difficulty and erected a wall using lumps of snow against the wind. Without sleeping bags to hide in, we sat in our suits of down, plagued by the jets of wind which penetrated the gaps between the blocks of snow. Doug chopped away with his ice axe at the hard snow, enlarging the cave and keeping warm with the activity. I tried to fill the gaps in the outer wall to shut out the draughts and dozed spasmodically as fatigue overtook me.

I became convinced that we had so badly miscalculated our movements that we had spoilt our chances of reaching the summit on this occasion. The cold seemed to reach my bones, and alternately I shivered and was gripped with cramps. I admired Doug's strength which enabled him to keep chopping away at what was now ice, only marginally enlarging the cave but able to keep himself warm. I picked away sometimes with my axe at what snow I could reach but my arms wanted to drop with fatigue.

We talked about Pete and Georges, unable to believe that they had been able to go much further. Partly we felt embarrassed at losing touch with them and partly we felt that it had been much more sensible to stop when we did and that the storm had interfered with our efforts to communicate.

The cold sapped our strength too, and at the first glimmer of dawn we left the cave, glad of the movement, to climb up and look for the other two. We had hardly started when we saw them emerging, 300 feet above us, from a hole in the snow beside the buttress of rock.

We met for a hasty consultation and agreed to descend to the large cave below 'the castle' where we had food and sleeping bags and could recoup our strength. It was a crestfallen retreat in the hard light of dawn back across the plateau and down to the reassuring comfort of the cave we knew.

Pete and Georges had discovered a crevasse alongside the rock buttress which they had used to hide in from the wind. This was why Doug and I had not seen their lights or heard their voices. They had tried to climb further – Georges had thought that the summit was not far away – but they had lost their way in the darkness and cloud and had retired to shelter in the crevasse.

Georges seemed deflated as if he bore the full responsibility for the plan which had backfired. Now we were all so tired we needed a good rest before going up again. Pete and Georges had caught sight once of the pinnacles on the summit ridge which marked a point where the first people to climb the mountain had emerged from the South-West Face. We knew for certain that that point was only 300 feet below the summit. Georges believed that he and Pete had been level with that point but Pete was not so sure. It seemed hardly credible that they could have climbed so high in a relatively short time.

We began talking of a change of tactics, considering using the snow cave or the crevasse near the rock buttress as a proper bivouac stop on the way to the summit. With a good rest there, taking up food and sleeping bags, we stood a better chance of climbing the last 2,000 feet. The long push from this snow cave was too much.

Georges was not convinced; he felt sure that he had been very close to the summit, as close as one often went to the summit of a mountain in the Alps where the objective was to climb a difficult route and the last few hundred feet of easy ground to the top made no difference to the validity of the ascent. It was obvious one could do it and it served no purpose to go those last few hundred feet for the sake of appearances.

He spoke in generalities as if, as a mental exercise, we could consider ourselves to have done what we had set out to do. We had overcome the main difficulties and in that sense we had completed the climb and had no need to continue right to the top when we could see that no more obstacles blocked the way. I was surprised that he and Pete could have got so close to the top but that only gave me encouragement that we could after all make it to the summit and it might turn out to be easier than we had feared.

We were all dead beat. Georges withdrew into his sleeping bag, remaining mute and unresponsive all day. Pete lay next to the inert Georges, near the tunnel entrance where the air was fresh. He tended the stove, producing drinks and food in such quantities that he became resentful of the passive gratitude from the rest of us, who made excuses to avoid working the stove ourselves. In the back of the cave where Doug and I lay, the air was stalest. I felt a certain claustrophobia in this icy tomb of our own making. The walls and roof were firm, but the weight of snow outside caused the ceiling to sink imperceptibly lower. Each day a few more inches of snow had to be scoured from the ceiling to save us knocking our heads every time we sat upright. The stove would only function near the entrance in the fresher air. Inside the cave the air was too thin, too stale or too cold to enable even a candle to burn. I wanted to sleep but the claustrophobia, the subconscious registering of the fear of suffocation, made my sleeping shallow and my rest fitful.

Doug mentioned the impression he kept having that there were more than just the four of us on the mountain and awoke memories of similar impressions in us all. On returning to the cave I had been unthinkingly waiting for 'the others' to arrive. Not Pete, nor Georges, nor Doug but an indistinct group of people whom I imagined were also on the climb with us. They were, I fancied, other members of the team and this impression of being part of a larger group, part of something greater than the little band that we really were, created a sense of reassurance as if someone else more capable, more perspicacious, was directing events and bearing the responsibility. The illusion created too a sense of harmony with the mountain. Pete recalled the very firm belief, as he was bringing up the rear on the way back to the cave, that he was not the last person at all. It was not a thought that needed verification; he was simply aware of the presence of someone behind him, just as firmly as he knew we three were in front of him. Discussing these impressions openly banished the phantoms from my thoughts, but the sense of harmony remained.

After a day of mute inactivity, Georges sat up and announced that he had decided to go down. It should have been a startling announcement but one's responses at altitude are dampened down as if all mental as well as physical activity has adapted to the need to conserve energy. All necessary effort is to be avoided and when Georges told us, directly and emphatically: 'I 'ave not enough juice left. It would be too dangerous for me to go for the summit. If anything happened I would not be able to get myself out of difficulties. I will go now, back to Base Camp, while I 'ave strength,' he evoked little more reaction than if he had said he did not want anything to eat. Someone reassured him that he probably had as much strength as any of us but that was a reason, he felt, for all of us to go down now because we were so exhausted. If we were entitled to decide to carry on he was entitled to decide to go down.

Georges often voiced aloud his thoughts; it was not unusual for him to come out with an idea radically different from any that had otherwise been suggested, but it was only his spontaneity which caused him to speak his mind immediately an idea occurred to him. In practice he was much more likely to have drawn closer to the majority view by the time any action took place. By morning I suspected he would have changed his mind. All of us had experienced such moments of doubt and the longing to end the toil by simply turning round and going back. Often I relied upon other people being at a different level of enthusiasm to sustain me when my spirits were low, just as I knew that at other times I was more confident and buoyant than others around me.

Doug, however, began to voice his own doubts, aroused by Georges's openly expressed decision. He wondered aloud at the purpose in what we were doing and whether, like the long-distance runner in Alan Sillitoe's novel, we would show more mastery over the game we had chosen to play if we were to turn back now that the goal was in sight. Doug had been on expeditions to big mountains more times than anyone I knew, but he was forever asking himself why he felt such a compulsion to climb them, and on the mountains he was forever questioning how he came to be away again, what it all meant to him and whether it would matter if he gave it all up.

Pete felt the impetus of the expedition threatened by the verbalisation of such self-analysis and appealed to me to discover where my resolve lay. The points at issue had all become very clear to him many weeks before when the injuries to his foot and then to his hand had made the possibility of not reaching the summit very real and had forced him to realise that reaching the top of Kangchenjunga was of paramount importance to him. The motivation he had had to summon up then to get himself walking and fit, and then to drag himself upwards with constant pain in his wrist, was not susceptible to any eleventh-hour uncertainties.

For myself, having been given back the chance of reaching the top when I had thought all was lost, I was keen too to carry on with the attempt. I did feel, however, that we needed a day or two of recuperation down at the tents on the North Col.

In the morning Doug woke us to say that he had had the most refreshing night's sleep full of dreams which had inspired him with the conviction that he should go on to the summit. He went outside to relieve himself and shouted in to us that it was the clearest of mornings and that it would be a pity to waste such a good day going to the North Col when we could use the good weather to go up again. This was the other side to the man wracked with doubts; this was the side of him which drove him on to climb more and more mountains.

It was a jolt to wrench one's thoughts upwards so soon again. We were low on food and had only one spare cylinder for the gaz stove. Our intention had been to descend to Camp 3 on the North Col to bring back up food and more fuel. Certainly the idea of going up again instead was more attractive than the long trail down and the climb back up to this cave, but I doubted if I had recovered enough to go all out for the summit. Pete was cautious too, torn between the opportunity of capitalising on this new enthusiasm and the risk of finally pushing ourselves to exhaustion if we were to meet bad weather and run out of food high up.

The discovery of a second cartridge of gaz tipped the balance. Upwards it was to be. Doug turned to Georges, who was still in his sleeping bag: 'Georges, would you like to come with us to the top?' He said it as if nothing would please him more than to have Georges's company.

'No. I am going down, but I think you should go for 'eet from here. It is better than delaying further.'

So we left to go upwards and watched Georges's figure dwindle to a speck. We watched until he was down the crest of the ridge to the start of the ropes at the top of the wall and we knew that he would be safe. It was the saddest of sights. Forever volatile, Georges was as easily despondent as he was enthusiastic. There was no ill-feeling. He had made a decision for himself and we for ourselves. He expected to get back to Base Camp that evening and he promised to light a fire as a signal to us if fine weather was forecast. No fire would mean bad weather.

Pete and Doug stood aside to let me break trail to the bottom of the rope leading up to the plateau. The storm which had caught us out the night before had covered the slope thickly with new snow.

'It's about time you broke trail to here, Joe,' said Doug, aligning himself with Pete in a self-righteous stance of having done their share of work other times when they had been this way.

The snow was knee-deep and though it was only 200 feet to the rope, my legs were leaden with fatigue. I reached the rope where it hung clear on bare ice and expressed my doubts to Pete and Doug about whether we had had enough rest. Pete was sympathetic to the idea that we should rest for another day but Doug wanted to press on and Pete was prepared to push himself to ensure that the chances of reaching the summit did not begin to dwindle once more.

Pete encouraged me on. He knew me more than anyone.

'Just make your way as slowly as you like to the cave in the crevasse. We should be there by early afternoon and you will get a good rest. You can make your own pace once we're on the plateau.'

Every inch of the 500 feet of rope up to the plateau was exhausting. My spirit seemed crushed by the impossible effort. On the plateau Doug was already far ahead, piling stones one on top of another to mark the way back in darkness or storm. If he had doubts about why he was on the mountain, they were not doubts about his strength, he seemed to have energy to spare. I hobbled along in company with Pete. We sat down often to rest, watching the afternoon clouds roll in, until Pete too went on ahead and I plodded with infinite slowness up the last incline to the snow cave.

Inside, Doug and Pete were already at work, levelling out the floor for us to lie on. I shovelled half-heartedly at the piles of ice-chippings, sending them down into the dark crevasse where the ice was parted from the rock wall.

A minor storm was sending showers of hailstones down the tunnel, so Pete sealed it with carefully fashioned blocks of snow. There was enough air, streaming up from the depths of the crevasse, for us to breathe comfortably.

We settled in for the night, Doug seizing the prime place, and promising to cook in compensation. His fingers still hurt too much, however, and he had to abandon the cooking to avoid the painful contact of snow on his bare hands.

Pete and I had less room, but it was better being squashed close together as we could share body heat. When one side of me grew cold, I would turn over so that I was warmed against the extra insulation of Pete in his sleeping bag.

At the arranged time of 8.00 p.m. we were reluctant to break open the protective cover on the tunnel to look for the light of the fire which Georges

had promised if the forecast were good. Any movement at all was dispro-
portionately tiring and therefore unwelcome. We resigned ourselves to
making our own judgement about the weather next morning.

I had a terrible cough which was caused by the heavy breathing-in of the
cold, dry air. My throat had become inflamed to such an extent that the
slightest irritation would send me into an inescapable, noisy bout of coughing, which Pete and Doug found alarming and I was concerned would keep
them awake.

We achieved a comfort of sorts. Doug, in the widest part of the cave, was
exposed to draughts which disturbed his rest. Huddled close to Pete, any
discomfort softened by the influence of a sleeping pill, I slept soundly.
Doug woke me to find the time, then again to ask for tablets to ease the pain
in his fingers and to help him sleep. But Pete was already fumbling for his
canister of pills and I dozed off again.

We were awake at 4.30 a.m. All three of us were slow and unenthusiastic
about stirring from the delicately achieved equilibrium between warmth
and cold. I started the stove, feeding lumps of ice into the pan and lying
back in my sleeping bag waiting for the liquid to heat. We shared a mugful
of granola, drank a mugful each of fruit drink and a mugful of tea, and then
there was no reason to delay further.

We left everything behind except a bottle each of water, spare mitts,
cameras and sweets. I thrust my share into my pockets but Pete and Doug
took their rucksacks. We burst out of the tunnel, pushing the protective
blocks aside. The sky was clear blue, mountains far below were in view as
far as the horizon, which was marked by the dominant shapes of Everest
and Makalu. A slight breeze was blowing but it was as perfect a day as we
had known on the mountain.

I needed to relieve myself before we started off and remember being
pleased that my body was functioning so regularly, even so high up and
under the duress of such effort and minimal diet.

We strapped on our crampons and moved off up a slope of snow, all three
of us on a length of rope 120 feet long. As soon as we started upwards I
felt the deadly fatigue again; we hardly talked, every breath was needed for
the strength it gave for movement. I could not know of the doubts Pete or
Doug might have, but in their silence assumed that they had none. I could
not imagine myself going on upwards all day if after every few steps I was
needing to rest. I resolved to go until I ground to a halt, then I would return
to the cave on my own, leaving Pete and Doug to continue together. I did
not want to hinder their progress, they seemed strong and purposeful, and
would turn back if I held them up.

On the earlier attempt overnight, Pete and Georges had gone straight up
a gully of snow and lost their way in the dark. Doug and I had talked about
taking a line which zig-zagged up through the rocky area, following two

distinct runnels of snow up to an unavoidable step of rock, the narrowest part of the barrier above. We took it in turns to go first, although we were moving together. The slope of snow was not steep but sometimes steps needed kicking in the crusty snow and this was tiring, so we shared the work, and as second or third on the rope one could easily rest mentally from the extra attention needed to decide which way to go.

At the step of rock it was my turn to lead. Judgement can be clouded at altitude and I distrusted the impression I had that this step of rock looked easy to climb. It appeared to be only about sixty feet high, and lay back in a series of slabby steps. Cautiously I set foot on the first holds, levered myself upwards and fingered each hand-hold suspiciously. I felt as if difficulty was personified and was going to grab hold of me at any moment. Pete safeguarded the rope below me, watching my every move and waiting till I reached the top of the step before starting up himself. Warily I glanced about; I had thought this was going to be as big a struggle as I had read that Nick Estcourt and Tut Braithwaite had had to break through the rock band on Everest, but it was no more of a struggle than was any other minute of survival at high altitude. If anything it was more interesting than the repetitive plodding up snow slopes and ice. I reached the top, where the rock shelved into snow bands which ran into the great diagonal swathe of snow, 2,000 feet across, towards a notch on the ridge 300 feet below the summit. That diagonal ramp of snow was clear of obstacles. My doubts had disappeared.

The interest and excitement aroused by solving what had been long considered an imponderable obstacle had subdued my feelings of fatigue. The weariness remained but the interest and desire to look over that notch in the ridge, down the far side of the mountain, to look round every remaining obstacle until we were looking at the summit, this eagerness to explore purely to see was what kept me going. I knew now that I could keep on putting one foot in front of another for as long as daylight lasted. No illness marred my feelings, only if time ran out would I turn back now. If my emotions had not been in a state of 'shut down' I would have felt enthusiastic. I turned and shouted down for Pete and Doug to come up.

They came up together, then Pete led on for a while. There were no stages, each of us led the way for as far as he felt able. Every few steps we stopped to gasp and pant for breath. We went at the pace of whoever was slowest, but the slowest was not slow enough. Every stop was welcome, something indefinable had taken over to keep us moving upwards when all stimulus was swamped by the distress of muscles and lungs starved of oxygen. An urge beyond description got us to our feet after every halt and made us go up a few more steps.

Doug went first for a while, but his painful fingers and feet which were growing numb slowed him up and he asked if he could bring up the rear.

We were well wrapped in red suits of down, so that to look at we were barely distinguishable, individual size and shape being lost in the rounded contours of the padding.

I took over the lead. Sometimes the snow was firm and the forward points of my crampons bit firmly at each step. Where soft snow was packed on the surface by the wind a kick was needed to bury the foot in the snow and make a step. Always we worried that this soft snow would slide away, taking us with it, but we had to climb up it in places. I set my sights on a rock protruding from the snow some distance away. The distance did not mean very much, it was impossible to gauge with nothing to give it scale. It was the time that counted, but that was difficult to judge too. Between one glance at my watch and the next, time would have moved on with little to show save a few, very few, steps upwards and a long gasping for air. The notch on the ridge below the summit was an inestimable distance away in the time needed. In memory there is little left save a series of cameos, telescoped together, of panting figures in red, or figures in motion, shuffling upwards, six steps at a time.

I reached the rock, the target I had set myself, with no idea how long I had been in front nor how far we had come. Doug asked for a halt. His feet were still cold and he wanted to warm them before they became numb and frozen. He took off his boots and I let him place his stockinged feet inside my down suit, on my stomach, where the warmth of my body restored feeling to them. Pete and I were benefiting from the use of the new boots made of plastic, with a thin foam inner boot, which we had found to be far more effective as insulation than the traditional leather double boots. Doug's feet were too large for his plastic boots and he was suffering as a result of having to use his old leather ones.

Pete led on. The notch on the ridge was appreciably nearer. It was early afternoon and shadows were lengthening towards us. He came to a patch of snow which hardly seemed to adhere to the icy surface beneath. He gathered all his strength and rushed upwards for fifteen steps without pause. Doug and I, caught unawares, struggled and choked in pursuit. Pete reached a rib of black, shaly rock alongside which he climbed and then the notch was in reach. He climbed to the crest, catching the sun as he moved out of the shadow, and shouted back in a cracked voice that the view was fantastic. I joined him on the rock where he was perched, with the South-West Face sweeping down below. It was at this point that the first people to climb the mountain had arrived in 1955, after ascending the South-West Face. Our route up the unknown north side was over; from here 300 feet of ground which we knew had been climbed led to the summit. It was 4.00 p.m. with two hours left before darkness.

Pete was looking content. We hardly communicated at all, but in these minutes of waiting till Doug joined us a little relaxation and self-congratulation was permissible. The weather had remained fine all day, the wind had not reached its usual ferocity, and now what had seemed an endless struggle was all but over.

It hardly seemed possible that we could reach the top from here and descend to the snow cave and safety before dark. We knew that we would be lucky to reach the cave, where we had left our sleeping bags and food, if we started back immediately. But the altitude or ambition or the innate drive which had borne us so far precluded rational decisions.

'Do you think we should press on?'

'I think so. Do you?'

'Yes. Let's wait till Doug gets here to make a decision.'

Doug hauled himself out of the shadows into the sun. We were only separated from each other by sixty feet of rope but it could take five or ten minutes to close that gap even on the easiest slope. Doug grinned broadly: 'That's it then. Cracked it. We'll never get up this last bit and down again before dark.' It was the voice of reason.

Pete said we would kick ourselves for the rest of our lives if we did not do this last 300 feet and urged that we go on. Doug was persuaded.

'All right. My turn to lead for a bit then, but I want a rest.'

We knew that the vertical interval was 300 feet but what that meant in distance we did not know. It was a chaos of rocks, snow and ice covering the slopes below the summit. A steep wall of rock barred the way to the summit cave. Joe Brown, a brilliant rock-climber, had forced his way up there with his oxygen turned to full flow on the first ascent. The second party of their team had avoided the steep rock by traversing below on bands of snow. We could not tell whether we were looking at a distance of one hundred feet or several hundred feet. Clearly we could not go on forever. Behind a huge spike of rock on the skyline we could see the foot of a bank of snow.

'Let's go as far as that snow,' said Pete.

'We'll go on until we have pushed the patience of the gods to the limit,' said Doug, and he began threading his way across the slope, over rocks, down a chimney and gently upwards.

Clouds were beginning to fill the valley. Jannu, 3,000 feet lower, was almost obscured by cloud, and behind it more clouds were banked up, resembling the mushroom-shaped columns of nuclear explosions. A storm seemed to be approaching.

We traipsed on, the time forgotten once the decision had been made. Up and down, wending an erratic path to no one knew where. Doug ducked beneath the projecting spike of rock and stepped onto the tongue of snow. With laboured movements he turned to face us: 'It's just up here. Fifty feet away.'

The snow bank was easy. The nearness of the much-longed-for summit inspired a last big effort and we stood all three of us on a prow of rock which jutted out from the snow dome of the summit itself. It was 4.45 p.m. Far below, Jannu drifted in and out of cloud. Everest and Makalu could still be seen standing above all else. To the east the mountains of Sikkim were softening in the light of the setting sun.

We had given no promises to avoid standing on the summit itself, yet none of us made a move towards the rounded dome only ten feet higher than where we stood. The obligation to respect what was sacred to another people was beyond promises. Doug tried to skirt below the summit to look down the eastern face but the slope was too steep.

We all took photographs and crouched down together as Doug set the time control on his camera to record the three of us against the summit. The dark form of an Alpine chough flew over us – an omen, a messenger of the gods whose home we were threatening to desecrate. The heavy cloud had risen from the valleys, homing in on the mountain where we stood. It was time to go.

'Just a moment while I take some black and white photos,' said Doug and we waited. I was impatient.

'We must get moving.'

'You'll be glad of these when we get back. Just hold on while I change the film.'

'Pete, start moving. It will be dark soon.'

It was 5.30 p.m. as we moved off. Half an hour before dark. As we made our way back to the notch on the ridge the belly of the heavy cloud now hanging over the mountain was aflame with the orange glow of the setting sun. The distant mountains were blanketed from sight by this apocalyptic curtain-fall. Darkness covered the mountain and the snow started.

We picked our way down the ramp from memory, glad now of the marks in the deeper snow showing us the way and vainly peering for traces of crampon points where the snow was hard. Doug was descending first. It was not easy to keep on line. All our instincts were to climb straight downwards but we had to stick to a diagonal line. I heard a cry in the darkness and felt a tug on the rope as Doug, deceived by the shadows cast by his torch, tumbled over a step in the ice to land in soft snow. I could sense a weary fatalism taking hold of me. I was becoming too tired to take sufficient care when every groping step in the darkness needed fullest concentration. Doug kept going off course. I could remember better the line we had come up but Pete's sharper eyes were able to pick out the slightest traces in the surface of the snow. He went first then and for what seemed like hours we climbed down by touch and luck alone, the weakening pools of torchlight often hindering rather than helping.

In the deep blackness below we saw the flickering pinprick of light from a torch at Base Camp, then fires flared in signal that our torchlight was observed and they knew that we were on our way back from the summit. It was no sort of reassurance, Georges was signalling from another life, and his pinpricks of torchlight would only have meaning for us if we survived.

What had been a breeze became a savage wind which flung snow in our eyes as we tried to see in the dark. Doug's hands were almost insensible with the cold and a note of panic and urgency marked his voice as he insisted on stopping to warm them. At the rear my whole being was tense with cold and as I waited to move on I wanted to plead with Doug to keep moving so that we could reach the cave sooner. Pete was too far away for me to see, careful and capable; I was confident in his ability to keep on the right line.

There was some confusion when we reached the rock step, until we realised where we were and the nearness to safety gave me strength for a last effort.

The slabby step of rock was slippery with the new snow, but I felt at home there, sliding down confidently on what I had climbed up so warily. Only a long, sweeping arc down the slope below remained before we were at the cave entrance. Doug disappeared inside to massage his hands back to life. I felt all the tension drain away and I paused outside to take off my crampons and coil the rope. I was warm now from exertion and I felt a reluctance to break the spell of these moments, savouring the fury of the elements lashing the mountain, knowing that for a brief interval we had been allowed to master it.

I chatted to Pete for some minutes. We were still at 26,000 feet with a long way to go before we were in complete safety but nothing could take away from us the fact that we had climbed Kangchenjunga, we had stood just a few feet short of the third highest mountain in the world and we had done it all ourselves, without a massive pyramid of support from other selfless workers who had paved the way for us. I thought of the lady who had become my friend, Mrs Beaumont, who had had such trust in first lending me support in efforts to come to the Himalayas. She had had confidence in us when we least felt it ourselves and I thought now that climbing this mountain would be a justification for her of all her earlier trust.

'Mrs Beaumont will be pleased, Pete,' I said.

'Yep, it's going to be great to get back, isn't it?' and we crawled inside to join Doug. It was 8.00 p.m.

I felt relief and cautious satisfaction that the hardest part of our task was over, but the relief did not help me rest. Though my body was weary, my mind was still stimulated by the long day's need for total concentration and awareness. Sleep was fitful, but without anxiety for the energy needed for another day of upward struggle.

The morning chores of making tea and packing sacks were undesirable duties postponing departure. The departure, when it came, was more discomfort, an endless trail for limbs moved by a spark of life from inside. Doug seemed to have strength remaining. He drew ahead on the plateau, while I hobbled on in company with Pete, finding the uneven ground awkward under foot. My muscles no longer had the power to hold my limbs steady, and I sank down to rest at every excuse, revelling in the moments of ease stolen from the time needed for the descent. It hardly seemed possible that the plateau should stretch on and on as it did, and I worried that Georges could well have been right, that we had pushed ourselves on to our physical limits in reaching the summit and now had not enough reserves of energy to bring ourselves back down in safety.

Doug disappeared over the edge where the ropes led down to the cave and gradually we too came to the end of the plateau. Doug had already been into the cave when we arrived and had retrieved all belongings left there. The ceiling had sunk more in our absence so that there was only two feet of clearance left. The dark cleft looked more claustrophobic than ever and did not invite entry for a last nostalgic visit. We were sheltered from the breeze beside the cave entrance and we lingered for a while, warmed by the sun and melting snow to make tea. The loss of 2,000 feet of altitude and the sweet tea restored some energy. We roped together and started down the ridge to the North Col.

The wind was stronger once we were out in the open, mist-like streams of snow scoured the ridge and stung our faces. The rope between us stretched in a taut bow as we moved together downwards, trying to keep pace with one another.

The tents of Camp 3 at the North Col were frozen to their platforms. We tried to free them but the fabric tore and we had neither the time nor the patience to ease them free. We decided to abandon them, packing all the remaining gear which we could not carry into two rucksacks to toss down to the glacier below, from where we hoped to retrieve it later. We had more to drink and debated what to do with the oxygen cylinder. It would cost as much as it was worth to transport back to Kathmandu so it was a choice of leaving it or throwing it down the mountain. I had never used oxygen on a climb and asked Pete and Doug what it was like. I said I fancied trying some before we abandoned the bottle but they discouraged me by threatening to put it about that I had used oxygen on the mountain when they had done it without. It was all in jest but I was put off the idea. Doug wanted to throw if off the ridge to clear the mountain and enjoy the spectacle but Pete was in favour of leaving it just in case someone might come this way again and find it useful. So we left it and dragged the two sacks of gear up to the crest of the ridge. We sent them off, sliding down the gully above the line of ropes, hoping that they would stay intact for recovery once we reached the glacier ourselves.

Our own sacks were heavy enough. We were clearing everything we could from the mountain as we would not be coming back up. The wall had changed in the week that we had been above the Col. There had been a change in the season as the year advanced more towards mid-summer and the ice of the wall had become softer and wet with the rise in temperature. The day was well on as we started down and the warmth of the sun had brought rivulets of water from the ice which soaked the rope, soaked gloves and clothing as we slid down. Sometimes I sucked up mouthfuls of the dirty water to slake my thirst. We had eaten little in that week and I could feel all the more the weight of my sack through the straps which cut into my shoulders from which the flesh had gone. More loose rock was exposed by the receding ice. I dislodged some inadvertently and saw some dislodged from above. When I reached the bottom, where the ropes ran onto the glacier, I freed myself and scuttled down to be clear away from more stones from above. I heard Doug shout but could not make out if he was calling a warning or venting his displeasure at the awkward descent. Then I caught his meaning. Suspended part way up the wall near to him was the shape of a red figure, arms stretched wide, legs together. I was shocked moment-arily as my mind seized on, then discarded as impossible, the thought that there was a body stuck to the ice. It was only a down suit, part of the gear we had thrown from above. I looked around me; a few hundred feet away were other objects. One of the sacks had burst open and the glacier was strewn with other items of clothing. The down suit had opened out and drifted on its own to catch on a rock projection. Doug eased himself across on the rope and tugged it free, so that it sailed on to the bottom of the wall.

I forced myself to go about gathering up the scattered objects, retrieving all but a suit of my own. There was no sign of Ang Phurba or Nima, whom we had asked to come to meet us. We took what we could and made a pile of the rest for them to collect.

It was 5.00 p.m. There was only an hour of daylight left, but the return to Camp 2 had only ever taken half an hour so we were confident of reaching it before dark. Pete insisted that we use the bit of rope we had remaining to tie ourselves together, cautious to the last, lest the mountain should strike back, swallowing one of us up in a crevasse just as we were thinking we were safe. We spotted the two Sherpas just as we were leaving. They were a long distance away and were moving very slowly. We were angry that they should be so leisurely when we were so tired. They would have seen us the moment we had started down the wall and could have been almost with us by this time. I started first; the snow was wet and deep. I looked forward to reaching the more level part of the glacier where the snow was usually firmer, but it never became firm. At first I was up to my knees, then up to my thighs, and sometimes I sank up to my waist and floundered helplessly trying to move forward when there was nothing solid to step on. I looked back at Doug and Pete, they were no better off following in my tracks. Doug seemed to sink in even further with his greater weight.

Sometimes a dark, bottomless hole appeared when I withdrew my foot and I was glad of the tenuous reassurance of the line attaching me to the other two. A couple of times I could see a crevasse in the way and crawled, spreading my weight over as wide an area as possible and lunging over the dark gap, in the hope of landing in the snow of the other side. Sometimes I could not tell that a crevasse lay hidden beneath the snow and I felt the stab of fear in my stomach as the ground gave way beneath me and I would throw back the upper part of my body to bury my sack in the snow behind, and wait, suspended over nothing, till I had caught my breath and could haul myself out.

This was the glacier we had walked up and down so easily, in snow at most ankle-deep, on a track well beaten by our own footsteps. We had usually worn the rope in accordance with the precepts of safety rather than because there were any clear indications of the dangers below. Now we could see that this whole glacier basin was seamed with crevasses and only the firmness of the snow had facilitated our passage in those earlier weeks.

We resorted to crawling in many places and dragged our sacks along the snow beside us trying to take more weight off our feet. Darkness was drawing on and in these conditions it seemed as if it would take us hours to get back to the camp. We realised now why the two Sherpas had not reached the foot of the wall in time to meet us, and saw too that this deep snow must stretch all the way to Camp 2. At the mound where the avalanche debris lay across our way the going was only slightly firmer. Ang Phurba and Nima were closer and to keep up my spirits I consoled myself with the thought that we would be able to walk more easily once we reached their tracks.

We were all wet and cold from contact with the snow. Doug complained bitterly as if the cold was singling him out for special attention. His fingers and toes were giving him great pain.

Unannounced, Ang Phurba and Nima loomed up out of the gloom, and I felt we were saved. We told them of the rucksacks of gear we had left for them to collect next day but they wanted to collect them immediately since they were halfway there and they continued on by the feeble light of an almost exhausted torch.

They gave us some directions but night came on and the wind brought snow. The going was slightly better but I lost the way and came up against a large crevasse. Their footsteps were indistinct in the darkness, but I remembered Ang Phurba's description and got back on course. Pete was better in the dark and took over the lead until at last we reached the camp.

The sole tent remaining was covered in snow and indistinct against the whiteness of the now furious storm. We almost missed it but had realised our error when Ang Phurba and Nima reappeared out of the dark, carrying the heavy sacks we had left. The speed with which they had gone up and come back emphasised how weak we had become and how little able we were to continue fighting against the elements.

Their arrival meant we could now surrender all duties to them. We three piled into the tent, making ourselves comfortable, taking off wet clothing and slipping into the luxurious warmth of our sleeping bags. We lay back, letting the two Sherpas hand back hot drinks and food to us, as the cosy drug of near safety made heavy our eyes. I fought off sleep for as long as they were administering food to us, enjoying the delicious sense of fatigue without responsibility. When all was finished we took a sleeping pill each, Ang Phurba and Nima squeezed into the tent, and we slept in such comfort and warmth as had been long forgotten.

We were woken at 3.30 a.m. by Nima with a cup of tea. He and Ang Phurba were anxious to be moving before the snow softened again in the heat of the sun. It was only the first stretch, down to our old Camp 1, where the snow was deep. It was not yet as soft as the previous evening and once onto the bare ice of the lower glacier we could walk freely. Only new streams of meltwater signalled the advance of the season and, once clear of the slopes from which avalanches might come, we knew we could relax. At last we were down off the mountain and could truthfully say we had climbed Kangchenjunga.

Doug's pace quickened again. I could not hurry, not even to share the good news with those at Base Camp. I needed to guard my strength to keep my footing on the unstable mounds of rocks over which we had to climb. Pete and I talked shamelessly of the cigarettes we would let ourselves smoke in arrogant defiance of all the doubts and anxieties which the mountain had inspired before we climbed it. Neither of us would confess to 'smoking' in normal life, and knew that smoking was antithetical to the excellence of health we needed to climb mountains. As a symbol it represented all that was forbidden to us, and having succeeded we wanted the forbidden.

I fell several times, too weak to keep my footing on the boulder slopes leading up to Base Camp. By the time I saw Georges rushing down towards us, my arms were cut and bloodied from these falls so that I looked to have had an accident. Then Georges was hugging Pete and then me, and kissing my cheeks, smiling his pleasure that we were back, successful and well. Doug had already confirmed what he had seen through the telephoto lens on the camera. He had seen us as three tiny dots under a magnification of twenty times.

'Did you get a photo of us on the summit?' I asked.

'No, I was so excited, I forgot. I am so glad. I felt I was up there with you. I am so pleased.'

Base Camp was a place of blissful ease and safety. There was a festive atmosphere which made an ordinary meal seem like a celebration. It was 18 May. Georges had sent down for porters as soon as he saw us on the summit. They were due next day. I calculated that we should be back in England by early June.

Suddenly the mountain had been climbed and all our attentions were focused in the opposite direction. There was a whole new variety of preoccupations of a lesser order of importance. I had a sore throat to nurse, stinking clothes to change, a beard to shave off. I had worn a beard for almost ten years so that I had forgotten what I looked like without one. I decided to shave it off at Base Camp so that it had time to grow again if I did not like what I found underneath. One of my toes was very sore and appeared black beneath the nail. I did not know if it was due to compression in my boots over a long period or the freezing cold of the previous night of floundering in deep snow with soaking socks. I wondered if the blackened toe-nail qualified me for the status of one who had had frostbite.

Even the simple food of Base Camp was too rich. For the previous two days we had eaten hardly anything and prior to that our diet had been minimal. No sooner did I eat something than I had to rush off to the toilet area.

This had been a long expedition and still it was far from over. The long walk back was unavoidable and once the thrill of returning to Base Camp had dissipated into normality I perceived how remote we were. At home, when distances are calculated in the hours of car or train or plane journey, it is hard to comprehend the isolation of knowing that only after many days of walking up hills and over streams will one reach a destination. It was difficult for me to conceive of life at home. We had been through depths of feeling and profound experiences which only we as a group had shared. I had become accustomed to facing my innermost being on my own, of coming to terms with hopes and fears, had realised where my real wishes lay in spite of the pain of reaching that place. The emotional and physical yearnings of the early weeks had been anaesthetised by the catharsis of the drama in which we had been the actors. I could hardly visualise what it meant to have a relationship with a girl. I looked forward to female company but without the urgency I had expected after so long away. The lovely village girl, Dawa, arrived as one of our porters and instead of the avid attention we had paid her on the way in no one took any notice of her. We were still influenced by the mountain which had dominated us and soaked up all our energies. In time, as the ascent receded into a memory, as we grew accustomed to knowing that we did not have to concentrate single-mindedly on the mountain any more, the ties of home would reawaken and wax stronger, drawing us irresistibly back.

In a way it was fortunate that the pull was not at full strength, or the isolation now perceived would have become unbearable with still many days, if not weeks, between us and the return home. We came back to full strength only gradually, feeling the punishment of the long marches for the first few days. Then we would stride on, making our own paces, until the evening halt. We walked long and hard. My feet were tender from the cold they had felt and every step was uncomfortable, but the air was rich, the days warm and the food plentiful as we passed through the lower valleys. We came upon our mail runner, long overdue, dawdling in his home village instead of bringing us the mail he carried. We paid him off and pressed on, retracing our steps along a pathway scarcely remembered after all these weeks, and down into a tropical valley, after nine days of walking, from where one last hill had to be crossed before we reached the road.

There was a compound of huts where a road-construction project was under way. A solitary Peace Corps worker in a village had told us that the foundation for the road was almost complete and sometimes lifts could be obtained over that last hill. Doug and I went into the compound and knocked on a door. A clean, white-clad Englishman opened the door to us.

'Would it be possible,' said Doug in his most persuasive manner, 'for you to save us any more pain in our feet by giving us a lift over the hill to Dharan?'

The face of the man, puzzled at our dishevelled appearance, lit into a smile.

'You must be the Kangchenjunga team. I'm sure we can arrange a lift for you. Are you in a hurry or would you have time for a spot of lunch with us before you go?'

SEVEN

Apocalypse

K2

I

My beard grew back by the time we arrived in England. Pete went off to Switzerland and Doug started immediately preparing to depart again. Georges came with his wife, Norma, to stay with me for a holiday. They were good company and I got to know a different side of Georges. When we were laughing and joking round the table he would stop me and ask a joke to be explained far more often than he had ever done during the expedition. I asked him how it was that he had understood things during the expedition and seemed to have lost that understanding. He explained that he had not understood many things but had not wanted to be a nuisance by interrupting all the time for explanations when everyone else was laughing, so he had laughed too, just to join in.

He became converted to music too and would walk in, if the flat was silent, with a 'Hey, Joe, let's put a record on,' and I came back late a couple of times to find that he had fallen asleep on the floor with music still playing.

Georges and Norma returned to Chamonix, where they normally spent the summers, so that Georges could guide and I tried to spend some time paying attention to the business of running a shop before becoming totally embroiled in preparations for the return to K2.

The ascent of Kangchenjunga mellowed into being an achievement that nothing could usurp. Above all the setbacks, the doubts and the pain which each of us had had to face, the fact of reaching the summit stood out and would remain with us forever. The ascent might not have brought peace of mind but it did bring confidence to go on further, to take on something new and more difficult. There was nothing lacking in that the objective so long striven for should not, once achieved, be sufficient in itself. It was in the nature of such objectives, and of us who sought them, that one horizon reached should lead to the next.

The ascent of Dunagiri had shown that two people was a viable team for a difficult Himalayan peak and the next logical step was to attempt Changabang by its West Face, which seemed to border on the edge of the impossible. Succeeding on it was in no way disappointing but as a mountaineer the essence of life is in the struggle, the contest against great odds. Climbing Changabang's West Face demonstrated the level of technical difficulty which could be successfully attempted even by a very small team. The challenge lay in even higher peaks. On Kangchenjunga the problem was clear, with no room for compromise: could our bodies cope with the lack of oxygen we would have to endure to reach the top? However erratic a course we each made in reaching the top, nothing could ever invalidate that we had done so, and each of us by the strength of his body alone.

To go on from there, to progress, the three of us who had reached the summit of Kangchenjunga were already planning to attempt a mountain which was higher, and a route to its top which was harder. The success on Kangchenjunga gave us confidence to dare to return without oxygen equipment to the West Ridge of K2 from which we had retreated in 1978 after the death of Nick Estcourt.

Then there had been eight members on the team and this time, for the renewed attempt, we decided to have a team of four. It was a bold idea to go as a foursome to climb the second highest mountain in the world, by a route which had defeated eight of us, but we rationalised that the mountain, although 28,253 feet high, was only forty-five feet higher than one we had already similarly climbed. The real problem was that the route appeared to have difficulties for most of the way, and the big unknown was whether we could continue to overcome those difficulties of buttresses, walls of rock and runnels of ice at altitudes where every step would be a deadly effort. And whether, where all movement is painstakingly slow, we would be able to descend safely if an accident occurred or one of us became ill.

The unknowns were what gave flavour and attraction to the idea, and we believed that we could safely avoid the slope from which Nick had been swept away by climbing a faint rib of rock directly to the crest of the ridge. This would bring us out above the camp where Pete and I had spent four nights confined by snow-storms, the way to which was menaced, we now knew, by avalanche danger.

The loss of Nick was not something I had forgotten, nor an incident whose impact had lessened. It was a tragedy which had become absorbed into experience, the memory of which was a constant reminder of the need for caution in continuing to follow a pursuit which owed much of its value and compulsion to the risks entailed. Without the danger it is hardly likely that the superlative performance needed to overcome the difficulties would be stimulated.

Pete and I had applied to the Ministry of Tourism in Islamabad on our arrival back there in 1978 for permission for another attempt on K2. A few months later Doug said that he too had come round to thinking of going back and we joined forces. On our return from Kangchenjunga in 1979 we started looking for a fourth person, and I was keen to invite Dick Renshaw, who had recovered completely from his frostbite.

Since Dunagiri he had regained the confidence which had been shaken by the possibility of losing his fingers frozen during that harrowing descent. In keeping with his nature, he had quietly pursued a very active life in the mountains, climbing in winter in the Alps, in Canada, in South America. Whilst his fingers were still recovering he had gone off for a trek across some mountain passes in the Karakoram range. A year after the mishap, the doctors treating him had managed to save all but a few millimetres of bone which had had to be trimmed from three finger-ends. The miracle had been that, when his fingers had been black with frostbite, he had managed to avoid infection through all that long descent, the walk back to the road, the journey to Delhi by crowded bus and train and treatment in a hospital where the nurses were too shy to wash him.

Now he told me he was much more careful with his hands, always taking several pairs of gloves, to ensure that he had a dry pair lest his hands get cold with the damp. He was delighted to be asked to go to K2 with us, seeming to see it as the answer to that blind love for mountains which I knew he had not lost. Since I had last climbed with him, Dick had become a vegetarian, and as such would complement Doug, who had so far been in a minority in his eating habits.

In the autumn of 1979, Pete went off on an expedition to a beautiful mountain called Gauri Sankar and Doug went back to Nuptse, which I had tried with him in 1978. I was relieved not to be going away again so soon. After three expeditions in thirteen months I savoured the prospect of almost a year at home. I knew that Pete was ambivalent about going off again so quickly, but an expedition is so complex to organise and is arranged so far in advance that alterations in the arrangements are hardly feasible. For once I had the chance to relax, to return to rock-climbing in Britain, to organise my life better, but the summer was gone, and the long, cold nights of winter drew in before I realised that the departure for K2 was only a few months away and that we had not raised any of the £16,000 we had estimated to need for the expedition. Most of the £9,000 we had needed for Kangchenjunga had come from our own pockets, and none of us had money left in such quantities. Expeditions to the Karakoram, in Pakistan, cost very much more than in Nepal and India because rates for the porters are much higher and the mountain regions are less inhabited. One cannot rely upon obtaining food or fuel in villages, even where they exist, so supplies for porters as well as for the expedition have to be purchased and carried for long distances.

Whereas Mount Everest is well known to the general public, and the wish to climb it needs little justification, the same is not true of K2, a mountain only a few hundred feet lower. Because the cost of the expedition was beyond our personal means, we needed to attract some form of sponsorship beyond the amounts we could expect from the Mount Everest Foundation and the British Mountaineering Council. Most companies, however, need more justification to act as sponsors than the wish to further a sport for its own sake. The sponsorship usually has to be seen as beneficial to the company itself. With climbing the mountains we were familiar, but in raising the money to do so we were amateurs. It was part of the conflict of any climber between the need to establish a reasonable life-style and the desire to have the freedom to climb. Often one has the means but not the time. We had the time but not the means.

A few weeks before we were due to leave, Doug had gone off to Australia and New Zealand on a lecture tour, Pete was living in Switzerland and Dick was based in Cardiff. Arrangements were well in hand but we were still £10,000 short of our budget. Because I was the only one of the team available, I was asked to appear on the BBC 2 *Newsnight* programme to talk about the expedition and from there more requests for interviews sprang up. Out of the blue one day the telephone rang and a Mr Swain introduced himself.

'I heard you speaking on the *Today* programme while I was driving to work. The company is Sadia Aerofreeze, and we make freezers. How much money are you looking for?'

The weariness with which I answered the many phone calls disappeared. We talked further and though he could not promise all the money we still needed, he was sure his company could be of assistance.

'By the way, how much will your total baggage weigh?'

'About one and a half tons.'

'Oh. We have a new model freezer which happens to be called the K2 model, and I was wondering if you could carry one to Base Camp to take some unusual photos of it.'

We agreed that since their freezer weighed a ton in itself, it was impractical for us to take one with us. I mentally tried to imagine the porters struggling with this object along the crumbling footpaths, over swollen rivers which we would cross by rope bridge and up the long Baltoro glacier with its unstable mounds of rubble and concealed crevasses. It brought home to me how little was understood by many people about climbing mountains. Mr Swain was not deterred, and the financial support of £3,000 which he offered on behalf of his company was of enormous help.

Of similar amusement was the request by Bass Ltd, whom we had also approached for support, to take with us some of their non-alcoholic beer. The beer had been developed for Saudi Arabia where, as a Muslim state, alcohol is prohibited. When it was realised that the beer had been brewed in a conventional manner, then had the alcohol extracted from it, the resulting alcohol-free beer was regarded as being contaminated still by the contact it had once with alcohol. Bass were left with vast quantities of the now unwanted drink and our visit to K2, itself the highest mountain in the Muslim state of Pakistan, was viewed as a suitable means of disposing of some of the drink. It was the only 'drink' we would be allowed to take into the country. Bass had long been associated with mountaineering in that they had raised a huge sum of money for the Mount Everest Foundation by a lottery run in their public houses. Peter Sherlock of Bass took an interest in our plans for K2 and promised to find what money he could.

From these two sources the sum needed was almost found and the final amount came with a request from *Newsnight* to send them back news reports, for which they would pay, during the expedition.

Only days before we were due to leave, the financial problems had been solved, and with £1,000 from each of us the total of £16,000 was reached.

I had another phone call before we left. It was Dick asking me when I thought we would be back from the expedition.

'I'm going to be a dad, you see. The baby is due at the end of August. We should be back by then, shouldn't we?'

We were due to leave on 31 April. August was four months ahead. Certainly we should be back, but Dick would be absent through the most trying time of the pregnancy and his girlfriend would have all the anxieties of knowing that Dick was out of contact, attempting a most difficult and dangerous mountain.

I had become friendly with a girl called Maria, whose brother was a climber but who had never appreciated the full implications of having a boyfriend who was committed to climbing mountains. The prospect of my being away for so long on this uncertain venture began to alarm her more as our departure drew near.

One afternoon I was in the process of booking our flights over the phone with a travel agent in London. Allen Jewhurst was visiting me for a few days. He had hovered on the fringe of involvement with mountains since he first took an interest in making a film of a climb. The march-in towards K2 in 1978 had whetted his appetite for the rough life of the mountains. Often he had hinted to me how much he would like to come on an expedition again. Now as I spoke on the phone he whispered to ask when we were leaving.

'Book me a ticket to Pakistan. I might come with you for a few days.'

I never knew when to take him seriously. He was impetuous in every-thing and I booked a seat for him, expecting to know for certain whether he was coming only at the last moment.

'It's "ma" business commitments. If I can sort them out I'd fancy a bit of sun. I think it's really lovely out there.'

He did come and flew with Dick, Pete and myself to Karachi. Doug was delayed a few days by his late return from New Zealand and planned to join us in Islamabad.

We had fifty bags and boxes of equipment and food, and expected endless hold-ups at the customs, but there was not a moment's delay. A truck was waiting at the airport, hired by us from England through the continuing assistance of my good friends, Mr and Mrs Beaumont. They had telexed our needs to the company office in Karachi and all was waiting for us. We threw all the baggage aboard, piled on ourselves and the truck drove off into the night.

We travelled for three days and nights across the Sind desert on the back of that lorry, and our whole world seemed to be centred inside those wooden walls, protected from the sun in the hottest part of the day by an awning tied above. Our rucksacks and kitbags provided uneven seating and the jolting progression of the lorry prevented any rest. From civilised, elegant airline passengers we were reduced in a matter of hours to bedraggled scarecrows, choked by the dust of the road, hanging onto the side of a wagon as yet another jolt flung us into the air.

The journey served to decondition us from the life of the West. By the time we reached Islamabad we had become attuned to the idea of being once more in the East. We made for the haven of the British Embassy residential compound where we had been invited to stay. Elspeth, a secretary whom we had met in 1978, had put her air-conditioned house at our disposal. After the bumpy ride it was an oasis of cool comfort where we could re-sort our equipment and complete formalities. Doug arrived, and together the five of us seemed to have taken over the whole house. There were not enough beds for all of us but Dick was content to sleep on the floor, telling us that he found the beds too soft for him. It had been almost five years since Dick and I had climbed together and had shared those bleak days when all our strength and life itself seemed to be dwindling away as we retreated down Dunagiri. He had not changed, still accepting with reluctance anything but the barest essentials for living. He stayed in the house only because we wanted to and he needed to be with us, but he accepted its comforts uneasily and suggested at one point that we should all bed down in the garage rather than crowd Elspeth out of her own home.

We divided up to attend to all the different tasks necessary before we could leave. Pete and I sat through the detailed procedure required to arrange a bank guarantee against the need for helicopter rescue, while Doug and Dick went off to purchase the 60,000 cigarettes needed as part of the rations for our porters. Allen relaxed by the swimming pool waiting for the formalities to be completed. He was not on the expedition proper and as such was not allowed to come with us further than the village of Dassu at the end of the first day's walk. He was disappointed but the regulations concerning movement in the mountain areas are very strict and even to obtain a trekking permit would have taken him several weeks.

We met our Liaison Officer, Major Sarwat, from the Pakistan army. It was a mark of the high regard in which our expedition was held that a major instead of a captain had been assigned to us, but we sensed that Major Sarwat was not impressed with our small group, with its lack of pretensions and its informality. Once again there was the dichotomy between the public image of expeditions, based on the well-publicised, large-scale ventures, and our own more intimate, loosely structured approach. I found I was comparing Sarwat with Captain Shafiq, who had been with us in 1978. He had been liberal in his attitudes and had seemed more of a companion than a supervisor. Major Sarwat seemed more rigid in his interpretation of the rules by which we had to abide. He was a strict Muslim and could not understand how five men could innocently stay in the house of a single girl. According to his religion such familiarity between the sexes was taboo. We had to get to know the man who was to be with us for many weeks and we each attempted to establish some familiarity with him. Major Sarwat was earnest and energetic in his wish to help the expedition to which he had been assigned even though it did not fit his preconceptions of what an expedition should be. Pete was the official leader but he did not behave like one. Amongst ourselves we came to a consensus on any decisions, but for official purposes one person had to have the title of leader. Major Sarwat needed one person to whom he could look for orders and the resolution of problems but Pete was as informal as any of us. He jested with the Major that we had friends in China to whom we would sell photographs of bridges when we returned home, but the jest met with the cold reply that the Chinese probably knew everything about the border areas anyway. It was as if the luxury of the Embassy quarters and our irreverent attitudes were a slight on the standard of living in Pakistan and an indication of a feeling of superiority in us. Our relations with the Major held little promise of being anything but a strain in the weeks ahead.

On returning from their shopping round, Doug and Dick discovered they had left the case of 60,000 cigarettes in the boot of a taxi, and had no means whatever of distinguishing it from any of the hundreds of ramshackle cabs which cruised the dusty streets. Doug regarded the mishap with philosophical resignation. Dick raged at his own stupidity and forgetfulness, feeling the loss as a personal blow to his normal sense of thrift. They reported the loss to the police without any great hope of recovering what would be an enormously valuable and untraceable booty for any taxi driver. But Mr Awan from the Ministry of Tourism rang the next day to say that the cigarettes had been handed in and Major Sarwat's face shone with joy.

'This day I am proud of my country,' he said with evident satisfaction.

At the airport, where we queued for seats on the flight to Skardu, there were two men from Hunza who made themselves known to us. One of them claimed to be a cousin of Quamajan, who had been with us on the 1978 expedition. We had written asking him to come and work with us again but his 'cousin' Gohar said he had come in his place as Quamajan now had a steady job as watchman in a government rest-house. Gohar was well over six feet tall, an unusually big man for the East. He was keen to join our expedition as high-altitude porter and with him was a man called Ali, who asked to be taken on as cook.

The men from Hunza have a reputation for reliability and resourceful-ness, but we did not wish to hire two full-time attendants without having a chance to assess their capabilities. In 1978 we had taken on a cook through someone else's recommendation and were subsequently disappointed in his performance. We did not want the same to happen again. The flight to Skardu was full anyway, and there seemed little chance that they would arrive there in time for us to sign them up. Our own seats had already been assured.

On the flight we noticed that Gohar and Ali had somehow managed to wheedle their way in and were sitting in a front seat, studiously avoiding imposing their presence upon us.

Little had changed in two years. The same motley assortment of ragged Baltis filled the baked mud compound outside the town gaol, jostling each other in the heat of the day, anxious to be hired. Similar police were in attendance, controlling the eager crowd. There was an order underlying the apparent chaos; there were groupings of men under appointed leaders and instead of suspecting, as in 1978, that this was another attempt to fiddle us, we found that these leaders were the instruments of control. We were no more admirable in our behaviour than we suspected them to be. We tried to reduce the number of porters we needed by increasing the weight of their individual loads, but the subterfuge was detected and we were diminished somewhat in their eyes.

We had learnt in 1978 that the men who congregated in Skardu, the men from Huche and Paphlu, were the most reliable as porters. They had to walk far to be hired and seemed to have more commitment to the work they took on than the porters from the villages along our way, who took it for granted that they would be hired. We tried to select all ninety porters we needed from the more reliable villages, but the local laws decreed that the work had to be equably distributed between several villages so that as wide an area as possible could benefit. We surrendered to the prevailing norms. Any attempt to change the order of things only meant more worries and frustrations for ourselves. In the end we knew we would reach Base Camp, no matter how trying circumstances might seem at times. Argument, discussion and compromise are all part of the tradition of these mountain areas and our Western ideas on efficiency and conformity were out of place.

The leaders of the groups of fifteen or twenty men were the Naikes, who expected to carry nothing, but were proud overseers of the groups. It was better to go along with this established practice, since it meant we had only five or six people to bargain with rather than close on one hundred.

We came together more as a group when we were held up by heavy rains in the village of Chakpoi only two days out from Skardu. Porters and team alike were confined in a muddy clearing waiting for the rains to stop before entering the Braldu Gorge. The track runs along the edge of the river for a number of hours and the hillside above is a steep slope of mud and boulders. The rain softens the mud and boulders are released, crashing down onto the track and threatening the passage of all below. In 1978, shortly after we had abandoned the expedition to K2, a member of another expedition in the region had been killed in the gorge by falling rocks and only a week previous to our present arrival a villager and a porter had been similarly killed. Only a couple of days after starting, we had come to a halt, worrying about the danger to the porters in our employ and the high cost of keeping them static for days at a time.

Allen had left us. He had gone back reluctantly but unable to come further, since Major Sarwat was with us as guardian of the laws of his country and so far had seemed unlikely to bend any rules. All four of us were sad to see him go. He was not overshadowed by the problem which affected all our thoughts, that of climbing K2. I felt that he was buoyant when we were intense, lively when we were reflective.

Since that first time in the mountains in 1978 he had come to know what to expect. The physical effort and discomfort had not shocked him into silence this time; on the contrary he seemed at home with the rough way of life. The weight of organisation was not a pressure on him but he had thrown himself into any work necessary to get the expedition under way. Each of us could laugh and joke with him because he seemed to possess a levity which the task ahead precluded us four from having. We said our goodbyes and I could see he was sorry to go. His heart was still with us. With him went some of the chirpiness of the expedition and I wondered if we were destined to have a serious time, since none of the four of us had Allen's gift for creating humour out of any situation. We seemed a more serious group when he had gone.

II

The porters hired a local holy man and made a prayer-offering with a chicken to halt the rain. They were as irritated as we were by the rain, since they preferred to complete their work for one expedition in order to rush back and work for another. 'Waiting days' were only at half pay.

When at last we exited safely from the gorge, the porters broke into song.

The sun came through the clouds and the heavy depression which had hung over the expedition lifted away. The song of the porters was a long traditional ballad of courtship and romance. The whole recitation takes several days but our porters would sing parts of it at night or on this occasion when there was cause for celebration. A dance was performed by a gaunt scarecrow of a man, partnered by a short, mischievous porter who called himself Mahdi. They danced in time to the song, performing an interpretation of the eternal confrontation between man and woman, a mime so well executed that we had no need of words to follow the story. I filmed some of it but the camera jammed and I was left to record in memory only the delightful scene. One of the Naikes, Ali Hassan, did a solo piece, revealing an unsuspected elegance of poise. His extended arms waved sinuously and his hands flicked expressively as he responded to the chant of the song. I felt that we were privileged to glimpse another side to the life of the people we were employing and that afterwards we had more rapport than on our first mutually suspicious encounters.

There was a slight tinge of green on the barren land we were passing through as if the heat of summer had not yet reached its full strength. Certainly the days were easier than I remembered. It seemed as if we were enjoying a spell of relaxation before entering the long, hard weeks above the snow line. Dick let slip details of the trek he had made this way in 1976 when he was waiting for his hands to heal. His two partners had turned back and he had taken over the tent and the food so that his sack weighed ninety pounds. He could not afford to hire porters but sometimes villagers had taken pity on him and carried part of his load for nothing or for a minimal charge. Once he had tried to cross a rotting bridge made from creepers, but the strands had parted and almost deposited him in the torrent below. He had a store of tales such as these which testified, if he could be enticed to speak, to a determination and resolution which assigned no value to comfort or ease. He busied himself about tasks in the evening which Pete, Doug and myself had grown accustomed to seeing done by the porters or the hired cook. He had not lost that self-sufficiency which made him do everything possible by his own efforts and which now made him uneasy to have a meal cooked for him or a cup of tea brought to his tent in the morning.

I knew the extent to which he felt uncomfortable at what he saw as undeserved luxury and I used to lead him on by exaggerated displays of laziness. I would ask for the sugar and let the cook put two spoonfuls into my mug, stir it and then pass it to me. Dick would look on in shocked disapproval, sometimes letting me know that I was living up to his worst memories of my indolence.

Pete knew how thrifty Dick was and he too would tease him with suggestions of extravagance. 'I don't want to spend more than £300 on presents in Islamabad on the way back,' he said to me once, knowing that

Dick was listening. And Dick, who could live for half a year on £300, responded with the expected incredulity at such profligate intentions.

For Doug, Dick was a welcome addition to the team. At last, after two years of enduring the scepticism and incomprehension of companions at his vegetarian diet, in Dick he had someone who was even more confirmed in the belief in vegetarianism than he was himself. Dick avoided eating not only meat but fish as well.

Ali and Gohar had worn down our resistance and by the time we were leaving Askole, the last village on the way, we had agreed that they should stay with us for the whole of the trip. Ali was to be cook and Gohar was to lend a hand with any load-carrying we might need.

There was none of the tension that had seemed to exist in 1978 between the expedition and the porters. I could not tell whether the porters had changed, had become more accustomed to the procedure of expeditions or whether we were more experienced and therefore more relaxed so that we did not suspect conflict where none existed. The only real confrontation came at Urdukass, a camping spot on a promontory above the Baltoro glacier, after nine days of walking. From here we had to drop down onto the glacier to find a way along its rubble-strewn surface for four days up to Base Camp.

The porters were demanding socks, footwear, rain capes and sunglasses before they would go onto the glacier. The supply of these items has long been a point of contention. In theory the porters have to buy them from the expedition, in practice none wishes to do so, preferring to keep all their wages for their other needs. If the expedition provides them free of charge, it is normal to see the porters walking barefoot, carrying the new footwear and storing the other items away to keep as new to re-sell later. Transportation alone of boxes of footwear, socks and clothing is very expensive and since the porters are expected to possess clothing and footwear for glacier travel we decided to hire only those porters who were equipped already.

At Urdukass it transpired that Major Sarwat had not after all translated this condition of employment and we were faced with the impossible demand to equip our ninety-two porters before they would go further. We had brought stockings and some cheap sunglasses, knowing that some such demands would arise however well equipped the porters all were, but the numbers we had employed were greater than I had envisaged when organising the gear. All told we only had seventy-five pairs of stockings and a similar number of sunglasses. Major Sarwat was insistent that I, as gear organiser, should solve the problem of finding another seventeen pairs of stockings. His demands seemed completely illogical as he knew how long it had taken to reach this place and how long therefore it would take to send back to Skardu for more stockings. I grew angry as Sarwat restated the impossible problem, looking to me for a solution. I knew that we would reach Base Camp and that some confrontation was inevitable owing to misunderstandings or cultural differences, but I did not like having to take part in what seemed an almost ritual scenario of argument, deadlock, ultimatum and capitulation. Pete intervened, playing the role of moderator but no more able to solve the problem.

Partly I suspected that such scenarios were as essential an ingredient in the lives of the porters as their ballads and mimes. The confrontation at Urdukass occurred during a day's halt agreed upon so that the porters could cook their food prior to the journey over the barren glacier. In 1978 the violent scene between our Liaison Officer and a porter, with the subsequent threat of a strike, had also occurred on a 'rest day', leaving one to conclude that arguing was all part of the entertainment.

The Naikes were the mediators and the solution to any conflict was in their hands. We were on good terms with them and Ali Hassan especially made a point of sitting with us and recounting tales, interpreted by Major Sarwat, about other expeditions he had been on. We were in sight of the colossal Trango Towers, granite monoliths which would inspire any climber. Ali Hassan had been with the British party in 1976 which had first climbed the Nameless Tower and he made us laugh with stories about the members of the expedition, all people we knew well. He had been impressed by the ascent of the huge tower but he remembered most the cameraman named Jim who ate enormous amounts for breakfast then after a few miles of hard walking would vomit up all his food and say he was hungry again. He would then eat more and repeat the procedure further on. It struck me how observant and humorous these people were and how much we could widen our experience if only we could speak their language.

He had been with the Polish women's expedition to Gasherbrum III under the leadership of a woman called Wanda. He thought she was a good climber but had problems as a leader. His favourite memory from that trip had been of crossing the Punmah river when all the women had had to be carried across by the porters. The Liaison Officer had wanted to be carried too until he saw his chance of carrying a woman across himself. Every couple of days, according to Ali, the women had crowded into a tent to have a good cry from homesickness. At one time the porters had gone on strike for more money (this was in the days before the rates were fixed) and Wanda had fled into her tent and cried. The Liaison Officer had discovered her crying and berated the porters for their unmanly behaviour. The porters decided to carry on.

As he was telling us these slightly scurrilous tales I warned Ali Hassan that Wanda was a friend of ours. He replied that he did not care if we repeated these stories to her, they were all facts, none were invented.

Wanda seemed, in fact, to have the leadership business sorted out. We suggested to Ali Hassan that going off and weeping in our tents might be a way for us to solve our problems. He said that we were welcome to do so if we wanted similar stories to be recounted about us to subsequent expeditions.

The impossible was achieved. Seventy-five pairs of stockings were divided between ninety-two porters and we carried on our way over the rough glacier. We had had a strange encounter at Urdukass with a French climber, Ivan Ghirardini. He is well known for his solo ascents of some of the most difficult routes in the Alps. He had permission to solo Mitre Peak, a small but steep mountain a few miles from K2. His wife, Jeanne Marie, though not a climber, was with him, intending to stay in camp whilst he was on the mountain. He asked, without preamble, if he could join our expedition to K2. There was no warmth in his manner, he seemed intense and serious, without any sign that he was pleased to meet us in this remote spot. It was not in our power to grant him permission to join us, for such a move could only be made, unless one risked expulsion from the country, with the sanction of the Ministry of Tourism in Islamabad. He knew this as well as us. Even so it was a strange request to make. There were many people whom we knew much better than this stranger whom we would have asked along if we had wanted a larger team. He had been on a French expedition to K2 the previous year which had been foiled just short of the summit. He wanted a second chance to climb it but he must have known how drastically it would alter our complex and carefully made plans for us to invite a stranger to join us.

He accepted our refusal and went off to ferry loads up the glacier. To save cost he was employing only one porter and spending several days going backwards and forwards to stock up a camp below his chosen peak. His wife stayed on the grassy spur of Urdukass, dining with us whilst we were there and content to continue the study of the only book she had, a book on shorthand and secretarial work. They had not long been married but it seemed a strange way for her to spend a holiday, camping in a remote, bleak spot while her husband was off climbing. We told her that Nepal was a much more pleasant Himalayan country for a holiday but she protested she was not on holiday, she was simply following her husband. The porters, influenced by all the taboos which circumscribed their relations with women, were intrigued to see a woman alone, with hair which to them was startlingly fair. The woman was a mystery to all of us and equally strange was her willingness to wait alone for her husband's return.

Mitre Peak stands at a junction of glaciers where we were to branch off to the north. It is an elegant peak but seemed too modest to satisfy the capabilities of the man we had met. The real motive for his presence in the area we suspected to be an intention to make a solo attempt on K2. Such a project would, we believed, be more in keeping with his past record and ambitions. It was a problem our Liaison Officer, as guardian of his country's laws, would have to face if the situation arose. Ghirardini's own Liaison Officer, he told us, had injured himself early on during the approach march and had had to go back.

Heavy snowfall made progress along the glacier miserable and difficult. On the second day on the ice the route was not always clear. I was walking with Gohar when we came to an awkward step. We turned back to circumvent it and Gohar, six feet ahead of me, disappeared from sight as the ground collapsed beneath his weight, revealing a crevasse concealed by the thick new snow-covering. There was pandemonium from the porters.

I could hear Gohar's voice inside the icy cleft and felt reassured that he was still alive. Dick was pulling on his climbing harness and I searched through the kitbags for a rope. Doug straddled the crevasse shouting reassurance down to Gohar and Sarwat shouted instructions, which no one heeded, as if he were commanding an army manoeuvre.

Dick made as if to descend into the crevasse almost before anyone was holding onto the rope he was attached to. Pete and I tried to pay out the rope in the disciplined manner of an oft-rehearsed climbing technique but the eager porters seized the rope, using the strength of numbers to hold the weight. Dick shouted up for us to pull and the porters heaved *en masse*. A shaken and bruised Gohar emerged from the dark hole. Dick was hauled up in turn and he told us that Gohar had been saved from falling irretrievably into the furthest depths by his rucksack which had wedged him in place twenty feet below the surface.

The dark mist and swirling snow increased the gloom which sprang out of the incident. Memories of accidents past and awful deaths in crevasses loomed large in all our minds. We reached Concordia, camping place for the night, cold from the wind and our feet wet from the deep snow. Gohar became silent and morose after his narrow escape and the porters, whose ragged clothing was poor protection against the weather, displayed a sullen resentment.

The porters carried their loads for the next leg of the journey but the stormy weather persisted. They refused to go any further. They had brought us to the foot of the mountain but we needed the loads carried up the Savoia glacier round to the west side to make a Base Camp at the foot of the West Ridge. They flatly refused. A porter had been killed the previous year on the edge of the Savoia glacier and Gohar's mishap had revived their fears. No matter how we tried to persuade them, cajole them, offer them three and four times the daily rate and promise to safeguard everyone over the dangerous areas, they were adamant. 'Please do not tempt us with money when our lives are at stake and we have families at home.' We gave in and paid them all off. Their viewpoint was valid but equally we knew that in 1978 hordes of villagers had returned, unroped, to loot our camps up to 20,000 feet on the West Ridge and that adamant as they were now, on another occasion a fine day would make all the difference to their willingness to go further.

The unexpected work which now fell to us had a marked effect on our plans to climb the West Ridge. Establishment of Base Camp near our chosen route took much longer than we had planned for and delayed our attempt on the ridge. When we were able to get to grips with it we made steady progress to 23,000 feet, with spells of bad weather occasionally slowing us down. We avoided the slope which had killed Nick in 1978 and reached the crest of the ridge. After following the ups and downs of the ridge we were forced back into the centre of the face when we came up to a steepening barrier of rock hundreds of feet high. A very difficult pitch of three hundred feet took most of a day to climb, but it linked us with an ice field in the centre of the wall. It had been my turn to lead on that pitch and I staggered into camp, an hour after the other three, utterly spent by the effort it had taken.

Time was running out for Doug. He had not anticipated being on the mountain for as long as we were going to need to succeed on this route. With more difficulties ahead, but much higher up, he believed we were too small a group for the siege tactics he was beginning to think were necessary. He had other commitments which were drawing him home, another expedition of which he was leader but which he would not be back in time for if we did not reach the top soon. He pressed for us to make an ascent of the route by which the mountain was first climbed, the Abruzzi Spur, on which we would not have to fix ropes and which we should be able to climb more rapidly than the West Ridge. None of the rest of us wanted to leave the West Ridge but Doug was going to have to leave soon anyway, so we abandoned the West Ridge for a second time. The Abruzzi Spur was not going to be an easy route at all. We spent three nights at 19,000 feet holed up in tents as storms lashed the mountain. We passed the time reading, having torn up the only book we had to share between us, and eventually we had to retreat. Doug had no time left, another life and another expedition drew him away; Dick, Pete and myself stayed on. For us, reaching the top of this mountain had come to assume an importance which outweighed any other obligations or considerations.

III

Tackling a mountain as big and difficult as K2 in a party of only three should have been a daunting concept but we had reached this point gradually so it seemed only a logical development. At Base Camp, back at the spot from where the porters had left, we amended our plans. Gohar and Ali were still with us, two mail runners periodically arrived after a round trip of ten days with news from home, and Major Sarwat was proving to be an encouraging and valued supporter of our efforts to climb the mountain.

Since the days when I had been perturbed by his serious demeanour and attention to the smallest of rules, I had begun to realise that he was wholeheartedly in favour of our expedition. In arguing with the porters he had worn himself out on our behalf to spur them on to help us. His job now was unenviable. He had to wait in attendance at Base Camp until we had finished the climb, however long it took. There was little for him to do, but he occupied his time reading and doing odd jobs about the camp. The vast pile of debris nearby from the previous year's French expedition provided a rich source of pickings for him. He unearthed several huge cylinders of gaz and put together a stove from discarded parts, providing for Ali a cleaner and easier means of cooking than the paraffin stoves we had brought. Sarwat always managed to appear immaculately clean when we were dishevelled and grubby. On the walk-in he wore a green tracksuit, appearing as neat and dapper as an athlete on a track. He preserved the ability to look neat and well cleaned throughout the three months of the expedition.

Ali had won his place as cook on the strength of his avowal that he had worked in an army mess. By the time we discovered that he had only been a waiter, we had not the heart to change our minds. The meals he cooked were excellent and he was always cheerful. Only when an aching tooth bothered him was he anything but busy and willing at every moment of the day. Gohar came to borrow some pliers to remove the aching tooth but we gave him some pain-killers and promised to send Ali to the Base Camp of a Japanese expedition three days away if the pain did not let up.

Dick had gradually come to accept that meals would be cooked for him. Ali as cook and Gohar as a general help liberated us from the daily chores and allowed us to concentrate our energies on the mountain. They were also company for Sarwat who, unlike many Liaison Officers, refused to slip back to wait in warmer quarters at Askole, insisting that his duty lay at Base Camp, to be on hand lest his help be needed. One day I noticed Dick, instead of jumping to do the job himself, passing a tube of Araldite to Gohar who was looking for some way to mend the cracked washing-up bowl. Misunderstanding Dick's instructions and gestures of mixing the substances together, Gohar started squeezing the tubes into the soup which Ali was busy stirring. The soup was rescued before harm was done.

We were waiting for a clearing in the weather before going back on the mountain. Little information could be obtained from the radio which Sarwat tuned in to each evening. A one-sentence forecast described the weather pattern for the whole of the country and we were having to make our own judgements.

On descending from the West Ridge, we had found Major Sarwat to be in a state of great distress. He was pleased to have our company again but it was a full day before he could be made to divulge what was upsetting him. I had developed a joking relationship with him, often being wildly outrageous in my comments so that he could see I was not serious. It was good for him to see that there were differences between the three of us so that when Pete took Sarwat's side in disapproval of some extravagant statement I had made, Sarwat could see that he was not an outsider to the group, that we regarded his opinion as of equal validity to any of our own. When the mail arrived and he received letters I used to tease him that his wife should still be writing and not have run off with someone else, an event which was a near impossibility in a well-regulated Muslim state. I remembered to enquire again what had upset him; he had not wanted to mar our return immediately by his own troubles.

He described the amazing confrontation he had had with Ghirardini, who had visited our Base Camp whilst we were away, and the arguments he had had with him. It seemed hardly credible to us that such antagonisms could have arisen to spoil the atmosphere of a region so remote that any encounter should be a welcome one of people who have a love of the mountains.

The same day that he recounted this tale we were visited by two American friends who had come to climb the neighbouring peak of Skyang Kangri. They had made their camp near to us and their jovial Liaison Officer, Tim, turned out to be an old friend of Major Sarwat's. We were sitting inside our large dining tent reminiscing and swapping yarns when Gohar's face fell, and a strange dismay seemed to possess him as two figures approached our tent. It was the Frenchman and his wife.

The ensuing scene was bedlam. The Frenchman vociferously insisted that he was prepared to forget the earlier arguments if the Liaison Officers would let him climb K2 on his own, and his wife offered her opinion and supported her husband's demands in a strident French which it was difficult to comprehend.

The scene seemed starkly out of place amongst the mountains, this confrontation and dispute, and the forcing upon us of a dilemma which had nothing to do with us but into which we were inevitably drawn.

Ghirardini wanted us to say that we did not mind him climbing K2 and he seemed to think he could manoeuvre the Liaison Officer into turning a blind eye to his activities. He intended to follow the ropes left in place by the French party the previous year. But we told him that we had no authority even to say that he could climb the mountain. We were in a foreign country and had agreed to accept their laws, whatever we thought of them.

The Frenchman had no time for such restrictions: 'If I see a beautiful mountain, I want to climb it. It is my natural response.'

There was some point in his assertions but his attitude was very simplistic and his peremptory manner did not inspire sympathy for himself or his views. Even Dick was moved to voice his disapproval of the man's attitude. In a quiet and sincere voice he said: 'But we all know what the rules are before we come.'

'I have no time for rules. They make me sick. I don't like coming to places with such rules.'

'Well there you are then. Don't come if you don't like it.'

'O.K.'

The man and his wife left to camp some distance away without saying whether he was going on the mountain or not. What should have been a period of rest before our return to the mountain had been more exhausting than if we had stayed high up in the worst of storms. I was keen to get back on the mountain but I felt annoyed at the waste of time and energy which had sprung from both meetings with the man. He was certainly an odd character and seemed to have the ability to introduce tensions and discord where none should have existed.

On 2 July Dick, Pete and I returned to the Abruzzi Ridge. Ali and Gohar came with us to the foot of the ridge, relieving us of the full weight of our loads until the climbing proper started. The trek round to the ridge took two hours, up through the complex maze of ice towers on the Godwin Austen glacier. There was debris from the camps of earlier expeditions at the foot of the ridge, including some oxygen cylinders and a decayed breathing mask. Pete turned on a bottle of oxygen to test if it still worked and sniffed at the oxygen: 'Smells good, do you want a sniff?' but Dick and I refused and Pete felt outlawed by our refusal even to sample the invigorating gas.

Ali and Gohar turned back from the small platform a few hundred feet up a rocky slope from the glacier. It had been on this platform that we had spent three nights confined inside our tents by storms during our first foray on the ridge. This second time we benefited from the knowledge gained during the earlier attempt and reached a camp-site on a snow shelf at the head of a couloir at 20,000 feet.

Our movements were slow and weary. We had expected ourselves to be fitter on this new attempt but it was six weeks since we had first reached Base Camp and although we were well acclimatised the effect of living at altitude and making strenuous efforts on the mountain must have had a debilitating effect. Our rucksacks were heavy too. We carried fifty pounds each, bringing up food for a prolonged assault and spare rope to fasten over awkward steps to facilitate our eventual descent.

Since the route had been almost climbed in 1939 and 1953, then finally succeeded on in 1954, we did not expect the difficulties to be too great. We reasoned that our technical skills were probably greater with the general rise in climbing standards since those days; the modern mentality now

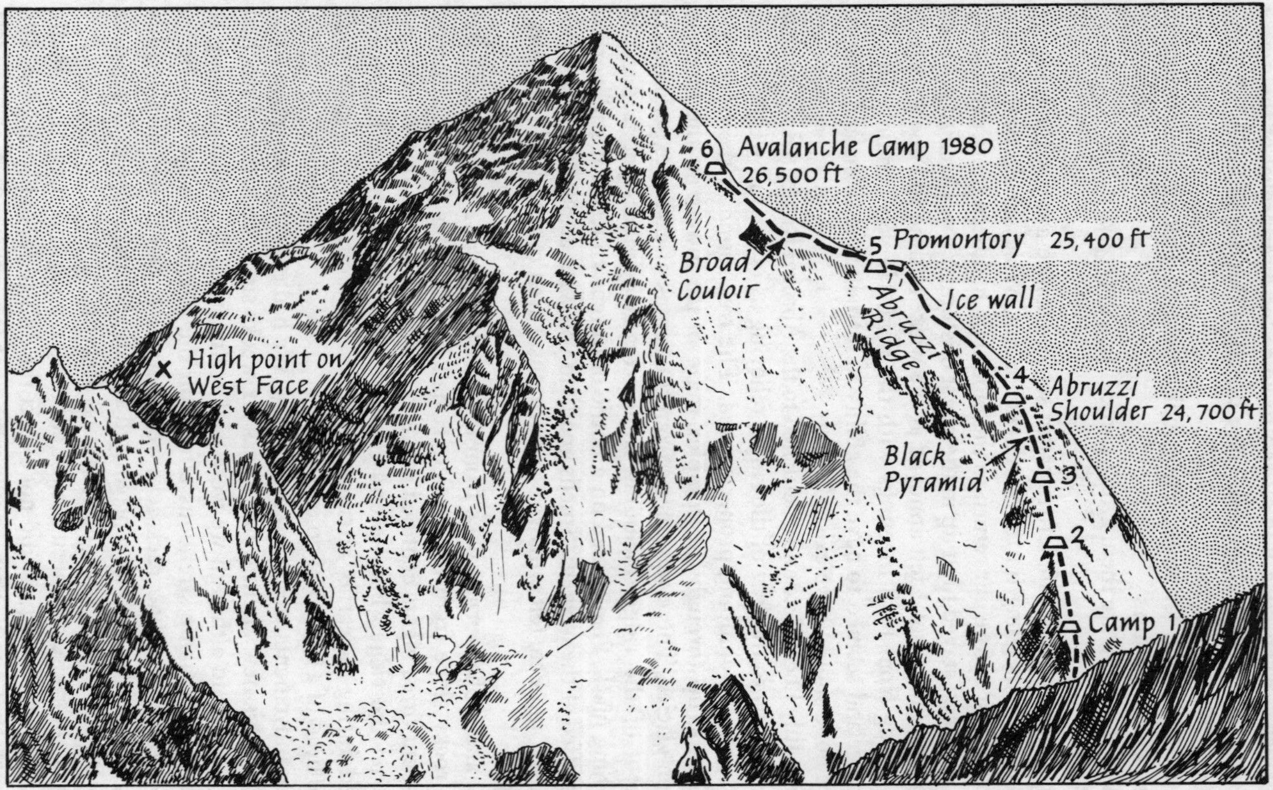
6 Avalanche Camp 1980
26,500 ft
5 Promontory 25,400 ft
Broad Couloir
Ice wall
Abruzzi Ridge
4 Abruzzi Shoulder 24,700 ft
Black Pyramid
3
2
Camp 1
High point on West Face

6. The line of ascent up the Abruzzi Ridge of K2 in 1980, showing also the high point reached on the West Face in the first attempt.

encouraged a more mobile attack on a mountain and our equipment was correspondingly lighter and better suited to this sort of approach. We could carry everything we needed for survival on our backs and, once fit and acclimatised, given that no obstacles caused long delays, we were now expecting to be able to start from the bottom of K2 and reach its summit in a matter of days.

We were not doing justice to the early pioneers. The route was extraordinarily difficult. Low down on the ridge, broken rocky slopes and snow couloirs were interspersed with awkward steps of rock. This was not unusual for the lower reaches of any route but on this ridge the difficulties increased as we climbed higher. Frayed remnants of ropes, sometimes over twenty-five years old, marked the route in places. Though only three expeditions had succeeded in climbing the ridge, the history of attempts, tragic accidents and hopeless retreats had left relics of former struggles along the way. We could always climb sections but were overawed by the perseverance which must have been needed in the days when ropes were made from hemp and when boots were heavy with the nails in the sole for friction. Our loads felt terribly heavy but they would lighten as we went on, as we consumed the food and left ropes on difficult passages. In those early days one rope alone would have weighed ten pounds, and much more when damp.

In theory, now that we were as acclimatised as we would ever be, we should have been able to climb the mountain in five or six days, even though it was the second highest in the world. We had worked out our projected camping spots on photographs and the stages into which we planned to break up the ascent.

In practice the difficulties were too great and our loads too heavy to make such methodical progress. The weather too played a major part and we became resigned to languishing in our tents for days at a time until the ferocious winds should diminish and the snow stop falling. We came to accept that we would have to climb in weather worse than we would normally have contemplated if we were to make any progress at all. Thus if it was possible to move we would climb up into the cloud, hoods drawn tight against the storm to explore the next section, fix short lengths of rope where necessary and dump food and gear up high ready for the next day when we would move up ourselves with the tents.

At 23,000 feet we spent four nights in the tents which were beaten flat by the winds, but the alloy tubes, forming hoops inside each tent, would spring upright once again when the storm allowed. Snow formed drifts against the tents but this was a welcome supply for melting into water.

We had with us two tents, weighing six pounds each. All three of us could squeeze into one but we carried a second lest one became damaged. During the enforced halt I had a tent to myself and Pete and Dick shared the other. I used to lie during the day with my rucksack packed, ready to evacuate the tent at any moment as the roof flattened against my body under the impact of the wind. I had used one rope to hold the tent in place, wrapping it round the poles and anchoring it to stakes driven into the snow. Pete and Dick thought I was better off then they and would shout to me to make them drinks of tea. For my part I believed my tent was more exposed and acted as a windbreak for them, whom I considered to have the advantage, expecting them to do the tea-making.

We had radio contact with Base Camp via a tiny, lightweight walkie-talkie. Major Sarwat could be relied on absolutely to pass on any information he could glean from the sparse weather reports on the radio. But K2 seemed to create its own weather pattern and the benefit of the walkie-talkie was the psychological advantage of a link with our Base. We had radio calls at 7.00 a.m. and 5.00 p.m. as a regular schedule, with a fall-back call-time every half hour after those times lest something prevented either party speaking then. We had brought lightweight walkie-talkies after realising on Kangchenjunga, when we had been separated and out of touch, just how useful they could be.

There were times when Sarwat was encouraging us on when the weather was clear at Base Camp and he could not suspect that the cloud, which he could see enveloping the mountain, was more than a light mist. From inside the cloud, for our part, we could not believe that the ferocity of the storms we were experiencing was having no effect at Base Camp only a few miles away.

On 8 July the weather allowed us to make our third camp. The ground was steep, complex and loose. The fresh snow further hampered us. We stopped earlier than intended as ledges large enough for a tent were infrequent. The third camp-site itself was only large enough for one of the tents. From there, however, we had a magnificent view across the border into the Sinkiang province of China and of Broad Peak, in profile, capped by plumes of cloud and coloured pink by the setting sun.

The most difficult part of all was yet to come. We knew of the Black Pyramid by descriptions from the earlier ascents but nothing prepared us for its sustained and improbable passages. The Black Pyramid is a distinctive area of dark, formidably steep rock, hundreds of feet high forming a rough triangle beneath a wall of ice. The rock was compact, with few foot-holds or cracks for pitons. This was one area where we took care to secure in place a life-line of rope for our descent. We did not have sufficient of our own rope to stretch all the way, so where the rock eased off into a slope of snow which ran up to the ice cliff we retrieved some remnants of ancient rope to use as a guideline.

Dick led the way up the wall of ice. I was pleased it was his turn in front, as the ice was hard and splintered at each blow of the axe. More remains of rope showed evidence of others who had passed this way but how the pioneers of the first attempt had climbed ice such as this I could not imagine. Dick went stolidly on. He had the ability to remain undaunted by any qualms about starting up such a repulsive section of ice, but he was exhausted by the time he reached the top.

There was an easy snow slope above and I went up it to scout around for our next camping site. Pete went off to the left and we had a heated disagreement about which way to go. The leftwards route proved best.

That camp-site, our fourth on the ridge, was the best so far. We had reached a shoulder of the mountain which went on upwards in an undulating incline of snow. We climbed up from the left edge of the ice cliff for another 300 feet to a level shelf, huge by comparison with any camping place we had so far used.

We had reached 24,700 feet. The effect of such sustained efforts at altitude was beginning to make itself felt, but all three of us were in good shape. For Dick it was the highest he had ever been. From this camp-site we could look over the edge of the ridge, only twenty feet away, at the precipice dropping sheer away down the South Face for 9,000 feet to the Godwin Austen glacier far below, and our Base Camp, invisible from this distance. Somewhere in this region two of the great tragedies in K2's history had taken place. In 1939 three Sherpas going up to rescue a sick American, Dudley Wolfe, disappeared. Bad weather closed in, preventing any other members of the expedition from returning to the mountain so that no one ever knew what had happened to the three Sherpas and the sick man. The second tragedy occurred in 1953 when another American, Art Gilkey, was taken ill from thrombophlebitis induced by inactivity due to the prolonged storms. The other members of the team attempted to lower him all the way down the mountain but, whilst the active members were recovering from a fall which had almost killed them all, the sick man disappeared from the side of the mountain. He had been wrapped in a crude hammock made from tent material and sleeping bag and was secured by ropes to the ice slope down which he was being lowered. On returning to continue the rescue his exhausted friends found the slope bare. The likely explanation was that an avalanche had swept him away but there was the lingering thought that he may have cut himself loose to relieve the others of a responsibility which would almost certainly have brought tragedy anyway.

The summit seemed within our reach, only one or at most two more camps, two or three more days and we could be on top. No illness or headaches had slowed our progress and there was every reason to hope that we could make it, providing the weather held out.

The next day, 10 July, the weather was magnificent. The sun shone in a clear blue sky, the snow under foot was mostly firm, and though the altitude made every step exhausting, forcing ourselves on was a discipline we had long since attuned ourselves to.

Before we left that spot on the shoulder we had sorted out only the bare essentials to take up with us. In a hollow in the snow we left the spare tent, extra food, a pan, spare gaz cylinders and any items of clothing we had found unnecessary. With the summit now in reach we intended to travel as light as possible.

The gentle incline of the slope steepened into a wall of hard snow topped by a cornice. We made for what looked to be a line of rope emerging from the snow. We were thankful for the direction shown by what we thought to be a relic from the past, but it was no relic, it was a shadow cast by the sun in a surface groove. We climbed on up nevertheless, me forcing a way past the overhanging cornice and Pete taking over to lead an unexpected wall of ice.

I hauled my way up the rope which he had led out and saw him striding upwards where the cliff fell back into a snow slope, into the sun and stopping to shout that he had reached the shoulder.

We came onto the end of a huge promontory jutting out from below the final 2,000-foot summit pyramid. The crest of the promontory was a broad, rounded plateau with hundreds of square feet of room in which to camp. The promontory rose gently towards a rocky escarpment which cut across beneath the summit, forming a narrow couloir of snow where it met the distinctive and enormous buttress of ice, the last barrier before the summit slopes.

Our fifth camp-site was at 25,400 feet, on the level plateau at the end of the promontory. The summit of Broad Peak was now only slightly higher than where we were, and most other peaks were much lower. I felt satisfaction at seeing the surrounding peaks dropping away below as we neared this mighty summit. We scrutinised and memorised details of the summit pyramid for the next day, trying to assess the remaining difficulties and the time we would need to overcome them.

But next day we were trapped in our tent once again by heavy snowfall and lashing winds. We lay dejected, with no means of passing the time except by daydreaming or cooking a meal. Our food was running short and after ten days on the mountain we ourselves were low in physical reserves. The illness which had afflicted Art Gilkey, arising from similar inactivity, preyed on our minds, and we discussed the pros and cons of continuing or going back down.

Over the radio, Major Sarwat was full of encouragement. He had come to have real faith in our ability after his early doubts about the likelihood of success for so unconventional a team. He exhorted us on as if he were a coach and we were his team of players. Reception on the little radio was poor but we could tell he was enthusiastic for us, mixing news of the weather with firm suggestions to press on.

By late afternoon the snow was deep outside and the weather showed no signs of let-up. I proposed that if the next day brought no improvement we should go down, recoup our strength and come back up with more supplies. Pete was against this idea and Dick was undecided. There were merits for both points of view. The summit was almost within our grasp and to go down now would set it back once again a long way from us. If the weather did clear, even if we had little food left there was a chance that we might be able to bring the expedition to a conclusion in one long, hard day of climbing, and thus avoid the uncertainty that a retreat all the way to Base Camp would entail. On the other hand there was the greater strength we would have in coming back up a route we now knew well after some rest and good food at Base Camp. With all the difficult passages prepared and little for us to carry except food, we could expect to regain our high point in perhaps four days. It is always hard to make a decision in such a situation, not knowing which will be best to achieve the desired outcome and not wanting to lose a position won against many odds. Though in reaching decisions we each propounded a more positive opinion than we actually felt as part of the process of thrashing out all possible angles on the decisions to be made, there was no conflict between us. Living in such close proximity to other people, when conditions are far from perfect, inevitably produces an abrasiveness of temper and curtness of manner, but we were all three experienced enough to recognise the tensions produced by the strain of the situation.

In the event, the decision seemed to be made for us. On the 5.00 p.m. radio call the Major informed us, with audible satisfaction, that he had picked up a detailed weather forecast. This had been transmitted for the sake of a Japanese expedition on Masherbrum, a mountain which we could see clearly in fine weather. The forecast, unusually specific in contrast to the norm, was for cloudy weather the next day, 12 July, with no wind or snow. The 13th was to be fine all day.

So the decision was clear. We would go up, using the day of cloud to reach a point as high as possible where we could camp in an advantageous position for the summit bid on the 13th. I slept with mixed feelings of excitement and reluctance at the test ahead. It was the nervousness of knowing that we were on the threshold of achieving something long desired and struggled for, but with apprehension about the test of strength, stamina and skill which the reaching of that goal would entail.

There was cloud next morning, thick and swirling up from a murky void which concealed the valleys below. We radioed down that we were setting off to make a sixth camp that day with hopes of continuing next day to the top. The wind was strong, blowing flurries of snow into our faces as we walked along the broad crest of the ridge. The forecast had said no wind but it did not strike us as unusual that high on the mountain currents of air should form localised turbulence. There seemed to be some snow falling as well as being blown from the surface under-foot, but even that was not a cause for concern in that such dense cloud could be expected to deposit a little of its moisture.

The ridge rose up gradually as we approached a wide couloir separating us from the main mass of the summit pyramid. The broad crest of the ridge sharpened into steep slopes and we picked our way carefully along one side, aiming for any rock which projected and offered a sense of security in the open expanse of snow. The crest of the ridge was to our right and to our left the mountainside dropped steeply away into a seemingly bottomless abyss of cloud.

We were roped together and moved simultaneously until we reached the couloir. The great channel was four or five hundred feet wide and had runnels scoured down it by the passage of avalanches. In the cloud above us we could sometimes glimpse the huge cliff of ice which guarded access to the summit slopes and which, we guessed, occasionally sent avalanches thundering down the couloir. The snow in the couloir was deep and instilled fear that it might give way at every step and that we would go tumbling down to the bottom of the couloir and be flung out into the abyss.

We aimed for an enormous boulder in the centre of the couloir which had clearly withstood the force of many avalanches. That was a halfway point, a breathing place from which to tackle the second part of the frightening gully. There was no technical difficulty in the crossing, the angle was gentle enough for us to walk upright, only using an ice axe for balance against the slope or to lean on in rest when fatigue forced a halt. Every step, however, was dogged by a presentiment of catastrophe, as if, out of the mists above, a white wave of death would engulf us. The altitude enforced its own pace of movement, but we urged ourselves on to reach the rocks at the far side with as few halts as possible. Only when we gained those rocks and climbed up out of that terrifying gully could we allow ourselves the frequent rests and slowness of movement which our oxygen-starved bodies were demanding.

I do not remember at what point in the day it became evident that there was a steady snowfall rather than an intermittent flurry of windblown surface snow mingling with light flakes from the cloud. It was early afternoon before we reached the safety of the rocks beyond the couloir and we certainly knew then that we were in another storm but we still had faith in the broader outline of the forecast and expected the next day to be fine. We carried on along a sharp, rocky ridge beginning to look for a place to put up the tent for the night. The altimeter told us that we had risen above 26,000 feet and, as on Kangchenjunga, we hoped to be able to climb those last 2,000 feet to the summit in one day.

It was another 500 feet before we did stop for the night. The rock ridge had few places where it would be possible to erect the tent and always we pressed on, enticed further by the illusion of a better ledge a little higher. The fear of an avalanche in the night kept us to the rocks well away from the snow couloir where we could have dug out a platform, and well away from the fall-line of any blocks of ice from the cliff above.

Pete seemed indefatigable. He led on in increasingly deep snow and Dick and I trailed behind, following his tracks but still not able to match his pace. Dick was experiencing the exhaustion of altitudes he had never before been to and that exhaustion worried him. The afternoon wore on and Pete still forged a path through snow as deep as his thighs. Time and again the promise of a ledge proved to be false until Pete forced his way up a shallow gully beside a rock and announced that he had found a usable spot.

With many more rests before closing the gap between us, the three of us stood on top of a rocky prow which stood out from the slope. All around more rocks protruded from the surface of the snow and a hundred feet above us stood a great wall of rock. The snow around us was anchored by the presence of so many rocks and the slope between the small prow of rock on which we stood and the great wall above was short enough to reassure us that no dangerous build-up of snow could form there. We believed the prow of rock to be safe for the night, but it needed two hours of work before we had chopped away enough ice to erect the tent. We tied the corners of the tent to aluminium stakes driven into the snow and hammered a couple of pitons into the rock as attachment points to give security to our precarious perch. We could ill afford the effort of cutting out the ice and it was night before we settled inside.

The ledge was barely wide enough for the tent and when all three of us tried to lie down inside, Dick, who was on the side of the tent nearest the edge, had to pad out the floor of the tent beneath him with the rucksacks. Half of his place in the tent was poised over nothing, but the alloy stays in the rucksacks formed a platform over that drop.

Radio reception was very poor. If the Major could hear us, we could hear nothing from him. Our location was probably as close to Base Camp as it had been at any time, and certainly in line of sight if the Major stepped out from camp a few hundred yards, but our proximity to the rock probably affected reception.

We were perched a mere 1,500 feet below the summit and, had it been a clear day, they would have been able to see us through the powerful telephoto lens from Base. The prow of rock on which we were camped was 500 feet up from the couloir we had so fearfully crossed. This couloir ran down for 2,000 feet before ending abruptly in the vast precipice of the South Face.

Across the slope from where we camped was the ice cliff which we would have to by-pass the next day. The rock wall above us spanned the rest of the slope, meeting the ice cliff at a narrow gully, the route past the cliff. That was the last remaining problem for us, and beyond we envisaged the slope easing off into the summit itself.

We hardly had energy left to make as many drinks as we needed; waves of sleep swept over me and I noticed that Pete and Dick too kept drifting off. Inside the tent, Dick was lying closest to the edge of the ledge, Pete was in the middle position and I was on the side closest to the ice and rock of the mountain itself, which we had exposed in chopping out the ledge. The tent was too narrow for us to lie all three shoulder to shoulder. Pete and Dick had their heads at the end of the tent nearest the tunnel entrance and I lay with my head at the opposite end. It felt airless inside the tent, lying with my head furthest from the door, and I fiddled with the vent, trying to let air in without an accompanying flurry of snow.

Outside, the snow was still falling thickly, the tent sagged a little under its weight and I could feel the pressure of snow building up between the tent and the wall of the mountain. I pressed against the side of the tent in an effort to close any gap and make the snow slide over the fabric and we talked about the safety of our situation with some apprehension about the persistent storm.

The snowfall was heavier than it had been all day and if it kept up we might find we could not make any progress next day, even if the day were clear, and retreat itself could be suicidal. We were stuck for the moment where we were, we needed rest and could not do much in the darkness anyway. We could not even find the energy to melt snow enough for more than one drink, in spite of all the knowledge we shared about the rapid deterioration in physical performance at altitude without plentiful food and liquid. We each went off to sleep without taking the customary sleeping pill lest we needed all our wits for any emergency which might arise from this storm.

I awoke to an instant awareness of the imminence of a sordid death. All was black, the tent was collapsed on top of us. A heavy avalanche of snow was pouring over the tent. I was lying face down, cloaked by the fabric of the tent, my body and limbs moulded and held in place by the weight of the snow, solid as concrete. I tried to rise, only my head and shoulders could move, but the snow crashed down on the back of my neck and my face was beaten inexorably closer to the ground. It was a brutal and implacable force of nature with no malice, which, impersonal and unfeeling, was bringing extinction. I felt awe at the power at work. There was no thought process, I was simply aware, knowledge without deduction, of all the implications of what was happening. I shouted to Pete and Dick by name; there was no reply. My arms were pinned down and I could feel, with my elbow, Pete's feet next to me, also pinned down. They were inert. Of Dick I knew nothing, could hear no sound. I presumed that they had caught the full force of the avalanche, had been struck by blocks of ice or rock, and were unconscious, if not dead already, and I knew I would not be long in dying too. The blows on my head from the avalanche went on and on, at any moment I expected the tent to be torn free and sent tumbling and cartwheeling for 10,000 feet with us inside, thudding into each other, resenting the blows from the others' flailing arms and legs, not the slow-motion impression of death as represented in films, a scruffy end, but not suffering for long before the impacts and collisions of the fall brought oblivion.

I felt no fear, only regret that our death should be so paltry and that we were to be extinguished without trace, because no one would ever know what had happened and there would forever be questions and guesses about our disappearance on the mountain, though our bodies would land only hours away from our Base Camp.

The blackness seemed to be inside as well as outside my head. Fire points formed jagged trails and then the blackness took me.

The snow had stopped falling when I came round. I realised that the tent was still in place – the snow anchors must have held it – my whole body was held fast by the weight of snow and only my head could move a little in a pocket of air. The air was stale, my breathing shallow from the crushing weight on my chest, and a slight panic that I would die now from suffocation began to form inside me. I could see nothing in the dark but I knew that in the breast pocket of my windsuit I had a penknife with which I could cut an air-hole in the tent. My arms were pinned beneath my chest but one hand was near the pocket. My groping fingers failed to find the knife at first, and my breathing came faster, the panic growing. Then I had the knife and, one-handed, tried to open the blade, but fumbled it and the panic all but overwhelmed me. I opened the blade at the next attempt and twisted my arm awkwardly so that my hand could force the knife into the fabric of the tent, inches from my face. My arm movement was restricted and the slit was only three inches long, but cold air came in and I felt relief that I could at least breathe. With Pete and Dick both gone I had to keep myself alive first before I could decide on my next move. Whether I could emerge from under the deadly weight of snow with only one arm partly free I did not know. Whether there would be any life left in Pete and Dick if I could ever get to their bodies I had little hope.

Breathing came easier, then I heard voices and I realised that Pete's feet were no longer next to me. The weight of snow came off my back. I could raise myself and I had my mouth at the slit in the tent, sucking in the air and shouting to them, immensely relieved that the impossible had happened and they were still alive. I was eager for more air but refrained from cutting at the tent more, since if all three of us were alive we might need it as our only form of shelter.

The avalanche had struck us in the middle of the night. At its first impact the tent had been partly knocked off the ledge before the snow stakes and the weight of the falling snow held it in place. Dick was suspended, in the folds of the tent, off the edge of the prow of rock, only the tent fabric preventing him from plunging down 10,000 feet of mountain. Pete had been pushed to the edge of the ledge where there was less weight of snow on him. With his head close to the tent entrance he was able to pull himself out. The prow stood clear of the snow slope still and the entrance to the tent was clear. He pulled Dick out of the tent and back onto the ledge where both of them shouted for me for long minutes, hearing no reply. This must have coincided with my blacking out. They had begun digging for what they presumed would be my dead body under a deep, solid mass of snow, and perhaps the gradual easing of weight from my chest had allowed air to enter my lungs and consciousness to return.

I realised that I was no longer against the solid wall of the mountain. The tent was still hanging off the ledge and the pocket where Dick had hung was full of boots, stove, food and anything else which had been loose when the avalanche struck.

We conversed through the slit in the tent while Pete and Dick dug clear more snow. My sentences were fitful as I sucked greedily at the air in between words, until I could sit upright and open the tent door.

I passed out to them their gloves and torches. When I had gathered my breath I made ready to join them outside but Pete suggested I stay in the tent to gather up all the loose objects lest we lose anything vital. Each of us functioned automatically as if we had rehearsed for such an event. Few words were necessary.

The snow-storm of the previous evening was still continuing. Now that I was alive I began to feel cold and uncomfortably damp. Outside, Pete and Dick scraped away at the snow, clearing the ledge once again. I groped into the pocket which had held Dick and pulled onto the ledge inner boots, and boots, and realised only then that they were still outside in their stockinged feet. I pulled the whole tent back onto the ledge and was able to slide back against the wall of the mountain now that the snow had been cleared away. I leaned back, surrounded by chaos, wondering what to do next.

A dull, hissing thud started up again, and the heavy blows of falling snow hammered once more against my head. I could not believe that there was snow left to avalanche again but the snowfall was so relentless that a new avalanche had formed already. I pressed myself back against the wall to prevent snow forcing its way between me and the mountain and prising me off the ledge. I held tight to the tent with all its contents, lest boots and other vital clothing were lost. I wondered if Pete and Dick would still be outside when it stopped.

This second avalanche brought home to me how helpless we were, how tiny and insignificant our lives were on this mountain. There was no harmony with these forces of nature; we were specks in this colossal and uncaring universe. In my icy tomb I was terrified, fearing another death by suffocation, but I did not dare try to move from my position, embedded in the bank of snow over which the avalanche was pouring. Even if I had managed to move from the frozen mould the avalanche would have whipped me away once I broke through the smooth surface over which it was now sliding. I waited, unafraid, for an outcome which I could do no more to influence; unafraid of what death would mean but horrified by the suffocation by which it was arriving.

Finally the pounding stopped. I shouted to find out if the other two were there:

'Pete, Dick? You all right?'

'Yes.'

They dug me free again. Pete had had the wisdom to tie himself with the rope to the pitons embedded in the rock. When the avalanche had struck he had grabbed Dick round the waist and held him all the while the snow was pouring down. We decided that the avalanches must be coming from the summit slopes above the great wall of rock one hundred feet above us. I passed them their boots and we took it in turn to dress properly and gather individual gear together. We had been sleeping fully clothed, only boots and gloves had we taken off, but it took time for each of us to make ready. We packed our rucksacks and waited for dawn, hoping against all hope that we would be spared another avalanche, for we could not move from the prow in the dark without risking ourselves even more on the open slope.

At the first glimmer of light in a sky still a heavy grey with cloud and snow I led off down, trying to keep to the rocks to avoid triggering off an avalanche and taking all three of us in it. But it was impossible to follow the rocks. Deep snow covered everything and my crampons slipped and caught on unseen projections. I decided to plough straight on downwards through thigh-deep snow, just trusting that we would survive. Inside I had a feeling of hopeless desperation and, as if some almighty power were manipulating us, I wanted to plead that we needed a break, that we had suffered enough, that no more avalanches should be sent down on us.

The three of us were on one rope 150 feet long but I could barely see the other two. I could hear Pete shouting and knew that he would be critical of my going straight down the open slope of snow, thinking me mad to be running the risk of starting an avalanche. Equally I knew without doubt that it was impossible to try to follow the exposed rocks when many more rocks lay concealed beneath the intervening stretches of snow. I had slipped and fallen many times in trying to keep near the rocks and thought that was certain to lead to an accident. I went down the slope of snow knowing the risk I was taking, knowing that we would be lucky to survive at all, hoping that if the snow did give way beneath me, Pete and Dick might be able to hold me if they were on firmer ground in the trough I had made.

I recognised nothing from the ascent. The swirling cloud and falling snow obscured all but twenty feet in front and behind. I ploughed on in the knowledge that if an avalanche came from above the rock wall again we would be wiped out whether we were on rocks or snow.

I reached the top of the rocky ridge we had followed along the edge of the couloir and recognised where we were. I tried to go along the crest of the ridge but the snow was too deep and I kept losing my footing. Pete agreed that we did seem to be better off in the deep snow, worrying as it was. I carried on down the couloir, down through that zone of fear, trying to keep to the edge and minimise the risk of being caught in the open. We glimpsed in the middle a huge boulder remembered from our ascent only hours before, and we cut across, feeling naked and powerless in the path of any avalanche from all the vast space above. We reached the boulder and took a diagonal line to the far side of the gully. The snow broke away at every step and I knew we were running risks which we could never expect to escape from if anything went wrong.

The previous day I had broken trail up to the edge of the couloir but could still recognise nothing. Pete seemed to be in a daze, his normally powerful self broken as I had rarely seen him and accepting being led. Dick plodded on, equally weak, encouraging Pete.

It was well after dawn but there was no sun, only blizzard; I kept my sunglasses off to see better and my eyes were stung by the driving snow and hail. I wondered if I would go snow-blind, and if I did which medication my doctor had said I should use, eye drops or amethocaine.

I was slow but Pete and Dick did not seem to mind. I kept asking directions and was told to follow the line of rocks. Gradually the angle of the slope lessened and I ground to a halt, bewildered by the whiteness around me and utterly exhausted now that we were out of the worst danger.

Pete forged on, knee-deep in snow, revived from his former aimless state. Dick went next and I brought up the rear. Suddenly I was very weak and could hardly keep up with the other two. I trailed along, repeating to myself the fact that it was not far along this almost level plateau to spur myself to keep on moving. I kept glancing to left and right trying to recognise features which would tell me where we were. I thought the snow ridge to the left was familiar, and the oddly shaped rocks to the right. We were roughly in the right place, but the smallest distance seemed too far to travel. I was falling over snow, and tried to force my pace so as not to be too slow and a drag on the rope for the other two.

Pete waded through an extra deep patch of snow, Dick followed and I found I had collapsed in the snow inadvertently. I heard Pete's voice:

'I think this is the place where we camped.'

I stayed sitting for a while, the snow was over my knees when I tried to walk, so I crawled over to join them.

It had taken us six hours to descend 900 feet. It was only nine o'clock in the morning but we were completely spent. We had brought down with us the tent which I had cut into and which had been further damaged by the avalanches, and to recoup some strength before continuing down we decided to put the tent up as best we could and carry on after a proper night of rest.

We had not strength enough even to level out the snow. We pitched the tent on a slight incline, hoping the weight of our bodies would flatten the snow sufficiently. The poles were bent and broken completely in one place. I bound an ice screw to the broken section, we drew the tattered tent over the misshapen framework and we had shelter. There were many vents and tears in the tent fabric but there were two layers of material and most of the holes were offset from each other. Little spirals of snowflakes came in but the main force of the storm was kept at bay. The wind battered the tent remorselessly but it stayed erect despite all the damage it had received.

Inside we lay on the sloping ground, wounded warriors resting from battle. Our weight did nothing to level out the snow beneath the tent floor, but we were too tired to stir again. We laid out our foam mats and pulled on our sleeping bags. Everything felt damp and we were chilled.

We needed food and drink but most of the food had been lost in the avalanche, as had the pan and spare gaz cylinders. We had only one cylinder of gaz on the stove and the pan lid in which to melt snow. Laboriously I melted handfuls of snow and poured the liquid into my water bottle. When it was full I heated the aluminium bottle on the stove and made a drink to share around.

I tried a radio call on the chance that the Major would be listening in but there was no reply. It was a gesture of hopelessness, wanting someone to turn to, someone else to take charge, someone with whom to share our catastrophe. We craved liquid but even the effort of melting snow on the pan lid was too much. I used my Swiss Army penknife to cut away the top of my water bottle and make it easier to push in lumps of snow. It made the melting of snow a little quicker but all three of us relapsed into a comatose state and if we started up from a doze, disturbed by the memories of avalanches and near oblivion, it was to stare dumbly about and to fall back doing nothing.

We found ourselves talking about our chances of coming back on the mountain until we realised how stupidly presumptuous such a notion was. Lying still, the pangs of hunger and fatigue forgotten in the dreamy state of rest after extreme exertion, we sometimes forgot the peril of our situation. We did not have all our wits about us, for when someone mentioned that we had not reached safety yet we all realised how much we had left to go through before we were off the mountain. The snowfall had not stopped since the previous afternoon, we had thousands of feet of mountain to descend, many open expanses of snow which would now be far deeper and more likely to avalanche than when we had come up over them. There were all the difficult stretches of rock which would now be covered in snow and in the thick cloud we would have trouble finding the way. Getting down would be a nightmare. With only one cylinder of gaz, perhaps three hours' worth, and little food, we could not afford to stay where we were. If we waited until the storm abated we ran the risk of being too weak to get down at all.

I had no spirit left at all. I wanted to surrender. If there had been any escape, I would have taken it; if it had been the same as in the Alps, where rescue by helicopter is possible, I would have called one in, but we were way above the ceiling at which helicopters can fly anyway. I mentioned my thoughts to Dick and he was appalled. He said he would not dream of getting off the mountain by anything but his own efforts.

At 5.00 p.m. I made the scheduled radio call. It took Major Sarwat a long time to comprehend my message:

'Our tent was destroyed in an avalanche and we are back at Camp Five.' Through the crackle of interference I heard him saying:

'I get that you have reached Camp Six and are going for another try. Is that correct? Over.'

I had to fight back the hysteria which was creeping into my voice. I could feel tears welling up in my eyes that we should be in such desperate straits and that there was no sympathy from below. The Major seemed pleased that we were sticking with the attempt to reach the top.

If the line had been clear I would have had no shame in saying: 'Please take pity on us. We are only just alive. We are trying to get down,' but I had to be blunt and clear; there was no means of subtle communication.

'The tent has been destroyed.' I exaggerated a little to get the meaning across. 'We are coming down.' At the same time I did not want to cause alarm.

Jeff and Mike, the two Americans who were camped near our Base Camp, were with Major Sarwat. When he had finally understood that there had been an avalanche and we were on our way down, he told us that Jeff and Mike were leaving and wanted to say goodbye. There was nothing that they could do to help us, good climbers as they were. They had no knowledge of our route and they would have been equally at risk from new avalanches if they tried to reach us. I did feel, however, disappointment that they should be going, even knowing that they were watching and waiting with us in spirit would have been a consolation. Obviously they did not know in what distress we were.

I understood from Major Sarwat something about them wanting to borrow our mail runners to be their porters. I consulted with Pete and Dick and they were equally aghast. I radioed down our refusal, feeling mean, but wanting the mail runners on hand for when we got down, if ever we did.

We all slept badly that night. I had pains in the back of my neck and realised only then that I had probably been concussed by the blows from the ice and snow on the back of my head rather than the suffocation.

It took a long time to get moving next morning. The storm still persisted. We packed our sleeping bags but abandoned the tent. I radioed down that we would like Gohar and Ali to come round to the foot of the ridge to meet us with food and a tent once we were off the mountain. If we were late getting off the mountain we could spend a night on the edge of the glacier and they could help us back to Base Camp with our loads. I promised to radio down every couple of hours to relay our progress and asked the Major not to let Gohar and Ali leave until we were sure we would reach the bottom of the Abruzzi Spur.

Pete led off over the crest of the ridge into a deep expanse of snow. He was making towards the ice wall which he had led the way up during our ascent. Dick and I waited, watching Pete making ungainly progress in snow which came up to his waist. He began expressing doubts about the feasibility of descending that way in all the fresh snow. Where the slope steepened he halted and finally shouted that he was coming back, to descend that way would certainly be lethal. He suggested we follow a route down some rocks. I looked about but did not understand which direction he meant. The cloud and snow limited visibility to a few yards.

He was a long time coming back, though he had only gone 100 feet on a gentle slope. The deep snow and absolute fatigue was affecting the movements of all three of us. When he arrived it was to snap at us for not moving.

'What's the matter? Don't you agree about the rocks?'

'No. I just haven't a clue where you mean.'

Pete had noticed a line of rocks a long way to the left of the ice wall he had led and it was this he was proposing as a safer descent. 'We should be able to get some anchors in the rocks,' he said, 'and in a few hundred feet we should be clear of the worst part.'

He went off into the blizzard and after 300 feet launched off down some rocks which disappeared into the mist and snow below. Dick and I followed, all three of us on the one rope. I marvelled at Pete's forethought and memory of this line, trusting that his sense of direction was accurate, because I could not visualise which direction we were facing.

Sometimes the rocks were very steep and Pete shouted his need for tension on the rope as he floundered and groped for foot-holds and hand-holds in the snow. When he could, he took up a stance himself, fastening the rope to a piton driven into the rock till Dick and I joined him, slipping and sliding, with little control over the unseen slabs and projections.

My hands were numb with the cold and my gloves soaking with the constant contact with the snow. We normally wore thin gloves under thick mitts with a waterproof cover. My inner gloves made my hands colder with the dampness, so I discarded them, and used only the mitt which kept my fingers together, generating more warmth. As the steps downwards went on and on, as the insane floundering, wet, cold and seemingly hopeless, persisted hour after hour, I knew then that we had been mad even to consider coming back up. I had had enough. Surely, I told myself, this was an honourable failure. Surely we had gone as far as could ever be expected. We had driven ourselves to the limit. I tried to make radio contact at the prearranged times but it was futile and the radio became packed with snow.

We could only see twenty or thirty feet at a time, and the descent seemed interminable. All the time my mind was full with the question of whether we were in the very place where Art Gilkey had been lost.

Eventually we came to the foot of a couloir alongside the rocks. Pete continued on in a diagonal line across a snow slope which I could barely distinguish in the mist. We tied two ropes together to give him extra scope whilst Dick and I still remained attached securely to the bottom of the rock ridge. The mist thickened and grew thinner by turns and after a while we could see that Pete was walking upright, facing outwards from the slope, and he was over the worst.

Together the three of us walked down the undulating slope looking for the small cache we had made, when we had left our fourth camp, of the spare tent, food and other superfluous gear. It was no longer superfluous. To descend 800 feet had taken us six hours. The afternoon was nearly over, there was no chance of getting off the mountain that day, and we badly needed to find the tent and food if we were to survive the night.

The white mist merged with the white snow so that it was difficult to distinguish one from the other, difficult to decide what was up, or down, or level. No shadows gave any shape to the slope. By sensation alone we knew we were on a shelf more even than the rest of the snow slope and we looked for any signs that this had been the place where we had once camped and had left the spare tent. The fresh, deep snow blanketed everything into a uniform whiteness.

We sat helplessly in the snow. There were hundreds of square feet to search even if it was the right place. Feebly we each poked at the snow with our ice axes, hoping to feel softness which could distinguish the buried tent from a rock or ice. Dick dug into a spot he was sure was the right location and uncovered a frozen turd, evidence at last that we were near, as we had not strayed far from the tent to relieve ourselves. We concentrated our search in that region and with mighty relief came upon the folded tent and the bag of food and spare gaz cylinders.

It was 3.00 p.m. Inside the tent we were able to relax a little more, reprieved for another few hours from the prevailing certainty that every step we took invited death.

On the radio I told the Major that we would not be off the mountain that evening and hoped to make it next day. Jeff and Mike had not left after all, and the Major had a surprise for us. He said he was passing the radio to a friend of ours and we heard a voice familiar in its expressions:

'Hey, you guys, this is Georgess. How goes it?'

It was Georges Bettembourg, who had been with us on Kangchenjunga, come to climb and ski down the neighbouring Broad Peak with a team of Frenchmen.

''Ow are you? You 'ave it difficult. When will you be down?'

It was the same old Georges, bubbling with vitality, questions pouring out, not waiting for answers. I could imagine him bobbing up and down, running back and forth with the radio, impatient with the reception and trying to find a better location rather than concentrating on the conversation.

Pete was equally delighted and somehow Georges's arrival at our Base Camp gave us new heart. He was a friend who understood our predicament, but we told him there was nothing he could do for us. Pete spoke with him also and in spite of the feeling that we were in a condemned cell speaking on a telephone line to a free man we were able to exchange some of the banter and chatter we had enjoyed the previous year with him. The warmth of his company was a bonus to look forward to on our return to life.

There was food and fuel sufficient for our needs but we only had energy to melt a minimum of snow. We wanted to start early next day to try to descend all the remaining ground before dark, so we settled down early to sleep. We all took sleeping tablets, but I swallowed two to make sure that the drug deadened any discomfort and gave me the rest I craved.

I had a night of disturbing dreams. I was in the Vietnam war on a battlefield, standing beside a Colonel Kurtz. I had seen him in the film *Apocalypse Now*. The battlefield was a muddy mess of broken buildings and broken tents. Inside the fabric of the tents we could see the forms of people moving, and the Colonel took out his revolver and shot at point-blank range at the rounded shapes that were people's heads. The film had astounded me with the carefree manner in which the characters courted death. They were shown surfing off a beach whilst bullets poured out of the jungle, dropping napalm on villages to the sound of music from loud-speakers mounted in the helicopters, and sailing up the Mekong river into ambush as they danced to a song of the Rolling Stones, 'Satisfaction', on a cassette deck. I woke with the same sensation of capricious flirtation with death, as if death was not final as we tended to think, as if death was not to be feared, otherwise why should people court it so playfully?

One last traverse across deep snow for 300 feet brought us to the top of the ice wall which Dick had led. Pete went first again as Dick belayed the rope. I sat and filmed Pete disappearing into the mist. I had recovered enough composure to use again the small movie camera we had with us.

The snow gave way at every step Pete made. He shouted impatiently, with annoyance engendered by the dangerous crossing, and I was glad of the excuse of filming not to be going first across the slope myself.

Pete abseiled down the ice cliff and as Dick followed him he dislodged some loose snow which caught Pete unawares. The snow knocked him from his footing and he fell fifteen feet to be held by the frayed strands of the old rope we had knotted in place where we had thought it least important.

There remained 7,000 feet of descent, more difficult than the open snow slopes, but safer. The rock buttresses were too steep to hold much snow and we could hurry across the open gullies to the greater security of more rocks on the far side. We abseiled down some sections and in others the ropes we had fixed in place hastened our retreat. There was little energy left in any of us now but we had hopes of survival greater than at any time in the last three days.

I felt no wish that we had never started on the mountain in the first place, but now that we were reasonably hopeful of living I resented the long days of hardship that remained before we could relax. Even when our future had seemed bleak, there had been no space in my mind for consideration of anything other than how we could extract ourselves from our predicament. I knew then that I could not pretend to myself that I should have chosen some other way of life because I had had doubts before and had returned again and again to the mountains. Dreadful as our situation was, we had chosen to be in it.

I radioed down our position every hour, unable to say for certain whether we would make it down before dark. Gohar and Ali wanted to climb up to meet us but I ordered them not to. I lost time in making these radio calls, sometimes waiting for the call time behind a ridge which would shelter me from the wind while I spoke, and Pete and Dick drew ahead.

We were on easier ground now which was transformed by the new snow. Even on level stretches I could hardly walk upright. Where tattered remains of rope from the earlier expeditions hung in place I swung down on them, careless of their age, too weak to ignore them as we had done in ascent, and hoping to be allowed to escape from this mountain.

As we came lower, the cloud became less dense and the snow wetter. Sometimes the dark valley bottom was revealed and I was disheartened to see how far away it was and how far ahead Pete and Dick were.

Gohar and Ali were on their way round to us and late in the afternoon

I saw their tiny figures on the ledge to which they had come with us when we had left all those days before.

It was dark before I reached them. By touch alone I felt my way down the wet rocks, guided by their torchlight. Pete and Dick were already there. The ordeal was almost over. I straightened up when I reached the platform for the last few yards but stumbled and was caught by Gohar who leapt forward. He and Ali pressed close, wrapping their arms around me and squeezing tight their welcome. They held me for a long while and I wept with relief, surrendering myself unashamedly to the care of these strong, capable men whom we had hired to work but whose concern and affection for us was beyond what money could buy.

They would not let us carry anything ourselves. We had to descend a few hundred feet to the glacier where they had tents and food. The rock under foot was wet and in places icy, but we were alive. Gohar and Ali were solicitous for our every move and shepherded us, as they would their children, down to the place where we would spend the night. They had waited for us for hours, in the cold, in thin clothing on that ledge, forbidden to come higher but reluctant to go back to the tents where they had left their warmer clothing.

At the edge of the glacier we three settled into one tent while Gohar and Ali cooked and served us from a second tent. We were thoroughly damp but we slept in the comfort of knowing we were safe, and that our responsibility was over. We did not even need to carry anything back to Base Camp.

Gohar brought us tea in the morning and Ali presented us with a tiny flower he had picked from the desolate moraine. The ordeal was over.

Our steps were weak and faltering, even on the level part of the glacier. Gohar and Ali carried monstrous loads, refusing to let us take anything from them. For Ali this was the first expedition he had been on and he was unfamiliar with mountaineering techniques, but he was proud to be needed and insistent on doing more than we would ever have asked him.

The weather was clear for the first time in an age as we made our way to Base Camp. There were clusters of people outside our tents and as we came up off the ice they were looking towards us. I felt uneasy at meeting people who would ask about and revive the pain of our ordeal and then Georges was running towards us, his face wide in a smile, and my eyes were brimming with tears. I stumbled into camp blinded by the mist on my sunglasses, glad that their mirror-like reflections would save me explaining the tears, and Major Sarwat was shaking our hands, pleased that his boys were back.

IV

Gohar and Ali had brought us letters when they came to meet us but I had not opened mine. I felt cauterised by the experience of being so close to instant death and then the strain of living for three days in the knowledge of how close we still were at every step. The experience had rendered unimportant the other anxieties of life. Having been given back my life I felt no urgency any more, as if I had all the time in the world. Every moment was to be savoured, every sensation treasured and valued more than ever before.

The afternoon was bliss, worries were all gone, we were in safety with food and drink to hand. We relaxed in our large dining tent. Ali worked away on one side preparing the food and drinks. We had the company of some of Georges's friends from the Broad Peak expedition who were making a film of the ski descent. We shared memories and news of mutual acquaintances and exchanged stories about anything except what had just happened to us. They must have sensed that we were in a state of shock and were careful with their questions. Their camp was an hour away and they left at dark to make their way back, leaving us to return to our own tents to sleep for the first time in two weeks without the pressure of each other's bodies in the night and alone with our disturbing memories.

Deliberately I steered my mind away from that area of pain. The thoughts were all there, the encounter with myself, the view over the edge of the abyss of death, were present at any time for me to examine, but I covered it all up, like a wound bandaged over. The tears were still there and, unless I occupied myself with mundane things, I found them welling up again in relief, self-pity, delayed shock, the closeness of death, the tears for life – I no longer knew.

Jeff and Mike persuaded us to let them borrow our mail runners so that they could get away. Their mountain had beaten them and they had no purpose in staying. None of us three even thought as far as making a decision about whether to leave or not. We had to summon porters to carry our gear back, since we had much more than Jeff and Mike, so it would take a fortnight for them to arrive anyway.

We did a hurried news report to fulfil our obligations to the *Newsnight* team and I found I was speaking a formula of words which I had learnt in order to describe the events, so that speaking about it would not penetrate to the anguish inside. I scribbled a letter to my girlfriend Maria and all that came out was the raw pain. I could not find words to pretend. 'Hope to be home soon,' I finished. A deceit so that she would not worry.

We lay about for three days, weakly making the journey between our own tents and the eating tent, tripping over the rocks which littered the way because the strength was almost completely gone from our limbs. We teased Dick about going to be a father soon and I wondered if Alf, the manager of Magic Mountain, would have gone off for his holidays before I got back. Alf was due to leave on 9 August, and I did not know if I would get back to find my shop closed by his absence. Dick's baby was due in the latter part of August. Pete was worried about the climbing courses he ran in Switzerland and whether, having taken bookings for them, the clients would be turning up to find no one to guide them. It was now 16 July. Even if we could leave immediately we would not get back till August.

I borrowed a book called *Shōgun* from the Broad Peak team and became absorbed in its 1,200 pages of battles, intrigue and romance in ancient Japan. It was the perfect escapist reading so that Pete and Dick grew annoyed at my unsociable silence. I read the book at every moment, all day, through mealtimes and at night until my eyes dropped shut with tiredness. The willingness with which the characters embraced death in accordance with their Samurai code and the readiness with which the Samurai inflicted death, as one might stamp on an insect, exercised compulsive, horrifying fascination.

Major Sarwat, as a devout Muslim, was observing the fast of Ramadan. He was enjoined by his religion neither to eat nor drink between the hours of sunrise and sunset. He used to rise before dawn and Ali would cook breakfast for him. Thereafter he would sit with us at mealtimes but eat nothing, impressing us all with his dedication and making me have second thoughts about the disrespectful teasing I had indulged in with him earlier on.

I took a bath in a large plastic drum retrieved from the debris at the site of the French Base Camp. Ali heated great pans of water over his stoves and filled the drum outside. I sat in the tub in the sunshine, in the lee of the tent, delighting in the sensual pleasure of hot water on my wasted body which had not seen daylight for weeks. The surface skin was all dried and came off in flakes. My legs were ridiculously thin and my ribs protruded noticeably from my chest. I had lost an enormous amount of weight.

It was as if we were convalescing, patients to be treated delicately, but at some stage we had to make a decision – whether to abandon our attempt on the mountain or go back for another try. We did not discuss it at all. For three days there was no mention of what we should do, then on the third day Pete suggested that it was time we got together to decide our intentions.

It was immaterial who spoke first. All three of us had decided, on his own, that what he really wanted to do was go back onto the mountain and finish the task we had so nearly completed. In spite of all the pressing commitments, in spite of all the traumas of the avalanche and the retreat, what we wanted most of all was to try once more.

There would be time for only one more attempt because we had sent for the porters and they would arrive on the 29 or 30 July. Once they arrived, we would have to leave, since we could not feed or shelter them for more than two days. We estimated that if the weather held good we could reach the top in five days of climbing now that we knew the route well, had prepared most of the difficult pitches and, if we were weak, we were at least perfectly acclimatised.

We prepared to leave but dysentery hit all three of us in turn and we recounted tales at breakfast of waking in the night to vomit all the previous day's food. When we should have been gaining strength we were being further weakened by illness. The weather was still unsettled.

Dick sorted out enough food for a week and we left on the fifth day for our last attempt.

On the days when we could climb we made steady progress but the weather deteriorated on the third day, an ominous cloud cap on Broad Peak bringing early warning of the change.

On 24 July we reached Camp 3 above the first big ice cliff and were stuck there for four nights. The raging storms kept us locked in the tent as the snow grew deeper against its sides. After three nights the weather was worse than ever and with little food left we decided to stay for one more night and then descend. Any longer and we would have no reserves at all. Dick's rations had been parsimonious in the interests of saving weight but we could not blame him as I had spent all my time reading instead of helping him to sort out the rations and Pete had spent his time writing.

On 28 July the weather was less poor than it had been so we went on, up the rocks down which Pete had led the way, avoiding the second ice cliff. We went past the plateau where our abandoned tent was flattened and buried in snow. I wanted to camp there again but Pete urged that we should press on higher whilst we could and Dick voted for that too since he would allow himself no easy option.

We crossed the broad couloir which we had trembled to cross in the deep snow a few days previously and, though it had snowed since, the slopes were swept clean by avalanche or wind. Instead of climbing up the ridge on the far side of the couloir we descended it a little and camped on the broad back of the ridge where it stood out proud from the mountain. There we were safe from any avalanche and in reach of the summit next day if the weather permitted.

But the weather did not permit. We lay all day as the wind battered the tent and heavy cloud obscured the mountain above. Sarwat radioed to us that it was fine below and we should press on but we could not stand in the wind.

We lay with stomachs aching with hunger, ruefully regretting Dick's estimate of the food. We had expected to reach the summit in five days and this was the eighth. The sparse rations had already been stretched to the limit. We were saving used tea bags to re-use them again without sugar or milk to add. We could not last much longer.

Dick was doing most of the cooking. He had the self-discipline to make himself wake up and start the stove in the early hours of the morning whilst Pete and I agonised over waking to a new day. We were all feeling the cold much more since we were all so thin and the prime place in the tent for warmth was the middle position where a person could benefit from the body heat of the two on either side. Pete bargained with Dick for this place, but I preferred to be near the wall of the tent where there was more fresh air from the vent.

We rose at 2.00 a.m. next day to start for the summit should the weather be fine but the cloud was still there and the snow persisted. The wind had kept us awake all night. We had arranged a special radio call for 2.00 a.m. and even Sarwat had to admit that from his location too the prospects were not good. It was beginning to snow and more cloud was coming in. We had to start down.

This time we were in control. We left at dawn and were down by 9.00 p.m., infinitely weary but met at the bottom by Gohar and Ali again, who took us into their care. The last time we had rehearsed this play it had been a tragedy, this time it was just a sad little scenario. We had tried to our limits and could do no more.

We had the satisfaction of seeing that the weather had not improved. Heavy cloud still hung over the mountain and we knew of the maelstrom which would exist inside it. As we neared our Base Camp we met friendly groups of our porters who had been waiting a couple of days for us to descend. We had used up all the time available to us, now there was none to spare for a rest. We packed up that day and left next morning for home.

V

I felt no regret and neither Pete nor Dick showed any of the soul-searching anxiety about whether we could have succeeded if we had tried harder. We had the satisfaction of knowing that we had tried to the utmost and that whatever had been lacking it was not anything in ourselves. I had a sense, which I knew the others shared, that we were not giving up in our efforts to climb the mountain but simply taking a break in order to attend to other things which were necessary, and we started going over dates and opportunities of when we could return. The mountain held a compulsive fascination and without needing to talk about it all three of us knew that we all felt the same.

The journey back was partly delirium. We had food to hand but our stomachs seemed to have shrunk and we could not eat enough to sustain ourselves for more than an hour. Already thin, my limbs were now wasted away and all three of us took to carrying stores of food to eat when weakness made our steps falter. Sometimes one of us miscalculated and homed in on whoever had been more foreseeing in acquiring bars of chocolate and tubes of sweets.

My brain drifted in an intoxication induced by the privation; exhaustion was like an old aquaintance. I wanted to get home as soon as possible but I could look at my wishes calmly without the agitation I would once have felt. I knew that this expedition had affected me more profoundly than any other experience in the mountains; I shared the feelings of the Samurai brought back honourably from his suicide and knew the exalted state he would have been in on his reprieve. A whole new life was mine, as if the past was no more. I felt beyond the reach of anything as if I had total self-containment. I felt wealthy, blessed with fortune beyond measure. The body I walked in was weak but it did not matter, the pain of movement was only another proof that I was alive, a sign of the new life. When we stopped for the night, an unplanned halt in the schedule of our return, it made no difference to my peace of mind. As in the euphoria induced by a drug, I could be content to pass the time contemplating the day going by.

We had not planned to halt for the night at Urdukass, the grassy promontory above the glacier, but we were force-marching the porters and they insisted on a rest. It was immaterial to me and Pete. We had both sat in the dust at Skardu airport for days on end in 1978 and we could not summon the energy to hurry now when we were most tired, only to spend the time we had gained in that squalid place. But Dick did not know the reality of our remoteness and the impossibility of hurrying out. He did some calculations and realised that every day was precious if he was to arrive in England in time for the birth of the baby. If at all possible he wanted to share the experience with his girlfriend. He began making promises of extra pay to the porters if they would do double and treble stages and told Pete and me that he would pay them out of his own pocket.

It was almost as if we were being whipped on as well. The days were intolerably long and one day I woke with stomach cramps and diarrhoea which made me run off behind boulders to relieve myself every few minutes. That day we had to ferry the porters on a rope bridge across the Punmah river and I lay in the shade, weak from the sickness, until they were all across and we had to move on again.

We reached Askole that night after dark. I trailed in last, hoping for a cup of tea but Dick, always so unassuming, had not presumed to ask the villagers. I was angry because I was so ill and shouted at Ali to organise some tea which he did in minutes from a willing house nearby.

I lay on the ground in the dark and heard voices calling me by name.

They were some Japanese whom we had heard, from our mail runners, were ahead of us and whom we had now caught up. They were asking for Pete and Dick too, so I left them to it hoping that I was concealed in the shadows, but I had been to Japan and they wanted to say hello. I rose weakly to shake their hands and was embarrassed to appear so feeble before them.

Later there were more voices asking for me and I ignored them but it was a man I had met in Tokyo and he would not be put off till we had met and talked.

We travelled together then and stayed in the same rest-house in Skardu. It was 7 August. Our party was booked on a flight for the 9th but it was the monsoon period when the flights are most unreliable and we knew that we could be waiting for days and weeks.

We hired a jeep and had a ten-hour ride over the roughest of roads to Gilgit and then a transit van down the Karakoram highway which was not officially open to foreigners. Major Sarwat was on our side now and he ignored the petty objections of the officious Deputy Commissioner in Gilgit who was insisting that we return to Skardu, but we came up against a landslide and did not reach Islamabad for two more days.

Elspeth was out but we had cabled her from Skardu and her house was open when we arrived in the evening. Dick phoned England and we heard him promising to be on a flight the next day. He left, without washing, for the airport to try to transfer his ticket but the offices were all closed and he returned to the bar in the British Embassy Club later that night and joined Pete and myself drinking to the luxuries of civilisation.

There was no means by which Dick could leave sooner than us. We spent the next day in a tightly scheduled series of visits to the Ministry of Tourism to undergo the routine debriefing, a courtesy call to the British ambassador and a lightning shopping spree for presents. That night we flew down to Karachi and boarded a plane for home.

It was the Pan Am 001 continuous round-the-world flight. I still retained the detachment which I had felt after coming down from the mountain. I wanted to return home but it was as if it were an intellectual concept, my emotions were still anaesthetised and I felt as if no hurt or anxiety could ever affect me; as if all extremes of pleasure and pain would be insignificant in comparison with the gift of life itself. Once on the plane I felt that I could just as easily stay on it until it had gone right round the world and I could disembark amongst the mountains ready to return to them once more. I returned to a girlfriend who could hardly recognise the stranger who disembarked to meet her.

Back in England, a few days after our arrival, Pete rang me asking for Allen Jewhurst's phone number. I had spoken already to Allen, whose tones of helpless concern told me how much his heart had stayed with us once he had left. I was vaguely puzzled and inquisitive after Pete phoned me to know why he had asked for Allen's number rather than asking me to pass on a message. Then Allen phoned me again:

'What's this about Boardman?' he demanded in his irreverent cockney manner. 'He says I'm to ring you and tell you he's getting married. Didn't you guys speak to each other on this trip?'

A day later the formal printed invitation arrived.

'Mr & Mrs Collins request the pleasure of the company of Joe Tasker at the wedding of their daughter Hilary to Peter Boardman. . . .'

The invitations, wedding, reception, had all clearly been arranged months beforehand and all through the expedition Pete had not said a word to us and had decided to go back up for another attempt knowing that there was every chance he might miss his own wedding. I realised then that the worry he had expressed for clients arriving for climbing courses before he was back had disguised his real concern at being absent on his wedding day.

Dick could not make it; his baby boy was born that same weekend. They called him Daniel, after the man who had survived in the lion's den.

Postscript

After the ordeal on K2, I felt, strangely, no sense of disappointment that we had not reached the top of the mountain, and I knew that Pete and Dick felt the same. We had done everything we possibly could to climb it. We had pushed ourselves to the limit mentally and physically and stayed at that limit for so long that we scarcely had strength left to drag ourselves back to normal life.

Physically we were completely run down and mentally I felt as if I was shell-shocked after a war. But the persistence remained, and I realised that I had changed or come to an awareness of self that was different from the perception I had had on first coming to the Himalayas when I had vowed never to return.

We had not reached the top of K2 but I saw more clearly than on any other climb that it was not reaching the summit that was most important but the journey to it, and though I would never have chosen such a trial as we experienced on that particular journey, having been through it I valued every minute.

Three of us had been united in a rarely experienced, single-minded determination, and when the going was difficult we had known we could rely absolutely upon each other. Since that first traumatic retreat from Dunagiri, descending with Dick, each of us almost oblivious to the other in our worlds of illusions and hallucinations, I had learnt how to cope better with hardship and exhaustion. I had learnt at least to recognise it for what it was and to separate the needs of reality from the fantasies of hallucination.

Many answers had been found to the questions I had had since first starting climbing. I knew now what karabiners were, knew why avalanches were lethal; I knew the mountains and some of the cities of the Himalayan countries so well that I felt at home in them; I knew that there was no closed circle of expedition people but groups of friends who chose to go away together as one would choose to go on holiday with people one knew, and now I had friends whom I knew I could rely on in the mountains, and would choose to go away with again, so that to someone starting to think about how to go to the Himalayas we too probably seem a closed circle into which there is no admittance.

I had never planned to go to the mountains so often nor to keep on going for a long time but I had come to see that there was something new and different there each time I went and that as long as that continued to be so I would continue to be drawn there. There are endless new challenges to face, endlessly alluring problems to solve, and difficulties to be overcome. Rather than being a matter of ticking off achievements or notching up a list of summits reached, visiting the mountains had come to be a way of life.

K2 had highlighted the extent to which we were prepared to push ourselves, and it must have seemed from the outside that we were suicidal or emotionless creatures. But we were only taking risks because the end we hoped to reach seemed worthwhile – reaching the top of the second highest mountain in the world purely by our own efforts – and so too with any objective in the mountains, the risks are only run because one believes the correct calculation has been made of how to avoid them in reaching a worthwhile goal. Rather than being suicidal, the climbers I know all love life and fight furiously to hold on to it, and the same restless energy and enthusiasm helps them overcome the problems of everyday life and is transmitted to those around them.

In some ways, going to the mountains is incomprehensible to many people and inexplicable by those who go. The reasons are difficult to unearth and only with those who are similarly drawn is there no need to try to explain. On returning from K2, we were planning to go back there some day soon, and there were other plans being formulated, other invitations being made to go to an unclimbed mountain in China, to attempt Everest in a small party, and for the foreseeable future, sufficient alluring prospects to keep on going back to the mountains again and again.

Chronology

The Eiger
Joe Tasker, Dick Renshaw.

1975　18–20 February　　　　First attempt.
　　　25 February–1 March　　Second and successful attempt.

Dunagiri
Joe Tasker, Dick Renshaw.

1975　30 June　　　　　　　　Permission offered for Dunagiri.
　　　5 August　　　　　　　 Dick passes driving test.
　　　6 August　　　　　　　 Departure overland for India.
　　　23 September　　　　　 Dick reaches Base Camp.
　　　27 September　　　　　 Joe reaches Base Camp.
　　　1–11 October (approx.)　Ascent and descent of South-East
　　　　　　　　　　　　　　Ridge of Dunagiri.

　　　End of October　　　　 Dick flies back to UK.
　　　End of November　　　 Joe arrives back in UK.

Changabang
Joe Tasker, Pete Boardman.

1975　December　　　　　　　First plans for attempt on West Face of
　　　　　　　　　　　　　　mountain.
1976　May　　　　　　　　　 Permission received for expedition to
　　　　　　　　　　　　　　West Face of Changabang.

　　　22 August　　　　　　　Departure from Heathrow for Delhi.
　　　7 September　　　　　　Arrive Base Camp.

16 September	Establish Camp 1 on crest of ridge at 18,000 feet. First half of route completed. Ropes fixed to top of ice field in middle of face.
29 September–2 October	Attempt to make progress using hammock bivouacs.
5 October	Meet two members and Liaison Officer of American expedition to Dunagiri.
7 October	Return to mountain.
15 October	Reach summit.
16 October	Accident on Dunagiri to American expedition.
18 October	Return to Base Camp and meet Italian expedition and Ruth of American expedition and learn of accident to four of their members.
19 October	Climb up to 20,000 feet on Dunagiri to bury bodies of four members of American expedition.
1 November	Fly back to UK.

K2

Joe Tasker, Pete Boardman, Chris Bonington, Paul Braithwaite, Jim Duff, Nick Estcourt, Tony Riley, Doug Scott.

1977	Autumn	Invitation to join K2 expedition in 1978.
1978	10 May	Fly to Islamabad, Pakistan.
	15 May	Fly to Skardu.
	18 May	Start of walk-in to Base Camp.
	1 June	Siting of Base Camp on Savoia glacier.
	4 June	Siting of Camp 1 at 19,700 feet.
	7 June	Siting of Camp 2 at 21,400 feet.
	8 June	Pete and Joe occupy Camp 2.
	8–10 June	Snow-storms.
	11 June	Reach 22,000 feet.
	12 June	Nick swept away and killed in avalanche.
	13 June	All back at Base Camp. Decision to call off expedition.
	14 June	Chris and Doug leave for Islamabad.

22 June	Rest of team leave Concordia for Islamabad.
29 June	Reach Skardu.
3–9 July	Various members obtain flights back to Islamabad.
September	Attempt on Nuptse, Nepal.

Kangchenjunga
Joe Tasker, Georges Bettembourg, Pete Boardman, Doug Scott.

1978	Autumn	Invitation from Doug to join Kangchenjunga expedition in 1979.
1979	13 March	Arrive Kathmandu.
	18 March	Start of approach march.
	26 March	Pete breaks ankle.
	4 April	Arrive at Base Camp.
	13 April	Establish Camp 2.
	15–21 April	Climbing and fixing rope on wall.
	27 April	Reach North Col. Establish Camp 3. Pete injured by rock-fall, descends to Camp 2.
	30 April	Pete returns to North Col.
	1 May	Joe descends. Pete, Doug and Georges climb ridge and dig snow cave, Camp 4.
	4 May	Pete, Doug and Georges camp at 26,000 feet on ridge above plateau.
	5 May	Tent destroyed in early morning. The three retreat all way down off mountain.
	9 May	All four return to Camp 2.
	10–14 May	Attempt to reach summit.
	15 May	Georges descends. Pete, Doug and Joe set off for summit.
	16 May	Reach summit.
	17–18 May	Descend to Base Camp.
	28 May	Reach Dharan.
	29 May	Reach Kathmandu.

K2

Joe Tasker, Pete Boardman, Dick Renshaw, Doug Scott.

1980	30 April	Fly to Karachi (Pete, Dick, Joe and Allen Jewhurst). Journey by truck to Islamabad (3 days).
	5 May	Doug arrives Islamabad.
	10 May	Start of walk-in.
	24 May	Arrive at 'Dump Camp' of 1978. Porters leave.
	26–28 May	Ferry loads round to Savoia glacier beneath West Ridge.
	5 June	Reach site for Camp 1 at 20,700 feet.
	16 June	Reach high point of 23,000 feet.
	18 June	Descend to Base Camp.
	24 June	First attempt on Abruzzi Spur.
	27 June	Descend to Base Camp. Doug decides to return to UK.
	2 July	Pete, Dick and Joe return to Abruzzi Spur.
	12 July	Reach camp (6th) at 26,500 feet.
	13–15 July	Avalanche and retreat.
	22 July	Return for last attempt on Abruzzi.
	30 July	In camp at 26,000 feet, decision to descend.
	31 July	Reach Base Camp.
	1 August	Depart for Skardu.
	10 August	Islamabad.
	11 August	Karachi.
	12 August	UK
	End of August	Pete gets married. Dick's baby born.

Index

Index

THE SHINING MOUNTAIN

MOUNTAIN

Two men on Changabang's West Wall

by

Peter Boardman

with material by

Joe Tasker

Contents

Changabang from the south–west

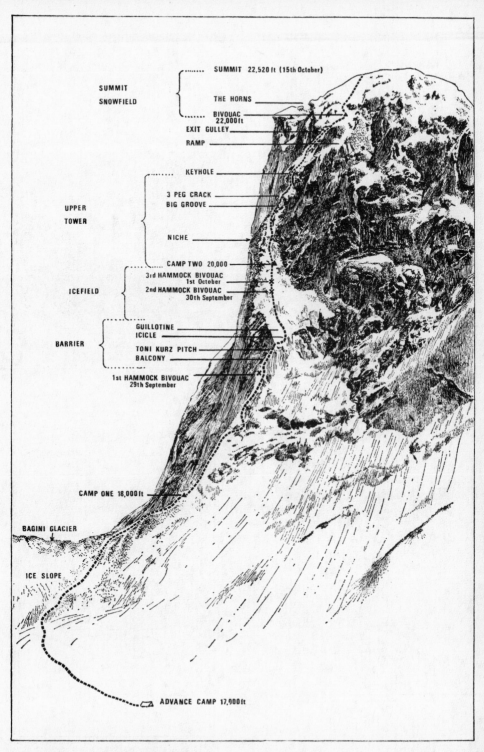

SUMMIT 22,520 ft (15th October)

SUMMIT
SNOWFIELD

THE HORNS

BIVOUAC
22,000 ft

EXIT GULLEY

RAMP

KEYHOLE

3 PEG CRACK
BIG GROOVE

UPPER
TOWER

NICHE

CAMP TWO 20,000

3rd HAMMOCK BIVOUAC
1st October
2nd HAMMOCK BIVOUAC
30th September

ICEFIELD

GUILLOTINE
ICICLE

BARRIER

TONI KURZ PITCH
BALCONY

1st HAMMOCK BIVOUAC
29th September

CAMP ONE 18,000 ft

BAGINI GLACIER

ICE SLOPE

ADVANCE CAMP 17,900 ft

The route up the West Wall

CHAPTER ONE

From the West

"SITTING HUDDLED BENEATH A DOWN JACKET, SHELTERING FROM THE sun, my back against a rock, I drank some liquid for the first time in four days. I was going to live. The photographs I took were purely a conditioned reflex; I would want one picture of this view, just as a reminder of the ordeal I had endured. The glacier, spread about before me like a white desert, was peopled by my imagination and over it hung the massive West Wall of Changabang, a great cinema screen which would never have figures on it."

Joe Tasker had survived Dunagiri and had returned to life to the west of the Shining Mountain.

Autumn days passed; meanwhile I was in the western world.

"Have you seen this letter?" asked Dennis Gray across the office of the British Mountaineering Council in Manchester, where we both worked. "What a fantastic effort," he added. I picked it up. It was from Dick Renshaw, who had just been on an expedition to the Garhwal Himalaya with Joe Tasker. The magnitude of their achievement jumped out from its few words:

Dear Dennis,

We climbed Dunagiri. It took us six days up the South-East Ridge. When we reached the summit, we ran out of food and fuel to melt snow into water. The descent took five days and we suffered. I got frostbite in some fingers and shall be flying home soon from Delhi. Joe's driving the van back.

Yours,
Dick.

P.S. Congratulations to Pete on climbing Everest.

I sat down, filled with envy. Dennis was already on the 'phone to the local press. "Incredible feat of endurance . . . Just the two of them . . . Tiny budget . . . 23,000-foot mountain . . . Far more significant than the recent South-West Face of Everest climb." I had to strain to hear the words above the clattering typewriters and rhythmic pumping of the duplicating machine. Beyond the plate glass windows, the red brick of the office block, the unkempt, lumpy car park, and the Home for the Destitute, I could glimpse the blue of the sky.

I stared dumbly at the trays of letters in front of me—access problems, committee meetings, equipment enquiries. Amongst them were invitations to receptions and dinners and requests to give lectures about the Everest climb—all demands to accelerate the headlong pace of my life. Their number diluted the quality of my work. 'Everest is a bloody bore,' screamed a voice inside my head. The previous evening I had given a slide show about Everest. It was as if I was standing aside and listening to myself. As time distances you from a climb, it seems you are talking about someone else. All the usual questions had rolled out at the end: What does it feel like on top? What do you have to eat? How do you go to the toilet when you're up there? Is it more difficult coming down? How long did it take you? Don't you think you've done it all now you've been to the top of Everest? What marvellous courage you must have!

Courage. Endurance. Those words drifted across the office and mocked my bitter mood of discontent. Meaningless. Courage is doing only what you are scared of doing. The blatant drama of mountaineering blinds the judgement of these people who are so loud in praise. Life has many cruel subtleties that require far more courage to deal with than the obvious dangers of climbing. Endurance. But it takes more endurance to work in a city than it does to climb a high mountain. It takes more endurance to crush the hopes and ambitions that were in your childhood dreams and to submit to a daily routine of work that fits into a tiny cog in the wheel of western civilisation. 'Really great mountaineers.' But what are mountaineers? Professional heroes of the west? Escapist parasites who play at adventures? Obsessive dropouts who do something different? Malcontents and egomaniacs who have not the discipline to conform?

"Will you answer this, Pete?"

"Oh yes, sorry."

Rita, one of the secretaries, was holding a 'phone out towards me. "Someone's ropes snapped, and the manufacturer says it isn't his fault."

"O.K. I'll deal with it." In the city, as on the mountain, there has to be a breaking point.

I had nearly died on Everest that September. With Sherpa Pertemba, I had been the last person to see Mick Burke, who had disappeared in the storm that swept over us during our descent from the summit. We had lost him on the summit ridge and it had been my decision to descend without him. But I had returned to the world isolated by a decision and experience I could not share. My internal resources had grown. At first, during the desperate struggle of the descent, I had a surge of panic. We nearly lost our way twice, and were constantly swept by avalanches in the blizzard, but then I felt myself go hard inside, go strong. My muscles and my will tightened like iron. I was indestructible and utterly alone. The simplicity of that feeling did not last beyond our arrival at Camp Six and the thirty-six hours of storm that followed. But I was to remember it in the months that followed.

Now back in Manchester, I was tired and depressed. My life had become dominated by one event. On Everest, the summit day had been presented to me by a large systematised expedition of over a hundred people. During the rest of the time on the mountain, I had been just part of the vertically integrated crowd control, waiting for the leader's call to slot me into my next allocated position. And yet, when I returned to Britain, as far as the general public were concerned I was one of the four heroes of the expedition, the surviving summiters. The applause rang hollow in my loneliness and the pressures of instant fame, although short-lived, made me ill. I yearned hopelessly for privacy so that I could digest the Everest experience. I longed for time to allow the thoughts which came to me in the early morning to take on form and meaning again.

I was now public property and, after eleven weeks away from the office, was left under no doubt that I had been allowed on my last expedition for a couple of years. I had sixteen committees to serve. Yet I felt in need of some new, great plan—some new project. I wanted to see how far I could push myself and find out what limits I could reach on a mountain. At the age of twenty-four there seemed so many mountain areas and adventures just within my grasp.

I was envious of Joe Tasker and Dick Renshaw's climb, not only because of the difficulty and beauty of the ridge they had climbed on Dunagiri, but also because I knew that two-man expeditions, in comparison with the Everest expedition, have a greater degree of flexibility and adventurous uncertainty and they generate a greater feeling of indispensability and self-containment.

Winter came; Joe Tasker walked into the office. He lived not far down the road, out of the city. I had not seen him since the early summer, when he had occasionally called in whilst organising his expedition.

"How's Dick getting on then, Joe?"

"He's got three black finger-tips—I don't know if he'll lose them or not. He'll be out of climbing action for quite a while. He flew home after three weeks in hospital at Delhi."

"Must have been an epic; how long have you been back?"

"Only a few days—the van died in Kabul and I had to hump all the gear home on buses."

A few weeks later it was Christmas time. I was at the end of days of travelling to meetings and lectures and was back amidst the telephones and typewriters, wilting under the headlong rush of urban life. Joe came in and sat down next to my desk.

Somehow, for Joe, the Shining Mountain had become more than just a backcloth to a hallucinatory ordeal.

"What do you think about having a go at the West Face of Changabang next year?"

I wished he had not asked so loud. Someone might hear him. "Yes, that would be good. Yes, I'd like to go; trouble is, I've just been off work for a long time on Everest—I don't think I'll ever get the time off for another trip next year."

Joe seemed surprised how readily I had shown my interest. I had agreed instinctively, flattered at his trust in me.

It was the Christmas party at the BMC and soon, upstairs in the pub, Joe was talking to Dennis. Then he came over.

"Dennis is really keen. He says, 'Leave it to me, lads'—thinks you might be able to get the time off, if the Committee of Management agree."

I didn't think they would, but kept quiet. I wasn't mentioning this to anyone. Joe's plans were sweeping me along.

There were now two fresh elements in my life. Joe Tasker and Changabang. I had never climbed with Joe, but was well aware of his reputation. We had met for the first time in the Alps in 1971, on the North Spur of the Droites. I was climbing with a friend, Martin Wragg, a fellow student at Nottingham University. We had started off on the route in darkness and had been intrigued to see two lights flickering a few hundred feet up the route. We passed them as dawn crept down the mountain—they were two English climbers who had been bivouacking—Joe Tasker and Dick Renshaw. 'Never heard of them,' I thought and climbed quickly on.

Martin and I were both too sure of ourselves, having climbed the North Face of the Matterhorn the week before. The Droites was badly out of condition, but we were young and inexperienced and kept on climbing as fast as we could. There was hard water ice everywhere, and I was forced to spend exhausting hours step cutting. But still these two climbers kept on close behind us. We couldn't shake clear of them. By late afternoon we had traversed onto the North Face, trying to find easier and less icy ground. It was snowing and I was exhausted. If the other two had not been behind us, or had turned back, we would have retreated many hours before. There were no ledges and Martin and I sat on each other's lap alternately through the night, while Joe and Dick bivouacked a little more comfortably a few hundred feet below. The following morning a storm broke and we teamed together to make twenty-two abseils back to the Argentière Glacier amidst streams of water, thunder and lightning. Once we reached the glacier, we split up.

I didn't see Joe for another four years.

During those four years Joe did a lot of climbing in the Alps, mainly with Dick, and steadily, in a matter-of-fact manner with complete disregard for the reputation of routes, achieved a staggering list of ascents, culminating in the East Face of the Grandes Jorasses in 1974 and the North Face of the Eiger in the winter of 1975.

After Christmas I went to North Wales to the hut of my local climbing club, the Mynydd, and confided to a friend about the Changabang plans—a blundering, stupid thing to do, for my girlfriend overheard me, and it was the first time she had heard the news. Before, it had been Everest that had obsessed me. By an almost mechanical transfer it was now Changabang.

I was living at home with my parents in early 1975. I asked Joe and Dick round to my parents' home for a meal. My mother, a keen reader of mountaineering magazines, laid on the full dining-room treatment. It was the first time my parents had met Joe or Dick. It was as if they were appraising Joe, examining the person who was taking their son away. Dick's fingers were still being treated and looked alarming. The unspoken question in the air was 'Joe's come out of the ordeal on Dunagiri without any scars—will he do this to Pete?' Throughout the meal, Dick was his usual quiet, polite self. Joe, however, was making digs and gibes about the size of the Everest expedition and the publicity it had received.

"I don't think the Everest climb was impressive as a climbing feat, but as an organisational one," he said.

I wondered if Joe must have resented the fact that I had been on Everest and not him. His achievement on Dunagiri had been formidable and far more futuristic in terms of the development of Alpine-style climbing in the Himalayas but, despite Dennis Gray's efforts, had received nothing like the recognition of the Everest climb. It was a naïve thought—I was being over-sensitive about Everest, and the sources of Joe's ambitions were a closed book to me. However it was obvious that rather than feeling satisfied with his Dunagiri climb, it was as if he still had an itch that needed to be satisfied.

After the meal Joe showed me the slides he had taken of the West Wall of Changabang, which he had taken from the summit of Dunagiri and from the Rhamani Glacier just above their base camp, as he had found melted water after the Dunagiri climb. Joe and Dick had been so exhausted and unbalanced by their descent that they had split up and descended the last 1,000 feet down different sides of the ridge. Joe had staggered beneath the wall alone. He had been beyond thoughts of climbing then. Vague plans only began to formulate in his head during the long journey home. Examining the slides carefully, I was impressed and daunted. The Face looked very steep and there were no continuous lines of weakness on it, only occasional patches of snow and ice between great blank areas of granite slabs and overhangs. This was Changabang.

Joe was not of the older mountaineering generation—on Everest I had felt in awe of the media images of climbers like Bonington, Scott and Haston—but here was someone with whom I could discuss the problems on equal terms.

"Where's this line then?" I asked.

Joe was taken aback. "Well, it just looks like an interesting Face—I mean it can't all be vertical—there's snow and ice on parts of it. Anyway, when you get close to a seemingly blank wall, there are usually some features on it." He mentioned ice slopes and pointed to shadowy lines which could indicate grooves and cracks. Our fingers hovered on the screen. Joe felt it was a crucial moment:

"Until I had a second opinion, I was not yet sure whether to regard it as a fanciful daydream or a feasible proposition. If Pete was sceptical about the feasibility of the project, the impetus would be lost and my belief in the venture would begin to wane. I wanted to draw from him some appraisal of the idea, but he was non-committal. I only realised slowly that his question arose not from doubt, but from interest—he was intrigued by the idea."

I knew I must go there. I began to wonder if I would come back from such a wild enterprise—to succeed seemed impossible.

"What do you think, Dick?" I asked.

"It looks as if it might go," said Dick. But then he did not have to try and prove it. My mind took a great leap and accepted the whole project.

This climb would be all that I wanted. Something that would be totally committing, that would bring my self-respect into line with the public recognition I had received for Everest. My experience on Everest had left an emotional gap that needed to be filled. The BMC had agreed that I could take another two weeks' holiday on top of my four-week allowance to go and attempt it. I longed for the summer to arrive, and saw the long, intervening months as time to be endured.

Meanwhile, Joe was doing most of the work for the expedition. The first problem was to obtain permission from the Indian Government to make an attempt. Some Lakeland climbers were planning a route for the South Face and already had permission. Joe set about trying to persuade them and the Indians to allow us to go. Neither was happy at first. Joe, however, had powerful friends in India and, despite an early discouraging letter from the Indian Mountaineering Foundation that said, "We do feel that a team of two climbers attempting a peak like Changabang will be unsafe", friendly persuasion was applied and the permission eventually arrived not long before we left. The Mount Everest Foundation gave us a modest grant, after several members of the committee had expressed the sentiment "that a team of four might be more advisable". All this was fuel to Joe, encouragement to his awkwardness when faced with obstructions. An iconoclast by nature, he had no respect for the cults and legends that surround personalities and preconceptions in the mountaineering world.

I met Ted Rogers, one of the Lakeland team, whilst out climbing on Stanage Edge in Derbyshire one weekend. I asked him if they minded us going to the other side of the mountain. After all, they had been planning their expedition for nearly two years. Our organisation, in contrast, was at the last minute. His reply was rather guarded.

"Joe usually seems to get his way," he said.

2

Chris Bonington was the patron of their expedition and he had told Ted that he considered Joe's and my plans as 'preposterous'. "Still," he added to us at a later date, "if you do get up, it'll be the hardest route in the Himalayas."

On occasion through the spring, Joe and I met to discuss our plans for the expedition. Joe had acquired a temporary job working nights in a frozen food distribution centre in Salford. Every night he was in a huge cold store for several hours, where the temperature was between $-15°C$ and $-20°C$. Much to the amazement of his workmates, who were always well wrapped up, he worked without his gloves on for most of the time, loading small electric trucks from the corridors of racking laden with frozen vegetables, meat, fish, ice-cream, cream cakes, chocolate éclairs—everything to cater for today's pre-packed way of life. It was not an enthralling occupation, but it meant that he was at home in the daytime and could attend to the work needed to organise the expedition during the day. He dashed about in a dilapidated car, stereo blaring wildly, his thoughts full of Changabang and his talk full of lurid stories about the complicated love lives of his fellow shift workers.

During snatched moments of spare time, I read books about the exploration of the area of the Garhwal, in which Changabang stands. I started by reading *The Ascent of Nanda Devi* by Bill Tilman, about the successful expedition to the highest mountain in India in 1936. I had the strange feeling that I had read it before. Then I realised that the book I had read before was Eric Shipton's *Nanda Devi*, in which he described the adventures that he and Tilman had met the year before, when they first penetrated the high ring of peaks that guard Nanda Devi and reached the Sanctuary at its foot.

They were the first human beings to reach there, and the story had a Shangri La quality to it, touching far back into the promised land of my subconscious. I had read the book when I was thirteen. Tilman's book jerked my memory and I re-read the book, in particular the passages where Shipton makes his first steps into the inner Sanctuary of the Nanda Devi Basin:

At each step I experienced that subtle thrill which anyone of imagination must feel when treading hitherto unexplored country. Each corner held some thrilling secret to be revealed for the trouble of looking. My most blissful dream as a child was to be in some such valley, free to wander where I liked, and discover for myself some hitherto unrevealed glory of Nature. Now, the reality was no less wonderful than that half-forgotten dream.

The words bumped around inside my head like a bell which had only just stopped ringing. Here was a subtle relationship between real place and mental landscape. I was becoming a willing victim of the spell of the Garhwal.

The mountaineer of today cannot hope to capture that feeling. Today's frontiers are not of promised lands, of uncrossed passes and mysterious valleys beyond. Numbers of ascents of many mountains in the Himalayas are now into their teens. Today, the exploring mountaineer must look at the unclimbed faces and ridges and bring the equipment, techniques and attitudes developed over the past forty years, rather than the long axe and the plane table. There are so many ways, so much documentation, that only the mountaineer's inner self remains the uncharted.

Changabang had been climbed for the first time in 1974, by a joint British-Indian Expedition led by Chris Bonington. Like all wise first ascensionists of Himalayan peaks, they chose the easiest, most accessible line—the South-East Ridge. In June, Joe and I heard the news that a six-man Japanese expedition had climbed the South-West Ridge. They had used traditional siege tactics—six climbers had used 8,000 feet of fixed rope, three hundred pitons, one hundred and twenty expansion bolts in the thirty-three days it had taken them to climb the South-West Ridge. This news was, for us, surprisingly encouraging. We were beginning to think—from the comments of other British climbers—that Changabang was unclimbable by any other route except the original. Chris Bonington had announced our plans to the mountaineering public at the National Mountaineering Conference, and this had provoked a lot of comment.

"You'll never get up that wall, you know," said Nick Estcourt.

"I don't think so either," said Dave Pearce, "but I think it's great that two of you are going to have a go."

"It doesn't look like a married man's route," said Ken Wilson, editor of *Mountain Magazine*.

We consulted all the British members of the first Changabang climb.

"You'll have your time cut out," said Dougal Haston.

Joe asked Doug Scott for his opinion of the chances of climbing the Face, looking for some sort of reassurance.

"Beyond the bounds of possibility, youth."

"Well, you've got to go and have a look."

"Yes, youth, you're right. I'd take an extra jumper with you though," then—two days later—'phoned Joe up to ask if he might come. We were bent on a two-man attempt and to have more would increase opinions and divide the purpose of the unit. Just two of us would make the dangers and decisions deliciously uncomplicated.

On one, well-oiled night in the Padarn Lake Hotel in Llanberis, Brian Hall staggered across: "I think it's great that just two people have got permission for a route like that—it shows that the Indian Mountaineering Foundation are at last beginning to move with the times. But if something happens to you it will mess things up for people who want to go on small expeditions in the future."

Meanwhile, Joe Tasker was asking Joe Brown about the difficult rock climbing he had just done at 20,000 feet on Trango Tower in the Karakoram. When he told Joe about our plans, the veteran Brown wrinkled his oriental eyes with a calm born of experience and said, "Just the two of you? Sounds like cruelty to me." The consensus of opinion was that we stood no chance at all of succeeding; only close friends thought that we would do more than make a noble effort before retreating.

Don Whillans, however, was encouraging. He himself had planned to go to Changabang in 1968, with a team including Ian Clough and Geoff Birtles, and Don lent Joe and me a number of pictures of the West Face he had acquired from various sources. He looked at one of them and, planting a stubby finger on the icefield in the middle said, "Well, you'll be able to climb that all right—you'll just have to get to the bottom of it, and then from the top of it up that rock wall above it." He ended by summarising the situation neatly:

"Well," he said, "there's three things that could happen: you could fail, you could get up it, or you could not come back. You'll just have to make sure you come back, won't you?"

It was obviously something special we were going to try and climb. Neither of us felt particularly immortal, or that our gifts transcended those of all around us. We would just need a lot of determination and steadiness of nerve. Also, it was clear, looking at the pictures, that if we were to be able to keep on performing, committed, high up on that wall for days on end, we would have to select our equipment with absolute care. High on the Wall, we would not be able to afford to carry anything superfluous. We had no detailed logistical plan, but were preparing for various eventualities.

Dunagiri, 1975. *Above*, Joe on the snow band entering the bottom of the rock barrier (DR). *Below left*, climbing the rock barrier (DR). *Below right*, Joe on the summit of Dunagiri (DR).

Changabang, 1976. *Above*, the massive inhospitable face of the West Wall (JT). *Below left*, first steps on the Bagini Ridge (JT). *Below right*, Pete approaching the overhangs of the Barrier (JT).

Pete coming up the steep granite wall. Changabang Camp 1 is the small dot on the left of the ridge below (JT).

Joe coming up the edge of the ice field, with the Rhamani Glacier, below, curling past Rishi Kot into the Rishi Ganga (PB).

Above, four-star recovery at Base Camp (PB).
Below, the first hammock bivouack, Joe suspended from 8mm terylene (PB).

Above, Joe at Changabang Camp 2 with Tibet beyond (PB) and, *below*,
threading himself through the Keyhole (PB).

Tragedy on K2, 1978. *Above*, Nick Estcourt leads the way up to Camp 1 at sunrise (JT). *Below*, Doug Scott re-crossing the slope now swept clear by the avalanche which engulfed Nick. Marks in the snow, lower left, are where Doug landed and stopped when the rope snapped (JT).

The Snow Mountains of New Guinea, 1978. *Above*, proud Dani warriors, the fiercest and most ruthless of the Irian tribes (PB). *Below left*, a Moni man with a locally made axe-head (PB). *Below right*, Hilary climbing through the mist above the melting ice of Carstensz South Face (PB).

One of the main problems would be bivouacking. There did not appear to be many ledges on the Face—certainly none more than a couple of feet wide. So we persuaded Troll Mountain Products, in Oldham, to develop some hammocks for us. Single point suspension hammocks have been in use for some years, on the sun-drenched high rock walls of California, but they had not been used at high altitude in the Himalayas before. Troll made us two pilot models with a canopy and Joe and I tried them out one night on Scout Crag in Langdale, in the Lake District. We waited till it was dark—the pub had thrown us out and everyone had gone to bed—before creeping up the field and fighting our way inside the folds of material. It was a bad night, particularly after it started to rain. When dawn came we packed up quickly, feeling rather self-conscious dressed in high-altitude suits and wearing double boots in early May. I met some friends walking up the path.

"You're up early, Pete," they said.

"Mmmmm."

Joe and I decided that Langdale was not the best place to test our gear. It was too wet, warm and crowded.

The thought came with a rush. We needed to try the hammocks out somewhere really cold. Already we had ideas for modifications, but the real test had to be in sub-zero temperatures to find out how effective sleeping bags were squashed within the nylon walls of the hammocks. What about the cold store where Joe worked? Since the lads on the shift already regarded Joe as slightly eccentric, the approach to the manager was made very secretly. He was bewildered but agreed, although he had worries in case there was an accident—yes, we could try out our hammocks by spending a night there.

By this time my girlfriend had given me up in disgust in the face of all this fanatical dedication. Joe took me under his bachelor wing, promising me an introduction to the Manchester social scene. We went to the pictures and then to the pub, where we sank a few pints of ale before picking up the gear from the house where two tolerant friends were harbouring Joe in between his travels. Before leaving we rang up the security guard at the cold store, to check that the manager had left the key for us to get in. He had not, and had not even told the security guard anything about our plans. It was 11.30 p.m. and the beer had not helped Joe's clarity of speech and, at first, the guard was disbelieving.

"What, two of you sleeping here, hanging from a million pounds' worth of frozen food?" Gradually, however, he was convinced, and the absence of the key would be sorted out. "Leave it to me," he said.

At the cold store it was the night off for the shift and the security guard was the only person there. We bribed him to keep quiet with a bottle of beer and he opened up the great fridge doors after we had donned all our equipment.

"I'll open it up at six in the morning," he said. "You can sleep in that corner if you want, above the ice-cream."

At first the cold was stunning. We stumbled and thrashed around, getting inside the hammocks, standing on crates of cheesecakes and holding onto pallets of ice-lollies. Soon we were lashed to the girders that held up tons of ice-cream, our feet swinging wildly above our heads as we tried to remove our boots. After about an hour we were settled in. Then Joe started moaning. He wanted to go to the toilet, having drunk too much beer. I told him gleefully that he'd have to wait until 6.00 a.m. I was Everest-trained, and had got my plastic pee bottle for emergencies.

It was a surreal night. The lights inside were turned on and the freezer hummed monotonously. Halfway through the night there was a great rumbling noise and I woke, convinced that the hammock was toppling to the ground with all the crates avalanching onto me. In a panic, I slid out of the hammock and dropped six feet, on to the ground, still inside my sleeping bag – to realise that the noise had just been the freezer generating.

At 6.00 a.m. Joe slipped outside to relieve himself and sat chatting to the security guard. The first member of the day shift arrived and went inside to start cleaning up. He walked up and down each aisle, sweeping the place clean. I was still inert in my bright red hammock – and the workman noticed its enormous sausage shape above his head and passed on; he went outside to Joe and the guard:

"Hey, what sort of new food's that, hung in the ice-cream aisle?"

Coming out from the icy confines of the store, into the grey summer's morning was like stepping into a hot bath.

After that session Joe took the hammocks to Troll and had them fully insulated. He even persuaded one of the young seamstresses there to join him inside one to see if they would hold the weight of two. Meanwhile, a friend of mine who works in an engineering factory, devoted some of his research time to turning out some aluminium spacer bars so that the hammocks wouldn't crush us and the sleeping bags. Pete Hutchinson of Mountain Equipment, another local Manchester firm, designed special lightweight down jackets and sleeping bags. He made them longer than usual, so that we could, in an emergency, get into them with our boots on. We told them weight could be a matter of life and death so, under our instructions, they used such thin material that the down found little difficulty in getting out. We were to be accompanied on our climb by floating fluff! As an outer sleeping bag for the hammocks, we took artificial fibre bags. These would retain their insulating properties after many days of condensation — we would not have any drying facilities on the route!

We spent another two nights in the fridge before we were satisfied. If anyone — climbers — asked us, "What's this rumour — that you're training in a cold store?" we would reply, "You must be joking!"

Joe and I also selected our climbing equipment with care. Ian Stewart, who had been one of the cameramen on the Everest climb, provided a one-piece suit and double boots for Joe. We decided to take full body harnesses, because we would be carrying heavy loads up very steep rock and would risk turning upside down without their support.

The possibility of an accident was one that worried us intensely. "I know it sounds horrifying, the idea of just two of you, out there alone," said Joe, "but once you're actually climbing it doesn't feel any more committing than when you're doing a big route in the Alps. Still, we ought to be prepared for emergencies."

I was worried in case I let Joe down, and he was probably worried about the same thing. I had been on a two-man expedition in 1974, to the Central Alaskan Range with Roger O'Donovan. At first, this had been very successful and Roger and I had made the first ascent of the South Face of Mount Dan Beard. After that we had attempted Mount McKinley, but had been forced to turn back when Roger had become ill. I was intensely disappointed. On a two-man expedition, if one of you becomes ill, or is injured, you have to give up and come home. There is no alternative. Alaska and the Himalayas are long distances to travel for that sort of disappointment to occur. Joe and I were determined to be prepared for any medical emergencies.

Joe knew a doctor, Andy Hill, from his student climbing days, and Andy helped arrange all our medical supplies. On the various medicines he supplied for us he labelled clear, idiot-proof instructions such as "For sore bum, three up daily". He had us practising stitching and injecting oranges, instead of each other. We also made a visit to a local casualty ward and, under the watchful guidance of nurses, plastered up each other's arms. We were taking our training seriously.

Joe couldn't understand why I wasn't becoming flustered about the

organisation for the expedition. I would just shake my head and pronounce, with irritating condescension, "It's nothing like organising for
Everest." Not that I had much to do with the organisation for Everest.
But now I was so wound up with my work for the BMC, dealing with
access problems, answering 'phone calls and letters, that I could only
provide Joe with occasional consultancy and encouragement. Also, it
was turning into one of the hottest summers in living memory in
Britain, and I was keen on doing some rock climbing. Joe's temporary
job in the cold store gave him a bleak, twilight existence and none of
his social hours coincided with anybody else's. He lived a half-life of
permanent semi-awakedness. At weekends he tried to adjust to being
awake all day, and then rush back to be at work for 10.00 p.m. on
Sunday night. We tried climbing together a few times, in North Wales
and the Peak District, but I tended to take the rock-climbing less
casually than Joe and kept out-climbing him and, at one point, we
decided on a 'trial separation' for a few weekends! I knew full well
that as soon as we were in the big hills Joe would click into action. Joe
was also confident that we could get on well together:

> "We often engaged in articulate gibing sessions with each other
> which often caused people to wonder that we should be going on
> an expedition together. On the other hand, it was useful to
> establish a good-humoured openness as a safety valve for when
> pressures should build up. If we could voice our thoughts it was
> likely that any tensions could be defined before they became
> destructive.
> "There were revealing moments, such as one weekend in
> Glencoe, when we were still warmly ensconced in our sleeping
> bags at 1.00 p.m. on a rainy afternoon, wondering which of us
> was going to have the drive to carry us up Changabang if we
> couldn't even get out of our tent on a wet, Scottish weekend.
> We must have shamed ourselves into action because we did reach
> the East Face of Aonach Dubh, to find that the rock was not too
> wet to climb on and completed three routes before the mad dash
> down to fit in a drink at the Clachaig before closing time."

I started doing some training runs. I had, by this time, moved into
my own home in New Mills in Derbyshire. This was right on the edge
of the Peak District, and there was only one row of houses between my
house and open moorland. Often, in the long northern light of the

evenings, I would go running up there, or I would go out with local climbing friends on the gritstone edges of the area. Gritstone always gave my favourite climbing, and I would turn to it for reassurance as to an old friend. Such evening exercise, after a long hot day in the office, helped to clear my mind; but only for a while. I needed to get away, to rediscover the clarity of focusing all my effort, concentration and skill on one big obstacle.

The thousands of tiny little pressures of urban life were closing in on me. Occasionally I had to make trips down to meetings in London. On one occasion, my train times dictated that I was early, and I strolled through Green Park and sat down under a horse-chestnut tree and wrote: "Life at the moment seems claustrophobic and narrowing, like Kafka's short story about the mouse being chased down a tunnel. It brings an increasing mixture of motives and complications. It's become an increasing struggle to rediscover a single-minded purpose and drive, and the freedom to move. Time races, absolutely races by, when you're in a job like mine. So many 'phone calls, little problems, papers to read, papers to write. Having a house, I suppose, multiplies the snags of life. Yet if I'm restlessly worrying about them, doing little jobs, continually concerning myself with all these problems, surely the spirit, the soul of life, will glide by unseen, as a deep current."

We booked a cheap flight to Delhi for the 22nd August. As the departure date grew nearer, the full consequences of going on a big trip to the Himalaya made their impact. I seriously doubted if I was going to come back. Joe and I threw a wild party at my house in New Mills, and invited all those who had helped us prepare for our expedition — and anyone else we could think of. An anxious curiosity not to miss anything kept us up drinking and dancing until daylight. After clearing the debris, we drove down to Charlie and Ruth Clarke's in London.

Charlie had been one of the doctors on the Everest expedition. His house exuded a relaxed calm. We had sent some food with the Lakeland team overland, some hardware with another overland trekker, and most of the gear by air. Now, we only had a few odds and ends to stuff into our rucksacks. Charlie, and Ruth, heavily pregnant, and Sheridan, their dog, reclined amusedly as we packed in their back garden under the hot sun. Four of my friends had come from New Mills to see me off. A young lady appeared at London Heathrow Airport to say goodbye to Joe. Once in the airport, the atmosphere changed and became tense and expectant. I couldn't think of anything to say to my friends. We had arrived at the last minute and the airline had overbooked on places. Jostling with many Asians in the queue, we were feeling hot and incongruous in our down jackets and double boots, which we were wearing to take precious weight out of our luggage. At last we got our places sorted out for the 'plane and stumbled through the barrier, with the inadequate sense that our last goodbyes had been awkward and self-conscious, and quite unrepresentative of our feelings.

I thought of these last vivid days in Britain many times during the weeks that followed. The memories circled around my mind as I walked up the glacier and lay down in the cold, during the long nights.

The Rim of the Sanctuary

22nd August–7th September

The humidity and crowds of monsoon August in Delhi sap your will to think and move. Joe and I were lying sweltering on grubby bunk beds in a doss house down Janpath Lane. Above us, a large fan hung from the cracked ceiling, swinging limply like a wounded bird. The manager of the place was unctuous and creepy — he didn't seem to trust us, so we didn't feel we could trust him. We wanted to move out as soon as possible.

Joe had stayed in a similar place on his way to and from Dunagiri the year before. The previous time I had been in Delhi had been with the Everest expedition, when we had stopped there for two days on the way back from Nepal. Joe and I were trying to climb Changabang on a budget of about £1,400, whereas the Everest Expedition had been sponsored by Barclays Bank International to a sum of £113,000. Then we had stayed in a five-star hotel, which cost 150 rupees each person per night. This time our accommodation was costing us seven rupees a night.

A girl came in wearing Indian clothes, talking in a London accent and scratching her backside. She had been living in a leaf hut in Malari with her boyfriend, surviving by rolling marihuana and selling it to westerners. She had come to Delhi for a gamma globulin injection against hepatitis.

"I've brought my own needle," she said. She had a slight figure and coughed heavily. Occasionally, during conversation, she would pause and rush to the toilet. "It's O.K.," she said, "I'm just being sick. I took too much opium in Old Delhi last night." She must have been about eighteen years old.

We walked through the streets. It was hot and muggy and sweat poured off us. A deep breath gave no ventilation. Everywhere were great placards and slogans, for India was at the height of the Emergency.

Their English language tricked us into half-familiarity and emphasised our remoteness from the problems of the sub-continent. 'Plant a tree', 'Only two children', 'Root out corruption', 'There is no substitute for hard work', 'Savings will help you'. Across the back of one crowded bus was written 'Talk less, work more'. Yes, I longed for action. For weeks now, in the preparation of our expedition, we'd had to tell people what we were planning to do and explain how we were going to do it. But deep inside, this had all felt hollow. I did not really believe that we were going to do the route at all. I wanted to stop talking and start some action.

Joe had some friends, Tony and Rosemary Beaumont, who lived near London. Tony Beaumont was one of the directors of an international company, Guest Keen & Nettlefolds, which had a sister company, Guest Keen Williams, with an office in New Delhi. This branch had helped Joe the previous year, and it had been friends of the Beaumonts in India who had presented our request for permission to climb Changabang to the Indian Mountaineering Foundation in person. Having raced in the Monte Carlo Rally, and taken part in ocean races themselves, the Beaumonts were in sympathy with the spirit of our project and we were indebted to them. So we went in to the office in Parliament Street, to renew acquaintances. J. D. Kapoor was there, beaming a welcome. Walking off the teeming monsoon streets into an air-conditioned office was like walking back into western reality, from the foreign into the familiar. J. D. accepted us immediately. He pressed a buzzer and refreshing drinks appeared.

"How can I help you?" he said.

It was a happy, friendly office and they helped us a lot, since there was a great deal of expertise there to assist us short circuit the bureaucratic networks of the Indian customs and excise. However, it still took us two days of trailing around long, impotent corridors of Kafkaesque bureaucracy to obtain the final papers that would release our air-freighted equipment from the airport. Everyone was always very polite and friendly, and presented us with cups of tea, but everywhere they would patiently explain away delays by saying that they were 'just adhering to the system'. If we complained they would just turn their eyes upwards helplessly and explain, "But it was you British who taught us these procedures." Perhaps my long hair and Joe's curly mop, and our denim jeans and plimsolls, did not give us the best appearance for obtaining co-operation from officialdom. One day we waited for two hours in the Customs office for a document to receive interminable counter-signatures. Above our heads hung a framed quote by Jawahar-lal Nehru: "I am not interested in excuses for delay, I am interested only in a thing done."

Modern India has many faces. It has its ghettoes for the rich as well as for the poor. One of the attractions for me about going on an expedition is that it brings a sense of purpose to travel and tourism. It is the experiences below the snow line, with the people of the country as much as the climbing, that one remembers on returning to the west. You see all the sides of a country if you are trying to get something done, or if you are actually trying to organise something complicated in it. You learn a lot if you have to try to arrange insurance, buy enormous quantities of food, move large amounts of gear by local transport and hire porters who speak only a Himalayan dialect. All this brings you into close contact with the country — a contact that is often closer than that of some of the people who live there.

We collected some gear that a friend had left with an upper-class Indian family. The woman of the house talked with the airs of a Kensington lady Tory, with the blinkered aloofness of aristocracy. I felt uncomfortable talking to her, because Joe was in one of his off-hand moods. He had switched off, and it looked rude. I murmured a few platitudes and eventually we escaped past the servants and guard dogs, out of the colony of rich houses, into a taxi and back to the streets.

We also borrowed some equipment that was mouldering away in a cupboard in the flat of an Englishman employed by a bank. When we went to collect it, we talked to this lone Englishman — he was about our age. He was losing interest in life in the heat and sweat, and was full of complaints about his flat. It seemed palatial to us. Servants were cheap and his salary was just spending money. His social life was confined to the insular English community in the capital. Occasionally, Indians asked him around for a meal, he said, but sooner or later they brought the conversation around to the possibility of a loan. He seemed to live an antiseptic life, away from the living warmth, smells and hospitality of village India.

It was always back on the pavements that the culture shock, the abruptness with which the aeroplane had transported us from the west, hit us. This was the real India — muggy, smelly, with small children pulling at my clothes, and pointing pathetically at their small baby brothers and sisters. Many impressions, memories, smells, sights and feelings of my previous trips to Nepal and Afghanistan returned; as if they had lain dormant, forgotten, during the rush of life in England.

Now everything flooded back and started to feel real—as though I had never been away or had been living two lives.

We went to a tea room and ordered a meal. It was the cheapest place in Connaght Circus and we had peered at the kitchen behind the curtain.

"We'd better stay off meat here," said Joe. Glasses of water came in. "Cholera cocktails," said Joe. We reeled off all the stock jokes of Europeans on the loose in Asia.

We seemed to be at a stopping place of the Hippy trail across India. Or, perhaps, the end of the trail for some. There were a few Australians and New Zealanders here—sporting stronger currency, but mainly Europeans and Indians sat at the tables. On the floor crouched an Indian, dressed in brown, sweeping a large wet rag across the floor. He moved it quickly around tables and people's legs. I watched him, fascinated. He seemed completely oblivious to life in the tea room above him. His vision went no further than the rag in front of him. I wondered what he was thinking about. Then a European approached us and started chatting. I talked to him. Joe looked suspicious. He was an Austrian and spoke very good English. Slowly, he spun out a long sob story about how he had ended up in New Delhi. His Embassy would not help him—they were besieged by such cases. All he needed was the train fare to Benares—he was pleading with us, as fellow Europeans, to help him. I was taken in, and was about to offer him some money, which we could not really afford to do. I have a fear of confronting people—a cowardice, perhaps. But Joe said to the Austrian:

"No, I've got absolutely no sympathy for you. There are millions of people in India who need help and money more than you, and I think it's pathetic for a European to come out here and end up in a state like you. What do you think the Indians think of us, when we come begging towards them. If I had any money, I'd rather give it to an Indian who really was in need."

The next problem, after the equipment had been extricated from Customs, was to find our liaison officer. The Garhwal Himalaya, the area in which Changabang lies, had been closed to foreigners for fifteen years owing to border troubles with China, and a dispute over grazing grounds on the Niti Pass, to the north of the Garhwal, had been one of the many issues that had started the cold war in 1954. Since the area was re-opened in March, 1974, expeditions other than those involving Indian mountaineers have only been allowed into the area if accompanied by a liaison officer—usually a member of the armed forces with some mountaineering experience. One of his duties, presumably, is to make sure the expedition does not stray over the 'Inner Line' (the area close to the Chinese/Tibetan border, inside which all travel is restricted), and to make sure that expeditions aren't working undercover, masquerading as mountaineering whilst photographing military installations or even, as is rumoured to have happened some years ago (although the device was avalanched), installing listening devices to monitor the Chinese over the border.

Our Customs papers, peak booking, and liaison officer had to be negotiated through the Indian Mountaineering Foundation. Mountaineering in India is still mostly done by the armed forces, and the IMF has its offices in the Military Defence block. To reach them you had to sign for a pass. They were situated in the corner of one overgrown block. There, Mr. Munshi Ram, the small, bald-headed, fussy secretary of the IMF, would beam a welcome and greet us in his high-pitched whine whenever we went around with some new problems. He found it difficult to accept the fact that neither of us wanted to call himself the leader. It did not seem necessary to us, since there were only two of us. He suggested that we took on a trekking and travel agent to organise the Customs entry and the transport and final porterage of our gear. The travel agents are parasites who profit from the slow wheels of the Indian systems and make a lot of money out of the most straightforward arrangements. They hover in the wings until their unfortunate victim is at his wits' end, trying to deal with the seemingly endless stream of problems, and then offer their help – at a price. But Joe had managed without them before and would manage without them again!

At last, at 5.00 p.m. on the 26th August, we met our liaison officer, Flight Lieutenant D. N. Palta, a pilot of the Indian Air Force. He had hoped to be returning to his wife and family in Chandigarh, 150 miles away, but had been diverted at the last minute to taking charge of us. In his early thirties, with a trim moustache, he was polite, well-spoken and serious, and from another world to Joe and me. He had a profound sense of duty to life and to the people of India that made me feel frivolous, anarchic and self-indulgent in comparison.

One of the obligations in having a liaison officer is that you feed and clothe him and pay for his transport. That evening Palta came around to our 'guest house'. He was visibly taken aback by the squalor we were living in, but said nothing. The boots we had brought for him were much too big and I felt embarrassed at the tatty clothing we gave him. It was functional, but was old gear that Joe and I had used in the past.

I felt uneasy that Joe and I were not living up to Palta's idea of 'an expedition'. As Palta left with his bundle of equipment, the manager of the 'guest house' tried to arrest him—he thought some illicit trading had been going on.

That night a rat ran over my stomach, quickly followed by another one in hot pursuit. Across the corridor, two emaciated Americans were talking. They were frightening sights of deteriorating humanity, all nerves and inarticulate, scattered intensity. A Canadian in the bed next to me was ill with a high fever.

The following day we went to the Superbazaar to buy most of our food supplies. There we trooped round in a trio, selecting rice, sugar and other basic commodities. It was useful to have three people there to carry things, but each acquisition became an abnormally complicated ritual of suggestion, agreement, reaffirmation, recalculation and further discussion. Joe and I were more used to dividing up tasks to be done and going about our separate ways to do them. With Palta there, eager to help, we felt we had to take note of his suggestions, otherwise he would feel shunned and dissatisfied.

The days when it was thought necessary to equip an expedition totally with food and equipment in Britain before it set out have now passed. Delhi has large shops, and few foods are unobtainable there. By the evening, we had everything packed into strong, cardboard boxes, rucksacks and kit-bags. We piled all the stuff into two taxis and careered towards Old Delhi railway station, surrounded by heaving carts, ancient buses and wandering scooters. One of the taxis brushed a man off a bicycle. There was a lot of shouting but no one was hurt. Soon we were back into the swirling chaos of hooting, shouting and screeching, where it was a matter of principle not to give way.

If we had been a big expedition we would just have hired one large truck, piled it with all the gear, and driven it three hundred miles to the mountains. Instead, we were to have the fun and excitement of moving sixteen items of luggage for that distance on various styles of local transport. It was a big money-saver, too, for now we were fairly money-conscious, calculating carefully so that we could get to the mountains and back.

All railway stations in India seem to have three times as many people in the booking halls and on the platforms than can possibly hope to squeeze onto a train. Among the crowds were whole families, just sitting or lying down, seemingly with nowhere to go. The poor lighting, dirt, the steam, the hooting trains and the crowds gave an atmosphere of turmoil. Some red-shirted porters rolled our gear onto a huge trolley and wheeled it onto our platform via two lifts and a tunnel under the lines. The tunnel was just on the water level, and there was water streaming down the walls to mingle with the heaving, sweating bodies of the porters.

"If Hell's like this, it must be quite exciting," said Joe.

I never ceased to be amazed by the number of people in the east. Thousands on the stations, on the roads, crowds and crowds melting away into the streets and darkness, sleeping on pavements and against walls.

The great steam train pulled us northwards through the night. The excitement, noise and dramatic strength, I remembered from childhood. When dawn came the plains of India were behind us. The early morning slanting light outlined shrub-covered foothills and ridges, and the air was cool. Despite the trials and tribulations of the journey, I was enjoying myself and feeling cheerful and relaxed. Now we were actually moving towards the mountains, all we could do was to meet each problem as it arose, as one of the early explorers of the Garhwal Range, Tom Longstaff, had advised: "The traveller must learn to live every moment in the present." This fiery, red-bearded explorer of the early 1900s had been the guru of the young mountaineers of the 1930s. Joe and I talked about him a lot.

From Hardwar railway station we went across to the bus terminus. There were large crowds of people around. As in most crowds, we felt that there would inevitably be people among them that we couldn't trust. When there are only three of you, it is very difficult to move equipment and guard it at the same time, so you start off with all the gear in one pile. Then someone carries part of it to where you're trying to get to, starts a second pile and guards it. That morning I was out-manoeuvred. Joe and Palta appointed themselves guards and I found myself rushing between the two of them, carrying all the gear.

In 1905 and 1907, when Tom Longstaff had led his expeditions towards the Nanda Devi Sanctuary, he had started his long walk to the mountain from the plains. In the 1930s, Bill Tilman and Eric Shipton had started only a couple of weeks away from the mountains at Ranikhot. Joe and I were travelling by bus to within a few days' walk of the area.

From Hardwar we caught the bus to Rishikesh. There we moved to the next bus station on a pony and trap. The trap was so heavily weighed down it threatened to lift the pony into the air. Now we were on the main Hindu pilgrim trail, moving north towards the three sacred shrines of Gangotri, Kedarnath and Badrinath. From Rishikesh we took the bus to Srinagar. Here we had missed the last bus to Joshimath and so checked in at a Government-run pilgrim shed. The man in charge of the shed insisted that we filled in forms, giving many details about ourselves. This was probably quite a reasonable request, but forms and papers and regulations make me feel uneasy, particularly when I am on a climbing trip. They seem so futile and obstructive.

"Some control of movement is necessary," explained Palta, "and every town has a Government health service clinic and supplies inspector."

Although there were only boards to sleep on in the shed, it was clean and had washrooms. India demands adjustment—slowly I was becoming used to being perpetually surrounded by crowds, gawping at us and following our every movement. It was taking me many days to adapt to this shift of continents and to start thinking clearly and feeling normal.

By afternoon the monsoon sun was hot and heavy. After a rest, and feeling lethargic in the heat, we went shopping. It took a long time. In Britain I avoid shopping whenever possible. I just dash into the nearest shop and buy the closest equivalent they provide to what I want. Palta, however, refusing to be hurried, insisted that we did a comparative survey of all the prices and quality of merchandise that the various shops had to offer first. In the bazaar, there were shops, stalls and areas created for every trade, skill and need. We walked past a barber, grain merchant, shoemaker and tea maker. We were in a time machine, moving back to Dickens and beyond, back to Hogarth.

The pace of life in Srinagar was slow. It took a long time to select and buy our graded grains of sugar—we hadn't any ration cards.

"Look, you chaps," said Palta, "I think you should sort all your food into man rations, otherwise you won't know how much to buy." The simplest calculations easily confuse me and I winced at this.

"We'll buy a big sackful," said Joe.

One shopkeeper, sitting cross-legged behind his wares, refused to sell us a can of paraffin. Palta translated the reason. "He says he is a god-fearing man and cannot sell us so much." Palta persuaded him by writing an official letter.

Joe and I had a matter-of-fact relationship. Joe's phenomenal memory for telephone numbers and names made me feel dreamy by comparison. We talked always about the next problem. We didn't often discuss any central issues of mankind. I was never quite sure if Joe was above or below that sort of intense discussion. He had studied to be a priest between the ages of thirteen and twenty-one—a restricted, cloistered existence against which he had eventually rebelled. But some motivation and belief must have been there once. One of Palta's first reactions, on seeing Joe's gentle face, curly hair and beard and blue eyes, was that he should apply for an audition for *Jesus Christ Superstar*! When Palta joined the two of us, it brought a shift in the topics of conversation. That evening, after tea, we discussed books, films and the value of mountaineering. Palta just couldn't understand why we were devoting all our time and energy towards climbing a superfluous rock in the middle of the Himalayas. To him, intelligent, highly trained and living in India, his country's problems presented all the challenges that an educated man could want. He had his country to defend against very real enemies, and a wife and family to support. Listening to him I felt very young. Perhaps Joe, I thought, three years older than me, would come up with something interesting to reply with. He didn't. A restless, confident individualist, he didn't offer any justifications. Perhaps he hadn't had to answer such questions before, or didn't feel any need to. But I had practice. Having climbed Everest and working for the British Mountaineering Council, I was used to explaining about mountaineering to people who knew little about it, to answering questions that sounded naïve to a mountaineer's ear. Also, attendance at numerous committee meetings had taught me to be a social chameleon—to smile and nod. I felt in the middle of this discussion. I knew we would soon be so interdependent that we couldn't afford to disagree too violently. Perhaps Palta was beginning to sense the seriousness of our objective, from the discussions that Joe and I were having together. I flinched as Joe explained to him that this climb would be, for us two, a culmination of many years of application and experience and that there was not the slightest possibility of him joining the actual climb. Palta was beginning to realise that he would be joining us in total isolation.

"It's a pity we haven't radios so that we can contact each other and civilisation," he said.

As I lay in my sleeping bag that night I, too, was beginning to realise. There would be no more ranks to throw at the mountain. Play it close to the wicket, a friend had said before we left home. Next door, many pilgrims were snoring.

It rained heavily during the night and became quite cold. In the morning, as we waited for the bus to Joshimath, there were thousands of flies crawling and buzzing everywhere, reminding me of the obscene imagery of *Othello*. Mist and cloud curled around the forested hills about us. Flowers and leaves dripped heavy with rain. I couldn't name any of them. Flora and fauna are so varied, immeasurable in India. There was a dappled variation of light and shade in the clouds, with horizontal breaks of watery light.

Palta wanted to talk about logistics. Dogs skulked, circling us. Gradually, more and more people and eager coolies gathered around. Their predatory manner was quite threatening—it felt like the last scene of Hitchcock's film *The Birds*. "Where have you come from?" "Where are you going?" "What is in these bags?" The same ritual questions rolled out monotonously and I answered them painstakingly. I remembered the story told by Bill Murray, leader of the 1950 Scottish Himalayan Expedition, which was the last British Expedition to travel beyond the Inner Line in the Garhwal. He tired of answering all these questions one day and snapped back, "Why do you want to know?" "So that I can help you," came the calm reply.

Soon the bus left to start its eight-hour, one-hundred-mile journey up the valley of the River Alaknanda to Joshimath, 6,000 feet higher. The journey was long and winding, up towards one of the sources of the Ganges. With gentle irony, the locals call the road 'the gift of China', since it was built to enable the Indian army to gain easy access to defend the frontier. The many people in Srinagar with a Tibetan look reminded us that we were nearing the crest of the Himalayas. Half of the Indian army is now guarding the northern frontier, and the road had only been open to westerners for three years.

"Hey, Joe," I said, "look at that bridge. I could take a photo of it and sell it to the Chinese Embassy—it might pay for the expedition." Palta did not know how to take the joke and firmly told us not to photograph it.

It was difficult for Joe and me, coming from an island which has not been invaded for a thousand years, to understand the sensitive political tensions of the Himalayas. Whenever we laughed we had to explain the reason. Palta's puzzled uncertainty made us think he was wondering if the joke was at his expense.

We were in the first-class seats, just behind the driver, which meant that our knees were just tucked under our chins rather than rubbing against our noses. As we set off, the bus driver—a very little man—informed us that the steering wasn't power-assisted and, with a grin on his face, pointed at the bends in the road as it twisted up the valley-side 2,000 feet above the river bed. "We lose about eight or nine buses down there every year," he said. Then he lit some incense at the front of the bus and waved his hand with a flourish. At that the entire bus started chanting prayers in unison. The most hair-raising of bends was heralded usually by encouraging reminders painted on the rocks at the side of the road, such as 'Life is short. Do not make it shorter.' Occasionally monsoon floods had washed mud and boulders across the road and these were being cleared frantically by road workers. As soon as there was a space cleared wide enough to drive through, on we would go. Joe and I would glance nervously at the door as the bus tottered on over such sections. There was a priest, a hen, and an old lady between us and the door. The driver glanced round and said, "Relax, nobody ever gets out when the buses go over."

The population inside the bus changed regularly, and we stopped occasionally for cups of tea. Up the valley ran the old pilgrim trail from Rishikesh—sometimes we could see it from the road. Many pilgrims, of varying prosperity and degrees of commitment, were in the area. Most of them today seem to catch the bus and make the trip in their holidays. We even met a Sikh from Cambridge. But there are many who walk. They seemed strangely detached. Some were dressed in red garments, others wore only a loincloth and were covered in white ash. The walkers had red-rimmed, far-away eyes and smiled and talked little. I tried to imagine where these pilgrims came from, and what significance the pilgrimage would have for them in their lives. The change of scenery alone must have been dramatic—to travel in the mountains after a life on the plains. The importance of their pilgrimage was in its physical act—in the effort they had to make.

In Joshimath the air was cool. For the first time in a week, I felt I could think clearly. We got off the bus next to the pilgrim shed and checked in there, before wandering up the main street. Joshimath is a pilgrim tourist town, perched high on the hillside above the Alaknanda. It consists of one main street of shops with corrugated iron roofs. Nearly every other shop is a sweetmeat and teashop. The mountains around were hidden from us by the monsoon clouds but, occasionally, long slanting rays of sunshine would break through. Above the town is a large military encampment that is self-contained, but down in the town we could see little of it. Joe had friends here—Mr. F. Bhupal Singh of the Neilkanth Hotel, and Yasu, a young local. We went to see them. Bhupal Singh welcomed us with a quick, kind smile and I felt an immediate sense of trust in him. Such openness is unusual in the plains of India, where politeness and formality, one feels, might be obscuring many motives.

In the evening we sat and discussed with Palta his role in the expedition. Palta had come with many maps and with a detailed brief for his role as liaison officer. These he was guarding carefully. Joe was, I felt, embarrassingly antagonistic towards the need for a liaison officer – he hadn't much respect for them. His liaison officer of the previous year had not lasted much longer than the first day's walk. We knew that one of Palta's instructions was to make sure that we didn't climb any peaks other than the one we had permission for. Joe and I spent a long time trying to tell Palta about the development of the world mountaineering scene, and how the trend was towards smaller parties tackling bigger and bigger mountains in a less formal style than hitherto. "Mountaineering is individualistic," we would say, "it can't be like an army exercise, it requires too much voluntary motivation." But Palta had only had a month's training in mountaineering, about five years previously, so it was heavy going. The same questions cropped up again: "I still don't understand how you chaps justify this climbing. What about your careers, the furtherance of humanity, your role in society and your duty to your country?" I muttered many reasons in reply—most of them rationalisations of ones I had heard other people give.

"It can develop your character," I said, "and make you more independent and hold things in realistic perspectives. The travel to the mountain as well as the mastery of mountaineering technique enlarge your experience so that you are more effective and interesting if you ever teach others, or even when you just meet people. Also, mountaineering has a pure exploratory strain in it—exploring human potential, doing things that nobody thought could be done before, finding things out about areas that are hardly known. It provides contrasts to help balance out the lives of people like us, who come from urban backgrounds. Anyway, I think any enthusiasm or interest is better than none at all. I find it so much easier to sympathise with people who are really interested and enthused about something—whatever it is—rather than without much interest in life, monotonously drifting. It was Eric Shipton's belief that a man is very fortunate and very rare, if he can truly say that he has found something profoundly satisfying in life which he enjoys utterly. And," I added defensively, "I enjoy mountains!"

Joe said little, and I was sure he was thinking, 'What a load of bullshit!' Perhaps I was trying to justify all this to myself. 'This sort of talk means more after a climb, not before one,' I thought, 'and we haven't done anything yet!'

We planned to spend two whole days in Joshimath, but we ended up spending three.

I awoke the following morning with my dreamland among the soft green hills of Derbyshire. The hooting of the pilgrims' buses brought me abruptly back to India. It had been a noisy night, with pilgrims coming and going and playing their transistor radios into the early hours. "What the hell can they find to jabber about all the time?" said Joe.

We spent two days sorting out the gear into porter loads of fifty pounds each, and buying rice, dhal, dried peas, pickles, curry powder and onions from the bazaar. Joe did most of the load-sorting—once he was involved in doing something, he tended to take over completely. Palta and I tended to stand in the corner of the room.

"You're a good worker, Joe," said Palta.

Also, a large spider had dropped from the ceiling to land somewhere amongst the equipment and neither of us wanted to be the one that disturbed it!

Joe was becoming irritated with Palta—though not openly. He felt that Palta always insisted that we did everything together, that every little decision—such as going for a cup of tea in the bazaar—demanded prior consultation and agreement. He could not bring himself to pretend that the liaison officer was not an imposition and that climbing Changabang was more important than Palta's feelings. Because of Joe's forthrightness, Palta regarded him as the Leader.

Joe and I were having some worries about finance, since Palta was—not unreasonably—insisting that we hired a porter to keep him company at Base Camp. This meant that we would have to clothe and feed another person.

Meanwhile, three of the South Face team had arrived, and we went out with them for a meal at our favourite café haunt, The Delight. It wasn't exactly five-star, and we amused each other by relating morbid anecdotes about stomach complaints, quietly keeping our fingers crossed and nervously glancing at the water and glasses for disruptive microbes. A bad gut could mean no climb. Joe and I were waiting along with them for their South Face truck to arrive, since two boxes of food and Gaz canisters for us were aboard it. The truck, and with it the rest of their team, was being delayed by a landslide further down the road.

This advance party trio had an air of solemnity which Joe liked to dispel. Being part of a larger group, their sense of purpose was more formal and they seemed slightly dazed by India. Joe knew them better than I, and often used to slip away for the relief their change of company gave him.

On the 2nd September we were all set to catch the 3.00 p.m. bus to the village of Lata, from where we would start our walk to Changabang. The South Face team had arrived and Palta hired a porter to carry our boxes on his head to the bus station. Then we discovered we had just done a dress rehearsal. Apparently the 3.00 p.m. bus had gone at 2.00 p.m., but had only gone five kilometres up the road on a private mission. It wouldn't be going to Lata until late tomorrow now. "Don't worry," said Joe, misquoting Kipling. "Here lies a man deceased, who tried to hurry the East." With that he escaped and sank into a chair in the back of a tea shop and drowned his sorrows with a sweet milky brew. Joe was always ready to relax if there was nothing else to do.

Later in the afternoon we went for a walk up through and above the military encampment. There, wearing our double boots, and much to the amazement of some local children, we climbed on some enormous boulders until we fell off among vicious stinging nettles. We were hoping to be able to see Nanda Devi, but the skies were cloudy and beginning to spit with rain. Eventually we found ourselves high on the hills in a sloping field full of apple trees and there a toothless old lady, with many rings in her ears, approached us. She held out some enormous red apples to us. They were delicious. She refused payment for them, smiled and stepped back to watch us move on. The gift of the apples was a simple, direct gesture which had been born of the hillside and not of the town and road we had left below us.

In the evening Palta took us to the Joshimath cinema. An earlier attempt to see the Hindu movie on at the time had failed because of an erratic electricity supply. The film lasted three hours and was called *Zameer*, meaning 'conscience'. It was about a millionaire who loses his son and finds him again. The film had song, dance, horses, a chase, some shooting and romantic love, all in an escapist, fantasy world. It was quite unlike the India we had seen in the previous week—there were no beggars and nobody was sweating. The hero and heroine seemed, to our western eyes, to be overweight—but being slim is not an attribute of beauty in India. "No wonder our small expedition is being judged poor and worthless because it's small," said Joe.

The theme tune had the little boy next to me singing his heart out, completely absorbed. It was to echo around my mind all the way to the glacier beneath Changabang. At the interval we bought some nuts from a stall outside, and ate them through the second half, in the dark. We only saw the grubs sheltering inside the shells when the lights went on. It was our last brush with the civilised fantasies of outside. Now we were moving inside, towards the Sanctuary.

At 7.00 a.m. the following morning, Joe was bustling about, assembling fifteen porter loads. By walking across the roof of someone's house from the pilgrim shed, we managed to place the loads directly onto the top of the bus. Now we had been joined by a Swiss trekker called Hans, who was intending to walk into the area at the same time as ourselves.

As we moved off I felt thrilled with the sensation of travel—always to move and never to arrive avoids many confrontations. I gazed at the view, thinking about other places I wanted to travel to, other trips I wanted to make to other areas of the world. The bus wound down towards Tapoban, a sprawling settlement of tea shops, a post office and a lot of mud. Here the high path which the pre-1970 explorers to the Garhwal had followed, joined ours after crossing the Kuari Pass. We could see another road winding up the Alaknanda valley, towards Badrinath, but now we had turned right up the valley of the River Dhauli.

History draws a false distinction between trade and exploration. It is facile to consider that the exploration of a Himalayan area started only when Europeans began to record their movements and discoveries there. We were now following a valley that had been brushed by the feet of the earliest tribes as a trading route between Tibet and India. At the head of the Dhauli lies the Niti Pass and at the head of the Alaknanda lies the 18,400-foot Mana Pass. The Mana Pass was the more extensively used. The first Europeans to cross the Mana Pass were Portuguese Jesuits in the seventeenth century, who were establishing a mission in Tibet. These priests were not geographers but, obsessed with their mission, travelled boldly, disregarding the time of year or the state of snow on the passes, putting their trust in God to guide them safely.

Soon after Tapoban we crossed the Rishi as it poured out of the Rishi Ganga. In 1950, Bill Murray had found there a square-slated shrine of Tibetan character, rigged by a score of tall poles from which flew strips of tattered cloth—offered in honour to the Seven Rishis who dwell in sanctuaries of the Rishi Ganga. These Seven Rishis, so the legend has it, are spirits who guard the sanctuaries of Nanda Devi, the bliss-giving goddess. I peered up the mouth of the dark and gloomy chasm, trying to glimpse some mountains and thought of the attempts made by W. W. Graham in 1883, and Bill Tilman in 1934, to enter the gorge by this place. It was only in the spring of 1976 that an expedition – the Japanese S. W. Ridge of Changabang Expedition, managed to force a way through this forbidding gash. They had to; the normal path was covered in deep snow and was, anyway, already crowded by the marches of the Indo-Japanese expedition and the Indian Trisul expedition. Today, at the mouth of the Rishi Ganga, is a military bridge and guard, and no sign of a shrine.

The bus dropped us and our loads by the roadside and very soon the headman of the village of Lata, Jagat Singh, appeared. He was very co-operative and wore a red flower in his fawn jersey. Soon Palta had arranged for fifteen porters to start carrying our loads the next day. Negotiations for porters is much easier in India than in Nepal and Afghanistan, as there is a fixed rate. It didn't take Palta long to settle with them. The men from Lata came down to have a look at their loads. Joe was pleased to recognise one of them, one of the 'untouchables' of the village, from the previous year. On the way back from Dunagiri, the winter snows had come early and nearly trapped Joe at Dibrugheta, on the Rishi Ganga. This porter, carrying an enormous load, had shown amazing navigational skill in a white-out. "He just stared into the mist and kept on going," said Joe, "and was right every time. I'd have had a hard time getting back over the top without him. I had to stop him rooting through the bags later on, though – he's still a rogue. I don't know his name – he only grunted to me."

One of the villagers, a large man called Tait Singh, was acting as shop steward. Many of them had bands of fleece twisted around their forearms and, with an air of dedication, were teasing one end of the fleece out into yarn onto the spindle, which they kept spinning by flicking it with their fingers. Joe and I had hidden our spring gauge (we both wanted to avoid the hours of load-haggling we had encountered on previous expeditions) and presented the loads as a *fait accompli*.

Fortunately, we managed to hire our porters whilst the South Face Expedition were still sorting themselves out. They had arrived at the same layby in their white truck – 'the ice-cream van', as one of their number, Jim Duff, called it. They were not a big expedition – by comparison, the Japanese had hired fifty porters in the spring, and the American Nanda Devi expedition had used over eighty porters and one hundred and twenty goats. The South Face team hired half their forty porters in Joshimath. Still, I could not help feeling pleased at our small, compact pile of gear compared to their long lines of labelled boxes, and I think some of the South Face team looked back at us in envy. Joe, however, was thinking that he would like to go on a larger trip sometime, with plenty of time and money to sort things out.

The next morning, the 4th September, we started moving in the pouring rain, up a narrow path that wound among wheat fields. After half an hour we passed through the village of Lata, which Bill Murray called the most wonderfully sited village he had ever seen in the Himalayas. But we could see little of the height and space around it. We could only see the village itself, its houses set back on stone terraces. Each house had its own courtyard and was half wood, half stone, with the families living on the wooden upper storey, reached by a ladder descending from a balcony. Their habit of salted tea-drinking, liking of ornaments and trinkets and often mongoloid faces, showed we had reached the fringe of Tibetan influence. Lata is fairly prosperous, since it is low enough to produce crops and hence it was comparatively undisturbed by the closing of the border, in contrast with the villages further up the Dhauli Ganga that lie within the Inner Line. The building of the road brought employment and, since 1974, the influx of expeditions has meant that many able-bodied men in the village have been employed as porters. These changes have brought some prosperity, but not stability. Much of the money from expeditions has been diverted to middle-men in Joshimath and elsewhere and, although the pay is good, the work is seasonal.

As we passed Lata, we met two students from Cambridge University, Rosemary Scott and Anthony Cohen. Rosemary had just finished a survey of the nutritional value of the diets of five of the sixty-five families in Lata.

Lata was the last habitation on our way to the mountains, and soon we were high above the village, following the ancient shepherd route into the Rishi. W. W. Graham, the enigmatic cowboy of nineteenth-century Himalayan exploration, had been the first European to find it. We were climbing around the back of one of the spurs that formed the mouth of the Rishi Ganga, and the day's walk involved about 5,000 feet of ascent up to Lata Kharak, a meadow high above the Dhauli at about 12,000 feet. We wandered up the path and, as the skies began to clear and the sun came out, we crossed a stream. "This is the last water till we get to the top," said Joe. By the stream there was an old lady washing, with such an enormous ring through her nose that it had to be supported by a clip in her hat. I asked her if she minded my taking a photograph. She did, and looked angry. Always, the westerner feels he has to possess everything, even if it's only a picture on celluloid!

I felt satisfied that morning, and relaxed. Adventures lose their mystery and worry once you are embarked upon them. Everything seemed to be taking shape. I was feeling happier than I had been at any time on the previous year's Everest expedition. The whole trip was purely ours; there was nothing superfluous. There didn't seem to be the built-in redundancy factor, as there had been on Everest. Also, I felt far fitter than I had the previous year—the running must have done some good. It was good to be walking into the Himalaya again. It felt as if I had always been there, and the year in between had been a dream.

From Lata Kharak, briefly, we had tantalising glimpses of the white snows of Bethartoli Himal and Nanda Ghunti across the Rishi Ganga. In the woods below there was a hidden spring. Nearby, living in a shelter, was a yogi. He was isolating himself from humanity for the summer, and hid from us in his sanctuary. Our porters crowded under a tarpaulin and lit a fire as the rain came in. Some of them had terrible coughs and were probably doomed to die within the next few years of T.B. I went for a wash—determined to be careful about personal hygiene and not to risk jeopardising the trip by illness.

In the morning, in the mist we moved up the ridge, over a pass and scrambled around the steep, twisting spurs on the other side until at last we reached Dharansi, the open ridge. Here there was a tent, and two shepherds, whom the porters greeted. They obtained a sheep from them and led the luckless animal all the way down the steep slope into the Rishi Ganga—it would provide their supper that night.

Below us we could see the 'stone and meadow' of Dibrugheta, which Longstaff had called 'a fragment of Arcady dropped amid chaos' where 'amid the vertical confusion of the landscape the horizontal instantly invited relaxation and repose'. We raced down in the drizzle. Flanking us towered great diagonal sheets of mica, sparkling through the mist.

At the bottom we found Hans, sheltering with his two porters in a cave blackened by bivouac fires. "That chap's having a ball," said Palta. Palta couldn't understand why two people wanted to go and climb a dangerous mountain, but he could see the sense and fun in wandering around an area, looking at the scenery. However, he was nonplussed that Hans had turned up without any permit, and simply walked into the area.

Whilst we were with Hans, a mail runner from the American Nanda Devi expedition arrived and announced that three members had reached the summit on the 1st September. We moved over the flower-strewn meadow to our camp site amidst tall pines and boulders of old camp fires. Unfortunately, the porters with our tents were hours behind and we had a long wait under our umbrellas. It was dark by the time we put up our tents. We asked Palta to light a primus stove, but he couldn't. 'No wonder he wanted a porter to help him at Base Camp,' I thought.

"When do you chaps usually do your toilet?" asked Palta. "In the morning or in the evening?"

Later, Joe muttered, "He's doing all right on the walking, but why do things seem so bloody complicated whilst he's around? Even the simplest tasks such as cooking and lighting a stove get confusing."

I was trying to be friendly, and to put him at ease, but it was hard work.

The next day we climbed steeply behind Dibrugheta. Joe reached the crest first. "Come up here," called Joe. "It's Big Nanda."

He knew how much I wanted to see that mountain. I arrived in time to see the summit of Nanda Devi through a hole in the clouds, rising above the sacred ground of her Sanctuary, surrounded by legend of inaccessibility. Far below us, the slender thread of the Rishi led our eyes back towards the mountain. It was a fleeting glimpse, for soon the mists closed all mountains from us.

We spent the day traversing the slopes 2,000 feet above the gorge. I was feeling quite tired, but was soon entranced by the thousands of flowers that littered the slopes. The sky was grey and it was the earth that drew my eyes to it. No wonder the Garhwal is called the Garden of the Himalayas. No wonder that F. S. Smythe wrote a book in 1938 called *The Valley of Flowers* about Bhiundar Valley, near Joshimath. The droplets of water that hung from the petals brought a freshness and immediacy. They were of all colours, and gave a gentler beauty to the fierce landscape on which they were scattered.

"What are you photographing those lupins for, Joe? They grow in everyone's garden back home."

The monsoon had swelled the streams that poured down the side of the gorge and which we had to cross. When we reached one very strong torrent, Tait Singh dramatically took immediate charge, stood

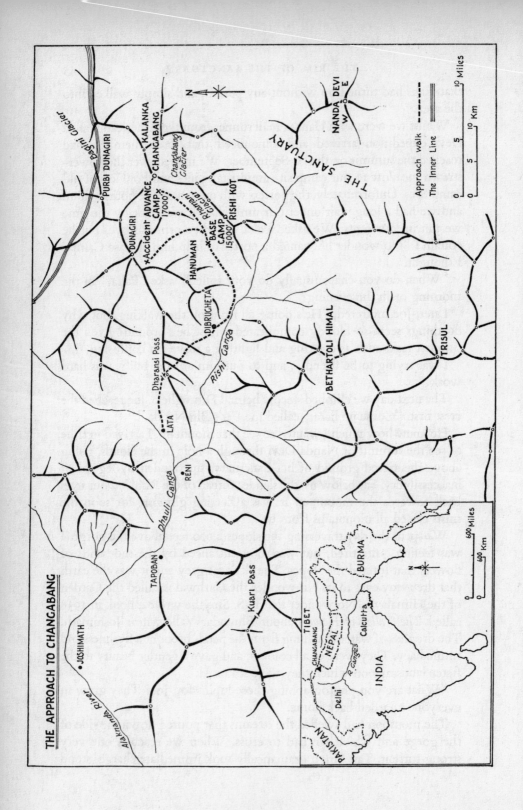

THE APPROACH TO CHANGABANG

N

Bagini Glacier

PURBI DUNAGIRI

KALANKA

CHANGABANG

Changabang
Glacier

DUNAGIRI

×Accident ADVANCE
CAMP×
17000'

Rhamani Glacier

HANUMAN

BASE
CAMP
15000'

RISHI KOT

DIBRUGHETA

Dharansi Pass

Rishi Ganga

NANDA DEVI
W   E
S

THE SANCTUARY

BETHARTOLI HIMAL

TRISUL

LATA

Dhauli Ganga

RENI

TAPOBAN

JOSHIMATH

Kuari Pass

Alaknanda River

N

Approach walk
The Inner Line

10 Miles
10 Km
5
5
0   0

PAKISTAN

TIBET

CHANGABANG

NEPAL

BURMA

INDIA

Delhi

R. Ganges

Calcutta

N

600 Miles
600 Km

in the middle of the current and helped the loads and people across. "The shop steward's proving a good lad," said Joe.

Below us, we could see the Rishi through the clouds. Occasionally we had to use our hands to scramble up the steeper areas—it was a long way to fall if you were careless.

It was a cramped camp site on a slope, and I was feeling irritated with Palta, who seemed particularly helpless, whilst Joe and I pitched the tents, slipped the polythene sheets together over them, and lit the stove. Our tents were still soaking from the previous evening. It rained again. Tomorrow we would reach Base Camp—the porters were making the six-day stage walk in four days.

Joe and I woke early. "Since liaison officers are sent to watch us," said Joe, "they ought to pay their way. This assistance/guide bit is rubbish!"

It was a lovely morning. The mist had gone and I was startled to see the exposed position of our camp site and the sense of space around us, as the Rishi Gorge was opening out to the Sanctuary of its head waters and glaciers. Now we were to turn up towards the Rhamani Glacier and Changabang. Palta had gone, as usual, for his toilet as Joe and I collapsed the tents and cooked the breakfast.

Palta returned with a startling ultimatum. Either we sent back for more fresh vegetables or he returned to civilisation with the porters. He said, "Look, you chaps, I will make sure you and your loads get to your Base Camp. But if I am not going to be any use to your expedition, I prefer to go back. Never in my life have I eaten such appalling food. I don't know if you have gained your ideas about Indian cooking from watching these people," he added, waving a hand at the porters, "but even my servant eats better food than you two do."

He was trying to force us to make the decision, but it was obvious he was unhappy and wanted to go home. I felt guilty about having brought so much beef with us. I had completely forgotten about the Hindu taboo about cattle. However, we had offered him all our lamb and fish. Also, I felt bad about Joe's earlier critical attitude. After all, Palta had only two days' notice that he was coming with us, and it had been two years previously when he had put his name down, volunteering his services as an expedition officer. But it was difficult for us to humour his fixed, class-conscious ideas and his proud intelligence—particularly for Joe, who was always quick to sense any form of pretension. In many ways, Joe had more regard for the tough resilience of the porters, cheerful in their poverty. From the start it had been clear that ours was not the sort of expedition Palta had wanted to be the liaison officer for. First he had bemoaned the lack of a radio transmitter; then he had insisted that we had a porter at Base Camp to keep him company. Now it was the food. He refused to be helped, and his stiff upper lip approach seemed to provoke unnecessary suffering. He just didn't understand the nature of the adventure. So we were to be alone.

Apart from my mind being preoccupied with Palta troubles, the morning walk was magnificent, with views of the wilderness in which we were to act out our adventure. Changabang was hiding until the last.

Unknown to us, that day, high on Nanda Devi, a tragedy stranger than fiction was occurring. At 24,000 feet, four American climbers had moved into a position to attempt a second ascent of the North-West Face/North Ridge. Up there, a blizzard was blowing and one of the climbers was slowly weakening from an abdominal illness. The following morning she died, and the three remaining climbers committed her body to the snows of the mountain. In 1948, Willi Unsoeld had announced that he would name his daughter after the most beautiful mountain he had ever seen. Willi was on this expedition with his daughter, and it was she who had died. Nanda Devi Unsoeld as a mortal, young and charming, had, so many Indians say, returned to her 'home' — she had been the goddess personified.

As our route twisted towards the Rhamani Glacier, we rounded a corner. Suddenly we saw it. In a slot formed by the ridges of Hanuman, the Monkey God, Kalanka, the Destroyer, and Rishi Kot, the fortress of the Rishis, soared the glistening milk white shark's-tooth of Changabang — 'The Shining Mountain'.

I rolled their names around in my mind. I pointed my camera at Changabang and took a progression of photographs — 28 mm, 50 mm, 75 mm, 150 mm, in a rush of lenses. As the mountain drew nearer it struck deeper, richer chords of awe within me. No wonder Tom Longstaff called Changabang "the most superbly beautiful mountain I have ever seen". F. S. Smythe's description lived — "a peak that falls from crest to glacier in a wall that might have been sliced in a single cut of a knife". The charisma given to it by its early sightings was fulfilled.

Joe was looking at me. "No anthems playing in my head," he said.

Slowly, the thought crept back — dared we presume to attempt to stand on its summit? Now I was seeing the West Wall live, after I had known it so well from photographs. Yes, the 'link pitch', the ramp of snow that we had first seen on the photographs taken by the Swiss mountaineer, André Roche, from the summit of Dunagiri in 1939, was still there, offering a possible line to the central icefield. Our attempt would be a bold enterprise, but I couldn't think of anyone I would rather make the attempt with than Joe. Soon we moved in amongst the moraines and Changabang lowered its head.

At 11.40 a.m. on 8th September, we arrived on the meadow where Joe had his Base Camp for Dunagiri the previous year, and all the loads thumped to the ground. It had been quite a gaspy walk—our altimeter read 15,250 feet. The mist swirled and hugged the ground, and the porters crowded eagerly around for the big pay-out. We handed out the notes and arranged vaguely that we would let them know when we wanted porters to help us ferry our equipment back to civilisation.

"I've nothing personal against you two," said Palta. And we hadn't against him. He left with the porters.

Joe and I sat amongst the boxes and kitbags and watched them disappear into the mist. "A bit of a lonely place to come for our summer holidays," I said to Joe.

"I was here for six days by myself, last year, after Dick had gone," said Joe. "I started imagining things towards the end."

We put the tents up. Then Hans arrived with his two porters. "I am here for two days," he said in his clipped Austrian accent. "Then I go to the Sanctuary."

Joe and I ate mashed potato and lamb slices for tea and shared our Christmas pudding, rum and custard with him. "This is the best dessert I have ever tasted," said Hans.

All other problems had stopped. Now we would contend with the universal elements—cold, height, rock, snow, all recognised and familiar. All mountains, all over the world, have something in common. I could feel at ease now we were among them . . . it no longer felt as if we were in India. I could understand it all.

4

CHAPTER THREE

The First Stone

8th–20th September

We took a rest day. It snowed heavily all night and then the snow turned to sleet. Our world was just our tents, some rough wiry grass, a tiny stream and then, through the thick drizzle, the boulders and dark earth of the moraine. I woke up eventually around 8.30 a.m., after twelve hours of much-needed sleep. I lay in the tent, stunned with altitude, looking at the blue nylon in front of my face. Joe and I were in separate lightweight tents and I was relieved to hear Joe move at last and put on the brew in the Base Camp tunnel tent. I didn't feel very hungry, but we managed to put down cold porridge and wheatgerm, followed by rice and pilchards. Joe prepared a jelly for teatime. I had a headache just behind my eyes and felt dizzy when I stood up. This, combined with worries about my stomach and a pain in the lower part of my back, made me feel a right old crock. Still, I knew that it was the general lassitude induced by the altitude that was giving me this hypochondria and, when I admitted anything to Joe, he said, "Well, you know what Shipton says—'No illness ever stopped a man who really wanted to reach a summit.'"

"How's the altitude affecting you?" I asked him.

"Oh, it feels just like home."

"Oh yes, just like after a night at the boozer."

"If you think I'm stoical, you ought to climb with Dick—then you'd think I'm a real softy."

Joe had had his appendix out when he was a child, and mine was still in. There seemed such a low chance of it giving any trouble, that I shut myself from the idea. But Joe loved to tease me about it.

"How's your stomach today, Pete? Any little twinges? Don't worry, I've got all the instruments here and the book to follow. It's only a minor operation, after all."

We crept back to our tents, under our umbrellas. I looked at mine with amusement. My Gran had given it to me for my twenty-first birthday. If she could see me now! I was reading, in between dozing in and out of consciousness, *Zen and the Art of Motorcycle Maintenance*. Joe was reading Gorky, *The Three*. We had a rather serious selection of books with us with which to pass the time. Also, apart in our tents, we were scribbling in our diaries little confessions about ourselves, and comments about the other. Joe was wondering if he was out of practice at high altitude exertion and suffering. Also he was commenting:

> "Pete is more relaxing than Dick to be with, but his doziness can be amazing at times. Not that he's lazy, he just doesn't think."

On the other side of the field Hans was crouching inside the shelter of his bivouac tent. He didn't emerge all day.

The sun was returning, the weather was clearing and so were our heads, and we determined to go up onto the glacier, look at the Wall and find a site for our Advance Camp. Hans was going to leave after taking some photographs of the area from a vantage point. After we had spent a couple of hours drying and sorting our gear in the sunshine, we said goodbye to him and left on our exploratory wander.

When we reached the top of the valley next to the moraine, about 1,500 feet higher up, we could see the whole of the cirque of mountains that ringed the Rhamani Glacier, with Changabang standing proudly at the end. A branch of this glacier turned towards Dunagiri, towards Bagini Pass between Changabang and Dunagiri, which Longstaff had crossed in 1907. We could see the route taken by Chris Bonington's team in 1974. They had arrived at the point where Joe and I now were. Martin Boysen, a member of that expedition, had written:

> We had come in hope of climbing the Western Face, a rock route which looked inviting on our faded photographs. We were now confronted with a precipice, the like of which I had not seen outside Patagonia: an enormous sweep of vertical and overhanging rock, plated here and there by ludicrously steep ice. The route we had originally contemplated was obviously so difficult it was laughable.

Instead, they chose to cross the steep ridge separating the west and south sides of Changabang, and climb the mountain from the other side. The point where they eventually crossed the ridge was Shipton's Col. In September, 1936, Shipton had reached that point from the other side, during his second expedition into the Sanctuary, and sat there for one hour, gazing at the white cliffs of the mountain.

Joe and I picked our way across the rough stone of the moraine at the side of the glacier, towards Changabang—two tiny figures in a vast amphitheatre of mindless snow and ice and granite. I was day-dreaming. 'Somehow, I don't feel alone in the mountains. Sights such as these make me flow with strength. All the time dormant mountaineering memories re-emerge, memories of a hundred situations and problems carefully solved. Experience helps me deal with the pain of altitude, with uncertainty, incredulity almost. Before a big climb I can rise above these things because I know them. I have felt them before. I don't feel at all confident that we'll get up that wall, but I know we're tackling this climb very thoughtfully and intelligently. Memories seem so logical, certain—events seem to have emerged so rationally and inevitably. Lines on photographs of mountains look so obvious and certain, and belie the agony that put them there. But here we are, at the foot of the Wall, with our climb before us, and there's absolutely no way we can predict how it will go. What does it say in that Zen book? ". . . You are never dedicated to something you have complete confidence in. No one is fanatically shouting that the sun is going to rise tomorrow. When people are fanatically dedicated to political or religious faiths or any other kinds of dogmas or goals, it always is because these dogmas or goals are in doubt . . ."'

A distant thin tongue of moraine stretched along the glacier, towards the foot of the West Wall. It looked a good place to set up our Advance Camp. The ground was rough. Often we had to cross gullies filled with enormous blocks of granite and we could hop from one to another. The sun had melted the ice on the glacier into crazy patterns and we crunched over them, sending collapsing tiny sheets of ice into tinkling submission, into pools of water and air. Across the surface of the glacier poured three or four streams, gaining force as the sun moved to midday. All the time, new angles of the West Wall presented themselves, and we stopped frequently—partly to gasp at the thin air, but mainly to stand and stare at the West Wall. As we walked we passed underneath the dramatic granite cliffs of the ridge between the Rhamani Glacier and the subsidiary glacier that stretches up towards the south side of Dunagiri. On the other side of the Rhamani, we could see the icy slopes of Rishi Kot and the line of steep cliffs that stretch towards Changabang, under Shipton's Col.

Soon Joe's Dunagiri route of the previous year peeped around at us.

It looked formidable—but mild in contrast with the West Wall which persistently drew our eyes. We discussed the Wall little, except to make occasional remarks about possible lines of weakness, breaking down its apparent impossibility into a series of logical steps. All its buttresses, its walls, its slabs, its cracklines, its patches of ice were becoming imprinted on our minds. Joe was as subdued as I:

"Monsoon ice and snow still coated most of the mountain. The photographs and colour slides, viewed in distant Britain, had held no hint of the massive, inhospitable atmosphere of this colossal wall. It confronted us like a petrified wave with ice dripping from its rim. My memory had faded in the intervening months since I had last seen it and I wondered what impression it was making on Pete. Neither of us expressed any anxiety to each other . . . I hoped we hadn't taken on too much."

At the end of the moraine we dropped our loads and looked up at the Wall through some binoculars a friend of mine had lent us for the trip. A great detached block that must have weighed about thirty tons seemed to guard one way through the overhangs to the icefield. The alternative route to the icefield, the link pitch, more towards the middle of the Wall, looked frightening. Perhaps it all was—as Bonington had said—'preposterous'. For the previous eight months, whenever we came across quotations or anecdotes which seemed to give us some encouragement, we would relate them to each other as a reassurance. The most notable was a quotation from Longstaff: "You must go and rub your nose in a place before being certain that it won't go." As if to reinforce his dictum, we could see Trisul, the scene of Longstaff's greatest achievement, far across the other side of the Rishi Ganga. In 1907, with Henri and Alexis Brocherel, brothers of Courmayeur, and a Gurkha, Kharbir, he climbed nearly 6,000 feet, in one day, to reach the top and then descended the same evening, some 7,000 feet, before camping for the night. They had climbed higher than anyone else had ever been at that time.

As Joe and I turned back down the moraine 'valley' to Base Camp, the setting sun was colouring the snows of Trisul. Behind us the suspended stone of Changabang was also glowing, with clouds drifting around it, asserting its height, their movement emphasising its stability.

That first day's walk onto the glacier was the first of six days' load carrying from the 9th–14th September, during which that day's pattern was repeated. We would wake with the sun and load about forty to forty-five pounds weight of gear in our sacks and cross all the glacial streams whilst they were low, in the early morning. We marked our route and the site of the Advance Camp with cairns, but after a while we found that they weren't necessary, as we soon recognised individual boulders. That helped. As we were pounding about with our heavy sacks on, from boulder to boulder, I was usually in a semi-daze, and my lips were blistering in the bright light. My thoughts were always wandering, and it was a relief not to have to concentrate too hard on the route-finding. I could distance my mind far away from the beast of burden that was my body. My mind would usually drift back home, to the last things I said and did with my friends. I had worried thoughts and laughing thoughts.

Apart from the second day, when Joe stayed behind at Base Camp to sort the gear out because he had a headache and diarrhoea and I went on my own, we always seemed to stick together, stumbling about, living in our own thoughts. I felt an inexplicable need to stay within about a hundred yards of Joe. I could still taste the disappointment that had ended my Alaskan climb and was worried about slipping and twisting my knee. I was turning into a hypochondriac, waking with slight nose bleeds and feeling slight pains in my shoulders and over my heart. I was much more physically or hygienically aware than I had been on previous expeditions. I was carefully changing my underwear, washing and combing my hair and cleaning my teeth and keeping warm and comfortable. I was constantly checking my pulse rate, to gauge my fitness and state of acclimatisation. I knew that Joe would feel hopelessly let down if something simple, but damning, happened to me. I wondered if he felt the same.

We would sit by the pile of equipment we were accumulating at Advance Camp and eat some chocolate and stare at the Wall, before going back down. We kept on seeing new possibilities, we were obsessed with looking at the Wall. Soon we had resolved a line to attempt. After taking as straight a line as possible to a col in the head-wall ridge of the Rhamani that melted into the West Wall, we hoped to establish a camp and attempt it from there by its left-hand edge. By doing this we would gain about 1,000 feet in height. The alternative of trying to find an ice cave amongst the icicles that swept over the great sweep of slabs below the link pitch in the middle of the Face, was unattractive and we decided against it. Reaching the icefield looked as if it would be a major crux.

After each walk we felt a little better acclimatised, and our times improved. It was good fun racing back down the glacier. We were always trying to photograph each other in stupid, compromising situations, such as becoming soaked in the afternoon meltwater streams, trying to topple enormous boulders like mushrooms on the glacier, and gripping great phallic pinnacles of ice. It was a battle of quick-draw cameras. The way and the views were becoming familiar. Their familiarity helped us to adapt, and reassured us.

Base Camp was always shrouded in afternoon cloud when we returned to it and we called it 'Bleak House'. But still it felt like home. Once we were back we would make a big meal and doze around, reading and chatting, talking about climbing and life back home. Joe, without a settled job to return to, was wondering what he would do on his return. He was tiring of his years scratching a living to support his climbing. I, on the other hand, having nearly always had a steady job or a place in college, was envious of his resourceful independence. Then we would begin to think of the next day's prospect of going back up 2,000 feet onto the glacier. Joe didn't like getting up in the morning.

"This load-carrying's harder work than climbing," he said. We wished we had kept a couple of porters on to help us with the slog of load-carrying, or had a liaison officer to help us at this stage—after all, we had been promised "one of the best climbers in India".

We had a folder full of photographs of the Face, and these provided moments of doubt and hope. But these moments were always personal. Conversation was cool and factual. For days we had been wandering underneath the Wall, prevented from attempting it by our own logistic snarl-up—the very thing we had wanted to avoid. Then we would retire to our sleeping bags, to our own thoughts and dreams. For months I had been building myself up mentally for the route. We were both working hard and building up a mutual trust and respect. I thought of home, of all homes I had ever lived in. Joe was reading *Nana* by Zola, with its depressing view of women. He dreamt about lots of people arriving from many directions. Don Whillans turned up, and then the American expedition we had heard was going to attempt Dunagiri. In Joe's dream it was an expedition of blonde, surfing girls from California.

On the 14th September, we finally left Base Camp. We put a little note in a polythene bag with a stone on top of it, just inside our tent doorway: "To whom it may concern", with a meagre message saying we were away, trying to climb Changabang, but should be back in a couple of weeks. Then we shouldered enormous, top-heavy loads weighing about seventy pounds each, containing all the remaining gear we thought we would need.

"I wouldn't want to carry this much in Britain, never mind up to 17,000 feet," said Joe.

It was late afternoon when we left and we were overtaken by darkness on the glacier, after watching the sunset move up the West Wall.

We put the little nylon tent up haphazardly, cooked some corned beef and mash and shrank inside our sleeping bags, out of the cold night air. The glacier was behind us for a while, we hoped. Above us, the sky was white with stars. It was an uncomfortable night—rocks were sticking into us, stonefall was rumbling from the two ridge peaks opposite Changabang. The moraine on which we were camped was creaking and groaning. When we woke up in the morning, the temperature was −14°C.

Whilst we were sorting out our food and equipment we discovered that something had raided our cache of food and, ignoring many other edibles, had prised its way under some plastic sheeting and opened a box of thirty-six Mars Bars. There were no wrappings or debris left, except the ripped box. Thirty-six, individually wrapped, two-ounce bars had disappeared without trace. There were no tracks in the snow—whatever had taken the bars had probably approached on the moraine.

"It's probably a small, nibbling animal," said Joe, "like what happened last year at Base Camp after Dunagiri. Every night something raided my food supplies—it carried off chocolate, Christmas cake, Mintcake—even my toothbrush! I tried to trap it for five days, but I never even saw it."

Perhaps it, or others of its species, lived on the glacier also. But still we could not work out how it had managed to carry off the separate bars.

"Whatever it was," said Joe, "can't have been that clever. It forgot to take with it the free voucher for some more."

We spent the day fiddling with our equipment, nailing and glueing our gaiters to our double boots, choosing the correct ratio of clothing to wear, sharpening and adjusting our crampons ready for action, not wanting to be caught unprepared. Everything had to be just right, and it always felt reassuring to feel at home with equipment, to identify with it, to have handled and fitted the familiar objects on which we were to depend so much. The tools of the craft. As the afternoon shadows lengthened, I was satisfied that the food and equipment were all ready, things were as near perfection as they could be, and now it was up to the feet inside the boots, the head inside the helmet, to perform. The first objective was to establish a camp on the ridge.

On the 16th September we set off in the shadows of the morning. The feeling of tenseness in the stomach, forgotten for some months, that always grips me as I approach the uncertain and the unknown, returned. The harnesses and crampons were put on, the ice axe and hammers slotted into their quick draw holsters. Soon there was just the crunching of our crampons in the snow and the enclosed feeling of hard breathing and heart thumping with the altitude as we moved across the edge of the glacier where it curled upwards towards the foot of the ice slope. Above us, the ice slope stretched in twisting runnels and gullies, up through rock buttresses to the ridge. As we kicked into the snow, the sounds of ice particles danced down the slope.

We crossed the bergschrund, where some snow had slid from above and bridged the gap. The angle suddenly changed and we tip-toed up the ice, hammer and axe in our hands, tapping gently into the ice for support. We were stepping from one existence into another.

"It seems in good nick," said Joe.

"No point in getting the rope out," I said, and we started on up—occasionally taking pictures of each other. The viewfinder could frame the steepness and the position, but not the effort the altitude imposed upon us. I would count ten or fifteen kicks upwards and then have to stop to gasp for breath until my head cleared. Without the rope, each could take the slope at his own pace, which turned out to be similar. I am a couple of stone heavier than Joe, and felt awkward as I looked at the lightness of his movements. I was worried, because in places the ice on which we were climbing was only about six inches thick. We were climbing on great sheets of it which were lying over loose rock and stones. Then, as I moved my weight up, the ice groaned and creaked.

All my senses went tense and alert. There was a sharp crack that bit my ears like a gunshot. I stopped instantly, inert with fear, imagining that a whole sheet of ice was breaking off, with myself on it, and that I was within a split second of plunging hundreds of feet off the mountain. But nothing happened.

"Did you hear that?" I asked Joe.

"Yes," he said, "I felt it as well. It should be all right though, it's just readjusting under our load. Anyway, there's nothing we can do about it. It's just a risk we'll have to put up with."

Soloing doesn't feel as isolated if someone else is climbing a few feet away, but now we quickly decided to move at least fifty feet apart to lessen the load on particular sections of the ice.

Whenever I stopped for a rest, I fixed my eyes on a rock on the ridge but it never seemed to come any nearer. It was intricate work, finding the most stable part of the ice slope. It was a thousand feet high. The early sun was moving now, warming Dunagiri, but seemed an eternity from us, on the west side of the mountain. Changabang was a tall mountain for the sun to creep around. I couldn't feel my toes at all — they were numb with cold. I was experimenting, trying out an idea I had heard was practised by American climbers in Alaska — wearing Neoprene socks as an insulating barrier. It wasn't working. I knew that eventually, when the sun touched us, I would have to take my boots off and warm my feet up again — toes left numb for many hours can quickly become irrevocably damaged. A silly mistake could stop the expedition.

For the final four hundred feet we turned into a shallow gully. The last few feet, now at an altitude of 18,000 feet, seemed endless. But then, suddenly, it was over. We were greeted by a rush of cold air as we reached the ridge. The Bagini Glacier appeared down the other side — often imagined, but now seen for the first time.

On our right was the vertical sweep of granite of the North Face of Changabang. That cold, dark ice-streaked wall never felt the sun. Its height reinforced its Gothic gloom. I hoped our route did not stray onto it. At its top were the 'Horns' of Changabang, on the Summit Ridge which we had seen on photographs of the South Side of the mountain. The wind was evidently stronger up there — flurries of snow spiralled madly around them, over four thousand feet almost directly above our heads. Another circle of mountains had appeared before us. The North-West Face of Kalanka soared in an icy arête directly to its summit — a new angle on what had previously always appeared to be the gentler sister of Changabang. Beyond that mountain was Rishi Pahar, Hardeol and then Tirsuli, the mountain that avalanched André Roche's Swiss expedition when they attempted it after climbing Dunagiri in 1939. On our left, twisting like the ramparts of a great fortress, was Purbi Dunagiri. To the north lay the Latak peaks, visited by the Scots in 1950. But all this was forbidden land, for Joe and I were right on the Inner Line. The border lay just behind them.

Beyond these white peaks, through the gaps between them, we could glimpse the brown plateau of Tibet. At last I had seen Tibet — on the summit of Everest, a horizon that should have been two-hundred-and-fifty miles had been dragged down to one hundred feet by a storm.

The view beyond the crest zone of Asia heightened our feeling of isolation. The tension of the climb disappeared as I breathed in the view. My feet were now planted firmly and my hand steadying me on rock, whereas before my life had hung on four crampon points and aching calves. Looking back down the Rhamani Glacier, Base Camp was a puny blue smudge on the moraine. New mountains were springing from behind ridges. Rishi Kot seemed to have ducked and, once again, changed its mood. Joe was relieved at my happiness:

"I had not experienced any urgency for a change of scene, but Pete seemed to find it oppressive in the Rhamani where our field of vision was restricted. In a way, I felt responsible for having brought him to the area and apologetic about its shortcomings. But now Pete was, for the moment, placated like someone with claustrophobia given a glimpse of open air and freedom."

Not far to the west, along the same ridge on which we were standing, was the Bagini Pass, which Tom Longstaff had crossed on an exploratory trip prior to the Trisul ascent. Accompanied by Charlie Bruce, the Brocherel Brothers and four Gurkhas, he had seen virtually the same view that we were gazing over now. At 10.00 a.m. on 22nd May 1907, on the third day after leaving their Base Camp at the foot of the Bagini Glacier, they reached the Pass after some hours of step cutting. They were carrying enormous loads, including rifles and ammunition and food for ten days. They didn't know what lay on the far side, except that the glacier melt-water that probably stretched down on the far side would eventually join the Rishi. They didn't know if they would enter the Inner Sanctuary, or if they were only entering the Outer Horseshoe. They didn't know, once they got into the basin of the Rishi, whether they would be able to get out again. They took a chance. Using primitive pitons and all the six-hundred feet of rope they had with them, it took them five hours to descend the thousand feet into the Rhamani. They had not, of course, any of the sophisticated ice-climbing gear that Joe and I were using. Longstaff regarded their descent as the only piece of climbing he had done in the Himalayas that would have been regarded as 'stiff' in the Alps. Over the following days, with ever-dwindling supplies, they managed to find their way out over the route that Joe and I had used to walk in. For Longstaff, it was "the happiest, most enchanting week I have ever spent in the mountains". They had reached about the limit of what was possible in the way of cutting loose from one's base. As a contemporary had commented, "Longstaff is one of those people on whom Providence smiles." Today, for Joe and me, it was an achievement sanctified by time, and had none of the competitive aura of the rush after the last great problems of modern Himalayan climbing.

I looked long and hard down the Bagini Glacier. The politics of the seventies would prevent anyone from following Longstaff's journey today. However, in 1907 Longstaff had wanted to go to Everest. Nepal was closed to all foreigners and Tibet, owing to the big power politics of that time, would not allow a big expedition in. So he had come to the Garhwal.

Joe and I were too far down the ridge and too far away from the Wall. We looked apprehensively at the cornices that hung over the ridge and put a single rope on between us. I moved delicately along the ridge, weaving over rock steps and around pinnacles. When the rope went taut, Joe followed and we moved together. This was exhilarating —the sculptured, windswept mushroom and rolling shapes of snow along the ridge had never felt the feet of man. It was satisfying to leave an intelligent line of footprints along them, threading the safest route. It gave the same excitement that I had as a child when, on a cold clear morning, after heavy snowfall, I had risen early and planted my tracks across the previously undisturbed snow-carpeted fields. Perhaps it was ego urging to dominate. I don't know, but it was enjoyable and made me feel alone.

The morning sun was now moving quickly down Bagini peak, a 20,000-foot shapely cone on the ridge which undulated from us towards Dunagiri. Soon it would reach us. First it started to touch Joe, then myself, forming a short twilight zone of about ten feet upon the ridge. I looked upwards to see the sun nudging over the South-West Ridge of Changabang, in a cascade of light over the West Wall, still in shadow.

"Timing our climbing with the sun is going to be critical on the route," said Joe. "It's going to be too bloody cold to do hard climbing in the mornings."

I looked at my watch. 10.00 a.m. It would be nearly two hours before the sun was properly established on the Face.

Suddenly the ridge started to rise steeply into the Wall. "We won't be able to hack a ledge for the tent any higher up than this," I said. I cleared some snow off a granite slab and started to take my boots off. My toes were white with cold and I warmed them with my hands till they were pink and tingling. The inner voice was ticking over — 'Look after yourself, don't exhaust yourself, eat well, keep warm, then you'll keep going.' A larger expedition would have given more comparison of fitness. I always expressed my worries and it seemed that I had more complaints, more physical ailments. I could never trick Joe into admitting a weakness. It was a game:

"Are *your* feet cold, Joe?"

"No, are yours?"

"Oh, no, it's just that my lace has come undone."

We were imposing ourselves on the ridge. We started to hack out a ledge, and the same feeling of reassurance that I had felt lower down on the ridge returned. What had been a bleak, hostile, windswept snow ridge we were turning into home. Even parts of our proposed route above our heads were beginning to look feasible, although a colossal banner of overhangs, 1,500 feet above us, cut across our view.

The descent was harrowing, but was brief, and we were carrying empty sacks, having dumped our loads on the ridge. We had taken three hours to climb up — it took us only one and a half hours to descend. As we walked back across the glacier towards our Advance Camp, it began to snow lightly. We had lost count by mid-afternoon of how often the West Wall had been in and out of its personal clouds. About ten times. The weather pattern seemed stable — but for how long would it hold?

We were exhilarated with our morning's climb. A detached part of me was becoming intrigued at how much I was enjoying myself. Once I could habitualise into climbing the Wall, perhaps it would seem no different from any climb I had done before. There didn't seem to be much objective danger on our proposed route, but we were going to have to give effort continually.

In the late afternoon I went for a walk by myself, to see if I could find the remnants of the Japanese Base Camp below the South-West Ridge. They had hidden the traces well, and it took some time to discover the blackened mound left after they had burnt their refuse. I rescued a polythene bottle full of paraffin from underneath a boulder, and picked up some sticks of bamboo that would be useful for anchoring the tent on the ridge. As I moved back around the shoulder, I could see our Advance Camp below and the stick-like figure of Joe next to the tent. He was cooking the evening meal. He looked bravely insignificant in the wilderness of peaks around.

I had an uncomfortable night and woke about three in the morning. I had been disturbed by the sound of distant rockfall. My stomach was rumbling and I couldn't get back to sleep. It was cramped inside the tent and I was huddled inside two sleeping bags. Outside the temperature had plummeted to −20°C. Then I heard a sound that made my flesh creep—a low growl outside. It lasted about thirty seconds. Then there was some sniffling, a scuttling noise, and I heard one of our pans knocked over. I did not dare move. After five minutes there were no more sounds and I felt it was safe enough to wake Joe. I nudged him.

"Hey, Joe, there's something outside the tent," I whispered hoarsely.

He didn't seem too concerned. "Don't open the door, you'll let the cold in." I agreed with him. If I opened the door, whatever it was was probably so timid that it would have run away at the sound of the zip. And if it didn't run away, and was not timid, we would probably regret having opened the door in the first place! However, after another ten minutes my curiosity took control and I peered outside. It was a brilliant moonlit night—the whole glacial cirque was bathed in colourless light. But there was no sign of anything living.

In the morning the fresh snow of the glacier from the previous afternoon was criss-crossed with tracks. They seemed to come from, and return eventually to, the northern corner of the glacier, beneath the Bagini Pass. One line of tracks paced backwards and forwards from the tent. The tracks seemed to have been made by a four-legged animal—it was difficult to gauge how big they were, or how many animals were involved, because of the loose powder snow. Bears? Leopards? Yeti? Mars Bar-eaters? We did not know the answer.

That day, the 17th September, we went back up to the ridge to ferry some equipment and to pitch the other lightweight tent up there. We would not have had the energy to carry anything heavier than light-weight, six-pound tents such as this. However, Bill Wilkins, of Ulti-mate Equipment (an American, whom we referred to as Ultimate Bill) was very worried when he gave us the tents. "Don't use them too high or in much wind," he warned, "they're just for backpackers." He had stitched a snow valance around them and this proved very useful as we perched the tent on the narrow platform. I became over-enthusiastic in enlarging the platform we had started the previous day.

"Look through this, Joe," I said. I had made a hole through the cornice and we could look down through the proposed tent floor at the Bagini Glacier, 1,000 feet below.

"We'd better move it a bit the other way," said Joe.

The wind rattled the tent but we tensioned it off on ice hammers, deadmen snow anchors and pieces of bamboo, and tip-toed gingerly back down the ice slope to Advance Camp. There, it snowed heavily for one and a half hours, and this stopped us getting on with all the little preparation jobs we had planned. When the snowfall stopped, Changabang looked plastered, as if it had just been creamed by a giant barber. But within half an hour it was clear again, having shaken the surplus layers off in a couple of enormous powder slides.

"Here in this endless and gleaming wilderness I was removed farther than ever from the world of man . . ." I closed the book of Hesse's poems and took a sleeping pill, hoping to avoid another disturbed night. As a result I overslept. Joe was always absolutely hopeless at getting up in the morning, and could never be relied on as an alarm clock. As a result it was late morning by the time we set off. The sun was on us, draining us. We both felt lethargic and were only managing about twenty paces at a time across the glacier. By the time we had reached the ice slope we had both decided, without any discussion at all, to leave the sacks on the snow till the morning, turn back and call it a rest day.

Joe and I discussed our proposed descent route from Changabang (on the assumption that we even got to the top of the mountain). Through binoculars we could see the fixed ropes that Bonington's team had used, still hanging from Shipton's Col. The idea of descending their North-East route and the popping back over Shipton's Col after having done the West Wall was appealing. With a bit of luck we might pass one of the camps of the South Face team on the glacier, and stop for a cup of tea. We had received various opinions from the first ascensionists about the feasibility of this plan. Martin Boysen thought "It should be all right". Chris Bonington changed his opinion from encouragement to dissuasion. "It's a very tricky ridge," he had finally said. "I'd go back the way you've come, if I were you. Better the devil you know than the one you don't."

It was a day of peace amidst days of effort, a lovely relaxing day. It was a jewel in my memory during the days that followed, the calm before the storm. There was little wind and just an occasional puff of a cloud in the sky. The only sounds were the creakings of the shifting rocks and ice of the glacier and surrounding peaks, and these sounds only accentuated the silence. The mountains were peeping through the mask of self-struggle that could so easily obscure them from my vision. I remembered a very similar day I had spent over four years previously with two friends in the Hindu Kush, during my first expedition to the Himalayas. It had been the day before we set out on the North Face of Kohi Khaaik. Three days later we had emerged on the summit, dehydrated and exhausted, above a very difficult and dangerous route, to face a long descent and a sixty-mile walk back to our Base Camp without food. Perhaps this, too, would be a calm day before our strength and will were tested.

Joe was relaxed on that day. "It doesn't seem as oppressive up here, as it could be with Dick," he wrote in his diary. "It's a bit more lighthearted." Sometimes I felt as if Dick was with us, Joe talked such a lot about their experiences together. He always talked of Dick's self-discipline, frugality and determination with a mixture of amusement and awe.

As the day wore on, Joe and I became immersed in our books. Joe was reading *Night Runners of Bengal*, and I became submerged in *The Odessa File*. They were easy books to read, and we escaped with them for a while.

After we had picked up the loads on the following day, the 19th September, and carried them up to the camp on the ridge, we were ready to move. On the 20th September we piled all the remaining food and equipment we would need into our sacks and climbed up to the tent on the ridge. Our food could stretch to about fourteen days and we hoped that would be long enough time to do the route. The loads were heavy, about fifty pounds each, and it was tricky work climbing the ice slope. It was our fourth carry there and, we hoped, the last time we would set foot on that slope.

We had a thousand feet of eight-millimetre terylene non-stretch rope with us, and a few old climbing ropes of our own. Our planned tactics were to run out all the fixed rope, returning to the camp every evening. We thought we probably had enough rope to reach the icefield. Then, after all the rope was fixed, we would set off with all our remaining food and the hammocks, pulling up the ropes behind us as we ascended. Working from our hammocks above the icefield, we would then run our ropes out again, up the upper rock tower, push on through to the summit and descend the other side. It all sounded deceptively simple.

Since it was only late morning we determined to start on the Wall that afternoon. We decided to lead four rope lengths at a time. In this way the one in front could get into the rhythm of leading, and the one following could switch his adrenalin off and rest his mind for a while. I had first go. I climbed without a sack, wearing my blue one-piece Everest suit and with all the hardware draped from my full body harness. Joe was to follow, carrying all the rope to be fixed in his sack.

"I've never used these things before," he said, fingering the jumar clamps that he was to use to climb up the rope after me.

"It's as good a place as any to learn," I said.

Keeping well to the right of the cornice, the climbing was straight-forward until I reached a point a hundred feet above the tent. The ridge was disappearing, curving into an ice-coated slab. I tapped a piton in a crack and teetered up the ice on the front points of my crampons. Scraping with my axe, I managed to clear a handhold, pulled myself up to it and mantleshelved onto it. Above it the slope became uniform again. It was hot work, kicking up it in the sun. By the end of the afternoon I had run out four rope lengths and Joe had led one—seven hundred feet of climbing. We had reached the foot of the Wall that stretched upwards to the barrier overhangs that guarded the foot of the icefield. We felt elated.

"At this rate, we'll be on the icefield tomorrow," said Joe.

"Somehow, a certain tension had been broken—we had started; the old familiar preoccupation with the problem in hand; gone were the fears and anxieties of the time when all we could do was look at and think about the mountain, not knowing what it would involve, what it would do to us . . . we estimated we could reach the summit inside a week."

Quickly, we abseiled down the ropes, straight to the tent door, took off our crampons and flopped inside. I suddenly felt tired. It had been good to start the climbing so positively, but the altitude had a draining effect. We nestled in our sleeping bags and cooked a meal of American freeze-dried meat, to which we added potato powder. After that we had some honey pudding, a piece of the fruit cake which my mother had baked for us, and some tea. For the first time ever, I took a Ronicol Timespan, that we had been told couldn't do any harm and might clear the sludge in our capillaries, by dilating them for eight hours. This we followed with a vitamin pill and a Valium pill to help us sleep. "We're a couple of high-altitude junkies," I said.

5

Neither of us believed that these did any physical good, but it was a reassuring ritual and a nightly ceremony.

It was cosy inside, once I had turned my mind off to the drop on either side of the tent. We had laid out all the ropes and the two hammocks on the floor of the tent, to insulate us from the snow underneath the thin ground sheet. The wind was continually blowing across the tent, rattling and flapping the nylon. It was a disconcerting noise and I felt uneasy about the siting of the camp. But there was nothing I could do about it and I drifted off to sleep.

CHAPTER FOUR

The Barrier

21st–27th September

A thin empty buzzing, like a bee trapped in a can, scraped at the surface of my consciousness. It was Joe's alarm wrist watch which we had placed on an aluminium plate between us. It was pitch dark. The wind over the ridge was flapping the tent rhythmically, powerful and threatening. Joe still seemed to be sleeping. My mind retracted and the immediate world floated off again.

My eyes sprang open. I looked at the luminous fingers on Joe's watch. An hour must have passed; it was 6.30 a.m. Cold dawn, a long way over the mountains, gave a hint of grey light on the inside of the tent. Thoughts tumbled in. The route! The time! Breakfast! I twisted my arms outside my sleeping bag, shuffled forward to the zip on the inner tent and pulled it down. I put my head torch on and looked at the thermometer: −20°C. The weather was definitely becoming colder. Pulling my gloves on, I unzipped the outer door where the wind met my face, whipping the flap into the air. I pulled my axe from the side of the tent and hacked at the snow wall of the cornice. Using the adze, I was able to break off large chunks of snow that rolled into the tent entrance. The fine powder and disturbed ice crystals spun round, stinging my face and pouring down my sleeves. I grabbed the zip and shut the world out again, then lit the stove. It was a fresh Gaz cartridge and the propane-butane mixture quickly started melting the bulging mass of snow I had crammed in the pan. Joe stirred briefly and turned over. I tried to doze as well, but the melting snow needed constant attention. Breakfast was on its way—all to be served in our one-pint plastic mugs—first a mug of tea, then porridge, then a tin of fish, then a hot fruit drink. The melting and cooking took two and a half hours. Joe just took the courses, muttering "Ta", his eyes moving in and out of sleep, cocooned in his own thoughts, pretending that the daytime had still not arrived.

As soon as the stove was out Joe allowed the day to start. "Don't worry, I'll be cooking the evening meal," he said.

"Am I expected to cook breakfast all the way up the route?" I asked.

"Why, do you want me to cook that as well?"

We could start moving around inside the tent in our one-piece suits and boots. Before leaving, we stuffed our pockets with sweets and chocolate to sustain us during the day. Outside on the ridge there was only room for one person at a time to put his crampons and body harness on. We had decided never to jumar up on a rope attached from the same anchor point at the same time. Joe was ready first and, since it was his turn to lead, he set off from the start of the fixed rope where it curled away from the tent door. It was 9.45 a.m. After he was past the first anchor I followed him.

We were both carrying sacks full of gear and rope and it was hard work. The terylene seemed soft and vulnerable as the teeth of the jumar gritted into it and I sank my full weight back on it. Dressed in all the high-altitude equipment, carrying a heavy sack, I felt like the lead weight used for testing ropes. And sometimes they snapped — I ought to know, as part of my job was investigating mountaineering equipment failure. These ropes had no standard — they were made for yachting. What would the BMC Technical Committee think of me? And what if a peg came out? I knew that low-stretch ropes such as these were not designed to take much of a shock load. I never seemed to trust pegs that I had put in, it was as if I knew their weaknesses too well. I wished someone else had put them in, then I could rely on them blindly! My mind and body were now completely alert to all the dangers, refreshed after the night's sleep. Above me, Joe disturbed the snow and it bounced down in spray and chunks. The wind and cold in the flat morning light were hostile. But I was a prisoner of my own ambition, and persisted on up the ropes.

Joe was waiting for me, perched on a step in the ice. He racked some of the hardware onto the rings in his harness and started to uncoil a couple of ropes. I emptied the remaining gear out of his sack into mine, and tied onto the same piton. It was a wordless ritual. Joe set off up the ice, tapping his axe and hammer in, moving his feet up quickly and neatly.

"You should be able to go straight up from there," I shouted, when he was about twenty feet above my head.

"The ice is really thin on the slab here," he said.

He made another move up and I could hear the sound of metal

scraping on granite. Then he started fiddling with his rack of pitons, selected a thin knife blade, and tapped it into a crack on a rib of rock on his right. 'Come on,' I thought, 'we've got a lot of ground to cover.'

"I'm coming down," said Joe. "I'll try it further over on the right."

"But there's reasonable-looking ground about ten feet above you," I said.

"I don't think this peg's any good . . ." said Joe.

It looked too far off the route to go to the right to me. 'I wish he'd stop messing about,' I thought. 'I'm sure I could bomb up there, he just doesn't like to commit himself to a hard move.' But I said nothing. Each of us had to look after himself beyond a certain point. It would have been easy to comment, but unfair unless I had tried myself. Thoughts could be brutal, they had to be, but only when they mature into constructive opinions should I speak them. The success of the climb was all that mattered.

It would be psychologically bad, at this stage in the climb, for Joe to relinquish the lead to me.

"O.K.," I said, and paid the rope out carefully as Joe descended below the peg. 'I'll have to get that out,' I thought.

Joe disappeared around up to the peg, tied my rope through a sling on it and I lowered myself down on it until I could move around the corner and up to where Joe was sitting. I untied from the rope and pulled it through the sling and back to myself.

"You should be able to get back on line by traversing back up through those blocks," I told him. I was feeling impatient, on edge, the idea of climbing the whole Wall above was worrying me, but I had to wait my turn.

Joe moved off, edging along a huge, seemingly detached block the size of himself as if he were walking the plank. The sun had now wheeled fully onto us and the rock began to seem more friendly. Whilst Joe pegged over a bulge fifty feet above me I sat on a sloping ledge. More of Tibet was emerging but I had no inclination to gaze. I still wanted to lead but, at the same time, was suppressing my impatience, part of me recognising it as irrational. It seemed to take Joe an age to lead the pitch. When I came to follow, it was the first steep bit of ground I had to jumar on the route and spinning out from the rock unnerved me. It was impossible to tell how difficult the climbing had been for Joe—I was just the following climbing machine that jumared and took the running belays out. I found Joe directly above the spot which he had failed to lead.

"I'll go down and swing the ropes around," he said. He descended the rope I had fixed in place and, after detaching it lower down, swung precariously around the edge of the buttress on it, whilst I protected him with a rope from above. Then he jumared straight back up to me and we straightened the fixed rope out.

"We'll probably have to do a lot of this sort of tidying up of fixed ropes as we go along, if we're going to stretch it to the icefield," I said.

The icefield. It seemed further away now than it had seemed the previous day.

Joe began to turn on the pressure in his climbing. When he realised how late in the afternoon it was, he quickly climbed 150 feet up the broken ground of rock and ice above us. It was a fast piece of climbing and brought us to the point where the angle of the slabs tilted from 55° to 65°. We were still 250 feet below the barrier of overhangs. We were getting near them, if only slowly. We could only live in the present and think of the next obstacle. If we kept on tackling the Face as a series of obstacles, each with its own solution, then we would have to reach the top sometime.

We fastened all our superfluous equipment to the high point and slid back down the ropes to the camp. The abseiling was fast and straightforward and we were pleased to arrive at 5.30 p.m. — it was still light. There would be hard climbing the next day, but that could have been next year for all we cared. Soon we had some hot drinks in front of us inside the tent and the comforting thought of twelve hours' rest ahead of us.

All that night and the next day the bitterly cold wind blew. By this time the alarm had twinged us into action. We were back into position and ready to climb by 10.30 a.m., having woken at 5.00 a.m. and moved off by 8.30 a.m. After taking his crampons off, Joe started up a long groove line that stretched up in the general direction of the overhangs. It was magnificent, hard, steep, free climbing, mainly jamming and lay-backing up the crack which was rough and ragged — rather like the famous beautiful granite of the French Alps. But Changabang's granite, not marked on geology maps of the area, had an air of mystery. It was this intrusion of white, coarse-grained granite that gave Changabang its miraculous shape, unlike all the mountains around it. It was so white that when he first saw it, Longstaff had thought it was snow lying on cliffs at an impossible angle. To us, it was so sound and rough to clasp, it was as if it had been made to climb on.

Joe belayed to a large flake of rock, high in the groove and I took over the lead. Many clouds obscured the sun; it should have reached us by then. Occasionally, to do difficult moves or fiddle with equipment, I had to take off my mitts and climb with just my under-gloves and fingerless mitts. There was a lot of ice in the back of the groove and I managed to smash most of it off with my short ice hammer. As the distance of rock between myself and Joe increased, I began to enjoy myself. This was what I'd come for. I had come for the physical thrill of climbing, not for swinging around on perilously thin fixed ropes. For a hundred feet of climbing I felt confident and light and indestructible. I felt relaxed, rapturously free from a sense of effort, pain and danger, and in total control. Even the altitude almost ceased to complicate my breathing.

The feeling did not last long. The groove dwindled out into a hold-less wall at the same steep angle. I had used nearly all my equipment up. Twenty feet above me, the Wall looked as if it relented, over at its right-hand edge, underneath the overhangs. If I could traverse diagonally up to that point, perhaps we could turn the overhangs through their right-hand side, where they looked as if they were at their narrowest point. I would be climbing right above the main Wall beneath the icefield—a near vertical drop of about 1,050 feet. My boots felt big and clumsy as I stepped away from the comforting security of the crack and balanced on two tiny footholds. Below me, Joe was waiting in the wind:

"That was my stint done. Pete took over the leading, up a groove towards the overhangs. Now we were on a real wall. There was no shelter from the wind. I shuffled about to find the most comfortable position on my footholds; Pete was out of sight in the cloud. I was cold.

"The cold had been driven right through my bones. The rope only moved out slowly; I shouted up to Pete that there was not much of it left, with no idea of what he was doing. Through a brief clearing in the cloud I saw him bridged across an ice-choked crack. There did not seem to be anywhere for him to rest. I was anxious. His calls to me were unintelligible, as mine probably were to him. Mist closed in again, more time passed. 'What the hell is he doing?'

"There was no rope left. I shouted to him, as well as a dry throat would let me. He must have realised what I meant. I undid the knots which tied me to the stance, in order to give him a little more rope; I hoped, that hope based on confidence, that he was safe and could not fall. With me untied, it would be very serious if he did.

"My whole physical being tensed with the cold, untensed and shook, trying to find some warmth. It was starting to snow. I interrogated myself with questions about our sanity — 'When will we stop this madness and get down to warmth?'

"'Come on, Pete,' I screamed in my mind."

I reached a thin crack with the tips of my fingers and tapped a soft steel piton into it. It seemed secure, so I used it to lever my feet and weight up until I could reach higher with my other hand. I scraped some snow away from the start of a depression in the Wall and curled my fingers around a hand hold. Trusting everything to this, I lurched up, my feet scraping against the rock and mantleshelfed on it. The effort had me gasping frantically for air. From there I hooked my ice hammer on an edge of rock and pulled up on that to teeter onto a sloping snow-covered shelf. I knocked in the only two pitons I had left. One of them seemed fairly sound so I yelled, "O.K., Joe, I'm there." Then I noticed it was snowing. I had no idea how long the pitch had taken me to lead, it was as if time had stopped, I had been so engrossed.

Within moments the clouds opened and deluged snow, then hail-stones. It was only mid-afternoon and we might have done a little more climbing, but the storm precluded anything except descent. I hammered in two more pitons and tightened and fastened the fixed rope I had trailed behind me. I had to knot two ropes together and then jerked back down them through the cloud to Joe.

"It's an impressive situation up there," I said. "We might be able to get around the overhangs to the right. There's quite a balcony to start from." And that's what we called it after that.

"I see you've fixed my two old climbing ropes," said Joe. "They should be all right, though I wouldn't jerk the yellow one too hard, I've fallen off on it a few times in the past."

We started abseiling quickly down, back towards the camp. The storm only lasted half an hour, and by the time we had reached the tent the evening sun was streaming through breaks in the cloud. Then suddenly, amazingly, the wind, which had been our constant companion all the time on the ridge, dropped completely. The tent stopped rattling and we no longer had to talk above its noise to each other.

We finished our evening meal with Christmas pudding and custard, to celebrate.

"I wish we had a cassette player up here," said Joe. "A bit of rock music wouldn't go amiss."

I was still scribbling diary notes onto bits of paper. I had left my diary on the moraine at Advance Camp, thinking that if anything happened to us on the Wall, then at least someone might find a record of what had happened to us up till that point. Also, I censored it—I didn't write about occasional disagreements Joe and I had, or worries I felt about the route. I thought, 'What if this is the last thing I ever write, and somebody reads it?' I find things said and done in the strange world of an expedition, once recorded, become inflated and can be easily misunderstood by the non-mountaineer or uninformed commentator, eager for 'the reasons behind the tragedy'. Joe was intrigued by my assiduous writings:

"I wondered why Pete wanted to preserve the situations, rather than use every conscious minute to savour them. He was usually full of apt literary quotations and when I told him that Graham Greene had said that a writer's greatest problem was not trying to remember, but trying to forget, he thought that I had made it up to excuse my laziness in keeping a diary."

My finger-ends had been chewed by the rough granite. We had to change our under-gloves many times because of this wear and tear. Fortunately, we had brought many pairs. I carefully put antiseptic cream on them, followed by plasters—I knew how easily infection can run amok when the flesh is weakened by exposure to the cold, having had a septic foot on the Hindu Kush expedition that had made my foot so swollen I could not put my boot on. I dusted my feet, massaged them and changed my socks before getting into my sleeping bag. Frostbite or infection could be our greatest enemy. It was only 7.30 p.m. by the time we settled down, and we were both asleep by 8.00 p.m.

The night closed my fitful dreams from the mountain, as if the climb on Changabang was just the surface of my life, irrelevant compared with my other life in the west. Only for a fraction of the time in my life was I climbing and my dreams were always about memories and situations and people at home.

The morning of the 23rd September was clear and still. We slept past the alarm, but still managed to move away by 8.00 a.m. I set off, jumaring first. The previous evening I had tied the two ropes knotted together below the Balcony on to the soft metal piton I had tapped behind the flake. This, I had hoped, would make it easy to ascend diagonally. As I was half way up Joe's frayed, old yellow rope, there was a little jerk and I somersaulted backwards. 'God, the rope's snapped,' I thought, 'I'm dead.' Rock was hurtling past and I glimpsed the glacier two thousand feet below. Then the rope began to tighten and stretch and spun me round into an upright position till I was yo-yoing up and down, hanging out from the Wall around the corner from the Balcony. At first I did not know what had happened. I gasped and then took brief breaths, looking wildly around me. The rope was still attached above me—the jumars had bitten deep into it, but the protective sheath was still uncut. 'I should be all right,' I thought. The knot on the rope above me had held, and so had Joe's old ropes. I looked up, along the line of the rope, trying to find the reason for the twenty-foot swinging fall. The peg behind the flake had come out. 'My fault,' I thought, 'I put it in.' Still, it had held my weight the previous day. 'Thank God I didn't fall on the eight-millimetre terylene,' I thought, 'even if it hadn't snapped, the jumars would have sliced straight through it.' At that moment Joe appeared around the corner, lower down the fixed ropes, about a hundred feet away.

"You're going slowly today. What are you doing over there?" he shouted.

"Oh, I just thought I'd go for a swing over this wall and see what it was like," I said. "The peg I put in half way up to the Balcony coming out, helped me."

"Christ," said Joe. "I thought I heard a little yelp and a clatter. Can you get back from there?"

"I can as long as the rope doesn't snap."

Fun is closely linked to fear. I began to slide the jumars slowly up the rope, trying to avoid any sudden sharp movement. After fifty feet I was on the Balcony. It had taken two and a half hours to reach it from the camp. The uncontrolled feeling of being flung about helplessly that the accident had brought, had shaken me—avalanches, falls, cars rolling, I had experienced them all in the past. Death could so easily follow that. The barrier of overhangs now stretched far out above our heads.

Over on our left, the overhang jutted out fifty feet from the Wall. The only line through it was an overhanging groove a hundred feet high. We couldn't see if there was a crack in the back of it all the way, and doubted if we had the equipment to climb it. It would be all arti-ficial climbing and might take us an exhausting two days. The only hope was to the right.

I racked a lot of equipment to my harness and dumped my sack on the Balcony next to Joe. It was difficult to decide what, and how much, to take. If I took too much, I would exhaust myself carrying all the weight and would be unable to do any free climbing—if some were necessary. Suppressing a knot of fear in my stomach, I moved to the edge of the Balcony. The exit from the Balcony was guarded by a seemingly detached block about four feet square. I had to use it. I slid a long knife blade piton in a crack that lay at the top of it, attached a long sling to it, and leant tentatively on it. It held. I leant on it with more confidence and looked around the corner. Below, the white hard granite swept downwards without a break or a feature to halt the eye. It bowed beneath me and I could not see where it eventually merged with the lower icefields that swept across the wall in curving bands. From here I could look right across the entire West Wall, to the South-West ridge. Great bold sweeps of rock with hidden amphitheatres and great barriers of icicles, hundreds of feet long, confronted me. I squinted at them, for the sun was moving over the South-West ridge into a powder-blue sky. 'Good, it'll warm up soon,' I thought.

I peered up at the overhangs above me. There seemed to be a ramp line that stretched diagonally right and upwards intermittently through a series of stepped roofs. The whole structure consisted of suspended blocks of granite on top of each other. I looked back at Joe, "There's some sort of line up there, sort of solid but detached."

I tapped a one-inch knife blade into a crack just over the edge of the first roof and clipped an etrier into it. I put my foot into it and gently gave it my weight, looking downwards and hunching my shoulders under my helmet in case the peg came out and smashed into me. I hopped in the etriers, it still held. So I launched out up the rungs of the etriers and pulled over the edge of the roof feeling very vulnerable. The first peg is always the worst—if it had come out I would have smashed my back on the Balcony. That sort of injury would have brought complications, for we were without the helicopter safety net-work that exists in crowded mountain areas. From the peg I made two strenuous free moves and locked myself into a little niche in the over-hangs by wedging my knees on one side of the niche, and my back against the other side. I was about fifteen feet above Joe, but could only see his feet from where I was, for his head was hidden by overhangs.

I was in the sunshine, but Joe was in icy shadows. Because of how he was tied onto the belay, he couldn't move into the sun. I saw one foot stretch out into the sunlight, then the other. He was trying to warm them up! He was painfully cold:

"Over and over again I asked myself what I was doing there, and made another promise that this would be the last time."

I was facing the wrong way though managed to twist painfully around and place another piton, just over the tip of the overhang above my head. At full stretch I patted it in, timidly. I had a morbid fear that the whole overhang would collapse with me if I shook it too hard. How did I know it would not? Nobody had been there before!

From there a sloping, uneven ramp, a foot wide, stretched upwards across the leaning Wall. It was plastered by white ice that was stacked along it, smoothing it flush against the Wall. Leaning out on the piton I started trying to smash the ice off with my axe. It was hard work. I hacked until my arms were exhausted and I could hardly open my fingers or lift the adze, panted until some strength returned, then started again. Eventually the hard ice at the back of the ramp came away and I managed to place a piton in it. This I pounded in as hard as I could, then used it to gain some height. Two more pitons higher up, the ramp stopped for a couple of feet and then bulged out again. Holding myself in balance with one foot on the ramp and one braced against the Wall, I reached across to where the ramp started again. The ice was too far away and seemed too hard to smash off. My mind was working quickly, absorbing all the tiny details around me, bringing movements into slow motion. In the white granite in front of my eyes were particles of clear quartz, silvery muscovite and jet black tourmaline. My attention floated to them; they emphasised my insignificance—emphasised the fact that I was fragile, warm-blooded and living, clinging to the side of this steep, inhospitable world.

My mind jerked back to the situation. There was only one thing to do. I leant across and hooked the pick of my ice hammer on the start of the ice, attached my etrier to it and began to ease my weight across into it. It was a long stretch, and I knew if I lost my balance the resulting sudden movements would pull the hammer off and probably some pitons as well. "Watch the rope, Joe," I shouted. He could have been a thousand miles away. 'If I fall now,' I thought, 'I'll swing right out into space and have quite a job getting back onto the rock—if I've the energy.' The hammer held. I put an ice screw in, above the hammer. It went in four inches. I tied it off before putting my weight onto it. I could see a foothold, the first one on the pitch; it was no bigger than the top of an egg cup. On my fingers, scrabbling for holds, I made two moves across and got my weight over it. If I was careful, I could rest and assess the situation.

What a place! I looked at my watch—I had been climbing for two hours and was bathed in sweat, although the rock and the air were cold. It had been some of the hardest climbing I had ever done. The air was soundless, emphasising the loneliness of my situation. Where would I go from here? Fifty feet above me I could see the massive detached block we had seen hanging below the icefield when we had examined the Face through binoculars from Advance Camp. We had called it 'the Guillotine'. No, not up there. The angle of the Wall had eased just off the vertical, and I carefully traversed for fifteen feet to the right, pain in my worn finger-ends forgotten, submerged in action. The rock became crumbly, and I had great difficulty in placing the only pegs I had left. I hammered in a nut, after excavating a little crack for it with my hammer, tied the rope off and shouted down, "O.K., Joe, come on. I'm there. Or somewhere. Gently does it." I was standing on one tiny foothold and my leg muscles were exhausted and quivery. I tied a couple of long slings to the pegs and stood in them.

Drained, but deeply satisfied, I hung there. It had been a struggle but I had made some progress—and was it not a struggle that I was seeking? Here, there were no spectators, none of that inflated, blown-up feeling of having everything filmed and recorded that there had been on Everest. The mountain was challenging our tenacity—but we would not give in.

Joe swung around the corner alarmingly. He was carrying an enormous sackful of gear that must have weighed fifty pounds. 'I hope those pegs hold,' I thought. Part of me wanted recognition for the piece of climbing I had done.

"Sorry it took me such a long time," I said, as he came across to the peg where I was hanging. Half of me meant that—the other half was fishing for a compliment.

"It must have been quite hard," he said.

No, we couldn't share out fears or achievements on this climb, we had to have a business relationship. If we opened up our relationship whilst on the climb, the mountain might exploit our weaknesses. We must present a united front against the mountain and swallow the subtleties of interaction. Self-preservation had to come first, even if this made us cruelly unsympathetic. Looking after my own life was evolving as a full-time occupation. I was tired, but did not offer Joe the lead. The icefield was in the top of my mind and I wanted to reach it.

It was a complicated manœuvre, changing over the belay with Joe, making sure, checking and counter-checking that each of us was still clipped on, and none of our equipment was in danger of falling off. The struggle, the sun, the situation and the altitude had dazed us into a dream. But the discipline within me recognised that this was the time a mistake could be made.

There was a groove above the belay, and I started up that. It seemed to dwindle out in the overhanging wall in the direction of the Guillotine. After twenty feet of straightforward artificial climbing, I thought I could see a line of weakness high on the right, where the foot of the icefield plunged over the wall in an enormous Icicle. I was climbing on a rib parallel with it. If I could reach the Icicle, climb the rock next to it, and then climb back onto the ice where it swept over the edge, then there might be a possibility of reaching the icefield. But to reach the Icicle I would have to tension down and commit myself to a long pitch. There was no time for that, the rock was already reddening with the sinking sun and we had to sort out the fixed rope through the overhangs. I clipped my rope through a karabiner to my high point and lowered myself down to Joe.

"You're missing some good atmospheric effects," said Joe.

I looked around and saw the mist billowing around the Wall.

"We'd better get down," I said.

We tied the rope off in six places on the pitch. "It'll be a grip going up and down through that lot, with all those pegs, knots and krabs in the way," I said.

"Yeah, a real Toni Kurz pitch," said Joe.

Toni Kurz was the Austrian climber who died on the North Face of the Eiger in 1936. Following the successive deaths of his three companions, he managed to rope down almost into the arms of a rescue party which, due to the bad conditions, was unable to ascend a small overhang to reach him. A knot in his rope jammed in a karabiner and he died of exhaustion whilst still just out of reach. A nightmare name for a nightmare pitch.

Back in the tent, after our meal, we scribbled our daily notes. "Someday, I'm goin' to get there," hummed Joe. A Carole King song. It was the only line either of us could ever remember. "I think it will be the key pitch," I wrote, "it feels a sort of psychological breakthrough for me; if that doesn't stop me, nothing will. But things are going very slowly."

Joe wrote: "It must be the hardest climbing in the Himalayas. Little niggling things seem to get on our nerves. I wish Pete was more considerate." Above us, the light faded off Changabang like sound receding.

Back the next morning, it was as if we had never left the arena. Refreshed after a night's sleep, I approached the Icicle in a different mood. Leaning down on tension from the rope, I cut steps across it, hoping that the ice was glued firmly to the rock. I kicked across some snow, onto the rock on the other side. It was a spectacular situation. One of my ropes hung over to Joe like the Golden Gate. A perfect crack split the wall above. I climbed it for twenty feet and suspended myself from some slings. It was a pitch that had been mainly diagonal and a tricky one for Joe to have to follow. Where I had tensioned down onto the ice, Joe had to lower himself and climb down, facing the possibility of an awesome pendulum swing across the void towards me.

"How am I expected to do this?" he muttered, then saw that he had no option except to have a go. A few neat movements and he was across.

Twenty feet above our heads, the Icicle appeared to change angle into a tiny little gully that crept down from the icefield.

"I'll climb up as high as I can above our heads, place a peg and tension across on the rope," I said. I put my crampons on, ready for the manoeuvre, knowing that as soon as I swung down onto the ice I would be committed and would have to climb—there would not be any room to change footwear, once started! The crack we were hanging from petered out fifteen feet above us. I hammered a peg as near to the top of it as I could reach, then tapped another peg in upside down behind a fragile flake of rock on the wall. Then I started leaning left-wards out on the rope. It was a hot, cloudless day—the best yet—and conditions were as perfect as they would ever be at this altitude for attempting this sort of hard technical climbing.

Watching my footwork very carefully, crampons grating on the rock and flashing in the sunlight, I eventually reached a point where I could just touch the Icicle if I stretched across with my ice hammer. I was arched across on tiny footholds and faced a big pendulum from the tensioned rope. Below me I could hear Joe's camera clicking. 'I mustn't mention it,' I thought, 'must call his bluff. But I hope he's holding the rope all right.' Then I spoke. "Watch the rope, Joe, I'm moving onto the ice." I swung down onto the ice hammer, hoping that it would not prise a lump of ice off and catapult me off as well. It did not. I smashed the pick of my axe in and kicked the front points of my crampons. They held also, but all my weight was on my arms. The cold discipline of ice-climbing technique moved into the front of my mind, not allowing hasty movements. First the axe, then the hammer, I tapped in above me, then the 'bunny hop' of bringing my crampons up until the adze of the axe and the hammer were level with my eyes. Then repeat. Thoughts of falling were now thrust to the bottom of my mind. I was committed and lost in movement. Then the angle eased. A rock jutted out of the ice and I smashed the ice from off the top of it and planted my foot sideways. I was nearly fainting from the effort. The oxygen debt that the previous few minutes had built up was blurring and fading my eyesight. The ice around me momentarily grew dark.

It gave a surge of relief to start moving up the shallow gully of ice, with my weight now over my legs rather than on my arms. I stopped at the first place I could make a ledge for both feet and brought Joe up. Once more we were trying to straighten out the line of the fixed rope and Joe managed to save a whole rope length by detaching himself and the rope behind him from all runners and belays since the stance at the end of the Toni Kurz pitch. This meant we could abseil straight down the overhanging rock next to the Guillotine, avoiding any detours. My four leads were now over and it had taken me nearly three days to do them. For me, the Barrier had been crossed, now the iron was returning to my soul; I was rediscovering that feeling of inner invincibility that I had felt on the descent from Everest. Had the climbing not been so utterly demanding, I could not have felt this way. Above us, the prospects seemed rosy, with the icefield stretching upwards for five hundred feet to the Upper Tower.

"I might as well get a pitch in," said Joe, and he swiftly moved up the icefield, crossing a few bulges where the rock broke through. Then, after 150 feet, he tapped some pitons in and abseiled back down to me. He seemed happy.

"Without stopping to talk about it, by some imperceptible transition of thought, it was clear that we could climb the West Wall, provided we could stick it out. The icefield had a symbolic

aura about it, and entering it was like entering other secret places —
there was the same air of privilege and mystery about it. I had the
same feeling about the Spider on the North Face of the Eiger."

Soon, we were winging down the ropes back to the camp. Whilst
we were on the first few abseils, the sun began to set. Cloud was
pluming off the entire length of the South-East Ridge of the pyramid
of Dunagiri. The sun had reddened this windswept cloud and it looked
as if the entire ridge were aflame, like a burning beam of wood. I saw
Joe below me, never slow on the draw with his camera, taking photographs rapidly. 'Typical,' I thought, 'he'll get all the best pictures.'
Seizing my camera, I tried to take a picture but the film was finished.
In fumbling to change films, I watched with dismay as the exposed
film slid between my fingers and bounced, at ever-increasing speed,
over the Inner Line and fifteen hundred feet towards the Bagini
Glacier. I lost film of two days' climbing that could never be replaced.
   "I got a good cover photo there," grinned Joe, when I reached the
tent. I just grunted. It had been a hard day.

   "I think about the soft things in life a lot" [noted Joe in his
   diary that evening. About the beauties of the sunset he wrote:]
   "They're phenomena only partially observed, and hardly appreciated, from a corner of my mind which makes me photograph
   them to look at some time when I can enjoy them."

So many things can happen in two days. Back home, I would have
been to a few meetings, travelled to many places, read the newspapers,
received and sent a stack of letters, used the telephone continuously,
perhaps watched television and been to the pub, played some records.
But here, all such communication, company and movement was
locked in the past. For two days on Changabang the only motivating,
all-consuming purpose had been to climb the Barrier.
   We now had three ropes left between us — once we had used those
up, we would have run out 1,700 feet, including all our climbing ropes.
It was a long way to jumar back up on the morning of the 24th
September.
   "It's a good thing we haven't much more rope," said Joe as we left.
"We've got to stop soon or we'll use all our time and energy up
jumaring. Also, if we keep on going backwards and forwards through
the Toni Kurz pitch and past the Guillotine, sooner or later one of us

6

is bound to make a mistake going past all those knots and pegs and unclip the wrong thing."

"We'll move up with the hammocks and pull the ropes up tomorrow," I said. "There aren't many camp sites up here."

Three hours later we reached our high point of the previous day. We were carrying very heavy loads, since we were taking food and equipment to leave at the high point in preparation for the big move the next day. The rope length next to the Guillotine which we had straightened out the previous day was exhausting, since we were hanging free. Here, we had tied off our climbing ropes and these, being nylon, stretched and bounced us up and down in the air like helpless puppets as we jerked our jumars up. I switched my mind off to the possibility of rope abrasion or anchor failure and kept toiling upwards.

To lead brings excitement and draws hidden strength; to follow relaxes, then enervates. The situations were spectacular and I was taking photographs furiously, to try and recapture the scenes of the previous day's dropped film. Joe moved quickly and dynamically up the ice and I envied him the liberation of movement that the change in angle of reaching the icefield brought. For the first time I felt closely involved with his leading, because there was much action to watch and, because of the scanty protection, the consequences of a fall would have been disastrous.

"The icefield was a bottle-green, repulsive colour, several hundred feet to the top. Rather than climb directly up the ice, I climbed to the left, where rock showed through. It was less fatiguing than tip-toeing up hard ice. The rock was poor and shattered if I tried to hammer in a peg. Frequently, as I teetered precariously up, I had to make wild moves to escape from a crumbling hold and grab something else, which might be only marginally more sound. All the time a prohibition on falling drummed inside my head. I was more exhausted from the nervous tension involved than from the physical exertion. From the top of a slab of rock I hooked my axe into the ice above, stretching as far as possible to reach beyond where the ice was just a veneer over hidden rock. By an awkward manœuvre, I put on my crampons and was now equipped to perform in the medium of ice for the last hundred feet up to the top rim of the icefield and the base of the huge upper tower of rock up which we next had to find a way."

Jumaring after Joe was a nightmarish struggle. I had to jumar up the nylon ropes for fifteen feet to take in the stretch before I could start gaining height. Joe was leading without a sack, so I was carrying all the equipment in mine, and it pulled me back continually. With the sack on my back, like a crippling symbolic burden of sin, every step demanded a conscious effort of will power. The settled weather was beginning to break up and clouds were swirling up onto the icefield from lower down on the Face. It was snowing lightly. But the weather was irrelevant to my enclosed world. I kept on collapsing for a rest on my forearm, hand gripping the jumar. The altitude was affecting me far more than it had done up until that point in the climb.

Joe was waiting for me at the top of the rope, looking around, watching my struggle. To my inner world he seemed remote, complete, disgustingly refreshed, seemingly unaffected by human weaknesses. Every time I collapsed I could hear his camera clicking as he took photographs of me. A great wave of emotion engulfed me. I remembered hearing some friends in Manchester commenting about Joe's lecture on Dunagiri. He had shown slides of Dick collapsed, flat on his back, on the summit ridge. They had thought it in bad taste. The camera does not lie—it is cold and factual, and unmoved. And yet the person behind the camera, clicking the shutter, seems to take on some of its qualities. Joe seemed to be obsessed with recording everything that happened, everything that I did. What was he going to do with the pictures? Give a lecture on 'How I took Boardman up Changabang'? In the heat of suspicion I gasped as loudly as I could, "If you take another picture like that, I'll thump you."

As soon as I had said it, the balloon of my ego deflated. When I reached Joe, I tried to explain. He was cold, perhaps shocked. I wished I hadn't bothered explaining, I lost respect. So I hardened—we had to stay within our shells to do this climb. Joe was astounded and appalled by the incident:

"It is true that we were on edge, but it amazed me that his anger should be so close to the surface. Under stress there are always a thousand assumed reasons for losing one's temper, but in one's mind it is clear that they are only the product of the circumstances and one holds back. Peter, for reasons which I did not understand, displayed his anger and I was alarmed that he should be so childish. I wondered if he was worried about his image after Everest, and whether he believed in all the bullshit which goes with being in the public eye.

"The incident was a minor one, and this was not the place for an argument."

By mid-afternoon, Joe had run out the three rope lengths. We put all the food, Gaz canisters and hardware we had brought with us into a green bivouac sack and attached it to the anchor. I set off down first. The clouds were boiling up beneath our feet and through them we could see the Rhamani Glacier in the shadow of encroaching darkness. Rishi Kot was shifting moods and colours with the moving clouds and setting sun. The lighting around us had a hypnotic effect. The relaxed feeling of sliding down the ropes without a burden, untrammelled and free, brought a sense of release to my mind, already dazed with altitude and fatigued after the day's effort. Nothing worried me, I felt that if the anchors came away or the ropes snapped I would just float down onto a cushion of clouds.

The big swing from the foot of the icefield, past the Guillotine, down a rope with an awkward knot half way, brought my senses back. *Tous les grandes chefs sont tues en rappels.* All the greatest climbers are killed abseiling! The phrase had been in the very first book on mountaineering techniques I had read when I was fourteen years old. The phrase echoed around my head as I lurched down through the Toni Kurz pitch. The discipline had returned, once more the knot and rope systems were being checked with constant care. The sun had disappeared and I descended through a cold and clinical world to the camp. It had been a long day, and we had been a long way up the mountain.

That night the wind started again.

At dawn, on the morning of the 26th September, I woke feeling tired and stale. The tent and the mountain were in cloud and it was windy. It did not take much discussion to decide to call it a rest day. But having made that decision, I felt uneasy. We were eating valuable food and, even more important psychologically, we were losing the upwards momentum we had sustained so far. Joe, however, once the decision had been made, resigned himself to it, closed his eyes and drifted off into a somnolent haze. At first I was surprised at his firmness, then I envied him. I decided I could only follow suit and engrossed myself in the gripping, escapist world of *Night Runners of Bengal*. An afternoon snowfall reinforced our decision and by dusk there was no change in the weather. After our evening meal, we set the alarm for 5.00 a.m., hoping that the big move would get under way then.

Breakfast postponed the decision. We were rationalising, trying to be realistic—and we were weakening. The weather was still uncertain and so were we. The mist had cleared from around the mountain but the sky was white with high clouds.

"It's almost impossible to read the weather here," I said. "I mean, if you saw cirrus like that in the Alps you'd think there was a monster front coming in, but here it's impossible to tell."

"It'll be a bit committing to be stuck up on the icefield, having taken all the ropes away, if really bad weather comes in," said Joe.

The problem was being thrashed out, openly and directly. We were both saying exactly what we thought.

"We could stay here as long as we liked if we had a string of porters bringing us food all the time," I said, "but I'm not sure we've got enough food up here to do the route anyway."

"There's bugger-all at Advance Camp," said Joe.

"Well, we're certainly low on sugar and bog paper," I said.

"That sounds critical," Joe replied. "Somebody might have arrived as Base Camp by now," he added.

"We've made steady progress every day—it'd do us good to have a change of scene. We could bomb down to Base Camp this morning if we set off now, pick some things up and then come back up to Advance Camp this afternoon. Then tomorrow we could quickly move back up to here and start the big move. We'd have only lost a day!" I had voiced the suggestion, but it had not been mine. It had evolved, naturally, from discussion as our decision.

Climbing down the creaking icefield was a new sensation of climbing concentration, after all the roped technicalities of the previous days. Once we were walking along the moraine, we were astonished to find ourselves feeling weak and beginning to tire. Perhaps our limbs were not used to horizontal walking—we were staggering clumsily from rock to rock. The mountain began to look remote and hostile. Through the binoculars, at Advance Camp we could pick out the line we had taken through the Barrier and up the icefield. The cache of the bivouac sack was the only sign of our visit we could see. It was a mere speck at 20,000 feet—3,000 feet above us, 2,500 feet below the summit. Our progress, our high point of which we had previously been so proud, began to look pathetically lower down the mountain the further we moved away from it. All the earlier doubts flooded back. The sun began to shine mockingly down on our retreat. We became hot and dumped some of our clothing under a rock before carrying on. Turning down the moraine valley, towards Base Camp, was like turning down one's home street. I could recognise every boulder. The Base Camp tent was tucked around a corner and it was impossible to see it until you were only a hundred yards away. Hungry for company, we lurched round the corner. No one was there. Even our note was undisturbed. Nobody had passed that way during the previous ten days.

We cooked an enormous meal, drained some of a bottle of Indian Lion Rum, and lay about on the grass. Nothing had changed, everything was as we had left it—except the little stream next to the tent had dried up. We agreed it was over-optimistic to think we could go back to Advance Camp that afternoon. Joe flopped back on the grass under the tent awning, leaning against a rucksack, his sun-hat tilted over his eyes, like someone on the sidewalk of some sleepy Wild West town at high noon.

"Just think," he said, "it was a year ago yesterday when you climbed Everest." I had not realised until then. Everest had dropped from my mind.

CHAPTER FIVE

Survival

28th September–2nd October

"I'd better have a wash and put on some clean underpants for the summit," said Joe. "You never know what might happen."

"You might get knocked over by a bus," I suggested.

We were trying to sort ourselves out for the walk back up to Advance Camp but the task was, as usual, expanding to fit the time available and it was three in the afternoon by the time we gained the impetus to leave Base Camp.

What day of the week was it? Ah, Tuesday. Tuesday, 28th September. That made it three weeks since we had arrived at Base Camp and nineteen days since Hans had left. Before leaving I unearthed my 'fixtures' diary. I glanced down at all the committee meetings I had missed in Britain and tried to link them with events on the mountain, hoping that the process would grind my fixation on our climb into some sort of framework of reality. It was as much use as reading an old newspaper.

As we reached the head of the moraine valley, snow started flying about in the air in showers and a cold wind blew up from the direction of the Rishi Gorge. We sheltered by an enormous boulder, about twenty feet high, perched on the moraine. Joe said he thought we ought to go back to Base Camp, arguing that the weather-pattern was completely unsettled and that Changabang had a lot more snow on it than before. I said that he was being influenced by the fact that we were in an isolated snow shower and we had a lot of them in the afternoons — that Changabang looked unchanged and, anyway, always shook off fresh snow quickly. We would never get up the climb if we lost our upwards momentum and kept on turning back at every opportunity. I was trying to argue the case rationally, but I felt guilty that we had wasted two days and, at the same time, felt an unreasoning impulse to get back into the mountain to see if the conditions could force us back down. It was a difficult situation and, although on the surface very calm, was the first tactical disagreement we had had. Neither of us knew if we were arguing from a balanced evaluation or an irrational urge. I had the morally stronger position because I was arguing for the more positive move. Yet I knew Joe well enough to respect his judgement, and quickly suppressed a momentary worry that his motivation was weakening. Perhaps it was I who was choosing the easy way out? Eventually, we decided to carry on to Advance Camp and to assess the situation from there. The decision had been made and neither of us referred to it again.

Once on the glacier, we were slowly overtaken by darkness as we searched for the clothing we had left under a rock on the way down the mountain. We had marked the rock with a cairn, but had forgotten which of the three parallel glacial moraines we had left them on. It took us an hour of wandering up and down before we eventually found them in the moonlight. It was bitterly cold.

"Bloody sweep searches," said Joe. "It's like being on a mountain rescue training course."

I was obsessed with the plot of *Night Runners of Bengal*. Thinking that we were coming back up straight away, I had left the book at Advance Camp. On arriving there I picked it up immediately. I didn't want to risk taking it up to Camp One and failing to finish it. It was too heavy to take on the route and I thought I might never see it again, since it was unlikely that we would be going back up the creaking slope to collect gear after we had climbed the route and descended the other side of the mountain. Joe was irritated at the waste of torch-battery power, for whilst he was preparing the evening meal, I was reading the end of the book to find out what happened. If the battery had faded, I would have been desperately concerned – I was so involved with the book that it would have been a mishap on a par with a small boy losing a bag of sweets. Changabang had made me vulnerable to roads of escapism.

The icefields on the slope up to the ridge camp were shrinking. Large areas of rock and rubble were uncovered. Where the ice managed to cover the rock, it was thin and unstable. It was a taxing climb, trying to select the safest-looking route up this increasingly dangerous ground. The relief on reaching the Ridge and wandering along it to Camp One was greater than usual.

We reached the Ridge Camp early and started the lengthy packing of all our equipment. We planned food for at least six days. Once we were bivouacking in hammocks, our organisation would have to be faultless. We sorted all the different meals into independent stuff bags, then marked them heavily in Biro — 'Breakfast', 'Supper', 'Brews', 'Day food'. One of the stuff bags we marked with a big cross and after much discussion, compiled a first aid kit for the climb, including Ronicol for frostbite, Dalmane sleeping pills and Valium tranquillisers, and some ampoules of Omnipon as a painkiller in case something disastrous happened.

Once we had packed all the food, two sleeping bags each, hammocks, fuel and the remaining hardware, our sacks were stacked so high they reached chest height when stood on the ground. They weighed about sixty pounds each.

Afternoon was well established when we eventually started. It was windy but no snow was falling. Innocently, we were encouraging each other forward on a wave of optimism, thinking it would take us only three hours to reach the top of the fixed ropes, including pulling the ropes in after us.

Joe set off first and I followed. It was soon apparent that the sacks were too heavy and that we were not well rested. After I had coiled three ropes from behind us and pulled another one up, I was very tired. With my enormous sack, and ropes draped all over my shoulders, I could hardly move my jumars. I was clipping them past a peg when a jerk wrenched me backwards and sideways. I grabbed the rope to steady myself. The stitching on one of the shoulder-straps of my ruck-sack had ripped undone — the sack had toppled over and was now hanging from one shoulder and my waist strap. It took a long, awk-ward time to improvise a new attachment. Snow was now starting to fall, wind whipped. Above me, five rope lengths up from the Ridge Camp, Joe was hunched against the wind, waiting for me.

I had done this before, in the Alps, in the Hindu Kush — stubbornly pushed myself into a situation and then watched myself trying to get out of it, fighting it out. I stopped, gasping with the load, and looked up at Joe, wondering what he was thinking, what motivated him. Perhaps I was just being over-dramatic, too subjective, and Joe was feeling calm, objective and factual.

We were both thinking upwards; to retreat for the night whilst only five pitches up, might have been an easy physical move to make then. But that would have been an impossible decision to make, for we had not yet hit the mountain with everything we had.

How else could we learn?

"We might as well stop here for the night," said Joe. "We'll never get up to the Balcony before it gets dark."

"We'd better try and get some food and drink down us before getting into our hammocks," I said, "and you have got the stove."

I was convinced that Joe, the master of Alpine winter and Himalayan bivouacking, would be able to sort out a meal and a comfortable night. I was sitting in slings; Joe was standing on the top of a rock spike. Calmly, and methodically, he unpacked the tower stove and pan and the brew materials, clipping everything on as he progressed. I watched, fascinated, as he clipped his blue polythene one-pint mug onto his harness. Blue harness, blue oversuit, blue mug—they all matched! I got my mug out and did the same. The mugs looked strangely incongruous, spattered occasionally with gusts of spindrift, hanging below our frozen beards. They looked pathetically expectant, like Oliver Twists in a queue. Joe hacked a little shelf out of the ice and balanced the stove on it. The Gaz was reluctant to light and spluttered ineffectively. Joe had a struggle melting the ice and snow, keeping the flame sheltered from the wind and balancing the pan over it. I noticed him burn a gaping hole in his mitt, but he did not mention it. 'If you've got a job to do, you just get on and do it.' I remembered he had said that sometime in the meaningless past. After two hours he served two lukewarm mugs of Oxo. We gulped them down within a few seconds. We could not stand the wind and cold much longer and decided to munch chocolate and marzipan for our meal, and to get into the hammocks as soon as possible. It was growing dark and the Salford fridge of our dress rehearsals seemed far away.

"I'll hang off the fixed rope and be the first floor," said Joe.

"The necky bugger," I thought. "He's going to hang all night off that eight-millimetre terylene. What if it gets chopped by a falling rock from above? He won't even have a back-up system."

The spike below looked much the safer alternative for me to hang from, although it would hardly feel like the ground floor. It wasn't my role to voice my worries to Joe—perhaps I was just thinking soft thoughts that didn't dare creep into his mind! Once I was fighting to sort out my hammock and its cowl, I was back in the world by myself. Joe was isolated four feet of vertical space away by his identical, but individual, struggle:

"Snow was everywhere. This was real—no simple exit through a cold store for a warm cup of tea, a chat with a security guard and a drive home for some 'proper sleep'. . . In the cold confusion I found that I was lying in my hammock with my crampons still on; they were tearing at the fabric. It was essential to fasten the straps of the canopy beneath the hammock, to keep the wind out—one of my straps snapped."

Everywhere there were bits of hammock, ropes and slings. It took a long time to get inside. The movements were exhausting and the altitude made me gasp for air—and there was not much of that available, once I had pulled the cowl down. I had only two karabiners and it was difficult to decide how to use them—to clip gear or myself on? Taking my boots off was absurdly acrobatic. I had to raise my legs vertically upwards inside the roof of the cowl to reach them whilst lying flat on my back. The thrashing movements that this entailed gave me the shuddering thought that if the stitching came apart, I would burst through the bottom and plunge two thousand feet. My life was hanging on the threads of an Oldham seamstress. Once the boots were fastened by their laces from a sling in the ceiling, I started worrying that one of the laces would snap. Without boots I would be helpless. I could not continue the adventure in stocking-feet!

The next problem was to unpack and shuffle inside the duvet and the two sleeping bags. In taking the terylene sleeping bag out, its stuff bag slipped between my fingers and fell out of the hammock. I yelped out loud, my nerves on edge. I was loud enough to reach Joe above the roar of the wind.

"What's up?" he shouted.

"Oh, I've just dropped my stuff bag," I called back, cursing myself for a typical, over-dramatic reaction.

After much wriggling and squirming, I got the sleeping bags pulled up round my shoulders. It had taken one and a half hours to get established. I nibbled some chocolate, trying to close off my mind to the situation. Unfortunately, we had taken our spacer bars up to the high point and left them there; with nothing to hold the sides of the hammocks apart, they held us in a vice-like grip, inhibiting breathing and movement. I took a sleeping pill, which helped me drift in and out of consciousness through the following twelve hours of darkness. Each time I woke, it was with a shock to realise where I was. On one occasion I had to poke my head out from beneath the cowl to breathe some more oxygenated air. I was greeted with a faceful of spindrift. Ten feet above me, I could see the hanging black sausage shape of Joe, and beyond that the dark outline of the Wall and Summit Ridges of Changabang. There was no problem of perspective on this mountain — it just towered over us. Beyond the ridges, clouds paced across the moon, hiding me from its light. Through gaps in the clouds I could see occasional pinpoints of stars. 'If you can see a single star, then set out!' went the saying. I hunched back inside the hammock, trying to conserve heat. A wry undercurrent of self-parody appeared in my mind and suddenly helped me realise that, against all reason, I was in control.

Dawn came to us independently:

"The night was endless, uneasy and cold; the hours to movement and warmth seemed infinitely long. Any change seemed
desirable, our situation could not have been worse.

"Showers of spindrift poured down, squirting through the gaps
between the cowl and the hammock, my feet were protruding and
were numb and I was very uncomfortable. But one can adjust to
almost anything.

"Morning was a subtle shift in the darkness to a greyness, then
light. There was no incentive to move. I was relieved that the
long journey through the night was over, but the world outside
was unattractive."

There was no relief from the powerful gusts of wind, which were playing with a myriad of ice crystals — throwing them up and down the Wall at random. It had stopped snowing but it felt as if it still was. The sun, if the clouds stayed out of the way, would not be on us until 11.30 a.m. The clouds were ominously dark over the Garhwal. I wondered if Joe would move. My mind was shirking from any deci-sion, but felt concerned at the same time because, going on the previous day's pace, we had an energetic day ahead of us.

"Hey, Joe," I shouted above the wind. "Shall we get up?"

There was no response. I shouted the same thing again — louder.

"What?"

"Shall we get up?"

"Yeah."

He sounded strange when he shouted, it was a side of his voice I rarely heard. I could not imagine him shouting except when compelled to because of communication difficulties.

I had imagined that Joe, being organised on bivouacs, would soon be ready. He had not much respect for my bivouacking ability. I always used to reply to his taunts at my disorganisation by saying that the only reason he was so experienced at bivouacking was because he always climbed so slowly and had to spend a lot of nights out on the mountains. That morning, I thought, I would dress and pack quickly. I slipped out of the sleeping bags and pulled on my boots above my head, after extricating them from the tangle of equipment that hung from the various loops inside the hammock. I left the duvet jacket on, it was so cold. I decided to pack my sleeping bags and tighten my boot-laces once I was standing up outside. Gently, I eased myself out of the end of the hammock and put my feet into the slings I had left there the previous day.

The wind was gusting up to about fifty miles per hour. I removed my outer mitts and, with my fingered gloves and fingerless mitts on, quickly stuffed the sleeping bags away, bundled the hammock into my sack and started doing up the laces of my inner and outer boots. I had had my overmitts off for about five minutes by the time I had finished. Then I realised—some of my finger-ends had gone hard and I couldn't feel them. I cursed myself—normally I was more careful than that. I tried blowing warm breath onto my fingers, but it was no use. Then I unzipped my oversuit and pile jacket and thrust my arms across my chest and my fingers deep into my armpits. Slowly, some circulation returned, but I knew some damage had been done. I had done something similar to my fingers on the South Summit of Everest whilst mending some oxygen equipment, but there the wind had taken one and a half hours to injure me; this time it had happened at more brutal speed.

Above me there was energetic pushing and bulging inside Joe's red hammock. It reminded me of the picture of Winnie the Pooh in the story where Wol's house falls down and Piglet is struggling, completely disorientated, underneath the carpet. After an hour, Joe emerged. He was completely dressed and packed, except for his hammock, and looked obscenely warm.

"I've got frost nip," I announced.

"What's that?"

"It's like what Dick got, except not as bad—I hope. Don't worry, it won't stop me."

Joe was winning at bivouacking.

I was embarrassed about my fingers. Joe was concerned:

"It could have been that the Expedition was finished. By all appearances the hardest half of the mountain was yet to come and a lot more damage could happen to Pete's fingers in the next few days . . . But his determination was an indication that in spite of any petty, irrelevant antagonisms and animosity, we had not lost sight of the fact that we were here to climb the mountain."

Our attempts to cook breakfast were a fiasco and soon had to be abandoned. We could not even light the stove. Hoping that it might be warm and sheltered in the afternoon, on the icefield, we decided to press on. We both knew about the debilitating effect that going for long at this sort of altitude, without food or drink, would have. Without six pints of fluid a day, we would become dehydrated and, without necessarily realising it, become weaker and start making irrational, potentially dangerous decisions. It's easy, when climbing at high altitude, to become blinkered, to hold one fixed purpose in your mind, but to be unable to allow any changes in weather or your fitness to influence you.

I jumared a rope length ahead of Joe. By the time I had reached the Balcony my hands were numb again. I knew that my only hope in retaining some use in them lay in painstakingly doing my best to warm them. For three-quarters of an hour on the Balcony, I blew on them, put them under my armpits, under my crutch. By the time Joe had arrived I knew that three fingers were virtually useless.

The sun had broken through the cloud and was shining down at me from the South-West Ridge as I started up the Toni Kurz pitch. Spindrift was cascading down the icefield and bursting over its edge. By the time it reached the beams of sunlight touching the edge of the Balcony, it was dispersed by cushions and up-draughts of air. It hovered all around me, in a million sparkling points of light, dazzling me as I looked over my shoulder across the sweep of the Wall. At first its beauty mocked me, like the forced gaiety of the tinsel finale of a television spectacular. Then it allured and drew me out of myself—this beauty was inhuman, but it was not petty, grasping or transitory. I could appreciate it, despite the hardship I was enduring.

Soon it was the sack that started to develop a personality. As I lurched up the Tony Kurz pitch it would swing about and catch on the overhangs, and then try to topple me backwards as I was stretching upwards to clip past a peg. I began to hate it for its obstinacy, its unwieldiness. I was sure that the weight of the sack, combined with mine, would pull a peg out or even snap the rope. As I moved around the last roof to join the ramp, I swung out uncontrollably and struggled with my feet to keep my balance.

"This is desperate," I yelled to Joe. "I'm going to dump some of the gear on this stance."

In a brief, shouted conversation, we agreed to take a couple of days' food to the high point, run out the three hundred feet of terylene rope we had retrieved, and then come back down and pick up the dumped gear and remaining ropes sometime later. Joe must have been feeling the strain too. By the time I had finished re-sorting the stuff sacks and had clipped some onto the stance to leave, Joe swung around the corner onto the rampline—he had left his cache on the Balcony.

The overhanging jumar by the side of the Guillotine seemed appallingly steep. The rope lengths up the side of the icefield seemed to last forever. I was moving up them so slowly that the stretch of the rope seemed to be absorbing all my efforts. The top of the ropes never came nearer, the ice never moved past my side and the ridges of the mountains around me did not become any lower. I was in a semi-daze and my movements were as jerky as a clockwork toy. The afternoon was slipping past. Clouds filled the trough of the Rhamani Glacier whilst we were touched with sunlight above them. But, scoured by the icy wind, we felt no warmth.

Late in the afternoon I arrived at the high point. The gear was still intact in the green bag. When Joe arrived he went straight into the lead. It was now nearly a week since we had gained any new ground and this had some thin taste of progress. The icefield was now petering out into the slabs that lined the foot of the Upper Tower. Joe reached the top of the ice and started climbing a crack that tilted diagonally across the slab. Since there were no holds on either side of the crack, he either leant along the crack, jamming his feet, or swung off onto the holdless slab below and, bracing with his feet against the slab, slid his hands up the crack. When he was fifty feet up it started to hail. Soon everywhere was white and I could hardly see him. Hailstones were bouncing and rushing down the slabs in torrents. I heard the sound of a peg going in. My eyes screwed up with the effort of peering up through the splintering hail at the dark shape of Joe, and I gripped the rope tightly. But he could look after himself. He lowered himself down and swung in next to me.

"It's just a shower," he said. "I'll get back up there tomorrow."

We pulled the hoods of our oversuits over our heads and leant in against the rock, looking down at our feet. Ten minutes later the hail had stopped falling from the sky, but on the mountain it was still moving. Changabang was shaking itself clear. Soon the shower was brushed away, just a memory for us, an irrelevance for the mountain.

There was nothing to discuss. A small rock buttress was sticking out of the ice. We moved ten feet apart and hacked ourselves steps in the ice and slammed in three pegs each, from which we proceeded to suspend our hammocks. We could now retrieve the spacer bars, so the hammocks would not restrict our breathing as much as the night before. As it was too windy to cook, we just struggled into our wobbling shelters.

We knew we were steadily deteriorating, but could not realise to what extent. There was no objective standard from which to judge. Vaguely, we assumed that if we kept on going upwards, things would right themselves eventually, and that the wind would drop soon. I was exhausted, but did not tell Joe and he did not tell me how he felt. That was the unspoken part of the game. If he did not give up, I would not. That night I dreamt of a warm, toasting, tropical beach with a hot sun high in the sky and not a breath of wind.

I do not know if it snowed or if it hailed that night, but the wind seemed alive, tearing and lashing us with spindrift. Avalanches rumbled past us, like distant trains in the night. Fortunately, we were on the left-hand edge of the icefield and missed their full force, being protected from the funnel above the icefield by the Upper Tower. At dawn they were still roaring past us. They were not killers though; Changabang was too steep a mountain to accumulate enough snow to crush us and sweep us off its sides.

The cold was seeping into my bones. It was not the cold of contrast that you feel in urban life, that makes you shiver when you move from inside to outside a building. This cold was gnawing at me from all directions.

"Shall we wait for the sun before we move?" I shouted.

Joe agreed. I knew I could not afford to lose the body heat that getting out of the sleeping bags into the morning wind would entail. Was I being decisive, I wondered, or was he just waiting for me to make the weak decision?

It was a long morning and the awaited sun brought no comfort. It was a false reprieve. Once we were out of the hammocks, I helped Joe shelter the flame whilst he melted snow over the stove to make a fruit drink. It took such a long time to melt that we did not wait for it to warm up, but drank it straight away. I levered open a tin of fish. Inside, the fish were frozen to their sauce and tasteless, but we forced them down our throats, knowing that if we did not at least try to eat, our efforts were doomed.

The day was moving into the afternoon and Joe finished the pitch which he had begun the day before, running out 150 feet of rope.

"Right," shouted Joe. It was the nearest word he ever used to the rigorous ritual of five climbing calls taught in the mountaineering centres back in Britain. When I left the stance, I realised I had been on the same few square feet of mountain for twenty-four hours. On reaching Joe I was disappointed to discover that he had found no ledges.

"Look," he said, "we're level with where the Japanese Ridge starts levelling out."

Our altimeter had stopped working many days before on the ridge, and we could only assess our progress by looking across at the mountains around us. With the scholastic documentation typical of Japanese climbers, the leader of the South-West Ridge Expedition had sent us a detailed 'topo' of their route, and we used this to assess our altitude. It was exciting how much just one new rope length opened out the view.

We had decided that I should run out the next and only rope length we had with us, but it was too late. "I'll lead it in the morning before we go back down to pick the gear up," I said.

"It's your turn to cook," said Joe firmly. "I've done all the messing about with the stove for the last two days."

I took the orders and he handed the stove over to me. We had some footholds large enough to stand on comfortably, and I tried to cut a sheltered perch for the stove in some ice on the rock at waist level. By the time I had the stove firmly upon this, it was dark. It took half an hour and a whole box of matches to light the stove in the wind. I managed to melt a panful of water but it would not get hot enough to dissolve the Oxo cubes to make a meat drink. So I chewed up two Oxo cubes in my mouth and spat them into the pan. Joe was trying to shield the stove with one of his bivouac bags, but the air kept on blowing around or underneath it. The freeze-dried meal—our favourite, Chilli with Beans—refused to boil and was quickly swallowed half cooked. It had taken two hours in the darkness to prepare a few mouthfuls.

An hour later we were lying in our hammocks. What was it I had been told as a child? If you cannot get to sleep, then just think pleasant thoughts, think about nice things. Dreams were a pleasant escape.

7

Soon I was back in a day during my school summer holidays. Outside it was pouring torrentially, with rain lashing the window and making me feel snug and warm and protected. There was no one on the streets outside. The world was indoors. I was lying on my bed, reading a book. Then the window smashed open with supernatural force; curtains flew and papers scattered everywhere. I woke up. The hammock cowl was inflated like a balloon, clear of the spacer bars and I was swinging out from the rock. The wind had veered and was now gusting from below. I fought my arms clear from the sleeping bags and grabbed the fabric which was billowing and crackling hysterically. With some spare bootlace, I reinforced the clips that were supposed to be keeping the cowl down. In doing so I lost so much heat I had to move quickly back inside the bags and resign myself to the wind blowing the cowl off my feet. I concentrated on wriggling my toes, hoping to fight off the cold. The spindrift seemed to have stopped finding us, perhaps because we were above the icefield, but the wind was veering and accelerating, snapping around us angrily, finding the chinks in our defences. It was an exhausting night and I could not sleep.

Three days and nights we had passed with virtually nothing to eat or drink. Surely we could not last much longer. At dawn something snapped inside me.

Descent was the obvious decision. I never thought otherwise. What would we prove by staying just to squeeze out another rope length? After it had taken me an hour to get out of my hammock, I stuffed it and one of the sleeping bags into the green bivouac bag to leave behind, and started to prepare to set off abseiling down. I knew if I stayed any longer above the icefield, even though the weather looked as if it might be settling, I would suffer from the exposure and frostbite that had already set in. Joe looked across at me.

"What are you doing?" he asked.

"I'm going down of course," I answered.

It seemed so obvious, all my instincts were telling me to get down fast.

"That's the bloody trouble with you," Joe exclaimed. "You're always changing your mind."

"You're joking, aren't you?" I asked, incredulous. "You don't think I'm going to do any leading after a night like that? I think we should bomb straight down to Base Camp, leaving as much gear as possible up here. We'll just burn ourselves out if we stay on the Wall any longer. We'll just need a bit of rope to abseil the section we've cleaned lower down."

"Just keep me informed," said Joe, and offered to go down first, so that he could sort out the ropes. My frostnip was making fiddly finger work difficult. We did not even discuss where we were going down to, but Joe had not argued:

> "Retreat was so welcoming. We were living from moment to moment. There was no promise of coming back, the way to live the next few moments was to descend, thaw out, eat and relax."

The icefield drifted past in the soft shapes of a dream; my mind was as numb as my finger-ends. I felt on the brink of fainting. Soon I was moving past the knot next to the Guillotine. It was a complex man-œuvre involving clipping the jumars above the knot, taking off the descendeur and placing it below, then replacing the jumars below the knot. I gathered all my concentration and started reaching into a grim recess of my mind. Yes, the iron was there if I needed it. The Toni Kurz pitch went slowly, but without any problems.

Quickly, Joe refixed the ropes down to Camp One, and I followed. Three rope lengths above the camp, I was changing over my descendeur past a piton anchor when it slipped out of my fingers. It bounced off, down the Wall. We had not any spares. I fumbled for some karabiners and clipped six of them together and across each other on the rope to form a friction brake.

The sun was warm on the tent when I arrived and Joe's feet were sticking out of the entrance. He was asleep.

"Where's the brew then?"

"There's no pan."

"What about the dried milk tin, that should do?"

I crawled into the still air of the tent. The sun had warmed the inside. It was the first time I had been in a warm atmosphere since we had packed the stuff bags there, three days before—it seemed a lifetime. We packed some snow into the tin on the stove. It melted effortlessly over the flame. Civilisation at last. I lay back drowsily. Then I started up. My fingers were shooting with agonising pain—the circulation was beginning to return. They throbbed, bringing tears to my eyes.

"Does it hurt?" asked Joe.

"Only when I larf," I said through gritted teeth, inwardly rationalising that the injury was not serious.

Joe was very sympathetic and dug out some Fortral painkilling tablets from the first aid kit.

"You're supposed to be able to crunch these like Smarties without much effect, aren't you?" I asked.

"Dick used them for his fingers and thought they helped," he replied. "You don't want morphine, do you?"

"No, it's not that bad. It's only like a bad dose of aches. It'll wear off in a minute!" And so it did; but my finger-ends felt very tender and I still could not feel the ends of three of them.

The blackcurrant drink, when it was ready, was the best drink I had ever tasted. I rolled it around in my mouth like a refugee from the desert.

As I stood up and moved along the ridge towards the ice slope, I tottered slightly.

"You all right?" asked Joe.

I was beginning to see a new side to his personality. 'He can be kind and considerate,' I thought. "I'm feeling a bit dizzy," I admitted.

Joe had a pill ready for every ill. "Here, try one of these Vertigon," he said. "I used them coming down off Dunagiri and they seemed to help."

The ice slope went past mechanically and I was past caring about its creaks and groans. Advance Camp was a haven when we eventually staggered into it. We polished off the only food that was left there—some rice and a tin of corned beef—and stayed for the night. Base Camp could wait. *Night Runners of Bengal* was lying on the groundsheet, where I had left it. I remembered that I had thought I would have returned to it over Shipton's Col. I opened it and read through the parts I had skipped past before. I lost myself by candlelight in the Indian Mutiny until my eyes closed to sleep. Changabang was far away.

CHAPTER SIX

Recovery

3rd–8th October

There was no breakfast on the 3rd October. All day stretched ahead, offering plenty of time to move down to Base Camp. Joe decided he would photograph the Upper Tower of Changabang as the morning sun moved onto it. The left-hand edge of the West Wall, the line we wanted to follow, was usually picked out in the morning if the clouds behaved themselves. He collected all his camera equipment together, and moved across the fresh snow of the glacier. 'The last time he was over there,' I thought, 'was when he was coming down from Duna-giri.' That was when he took the photographs of the West Wall that were to fascinate him so much later. He had taken them automatically, whilst hallucinating through lack of food, just as some sort of a record. To him and Dick on Dunagiri, Changabang had been simply the mountain that prevented the early morning sun from reaching them. Now it was the mountain that nothing would stop him from climbing. He was so confident that we would climb the Upper Tower, he was recording the scene before the adventure occurred. 'That's profes-sionalism,' I thought, and admired him for it. I was impressed that he was already thinking about climbing, after our recent epic, when all I wanted was a rest. As he moved further away into the distance, the tracks behind him wavered around haphazardly in the snow. 'He's not completely fit then,' I thought with relief.

It was half past eleven before I moved off along the familiar route back to Base Camp. 'Perhaps the Americans will be down there,' I thought, as I turned down 'our valley'. There was a strange feeling about the ground as I walked down by the side of the moraine, but I couldn't decide whether or not all the scuff marks had been made by Joe and me previously. Perhaps some animal had made them. Small stones had been disturbed in places; every few feet I noticed something subtly different. I felt rather apprehensive as I turned around the corner to Base Camp. As usual, the mist was down and Bleak House looked eerie as I approached it. Nothing was disturbed. Not even our message to passers-by had been moved. I rummaged through the boxes and eventually rooted out a much-missed Mars Bar, and gobbled it down. I had been longing for it!

The brew I had put on the stove was just beginning to come to the boil when Joe arrived.

"Did you notice anything different about the valley on your way down?" I asked.

No, he had not. We cracked open the bottle of whisky and lounged about, both feeling chatty and relaxed but 'spaced out' after the effort of the previous days. I washed and bathed my fingers in antiseptic solution and bandaged them up, whilst Joe cooked a meal. I started on a course of Septrin to ward off infection. Unlimited food, unlimited brews—this was Heaven. We had brought the smallest and most effective primus down, and this purred continuously, producing a succession of drinks, steamed puddings and large meals.

The relaxation and 'restoring' of our stomachs continued all the next day at Base Camp. Without discussing the future, we savoured the security, warmth and ease of life on level ground.

Joe was a master of the anecdote. He would deliver one in a relaxed, comfortable way, and it nearly always had a subtle little twist or point at the end. They were never particularly self-revealing, although he always emerged in them as the normal person who gets involved in weird and wonderful places and events, or in dangerous situations. On the 4th October at Base Camp he prattled on amusingly between bouts of eating and reading. He always refused to philosophise, to try and draw any hard kernel of moral or ethical point from his stories. It was as if he always fought shy of intensity in conversation. I did the same. His stories stood alone. The rest was up to me. Often he would repeat a story I had heard once, or even twice before, or had read in one of his mountaineering articles. I did not mention it to him—I was probably doing the same! We rarely probed each other about details of our private lives—if either wanted to mention anything, it was up to him. I envied Joe the number of contacts he had gained in the mountaineering world, that he had acquired on the sheer strength of his achievements and personality. He was truly 'one of the lads'. I had come to know people, I sometimes felt, more through my position as National Officer of the British Mountaineering Council. I could never seem to get involved in the close-knit mateyness of the climbing social world, which always seemed to be designed to repress as much as it expressed.

Joe was a strange mixture of ruthlessness and consideration. Occasionally he would make extraordinary gestures of thoughtfulness. However, there were just two of us; we had to share tasks, and often by confrontation, he would manipulate me into doing something—small things, like fetching the water or cooking the next meal—that I would otherwise have sat back and hoped he would do. He used to tease me as a hot-house climber, somebody who had all the lucky breaks and never really had to suffer, saying that I had acquired a knack of getting people to do things for me. Well, he was not going to have any sympathy with that, and I knew it. I used to dread giving him justification for complaint. The problem was, I tended to sit lost in thought and, if there seemed to be little to do, not to think or act dynamically until the last minute. Joe seemed much more competent and organised around the camp.

There was always an 'edge' to the relationship between Joe and myself. With brittle over-familiarity, we joked at each other's expense, always on the verge of direct damning comment. Joe managed to take this less seriously than I:

> "There was a non-co-operative hostility towards each other in things which did not matter. If an argument became too heated we grew accustomed to using the catch-phrase, 'Don't worry, it will be all right when we get back.' It was a code which meant that we both acknowledged that any tensions were due to our unusual circumstances."

It seemed that neither of us ever opened up completely. There was always a tension that held us apart and this helped us retain our individuality. We had enormous respect for each other's climbing ability. This, for me, was a marked contrast to the most demanding climb of my youth, in the Hindu Kush, when I had felt utterly alone. Then I was the only one in the party with the combination of skill and drive to pull us out of the situations we ignorantly got ourselves into. With Joe, I knew I could relax when he went into the lead, for he was so motivated that he would get up the piece of rock ahead.

On that day, however, the climb was hardly mentioned. Joe talked, as he rarely did, about his childhood and his home. He came from a strong Catholic family, and his father was a caretaker at a local school in Middlesbrough. He was the eldest son, with four brothers and five sisters. Before leaving for the climb he had spent a brief weekend at home. He had not, of course, made the point to his family that it might have been a last farewell. They had been glad to see him. They would have preferred him not to go off on such risky undertakings, but had long since ceased trying to dissuade him, except by the occasional subtle suggestion that he might occupy his time more fruitfully. When he had started climbing it had been their strong disapproval he had found worrying—it had shaken his confidence. As time went on they became used to the fact that he kept coming back in one piece from climbs in the Alps. They started to see that there was more to climbing mountains than running risks for risk's sake and they took more interest in the climbs he was doing. For earlier climbs, Joe's mother had given Joe medals of different saints to take with him; for Changabang she did not. For the first time she said as he was leaving, "Enjoy yourself", rather than, "Be careful."

Between the ages of thirteen and twenty-one, Joe had trained at Ushaw College to be a priest. He related strange, wryly amusing stories of the cloistered isolation of the place; the tensions and anomalies that exist in all residential institutions were even more emphasised there. For eight years he had been deprived of contact with the outside world, deprived of newspapers, television, alcohol, the company of women. Religious services had been held seven times a day, starting at six in the morning. As Joe had grown through his teens, he had started having more and more confrontations with the authorities at Ushaw, rebelling strongly against the restrictions that, to him, came to seem meaningless. He became entangled in a major row one Christmas when he and a fellow pupil sneaked off to a nearby plantation and returned and erected a Christmas tree. Institutional life was not for Joe, he felt that if he let go and sank into the flood of the organisation he would lose his identity and become slowly and irrevocably changed. Then he discovered climbing, in a quarry near the college. His early climbing was done without any instruction. He did not have many friends to go climbing with and often went soloing. His friends had always regarded him as physically lazy, and he could never be enthusiastic about conventional sports with formalised competition. But in climbing he found something different. He was frightened, yet fascinated by it. It was so irrational and pointless that his rebellious awkwardness found an outlet in it.

Joe left Ushaw and went to University to study Sociology. Seven years later we were trying to climb Changabang, and it seemed to me that Joe was still reacting against his days at Ushaw. His moods varied, even during that day at Base Camp. He would drift out of a chatty mood and start looking serious and intense. His intensity frightened me and I wondered if I had the same quality—if it was necessary to have that quality to climb Changabang. Was he prepared to accept a greater level of risk than I? Joe did not seem to be as happy all the time as I felt when I was in the mountains. I wondered if he was worrying about the fact that he did not have a job to go back to when we returned to England. He was still the rebel. Perhaps this mountain was purging something inside for both of us? I thought of the shores of the coasts of Scandinavia that are still rising a few inches every year as the earth's crust readjusts from the weights of the ice age, although that was many thousands of years ago. Joe seemed like this, continuing to readjust. Would he always be like that?

In the late afternoon we settled down to reading. Joe was now reading *Zen and the Art of Motorcycle Maintenance*. I had found it a radical, disturbing book, but one which needed far more academic discipline to absorb than I could muster on an expedition. Joe just dismissed it completely. It was as if he felt he had wasted enough years discussing the finer philosophical points of life. He wanted action, the total involvement of climbing. It was one of the few things that brought him satisfaction.

Joe saw himself as very practical and down to earth. I was more romantic and idealistic. Joe saw in me many aspects of what he was trying to put behind him, to escape from. As a result, some issues and feelings that were of greatest importance to me, I could not discuss without embarrassing us both.

I was reading Zola's *Germinal*. Reading a book helps me, particularly as it had absolutely nothing to do with mountains, but can transport me into a different world. Obsession is always a danger for the mountaineer—I found that reading for long hours during that afternoon restored some sort of normal balance to my thinking and values. It was because I was involved in the bleak world of strong contrasts, between fear and exultation, danger and security, between life and death, that the finer balances of hopes and fears of people living hard-working lives began to take on new meaning. The grim struggle of the miners in northern France against appalling working and social conditions involved me deeply, and threw a question mark over our adventure.

Unlike the miners in France and, almost in the same way, unlike the people in the Garhwal struggling for daily survival against harsh physical conditions, Joe and I were here seeking a survival situation. We had been struggling for survival not because of force of circumstance, but because of a deliberate choice we had made. Our adventure was a pampered luxury that we could afford to enjoy, it was pure self-indulgence. As the mountain writer, Geoffrey Winthrop Young, once wrote, "Our poignant adventure, our self-sought perils on a line of unreason to the summit of a superfluous rock, have no rational or moral justification." This was an honest thought I do not think Joe would have accepted. As I read, the crowd scenes in *Germinal* scattered and thundered around my mind, and self-questioning and Winthrop Young faded into the background. My headtorch was broken. Joe mended it and I read on. Zola was reaching out over a hundred years to hold me in thrall in the dark days of northern France. Meanwhile, outside the tent the weather seemed to be settling. The moon rose strongly over Rishi Kot. At 10.30 p.m. I finished the last page. Thoughts of the Shining Mountain had waited for a day.

On the morning of the 5th October, our minds slowly returned to the problem. Joe and I had booked our return flights to London for the 18th October. We knew now that if we went back up the mountain we would miss the flight. If we missed the flight, we might have difficulty in obtaining seats on another one. We would not be able to tell our parents of our change in plan, they would be expecting us and would immediately start worrying. Even if I caught the 18th October flight, I would be two weeks late for work. If I arrived back even later, it seemed probable I would be out of a job. But there was no thought of abandoning the route. We were committed to getting up the climb, even while we were down at Base Camp. The decision had been made without question, and it had been an easy choice, to risk our lives 6,000 miles from home. The two of us had developed into a powerful, intense unit, a compound being with a single motivation—to climb Changabang's West Wall. If we had been on a bigger expedition the whole situation would have been much more complicated. It would most likely have been more lighthearted, too. There could have been more scope for the good-natured gibes that always accompany a group of easy-going climbers. That we should climb the West Wall was now becoming the most important thing in the world. Nothing would stop us. The steady pressure of risk, that had forced us into being alert for weeks, had generated an intensity that, during moments of reflection, was frightening. The whole venture had become bigger than our lives. Yet, at the same time, our combined abilities seemed to have made a third, invisible quality outside ourselves, in which we had implicit faith.

Joe sensed the menace of the unfinished task ahead:

"We both wanted to go and finish it. I was surprised at my own persistence. There was no joy left in it—just hard work remaining; an ordeal in whose value we had to believe during this period of darkness and discouragement, believe without any glimpse of the satisfaction there would be in having completed the climb."

The autopsy was thorough. We discussed over and over the mistakes we had made during the three nightmare hammock nights on the Wall in the storm. We went back over the equipment used and tactical weaknesses. We had been defeated because the hammocks had not been satisfactory in the bad weather we had encountered. We had not been able to cook and, hence, eat or drink properly for four days. We would never be able to climb the Wall if we could not cook. Also, getting in and out of the hammocks had been a debilitating struggle at altitude and it would have been only a matter of time before we dropped some vital piece of equipment. Perhaps the main disadvantage was our being almost completely isolated from each other the whole time. There had been none of the relaxed, easy discussion that could occur in the evening when we were in a tent together. We had been many feet apart, unable to communicate, locked in our own thoughts, buffeted by the wind in isolation. It had been impossible to use any light-hearted banter about the situation, to bring it into perspective. We discussed the possibility of taking the inner from the tent at Advance Camp with us, and trying to hack out a ledge at the top of the platform to pitch it on. To reinforce this tiny tent, we could take with us some of the thin bamboo poles left by the Japanese at their camp at the foot of the South-West Ridge. We would just have to keep our fingers crossed that we could make a ledge wide enough, and that the fabric would withstand the wind and snow.

It had been becoming steadily more windy at high altitude all the time we had been in the area and we revised our thoughts about the clothing we would wear for our return to the Wall. Even at Base Camp, it was much colder than it had been a month earlier. Joe unearthed an extra duvet we had brought with us for the porter who had been going to stay at Base Camp with Palta. I decided to take my Everest one-piece down suit.

We knew that this attempt on the Wall would be our last and that it would be a race against time. The previous year the winter storms hit Joe while he was walking out of the area on October 15th. Clearly, it could be suicidal to risk being caught out on the mountain too late into the month. As we had only enough lightweight freeze-dried food to last a week, we decided to take our primus stove and pressure cooker up to the ridge camp, so that we could cook our local food of rice and dhal up to the last possible moment.

As we sorted through our equipment, we found our folder full of photographs of the Face. We studied these for an hour, and tried to convince each other that all that separated us from success was just over a thousand feet of difficult climbing. Joe packed a few of the photographs in the medical box. The route finding on the Upper Tower looked as if it would be tricky, so we would need these on the route to refer to at night, to gauge our progress and direction.

The biggest decision which we had to make that morning was whether we were still going to stick to our plan of going down the other side of the mountain, if and when we had climbed it. The idea of descending the ridge on the other side whilst in the sort of state we had been after the hammock epic worried me. Also, I thought that the South Face expedition had probably left the Changabang Glacier on the other side by now and would not be able to help us if we tried to descend in a bad state. However, the alternative of coming down the West Wall was not much more attractive, apart from the fact that we should be able to retrieve our equipment. We would have to abseil all the way down the Wall—most of it without fixed ropes to guide us.

It was a difficult decision to have to make and we decided to put it off until the following day, when we would go across from Advance Camp towards the foot of the ropes leading up to Shipton's Col. There, we hoped to examine the state of the piton anchors, in case we had to come down that way, and also try to retrieve some rope to string along the lower part of our route, in case we returned via the West Wall.

We had done so much climbing in the previous few weeks that much of our equipment had been badly damaged. Joe spent all morning mending his gaiters, stitching, glueing and tacking the tattered bits back together. Our woollen mitts needed darning, our oversuits patching, our crampons sharpening; buttons needed sewing back on. It was enjoyable therapy. As usual, our departure time dragged on into afternoon, and we decided to have lunch before we left. We rewrote the message to leave outside the door and destroyed the optimistic one we had left there on 28th September.

The pressure cooker was hissing vigorously away and Joe and I were lying around on our ready-packed sacks when, simultaneously, we saw a figure coming down the moraine valley. We were astonished. My pulse raced. This was a situation I had forgotten how to deal with — other people! I put the zoom lens on my camera and took a few pictures of him discreetly as he reached the level of Bleak House meadow. Joe, also, had his camera out, but kept on coolly clicking away openly as the man approached.

"Hallo," we said eagerly.

"Hi there." He was American. He did not seem at all surprised to see us.

We soaked up his news avidly. He was called Neko Colevins, a member of the South-West Ridge of Dunagiri expedition. There were nine Americans, one Mexican and an Indian liaison officer on the expedition. He was rather vague about their progress on the mountain. Apparently they had arrived at their Base Camp about a week previously.

"Where is your Base Camp?" I said.

"About a couple of hundred yards down there around the corner," he replied.

"Effin' hell," said Joe, "that's typical of the porters. Lazy lot. They conned you to have your camp down there so they would not have to carry the gear up here."

Neko seemed very self-assured about their expedition and talked in round terms about it. I offered him some of our lunch, which was now ready—he seemed surprised and quickly declined, and proceeded to talk a lot about the freeze-dried food they were eating on Dunagiri. He had organised its acquisition. We told him about our route and our hammock epic, but he did not seem particularly interested.

"Oh yeah, we knew you were here, of course, we've been walking backwards and forwards for days. Oh well, I'd better move on. The leader of our expedition is coming now. He'll be here soon. He's bringing down our Indian liaison officer who ain't feeling too good. The height, I guess." Neko moved off down the valley and disappeared around the corner.

"He had nice new gear, didn't he?" I said.

"He seemed a bit old," said Joe.

When our next two visitors arrived, we were ready for them.

"I'm Graham Stephenson," said the tall man, "from Los Angeles." He was bearded and in his mid-fifties. "And this here's our liaison officer, Mandip Singh."

Mandip Singh did not look very well. I asked Graham why they had chosen to climb Dunagiri. Apparently Eric Shipton had given a talk to the Sierra Club whilst on a lecture tour of the States, and Graham Stephenson had asked him at the end of the evening if he could recommend a good peak to climb in the Himalayas. Shipton, who attempted Dunagiri in 1936 with the Sherpa Angtharkay, recommended the South-West Ridge, that he had so nearly climbed, as a reasonable objective. We asked Graham about other expeditions in the area. He told us of the death of Nanda Devi Unseold, and that some Italian climbers were due in the area soon, intending to climb Kalanka. We absorbed the news avidly, it was like arriving in the Chamonix camp site, fresh from England. Joe was swearing obscenely whenever he spoke. I do not think he realised. We had been alone together for so long that our language had deteriorated—there had been no one to offend. I was embarrassed. Graham was confused, but courteous. We showed him a picture of Changabang and indicated our high point. He was impressed. We wished him the best of luck and he said he would see us later, when we were down from the summit—they were planning to leave around the 12th October. Then he left us, taking Mandip Singh down with him.

Joe and I sat for a few minutes, savouring the minutiae, every word and gesture, and hint that had been said and made during the previous half hour. The whole tenor of our conversation, of our relationship with each other, changed. We no longer felt isolated as we had been for the previous twenty-seven days. We were almost performers again —someone knew what we had been doing. The mountains had people in them. As we shouldered our packs we continued to discuss the meetings endlessly, digesting all the nourishment from them before they became a mere memory.

"Did you see that Chouinard ice hammer Stephenson had?"

"It looked brand new."

"I wonder if they realise what they're tackling?"

"He seemed as if he'd been around a long time though."

"It's difficult to judge American climbers—there are so many types.

Have you heard of the gear freaks, the 'Sierra Cup' types—people who buy these aluminium cups that burn your mouth and hang them from their waists?"

"Communication between different areas and groups of climbers in the States is so bad that there is very little interrelation of climbing standards. Each little group creates its own experts."

"And I thought they were going to be Californian surfing girls."

We were assessing the people we had just met, making gross generalisations. We were full of a sudden confidence generated by the contrasting boldness of our own adventure. We had summed them up as if they were opponents. We were both well practised at assessing climbers, by the way they talk about climbing and the equipment they choose. In particular, I had learned from instructing with a mountaineering school in the Cairngorms, how to categorise people quickly before going out for a day on the mountain with them. We had judged them solely in the narrow terms we ourselves prescribed.

"They must have had a lot of porters," said Joe, as we walked up the valley.

Now I realised that I had not been imagining all the scuff marks on the ground before. They had been caused by the passing of the feet of the porters hired by the Dunagiri expedition to help them establish Base Camp. But our ways parted. The tracks turned left up the glacier towards Dunagiri, and we turned up onto the moraine towards Changabang.

We were talking to each other unguardedly, chatting naturally all the way up the glacier, even though we were approaching seventeen thousand feet. We felt perfectly acclimatised, and fit. We were at that optimum point of acclimatisation, after about four weeks at high altitude, which seems to precede the onset of gradual deterioration.

The sun set whilst we were half way up the glacier, and we sat for half an hour and watched the shadow line racing up the Western Wall. The longer retracting rays of the sun turned the upper part of the Wall through gold to rich red. Then the light faded and froze and we began to shiver. As we picked our separate ways over the ice towards the tent, the moon took over the lighting with silver brightness. It was Bill Murray who had described moonlight as the eye-fang: "Changabang . . . shone tenderly as though veiled in bridal lace . . . seemingly as fragile as an icicle; a produce of earth and sky rare and fantastic, and of liveliness unparalleled so that unaware one's pulse leapt and the heart gave thanks—that this mountain should be as it is." Happiness was welling inside me, and I wondered if Joe felt as deeply content as I. Surely the radiant fall of night stirred his imagination too?

On the following day, the 6th October, as planned, we went across to the ropes hanging from Shipton's Col. After rice pudding for breakfast we left at 11.30 a.m. and enjoyed moving off the beaten track of our route up from Base Camp to explore a new corner of the glacier, to get to know the area better by seeing old familiar mountain shapes from new angles.

There was a long snow slope to the foot of the Wall below Shipton's Col. It felt good to move finally up to it, unburdened for once from the heavy, crippling sack that had accompanied nearly all our other efforts in the previous weeks.

We were disappointed when we arrived, for the ropes hanging there looked as faded and unreliable as washing lines. There was some old polypropylene, white and bleached by the sun. Next to that was some red nylon line. In the autumn of 1974, after the Indo-British Changabang ascent of the spring, an English expedition led by John Prosser had attempted Kalanka. They had been unable to persuade their porters to take their gear round into the Nanda Devi Sanctuary and up to the Changabang Glacier to the foot of Kalanka, because of the extra three days' walk it involved. Instead, their porters had dumped them in the same place as the Bonington expedition. There had, therefore, been a painful re-enactment, with a smaller team, of the trip over Shipton's Col. In the lower places they had reinforced Bonington's polypropylene with their nylon rope. Later, however, hampered by bad weather, an extended supply line and a tight time schedule, Prosser's expedition failed on Kalanka after running out some fixed rope up the mountain. Joe and I looked at the rope. In many places it disappeared, and then reappeared behind feet of ice. We scrambled a hundred feet up. We could never trust this rope. If we came over from the other side, we would have to arrange our own abseils.

"We must be really close to the others," said Joe. The South Face team Advance Camp must have been just over the other side of the col. We shouted their names—but it was only a gesture.

There were a few pegs not yet buried under the ice. It was a haunting thought—hands I knew had placed those pegs, two and a half years ago. I wondered if it had been Martin, or Doug, or Chris, or Dougal. All had been my companions on Everest since. It was an archaeological dig of mountaineering history with a difference—I had known the hands that had used the tools we were uncovering. We cut some lengths of rope.

"We could always use some bits as a sort of handrail in an emergency," I said.

A peg that Joe was holding onto came out as he descended – it was an incidental near miss. "It's bloody dangerous just existing in these hills," he said. But we had reached no decision about the descent route – it would evolve in time.

Back on the glacier, we played with our camera equipment and joked about expedition filming. With sardonic humour, we imitated the commentaries and format that they entailed. I said, in a deep, confident mid-Atlantic accent: "Those reserved young men, quietly avoiding the crowds, sitting in a peaceful corner of the glacier. No one could notice, would have noticed the intensity of their planning, the careful sorting of their equipment, and their long, hard looks at the mountain behind them – the mountain that was not only going to test the uttermost of their skill, stamina and courage as mountaineers, but of their whole moral stature as men."

Joe laughed. We considered having a formal expedition photograph but our tattered equipment and clothing made us look too much like bandits. Also, we had no flag to raise. We talked of how summit moments were treated. "He kicked a foot onto the summit and, with a whoop of joy, raised his axe to the skies in a wild, primitive gesture of triumph."

As we walked down the glacier, Joe started leaping about making wild, primitive gestures, whilst I photographed him. It was a quarter past three when we arrived back at Advance Camp.

I had filled my mind with many little tasks, which occupied the rest of the afternoon—'equipment fiddles' I called them. I taped my jumars – I had heard that certain sections of them can break, as they are made of cast iron. Joe's were already taped – he had borrowed them from a young lady who knew about such dangers.

As the day ended, Joe went off for another walk:

"The setting sun cast a rosy tint on the upper half of Changabang's West Face. I wanted to capture it on film and, as the shadows lengthened, I left the cooking and raced across the glacier towards Bagini peak. I stopped, waited, moved off again looking for the best vantage point. The moment and colour was not quite right – I waited. A cloud drifted past. The mountain was bathed in pink, but the summit was obscured by cloud. The cloud became thicker. A brief gap revealed the summit. I took a

8

couple of shots, but they were not what I wanted—only a pink blur through a hole in the cloud. The chance would not occur again during the Expedition. I set off back; I was cold now and I seemed to have travelled a long way from the tent."

For supper we ate our, by now, standard meal of spiced corned beef and rice, followed by our favourite calorie-packed dessert, Christmas pudding and custard. This was followed by our evening pill-popping ritual of multivitamins and Ronicol.

Dusk was my favourite time. It always changed my mood and often the topics of conversation between us. It acted like a magic mirror, as if the past, present and future were meeting in my mind. It set in motion the symbolism of my nature. I was finishing writing my diary up from the previous few days:

> I'm always in a state of suspension when I'm trying a route, and this is no exception. At least I recognise the feeling. Joe seems at times a bit depressed. All this cloud moving down the valley is upsetting, after the weather appeared so windless and settled. Still, we'll see— after the alarm has gone off at five-thirty tomorrow, and it's my turn to steel myself to the cold and to light the stove. And now to thoughts of the past—memories, people, places and events, and to the future, to plans—after we get up this route and, who knows, we might do that! The determination's there. 8.47 p.m.

On the next day, 7th October, we moved up to the Ridge Camp, which we now optimistically called Camp One, in the hope that we would soon be establishing a Camp Two on the icefield. I was going to leave the tiny notebook of my diary at Camp One, to save weight, because I did not think I would feel like writing it higher up the mountain and I did not want to risk losing it, either by dropping it, or with our bodies as the only record of our adventure if an accident were to happen. I knew that the final round with the mountain was imminent, and was feeling increasingly nervous and excited. The 7th October was the last day I was able to scribble notes about any fact, beauty, or doubt.

> 7.15 p.m. Camp One. It never thunders and lightens in the Himalayas? It never snows at night on Changabang? These I now know are myths. Joe's done the cooking (we've humped the pressure cooker and primus up here). I had a load of 50 lbs. this morning!

Woke up (alarm) around 5.30 a.m. and had a couple of brews and porridge. We've brought the Advance Camp tent inner up with us, also a load of food and the little stove. So we had a lot of packing to do. Away around 8.45 a.m., wearing our windsuits – which we were glad of when we reached the Ridge. I'm feeling fit – hence hungry all the time.

When we arrived here we sorted the tent out – which seems to have sunk! Incredibly stable though, considering how long it's been up. We had dhal with some rice I'd brought up frozen in a poly bag – cooked last night. We've enough fuel up here to last for days. I re-dressed my thumbs and fore-fingers and spent a tedious afternoon mending my overboots – finished off the strong twine, Evostik and Araldite. Worked from about 1.00 p.m. until 6.30 p.m.! And now my head aches. Just eaten corned dog and rice – as usual, but it's filling – followed by a cuppa and Mars Bar.

But the main thing to write about is today's weather – such a contrast to the last three or four days' still sunshine. Early this afternoon, a dramatic two-hour electric storm – and after I'd been telling Joe that you don't get storms like the Alps in the Himalayas. "Is it the Chinese then?" he asked. When it cleared, it just moved back like a curtain, leaving the whole valley down to the Rishi plastered in snow. Perhaps it's the same as 'Termination Dust' in Alaska – the first snowfall of the winter season and a sign that summer is over. And now there is a very violent wind, rattling noisily, with occasional lashings of spindrift. All reminiscent of our days a week ago in the hammocks. Still, we are secure down here in the tent – glad we're not up there, but rather apprehensive about how we're going to build an effective shelter up there when we go up.

It's quite chilly – I'm glad I've brought my down suit. Our route seems to be in a very exposed position. 7.55 p.m.

There followed an uneasy day, which held us in a void. We discussed whether to move – as always, each of us took opposing points of view and tested them out on the other. Joe was for staying and, after a few minutes, it was evident that he was right. We had woken late and it was blustering outside. It would be madness to risk being caught out on the ropes again – particularly since we had not even brought the hammocks with us. We had left them at the high point on the ice-field. We resolved to leave very early the next day, whatever the weather.

"Ah well," I said, "we can eat the other half of that Christmas pud in comfort."

By mid-morning, the weather turned out not to be as bad as we had feared. It was too late to alter our decision. We had brought some books up this time. Joe settled back to read *Germinal* and I tried to start Stein-beck's diary. Some publisher had decided to print verbatim all the warm-up pages that Steinbeck wrote every morning before he started writing seriously. It seemed a bore, snapping and biting at trifling worries and obsessions about his accommodation and family. I felt that Steinbeck had been cheated by the publisher and that he would never have allowed such material to be printed if he had been alive. Having brought this book to such a remote place, I felt in a position to judge quickly and harshly many values of the civilisation that had governed it. Filled with the hubris only wilderness can bring, I stuffed it to the back of the tent. The books we were reading always had a strong effect on our moods—it was as if they brought new personalities into the tent.

For the rest of the day I pottered about sorting the tattered bits of rope we had recovered from Shipton's Col. My mind was too busy thinking itself up the sides of the mountain to concentrate on subtleties. Back home I had never been very practical, I could never see the point of wasting time on tasks that I knew other people could do much more quickly than I. Here it was different—there were no helpers. Four years before, I had been on a one-year outdoor activities course at Bangor University, and part of this course was learning to sew and make equipment. Over the year, I had produced a misshapen pair of overtrousers, and cut out the pattern for a rucksack. I had kept the unfinished rucksack material for mending purposes and had brought it with me to Camp One. For three hours I cut out strips of it and sewed lengths of polypropylene to them. These would be the marker flags with which we would guide ourselves on our descent, if we decided to come down the West Wall. At the back of my mind, I was coming round to thinking that would be the case. When we picked up the ropes as we went up the next day, we would leave most of the anchor pegs in place. If, when we eventually came down, some of them were hidden by overhangs, or by mist or storm, then the blue flags would help us find them. I knew from personal experience how important markers can be. On the descent from the summit of Everest, I would never have survived if I had not stumbled across the near-submerged shape of an oxygen cylinder marking the end of the fixed ropes. Lying beside me in the enforced closeness of the tent, Joe was feeling depressed:

"I was not feeling well for some reason, either just general weariness or something I had eaten. Camp One was becoming a little squalid. I hoped my anxiety was simply due to our bad experience in the hammocks. I reasoned with myself that Dick and I had spent ten nights bivouacking on the Face of Dunagiri only a year before. But my earlier enthusiasm to be back on the route seemed to have tarnished. I was back in the old going through the motions routine, doing what I was there for without knowing why.

"In the confines of the inside of the tent we were aware of every movement, action, thought even, of each other. There was no argument, no need for words, the mute passivity, clipped and curt responses, non-volunteering 'find out for yourself' attitude, were sufficient indications to each other of our feelings.

"For a full month, we had been alone together, working virtually every day, the whole burden of the Expedition resting on both of us. We could not succeed alone, we needed each other."

When I had finished making the marker flags, I started reading *Nana* but the light was fading and I was so wound up for action that I could not concentrate on Zola. If we could move up and establish a well-stocked and secure camp at the top the following day, then battle could commence. This was like war: we were living under constant threat and danger, our cunning and stealth were being stretched as exactingly as if we had been commandos beyond enemy lines. Except here there could be no victors or conquered—but perhaps we could sneak up and down whilst the enemy was sleeping?

CHAPTER SEVEN

The Upper Tower

9th–13th October

Camp One shrank below me, a blue dot on the curve of the ridge that swept from far beneath my feet towards Bagini Peak and Dunagiri. The only sounds were the wind whipping the corners of my down hood, and my own heavy panting as I pushed and pulled myself up the rope with the jumars. I was returning to the problem, feeling strong. Everything around me was pure in the light of receding dawn. The fresh powder snow, the harsh crystalline granite, the air itself, seemed newly created. There was even a terrible cleanliness about the danger to which I was exposed.

Two hundred feet below me, Joe was fixing a few short lengths of the rope from Shipton's Col, over the rock steps above Camp One. He had agreed to continue up behind and do the finger work of dismantling the fixed ropes beneath the Balcony and bringing them up with him. To compensate his extra burden, I was carrying all the down epuipment.

It had been the earliest start we had ever made on the mountain. I had not slept well. I had kept on waking up and thinking about the route. At three in the morning I had decided I was certainly not going to get any more sleep. Silently resenting Joe's peaceful doze, I had leant out of the door in the darkness and smashed some snow off the ever-retreating section of the cornice outside the tent and put the brew on. 'Typical!' I had thought. 'I bet he hardly stirs for another three hours.' And he did not. Nevertheless, we had moved off by half past six, at first light.

The plan was to pull up all the six terylene ropes hanging below the spike beneath the Balcony, where we had spent our first hammock bivouac. These, combined with the ropes on the icefield, ought to be enough to fix the Upper Tower. In this way we could still leave two ropes tied through the overhangs. We knew that if we retrieved these, we could never get back again. We had mused morbidly that it was retrieving the rope after the first crossing of the Hinterstoisser traverse on the Eiger that had cut off the retreat and precipitated the tragic deaths of the four climbers in 1936, including Toni Kurz. Joe and I were not prepared to cut off our retreat completely. If the hammock plan had worked, then we would have moved slowly up the mountain, stopping whenever we finished the day's climbing. But now, if we could establish the tent on the icefield, we would have to work every day from there, and take all the risks of jumaring and prusiking that it entailed.

I was astonished how smoothly the jumaring went. I was carrying two long sticks of bamboo that we had rescued from one of the Japanese expedition camps. I had pushed them as far as possible to the bottom of my sack. Now their ends wavered in the air above my head like bizarre antennae, as if they were rendering mysterious aid to my progress. I was wearing my one-piece down suit, yet even when the sun came out I was not too hot. The weather was steadily becoming colder. As I negotiated the vertical jumaring onto the foot of the icefield above the Toni Kurz pitch, I was bouncing about as usual when I ripped a large tear in the suit. For the rest of the journey up the ropes, I was accompanied by a trail of down, which rose, hovered and plummeted on the up-and-down draughts of air that sailed around the West Wall. Now, instead of staring glumly at the ice as I recovered between bursts of effort, I watched feathers soar hundreds of feet, with the intensity of a child at a balloon competition at a fair. Yet this was a more expensive game. I decided, and determined to wear my oversuit on top of my down suit in the future.

I reached the high point at half past two in the afternoon, thankfully to find that all the equipment, food and fuel we had left there was still intact. Combined with the food and fuel we were bringing up with us, we had a week's provisions — or ten days in an uncomfortable emergency. We were still feeling fit and fresh. I knew that I had lost a lot of weight, and that my body had become hardened and sinews become wiry with the effort of the previous few weeks. And I knew, also, that this feeling might not last for long. However, for the moment my mind and body felt in perfect accord, as if my will could force my limbs into any situation, as long as it entailed reaching the summit of the mountain.

The critical problem then was to find a site for us to pitch Camp Two. I unclipped from the rope and started soloing around the mixed ground above the fixed rope. After climbing about fifteen feet, I came to my senses and decided to clip back on. It was stupidity to deny myself some sort of chance if I were to slip. Joe was still a long way behind me on the icefield, so I pulled through fifty feet of the spare rope we had left up there and tied on to it. Then, with more confidence, I started climbing. I ran half the rope out, by which time Joe had arrived. Joe belayed me and I looked at all the area within seventy feet above our high point. Every time a line of rock promised a ledge, on inspection I always found its top stacked steeply with hard water ice. I crept back to Joe. I could not talk to him because of the wind, until I had reached him.

"Well, there aren't any good ledges. We might as well try and hack a platform out of this bit of ice as any other."

We tied off to fifteen-foot lengths of rope and started slicing into the ice with our axes.

We set about the work with enthusiasm. This was mountaineering at its most basic; serious play. As a child I had loved building tree-top dens and digging dug-outs. This was similar elemental home building, except the difference was the situation and the materials. Now we had the threat of bad weather and avalanche hanging over our heads if we did not do a good job. Secure shelter would make the difference between success and failure.

The ice-cutting was exhausting work. We hacked furiously until stopped by shortness of breath or cramp in the forearms. We soon hit the rock of the slab under the ice, and this forced the limit on the width of the ledge. By the time the sun was sinking into the cloud beyond Dunagiri, we had enlarged a ledge six feet long, two feet six inches wide at one end and tapering to two feet at the other. Whilst I tensioned the tent off from a system of nuts, spikes and rock and ice pegs I had fixed above, Joe lashed two sticks of the Japanese bamboo together and bent them across the entrance like a hoop. He improvised guylines from little stones knotted into the walls of the tent and hammered our hammock spacer bars into the ice for tent pegs.

Before the afternoon sun disappeared, I finished off the pitch I had started leading earlier. The climbing was quite awkward, but it was mere scrambling compared to that beneath the icefield. My thoughts raced ahead with the hope that the Upper Tower would be quickly climbed if it were all like that.

The last rays of the sun had moved off the Wall high above us and 'home' was ready.

"There doesn't seem to be much room in there," I commented.

"We'll have to tie on well," said Joe.

"Yeah, that's a drag, we'll have to leave part of the tent open to let the line through. And we'll have to keep our harnesses on inside our sleeping bags."

We had left our full body harnesses at Camp One, and put on our sit harnesses, hoping to save weight and also because the full body harnesses got in the way of the pockets of our oversuits. Now we regretted having made this decision, for the point of attachment of the sit harnesses was so low down. Outside the tent there was a chaos of equipment, slings and ropes, and after we had sorted them out the question that had been in the backs of our minds came out into the open. "Who's going to sleep on the outside then?" If Joe was still insisting that I cooked breakfast, then I was not going to give in on this question. To my surprise, he agreed to sleep on the side of the tent overhanging the edge.

"Only for a couple of nights, mind you," he said.

The tent was so cramped there was only room for one of us to sort himself out at a time. I went in and laid the insulating mats and the hammocks down, took off my boots and got into my sleeping bags. Joe squeezed in and did the same.

"Christ, my knees protrude over the edge," he said.

"Isn't it cosy?" I said.

"Good job we've got our pee bottles with us," said Joe. "I wouldn't fancy getting up in the middle of the night for a piss!"

"Make sure you pour it out on the left-hand side, we don't want our cooking ice polluted," I said.

We wedged the stove in between the soles of my boots in the tent entrance and put a brew on. The wind did not seem to be penetrating the thin fabric.

"You taking Dalmane or Valium tonight?" asked Joe.

"Dalmane, Dalmane, all around my brain, please."

Saturday, October 9th. I had missed the BMC Peak Area Meeting! The improvised tent was protecting us—the problem of shelter had been solved, and my heart warmed to the action to come.

We had decided that on the Upper Tower we would do two leads each in succession. We expected to go just as slowly on the Upper Tower as we had done below and had found that leading four rope lengths each was too much—two days' consecutive leading had been exhausting, and if you were seconding, you lost a feel for the action.

The next day I was intending to run out another rope length before Joe took over.

It was an exciting change to start climbing in the cold of the morning, straight from the camp and without any jumaring. But the optimism of the previous afternoon was short lived.

The only line that offered any feasibility of progress was a bottomless groove that was guarded from me by a bulge of ice. As I moved up to the bulge I started feeling tired. The climbing became hard and the wind and cold were sapping my strength. I was now wearing both down and nylon Ventile oversuits—far more than I had ever found it necessary to wear on Everest the year before. With my overmitts off and dangling from my wrists, and wearing only the pairs of gloves underneath, my fingers quickly became cold. I wanted to avoid making them colder by trying to put my crampons on. I traversed left on the rock to below where a bulge turned into a rock overhang. This was slit by a ramp, which I managed to step onto, and I traversed across to the side of the ice that filled the back of a hanging groove. Rather than put crampons on, I tapped a drive-in ice peg into the ice. It went in a couple of inches before stopping against the rock underneath. I tied a nylon rope sling around it where it came out of the ice, and stepped into it. Then I repeated the same movement further up the groove twice, before I could bridge out with my feet on either side on to rock. A few feet of climbing and I had reached the top of the groove.

The groove was capped by a six-foot overhang. I saw one ledge eighteen inches wide over on the left that ran around the corner onto the North Face and, after shouting a few warning words to Joe, I crawled along it. The wall above me bulged out and I was virtually on all fours. The ledge was in a horrifying position, without the ice-field to soften the view downwards. Below me was a sheer drop of four thousand feet onto the Bagini Glacier. By curling my fingers around narrow sideholds, I braced myself sideways and peered round the corner. We had seen, through our binoculars from the glacier, a long slanting groove line high on the edge of the Upper Tower between the West and North Walls. It had been the only obvious feature on the Upper Tower and we had hoped it would offer some straightforward crack climbing. We had called it 'the Niche'. Looking upwards now I could see it, and it scared me even to look at it! The corner was vertical, ice-smeared and two hundred feet high. I shouted down to Joe.

"I've seen the Niche. It's around the corner. It overhangs the North

Face and looks bloody impossible—to reach it, climb it, or get upwards from the top of it. We'll only get up if we climb the right side of the Upper Tower for the next few pitches!"

It was a measure of our trust in each other's climbing judgement that Joe accepted all this immediately, without demanding a look of his own.

The right-handed exit offered the only option—a fifteen-foot leaning crack. I tried to climb it by artificial aid, but none of the pegs or nuts I had with me would fit the crack. 'Don't be such a chicken,' I told myself inside. 'If this was on gritstone you'd bomb up it. It's obviously a lay back crack and doesn't look as if it'll play any tricks. Just take a few deep breaths and fight up it.'

I felt as if I had lead in my boots and my weight had doubled as soon as I swung my weight onto my arms. Half-way up the lay back, my fingers started to unfold from the edge of the crack so I rammed my fist round and into the back of the crack and squeezed it in a hand jam. I locked my arm straight from the jam and hung there until my breathing returned to normal. Then I returned to the lay back position and fought, with continually draining strength, upwards. My fingers curled over the edge of the arête that bounded the top of the crack. The arête rocked a little—it was a granite block of dubious quality. But I was past caring about that. One last heave and I swung up onto some footholds and gasped for air. A momentary feeling of nausea welled up from my stomach; I thought I was going to vomit. I managed to bang a peg in, tied the rope off and shouted down into the wind to Joe that he could start jumaring.

'That would have been quite a respectable grade on gritstone,' I thought, and resolved to avoid such strenuous climbing in the future. I looked down past Joe at the buff-coloured tent of Camp Two, now two hundred steep feet below. Beyond that was the sweep of the ice-field and then nothing. The Wall seemed to breathe in under that. There was only the Rhamani Glacier, and the tiny dot of the Ridge Camp Ore was just visible. Joe was dangling beneath me, all arms and legs, braced across the groove, hanging from a thread. He was unscrewing the ice pegs.

"A pity you'll miss the lay back," I said.

It was an uncharitable sentiment which back home on rock I used to relish when I watched seconds struggling up something difficult that I had led. Joe heard me from beneath his layers of balaclava, helmet and hood.

"It looked quite hard," he muttered. With a few upward strokes of his jumars, he had joined me. Now it was his turn.

With confident balance, Joe moved up a few feet above my head and then traversed diagonally rightwards under a line of overhangs, placing his feet carefully on a narrow sloping granite shelf. He placed a runner around a spike and looked around, obviously enjoying himself:

> "The climbing was delicate and thrilling, tip-toeing up the edge with stupendous exposure below. At the end of the shelf was a magnificent groove, steep and reminiscent of a Scottish climb. I put on my crampons. I found it hard, but on the right side of the borderline. Rocks frozen in place provided welcome holds and, when loose, added an extra thrill to the climbing. I was bridged across the icy runnel for most of the way. It was just the kind of pitch I enjoyed most, varied, intricate, uncertain."

I was watching the progress of the sun. The shadow crept back towards me imperceptibly, but inexorably. It had long since moved down the Bagini Peak and past Camp One. As the Wall steepened, so its speed increased. For a few moments I could see the icefield crystals shimmering in the sun's halo above the windswept South-West Ridge. Then the sun came out and the shadow ran away up the Wall. But the wind and the altitude were fighting away the warmth that should have come with the light.

The rope stopped moving, and there was not much of it left. The restless wind swept our shouts aside and threw them around the mountain. I decided that Joe must have tied on. I pulled on the terylene rope. Yes, it seemed secured. I shouldered the sack and moved off.

I was tense with concentration as I crossed the shelf that Joe had appeared to stroll across with such ease. 'Perhaps my boots are too big. Perhaps it's the weight of the sack. Perhaps I'm having an off day. I wish he'd put more runners in, I might swing off,' I thought. The thought that Joe was climbing well, was not allowed. I swallowed my moans.

The groove up which he had disappeared looked as if it had been fun to climb, with a succession of spikes to haul up on—held on to the mountain by hard water ice. But now I had swung into the line of the rope and was jumaring past them. Above the groove there was some easier angled rock and the rope whipped back left around the edge of the Upper Tower. I followed it and found Joe standing at the bottom of an overhanging groove that split the edge of the mountain for about three hundred feet. We both hoped it would not be necessary to climb that, and called it the 'Big Groove'. However, the alternative over on the right did not look much more attractive—massive blank walls stepped by overhangs looming upwards for over five hundred feet confronted us.

"There might be some easier angled ground on the left between us and the top of the Niche," said Joe. And he disappeared round the corner, leaving me standing at the foot of the Big Groove.

For two hours, Joe fought a hard and cunning battle with the rock and ice of the North Face on the left of the Big Groove:

"I came to a long, slightly overhanging crack. I chose to look further left. The crack was feasible but would have been very strenuous. Another corner had a tongue of ice running up into it— this seemed a better proposition. The ice was steep, a lot steeper than it had looked from below and, as I gained height, the tongue of ice became narrower and thinner. I had difficulty in maintaining my balance. I hammered a thin blade piton into a crack above. It only went in an inch, but gave me a little more support. I wondered whether to come down and try the other corner. It would be time-wasting to start again; I could see nothing of Pete. He would be wondering at the slow movement of the rope. I hoped he had secure hold of it. The next few moves would depend on everything working together just right.

"I hammered the pick of an axe into the ice; carefully, I balanced up and stood on the head of the axe protruding from the ice. Gently I reached down and undid my crampons. With my boots free of the crampons I stepped up onto small footholds on the rock, feeling strangely naked. I bent down and yanked out the axe.

"There were some delicate moves to make on the rock, but the friction of the rope pulled me back. I had to strain furiously to pull sufficient rope through to allow me to move up a few feet.

"Above was another ice slope. It seemed like a haven of security. On the rock I had been exposed and vulnerable. I drove the pick of my axe into the ice and went through the procedure of refixing my crampons.

"With my crampons on, I climbed up the ice to a grotto where I could see some boulders to which I attached the rope, and relaxed."

It was obvious that this lead had been desperately hard and, for Joe, the most demanding of the climb so far. I found it very difficult leaving Joe's last runner without swinging off further over the North Face like a pendulum—a sixty-foot swing could do a lot of damage and I would have difficulty getting back. I felt mentally and physically tired when I reached Joe. "It's getting late," I said.

Joe, full of accounts of sliding feet and frightening hops with ice hammers, was obviously thirsting for more action. It was 4.30. We had not far to descend back to the tent, but we knew it would start getting dark at five. There were seventy feet of steep ice above us on the North Face. It was my turn to lead but Joe was obviously more in tune than I. He set off up it, after agreeing to stop at five. He climbed it carefully but quickly and hammered in two pegs. The shadow that had climbed upwards six hours before was now returning. It was good to have snatched those extra feet at the end of the day. We swung quickly down the ropes to Camp Two, feeling happy. Things were going well.

Back in the tent, we peered at our photographs of the Face, trying to calculate our latest high point. We knew that we could not continue up the North Face any further, for we wanted to reach a feature which we had named 'the Ramp'—a thin line of snow that appeared from our photographs to stretch down from the summit snowfield, through an area of steep rock to the top of the Upper Tower. If we became committed to the upper section of the North Face, we would inevitably miss that exit. We only had five lengths of rope left which we could fix in place. After that we would have to climb away from our lifeline, and the Ramp seemed to be the only feature that would not trap us on the Wall or dangerously slow us down, but would offer us a slim chance of success. So the next day we would have to try and regain the crest of the Upper Tower above the Big Groove. And that would be my task.

It was morning.

"Bloody hell, no lumps of ice left." I swore violently.

Joe's eyes shuttered open briefly. "What's up, hasn't it been delivered?"

All my pent-up fears and frustrations were being released in curses into the morning wind. I had forgotten to break any ice the night before for the breakfast cooking and, in the darkness, was having to stretch out and claw at the ice hanging above the tent. Slowly, I accumulated a pile of ice chips on the side of the level patch outside, shouting loudly and angrily at the fragments that splintered off into the air and bounced down the mountainside. Back inside the tent, I tried to warm myself up again and started melting the ice, chip by chip. "I'll be glad when we've got up this mountain!" I mumbled, as it started becoming lighter. "I'm fed up with this view, I hope we can see Nanda Devi from the top."

The reality that soon I was going to have to do two hours of frightening jumaring was gnawing at me and I was irritable. I crushed thoughts that Joe, lying snoozing peacefully, was deliberately obstructing my cooking, and felt embarrassed about my morning moaning. I had not been shouting at him; I wanted to say I wasn't blaming him for suggesting this climb, for not cooking breakfasts. I was just exploding with the tension and shouting at everything—it did not mean anything and I was all right now. But our conversation had died to a basic minimum. I tried to rouse him with some talk about how settled the weather was. I felt that we ought to talk about something. But Joe hated small talk and platitudes, and felt as if I were treating him as if he were on one of the BMC Committees. He preferred to keep his brain ticking over in neutral.

It was the lonely hour of dawn. Joe went down to the icefield to pick up three ropes which we would need for climbing on and fixing on the Upper Tower. We had done a lot of diagonal climbing backwards and forwards the previous day, and I went up to straighten out the first three rope lengths. By removing the first two anchors, I hoped to be able to save a hundred and fifty feet of rope for higher up. It all seemed feasible in theory. On reaching the second anchor, I wanted to swing the rope into line below Joe's shelf pitch. I took the peg out and leaned sideways on the rope. But I had miscalculated the distance I was going to swing. Time closed up before me, like the progression of incidents in a split-second dream. I was soon hurtling through the air with a momentum that would not have been out of place on an Outward Bound ropes course. Too late I tried to spin my legs round to take the impact, but was not fast enough and I crashed into a wall, vertically below the next anchor, with a sickening thud that squeezed all the wind out of me. I had swung forty feet—half a pendulum, stopped abruptly by a rock wall.

I wriggled as much as I was able, whilst suspended from my jumars. No, nothing seemed to be broken. My mind shrugged grimly, 'Well, I'm still here.' I looked down at Joe, a tiny dot on the icefield. He probably had not seen my mishap, and why should he bother about it anyway? There was nothing he could do. We were further apart than we had been for a long time.

It was strange deciding the line of the ropes, by myself, after days of deciding all tactics by consultation. I laughed at how dependent I was becoming, and moved on. I chose to keep the line of the rope going through Joe's groove in the overhangs, so as to avoid any overhanging jumaring. Soon after eleven, I was established at the previous day's highpoint and waiting for Joe, feeling determined to maintain the momentum he had set in his lead the previous day.

The problem was to try and move back right to the edge of the Upper Tower. There was a line of cracks stretching across a steep wall in between us and the sky line. Guarding any entrance to them was an enormous flake. It was angular and about ten feet across, and it was possible to see light behind it in places. It seemed to be glued to the side of the mountain by a few patches of ice. Wearing my crampons, I front-pointed up to it and thumped it hard with my hammer. 'BOOMM!' it replied threateningly.

"What do you think to this, Joe, do you think it'll be safe? It might skate off with me riding it."

"Oh, it'll be all right," he replied. "It must have been there long enough. Anyway," he added reassuringly, "it's not my lead, is it?"

Nervously, I draped a sling over the top of the spike, as if I were conferring a holy order. I curled my fingers around the edge of this spike and swung my weight onto it. Nothing moved, except my mind, which was whirring with thoughts of the sweeping action this great tonnage of rock would have on us if it decided to detach itself. What would Joe do with me if I broke my back up here?

I slotted the front points of my crampons into a tiny lip of granite on the block and edged across. Leaning across the wall I could just reach a crack about two inches wide. At full stretch, I managed to prod a large bong peg into it, and this I patted in until it seemed to stay there by itself. Using this as a hand hold, I traversed out a little further. I reached high above my head with my hammer pick and hooked it into a little niche in the rock, then, pulling myself up onto this, made a lunge with my feet for a foothold on the edge of the buttress. Gently, I eased my weight over my feet until I was in balance. The foothold was a good one and I relaxed, detachedly amused at myself for reaching such an extraordinary position.

The sun had moved onto us whilst I had been climbing and I could see my shadow silhouetted on the rock above Joe. Beyond his self-absorbed form hanging in slings, I could see the forbidding sweep of the North Face and the brown lines of moraine on the Bagini Glacier, far below. I was directly above the Big Groove, and could now see parts of the West Wall again. I leant across and screwed a good hand jam into the top of the crack at the back of the Big Groove, and bridged across. A few feet above, the Big Groove reached an apex, like a pea pod, and I swarmed up to it. Above this, there was a ten-foot-high iceslope and I planted my ice axe and hammer into this and pulled up until I was teetering on the ice with my front points. My calves were quivering with the strain and I battered the ice with my axe until a foothold splintered into existence and I could rest my foot sideways. Above me, the Wall reared up again, split by a thin crack. Longing for security, I pounded three pegs into it, a blade, a soft steel blade and a leeper. These three pegs provided a welcome refuge after the sixty feet of instability beneath me.

Joe jumared up to me and we quickly discussed the situation. We had generated such unified intensity of purpose that whatever Joe said I had been thinking at the same time. Yes, we would straighten the fixed ropes the next morning. Yes, the next pitch should bring the Ramp into view. Yes, the crack looks the best line to follow until I can tension around the corner. The wind and the sunshine were forgotten.

The crack line became continually thinner, but there were no other features to use to climb this blank wall. After twenty feet, it faded out among the granite crystals. I leant down and sideways until it seemed every muscle in my body was taut. My balance was wobbling on the point of swinging me round and off the rock like an unfastened barn door in a draught. I was able to place a one-inch long knife blade peg in upside down, and this enabled me to reach another crack line which took me around an arête into a groove. For twenty feet I was able to establish a pattern of movement as the pegging became straightforward, and there was no hope of free climbing, since the rock was either vertical or overhanging. However, soon I was running out of equipment and above a short overhang I could see the back of the upper part of the groove gleaming with bulging ice. 'Nothing's ever simple,' I thought. I took out two pegs I had used below me and placed them, and then knocked two ice pegs into the ice-filled crack. As I moved my

9

weight onto them, I was not quite sure if it was the rock, ice or just a lot of luck that held them there. Now I only had small angle pegs left, and there were no ledges in sight.

Our route seemed to be forcing us up into ever more bleakly exposed fly-on-the-wall situations. However careful we always were at retrieving pegs, there were always some that were dropped or were left behind, and now we were running short of many sizes. The three angles that I had hammered in did not inspire my confidence, but I convinced myself that, on the law of averages, one of them would stay in, and I tied the rope off. 'Joe can sort it out from here in the morning,' I decided.

"Can you see the start of the Ramp?" shouted Joe.

"Yes, I think so." I returned to him, de-pegging as I descended and it was nearly dark when I reached him. We were late and, for the first time, I realised the full consequences of the loss of my descendeur as I struggled down with my complicated karabiner brake, past pegs and knots. The difficulty of this descent was a harbinger of the nightmare descents to come.

Dawn, the following morning, was the time of reckoning. I was going to have to go to the loo. I had been fighting this moment off all the previous day. Crawling out of the tent was a problem in itself, there were so many things I could knock over, including Joe and the tent. Only one person could move at a time and it was my turn. I imagined that I was at the fairground, trying one of those games where you have a circle of wire in your hand which you have to thread along another meandering piece of thicker wire without touching it. If you do touch it, a buzzer rings and you lose your money. Joe, the tent door, the pan on the stove, I thought, would all buzz loudly if I touched them as I threaded myself past them. Once outside the tent the game was just as delicate. On the third night, in Camp Two, we had not bothered to tie ourselves on whilst we slept, because the criss-crossed ropes inside the tent made the simplest movement too complicated. Once outside, however, to move anywhere you had to climb, and it was important to tie on. We had cut a line of steps underneath the tent and these I followed until I reached the back of the ledge. There, leaning out on the rope, I wrestled with the specially-designed zips of the oversuit, down suit and polar fibre undersuit. As soon as they were undone, my trousers started flapping agitatedly upwards, like medieval streamers in the bitter wind that was rolling up the Wall. Occasionally, my face or backside was lashed by a volley of spindrift or a flailing zip.

The whole bizarre procedure took half an hour and, at the end of it, the word 'masochism' had taken on a new meaning.

We had decided it was Joe's turn to go up the fixed ropes first that morning, and this gave me a feeling of relief—we were sharing the risk. Joe was to go up and straighten the fixed rope and sort himself out at the high point of the previous day. The first one up always took the risk that the wind might have frayed the rope against a sharp edge of rock somewhere. Nevertheless, following him I was still apprehensive, even though he had tested the rope and anchors like the jester sampling the king's food for poison. When we had climbed the rock below the icefield we had thought it steep, but it seemed that now the Wall was rearing even steeper. The jumaring was correspondingly more exhausting. My thoughts, refreshed by the night's sleep, were alert to all the dangers. I was delayed by still having some rearranging of the anchors to do on the ropes above Camp Two, and when I arrived at the foot of the Big Groove a shock was awaiting me. Joe had de-pegged the anchors from the three rope lengths above me and, on reaching the three peg crack, he had swung all the rope round in a great loop like a four hundred-foot skipping rope until he had lodged them in the Big Groove. Then he pulled them up tight. As a result I was confronted by nearly two hundred feet of eight-millimetre terylene rope hanging out from the rock down towards me.

'Joe's put it there, so he must be prepared to jumar it,' I thought as I started up, the competitive urge the only motivation. All the instances I had ever known of ropes snapping flashed through my mind like slides on a projector on autochange, interspersed with pictures of me spread out in the air in the apparent standstill of a free fall. 'Still, at least terylene doesn't saw up and down,' I thought. But as I got higher, this rope started to shudder sideways on an edge of rock at the top of the Big Groove. The apex was far away. I moved very stealthily, trying not to jerk the rope, looking at my jumars, eyes focused only on the umbilical cord that held me. The uncanny double-take, a constant companion at altitude, moved in. Was my mind here? My body seemed to be, but my mind felt free and uninvolved. Suddenly it was the top of the apex—there was the short ice slope, Joe, and the three peg crack. Joe was preparing to jumar up the last pitch to our high point.

"That last bit was exciting—it's in a good position," I said.

"It's saved a lot of rope," said Joe.

I knew that we could not afford to go up and down that length of rope many times without it wearing through, but did not mention it. Joe could see it as well as I, and he would find out all about what it was like to jumar the Big Groove when we next came back up! But did he worry as much as I did? I was filled with envy—I was seeing his existence from my separateness, and it seemed to possess a coherence and unity that mine did not.

I followed Joe up to the high point I had reached the previous day. It was a tangled procedure, interlocking me onto the hanging belay. I noticed he had only clipped into two of the three angle pegs I had placed so apprehensively before.

"Why have you only clipped onto two, Joe?"

"They look all right. Two should be enough," he said.

I hastily clipped into the third one. Pegs always give an illusion of safety if you have not put them in yourself.

The sun was filtering around on to us, as Joe set off in the lead. At first the climbing was almost identical to that of the pitch before. Joe did a few feet of pegging until the crack disappeared. He drove a blade peg until it stopped half way, and then passed the climbing rope through a karabiner on the peg. As I held the rope taut he leaned across rightwards, his weight supported by the tension in the rope. Using tiny flakes on the slab, he pulled himself across to the arête. Soon all that I could see were his left hand and foot, scything the arête. It was a fascinating puppet show. The hand and the foot jerked up and then scuttled down. Up, and then down. Up, and then down. Then suddenly they disappeared.

Around the corner, Joe was having a grim struggle:

"From the arête I could see a groove with a crack in the back about six feet away. The groove continued upwards towards the corners above.

"I pulled myself round the arête. The rope was horizontal between my waist and the peg; it was still holding my weight. I tried to reach the groove but as I stretched further right I tended to swing away from the rock. There were no holds big enough to hang onto; I relied on friction to keep me in place. Moving further rightwards round the arête was to move beyond the balance of friction maintained by the rope taking much of my weight and the rugosities of granite beneath my boots and hands. If I parted company, I would swing back twenty feet and the peg would probably come out.

"I juggled with the precarious balance for a while, stretching slightly further each time by clinging to tiny flakes discovered by my groping fingers. My body was almost horizontal and still I could not reach the groove. I glanced at the rope—it was rubbing, every time I moved, up and down the sharp edge of the arête. There was a sense of detachment about this observation; I wondered if I would reach the safety of the groove before the rope was cut through.

"I was quite exhausted by now and as a final resort took a nylon sling from around my neck. It had an aluminium chockstone on it, which I threw towards the crack. It lodged there first time, and I pulled myself to the crack on the nylon tape. The groove was overhanging; I didn't look down to soak in the atmosphere, but hammered in a peg immediately, fastened myself to it and rested."

A few feet of free climbing took him to a large granite block, which he flopped his arm around and rested again.

From the block Joe could see on his right an enormous hanging corner, two hundred feet high. Above that hung tendrils of ice, signifying the start of the Ramp. Towards the middle of this corner, across an overhanging wall, ran a two-foot wide sloping ledge, thirty feet long and banked high with ice. Joe gingerly put his crampons on and kicked his way across it until he was barred by an overhang. This he pegged over. Then he hammered two pegs in to hang from, and waited:

"I shouted for Pete to follow. When I remembered to examine the rope which had been wearing away on the arête I saw that it had been half cut through. I felt a lot more frightened now that I was safe and just thinking about what could have happened, than what I had actually been when involved with the situation. I cut away the frayed part and re-fastened the good rope to my waist."

Joe's tension traverse was difficult to follow, and I moved the diagonal line of his ropes by a series of swings as I knocked pegs out. It was acrobatic, and I felt like Tarzan swinging on a long vine that kept on snagging amongst twigs and branches. When I reached the big block, I peered around the corner and could see Joe, roosting forlornly above the overhang, like a big black hooded bird.

"Where are you going from there?" I shouted.

It looked like a dead end to me. The corner above him that stretched up to the Ramp would take a whole day to climb, if it was possible at all.

"Don't worry," came the habitual reassurance, with its over-emphasised, patronising tone. "I can see a way."

Feeling thankful that he did not sound frightened, I tightened up the rope along the ledge like a handrail on a catwalk, and set off along it. I had decided not to waste time putting my crampons on and my feet felt very insecure in the footholds Joe had hacked in the ice. Most of my weight was on the rope, which felt even thinner than normal, since it was stretched sideways. I remembered that the breaking strain of the rope was even lower when it was stretched horizontally. It had started to snow, and Joe was busily recording the dramatic situation and the snow and cloud effects with his camera.

Joe was right, there was a way out. Between the overhangs, and out of sight from below, a stepped corner reached up leftwards for sixty feet back to the crest of the Upper Tower. "Good route-finding," I complimented him, wondering if he had been led there by his sixth sense, blind luck or just because he could not climb up anywhere else. At first the crack in the corner was blind and he reached another crack on the left wall by a tension traverse. This crack he followed into the corner, and proceeded to climb it by a series of delicate free moves. After an hour he reached the crest. "Can you see the Ramp? Will it go?"

"Yes, it only looks one rope length away. Hurry up, it's a hell of a way down and it will be dark in a minute."

The snow shower had passed and rock was turning red around us. But I felt relaxed. I took some pictures of Joe, varying the exposures so as to catch the lighting.

"Hurry up, there's no time for taking photographs." It was the first time Joe had sounded angrily impatient.

"Don't worry," I shouted back. "You'll be glad of them when you are an old man!"

It was another diagonal swinging pitch to follow. I retrieved all the pegs and nuts so that we could fix the edge out straight down the overhanging wall to the big block. Joe was perched on one foothold and I hung off the slings of his spike belay whilst he sorted the equipment out for his descent. I had taken half an hour longer than he did the day before to descend back to Camp Two, because I had to use a karabiner brake.

"Don't forget to put the brew on," I reminded him.

"See you soon," he said as he reeled off down the rope and out of sight.

Irrationally, I did not share Joe's sense of urgency. I looked up and saw an overhanging groove reaching up to the Ramp. For me it was a golden line of promise through an area of turmoil, as if parted by the rod of Moses. At the top it was crowned by an enormous block of granite bridging across the walls of the groove like a beam across the corner of a roofless house. Perhaps we could peep beneath the crown? Nothing could stop us now.

The rope that had been my tormentor in the harsh light of early morning awareness, had now become a friend. I was descending in a trance. The swooping slides, the dancing traverses and swings, were part of the pattern deeply hidden within the game of the descent. The complicated procedures for passing knots and pitons were factual procedures to be mastered as part of the choreography. The consequences of a mistake were forgotten. The emphasis of progress and the numbness induced by the cold, altitude and fatigue had put me in a state of reverie. A fantasy world had grown around me assuming nonsensical names and nationalities. The knots in the rope I called 'cows', the pegs became 'Americans', the karabiners at my waist all took the names of different girls. I was a big spider scuttling down.

There was a blue light inside the tent, telling me that the stove was purring. The brew was on. I crouched in the darkness, sorting and clipping my equipment to the slings outside, ready to crawl in for shelter.

"I nearly left you to finish the climb on your own, whilst I was up there," said Joe. He was shaken and unnerved.

At the point where there were three pegs together, the rope was criss-crossed between them. Whilst Joe had been passing this section, he had realised something was amiss, and had noticed that his jumar had become unclipped from his waist, his descendeur was in his right hand and all his weight was hanging from his left hand on the jumar.

"It was really weird, odd thoughts kept on spinning round like 'Is this it?' and 'Is Pete going to have to finish the climb on his own?' and 'I don't want to drop my descendeur.' Eventually I fumbled a nylon sling from my neck, wrapped that round the rope and put my arm through it, so that I could get myself clipped in."

Joe said little as we ate our evening meal. It was the usual Oxo with freeze-dried meat and mashed potato and a cup of tea, followed by a nibble of chocolate. I dozed out of his way, as he cooked. What a day it had been—from doubt and fear to resolution. Then from intense effort to joy—all the emotions of a lifetime had been carried to my heart with extraordinary power. Yet our conversation reflected no more than a quiet, calculated hopefulness. In the morning we would move away as early as possible, pack food for two days, and push, alpine style, for the summit.

It was as if our subconscious was plugged into the same internal clock. We both woke late, having already made the decision whilst we were asleep to have a rest day. Now we were waiting for the other one to suggest it. Eventually I asked Joe what he thought about the idea since I had to decide whether to start cooking or not.

"I'm glad you suggested that," he said. And we laughed and slid back onto our imaginations, comforted by the thought that we could wait for the sunshine before starting the cooking or venturing outside into the wind to go to the toilet. That morning at least our internal clock could rest unwound.

During the afternoon, I started to feel claustrophobic inside the tent. When crawling out I accidentally knelt on some of Joe's camera equipment. He snapped at my clumsiness. I had not understood until that point his enthusiasm as a photographer. He had brought his lens tissues and brush up with him and was fastidiously cleaning his equipment.

"I had to buy my cameras," he said. "They weren't given to me, you know."

I had been given an Olympus OM1 camera for the Everest climb, which I had brought up with me, fitted with a wide-angle lens. But I wasn't lavishing it with the attention that Joe thought it deserved. As usual, Joe's precise, orderly approach to bivouacking and equipment made me feel muddled and clumsy, like a small boy told off for touching in a china shop. Some people judge mountaineers by their speed, and by the difficulty of the rock they can climb. But on Changabang the real test was more how efficiently you could put a brew on, warm your fingers or take your boots off.

Outside I drank in the view in the afternoon sunshine. All the mountain shapes nearby were so familiar. Was that the Holy Kailas I could see, I wondered, looking at a solitary white-topped mountain above the distant brown plains of Tibet? Kailas—the throne of Shiva, the precious ice mountain, the crystal one, the centre of the universe. The waters of Kailas fed some of the greatest rivers of Asia and before politics and a war changed borders and religions, thousands of pilgrims travelled to walk or crawl around it. To me it was a white signpost to a forbidden land. Soon, I thought, I would see Nanda Devi from the Summit Ridge, and we would have worked hard for that view. It was now the 13th October, and soon the winter would come. We had not much time.

As I began to squirm back inside the tent I noticed some dark stains on the snow just outside the door, where Joe had been coughing. He had been spitting blood. Since he had not talked about it to me, I decided not to mention it. Inside the tent he was lying in his sleeping bag with an ecstatic look on his face.

"What's making you look so pleased with yourself?" I asked.

"Ooh," he said, "have you felt the tent fabric? It's sort of billowing down over my face, and when you touch it it sort of bulges in soft round yielding curves. Ultimate Bill says that it's the same material used for making women's underwear."

The rest of the day floated past in idle banter. Changabang did not worry us any more.

CHAPTER EIGHT

Beyond the Line

14th–15th October

> White hovers away and near
> Brushing and sliding a solution above fear
> In clouds that pierce and sway
> Through solids inside, beneath and away
> As feathers of needles
> Caress in a groan of silver
> Who am I here? Alive yet apart
> Without and within the wings of the earth.

Outside the night roared. Winds were breaking around the great white rock of Changabang, and then retreating, drawing in their breath with anger, gathering their frustrated powers beyond the mountain, to return again through the darkness. And the mountain rolled on. Only dreams of the summit helped us cling to its side.

It was three in the morning, and pitch black. "It sounds bloody awful out there," said Joe.

It always did from inside the tent—the crackling walls seemed to be shaking with the constant threat of imminent disaster and were turning the tent into a sound box. Joe was still lying on the outside, and only the bulging nylon of the walls was holding him in place. When the wind gusted violently, the side of the tent tried to roll him over. Fortunately, I had chipped the ice ready for melting for breakfast, the night before, and soon had a pan on the stove. The flame of the stove reasserted our defiant right to be there. The tent walls moved the air inside, and the flame swayed slightly from side to side, as if it were continually slipping and righting itself—shaken but always recovering its balance.

We were ready to move at half past six. We had very little equipment, just a climbing rope, a sleeping bag and a bivouac sack each, and a stove, a pan and a little food.

"It's going to be a long, cold haul back up there," I said. "Do you want to go first and sort out the rope just below the high point? Then you can get belayed ready for me to lead the top pitch. The Big Groove jumar might get you buzzing."

Joe agreed and I was thankful. I did not want to be the first to jumar the Big Groove, and wanted him to find out what it was like.

The wind was gusting up to fifty miles per hour, and it was agonisingly cold. Every fifteen minutes I had to stop in my jumars, undo the zip on the front of my oversuit and down suit and thrust my hands deep under my armpits, gripping my fingers firmly under my arms. 'If this goes on any longer I soon won't be able to warm them back up again,' I thought. It demanded a disciplined effort to recognise when my fingers were reaching the danger zone, because many of the ends were numb already.

Joe had forgotten to tighten the rope below the high point – it had been a misunderstanding. Still, it did not matter. We had an old hawser laid rope which we thought would reach the Ramp, and probably would not need any more. I took off my sack and left it with Joe, and set off up the pitch. A day's climbing was ahead, and we had no idea where we would be at nightfall. A day to hold in the front of my mind, to pace myself through. But the immediate problem was the Groove.

There was a lot of ice on the rock but I wanted to avoid using crampons. First I had to reach the foot of the Groove by crossing its right-hand wall from Joe's stance. There were some good incut holds for my fingers, and soon I was fifteen feet above his head. However, my fingers had lost all sensation again; I clipped an etrier in to a spike runner, stuck both feet in it and tried to warm them up. I knew I could keep on climbing with numb fingers, but that would do permanent damage, and we had a few days to keep going yet. If Joe resented having to wait in the cold during my re-warming antics, he never complained. However, this was the first time we had been forced to do desperate climbing out of the sun – it was a good excuse.

A flake of rock curved into the Groove and I hand-traversed across this, finding little flaky holds on the granite beneath to support my feet. Soon I was poised next to the Groove, uncertain whether my legs would stretch to a small foothold on the other side, if I launched myself across it. I took a deep breath and, feeling as if I were stepping from a secure quayside into an untethered rowing boat, lunged across. My foot missed the hold but, with my hands, I steadied myself against the left-hand side of the Groove, and eased myself carefully into a bridging position. After twenty feet the Groove moved from the vertical to overhanging. The right-hand wall had become blank and I could no longer bridge across. I placed a nut in the crack and clipped into it, gasping for oxygen. I twisted my head back and looked around.

It was the most amazing, exhilarating situation I had ever been in. I looked down and across at Joe, who was hanging on the edge of space. Directly below me almost our entire route fell sheer away. Over a thousand feet below was Camp Two, and yet the Upper Tower was so foreshortened beneath me, and the air so clear, it felt close enough still to be our home. Beyond the icefield, the undulations and peaks on the ridge between Rhamani and the Bagini Glacier were flattened by the perspective of my height. The ridge drew a vertical line across the earth beneath my feet between light and shade, white and brown, known and unknown, explored and forbidden. The black spot of Camp One on the ridge was the only sign of our passing in that wilderness. The rock of the Groove seemed poised on the edge of the mountain. I was directly above that tent nearly four thousand feet below. For a moment I was speeding through the skies above the wrinkled world.

Above me, a great arc of colours stood across the sky in a rainbow around the pool of white light of the hidden sun. The ice crystals in the air of the upper atmosphere were forming a halo around the sun, the classic herald of an approaching front. I wondered if Joe had read the signs as well, and when the storm would arrive; I hoped it would not be a big one.

The big block crowning the Groove was suspended above my head. I leant out on the nut I was hanging from and pushed it. It did not tremble, so I moved up onto another nut higher in the Groove, pulled a leg clear and kicked it. I did not want to dislodge it in case it chopped the ropes or hit Joe. It probably weighed half a ton. Since there were no signs of it moving, I decided it would be safer to try and squirm behind rather than risk levering it away by pulling around its outside.

As soon as I had wriggled my shoulders through the hole my feet swung out into space. After a lot of undignified wriggling and heaving, I suddenly popped out onto some snow. From above, the block seemed to be balanced on a perch that defied gravity, and I quickly moved my weight off it. I looked upwards and saw snow, the easiest angled snow I had seen for four thousand feet. I had popped through the Keyhole that, at last, seemed to have opened the door to the climb—surely nothing could stop us now?

"I'm on the Ramp," I yelled into the wind.

Within seconds the sun moved onto me, to help match an outer with inner warmth. I tied off one of the ropes for Joe to jumar up, and started hauling up my sack. As Joe neared me, he had to take his own sack off and attach it to mine, so that he could squeeze the sacks and himself separately through the Keyhole. He was pleased to join me in the sunshine.

> "Reaching the Ramp was tremendous. That was the real conquest, the imponderable difficulties were over—the summit was 1,000 long, cold, weary feet away."

The sun was weak and watery, but now we had movement to warm our limbs. We shed most of our hardware and took with us two ropes and a handful of pegs, slings and karabiners. We were still adhering to the pattern of leading two pitches each at a time, and I quickly set off, kicking steps up the snow above us, plunging the spikes of my axe and hammer with a steady rhythm. It was a joy to be able to move so freely, to begin to gain height with such ease. Dumping most of the hardware had made a big difference.

Another buttress of rocks towered above us, rearing its head between us and the summit slopes. The snow I was climbing was powdery and unstable, and I decided to aim for these rocks to gain the security of a rock belay. To reach their nearest point, I had to climb diagonally across the slope. I touched the rock at the same moment the rope stopped coming to me from Joe. It had just been long enough.

Joe soon joined me. We had left the jumars behind and were now climbing in the Alpine style with which we were familiar, moving as a fluid, integrated unit, our sacks geared for survival. We had cast off from the fixed ropes and the rope between us had been demoted from master to servant; for a while, at least, the mountain would be our total support, and we were reprieved from the hanging, fragile line. The leader and the second could share the climbing movement, no longer were we jumaring past the verticality of each other's achievement. The movement had become all-important. The afternoon was ticking past —we were committed to the summit and our speed would be our only defence.

"This must be the Ramp," I said, "and so we ought to keep on traversing right. It should curve up through this buttress on to the summit snowfield."

Joe, however, thought we should go straight up, following a more direct gully line through the rock buttress. "It looks all right, it'll be much shorter, and it'll be easier to abseil down," he said. Also, he didn't like the state of the snow, and considered that a lot of traversing without the assurance of there being good rock belays would be more dangerous. I was worried that the gully might be too difficult, and that we would waste too much time on it. But it was Joe's lead and so it was his decision to make. After taking a few slings from around my neck he moved off and, after hugging the foot of the rock, led a difficult diagonal pitch over mixed ground up into the gully.

The upper section of the gully was out of sight from us, hidden by an ice slope fifty feet wide, that bulged at eighty feet. Joe pulled over a short rockstep and climbed steadily on the ice up to and over the bulge. Many ice fragments started falling down and the rope stopped moving out so evenly. The texture of the ice had changed from being white, aerated and firm to black, hard, unyielding water ice. Joe climbed for thirty feet up this sixty degree, steely surface towards the left-hand side of the gully at a point where the gully walls closed in. As he climbed he tried to protect himself by hammering in ice pegs. The ice was so hard that it splintered after the ice pegs had entered more than a couple of inches, and he had to tie them off. They offered him little more than psychological protection. His axe and hammer picks and crampon points were blunt after all the previous climbing and demanded heavy swings before they penetrated enough to offer any support. It was mentally and physically an exhausting pitch, and by the time Joe hammered in a rock peg, he had cramp in his forearms and calf muscles. He managed to nick a small foothold in the ice to stand on, and pulled the rope in.

"I found that quite hard," said Joe when I eventually reached him. There was not much room, and I found I became spread-eagled around him, with one foot on the ice and one foot on the gully wall. I had enjoyed the pitch immensely. It had been the first time on the route I had been able to relish hard technical climbing under the safety of a top rope.

"Excuse me," I said, since I was half hanging from his harness in my attempts to pass him.

"It's about time you had a wash," said Joe.

I returned to the original subject. "Yes, that last bit was rather tricky. Where do we go now — over there on the right?"

Joe agreed, he had been weighing up the next section whilst I had been climbing. On the right at the back of the gully was a line of apparent weaknesses in the broken ground, where the rock and the ice met. It was impossible to judge its angle and difficulty from where we were.

Trying to appear as confident and forceful as possible, I took a few deep breaths and vigorously front-pointed for fifteen feet across the gully until I could brace a foot across a spike and scrape my other crampon against the ice until I was in balance.

For me, it was a perfect pitch. Every move was intricate, technical and yet I could recapture my balance after every two or three movements. Every technique I had ever used was tested and applied, half consciously — bridging, jamming, chimneying, lay-backing, mantle-shelfing, finger pulls, pressure holds all followed in a myriad of combinations. The struggling rope acrobatics of the Upper Tower were forgotten, for this was mixed rock and ice-climbing at its finest. I felt in perfect control and knew the thrill of seeing the ropes from my waist curl down through empty space. I was as light as the air around me, as if I were dancing on tip-toes, relaxed, measuring every movement and seeking a complete economy of effort. Speak with your eyes, speak with your hands, let it all flow from your heart. True communication, true communion, is silent. Chekhov once said that when a man spends the least possible movement over some definite action, that is grace. This was my lonely quest, until the jerk of the rope reminded me that I must stop and secure myself — and that I had a companion. Looking back at Joe, I realised how late it had grown. The gully had turned into a golden amphitheatre, poised on the edge of darkness.

It was an awkward pitch for Joe to follow:

"The rope was pulling me rightwards; I had to climb into the back of the gully but was pulled off balance each time by the rope. I shouted to Pete but he did not seem to hear and I could not pull any slack down. With a fervent prayer that he had a good belay, I swung on the rope across the gully and grabbed the rock on the other side."

Our awareness of each other, and our strength, flowed between us in waves. Now, when Joe arrived, I realised with an almost physical sense of shock that he was tired. For a few moments the mask of silence between us fell aside. Nearly three hundred feet above us, the gully seemed to finish in a crest against the summit slopes. There were no ledges where we could spend the night around the narrow snow slope, broken by rocksteps, above us.

"I'll take us to the crest if you like," I said.

"Yeah, I'm a bit tired," said Joe.

I was filled with urgency, and determined to stay in the sun until I reached the crest. It was an invented game, to pluck us from the grasp of darkness. It gave me a surge of strength, keyed up as I was by the rhythm of the action. The gully was sheltered and, as I churned upwards with my feet, the powder snow poured straight down. The air was becoming colder but the light was warm and red. The sun was pushing me upwards as if I were soaring on particles of solar light.

Ten feet beneath the crest, I plunged a deadman into the snow and pulled the rope in, but Joe was already moving. I saw his red helmet bob over a rock step, lassooed by the evening light. For the first time since I had followed Joe's pitch up the gully, I could look around me. But night was quickly closing its doors and only the sun held my gaze. It was a glorious sunset that spread its calm into me and abstracted me from the time and space below us. Numb toes and racing heart were forgotten. But these were moments I could not savour. The advent of Joe, darkness and cold stopped our upwards motion. We had to bivouac.

The crest of snow where the gully met the summit icefield was on the edge of the mountain. We reckoned we were at 22,000 feet—with about 500 feet to gain to reach the summit. As soon as we moved onto the crest, the whole atmosphere of the evening changed, for we moved from the shelter of the gully into the wind. The wind was blowing agitatedly across the crest, as it accelerated around the top of the mountain. The temperature was plummeting as the sun disappeared.

"We'll have to stop here," I said, "we might be able to dig in." I felt unusually assertive, as if it was my job this time to organise the bivouac. I fixed up a belay line to some nuts and a piton I had placed in a rock that poked out of the snow, and we both tied on to it. I traced out the area of snow that we ought to excavate, with the pick of my axe, and Joe started digging at one end and I at the other. It was becoming colder by the minute, and soon we were digging with the feverish haste of gold-crazed prospectors, using feet, hands and axe, and throwing up clouds of snow into the wind.

Rock was disappointingly near the surface, and our hopes of a snow-hole faded. Eventually we managed to gouge a tiny platform. We were now dangerously cold and it was vital to warm ourselves up. We had brought two small bivouac bags with us in case we had been unable to find a ledge and had to bivouac separately. This meant we had no shelter large enough to cook inside, out of the wind. There would be no evening drink or meal.

"It's your turn to sleep on the outside," said Joe.

"Are you keeping your boots on inside your pit?" I asked him. Yes, he was. We only had our two-pound, lightweight sleeping bags with us, and would need as much warmth as possible.

With his habitual bivouacking speed and catlike search for comfort, Joe was soon ensconced in his green cocoon.

"Our values had sunk ever further. Tonight, bliss was cessation of activity, a place out of wind and warm sleep."

I was struggling with my sleeping bag, feeling angry at my own comparative ineptitude. I felt very insecure, as if I were only preventing myself rolling off the shelf by keeping my muscles tense. I was lying on my side, facing into the slope which was not quite long enough for me. My feet were poking out over the crest and the wind was tearing at them so fiercely, it felt as if there were no layers protecting them.

Joe seemed to gain a few inches of the ledge every hour. An irrational, miserable little corner of my mind started resenting him. 'I bet he's really warm. I bet he's fast asleep. Why does he always seem more comfortable than me? Why does he need so much room?' Every time I dozed off and relaxed, my back and leg muscles would jerk back awake as gravity started to topple me off the ledge. There is a bivouac story of a climber who stayed awake all night so as not to wake his sleeping leader who had slumped against him. Well, that was not me — and I had had enough.

"Hey, Joe, you're pushing me off!"

"Oh, sorry." He sounded wide awake, and immediately made some room for me.

I must have fallen asleep. I pushed the tiny hole left where the drawcord had been drawn tight at the top of the bivouac bag, round to my eyes. It was still dark. It was even colder, and the wind felt as if it were blowing through me like a sieve. Then I realised. My feet. I could not feel my feet. I fought the overwhelming desire to flop back to sleep again, and struggled into the foetal position and started taking my boots off. One foot, and then the other; I tried to warm them alternately by pushing both hands down the sock and rubbing and holding the base

10

of the foot and then the toes. It took two hours to bring the feeling back into them.

Dawn meant nothing to us and we were not ready to accept it. I was wincing uncontrollably with the cold.

"Shall we wait for the sun?" I bawled into my bivouac bag, hoping that the sound would manage to escape somehow through the hole above me.

"Yeah," came the strains of a reply. "We should be on the top in an hour or so from here."

I was too cold to think. Two hours later, however, the bivouac king was bored.

"I'm making a brew," he announced, the trade union job differential forgotten. An hour later, a lukewarm mugful of something nondescript was thrust through the gap and I downed it in a couple of gulps.

"The sun's out you know," came the second announcement. And so it was, but all its power was filtered by a high veil of cloud, and it was not warming the day up as we had hoped. I counted up to ten, steeled myself and started getting up.

"Could you tie my bootlaces, Joe?" I knew if I tried to do it my fingers would never recover.

Joe stooped down without a word and tightened them up for me. I felt like a pathetic little child—but Joe did not take the opportunity to throw a gibe. 'He must have had a lot of practice doing this for all his little brothers and sisters,' I thought.

"We'll leave all the gear here, shall we?" said Joe.

So we were not going to descend the other side. "We'd better take a rope and a couple of deadmen," I said. And we were ready.

It was as if I had done all this before, in a dream, but now I was in the dream itself. We quickly climbed through a short rock step above the bivouac site and started moving together up the 50° snowfield. Joe was in the lead.

"I wanted to get it over with. The romance for me was gone . . . the fatigue of altitude and exertion were familiar and not disconcerting. I never looked back to see how Pete was doing, whether he was moving faster or slower. I could feel the rope tug at my waist and I would wait, but did not know if it was Pete on the other end or whether it was just dragging in the snow . . . The 'Horns' of Changabang were now below us and faintly, in the depths of my consciousness, was the awesome thought that at long last we were clawing our way up a slope, poised breath-takingly above the precipice of the West Wall, 5,000 feet above the glacier. A few points of metal on our boots, a couple of metal tools in our hands and a rope tying us together, were all that were holding us in place."

The light, like an over-exposed photograph, now had no warmth, no colour, no perspective and the snow could have been of any angle—except my gasping breath and heavy feet told me of its height. The wind bowed my head. My eyes were lowered to the moving ground. Wind buffeted, powder snow scurried past in an endless stream. The standstill feeling had returned, which I had felt so many times before when climbing on snow. I was inside a shell that moved in slow motion, with a steady mechanical high-lifted step.

I was blinkered in mind and vision. Clouds were surrounding us. This was Changabang, soon I would be able to see its other side. Would I be able to see Nanda Devi and the Sanctuary of my childhood dreams? It seemed simplest to stay in a single, intense thought, to feel the prospect of a wider horizon draw me like a magnet towards the summit ridge. The memories of a month's struggle on the West Wall lay beneath my feet and the summit was the distillation of all my hopes.

Joe was sitting on my horizon line. He had reached the ridge and was pulling in the loops of rope between us. For the final fifty feet there was a wind-carved crust of hard snow on top of the powder, which collapsed under my weight. I steadied my impatience and kicked through it carefully. Joe was as relieved as I was excited at the view. "Don't worry, you can see it," he said as I arrived. It was as if he would have felt responsible if I could not but, so reliable, had managed to arrange a convenient break in the clouds. And there it was. Nanda Devi, the bliss-giving goddess.

Clouds plumed horizontally from its summit above its shadowed North-Eastern Walls. These 8,000-foot walls formed a vast, forbidding amphitheatre of swirling mist. To the west, however, the sun picked out a silver track along the Northern Ridge that threaded its way to the main summit. And the summit was clear. Below the spaciousness between our spire and the twin-peaked mass of Nanda Devi, stretched the upper arms of the promised land. Long, orderly brown moraines lined the sides of the glaciers, as if fashioned by giant hands. It was the 15th October and winter would soon cover all that wilderness. No man slept there.

The summit, the highest point on the whole of the ridge, was thirty feet away.

"You might as well move across," said Joe. The top was only a few feet higher than the point where we had reached the ridge.

I thought we would at least shake hands, but Joe did not make any gestures. I wondered if he felt he had just done another climb and that life would just go on until he did his next one. Perhaps wiser than I, he had already started focusing his concentration on the problems we were to face in the descent—perhaps to touch each other would have broken the spell of our separateness. I took some photographs of him sitting on the ridge, with Nanda Devi in the background. His beard and mouth were encrusted in ice and his mirror sunglasses hid any feeling in his eyes. In the mirrors I could see my own reflection. How could I ever know to what depth he was retreating? His few words seemed so inadequate. I could not know if practicality did rule him, or if he was concealing his emotion. Was it that we had different attitudes to expression? Or were we really living at different levels?

It was difficult to judge the size of the cornice and we belayed each other and peered alternately over the edge and down the upper ice slopes of the South Face. We could see about two hundred feet, and then the Face cut away into the unknown.

"There don't seem to be any tracks anywhere," I said, "perhaps the lads haven't done the South Face."

I was glad there were no tracks, for they would have taken the edge off our isolation. To the north-east, we could see Kalanka Col, with Kalanka rising from it. Beyond that more white mountains, and I photographed them, determining to discover their names later. But they were tame to our eyes, after the vertical world we had left beneath us. I wished we had decided to descend the other side, to bring a new dimension to our experience of the mountain.

I sat in the snow and changed the film in my camera. But now Nanda Devi and Kalanka were obscured by cloud. "Have you seen over there?" asked Joe.

The storm cloud which had been darkening the northern sky over Tibet all day, had suddenly grown and was moving towards us. The coming of the storm had been announced by signs in the sky, twenty-four hours before. Now it had arrived.

I did not want to leave and hated the prospect of descending the West Wall. The sight of the other side had liberated my spirit. The isolation of our situation, and the size of the wilderness beneath us, intensified our strength. For a moment I felt omniscient above the world. But this feeling of invincibility was an illusion of pride, for we had yet to descend. It was two in the afternoon and we had been on the summit for half an hour when the first snow flakes began to fall.

CHAPTER NINE

Descent to Tragedy

15th–19th October

"We might as well unrope for the first part of the descent," said Joe.

"What—with this storm coming in?" I was incredulous.

"Well, there's not much point in keeping it on if we're not going to belay. If one slips, he'll just pull the other one off."

"I prefer to keep it on and move together, so that it's there and ready in case we come across any tricky bits," I said.

"Well, there aren't any tricky bits and we'll have to abseil as soon as we reach that rock step above the bivouac," said Joe.

"All right then, but you go first and I'll carry the rope," I agreed. 'If he can do it, so can I,' I thought. Although I could understand Joe's cool rationale, I was repelled by the idea of soloing above the five and a half thousand feet of the West Wall of Changabang. On the summit Joe had become assertive, whilst I had been preoccupied with the view and our arrival. A wave of purpose had rippled between us and I was happy that he led down.

I finished coiling the rope. Joe quickly moved back along the ridge and started down our line of tracks that stretched down the snow-slope. As I looked across at him, I could see under the cloud the familiar sight of the Rhamani Glacier, twisting down towards the Rishi Ganga. The walls of the Rhamani before had oppressed me, but now we moved above them, and they were reduced to geographic details. The moraines of the Rhamani, that broke through the ice like the bones of the earth, were now the highways of our return. The beginning of the dark sheltered vegetation of the Rishi Ganga was a promise that sprang from a kindlier planet. There, only treetops would be swaying.

The snowslope was easier to climb down than I had feared and, in descent, the altitude had lost its enfeebling effect. Soon the falling snow had imprisoned us in mad, whirling whiteness and we kicked and plunged downwards with increasing urgency. Joe reached the rock step and hastily fixed a sling. I uncoiled the rope and we flung it below us. It snaked out into the cloud and writhed down among the falling snow and spindrift. The air and snow around us were in constant downward dance, and as we slid down the ropes we joined their momentum.

As we picked up our sacks and sorted our gear at the bivouac site, spindrift was pouring everywhere, into our sack, into our gloves and down our necks. We were retreating under bombardment. The hardware was so cold it stuck to our gloves. 'Let's get the hell outa here,' echoed a thought in a voice like a John Wayne movie, and with it came the return of the strange realisation that I was actually enjoying myself.

The next two abseils went quickly. By the time I arrived next to Joe, he was fixing the anchor for the next abseil and he threaded it through as I pulled one end of the doubled rope down. The previous time we had used this abseil procedure had been five years before, when we had first met in the Western Alps. Now it was automatic.

We had reached a point half way down the steep pitch I had led the previous day. As I swung down the rope towards him, Joe said, "If I direct the rope right, we should make it in one go to the bottom of the gully from here." He was perched on a couple of footholds and I held on above him. After I had pulled the ropes down I saw his anchor. He had tapped a one and a half inch knife blade into a thin diagonal crack in a rock inlaid in the ice. It had gone in about an inch of its length. And he was about to slide off on it!

"You're not going to just abseil off that are you?" I was aghast.

"Can you suggest anything better?" he replied coldly.

We had left most of the pegs at the top of the fixed ropes and now only had two left with us. The other one was of the wrong size. I could not suggest anything better, and off he went without an upward glance. I clung on to the peg with one of my hands, hoping it would not lever out. Joe did not seem worried:

"I believed that the piton was just adequate to take our weight. I had the impression that we would be all right. We had put everything possible into making sure it was safe, we could do no more; we needed now a little bit of luck."

Joe, out of sight beneath the bulge of the gully, shouted to me that he had reached the snow, and that he was swinging across to the side of the gully to fix an anchor. I was still frightened about the peg, because of my extra weight. However, I knew that once Joe had tied off the end of the rope there was chance of a fall being held after 300 feet.

I went springing over the bulges, and the sun started fighting through the snow clouds. The storm was passing and I knew that with the improving visibility we would find the end of the fixed ropes. But it was a declining sun and brought to the amphitheatre lighting identical to that of the afternoon before; except we had reached the summit in between, and now golden particles of snow were falling through the light.

Reaching the fixed ropes felt like coming into the mouth of the harbour out of a storm-tossed sea. Our faces and clothing were encrusted with ice from the struggle. As we arrived, it stopped snowing but, unfortunately, it also became dark.

"Go and get the brew on, Joe," I said. We had eleven hundred feet of abseiling to do. It would be too dangerous to try and retrieve the rope, and, so, sadly, we would have to leave it behind. Joe went first:

> "We did the long, lonely abseils in the dark, without seeing or hearing each other. There was just an awareness, a mental, psychological bond between us . . . In the thirty-six hours since we had been on the ropes they had been, in parts, affected by the wind. One anchor point on the big flake had lifted off. I had to haul, drag and claw my way back onto course. I replaced the anchor point to make it easier for Pete . . . Then on down, with my hands stiffening into cramp with the strain of hanging on, finding my way by touch and memory."

We had climbed the West Wall when nobody had thought we could do it, and now I was grimly determined that the mountain would not have the last word. Every knot, peg and ropelength that I unclipped and clipped and heaved my way past was another piece of mountain that could not capture me. Every foot I descended was taking me further away down the mountain that was now an enemy that was trying to cheat us. The circling voices, faces and names returned, accelerating around in my head.

The descending traverses that reversed the tension moves were desperately complicated to negotiate, because the rope was tied off in so many places. I was thankful to reach the three peg crack above the Big Groove. On reaching the top peg I leant down and clipped an etrier into the lower peg and put my foot into it. Then I clipped my waist into the middle peg with a fifi hook and leant out on it and extricated the karabiner brake from the rope above. Suddenly I was being propelled backwards, flopping over head-first, as helpless as a rag doll. 'I'm dead. How did that happen? Thwack!' I was winded but I had not fallen. My foot had caught in the etrier. Without a thought, I scrambled and pulled myself upright. The middle peg had come out. It was one that I had put in. 'Well, I'm still here – better get moving.' This was not the time for prayers of thanksgiving.

Wind and cold were forgotten. The rope in the Big Groove only had to hold my weight once more: and it held. Long engraved disciplined skills took me past obstacles and my detached mind was half-surprised at my progress. Trained homo sapiens, the tool-user, had taken over.

Far below me, Joe had reached Camp Two:

"Half-way from the summit, half-way to safety. As usual, I hacked some lumps of ice and put them near the tent doorway, then tumbled into the tent, feeling more exultation than I had ever permitted myself on the summit.

"Warm inside my sleeping bags, revelling in the sensual ache of relaxation after exertion, I melted ice, preparing a hot drink for Pete when he came in. Without a descendeur, it usually took him much longer to descend than it took me to have the water hot. I listened for him, full of things to say for once, wanting to share the satisfaction of knowing we had succeeded. He seemed to be taking longer than usual. The water was hot. For some curious reason, I delayed having a drink myself until he arrived.

"I waited. There was no tell-tale jangling of hardware to herald his approach. I looked out into the blackness. Not a sound. I called out. Nothing.

"Back inside, I mentally went over the last hour – one and a half hours – to see whether I could recall any sound which might have been Pete falling. With this, I admitted the possibility to myself of what might have happened, but could recall nothing.

"Still there was no sound. I asked myself what the hell could I do? I longed to hear the sounds which would banish these morbid thoughts from my mind.

"Then the sounds came – a rattling and jangling, a scraping of crampons on rock; not in the sudden rush of catastrophe, but slowly, in control. My fears vanished, but I could not find again quite the same exultation which I had wanted to share two hours earlier."

I saw the fragile, flapping nylon of Camp Two, fifteen feet below me in the darkness. It looked deserted but I knew Joe would be inside, crouched over the stove. Then, far below on the glacier, I saw a green light.

"Hey, Joe," I yelled excitedly. "There's a green flare on the glacier. Can you see it?" But he was too late, for by the time he got his head out the tent door, the light had faded. "Pass me your torch, Joe." I flashed it back down towards the glacier, but there was no reply. I insisted that I had seen it, but Joe was guarded—like a doctor suspecting a patient of concussion.

Inside the tent we talked compulsively, our minds unwinding the elation of success. We laughed unashamedly at the terrible warnings other climbers had given us. For two hours our egos reigned supreme. We were not off the mountain yet, but the dangers below us were all on known ground.

The morning sun thawed us slowly into action. There was no sense of urgency. The view from the door seemed as friendly as a loved and familiar face. It was not the mountains around us that had changed, but our attitude to them. The cold camp we had left with tense resolve two days before was now a warm and comforting haven. We talked on the surface, but there was no need to express the deep contentment that flowed between us. There was no need for blunt confrontation any more, because all the important decisions had been made.

"I suppose we'd better get moving, or we'll get benighted again."

"I don't like the idea of having to hump all this stuff down on our backs."

"We could always roll some of the gear down from here, it'd only bounce a couple of times before landing at the bottom of the Wall, and there aren't many crevasses for it to go in."

"Yes, and it'll be fun to watch too."

"We'd better hang onto our survival gear though, just in case the stuff disappears."

We rolled up the superfluous equipment including the tents, the hammocks and the three remaining Gaz cylinders we had left, into red stuff bags and strung them together until they looked like a string of floats for lobster-pots.

"Remember to let go of them when you throw them."

"I wonder what the Mars Bars-eater'll make of these when they plunge out of the sky and land around its ears."

The stuff bags slid off down the icefall with the confidence of an Olympic ski-jumper, launched out above the Barrier, hung momentarily in space, and disappeared from view.

I had to rebandage my three fingers that were most damaged. Once again, Joe offered to go first and rig the abseils on the icefield. He would find it easier than I to find the anchors we had left behind, since he had led this section of the climb.

I am always scared unless I am abseiling off at least two pegs, even if one apparently is a perfect placement. But it did not seem to bother Joe to abseil off just one. Halfway down, he set off on another solitary knifeblade. It was flexing as he went down. This time I was not going to say anything, but I unclipped from it, so that I would not be pulled down after Joe if it came out. At that moment, Joe looked up and saw what I had done.

"Well, if it does come out, you'll be a bit stranded up there without a rope," he shouted cheerfully.

"I'd take my shirt off and wave for help," I shouted back.

Fortunately it was an obedient peg, and stayed where it was to Joe's apparent confidence and to my whispered incantations. I suppressed my worries and drew strength from his attitude. I did not know whether this bluffing of each other was based either on mutual deception or on mutual support. It was like being in a platoon of soldiers, in which nobody really wants to fight, but everybody is doing what he imagines his comrade expects him to do.

Soon we were at the bottom of the icefield and Joe disappeared down the overhanging wall next to the Guillotine. It was half an hour before he shouted for me to come on down. As soon as I moved down over the lip of the icefield I saw the reason for the delay. The abseil rope had not been long enough to reach the end of rope we had fixed through the Toni Kurz pitch, and Joe had found himself dangling and sliding towards the loose ends whilst still a few feet out from the rock. He had tied some slings together and, after knotting them to the end of the abseil ropes, he had swung in and grabbed the peg.

I found it difficult to retrieve the ropes. Joe pulled me into the rock with the slings on the end of them and held me there whilst I hammered in some pegs. I then hung off these and pulled the ropes through and then abseiled from there down to Joe.

"I'd better go down the Toni Kurz pitch first, in case I get tangled up in karabiners and need to be extricated," I said.

"Don't worry, Uncle Joe'll look after you," came the reply.

It was the first time on Changabang that I had abseiled whilst wearing such a heavy sack. Halfway down I lost my balance and turned completely upside down with a squeak of fright. I hoped that Joe had not heard it, and painfully righted myself. I floundered and thrashed about, trying to unclip and clip the mess of karabiners around my waist so that I could pass the pegs, hoping that I was not unclipping the wrong ones. The torques and tensions the heavy sack had introduced were enormous, it felt as if I were trying to couple up the trucks of a heavy goods train single-handed. But I reached the Balcony before I realised that I could have saved a lot of energy.

"It'd be best to come down on your jumars, Joe. It'd make it much easier getting past the pegs. It's bloody desperate if you try to abseil."

The afternoon had rushed past, and granite was turning red around us as Joe bounced into sight around the overhangs.

"It looks easy angled down there," he said, looking past me at the rock below us. I looked round at it. Yes, compared to the rock and the risk of the Upper Tower, its angle looked gentle. And to think how awe-struck we had been on those early pitches! If only we had known what was to come – how our sense of judgement had changed.

"We'll have to find all the abseil placements in the dark now, though," I said. I was cursing myself for the conceit of our leisurely morning. We had completely underestimated the time the descent would take. 'Why does everything always turn into an epic?' I thought. 'Why can't anything be simple?' Then Joe announced that while he was overseeing my descent, his descendeur had become unclipped from a karabiner and had bounced down into the shadows. A nasty thought sneaked into my mind and had its say before I slammed the door on it. 'At least he'll find out how desperate it is abseiling with all these karabiners.' It did not matter now who went first, we were both equally slow.

As quickly as we could, we made three abseils in the waning light and were five hundred feet above Camp One when it became dark. The remaining problem was to find convenient abseil points on this mixed ground of snow and rock without straying so far to our right that we went over the North Face, or so far to the left that we missed the ridge altogether. The short sections of rope that we had gleaned from Shipton's Col and hung over some of the rock steps were hidden by the darkness.

One hour after nightfall, the wind started to carry snow with it. Steadily the wind became stronger and the amount of snow in the air increased. Now we had reached the change in angle where the ridge started out of the Wall.

"You'd better go down first," said Joe. "Your eyesight's better than mine in stuff like this. My contact lenses aren't infra red."

"It's finding the point where we go down through that first rock step above the camp that's going to be the tricky bit," I said.

We decided that we would move together, to save time, and I would go first and place as much protection as I could.

I kicked off down the slope. The visibility was so bad that I could not see Joe after the first ten feet. I was scared that I might go through the cornice, and tried to sense that I was just below the crest of the ridge by the angle of the snow. After seventy feet I placed a deadman snow anchor as a runner and, after ninety feet, I stumbled across the blackness of a short rockstep with one of our pegs and marker ribbons in it. I clipped the rope into this and kept going. Soon I felt the rope tug gently, as if there were a fish on the end of the line. Then it slackened off again. Joe was coming.

It was a bitter ordeal—feet frozen, legs shaking with cold, bodies screaming 'no more!' Yet we were completely in control, treading the fine line that separates the difficult from the dangerous. It was impossible for us to feel tired whilst we still had one more obstacle to overcome. We knew we were probably only a couple of hundred feet above the camp, and thrilled to the action, for success could not be far away. I was playing to the audience of my mind. The situation was drawing from me the utmost of my skills and strength, and yet more seemed to rush in to compensate, as if I had been created to struggle through to life. 'If I've got any sixth sense, it had better start working now,' I thought. We were so keyed up by our tantalising position that nothing could have stopped us from finding the tent.

"The rock step must be just below." Joe's voice was muffled by the snow and wind.

I moved down and a few feet below me the slope sheered away. I lowered myself down from my ice hammer and axe, and lunged at the ice below with my feet. It was like kicking concrete. The crampons bounced off hard granite beneath the ice.

"I'm just above it now, I'll traverse around till I find the polypropylene," I shouted. If only it were daylight! Then I recognised something about the way the black outline of rock curved into the slope. I stepped down and brushed away the snow. I could feel two pitons and a length of polypropylene rope. I clipped into them and belayed Joe until he joined me. We quickly rigged an abseil and sped off down it.

"We'll pull the rope down in the morning."

The dark shape of the tent loomed up in front of us through the drifting curtain of snow. We tumbled inside. It was 9.15 p.m. We had been descending for three hours in darkness. We prepared a quick meal with the scraps of food that were there. The air inside the tent quickly warmed up. We started to feel drowsy, and soon flopped into exhausted sleep.

It had been the 17th September, exactly one month before, when we had erected the tent at Camp One. Now it had sunk deep into the snow of the ridge and, in the morning, we hacked it out and packed up all the equipment we had accumulated at the camp.

"To think we carried all this lot up," said Joe, as he thrust the pressure cooker into the top of his bulging sack. I chipped out the sweet papers that were inlaid like a mosaic under the groundsheet.

"We could always do another trundle," I suggested.

Joe seemed slightly shocked. Dropping anything, whether it's part of the mountain or equipment, is frowned upon as bad practice in the crowded Alps, when it is likely that you will hit someone. This accounted for the sense of guilt we had felt when we dropped the gear down from Camp Two. We both peered over the edge of the ridge, like a couple of small, mischievous boys planning to drop something on a train.

"We'll have to throw it well clear of these first rocks," said Joe. We wrapped the tent and our outer sleeping bags and duvets in the foam mats and hurled them into the air. Long seconds later, many objects appeared back into our view on the glacier a thousand feet below. Our carefully tied parcels had disintegrated and now all our jettisoned belongings were running all over the glacier like startled sheep. We tried to watch them all until they stopped, memorised their positions and then shouldered our sacks. We then climbed down the ridge and, taking one last look towards Tibet, started to climb down the ice slope towards the Rhamani Glacier.

It was an effort to summon the concentration to descend the ice slope. Our crampons were worn into blunt and stubby points and hardly bit into the ice. The slope had disintegrated beyond recognition and was still poised on a layer of loose rubble that threatened to behave like ball bearings and roll the sheets of ice off. Joe moved quickly below me, to get out of the way of the stones I was dislodging. He was down it half an hour before I was and, as I descended the last dangerous section, I looked down at him collecting our fallen belongings, envying his safe world of the glacier. At last I was stumbling over the lumpy avalanche debris at the foot of the slope. 'Nothing can kill me now,' I thought as I walked across the glacier to help him.

"It kept us on our toes till the very end didn't it?" said Joe.

We managed to find nearly all our equipment. The Mars Bar-eater had covered the glacier with more of its tracks whilst we had been on the mountain, and now we added to them in our search. Our full body harnesses and the tent had disappeared.

"We'll come back and look for them in the morning," I said.

"It kept us on our toes till the very end, didn't it?" said Joe.

There was only a tin of corned beef to greet us inside the tent at Advance Camp, and we soon demolished that. Now that we were safe, thoughts of food started to obsess us. It was eleven days since we had eaten our last big meal at Base Camp. However, we knew that we could manage another day without much to eat. There would be plenty of time to celebrate later. It was a marvellous luxury to slide into our sleeping bags before it was completely dark, and to fall asleep without the fear of rolling over.

We woke up hungry, but there was no breakfast. I decided to start on a course of Ampicillin to prevent my fingers from rotting.

"Who's the junkie now?" said Joe, as I took the first pill. "I bet they haven't any calories!"

It was the 18th October, the day the flight we had booked left Delhi. Our parents and our friends would be starting to worry about where we were, since they were expecting us on it. They would not have heard from us since we had sent letters back with Palta for him to post for us, early in September. Obviously, it was a priority to reach Joshimath and send some telegrams. Also, we were bursting to tell someone we had climbed the West Wall. We wondered how the Americans had fared on Dunagiri, and if there would be any of them around at Base Camp. Joe was longing for a change of company as much as I:

"That would be good, to go and relax amongst other people
. . . Able to laugh and joke in the knowledge that I had earned
the right to laugh completely, that it wasn't a false façade I would
be projecting. We had earned the right to relax."

We had wound down from the effort of the route into a lazy passiveness, when it came to turning our talk of descent into action. Food is fuel and we had none, and our stomachs were rumbling as we walked up to the foot of the West Wall to look for the gear we had lost. Joe saw the harnesses, half buried by snow inside the bergschrund, and lay flat across a snow bridge so that he could lever them out with his ice axe. There was no sign of the tent and, after extensive searching for it, we assumed that it had disappeared down a crevasse.

The amount of equipment at Advance Camp seemed enormous, after we had taken the tent down and accumulated it all in a big pile. We realised that we would not be able to carry it all back down to Base Camp that afternoon, and determined to return for the remainder the following morning. We did not contemplate leaving any behind.

"Ever a little further . . ." muttered Joe, as he hitched his sack up.

"It's 'always a little further', actually," I said—the title of a book by Alistair Borthwick, from a line in a poem by Flecker.

"Pedant," said Joe. "Typical English student!"

The sun was low in the sky by the time we left the moraine of Advance Camp. Imperceptibly, the days had become shorter with the coming of winter. Our departure offered a scene that would have gladdened the heart of any film producer, had he been there. Our sacks were piled high on our backs and the sun was glittering on the ice of the glacier, casting our long shadows into the shadows of the mountains around us. We crunched downwards with slow, wandering steps, whilst white-walled Changabang loomed high behind us, cold and aloof, looking as awe-inspiring as it had on first sight.

It was dark when we reached the top of the valley. I always regarded Base Camp with a strange mixture of feelings, for it was both a welcome home and a misty Bleak House at the same time. It had been a refuge of recovery, but also a hiding place after defeat. Now I was in a silent mood of trepidation, although we had both just been complaining to each other about being ravenously hungry. As the angle of the descent changed, and our feet started thumping the soft earth of the moraine instead of harsh grey ice and stones of the glacier, Joe suddenly stopped.

"Can you hear voices?" he said. We both listened, but there were no living noises in the eddying air. "I'm sure I heard something. Oh well, perhaps not."

We were walking closely together, as if for security. A few hundred feet lower down, I was convinced I could smell woodsmoke. Then we both definitely heard voices. Our pace quickened involuntarily. We rounded the boulders abruptly and saw a hillside aglow with lights and fires. Our forty days of self-imposed isolation had ended and we were back in the world of people. We shouted hallos. No reply. We became dubious. "Perhaps someone's raiding our tent," I said.

We approached with caution. Nothing seemed out of place. The tent was still fastened up. The note was still underneath the stone. We dropped our sacks and hurried, tripping and falling, and a little uncertain, across to the fire. A large tent loomed up; there were lights inside and voices chattering away. "They sound Japanese," said Joe. I pulled back the flap.

The inside was bright with candlelight, and I saw a blur of red sweaters and dark, bearded faces. It was a big tent and they were all sitting around the sides. In the middle of them was a table made of boxes, with an enormous primus stove belching away with a large pot on top of it. Everyone shuffled around and room was made for Joe and me. Rabbi Corradino introduced himself as the leader of the Italian Garhwal expedition, from Turin, and then introduced his seven fellow-members. Joe and I found ourselves sitting next to a woman, who told us she was from the American Dunagiri expedition. Cups of hot tea, biscuits and Italian cheese were thrust into our hands and we chatted in a mixture of broken French and English.

The Italians had come to climb Kalanka, but their porters, disliking the idea of the long trek around into the Sanctuary and up the Changabang Glacier, had brought them here to the foot of the Rhamani. The Italians had tried to cross the ridge but had not realised the circuitous manœuvres that the Indo-British expedition had made to cross Shipton's Col. Two of them had reached the ridge by a snow slope between Shipton's Col and Rishi Kot, but the other side had been too difficult for them to contemplate descending. Then the expedition had seen signs of fixed rope on the Japanese route on the South-West Ridge and, hoping that it was all in place, had been across to attempt a second ascent. However, the ropes had stopped after a few hundred feet and so they had not got very far. And now they were going back and their porters were due in two days' time. It had not been a very successful expedition for them, but they did not seem too bothered.

Yes, they knew we had climbed the West Wall, they had seen us coming down. Had they any news of the South Face expedition? Apparently they had reached the summit about ten days before we had, by a new route on the south side, although they did not think it was the actual South Face. We were hungry for more news, and our achievement and experiences were changing in value to us, for the outside was bringing new perspectives. I had organised a climbing trip to Britain, the previous year, for eight Italian mountaineers from all over Italy, and now I repeated their names to them. Yes, they knew them all, and it was good to talk about mutual friends. Joe they knew of by his reputation, mainly because of his second ascent of the Gervasutti route on the East Face of the Grandes Jorasses. It was an ascent that had been widely acclaimed in Italy, and an article by Joe about it had been published in an Italian mountaineering magazine.

And what of the Dunagiri expedition? Had they climbed their mountain? Why was the woman next to us the only American here? Where were the others? We thought that they would have left days before. Had they been delayed? The American woman, Ruth Erb, had a quiet voice and it was difficult to hear her against the background hubbub of the Italians.

"We had an accident," she said.

"I'm sorry to hear that," said Joe. "Was anybody hurt?"

"Yes, four of us were killed three days ago. I'm the only one left."

Slowly her words penetrated our bemused confusion of fatigue and elation. I winced as if I had been slapped in the face. Had we heard correctly? Her voice seemed so calm, so measured, it seemed to belie the content of her words.

"Was anyone related to you?" asked Joe.

"Yes, my husband."

"How did it happen?" I asked, suddenly unsure of myself, not knowing if she would want to talk about it. Our happiness, our intoxication at our success, started to feel inane.

Ruth talked objectively, as if with an enormous effort she was holding the full implication of the tragedy off from her consciousness. On 12th October they had established a camp at 19,850 feet, at the foot of the rockstep on the South-West Ridge. By the 15th, the day Joe and I had reached the summit of Changabang, six of the team had to leave because their available time was growing short or for various other reasons. Ruth had stayed at the 19,850 foot camp while the remaining four climbers, Graham Stephenson, the leader, Arkel Erb, John Baruch and the Mexican climber, Benjamin Casasola, had set out to establish a camp on the ridge above, from which they hoped to reach the summit the next day. On the afternoon of the 16th, Ruth had been watching Arkel and John descending the snow ridge between 21,000 and 22,000 feet, when she saw them slip and fall. They had appeared to be trying to brake their fall with their ice axes on the slopes but had failed, and had disappeared from view. They fell about two thousand feet. Ruth had moved to a point on the edge of the ridge where she could look down onto the glacier below, and saw not only the bodies of her husband and John, but also those of Graham and Ben.

Ruth had spent the next two nights alone at the camp, hoping that the expedition porters at Base Camp would come up to see what was wrong and to help her down. The previous day, the 17th, she had noticed someone about a thousand feet below her. She had shouted and whistled and thought he had heard her, but was shattered when he went back down. However, the man (Yasu) had gone down to Base Camp to get help. He had found the Italian climbers and that day three of them had gone up with Yasu and helped her down. She had arrived at Base Camp one hour before we had.

Joe stumbled out of the tent, in search of Yasu, who was a good friend of his. For me, the Italians had drifted into the background. They were tactfully talking amongst themselves. I asked Ruth if she had any children. She had a twenty-two year old son. Had she thought what she was going to do now? She hoped there might still be some members of the expedition in Delhi, and would leave the mountains with the Italians. However, she was worried about the bodies. Someone ought to go up and find them. I felt overcome with the pain of listening to her and hardly dared look at her face. I told her I was going to get something to eat and left the tent.

Outside, I stretched upwards into a clear, starry night. I shivered from the cold and went to our tent, which was still in darkness. Joe appeared.

"Hey, Pete, come over here to Yasu's tent," he said. "He's got masses of food. His mate Balu's here from Joshimath."

We wanted to talk the whole thing over together, and as we walked over to Yasu's tent Joe told me what he had been able to find out. Yasu had been able to see the bodies in the distance on the glacier, below the South-West Ridge, and they wanted Joe and me to go back up to them the next day. Joe's knowledge of the geography of Dunagiri would be a great help.

"Yasu was incredibly pleased to see me," said Joe. "I think that since they'd acted as agents and negotiated porters for the expedition, they feel responsible about the whole thing. I don't know how experienced they are, and they seem a bit subdued. Yasu's only about twenty and Balu must be around the same age. Somebody has to take decisions for

Ruth at the moment, and its easier for us to discuss with her since she speaks English."

Yasu gave me some packets of freeze-dried food that the Americans had left behind. "They have no need of it now," he said.

The stream that flowed through the meadow had dried up and Joe set off up the hill to fetch some water. I flopped inside the tent with a confusion of thoughts racing through my head. I put on my down suit and lay down, looking at the pattern of the candlelight on the tarpaulin of the shelter. It was half an hour before Joe arrived.

"Haven't you got the primus lit? What have you been doing all this time? I had to go bloody miles to get the water." He was furious.

I shook myself into action and rushed about, lighting the stove and preparing the meal whilst Joe crouched outside self-righteously. Yasu had come over to talk to Joe and I saw the teeth of his smile gleam in the darkness.

"You know the Monkey God, Hanuman? He has servants who are also monkeys and who rush about and do everything for him. Just like Pete is for you!"

Joe had quickly focused on a plan of action. I was amazed at the speed with which he had absorbed all that had happened, and had decided exactly what we had to do. We would leave at seven the next morning with Yasu and Balu, climb up to Dunagiri and reach the bodies. If it seemed the best thing to do, we could bury them in a crevasse after collecting as much of their personal belongings as possible, and after photographing them in case there were any legal problems about proving their deaths. We considered walking up the Changabang branch of the Rhamani Glacier, and collecting the rest of our equipment afterwards, but realised we probably would not have enough time. Joe went and consulted Ruth about the plan. She was desperately anxious that the bodies should not be just left on the glacier. She could only speak for her husband, but felt that the other relatives would, if they knew, entrust us with the task and the decisions that would be involved.

I was in awe of Joe's honest compassion and the direct simplicity with which he had immediately offered to help. How crass my bumbling professions of sympathy seemed in comparison!

"It could be a bit gruesome," I ventured.

Joe just shrugged a sigh. "It's just something we've got to do," he said.

Before we finally settled down and tried to snatch some sleep before the morning, a new sort of conversation started up. The crazy hours of the evening had shaken us out of a groove into a frank realisation of how deeply we understood each other, and what a solid team we had become. Now that we had met other people and climbed the mountain, we were no longer so committed to each other. The squeamishness with which we had previously steered conversation away from discussing our relationship was forgotten. However, our conversation was not painful or probing — it was a frank development of ones we had had before. The darkness suspended time and made it easier to say exactly what we thought of each other. We discussed our experiences on the mountain, revealing our moments of greatest effort and deepest depression. We both agreed that it was the hardest route either of us had ever done, or particularly wanted to do. We told each other exactly what judgement we had reached about each other's abilities.

"You're a funny bugger," said Joe. "I mean, back home your job thrusts you into the limelight and you have to be diplomatic with all these different types of people, and yet somehow everyone seems to like you because you don't pose a threat, you're so mild and trusting and seem so naïve — and yet when you're climbing it's a different bloke. You're confident and can be bloody arrogant."

Joe said that he had been surprised at my persistence, and that he thought I was probably a bit stronger than he was. I told him how much better I thought he was at looking after himself, and how much I had learned from him. "I don't think I could have done the climb with anyone else," I said.

"You scratch my back, and I'll scratch yours," said Joe. The conversation had only been a momentary thaw — we could not resist teasing each other for long. "I didn't think I'd have anything to teach a Superstar," said Joe. "They'll be expecting great things from you on K2 now."

He knew that he was just as good as I, if not better, and he gibed me slightly about the fact that I had climbed Everest and had been asked by Chris Bonington to go on an expedition to K2, the second highest mountain in the world, in 1978. I mocked Joe in return, sharing his amused distrust of the outside world's attitude to mountaineering achievement.

"Never mind, Joe," I said. "You can relax now for a bit. You've made the grade. You're bound to hit the big-time soon and join the hall of heroes."

"No thanks, it sounds a real rat-race."

Strong moonlight was filtering through the tent. I looked at my watch. 5.30 a.m. I had hardly slept and since I was feeling thirsty, I decided to put a brew on. We had no water left, so I crawled past Joe and out of the tent, past the still-sleeping tents nearby, and walked up the river bed in the hillside towards the sound of running water. It was a long way up and I did not hurry, but savoured the calm, colourless light of the moon that seemed to flatten the ground around me. When I found the water it was a dark pool, and I had to stoop deep into the ground to scoop it out. As I descended, carrying icy water that slopped painfully over my fingers, the sky was becoming lighter and the ground was gaining relief. I saw the figure of Joe standing outside the tent. "I couldn't sleep either," he said.

We ate some porridge and then Yasu and Balu arrived. Soon we were ready, and the four of us set off over the frozen ground towards the moraine valley and Dunagiri.

It had been many days since we had seen the morning sun on night-frosted grass, and we stopped to enjoy its arrival as we neared the top of the moraine valley. The sun helped to warm our stiffened limbs. The days at high altitude had taken their toll and our muscles had shrunk into stick-like arms and legs. Once at the top, we turned left up the Dunagiri branch of the Rhamani Glacier. It was of a very different character to the Changabang branch. Here, instead of massive blocks of milk-white granite, the moraines were of dark reddish brown smaller blocks and shale. We climbed these steadily onto the glacier. It was a relief not to be carrying heavy sacks and we moved over the ground quickly.

The route was well cairned and it was not long before we passed the Americans' Advance Camp. All that remained of it were two derelict boxes on the moraine and an American flag, erected on a tall pole. The flag had no meaning, its sadness lay too deep for comment and we moved on.

As we gained height, the moraine we were following dwindled into the snow of the glacier. We followed the tracks of many footprints in the snow as they wound past crevasses up the mountainside. We were following the outside edge of the glacier as it curved around from the cirque formed by the South-West and South-East Ridges of Dunagiri. On the inside edge, where the corner was much tighter, the glacier had been squashed and jostled into an icefall. Once we were above the level formed by the bulge of this icefall, we could see the whole southerly flank of Dunagiri. The great sweep of the South-West Ridge nearly filled the entire skyline and it was stepped by the projected ends of layers of rock that inclined downwards from left to right beneath the snow of the flank. The mountain was considerably foreshortened because we were so near its foot. The South-East Ridge, which Joe had climbed the year before, looked deceptively easy angled.

Yasu pointed to where the bodies had landed. They must have fallen from a point much lower down the ridge than we had expected from Ruth's description, and we would have to go up a tongue of glacier, skirting through an upper icefall below the lower part of the South-West Ridge. We scanned the area through our binoculars and picked out the tiny dots of the bodies and scattered equipment below the bergschrund. They lay just above a heavily crevassed area.

At midday, we reached the tent that the expedition had established on the glacier, before their route had turned up to the foot of the South-West Ridge. We looked inside and found some books — one of them in Spanish, and evidently the Mexican's. Also, there was some food, and amongst it some peppermint indigestion tablets. I had a queasy feeling in the pit of my stomach and took a packet and started chewing them. Balu said he was feeling ill, and dropped behind. Soon after he had left us, the slope we were climbing steepened.

"Balu has my crampons, will I be safe without them?" asked Yasu, who was trailing behind us.

We were just about to put our crampons on, and told him he would not be safe. Joe and I climbed over a bulge in the glacier and both Yasu and Balu dropped from our sight.

"I think they're both a bit superstitious," I said. But my plodding pace lacked the forceful purpose of Joe's stride and I lagged behind him.

This was not like the death of Mick Burke; I had not known these climbers, they had not been my friends. I had been on mountain rescues before, and knew what bodies looked like after they had fallen a long way. I had nursed a dying man by a roadside after he had been knocked off his bicycle. But this was different, just as terrible. We were alone, in the sunlight in the middle of a wilderness of mountains, and the drama of the situation overpowered my attempts to rationalise my frame of mind into the matter-of-fact, hardened attitude of a hospital casualty officer. The fact that we had not known them seemed to add to the sense of pathetic waste. Every piece of scattered equipment seemed to unfold an aspect of the tragedy as we walked past it. The bodies were close to each other, still roped in pairs, at 20,000 feet. On reaching them we saw that they all had severe head injuries and must have died instantly. There was no indication as to how the accident had occurred. We gathered all the pieces of equipment from the slope and went through their pockets and rucksacks for items that might be worth saving. Only John Baruch, the nineteen year old boy tied to Ruth Erb's husband, had a diary in his rucksack. It was soaked in paraffin from a smashed bottle, also in the sack. I put it in my rucksack to give to Ruth. It was not my business to read whatever story was told inside it. "He seems a good-looking lad," said Joe.

We agreed to slide two bodies each down the slope, using the ropes to which they were attached and to bury them in a crevasse. Joe took the bodies of Arkel Erb and John Baruch and I took Graham Stephenson and Benjamin Casasola. The bodies were twisted and stiff and it was awkward and dangerous sliding them into the narrow neck of the first crevasse we came across down the slope.

We couldn't judge how stable the edges of the crevasses were. "Watch what you're doing, Joe!"

I was feeling sick and Joe, noticing I was fighting back tears, came over to help me. But this was an overwhelming sorrow that weeping could not symbolise. "I suppose we ought to say a prayer or something," I said. We had never discussed religion or beliefs before.

"We'll stop for some moments," said Joe.

All around us, the peaks of the Garhwal glittered in the late afternoon sunshine, Changabang, Rishi Kot, Nanda Devi—we were seeing them all from a different angle, and this fresh perspective heightened the impact of their beauty on us. Our sense of the area fell into a new pattern. The deaths of the four climbers had made us feel alive with every breath. This was the sensation of life—the sense that we remained. The four climbers were now part of the Rhamani Glacier, and 'Rhamani' meant 'Beautiful'. The legend told that the Rishis were troubled by bad people and demons, but they came to this place and found a refuge. Surely there could be nothing mean or sordid about death in such a place?

We trudged down, into the gathering shadows. Yasu and Balu had packed the equipment at the camp and, when we arrived, they looked at us as if we had come from the moon.

It was long after nightfall when we approached Base Camp. There was a great fire burning and around it many people were silhouetted. It was the Italians' last evening, and their porters had arrived, ready for the departure the next day. The porters had just finished singing a song of the Garhwal, and the Italians had launched into a song of the Dolomites. Joe and I walked into the light of the fire and the singing stopped abruptly. I was sorry—we had not wanted to stop it. I felt all the eyes of the Italians and the porters on us. We went over and talked to Ruth. There were the lines of tears on her face.

"I'm sorry about these," she said, brushing them away, "all that lovely singing made me kind of forget myself."

CHAPTER TEN

The Outside

20th October–1st November

We wanted to be home. The intensity and single mindedness of purpose that we had generated in our adventure were ebbing away. The immediate priority was to get word of our safety back to our relatives and friends in Britain. Also, I started to worry about my job, since I was three weeks late for work at the BMC. The Italians did not have enough porters to help us; some of them were already being used to carry the American equipment and we could not move ours straight away because there was still about fifty kilograms of it up at Advance Camp. We decided that one of us should go out immediately with the Italians and Ruth, to Lata, send five porters back from there, and then go on to Joshimath to send telegrams.

Joe had spent six days by himself in the same place the previous year, not knowing if the porters whom Dick had promised to send were going to come or not. He did not relish the prospect of a repeat performance. I did not mind staying behind, and looked forward to some quiet, undisturbed hours during which I could recover my thoughts. Although I wanted to be home, I dreaded the noise and bustle of the return journey, which I knew would bring complications before it brought comforts. Early on the 20th October, the morning after we returned from Dunagiri, the porters were rushing around the Italians, trying to get everything ready to leave. They wanted to reach Lata in two days, in time for the Diwali Festival. We negotiated with Tait Singh, who had been so dynamic on the walk in, that he would return as soon as possible with three Lata men. He realised that there was no time to lose, since a winter storm would make the whole route impossible. I thought the return journey should take them about five days.

Yasu, Balu and the porters were very worried that I was intending to stay at Base Camp alone, and urged me to come with them. They seemed superstitious about the deaths of the four climbers on Dunagiri. But having been there and buried them, I did not share their sense of mystery. The Italians gave me some potatoes and biscuits and shook my hand. As soon as they started moving away, all the individuals I had just been talking to seemed to melt into the crowd of thirty people. 'It looks quite a horde,' I thought, as they walked down the meadow. I stood and watched them until all the dark woollens of the Garhwalis and the red sweaters of the Italians had disappeared down and round the corner between the moraine and the flanking hillside. It was many minutes before the noise of their shouting and laughing died away. Joe threw a few pieces of equipment into his rucksack and was ready.

"See you soon."

"Cheerio for now." He hurried away, trying to catch sight of those in front, looking fit, strong and capable. It was a beautiful day. Silence surged back around me.

The expeditions had wreaked havoc in the area. There was a litter of discarded and broken equipment, and tent platforms hacked out of the slope with stone walls built around them. Now I was alone it looked like vandalism. I spent the morning tidying the meadow up and lit a big fire of rubbish. I was worried about spending the long hours of darkness inside the tent without any light, for our supply of candles and batteries had long since run out. Fortunately I found some candles whilst rummaging around the Italian camp. Once the meadow was as near to normal as it could be, I started feeling more relaxed, for now there were no distractions. I started sorting out our equipment, and found the medical box and a mirror. I bathed and bandaged my finger ends and trimmed my beard. It was the first time I had seen myself soberly for weeks. I sat on a kit bag just outside the tent, under the tarpaulin that we had arranged as a large awning over the entrance, supported by an improvisation of sticks and tent pegs, line and boxes. I felt like Robinson Crusoe, for I had built the boxes up around me into a protective wall. I had stocked up inside with food and two big Italian tins full of water, so that I would not have to wander in search of the stream at night.

At dusk I started to feel slightly threatened as the shadows closed in around the tent. I decided to light the primus stove and make myself a mug of tea, hoping that the flame and purr of the stove would dispel the sense of loneliness. It was the small primus stove which we had bought especially for the expedition, and had used constantly at Advance Camp and Camp One. As usual, I put some solid fuel on the preheating cup and lit it, closed the valve, gave it a couple of pumps, put a pan of water on top and waited for it to light. As I was rooting out the sugar and teabags, I heard a bubbling, rasping noise and turned around. It was the stove, behaving rather erratically: little blue flames were coming out of the point where the top unit is screwed into the bowl. Then a swirl of flame started to come out of the safety valve and pump. 'I'd better leave it outside,' I thought and put it on the grass near the entrance. I watched, fascinated as flames started to lap all around the stove, gaining size rhythmically as if fanned by bellows. 'That's getting a bit too dramatic,' I thought. 'I'd better kick it farther away.' I started to get up. There was a flash and the air was filled with flame.

When I came to, I didn't know where I was. It was completely dark and my face was smarting with pain. 'I'm blind,' I thought. I reached up instinctively. I was enveloped in fabric and I realised that I had been blown back into the back of the tent which had collapsed on me. I struggled out into the night and knew immediately that I was not blind because I could see the burning remains of the stove. I threw some water over it to stop the fire spreading. I felt myself all over, and decided that I was not seriously injured. I lit a candle and found the mirror, and looked at my face. My beard had virtually disappeared and my eyebrows, eyelashes and the front of my hair were singed. My neck and wrists were slightly burnt and I cleaned and dressed them. 'How ironic,' I thought as I recovered the tarpaulin from where it had landed and re-erected the boxes and shelter, 'to have climbed Changabang and then to have nearly been killed by an exploding stove at Base Camp.' All that remained of the stove was the mangled, steaming wreckage of its base. The top part, pump, legs and panful of water had been blown into the night. I was determined that the incident would not upset me and managed to extricate a stove left by the Italians, and tried to light that. It gave off a sooty, weak flame but at least—I hoped—seemed fairly safe. It was a long time before I had cooked and eaten an evening meal, crawled into the tunnel tent and painstakingly fastened the door, shutting out the night. It was a slow, lonely discipline the next day to summon the energy to climb back up to Advance Camp and I did not leave until midday. I was feeling very weary, and hoped that Joe was faring better on the walk out, and that he was feeling more wound into action than I. I did the walk as quickly as I could push myself, but still could not carry the load back down before it went dark. I ate a cold meal of Italian biscuits and cheese before dropping asleep from fatigue.

The next morning I felt more enthusiastic, because I knew it would be the last carry I would have to do. I left much earlier, determined to return in daylight. The fact that I was alone and dreamily tired made me feel self-conscious, as if I had been on a stage too long, walking in front of a giant insubstantial backcloth of mountains. The previous day I had felt in a grim mood, and had stared only at the ground. But now the persistent sight of Changabang once more took my breath away. Had I really been up there? Well, I need never go there again. At Advance Camp I packed the remains of the equipment into my sack and collected all our rubbish together. There was a bottle of paraffin left and I poured the liquid all over the rubbish and then set it alight. Flames leapt up and licked the sky. I tended the fire for a while, until I was sure that everything would burn into disintegration. Then I knocked over the cairns that had marked the site of our camp and guided us towards it across the glacier. I was determined, if at all possible, to leave no sign of our passing. As I walked away across the glacier I kept on looking back, to see if the fire was still burning. There was a sacrificial quality about leaving it burning beneath the West Wall; the flames seemed to be stranded on the moraine imbued with life.

That night I had a terrible dream. I was at a party and did not know anyone and people were dissecting each other coldly, clinically, in fun and without any trace of fear. In my dream I cried out in horror. I woke up, mouthing dumbly into the darkness of the inside of the tent.

When I awoke in the morning, I looked at the date on my watch. It was Saturday, 23rd October, the day after the great Hindu Festival of Diwali. 'The porters'll probably arrive tomorrow evening,' I thought. 'I bet they can't drag themselves away from all the drum beating in Lata.' I got up and made myself some porridge. Then I found some pliers and levered off the supergaiters that were nailed around the soles of my boots. It had the nature of a symbolic act, for nothing would induce me now to leave the ease and safety of low altitude to go amid the hazards of the glacier and mountain where I would have to wear them. I filled out the rest of the daylight vaguely sorting out the equipment into porter loads—the only important task left. My mind was marking time and I just wanted to leave the mountain. I was yearning for the contrasts of home in Derbyshire. The longing I felt was not for any particular things. It was nostalgia that defied analysis, but was just there, as a dull ache.

In the evening I decided to cook some of the Italian potatoes but was too scared of risking another explosion to use the pressure cooker. I had forgotten how low the temperature of boiling point is at 15,000 feet and, after boiling them for over an hour, they were still hard. Nevertheless, I ate them.

I had been so intensely caught up in the climb and descent and aftermath, that I had not written my diary for sixteen days. Now I got out a piece of paper and tried to reconstruct the main events of the missing time. As the evening went on, I was looking at my watch, thinking what time it would be back home. It was the evening of my local climbing club, the Mynydd's dinner—the first time I had missed it for years. As I lay in my sleeping bag, the numb parts of my fingers and toes were tingling with growing nerve ends and improving circulation. Yes, I had a lot to be thankful for, and there would be some good booze-ups when I got back.

I woke suddenly, sure I had heard a shout. It was daylight, 9.00 a.m. —I had overslept! Yes, there it was again, a great, long drawn out shout that echoed around the mountains. Excitedly, I struggled out of my sleeping bag, pulled on some clothes and rushed out of the tent in the full light of the early risen sun. I could see no one. It was as if the sound had come from the mountains themselves. Then I heard the babble of voices and, moments later, the porters rounded into view, moving very quickly over the frozen ground.

First I felt delighted, then guilty, as if Joe were telling me off for being dozy. The five porters had arrived a day earlier than I had expected, and I had not got the loads ready. I rushed around, flinging things into boxes, for it was evident that Tait Singh was in a hurry and the other Lata men jumped about as he ordered them to help me. The tent was suddenly ripped up from the ground and shaken inside out and disappeared inside a kit bag. My packing stopped abruptly, so that I could ensure that they did not pack my books and other things I would need for the journey out. I was impressed to hear from Tait Singh that they had left Lata only the day before, and had bivouacked just below the left turn up the Rhamani. And tonight we could reach Dibrugheta!

Before we left, Tait Singh handed me a note which Joe had written to me on his arrival at Lata.

Dear Pete,
    The porters will bring the gear to Lata for 640 rupees and Tait Singh will bring it to Joshimath if we give him one of the tarpaulins.
                                                                            Joe.

I laughed. I was used to Joe's ways now. No news, no platitudes, just a statement of fact—and why not? All this adventure was perfectly normal was it not?

The porters were happy, because their loads were light, and I was happy because I was leaving. The descent to the side of the Rishi swept past and soon we were picking our way along its side. It was good to be alone with the porters, because I could laugh and joke with them in a more relaxed way than when I had been with Palta and Joe. Also, they seemed to have gained respect for us now we had climbed the Shining Mountain. We were no longer just some more western trekkers to fleece.

Now the flowers had gone and the Rishi Ganga had faded from greens to mellow autumnal tints. What had been misted over on the walk in was now clear. I could see the whole height, now, of the mountains on the other side of the Rishi as they rose from the warm forests of the river bed to their high snows. Behind us, standing at the head of the gorge like a sentinel, was Nanda Devi. Details of the ground, shapes of rock, and patterns of tiny gullies, areas of level ground encouraging a rest, had lain dormant in my mind for many weeks, but now rose up to be remembered. The change in visibility was a revelation and it was only these little details that anchored my sense of place.

That night we reached Dibrugheta. I was going to sleep out in the open, but Tait Singh insisted that I slept in the 'member tent' and he quickly erected it. The porters built a fire and sat around it. The flames held their eyes into the night. The temperature was way below freezing point and they did not have many blankets with them. I took a gulp of the tea they had made and nearly scalded myself. We had descended 8,000 feet that day and, for the first time for nearly two months, I was drinking tea that had reached something near the usual boiling point temperature. I could not gulp it down, but had to sip. It felt as if I were learning to taste again.

There were also hostile signposts to the life to which I was returning. The track had been beaten even broader by the passing of expeditions back from the Sanctuary. And along it was a trail of metallic foil, tins, empty Gaz cartridges and food wrappers. I could see from the wrappers which expeditions they had come from. And now the Indian Government is mooting plans to build a catwalk through the mouth of the Rishi Ganga, to make the area even more accessible for tourism and hunting. Nature's best defence that held back explorers until the 1930s cannot withstand the might of bulldozers of the 1970s. And what will happen then to the Sanctuary of Graham, Longstaff, Tilman and Shipton?

Many tales and legends, linked through all cultures, carry poignantly within them a sense of loss, of a glory that has gone, an Eden unrecovered and yet also convey the implicit promise of renewal, return, recovery, the Eden which will again be found. Perhaps the Sanctuary of the Bliss-Giving Goddess would one day recover from its imminent devastation—but in what way I could not guess.

As we climbed steeply up the slope towards Dharansi Pass, the porters were reacting differently to the effort. Dharam Singh, sporting a brown balaclava and yellow anorak from the American Nanda Devi expedition, was always in front, effortlessly singing at the top of his voice whilst climbing the steepest sections. Tait Singh, always the leader, decided when to rest. Immediately they would dump their loads with a whistle of relief, and light a beedi or leaf cigarette. The beedi finished, he gave a sharp nod of command and they jumped into action. They had a good rapport with each other and worked well as a team. They were forever laughing and chatting together, as though they had just met after a prolonged absence. I could not understand the language of their banter, but slotted them into caricature—one big, strong and aggressively reliable, one cheerful and worldly, another with a sharp, dry wit and a wizened face. One of them, the dozy fall-guy, was always lagging behind—he had a deep, rattling cough and seemed ill. I think he had T.B. He was probably in his late thirties.

On the ridge we paused for a while. Dharam Singh unfolded a grubby teacloth and handed me two chappaties. "Packed lunch," he announced.

The view was fantastic and I felt I had seen it before with the same amount of fresh snow covering. Virtually the same panorama was in the long, fold-out photograph in the book *Five Months in the Himalayas*, which had been written by Arnold Mumm about Longstaff's 1907 expedition. I asked the porters the names of some of the more distant peaks to the north and west, but I could not decipher their words and they disagreed with each other. To the east, I could see Dunagiri from a new angle. It looked deceptively low and accessible. Having climbed the West Wall of Changabang, my whole attitude to these mountains had changed. I thought continually of the early explorers of the Garhwal. In earlier days a trip to the Himalayas had involved far more in travel. The boat journey to India had given those expeditions a different attitude to time. It had only been worth the effort of coming out if you had a six-month plan including many objectives. In 1939, André Roche's Swiss expedition had attempted many peaks in three different areas. In 1950, Bill Murray's Scottish expedition had walked around three ranges. As Eric Shipton had said, "A lifetime is not enough to absorb the wonder of that country." The experiences of modern politics would, of course, now prohibit such wandering. But Joe and I had spent forty days clinging to one side of one mountain. We had exalted the idea of climbing the Wall. For two months, it had given us something to believe in. It had acquired a permanence—a hold on our lives. As I took one last look at Nanda Devi and the white rims to the great space around me, I could not help worrying that our single-mindedness had been unhealthily tinged with fanaticism. 'Monomaniacs, that's what we are,' I thought. 'We've proved nothing that hasn't been proved before—if you want to climb something enough, you'll end up climbing it. Perhaps I'll go round a mountain in the future, instead of pushing an irrational way up one of its sides.'

The porters had left, moving nimbly over the icy slopes of the north side of the ridge, down towards the first trees that promised the hillside above the Dhauli Ganga. My legs felt emaciated and my knees were rattling together as I jolted in hot pursuit to rush down the 3,000-foot slope to Lata.

Little boys and girls peeped shyly from doorways—they were the first children I had seen for two months. Below me, on the stone-flagged courtyard, Tait Singh's wife was threshing grain, ready to be stored for the winter. That night I slept on Tait Singh's balcony. The festival was still in progress and, late into the night, I could hear the throb of drums and the wild cries of dancers.

In the morning the porters turned up again at Tait Singh's house and carried down the loads to the roadside. It was eight o'clock, and Tait Singh and I sat on the boxes waiting for the bus. But the bus was full, and the next three buses also refused to stop, as did every vehicle that passed us. For the following eight hours we sat by the roadside. The sun moved onto us and moved off. High above the opposite hillside, a great lammergeyer, with a wingspan of at least nine feet, wheeled and swept effortlessly backwards and forwards, hunting the ground below it. I admired its self-discipline, but drew no comfort from it. During the day a succession of characters, families, flocks and herds

12

walked past us at biblical pace, in marked contrast to the roaring dirt of military jeeps and wagons heading to and from the north.

By four o'clock the vehicles were becoming less frequent, when a truck stopped in front of our desperate flaggings. Tait Singh pleaded with the driver for ten minutes. Instead of just slamming the door, as had happened before, the driver eventually agreed to take us as far as the military camp near Joshimath. I found myself sitting next to a Sikh soldier whose mouth was masked by a fold of his turban to keep out the dust that billowed into the back of the truck. On the way we stopped for petrol at Tapoban. The soldier spoke some English. He came from the plains, and was just going home for two weeks' leave.

"Do you like being in the mountains?" I asked.

He laughed. The question was a foolish one. "My family lives in the south," he said.

Once more we were by the side of the road, but this time we were outside Joshimath. There were soldiers everywhere. Tait Singh looked slightly lost, and it pained me that someone who was so competent on the hillside and respected in his village, should be swept up by a civilisation that seemed to reflect him as a simpleton. I offered to walk to the Neilkanth Hotel, and to send back some porters to help carry the gear.

As I strode through the main street I started to feel, for the first time, unkempt and strangely dressed. But no one was noticing me and I felt confident. So this was the outside—were its preoccupations off-centre or were mine? Did I need it? It was twilight, transistor radios were blaring and naked bulbs were flickering dimly in the shops and sweet-meat stalls. It was crowded, and I had to jostle past through the crowds of shoppers, pilgrims and beggars, carts and dogs. My senses were stormed by a confusion of images, intense, momentary 'takes' freely flashing by the corners of my eyes.

I walked into the rest house. Joe was there, looking washed and rested. I was still carrying with me the wilderness of mountain life and the aura of one newly returned amongst people.

"Where's the gear?"

"Don't worry, Tait Singh's waiting with it at the top of the main street." I was pleased with myself—I had actually done something without Joe's initiative.

"That's a relief, I thought you'd got stranded on the other side of the Dharansi Pass by all this fresh snow."

"No, it was O.K., actually—most of it must have fallen on the other side of the Dhauli Ganga. Did you send the telegram?"

"Of course."

"To the BMC and to me mum and dad?"

"Yes, don't worry."

We had not seen each other for a week, and we talked incessantly, bringing each other up to date. Joe had been in the outside world for five days, so more had happened to him, and I soaked up his ramblings. His words tumbled out.

"It was bloody desperate getting here. I felt really fit after I'd left you, but Ruth had quite a hard time and I stayed with her. We camped at Dibrugheta and I was determined to catch the last bus to Joshimath, so I ran ahead of all the others on the descent to Lata. I just got to the road in time to see the last bus disappearing around the corner. So I kipped by the roadside. But of course, the next day was Diwali and it took me ages to get on a bus. I got the telegram off, virtually straight away. That first American we met, Neko Colevins, came up here to meet Ruth—he was still in Delhi when he heard about the accident. Some bastards have broken the news of the deaths worldwide, so that families'll hear about it over the media in the States before they're told. Ruth'll be swamped by reporters when she reaches Delhi—it'll be a hell of a strain for her. The two of them left two days ago. I had to go to the Police with them and make two statements. The Italians left this morning. I went to Badrinath with them a couple of days ago on the bus. It was an amazing journey, crammed packed with pilgrims, all spitting red betel juice out of the windows like blood. Oh, and I met Jimmy Duff—they didn't do the South Face—got to the headwall and ran out of time, so they did a new ice route to the right in a four-day round trip. Pretty good effort, eh? They reached the top on October 2nd, so they must have done the route during that bad weather, whilst we were in the hammocks. The big snow storm whilst we were at Camp One must have blotted out their tracks on the summit, so that's why we didn't see them. Oh yes, and you've got some letters."

I seized the bundle greedily and Joe went off to ask Bhupal Singh to fix me some food and to send some porters to help Tait Singh with the gear, and to buy the bus tickets for the next morning's return to Delhi.

Tait Singh arrived and we had a long argument over the money we owed him. We knew he was not well off, but he had put up the price and we felt we had a responsibility to future expeditions to the area, and ought to be hard bargainers. It had only been the large-monied expeditions of recent years that had disrupted a long-surviving tradition of fair dealing by distributing lavish baksheesh and thus sowing the seeds of greed. We wanted no part of that. I hated the confrontation, because Tait Singh and I had shared such a grim day together. Eventually, Bhupal Singh smoothed a compromise by paying Tait Singh a few extra rupees out of his own pocket, and everyone shook hands.

It was a long bus ride. In the early morning the bus side-slipped down and around the steep bends, blaring at the migratory families and livestock that were strung along the road. The inhabitants of the high villages of the north were descending to the Chamoli district for the winter, carrying with them their pots and pans and valuables. As we roared past, little boys hurried their goats and sheep to one side with their sticks, and old men stood, staring impassively. On mothers' backs were child-shaped forms, swathed in cloth, waking and sleeping to their life on the move.

After twelve hours we were down onto the plains and into the heat.

"Back into Coca-Cola country," said Joe.

In Rishikesh I bought a newspaper and we met another European, dressed in Asian fashion. "You guys know a place to hang out for the night?"

"Sorry, I don't," I replied. "We're just moving through. Are you going anywhere in particular?"

"No, I'm just travelling around, stopping wherever it takes my fancy."

"That's hardly wandering in the Shipton style," I said to Joe when he had gone. "But then, there's a shortage of blanks on maps nowadays – that's the problem."

The bus journey seemed interminable. We hung on through the night for another six hours, sitting upright on scarcely padded seats, in silent agonies of piles, diarrhœa and stomach pains.

"Never thought I'd be glad to see Delhi," said Joe.

We must have smelt – only money persuaded the Y.M.C.A. to let us in. It was four in the morning and we flung our skinny frames under hot showers. Old skin peeled off my fingers and new skin appeared underneath.

Five days later we arrived at London Heathrow Airport and a Swiss diplomat from Kuwait gave us a lift into the gleaming lights of central

London in a taxi. We had a few hours to kill before the overnight sleeper left for Manchester, so we found Charlie Clarke, on night duty at his hospital.

"Can I use your 'phone?" I asked.

"He's going to 'phone Dennis, to find out if he's lost his job," explained Joe.

The Yorkshire twang of Dennis Gray, General Secretary of the BMC, answered the 'phone. "Peter Pan Boardman—am I glad to hear your voice? Come back, all is forgiven."

Charlie told us that his wife, Ruth, had had another little girl and we told Charlie all about our adventures. Joe and I had thrashed out our opinions about the climb so closely that they had become almost identical, as if we were presenting a solid front to the world.

Charlie sniggered. "You two both give exactly the same answer to a question—it's like talking to the same person."

"Don't worry," said Joe, when we were on the train, "it'll wear off. You'll regain your sense of identity. It's only your sense of humour that's the same. That's why I asked you along in the first place."

"The next time I go on a two-man expedition," I said, "it's going to be a two-person one. I've had enough of tough-guy talk and cold toes. I'm going to find a young lady and go to the tropics."

"Mmmm yes," said Joe, "that'd be a pleasant change."

When we left the platform at Piccadilly station in Manchester the following morning, we saw a line-up of men in blue overalls sitting on a bench in the entrance hall. The entire night shift from the Salford deep freeze had come to meet us. Our grins matched theirs.

That morning I was back in the office.

Chronology

December, 1975	Plans for Changabang West Wall first mooted.
May, 1976	Permission to attempt Changabang as a two-man team received from the Indian Mountaineering Foundation.
22nd August	Flew from London Heathrow.
23rd–28th August	New Delhi. Meet liaison officer Flt./Lt. D. N. Palta and collect together equipment and food.
29th–30th August	Train to Hardwar and then buses to Joshimath.
2nd September	Bus to Lata and organise porters for the approach walk to Changabang.
7th September	Arrive at Base Camp (15,000 ft.). Liaison officer leaves with the porters.
9th–14th September	Carry our equipment up to Advance Camp (17,000 ft.) beneath the West Wall.
16th–20th September	Establish Camp One (18,000 ft.) on the ridge between the Rhamani and Bagini Glaciers; carry our equipment up to it and lead five ropelengths.
21st–25th September	Climb the Barrier and onto the icefield and run out all fixed rope from Camp One.
26th September	Bad weather—Camp One.
27th September	Descend from Camp One to Base Camp to replenish supplies.

28th September	Return to Advance Camp despite tactical disagreement owing to bad weather.
29th September	Climb past Camp One to bivouac in hammocks below the Balcony, pulling up fixed ropes behind us. Bad weather.
30th September	Boardman is frostnipped in fingers. Continue up fixed ropes to high point of 25th September. Attempt to gain height stopped by hailstorm. Second hammock bivouac.
1st October	Third hammock bivouac after one rope-length. On the verge of frostbite and exposure.
2nd October	Abseil back down to Camp One and then retreat to Advance Camp.
3rd–4th October	Recovery at Base Camp.
5th October	Briefly meet Neko Colevins, Graham Stephenson and Mandip Singh of American Dunagiri expedition. Return to Advance Camp.
6th October	Advance Camp. Reconnaissance to the foot of Shipton's Col.
7th October	Return to Camp One.
8th October	Rest day at Camp One.
9th October	Pulling fixed rope after us, we regain high point of 1st October on the icefield, hack out a ledge and pitch an improvised tent — Camp Two (20,000 ft.) and lead one pitch above it.
10th–12th October	Fix 1,000 feet of fixed rope on the Upper Tower.
13th October	Rest day at Camp Two.
14th October	Reach top of the Upper Tower and climb gully through rock step above it. Bivouac at 22,000 ft.

15th October	Reach summit of Changabang (22,520 ft.) at 1.00 p.m. and abseil down to Camp Two.
16th October	Abseil back down to Camp One—reached three hours after nightfall. Unknown to us, accident occurred on Dunagiri Graham Stephenson, Benjamin Casasola, John Baruch and Arkel Erb fell 2,000 ft. to their deaths.
17th October	Descent to Advance Camp.
18th October	Run out of food. Recover jettisoned equipment. Descend to Base Camp to meet Ruth Erb, Yasu, Balu and Italian Kalanka expedition.
19th October	Climb to 20,000 ft. on Dunagiri to bury bodies of the four members of American Expedition.
20th October	Joe leaves Base Camp with Ruth Erb and the Italians.
21st–22nd October	Pete collects equipment from Advance Camp.
23rd October	Joe reaches Joshimath and sends telegrams.
24th–26th October	Pete returns to Joshimath with equipment.
28th–31st October	New Delhi.
1st November	Fly back to Britain.

Index

Index

SACRED SUMMITS

Peter Boardman

CONTENTS

ACKNOWLEDGMENTS

Eunice Tietjens' poem, 'The Most-Sacred Mountain', appeared in *New Voices* edited by Marguerite Wilkinson for the Macmillan Publishing Company.

The drawing of the Carstensz Glacier is based on two photographs, one taken by J.F. Wissel on A.H. Colijn's 1936 expedition, and the other in 1972 by Richard Muggleton and reproduced in G.S. Hope, J.A. Peterson, V. Radok and I. Allison's *The Equatorial Glaciers of New Guinea*, A.A. Balkema, Rotterdam, 1976.

THE MOST–SACRED MOUNTAIN

Space, and the twelve clean winds of heaven,
And this sharp exultation, like a cry, after the slow six thousand
    feet of climbing!
This is Tai Shan, the beautiful, the most holy.

Below my feet the foot–hills nestle, brown with flecks of green;
    and lower down the flat brown plain, the floor of earth,
    stretches away to blue infinity.
Beside me in this airy space the temple roofs cut their slow
    curves
    against the sky,
And one black bird circles above the void.

Space, and the twelve clean winds are here;
And with them broods eternity–a swift, white peace, a presence
    manifest.

. . .

But I shall go down from this airy space, this swift white peace,
    this stinging exultation;
And time will close about me, and my soul stir to the rhythm
    of the daily round.
Yet, having known, life will not press so close, and always I
    shall feel time ravel thin about me;
For once I stood
In the white windy presence of eternity.

EUNICE TIETJENS

ONE

SNOW MOUNTAINS OF
NEW GUINEA

I

SACRED SUMMITS

30th November – 5th December, 1978

It was the last day of November. It was a quiet uncluttered day, and over ten years since I had last stood on this mountain. Then I saw only an exciting, jagged blur of sweeping snow and rock shimmering in summer heat, and dark hazy valleys twisting away below and beyond. Now I saw with different eyes, with a sense of intimacy, almost possession.

Each mountain I could see from the Aiguille de Tour held a different adventure shared with a different friend. Memories, trivial and moving surged inside me. Time had not diminished them. I saw tiny figures of the past picking slowly across the snow and heard their voices. Among those mountains I had found a kingdom that had seemed infinite. Although a newcomer, I had felt apart from the tourists. I was one of the climbers who lived in the woods. First I had climbed urgently, to escape, rather than to search for something that I loved – the absorbed, animal struggle up the crack at the top of the Aiguille de Purtscheller when I was seventeen, the storm on Mont Blanc, when the snow covered our tracks, the lightning shocks on the Gervasutti Pillar, dawn on the Frendo Spur, and the heights of freedom and happiness, emerging into the evening above the precipices of the Dru. And more gentle, recent memories of just a few months before, a walk across the Trient Glacier with my mother and father, and a traverse with Hilary of the Aiguilles d'Orées, the needles of gold.

Different memories of early mad rushes to fill up my postcards home with lists of routes I had climbed, to tick off the hardest routes as if they were a shopping list, and of later calm, when I discovered the long ridges and filled out the landscape within my mind, seeing these mountains from all sides, in all weathers, and understanding them.

Many people know these mountains – some grow to love them, others try to rape them.

13

It was cold, and humanity huddled in their oases – dark smudges below the thrusting white snows of winter's defence. The ski season had not yet started and the new, packaged human colonies above the snow line had not yet awakened. Man the exploiter and nature for some moments stood apart.

In the east a distant spire rose from a crown of rock. The Matterhorn. Eight years earlier, and again three months ago, I had stood on its summit. Little more than a century ago, the natives of its surrounding valleys felt an invisible cordon drawn around it. To them the Matterhorn was not only the highest mountain in the Alps, but in the world. They spoke of a ruined city on its summit wherein spirits dwelt; and if you laughed, they gravely shook their heads. To them the mountains were to be feared and suspected as haunts of monsters, wizards and crabbed goblins – and the devil. Something had gone wrong. In earlier times the Matterhorn, the Alps and the trees, rocks and springs of Europe were loved and respected as sacred places. Man had felt his links with them. But then he had broken with this heritage and had buried this delicate magic of life.

I thought of another mountain with a Matterhorn shape, thousands of miles away in the Himalayas. "Menlungtse, Menlungtse looks like that, I must look at the photographs." The wind veered beneath the cold dark blue sky and I turned my back. There were the tiny rock spires above Leysin, where I lived. And the sun swung down to the west, picking out the deep line of my tracks etched across the glacier below. Shadows grew on the mountain and a great silence was descending too. I knew the mountain, earth set upon earth, would remain silent, long after I had stopped. For some moments I listened, with a still open soul, until I had to turn from a surging feeling of love, before it overwhelmed me. Dear old planet, stay awhile, wait for me. Now I had to go down also.

Four days later she sat next to me in the car. A quick ready shy smile behind a cupped hand and an uncertain, beautiful voice – and we were going on an adventure together! We wound through the ground-hugging fog of the Jura, the headlights beaming a moving wall of white.

We curled out of the mist, and on to the plains of France. The car winged like a bird through cold night air past snow-covered fields, following the arrow of the autoroute to Paris. Hilary's face was softened by the darkness and she was wrapped in her own silence.

The headlong rush of the car brought plans juggling in my head. Two expeditions to the Himalayas were projected for the coming year. In the spring there would be Kangchenjunga – the arrangements had been made with a casual air in a pub a month before. To attempt this, the third-highest mountain in the world, four of us would leave for Nepal in March. Then, in the autumn, I would return again to the

Himalayas to attempt Gauri Sankar, the finest unclimbed mountain in the world. And in between these highlights, I would have to make some money. Peaks in Nepal have to be booked many months before you can approach and attempt them, and my life was booked up in advance. I was on a conveyor belt, carrying me from one booked peak to another. In my mind I tried to stem the rush of these pre-determined commitments and to think clearly, but stopped at the question "Why on earth should I fling myself into all this? What was the rush?" I could not answer. A tiny, not-yet-drowned part of me stood helplessly as the flotsam crashed past, squeaking, "I'd rather not," and "If you don't mind," and "Help!" like Alice wallowing about in the pool of her own tears.

The Snow Mountains of New Guinea, the mountains of the Stone Age, however, could not be booked and that was where Hilary and I were going now. Not only were we uncertain about reaching their summits but also uncertain that we would even reach their feet.

In Paris, our friend Marie, a painter, said: "Mountain climbing, brutal dangerous mountain climbing is too extreme for me to express. But exploration I can understand. You go not for the people, not for the mountains, but for them together. Climbers, they are lucky in that they have mountains to justify journeys across continents."

Projects, hopes and resolutions jostled in my brain, clamouring for attention. I could not wander from day to day. I had to plan. The Victorian explorer, Tom Longstaff, always warned his protégés: "Once a man has found the road, he can never keep away for long." The germ of travel was working inside me like a relapsing fever.

2

TROUBLED PARADISE

6th – 22nd December, 1978

"We saw very high mountains white with snow in many places which certainly is strange for mountains so near the equator." So wrote Jan Carstensz the Dutch navigator, in 1623 as he sailed on the Arafura Sea, between New Guinea and Australia. Snow mountains in New Guinea? Nobody believed him when he returned to Holland. Centuries later the mysteries of these mountains are still being unravelled. At 16,020 ft. (4,883m.), the highest peak in South East Asia and the highest point in the range has been named after him, the Carstensz Pyramid.

At some time during their careers, all great explorers are monomaniacs – imagination seized, they identify with a mountain, a pole, a blank on the map, then gather will and energy together to fling themselves in effort after effort towards it. The history of exploration is punctuated with the intensity of such relationships: Scott and the South Pole, Mallory and Everest, Shipton and Tilman and Nanda Devi, Bauer and Kangchenjunga, Herzog and Annapurna. The Snow Mountains of New Guinea have obsessed two great explorers – A. F. R. Wollaston, who tried to reach the mountains from the south early this century, and the devoted and energetic New Zealander, Philip Temple who, in 1961, became the first explorer to approach from the north. Both were fascinated by the unique isolation of these mountains.

However, even in the late 1970s, very little was known about the Snow Mountains in the mountaineering world. The allure that had attracted Wollaston and Temple was still there. These mountains were far away from the main mountaineering regions, they were difficult of access, usually covered in cloud, and rose from a strange uninhabited plateau surrounded by jungle, swamp and tribes of primitive peoples still living in the Stone Age. In the autumn of 1976, these isolated mountains had slowly begun to take hold of my imagination.

16

Whilst Joe Tasker and I were climbing the West Wall of Changabang in the Himalayas that autumn, we often talked, during the forty days of cold struggle it took to climb the mountain, about how it would be so much more pleasant to go to a mountain range in the tropics. We longed for the excitement of travel in an unknown land as a change from the lonely black and white struggle of extreme climbing. But it would have to be the right place, with the right person. Half in fun, we made a pact to find two young ladies and go to New Guinea together.

I was lucky, I found the other half of my expedition very quickly. The first public slide-show I gave about Changabang was at Belper High School. The lecture was organised by Hilary Collins, who ran the school's Outdoor Activities Department. We had met before in 1974, when she attended a course on which I was an instructor at Glenmore Lodge in the Cairngorms. Not long after the lecture we went rock climbing together for the first time, at the Tors in New Mills in Derbyshire. I fell off, clutching a large flake of rock that had come away with my weight. Hilary managed to stop me with the rope after I had fallen thirty feet – a good achievement considering she was only two thirds my weight, and I had nearly hit the ground. It boded well for our relationship. Over the New Year of 1976/77 we went climbing together again in Torridon in North West Scotland. All the girls interested in mountaineering I had met previously seemed either aggressively fanatical, or obscenely healthy, noisy, strong, rosy-cheeked types, inseparable from their anoraks and bobble caps. Hilary was different, and we shared a passion for mountains rather than climbing for competition or health. She had a commonsense, hard working practicality that I lacked. We were compatible. She was talking about going on a trip to the Himalayas when I suggested she came to New Guinea with me. She agreed. Then she started a new job, teaching geography and biology at a private school in Switzerland.

On the 9th January, 1977, I began writing a lot of letters – to Papua New Guinea, Australia, Indonesia, Hong Kong, America, West Germany and Holland, with the intention of following up all leads and of piecing together, like a jigsaw, a picture of the Snow Mountains of New Guinea. I devoured all expedition reports and all the books I could find on the area: *Pygmies and Papuans* by A. F. R. Wollaston, *Nawok!* by Philip Temple, *I Come From the Stone Age* by Heinrich Harrer and *Equatorial Glaciers of New Guinea* by Melbourne University. I also read many evangelical books by American Fundamentalist Protestant missionaries, describing their work in the highlands around the mountain. Unfortunately, the most comprehensive books were written in Dutch, including the tantalising *To the Eternal Snow of the Tropical Netherlands* by Dr. A. H. Colijn. This book described the 1936

Dutch expedition to the mountains and had very useful aerial photographs. All this research was immensely satisfying. New Guinea was completely outside my previous expedition experience, and every piece of information I gleaned and stored was, for me, a little inroad into a dark unknown.

On 17th January, Dougal Haston, with whom I had climbed on Everest, was killed in an avalanche whilst skiing above the village of Leysin in Switzerland. The mountaineering politics I was involved in at the time, in my work for the British Mountaineering Council, suddenly seemed petty when I heard the news. I went to Dougal's funeral. By coincidence, the school where Hilary was working was in the next valley, and she was able to meet me at the station in Leysin. The service, the coffin, the grave, the blue sky, deep snow and the mountains, and my walk away, hand in hand with Hilary beneath the tall trees, all combined to make one of the saddest, most moving days of my life. I had come as a pilgrim, to reaffirm a faith in extreme mountaineering, but felt only doubt. Many people said that Dougal had been doomed – that he was an Ahab after a White Whale, that his life had a restless, fanatic pace, and that he had been bound, sooner or later, to over-reach himself. To me he had seemed indestructible, and his death was a sudden shock. Nevertheless, our New Guinea plans were a comfort, for they were a step off the conveyor belt of a career of a professional high-altitude mountain gladiator, and a step towards a wider emotional development.

At Easter we met Jack Baines, the leader of R.A.F. Valley Mountain Rescue team in North Wales. Jack had been to the Snow Mountains in 1972. An effusive talker, he was positively garrulous about New Guinea. It had been the greatest experience of his life. He brought seventeen hours of tape recordings and, as he bubbled a commentary, his enthusiasm caught us and we absorbed his every word like blotting paper. Jack kindled in us a fire of enthusiasm for the Snow Mountains that was to burn steadily for the many frustrating months that were to pass before we finally saw them. We planned our departure for July 1977 and, as time passed, our New Guinea file became thicker. The mountains were appearing in my dreams. However, I would never really be able to believe in their existence until I saw them for myself.

New Guinea is divided into two halves – Irian Jaya and Papua New Guinea – by the 141° line of longitude. The highest mountains, and the only mountains with glaciers, lie in the western half, Irian Jaya, which used to be a Dutch colony but is now controlled by Indonesia. The whole of the area is under military control and previous expeditions advised that we would have to keep a very low profile and travel as tourists, rather than as an 'official' mountaineering expedition. I wrote to the British Embassy in Jakarta asking about access to Irian, and within a few days the whole situation was taken out of my hands. One of the staff at the Embassy, coincidentally, was organising an eleven-man joint Indonesian–British expedition to the mountains at the same time, and Hilary and I were embraced into their ranks. The Deputy Chief of the Armed Forces of Indonesia had agreed to be the expedition's patron. Since most of the positions of power in Indonesia are held by army officers, it seemed that all our problems were solved.

On the 6th June, however, our expedition was cancelled. Apparently there had been some trouble in Irian Jaya, and outsiders were not welcome. A proposed visit by the American Ambassador to the copper mine south of the mountains had been cancelled. Most of the missionaries in the interior had been flown out.

Quickly we changed our plans and spent a month climbing in Kenya and Tanzania, reaching the summits of Mount Kenya and Kilimanjaro. This, however, was mere 'tropical training', compared to our determination to go to the Snow Mountains of New Guinea. We planned another attempt to reach the area during Hilary's Christmas holidays in December, 1978. There is no settled weather season in Irian, but we hoped that this choice of date would give time for political problems to calm down. For seventeen months we traced and contacted people for first, second and third-hand reports of what was happening in Irian Jaya, and kept our eyes on the papers. Reports were conflicting. While the Indonesian government said its troops in West Irian were merely settling tribal disputes 'over trifling matters like dowries, cattle and women,' the Free Papua Movement was claiming the Indonesian Air Force had napalmed the jungle villages which gave the guerillas their chief support. It did not help us that the Carstensz Pyramid was so near the Freeport copper mine at Ertsberg, a prime target for guerilla attack. We were told it had had its pipeline blown up in 1977 and a helicopter shot down.

By November, 1978, however, the trouble in the Carstensz region was thought to be largely over and we were encouragingly reassured that in Indonesia all things are possible, regardless of what officials say in the first place. So Hilary and I decided to go to Jakarta and try to sort things out from there. But as we arrived, at the first stage of our journey, Charlie and Ruth Clarke's house in Islington (on the 6th December), we were no more certain that we would ever reach the Snow Mountains than we had been when the idea first germinated, two years before.

The Clarkes' home has one of those rare generous atmospheres that allow you to walk in, struggle past the dog, cats, toys, children and put the kettle on to make a cup of tea. Ruth's dramatic manner and Charlie's air of detached nonchalance provide hours of entertainment – they could play themselves on television. When Charlie asked

Ruth's father for permission to marry her, he was told: "Good God, you must need a psychiatrist," which was fortunate because she is one – and he does.

Their house has become, over the last few years, a climbers' London Base Camp. Climbers' wives, girl-friends and widows find a comforting haven there, professional freelance climbers use it as their London office, and expeditions use it as their springboard – the last night before Heathrow, and on their return for the first bed and bath they've seen in weeks.

Chris Bonington and his road manager were there, in London on a lecture tour. I got out some photographs and unfolded the large Australian 'Operational Navigation Chart 1:1000,000 1968', on the kitchen table. I described our journey to them all.

"From Jakarta we'll fly to this island here, called Biak, and from there to Nabire on the coast of the mainland. Then, we'll charter a light plane to Ilaga, just five days north of the mountains, and walk in. See these large white spaces, 'Relief data incomplete'. It's very difficult to map the place from the air, because it's always so cloudy."

"Blank on the map, eh?"

"Where are these gorillas?"

"Ooh look, they wear those things on their dicks."

"I'm worried about you two, I hope you'll be all right by yourselves."

The telephone rang. It was Bernard Domenech from Marseilles. He and another French climber, Jean Fabre, were also going to try to reach the Snow Mountains. We had heard about each other's plans during the summer, and had met in Chamonix. Now we exchanged last-minute details. We had agreed not to travel together, since a group of four would attract more attention and imperil our chances. However, we hoped to see each other in the hills.

"We're leaving next week. See you somewhere perhaps," he said.

Hilary and I spent our last day hunting through London shops for mosquito nets and silica gel bags to keep our cameras dry. Her hands moved quickly and intelligently as she squeezed vast piles of equipment into our rucksacks, after carefully hiding our ropes and climbing hardware at the bottom – we were to travel as tourists.

"Just think – that biscuit you're eating'll come out in Indonesia," Ruth said.

"Or over Bangkok," said Charlie.

On the 8th December we left Heathrow for Frankfurt – the first leg of our journey to Jakarta, the capital of Indonesia. Frankfurt was gripped by a fierce winter storm and we were delayed there for six hours whilst ice was cleared from the runway. Free drinks were provided and a boozing team developed, mostly comprising Welsh

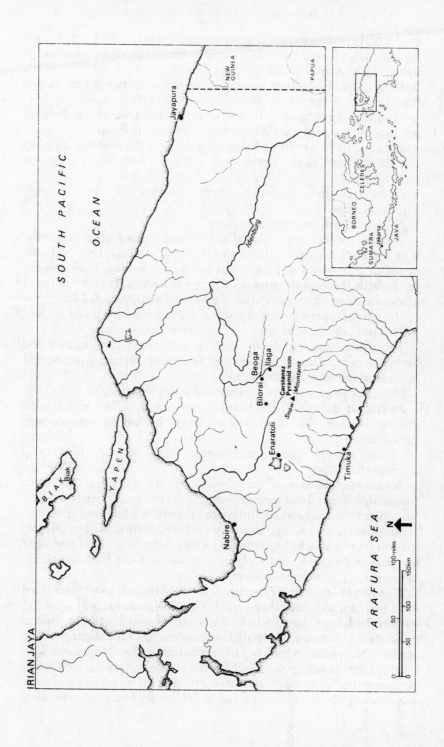

rugby players who started singing songs. When at last we settled back into the DC10, night had fallen and most of the rugby players fell asleep. Hilary and I sat on the port side. As we took off there was a loud bang and flash from the engine on the wing next to us. A few minutes later we heard the deep growl of the captain's voice:

"Ladies and gentlemen, the port engine has just blown up. We shall go up to 20,000 feet, eject all our fuel and return to Frankfurt."

The careful delivery in a foreign accent gave the message an extra impact of uncertainty. There were a few nervous titters from the passengers.

"How many more engines are there?" I whispered.

"Two I think."

"These things don't glide do they?"

We saw the fuel being ejected as the wing lights flashed. Then the long descent began. It was difficult to believe that this brightly-lit tube containing hundreds of people was not on the ground, but plunging earthwards through the night. I felt my pulse rate. It was soaring. I glanced at a few passengers to see if they were as nervous as I was. Two rugby players were fast asleep. Hilary and I put our boots on and stuffed our pockets with money, cameras and passports.

The plane bumped down, and as we landed fire engines and ambulances raced towards us from all directions and strung out behind in a line of moving, flashing lights.

"He can't just reverse two engines or it'll spin round."

At last, at the end of the runway, we stopped. Everyone started talking at once. The two rugby players behind us yawned and stretched.

"Where are we?" one of them asked.

"Frankfurt."

As we stepped out of the plane we heard the pilot confess to someone: "When the engine exploded, I did not know whether to try to stop or to keep on going and try to take off. We just got up."

So ended the second of the twenty-six take-offs that were to carry us to Irian Jaya and back. It was an unnerving beginning. Two days later the port engine had been replaced and we took off from Frankfurt again, this time without incident.

This was Hilary's first expedition. On the previous two expeditions I had been on, to Changabang and K2 in the Himalayas, my climbing partner had been Joe Tasker. We were of equal abilities, and a poker-faced, competitive edge to our relationship gave impetus to our efforts. I had relied on Joe's organisational drive a lot. Now I was with Hilary, I felt more responsible about the whole thing. I worried about obtaining the *Surat Jalan* (travel permit) and all the travel ahead of us. It was awesome going into a big Asian city for the first time, knowing no one, with so much to do. Still, one obstacle had to be taken at a time. I opened *Teach Yourself Indonesian*, and tried to learn some words.

Jakarta seemed many cities rolled into one, with tall international skyscrapers pushing into a hot, drizzly sky and contrasting with the tight cluster of small houses – the kampongs – where most of the people lived. Waves of tiredness washed over us in the sultry heat as we tried to find the correct police office initialled M.A.B.A.K. When eventually we arrived it was closed for the day. It was the first encounter of an eleven-day trail through corridors of officialdom. We went to the Garuda Airline office.

"Can we have a flight to Biak, the day after tomorrow?"

"Let's hope so," smiled the girl behind the desk. At five-foot-two, Hilary seemed tall beside the tiny Javanese girls.

The next morning we went back to M.A.B.A.K. It was the start of a busy day. Nobody seemed deliberately obstructive, but nobody wanted to take the responsibility of saying yes or no.

"We are tourists and we want a Surat Jalan to visit Irian Jaya. We would like to go to Biak, Nabire and Ilaga, if possible?" I said.

"Ilaga, in the interior? You must apply to the police in Biak for permission to go there, I can give you a Surat Jalan to go to Biak and Jayapura only. Will you come back at 2.00 p.m.?"

At 2.00 p.m. the permits were ready and, elated, we went shopping. Jakarta supermarkets contained all the lightweight foods we needed – at expensive prices. Fortunately, the Indonesian rupiah had been devalued by thirty per cent a few weeks before. Everyone in the shops grinned helpfully.

Early the next morning the domestic airport of Jakarta, Kemajoran, was in apparent turmoil and hundreds of people were waving and thrusting with tickets in their hands. Nobody spoke English. I tried to persuade Hilary to check in: "They won't push a woman," I said. We strained to hear the words that would tell us our flight was about to leave.

"Why did Sukarno change all the place names? We didn't learn those in geography at school."

"Ujung Pandang, Amon, Biak."

"That must be us!"

At Ujung Pandang, which used to be called Makassar, we changed planes in the shimmering heat and were soon flying through towering clouds above coral islands. When we landed on the island of Biak that afternoon we saw our first Papuans, smiling in yellow uniforms as airport porters. They looked African, with their black skins, woolly hair and broad noses and feet, but apparently they are not closely related. They have no affinity in language, culture or race with the other peoples of the Pacific, the Malayans and Polynesians, and have only tenuous links with the Aborigines of Australia. Although the Papuans were not tall by European standards, they seemed huge to the tiny Indonesians, and Indonesian legends are full of conflicts between the good princes and the 'giants' who inhabited the jungles. The Papuans of Biak speak one of the hundreds of languages of New Guinea – the world's most complex linguistic region.

We found a large, damp hotel near the airport. It used to be popular in Dutch days. Now, many Papuans wandered around it doing little jobs, as the whole mildewed edifice seemed to be crumbling around their ears. These were the lucky ones. There were many others still roaming the town who had also come from the mainland looking for work. We were the only guests in a large dining room. Outside we could see hot steamy coral and the blue sea. Small lizards ran around the walls. In one corner was a bar with no drink behind it, and in another stood a large Christmas tree with cotton wool and flashing lights. A cassette player was blaring out old Beatles' numbers and traditional Western Christmas carols to Indonesian words.

There used to be a Biak legend that vast wealth would one day arrive from the East. After the Second World War, the Japanese departed and generous Americans, rich in material things, arrived. It seemed that the prophecy had been fulfilled. But now they, too, had gone.

In the morning we were interviewed by a policeman. In his immaculate uniform he looked firm and tough. I remembered what a climbing friend, John Barry, had said about Indonesians: "Bloody good scrappers". He had fought against them as a Royal Marine in Borneo in 1964.

We presented a list of the villages north of the mountains: Bilorai, Beoga and Ilaga. "We want to fly to them from Nabire," we said. "We want to see the people who live there."

"I can only give you permission to go to Nabire. You must ask there about places further on."

Our Surat Jalan was duly stamped, and the immigration office extended our visas.

"Things are going too well," I said, "we haven't had to bribe anyone yet."

At an efficient little travel agency run by a Chinese – always the business men of South East Asia – we booked places on the scheduled flight next morning to Nabire. The travel agent warned us that we would not be able to charter a plane in Nabire because there was a fuel shortage in the whole of Irian Jaya. We decided, nevertheless, to take the chance.

There were only four other passengers in the Twin Otter. We veered around enormous clouds towards the mainland of Irian Jaya.

The tiny outrigger canoes of Biak shrank to specks on the ocean below us. We crossed the island of Yapen in a few minutes. Isolated tall trees reached out of the dense jungle and there were no signs of human habitation. The clouds became thicker. We could see the long finger-nails of the pilot's hands on the controls.

"I hope he knows where the coast is," said Hilary.

Then we saw the long airstrip pointing out to sea, first built by the Japanese during their years of occupation. On the shore a white ship with a rust-stained hull was being unloaded across the surf by tiny figures in little boats. Behind the flat town of tin roofs rose a steaming jungle.

Once we had landed, would-be helpers buzzed around us. A small lively European with a goatee beard stepped through a milling throng, shook our hands and introduced himself as Father Tetteroo, a Francis-can missionary.

"I am saying goodbye to a Sister who is leaving on the plane. Come round to my little house this evening for coffee. It is next to the airstrip. Everyone knows where I live."

A friendly but insistent policeman perused our Surat Jalan, and this inspection attracted an even larger crowd of onlookers. We were whisked away to the only hotel in the growing town of fifteen thousand people.

The hotel manager spoke good English – his father was Dutch. He asked if he could help us. I told him we wanted mainly to go to Ilaga.

"Why?" he asked abruptly. His manner was grave and stern.

Momentarily, I dropped my guard, and forgot our strategy, con-fessing that we wanted to go to the Snow Mountains.

"Impossible. Impossible," he repeated adamantly.

The whole area was closed. Only two weeks ago a missionary at Ilaga was 'taken'. He did not even think it worth asking the police, but eventually agreed to introduce us to them. As we walked with him, he puffed at a pungent cloves cigarette and remarked that he used to be the Chief of Police. We had lost the chance of secrecy.

At the police post we discovered that the Chief of the Nabire Police was not there – he was in Biak. So we went round to the house of the second in command. I produced my Australian map – it was the best they had seen – and systematically asked about all the other approaches to the mountains. We all sat at a table and chickens scratched around our feet. It was difficult to follow the gist of the conversation, because they were laughing and smiling at the same time as stone-walling our plans. Had I been to the Himalayas? I showed them a little photo of myself on the top of Everest. But why did we want to go to the mountains of Irian? Was there gold there?

25

Anyway, it was impossible; we could not approach the mountains from the north. However, the southern approach via the Freeport Indonesia copper mine was in another police district – they offered to ask the Jayapura authorities to see if they would allow us to use that way of reaching the mountains.

I knew that even if the Jayapura authorities allowed us to go to the south, the people at the mine had already refused us entry in response to an earlier request. We had heard at Biak that when the guerillas blew up their pipeline, the mine had been put out of action for three months. It seemed most unlikely that tourists would be allowed now.

In the evening we went round to see Father Tetteroo, the man we had met at the airport. He was among the first group of missionaries to come to the interior, in 1937. He knew Colijn and Wissell, who had explored part of the Snow Mountains in 1936. In the early days, he and other priests had crossed the jungles of Irian on foot, often travelling for months at a time with a couple of porters. Very few of the tribes they met had seen Europeans before. He had not heard about Pearl Harbour until a month after the raid had occurred. He had been in a Japanese Prisoner of War camp for three and a half years – a camp which had been bombed mistakenly by the Allies. He delighted and fascinated us with his insights about Irian. His stories were simple, like parables, and directed outwards with a lively sense of fun – and mischief.

Father Tetteroo was sixty-seven years old.

"Why should I go back to Holland, where I shall be retired? I prefer to stay here and help life wherever I can. I shall stay here until I die."

He was full of joy, as if he would bounce back no matter how hard life knocked him. He lived simply. When we left him a present of a large bunch of bananas had appeared on the porch. He did not know who had left them there; it could have been anyone in Nabire. We walked back across the airstrip, feeling selfish in our pursuit of the mountains. We could absorb so little, compared with the lifetime experience of a missionary. In the distance, lightning flashed beneath anvil-shaped clouds.

"Ah well, it was worth coming, just to meet him."

"Perhaps we should make the best of a bad job and try to get to those mountains in Borneo."

"We could go on a trek somewhere in Irian where there are no problems – then we would at least meet the people."

But we were sad at heart.

All this way, all this money, to be refused on the doorstep of the fabled mountains. We decide to stay till Monday and give the police another try.

Next morning they seemed to relent. As long as the Jayapura

authorities agreed, we could fly to Bilorai and walk out via the mine. No political troubles in the interior were mentioned, but we guessed that the main problems near the mountains were north east of them, in the Ilaga Valley. Bilorai lay to the north west. Obviously, the Indonesians would not want to risk the international outcry if two Europeans were kidnapped as a symbolic protest by guerillas. The police promised to radio to Jayapura immediately.

Caught up in a mood of optimism, we went to see Tom Benoit, a pilot who serviced the Catholic missions in Irian. An American from Minnesota, he lived in Nabire with his wife Mary and two little daughters – with another on the way. He had flown over ten thousand hours in Irian.

Tom was short and stocky, relaxed and practical, and wearing a pair of long garish surfing shorts. "He likes to help people," Father Tetteroo had said of him. I asked him if he could squeeze us in on a flight to Bilorai. I was very aware of using people, capitalising on their open goodwill, and I apologised.

"Somebody's got to climb mountains," said Tom. He could fit us into his schedule on Monday morning. "I'm rather busy at the moment. One of our pilots – an Indonesian – disappeared a few months ago. He got lost in the clouds and flew into a mountain."

"We're white parasites waiting for permission for our own ego trip," Hilary whispered to me after we had left.

Nabire slept during the hottest part of the hot day. When the shops reopened, we went provisioning to the blare of a loudspeaker van bellowing the name of the evening film at the cinema. The shops, mainly owned by Indonesian small traders from all over the archipelago, stocked a wide variety of Western goods, and we bought food for three weeks.

Over the centuries a trickle of Indonesians had settled on Irian's coasts, leaving the interior's forbidding jungles to the strange Papuan tribes they had found there. However, the shopkeepers of Nabire had arrived in the wake of a more recent influx of immigrants, resulting from the Indonesian government's transmigration scheme. This scheme arose initially from President Sukarno's opposition to birth control, and was aimed at relieving the population problems of farming in Java, and also at increasing the strength of Indonesia's ethnic toehold in Irian. The government wished to make the moves as attractive as possible to the Javanese, and offered transportation, land, the corrugated iron for a roof, and sufficient food until the first harvest to those families who agreed to relocate. If the transmigrants become homesick, however, the return ticket is discouragingly expensive.

In the evening Tom showed three home movies he had taken in Irian. They whetted our appetites.

"This is Bilorai a couple of years ago," he said.

"Sure you don't mean three thousand years ago?"

"You won't find them much changed now."

Bad news arrived the following afternoon. The police had received an instruction from Jayapura that we would not be allowed into the interior until we had received authorisation from two organisations, LAKSUSDA in Jayapura and LIPI in Jakarta. To obtain this we would have to fly a circle – a thousand miles to Jakarta and then over a thousand miles back to Jayapura at the other end of Irian Jaya. Hilary and I started miserably snapping at each other. Now we had tasted Indonesian bureaucracy, we knew that, even if we could afford the travel, we could never obtain such documents. Next week the rules would probably be different. Our pile of recently-bought food and all our packed equipment in the corner looked pathetic – mute but lucid witnesses to the state of our fortunes. We would return to Biak the next day.

Dawn was the best time in Nabire, and we made the most of our last few hours there. Despite our setbacks, we felt affection towards the Indonesians as we watched the transmigration camp come to life. When the first rays of light sprayed skyward through the tall trees, the jungle chorus started as if at the signal of a baton. The noises faded just as suddenly when the sun appeared. There was a roar of engines as Tom took off on his first flight. We walked along the road to the settlement and were soon walking against the tide of hundreds of people, on scooters and on foot going to school, to work in the shops, government offices and at the airport, and perhaps just going for a walk like us. Everyone greeted each other and us gaily with shining eyes and contagious smiles. "*Salamat pagi!*" Our faces became fixed grins. We walked to the Javanese market, past houses on stilts, fields of maize and bananas, a mosque, and a few cows, goats and dogs. Then we returned to the hotel for breakfast.

The manager came up with another straw of hope to clutch at: "At Biak you must go and see Mr. Engels, who owns two hotels and a building company and exports wildlife to European zoos. He is a very powerful and influential man. He will help you to ask the Major General for permission to approach the mountains via the mine."

At the airport building there was a confusion over the tickets. We pushed our way on to seats in the aeroplane. Our precious dollars were melting into flights and hotels as the days ticked by.

"If we want to move away from problems, I think we'll have to move away from Indonesia," said Hilary. The flight between Nabire and Biak had lost its excitement now.

At Biak we checked into one of Mr. Engels' hotels. It had a vast, extravagant painted Toroja roof, built of thousands of matched pieces of bamboo laid one upon another like tiles, sweeping up in a great curved prow at either end. A legend says that the design of the Toroja roof reflects a folk memory of the ships in which the distant ancestors arrived from China.

Mr. Engels had a strong personality. He gave us a rapid resumé of his life history and sent us to the Freeport office with his son, William, but all in vain. Even when I phoned the mine direct, the word was a firm but polite no.

"Come back next year, I shall organise everything for you," promised Mr. Engels.

Eventually we decided to do the one thing nobody had suggested, fly to Jayapura. At least then we would have tried everything.

We pressed our faces against the windows of the aircraft as it followed the coast, gazing longingly at the jungle, which harboured unknown wandering tribes of sago eaters. These people, we had read, hunted and collected food from the sago forests and occasional small-scale shifting cultivation. They had no contact with white people or administration, and spoke their own languages. Sometimes they traded in this jungle, leaving and collecting stone axes, salt and cowrie shells in traditional clearings, without ever seeing the tribesmen with whom they were exchanging goods. Through the jungle wound great meandering rivers which left a trail of oxbow lakes and emptied many channels into the sea.

Jayapura was once called Hollandia by its Dutch administrators – a name flashed around the Western world when General MacArthur spearheaded a battle against the Japanese there in 1944. Even now the rusting hulk of a partly-sunken Japanese transport ship projects out of the town's beautiful blue bay. The change of place names reflects the tide of political fortunes. Hollandia has been re-named Kota Baru (new town), Sukanapura and, recently, Jayapura. Meanwhile, West New Guinea has been known as West Irian and Irian Barat and has only in 1973 become Irian Jaya (literally, Irian Victory).

Before landing, the plane circled over a landscape as gentle as a Chinese watercolour, open pale green hills, red volcanised soil and large blue lakes whose shores and islands were clustered by houses built over the water on stilts. "At least it's a change of scenery," I said. Hilary was busy taking photographs for her geography classes.

Jayapura's airport is twenty-eight miles out of town, so before leaving I decided to investigate the possibility of flights to Bilorai, and left Hilary guarding our equipment. First I went to a large hangar run by a missionary alliance of the twelve different Protestant sects who operate in the highlands. Two tall Americans with crew-cuts ignored me, but eventually I found an office with two Indonesians inside it. The conversation lasted about a minute. There was no possibility of chartering a plane until the second week in January. Christmas was coming and they were too busy to have anything to do with us.

I decided to try the Catholics. A small boy pointed out a house where a Catholic pilot lived, but nobody answered the door. I walked back to Hilary, feeling as helpless as I have ever felt in my life and tiring of the indignity of asking people for favours. We found the large brown police building where our fate would be decided next day, and went away to type a letter to take with us describing what had happened so far. We looked for someone to translate it, and met Father Frans Verheijen, who agreed to come to the police building and help us. There was a pragmatic, straight-talking air about him, of someone used to getting things done – a quality he shared with the other Franciscan missionaries we had met. Next morning we followed him in, past guards and secretaries and along corridors until we were outside the room of the Chief Intelligence Officer of Irian Jaya.

"Wait outside," said Father Verheijen. We sat down, trying to gauge the mood from the ebb and flow of conversation next door. Hilary had her fingers tightly crossed. Long minutes passed and eventually we were summoned in.

Politely, we were shown our seats. Humbly we looked across at two immaculately uniformed Indonesians sitting beneath a large map of Irian Jaya. One of the men was holding an ominous-looking folder full of papers. Evidently it was the mountaineering file, because he recited the familiar words of the letter, written one and a half years before from Jakarta, cancelling our previous expedition plans. It was the last official – and thus definitive – statement on mountaineering expeditions "until I have better news from Irian Jaya." Red rings around many of the districts indicated trouble spots. The village of Bilorai was in an all-clear region, but the area south of the mountains was clearly 'no go'. We were told that an agreement had been reached to allow us to visit Bilorai as tourists, but we were to promise not to go to the mountains. If we went near the mountains, we would be thrown out of Indonesia. The police considered all scientific, surveying and mountaineering expeditions to be forbidden. We were issued with new Surat Jalans, and asked to sign them after these conditions had been typed upon them. We agreed. Everyone smiled and we left.

We blinked in the sunshine outside and thanked Father Verheijen, who rushed off to attend a meeting. He had used all his powers of persuasion and influence, and lain his integrity on the line – and that of the missions he worked for – to help us, two complete strangers.

"We'll see the people at least," said Hilary "and perhaps we'll be able to see the mountains from a distance. But if only they hadn't found out we wanted to go to the mountains!"

"Let's just see what happens," I said. "Anyway, the next problem is to try and get a flight organised."

Back at the airport we found a commercial charter company with one Australian pilot. Although he was away for the day, there seemed a possibility that he could fly us – until we calculated the price. We could not afford a thousand U.S. dollars. We trailed round to the Catholic pilot's house. His flight schedule was stretching him to the point of tears. He told us that in Irian the Catholics had only two pilots with four planes, but they had enough work to keep six busy. However, he had a suggestion to make. The Seventh Day Adventists had a grass strip a few miles away, and maybe had more spare time to help. He didn't know much more about them, except that they had split from the main Protestant missionary alliance owing to a disagreement about which day of rest to take at weekends – the Seventh Day Adventists refused to fly on a Saturday but, unlike the other sects in the alliance, they were willing to fly on a Sunday.

Eventually we found the strip, carved out of the jungle. Next to it were two modern houses and a hangar. The property was lavishly modern and well-cared for – evidence of the support of a wealthy religious commitment. We were nervous.

"Watch out for the death-adders – stay away from the long grass." The wives of the sect's two pilots were listening to their husbands conversing on the radio. "They'll be back in a couple of hours," one said. "I'm sure they'll try to help you."

We went for a long walk along a narrow road through the jungle. We joked and flirted, trying to fill in time. Then, within minutes of each other, two tiny, snub-nosed Cessna 185s flew in noisily over the trees, arriving from opposite directions. We walked with slow steps to the hangar, bracing ourselves to bother people again. What would my response be, I thought, if a couple of strangers walked up to me in Leysin after I'd spent a hard day on the hill, and asked me to drive them to Geneva? I need not have worried.

"It sounds like you need a bit of luck," said Ken.

"I'll fly you in tomorrow morning," said Leroy. "Be here at 5.00 a.m., I'm going to Jayapura right now – do you want a lift?" The old American frontier spirit of help and co-operation had not died in the new age of competition. The tide seemed to be turning.

We had left most of our food in Biak – it was costing too much to pay the excess baggage every time we flew. Now we had twenty minutes before the shops closed to buy our rations. We found a large shop with a lot of Australian food displayed, and dashed from shelf to shelf until we had accumulated a large pile on the counter before an amused shop assistant.

"I hope we haven't forgotten anything."

31

"Look up Indonesian for 'bulk-buy discount', Hilary. You've got the dictionary."

Leroy had not flown to Bilorai before, and before taking off we listened apprehensively in the half-light of the dawn as he discussed with Ken where it was:

"Turn right at Ilaga . . ."

I wondered if climbers discussing a route up a mountain sounded so casual. Then God was addressed very directly, in a strong clear prayer.

We flew along a compass bearing into the interior.

Already, the crisp morning air was being invaded by the first wisps of cloud floating up and starting to gather in bulbous shapes. After crossing some low mountains we approached the vast plateau of the Idenburg River. Below us stretched a dense jungle of sago swamps.

"Where would you land in an emergency?" I asked.

"I'd look for a river," he said.

"Where are the Snow Mountains?"

"Over there somewhere – I've only seen them twice; usually they're in the cloud. Mind you, I've only been flying in Irian for nine months."

The river took a hundred detours, but our direction was straight. We surrendered ourselves to our pilot's skill. Clouds picked out ridges in the dark green below. The ground started to move up towards us until we were enclosed in steep-sided valleys, skimming ridges, searching for the needle of an airstrip. After two hours of flying we still had not found the landing ground; we were peering in all directions and we had our maps out. Leroy admired them – they were better than his. I wanted to spend a moment inside his head, so I could find out how worried to become. Then Hilary saw it – a dark brown, unmistakable stretch of level ground above a tin-roofed hut. It was the first sign of habitation we had seen.

We wheeled around and I saw many dark figures race up a track towards the airstrip. As we landed, small grey pigs ran squealing out of our way.

"I'm going to Wamena to pick some people up for Christmas," said Leroy. "I'd better go now, before these clouds become any bigger, and the mid-day winds pick up."

The plane was out of sight within minutes. The Time Machine had dumped us. Hilary and I sat down and waited for the reception committee to arrive.

3

AMAKANE

22nd – 28th December, 1978

We were looking at the figures painted on the wall of a cave come to life. Our eyes turned and darted in their sockets like tropical fish. A large crowd swarmed around us. Men of all ages wearing nothing but long yellow penis sheaths were waving bows and arrows. Women in grass skirts peered from behind. All our baggage was picked up and people started carrying it off down the hill. I had not done up my briefcase properly; the contents fell out and I rushed around in a panic picking up the papers.

"Hurry up, let's get after them," yelled Hilary.

We are half-scared, half-thrilled.

A few hundred yards down the hill the mob stopped and our equipment was put in a pile. We were relieved when a European, in his mid-thirties, appeared and introduced himself as Jan van der Horst.

"Welcome to Bilorai! Excuse me, I have not spoken English for a long time and am a little rusty. I am just here for a few days over Christmas. I work in Enaratoli now but used to live here. Would you like a look around?"

We hesitated, not wanting to leave our equipment unguarded. "Don't worry," he said, "you can trust these people. They will not harm or cheat you." He plunged off into the undergrowth and we steamed after him. It was the start of a vivid afternoon.

"Walking is hard work in this country. I weighed eighty-four kilos when I first came to Irian – now I weigh fifty-six."

Eagerly we peppered him with questions – first about himself. He had studied for seven years at university – maths and chemistry and then philosophy and theology. Working as a priest, he ran a school for

33

children with behaviour problems before coming to Irian when his bishop asked him to. He could speak several languages – Dutch, German, English, Indonesian; and the language of the people of Bilorai, the Monis.

"The Moni language is very difficult – it has twenty-eight tenses. I can use six or seven and they seem to understand what I mean. Before I learnt it, I had to use a small boy, who had been to school and understood my Indonesian, as an interpreter. Sometimes this was embarrassing, particularly when talking to the older people. Now, however, I can ask the questions that I want."

He was at the moment trying to learn the language of the Ekagis who lived in the west, in the Paniai Region, around the Wissel Lakes.

After a few more questions Jan warmed to describing his work, and the culture he lived in, with the eagerness of an expert lost in his subject. "When I arrived I did not talk about religion for a long time. I wanted to understand the people without preconceptions, without automatically condemning the beliefs and lifestyle I found. I soon learnt that their social norms and rites have the same right to be respected as our own. I had done courses in agriculture and medicine before I came, so I was able to help. Not long ago infant mortality was seventy per cent. Now it is thirty per cent. But that isn't everything. What I really want to do is to raise their level of consciousness in a Moni way to prepare them for their inevitable future contacts with the outside world. I am trying to help them settle their problems themselves and not trying to see how many people I can baptise in as short a time as possible."

I did not comment, for I too had much to learn and absorb.

We slid down a muddy track. Little boys were running backwards and forwards around us, like lively dogs out for some exercise. One of them was firing arrows into the trees, for fun. Jan showed us the different arrow heads:

"This one for birds, this one for rats, this one for pigs, and this one for people. They still have not developed flights for them – perhaps so that when they aim at each other they are not too accurate. There is a delicate balance here between chance and competence."

We arrived at a rectangular wooden hut. Smoke was filtering out of its roof which was thatched with grass and sedge. "The smoke keeps the roof tarry and waterproof," said Jan. "It rains every afternoon here." Inside, the floor was raised eighteen inches off the ground and six Monis sat on it. They were eating steamy jungle greens – it looked like spinach.

"*Amakane*," they all grunted. Then grinned.

"That's a good word to learn," said Jan. "It means Hello, how do you do, that's good, thank you and goodbye."

"*Amakane*," we said.

"They have no cooking utensils," said Jan "and so never have hot drinks. They cook sweet potatoes in the fire and greens in a pit with hot stones – sealed by large leaves like a pressure cooker."

We passed a longer hut. "That's where the richest man in the area lives," said Jan. "He has six wives, many cowrie shells, and his pigs live inside that enclosure. Each wife has a separate room, and their children sleep with them until adolescence, when the boys move into the father's room. But not many men have enough cowrie shells to have many wives."

We saw a tightly-woven fence about six feet high. "Sometimes wild dogs can jump the fences," said Jan. "They like to eat pigs."

The Monis did not have village structures, but since the airstrip was built they had been slowly beginning to settle higher up towards it and the mission and government huts. The valley sloped two and a half thousand feet below the airstrip and Monis who lived lower down tended to class all the Monis, missionaries and Indonesians who lived higher up as 'them up there'. "Whenever there is a local dispute," said Jan, "they think we are automatically on the side of those higher up. When the mission was lower down it was the other way round."

"How do they know what water is safe to drink?" I asked.

"They know exactly where the good water is," said Jan. "You see they are not stupid. They are just as intelligent as anyone else, but they use their intelligence for different things. They know the names of all the pigs around, they can identify and recount the age and history of their cowrie shells, and when there is a local war, they know exactly who is on their side and who is not. They know the names and properties of hundreds and hundreds of plants, and can identify all the seventy species of sweet potato . . ."

We came to another clearing and saw an old man crouching next to a pig. The pig's eyes were contentedly closed, and the man was affectionately stroking its stomach.

"*Amakane*," we said.

"He's the oldest man in Bilorai," said Jan. "He's about sixty-five years old. Of course no records have been kept until recently, but the average life expectancy of these people is just under forty." At 6,000 ft. it was too high for the malarial mosquitoes that had plagued us in Nabire. However, civilisation had brought TB to Enaratoli in the west and the Baliem Valley in the east. There had been a lot of goitre problems in the area owing to the lack of iodine but recent injections had cleared this up – with the side-effect of giving the cured a soaring I.Q.

"What sort of concept of time have they got?" I asked.

"They remember two or three generations back, although nothing precise, beyond morning, afternoon and evening and two or three moons. Of course, they have no seasons, although they carefully rotate their fields. You see that sharp pointed mountain over there in the east? No one has been there. But they have noticed that for half the year the sun rises on one side of it and for the other half of the year on the other side."

Another man in the clearing was smoking a cigarette made of locally-grown tobacco, rolled in a pandanus leaf. He was smoking it through the side.

"The tobacco was here long before the Europeans came," said Jan. "Here, try it."

I coughed and spluttered with the thick acrid smoke – a great joke. The man showed us a cowrie shell, which he prised out of a tightly woven purse. The shell was filled with beeswax and the man pointed to its teeth, its mouth and gums and its backside. It would have bought a small pig.

A woman nearby had lost the top two joints of three of her fingers. "They were cut off by her parents when she was a child to express grief when one of the family died," said Jan. "It is a sort of adolescent rite. The funny-bone is knocked, as an anaesthetic, before amputation. This tends to be the only time, nowadays, that they use the stone axe."

The same mutilations are depicted on the walls of caves in France. I tried to imagine how a child could submit to such an ordeal – the grim symbolic mood cast by the spell of the ceremony, the suffering of the amputation, and the mixture of pride and relief the child must have felt to come out at the end of it all.

We passed a lot of planks placed carefully against a large tree. "There is a female symbol behind there," said Jan, "and it marks the boundary between those above and those below." Lower down the hill, away from habitation, was a sacred grove of trees with a broad swathe cleared from jungle around it. "No one is allowed to enter that," said Jan, "spirits and ghosts are supposed to live there. The Monis used to put their dead in tree houses for the birds, but now they bury them, particularly near the missions. They believe that the ghosts of dead people are around all the time helping or playing tricks. Sometimes whole forests are forbidden because they are said to be full of spirits. But also they have a word 'Ebu', which means many things – blood, earth, life-energy, Supreme One, nature. If a man steals an axe, then the Ebu knows."

Did he know what the Seventh Day Adventists believed in?

"The same God as you or I," he snapped.

I asked for that, I thought, from such an aggressive, committed intellect.

"Many Monis come to church, and sing Moni hymns. You can decide how Christian they are," he said.

I asked him about the penis sheaths – they were obviously important. What did they wear them for? Was it to affirm their virility, or to protect them from bad spirits?

"They feel naked without them – any other reasons have been forgotten, and now they wear them for modesty only. They come in all shapes and sizes and usually they have a wardrobe of one or two others. And it's easy for them to change styles – they just go into the jungle and cut a different shaped gourd."

We started walking back up the hill. Jan studied for four hours every day and we did not want to interrupt his schedule. I asked him when the airstrip was built.

"1967. It took three hundred men six years to carve it out of the ridge. These people saw jets a long time before they ever met Europeans – they have some amazing stories about them. The first wheels they saw were on aeroplanes. They accept outside phenomena very quickly – although seeing things, of course, from their own point of view. Nowadays, when an aeroplane goes overhead they hardly look up."

"Do they use money yet?"

"They have started to do so over the last three or four years. It is very important that they learn about money, otherwise they will be cheated if, in the future, they trade with the coast. Of course there are about eleven thousand people in the valley, and a few other places with airstrips like this, and I suppose about a hundred people in Bilorai earn a wage of some sort – doing jobs for the mission and the government, and maintaining the airstrip. The rest of the people work in the gardens, and they are very clever and successful agriculturalists. They are lucky in some ways, too, because they are not troubled by seasons, drought, floods or pests. It is not an easy life but a good one – unhurried but purposeful."

"We ought to check in at the government post," I said, "and tell them we're here."

"The place is empty, there's no one there," said Jan. "You see we had a war here about two weeks ago, and all the Indonesian police and teachers escaped to Enaratoli. They were worried that the emotion of the battle would boil over on to them."

"Why did the war start?"

"It was between the Monis of Bilorai and those of Titigi – a place about two hours' walk down from here, but further up the valley. It started when a man from Bilorai was drowned in the river near Titigi. The Bilorai Monis thought that a Titigi ghost had pushed him in. You see, if an accident cannot easily be explained by commonsense, they accept that a ghost is involved – even if it is something as simple as tripping up. Anyway, casualties have to be even, and a ghost will not rest until he is avenged, so a battle was arranged on a sort of no-man's land halfway between the two villages. Of course an inter-clan war is not as serious as one between tribes and, unlike the Danis in the east, the Monis do not damage property or harm women and children; they do not forget themselves and go mad with slaughter. The battle is an elaborate, stylised event, so there are a lot of women and children watching from a safe distance – like a football match. They know the names of the people on the other side, and shout insults and taunt each other. Whereas the Danis use spears, these people only use their inaccurate bows and arrows. They crouch very low when fighting, so that they are not injured in the chest. In this last battle, nobody was killed but about forty were injured – some of them quite badly. Many of them think that the risks involved in fighting the battle are not as bad as if they ignored the unavenged ghost. But they have never harmed me – I once walked through a fight, and they stopped firing when I was in front of them, but started up as soon as I had passed.'' Jan explained that he had been trying to call a meeting between the two sides, not to shout at them for their sins, but to encourage them to discuss why they had fought each other. However, those little wars brought so much excitement, it was unlikely that they would stop. I did not ask Jan whether he thought they had a function as population control.

When Jan had gone, Hilary and I discussed what to do. It was a moral dilemma. There were no police around to stop us going to the mountains, so should we take a chance? No one had spoken of guerilla warfare, and the Monis seemed friendly towards us. But if a police patrol did stop us, and saw the statement on our Surat Jalans, we could be in trouble. The consequences of becoming entangled with a guerilla unit were unthinkable. To know what is right and not to do it is cowardice. But what was right? Missionaries seemed to be able to wander about without being kidnapped, as did Europeans at the Freeport mine, so why couldn't we? In the Himalayas one respects a government's ban on climbing mountains in politically sensitive areas because there are so many open areas to choose from. But here, in Indonesia, there was only the one area, and I was sure that the Indonesian authorities did not understand the innocuous nature of mountaineering. We were not journalists out to sensationalise Irian's problems to the outside world, we were not spies or mineral prospectors. We were not going to do anything dramatic, like Mrs. Wyn Sargent, the American anthropologist who reached the world's headlines and upset the Indonesians by becoming the fourth wife of a tribal chief in the Baliem Valley. And we were so near the mountains; the idea of repeating the same effort and expenditure in trying to reach them in another attempt in the future was appalling.

I was so determined to climb in these mountains that I would break a promise to do so. We would go.

"We must make sure we don't involve the missions at all, though," said Hilary. We would be on our own, with our Indonesian dictionary, the knowledge which we had gleaned in our reading before, and what we could try to understand as our adventure unfolded.

No one from Bilorai would come with us as porters to help us carry our equipment to the mountains because everyone wanted to stay for the Christmas celebrations – and also did not want to go through or near the enemy territory of the Titigi Monis. We decided to go down to Titigi and see if we could obtain porters there.

A broad muddy track stretched down to the other settlements. Jan had said it was the best track in the area. The next day we slithered down it, past the huts of the empty government offices and school and away from the cultivated area of Bilorai, through the jungle and out into a broad clearing on the hillside. This was the neutral zone between the two clans, where the prearranged battles were fought. Here we met some Danis, proud warriors with bows and many arrows, pig tusk ornaments and painted foreheads smeared with pig fat and soot. The Danis, fiercest and most ruthless of the Irian tribes, could travel outside their own areas with impunity. Although they had internal feuds of their own, they were not involved in the local war between Bilorai and Titigi and were free to move between the settlements. They appreciated our 'Amakane'.

As we crossed a side stream in the river bottom by a recently-built bridge, a group of distant figures by the main river rose, tall and lithe, to follow us. They kept a hundred yards behind us, with the intimidating stealth of a band of Red Indians stalking two white settlers.

"Retreat's cut off," said Hilary under her breath.

In Titigi a large crowd of men of all ages, from two years upwards, accumulated under a tree to discuss our proposals. The worn ground told us it was an habitual meeting place. The first hopeful sign was four large pits dug in the ground and lined with leaves: the sign that a festive occasion had occurred.

"*Hari Natal*," someone said. Some aspects of Christianity were evidently widely spread through the northern highlands, but the religious calendar was flexible. Titigi had already celebrated Christmas two days before, and there would be no problem about obtaining porters. The trip would be an opportunity for the Monis to make some money from us, and to trade with the tribes south of the mountains, and perhaps obtain cast-off loot from the copper mine. They had only one misgiving, and Hilary was upset when they expressed apprehension about accompanying a woman of unknown endurance on such an arduous expedition.

We could not distribute loads heavier than ten kilos for each porter because Monis eat vast quantities of sweet potatoes each day, and they would have to carry sufficient food for the journey. A fee was fixed and we had far too many volunteers – we wanted eight, picked ten and ended up with eleven.

We plodded back up the hill to Bilorai. Hilary quickly packed up our equipment into ten-kilo loads, whilst I sorted out our papers, maps and films. Ten young boys picked up the gear and ran off down the hill, whooping, shouting and barking like excited dogs. Two old ladies carrying large bales of grass up the hill were almost knocked over in the exhilaration of the rush – they were muttering bewilderedly when Hilary and I jogged past. At no-man's land we were met by the men from Titigi, and the boys from Bilorai quickly withdrew.

We were confused by the blur of faces. "I'm sure they aren't the men we took on," I said.

The eleven men of the grinning armed escort drew their bows like a firing squad. We persuaded them to point their arrows in the air. It was evening by the time we had arrived in Titigi and anxiously checked and reassembled the loads. We gave out mirrors, which caused hoots of merriment. The Monis chanted and sang late into the night, relishing the last hours in their homes before starting on the journey. Because of the loss of altitude, it was much hotter than Bilorai. I was excited and did not sleep well.

"Happy birthday Hilary." It was Christmas Eve. Two of our porters were now wearing shorts and vests rather than just penis sheaths – or *kotekas*. They had received the shorts from the Indonesian authorities in 1971 under Operation Koteka – a short-term plan to bring clothes and western culture to the natives within Irian. These muddy torn clothes looked less dignified and less healthy, without the pride of a secure culture. We had some spare rucksacks and the men, never having seen such contraptions before, spent a hilarious time putting them on. They stuck their hands straight up in the air, whilst another jumped up and tried to lasso the upraised arms with the straps. Soon the sacks were coated with greasy soot from their smoke-blackened bodies. The rest of the gear they either put into their string bags, or just carried in their hands. After prolonged goodbyes to their friends and families, the porters eventually set off at a fast pace through the terraced fields.

At the last huts, a husband and wife, busy splitting logs into planks paused to grin at us. Nearby, sweet potatoes grew in gardens of individual mounds, set two feet apart. We stopped by a field of sugar cane and tried to emulate the men as they dextrously stripped the cane with their teeth. They had brought pre-cooked sweet potatoes for trail snacks, and ate different varieties for breakfast, quick nourishment, lunch and dinner.

We tried to follow our direction on the map in *The Equatorial Glaciers of New Guinea*. The information for this had been provided by Bob Mitton, a geologist who had perhaps travelled more of the paths in Irian Jaya than any other foreigner. His fascination with the country had led him to learn Dutch, so that he could read more about it. We calculated from the map that we were following the most direct route to the mountains. On this first day we were following a 'major track' which, according to the map, climbed out of the bed of the Weabu River and then across two steep slopes separated from each other by a swampy plateau, to reach a ridge-side at 9,100 ft. Then it descended to the Kemabu River Valley. This was a horizontal distance of eight miles, and was to take us eleven hours without stopping. The jungle demanded maximum effort for minimum distance. After a few minutes walking we voiced suspicion about what the next day's 'minor track' would be like.

The porters knew the route. They wound their way through the jungle with the nonchalant ease of trained gymnasts. Following them, even though we were only carrying cameras and lightweight anoraks, we felt as if we were trying to break a world speed record on an Outward Bound assault course.

The dark, fetid jungle was a sudden change of atmosphere from the open, garden valley of the Monis. The canopy above us dripped. Mud, roots and vines, dead leaves and trees, fallen and upright, were strangling and struggling with each other. Our footfalls were softened and sucked into the mud, and no birds sang. No doubt we were surrounded by animals, birds, snakes and insects, but our eyes and ears were not attuned to detecting them. We ducked under fallen trees and balanced along sloping greasy logs for fifty feet at a time, nervously glancing at the intangible depths of decay underneath.

"I wish we had crampons on," said Hilary.

We waded along the beds of streams and wobbled across natural bridges of splintered jigsaws of vegetation. Branches swung at us, thorned vines hooked at us and pulled us back and greasy steps seemed placed with the hidden precision of banana-skins in a cartoon prank. The ground was never flat, but was a succession of steep, slithery, vegetable barriers. It was similar to caving, except that the effort was even worse and occasional glimpses of daylight told us that we were still above ground.

Soon we were battered and scratched and tiring with the use of half-forgotten muscles in the constant crouching and bending. The many slips and falls turned our legs to jelly. Hilary, being a foot

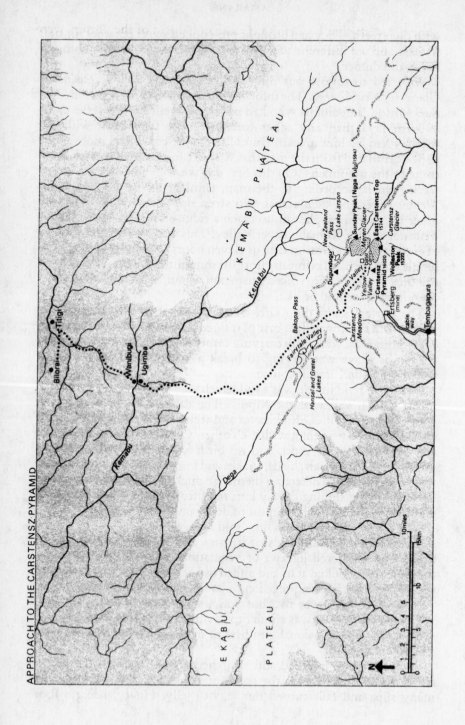

APPROACH TO THE CARSTENSZ PYRAMID

EKABU PLATEAU

KEMABU PLATEAU

Kemabu

Kemabu

Biloral

Tiligi

Wanibugi

Ugimba

Dega

Bakopa Pass

Fairytale Valley

Hansel and Gretel Lakes

Carstensz Meadow

Dugunduguo

New Zealand Pass

Lake Larson

Sunday Peak (Ngga Pulu) 15947

Meren Glacier

East Carstensz Top 15344

Carstensz Glacier

Base Camp

Meren Valley

Yellow Valley

Carstensz Pyramid 16020

Wollaston Peak 15322

Ertsberg (mine)

cable way

Tembagapura

N

10 miles

15 km

10

5

6

5

4

3

2

1

shorter, seemed to be faring better than I. Most of the porters were even smaller. The path, I decided, was not designed for people six feet high. The Monis ran down logs, gripping effortlessly with their prehensile toes. We blundered along, our eyes glued on the zigzags of the men in front. They, however, were chatting and looking around as if out for an afternoon stroll. We were grateful for the occasional stops, when the men paused to chew potatoes and to fish dry tinder out of a spare *koteka* to light cigarettes. I vowed I would never be impatient with a mountaineering beginner again.

The Monis took us in their care. To us the interminable jungle looked all the same and if we could not see them for a minute we became lost, but if we waited another minute one of them came back to look for us. Whenever I slipped on a log or teetered on a river crossing, a rock-like, steady grip held my arm from behind, although I had heard no one coming after me. One of the older porters, who had a perpetual runny nose (we called him Sniffer) and a short bulky *koteka*, became particularly concerned for Hilary's welfare, and doggedly hung on her heels. "You never look after me like that," she said. Hilary bewildered the porters by constantly changing the combination of jumpers and anorak she was wearing to adjust to the humidity.

The porters liked disposable ornaments and, as the mood took them, they picked up blades of grass and various other small bits of the jungle and put them through the pierced holes in their noses and ears, or made them into armbands. This was a change from the safety-pins and biros the Monis used near the missions in Bilorai.

At two in the afternoon it started to pour with rain, and did not stop for six hours. We put on our cagoules, but were already so wet with mud and perspiration they did not make much difference. The porters unfolded long pandanus-leaf raincoats – a simple long rectangle fastened along two sides, exactly the same as is used by porters in Nepal – and hung them over their heads. Two of them put on our climbing helmets, and became very attached to them. The rain was to start progressively earlier each day for the following eleven days.

I was engrossed in the ground immediately in front of me and suddenly came face to face with a ferocious-looking Dani coming in the other direction. I flinched as he shrieked in astonishment. Then he shouted with delight when he saw Hilary. "*Amakane*," we all said. It was the only encounter of the day. Very few Europeans have ever been harmed in Irian, and one of the reasons for this must have been the tradition of fair dealing by the missions. However, at first it was easy to imagine hostility before we recognised their trust.

When we crossed the final ridge at 9,100 ft., the porters started up with high-pitched cries of two or three notes – their own code for sending messages over great distances. Far down in the Kemabu

Valley, eleven hundred feet below, came answering cries. The porters were calling: "We're coming from Titigi – light a fire, give us some room, we're coming to stay for the night."

It took us an hour and a half to descend, and it was dusk when we reached the first habitation. We stopped in a clearing with two circular huts made of upright planks. One of them was full of women, children and pigs. The other one, the 'boarding house', had smoke steaming through its thatched roof but was empty, and the porters dived in. I followed them. A fire was burning in a box full of sand in the middle of the floor. The room was dry and warm, but I could not stay long in the suffocating smoke. No wonder most of the porters had bad coughs! Tents were colder, wetter, but less claustrophobic and more healthy. Despite the rain, a curious crowd of locals peered at us until long after dark.

"You would stare if two Martians camped in your back garden," I said to Hilary. We felt like zoo exhibits.

Hilary was upset that I had not offered to cook her birthday meal. I argued that I was sorting the films out. Eventually we ate instant spaghetti and a Chinese tin of pork and a Christmas pudding carefully nurtured all the way from England. Whenever we took food out in front of hungry, watching eyes, we felt guilty. For this reason we did not eat during the daytime, in front of the porters. We wanted to give them some, but our precious rations were so stretched that we had not enough for an emergency or to hand out.

The porters seemed to have skins of leather, but they liked having their scratches fussed over by Hilary, who became chief plasterer. They decided she had magical medical powers. Hilary was relaxed company – a lovely change from the usual tough-guy talk with 'the lads' on a Himalayan expedition with a big, serious mountain dominating the horizon all the time. Our mountaineering, I hoped, was going to be relaxing after all the hard work in the jungle.

Below us, the turbulent Kemabu River divided two settlements at the point where we had to cross it. On the far side, to the south, lay Ugimba, a sprawling Moni settlement of predominantly rectangular huts, and on the side where we had arrived was the more cohesive unit of circular Dani huts – Wanibugi. Across the river between the two places was a magnificent rattan suspension bridge built without nails or modern tools. It had to be replaced every few years as it rotted.

On Christmas Day it was my turn to have a birthday. We decided to open all cards in the evening, for we had problems to take our minds off the day's religious and festive significance. Two of the porters were deserting us. One of them, the leader the previous day, had a badly swollen leg. The other was complaining of toothache. We gave the first some antibiotics and the other aspirin and looked around, hoping to recruit local substitutes. Eventually we found two Danis – one tall, with a competitive air and very greasy face, and the other wearing a bizarre collection of loot from the copper mine – old wellington boots and sunglasses and a yellow waterproof construction worker's jacket. The purpose of some Western goods must fascinate them, for in 1974 Bob Mitton had found in this place a large marquee, erected but unused and weighing fifty-five kilos, which must have been carried for at least three days' walk from the mine.

No sooner had we acquired two new porters than all the others ran off down the hill, leaving us standing in the camp site with all the gear. Suspecting mass desertion we shouted after them, but they kept on going. In despair we gathered all the gear on to our backs and under our arms and followed them. By the time we had staggered and slipped through the mud to the suspension bridge, one of the porters spotted us and came back. I went with him across the river to Ugimba to investigate the cause of their rapid departure. After I had primed myself with a few words of Indonesian, I soon found out. They were simply obtaining sweet potatoes for the rest of the journey and soon returned to pick up our equipment.

Ugimba was high enough for the morning to be cool. We were surrounded by little children, huddling themselves to keep warm. Two women were weaving net from bark, to make carrying bags. They still had enough finger ends to do it; often of necessity it was a man's job. They paused to touch Hilary's long hair – she was probably the first European woman they had seen.

Our eyes, accustomed to scanning the open spaces of mountains and networks of city streets, could barely discern the minor track we were now to follow. If we had been left alone, we would still be there. The porters, however, managed the terrain with the air of detached confidence of a London commuter on his way to work. The tall Dani from Wanibugi seemed eager to demonstrate his local knowledge and jungle mastery to us and the Monis, and he set off at a half run. "We'll give him a heavy load tomorrow," said Hilary as it started to rain. We bent double through the undergrowth and waded and crawled through the murky waters of a stream for hundreds of yards.

We were heading into a deep, vegetated box-canyon, with thousand-foot walls. How were we going to reach the plateau from here, we wondered? The Dani sprinter started climbing up a wall of vegetation that made us gasp. When we followed him we found a hidden staircase of holds clipped and scraped out of the network of roots and mud. With the weight of thirteen of us on it, the tree ladder trembled. We forgot the rain and did not notice the leeches between our fingers until we reached the top.

It was like popping over the top of a crag climb in England. We breathed with sudden relief as we reached the horizontal. Our eyes adjusted from the darkness of the forest. The sense of space was exhilarating after the jungle prison. At last we were able to walk a few steps without tripping and slipping. Outcrops of white carboniferous limestone hinted at the mountains far ahead. But we could see little of the future, for the plateau appeared and disappeared in swirling mist. However, the view opened out below, and a general discussion began as to which way we had come, and as to where we had crossed the ridges the day before. The porters had found their way through the jungle without discussion, but the total picture of their route from this airy viewpoint was hotly disputed.

The rain only collected in a few places on the porous plateau, and we worried that the porters would stop far from a water supply that night. Sweet potatoes seemed to provide them with most of their fluid, for they rarely drank, whilst we were always thirsty. However, they found a lean-to shelter not far from a spongy spring. Within minutes they had their bivouac organised, with the roof mended and a fire crackling. The height gain had brought a sharp drop in temperature and some wind. Wrapped in warm woollen clothes, we sat around the porters' fire and opened our damp, smudged cards.

We were ten hours ahead of the festivities at home. Instead of opening Christmas presents, we were protecting our belongings from the rain. Life was a perpetual opening and closing of polythene bags. Outside frogs croaked in unison.

Dawn brought a new world. The sunshine turned the grass to gold and the bushes and cobwebs were fresh with yesterday's rain. We twisted and wriggled through them along the side of a spur until the thin track veered up on to a natural clearing on the crest. From here we could see the line of the scarp cliffs of the Ekabu Plateau, stretching away to the west – its pillars edged sharply in the morning sunlight. I was enthralled by the sight of the high ground. In 1962 Heinrich Harrer exclaimed of the same range, "Everything an explorer ever dreamed of could be satisfied here." He had christened the valley next to our route 'Fairy Tale Valley' and called the lakes in it 'Hansel and Gretel'.

We dropped from the spur and wound across two grassy marshes to reach a limestone pavement. "It's just like the Pennines," said Hilary, busily photographing the clints and grykes, "and higher up there's giant groundsel and lobelia like there is on Mount Kenya and Kiliman-jaro." She was noticing more than I was.

My left knee was becoming painful – I had stretched a tendon in its side. Our tennis shoes were being ripped by the limestone. The porters did not notice the razor-sharp edges. Their feet naturally slotted into the best places, as if they had spent a lifetime practising the route in the dark. Hilary, being of similar size, followed one of them and placed her feet identically. I tripped and stumbled behind.

A natural dry rift, punctuated with caves and sinkholes, cut a swathe across the grain of the high plateau and we realised from the map that this would lead us to the Bakopa Pass at 12,000 ft. The valley retained vegetation but the limestone on either side stretched white and bare. The Monis called the plateau 'Tugapa', comparing it with a flat hairless skull. I savoured the rest when the porters stopped to cook some sweet potatoes.

"Which porter's got the bandages, Hilary? You did the packing." I was not used to things going wrong with myself and was tired and grumpy. I blamed my fatigue on the jungle, and on the two weeks we had spent trailing through Indonesian bureaucracy. Hilary diagnosed my injury as "just New Guinea knee, a well-known missionary complaint." The afternoon rain swept in and the valley seemed endless.

After a quick discussion, the porters stopped, although it was still only early afternoon. We had reached the last water, and so we would have to wait until morning before committing ourselves to crossing the Bakopa Pass. They split into three groups and used bracken to light smoky fires under rock overhangs.

Perhaps, like the Australian Aborigines, the Papuans have a very efficient system of heat exchange between the outgoing arterial and incoming venous blood in their arms and legs. But physiological advantages were not enough. The temperature was below freezing.

"*Dingin, tuan*" said one of them. It was the first complaint of the cold we had heard. We felt guilty in our down sleeping bags. We lent them all our spare clothes and wished we had brought more. Their teeth and the whites of their eyeballs gleamed in the low firelight. They crooned monotonous chants into the night, and started talking long before dawn.

We never identified the Bakopa Pass, because the path undulated across the plateau. The Dani in the yellow raincoat kept on racing away to the next in the procession of cols. He stood there waiting for us, barking with a mixture of fun and impatience, amid a desert of bare rocks. He had taken off his sunglasses in recognition that the weather was bad. Across the plateau we caught our first glimpse of a giant dark fin of rock scattered with fresh snow – the North Face of the Carstensz Pyramid. It was a very long day before we saw it again.

We were losing height, and the plateau was behind us. At the point where the path began to plunge downwards from the pass stood a wooden platform on poles. Inside was a half-decomposed body. I was curious. Air burial was also practised in Tibet, and many American Indian tribes exposed their dead on scaffolds, because Fire and Mother

Earth were both sacred and so bodies could neither be burned nor buried. The porters said it was a Dani who had died of cold.

The two sprinting Danis started a race downhill and as we limped after them I became increasingly worried that we were losing too much height. I had anticipated a high-level traverse across to the Meren Valley in the midst of the Snow Mountains, but high cliffs barred our way and forced us ever downwards. When we came out of the mountain cloud and looked at the valley to the south, my heart sank to my muddy feet.

We were seeing the most extreme cultural confrontation in the world. One thousand feet below we saw great white buildings blocking the narrow neck of the valley, beyond the dull green swamp which we knew from our map to be the Carstensz Meadow. We could hear the hum of generators and the sporadic roar of giant earth-moving machines. High floodlights pierced the mist like alien eyes. It was the Freeport copper mine – Ertsberg. We had not realised it was so big and so near the mountains and that our approach would be so close.

Army patrols! Surat Jalans! Detection! Arrest! We stumbled and ran in near panic, trying to stop the porters from being seen. It became apparent that to reach the mountains we would have to pass within eight hundred yards of the high wire fence that surrounded the mine. I wanted either to rush up into the mountains immediately, or to wait in hiding until nightfall. However, most of the porters were out of sight, unaware of our worries, and the remainder were struggling far behind. We caught up with the front runners at the foot of the hill, at a little bivouac hut improvised out of corrugated-iron salvaged from the mine.

The two porters who wore shorts had produced shirts out of the depths of their string bags, and were dressing. They announced that they and two others were doing down in the cable car to Tembaga-pura, the mining town far below the copper mine, Ertsberg, to obtain some food. Their sweet potatoes were 'habis' – finished. It was beyond their comprehension that we wanted to avoid a visit to Tembagapura, a town full of people of our race and colour. Apprehensively, we watched the four figures cross the two swamps and two rivers to the first outbuildings of the mine. By this time the remaining seven porters had arrived. We told them to stay inside the bivouac hut.

An hour later the two clothed porters returned with instructions from a 'Commandant' that we were to pack up all our things and to come across to the mine immediately. I pretended not to understand the message.

"The other two must be being kept as hostages," said Hilary. "If we go over there we'll be arrested and thrown out of Indonesia." Once again, we told everyone to stay put.

The hide and seek manoeuvring forced a new initiative from the Commandant. Two figures left the mining perimeter and came towards us – soldiers with guns. Hilary and I, as well as the porters, became very agitated.

"You stay here with the gear and the porters. If we all go down there we'll never get back. I'll go across and talk to them," I said to Hilary.

I met the soldiers when they were a third of their way from the mine. One of them was the Commandant himself. He had dark, curly hair, a moustache and wore a green uniform, and smiled with the panache of a South American bandit. They seemed to be friendly. The Commandant spoke a little English. I told him that we were just walking in the mountains and had no intention of visiting or going near the mine. He asked to see our Surat Jalans and glanced over them. I was calm now, and wondered if he would discover our guilt. I looked at his face for the change in mood when he saw the indicting 'no mountaineering' clause that had been written in by the security authorities in Jayapura. Either he did not see it, or he misunderstood, for he said nothing about it. But I could not be sure. He offered lodgings inside one of his guard huts. Politely, but insistently, I declined. He insisted that the porters spend the night there and ordered the sergeant to accompany me back to the camp-site and to wait there until 6.00 p.m., when it grew dark. I returned to Hilary under armed escort. She thought we were being arrested and I thought we might be. The sergeant dispatched all the porters across to the mine, firing his rifle wildly into the air as if trying to provoke them to stampede.

Hilary and I entertained the sergeant until dusk, plying him with cups of tea. We were uneasy about him and did not trust the casual way with which he fingered his rifle. We told him that we wanted the porters back early in the morning, and would he make sure they were released? At 6.00 p.m. we heard a rifle shot from the mine and, turning to go, the sergeant fired some answering bullets towards the mountains. "My Commandant is very stupid," he said, and he winked.

"What a cowboy," muttered Hilary after he had gone.

I woke at two in the morning, thinking it was dawn. It was not the sun, but the floodlights of the mine, casting a yellow light across the valley and turning night into day. Instead of the chatter of the Monis, I could hear the throb of motors.

Hilary and I were packed and ready to move by 6.15 a.m. We had no idea how long the walk up the Meren Valley into the mountains would take – our sense of scale was deceived by the cloud and by the size the mountains had assumed in our longing imaginations. At 7.30 a.m. there was still no sign of the porters.

"What if the police have taken them all down to Tembagapura," said Hilary. "We may never see them again!"

I went across to the mine to investigate. Two hundred yards away, behind a wire fence thirty feet high, white men sat astride great caterpillar-tracked, ground-eating machines. But before I could make contact with them, I was greeted by the Commandant from the door of the hut. The interior walls were covered with graffiti and pictures of Javanese beauties. Four booted soldiers sprawled across bunk beds and an electric fire glowed in one corner. In the other, huddled together, were our porters; they had crushed themselves into a tiny space and were a sea of worried upturned faces. They were silent and their eyes were startled and constantly moving, as if they had been cornered in a manhunt. I tried to encourage them with a smile, but they did not even flicker with recognition. They were thousands of years away from the carefree laughing, hooting and barking of the previous days.

"Have the Monis eaten anything?" I asked.

"Who? Oh – these people?" Yes, they had.

I counted the heads. Ten. Where was the eleventh? He had gone down to Tembagapura with the sergeant and would be back about 10.00 a.m. Then the Commandant ordered all the porters out of the hut, and they stood outside in a group, shivering from the sudden change in temperature. He offered me apples, cake and tea, but I was anxious to return to Hilary and tell her of the latest developments. He insisted that he came with me, put on a dark beret, immaculate white gloves and his pistol belt, and appointed two of the porters to accompany us.

The Commandant was very unfit and complained constantly of the cold; he stopped every twenty paces and rubbed his hands together. "It ees warm at my home in the Moluccas," he explained. The morning sun was moving on to us but failed to warm him. He contrasted strangely with the two naked porters, but was too preoccupied to notice it himself. Four hundred yards away from his hut, he admitted that he had never been this far from the mine before. The walk took a long time, and Hilary came to meet us, unable to stand the strain of waiting.

"I think it's O.K.," I whispered. I gave her a green apple – her favourite fruit.

The Commandant was amazed to see the shelter, and warmed himself by the fire. Then he started writing an official document.

"What's he writing?" whispered Hilary. "A parking ticket?"

"Zees my address – now you take photos of me and send in letter." He put his arm around Hilary "You don't mind?" he asked, flashing a smile. I took a photo. Then he put his arm around me and Hilary took a photo. We all wore fixed grins.

At 9.30 a.m. all eleven of the porters came over from the mine. They had obtained some cooked rice from Tembagapura and were carrying it, wrapped into tin-foil packages. The sergeant with his rifle trailed far behind them. Thirty minutes of baffling uncertainty ensued. The porters refused to go any further. Hilary had grown to trust and respect them deeply, and their sudden reversal in behaviour shocked her. She lost her temper. She pulled all the loads out of the shelter and shouted at them to go away – she and I would carry the gear into the mountains ourselves. I asked her to calm down, telling her that porters always go on strike from time to time – it was traditional. The Commandant, impressed by Hilary's anger, decided to take over on our side. "Excuse me, speak little English, I speak Indonesian with zeeze men. I tell them Christus says they must help you."

After five minutes we learnt that it was all a misunderstanding. The porters were demanding ten thousand rupiahs for food. Such was our communications problem. I had told them days before that they would receive two thousand each when we reached Base Camp. All seemed settled, and Hilary stormed off across the marsh of the Carstensz Meadow whilst I agitatedly dispatched porters off after her. I thanked the Commandant for his help but it was a relief to move away from his jurisdiction and out of sight of the mine.

We climbed up into the hanging valley of the Meren, beneath steep limestone walls two thousand feet high. These slopes had been climbed in 1936, by the Dutch explorers Colijn and Dozy, after they had penetrated the southern jungle from the coast. The two men had found untracked, virgin ground. Forty-two years later we were following a muddy path flanked by boulders on which had been sprayed Indonesian graffiti. Rounding a corner, we came face to face with a human skull perched on top of a pole – a forceful reminder that we were in New Guinea.

"They must come up here from the mine for Sunday afternoon picnics," said Hilary. "I can see a glacier."

In the distance, part of the snow cap swept gently down into the Meren Valley, along the backs of the steep north walls of the range. It was a desolate place. We walked along fresh moraines. There was no vegetation. We passed two of the three lakes which gave the valley its Dutch name. Beside the third lake we found four big oil drums, left by the Melbourne University scientific expeditions of December and January, 1971/72 and December – February, 1972/73. The porters stopped. A brisk wind blew across the camp-site and it started to hail.

We had decided to keep two of the Monis, Fones and Ans, with us. Since the Base Camp was on a trading route from the north over the only gap in the ice cap -- the New Zealand pass -- we did not want to risk leaving our equipment unguarded whilst we went climbing. We also hoped that keeping two would ensure that their friends returned to carry our equipment back to Bilorai. We wanted the rest of the porters to wait for us south of the mountains for seven days before rejoining us. Communicating the plan was a difficult task. I counted by sticking my fingers up, whilst the Monis brought their fingers down across their palms. Eventually I tied seven knots in a string and told them to untie one as soon as they woke each morning. Now Hilary and I took a turn to feel hungry. We watched them eat their packed lunches, fingering the rice out of the foil and sheltering from the hail behind their pandanus-leaf coats.

Before leaving, two of the Monis picked old tins from the ground and rushed up to the glacier with our ice axes, returning with the tins full of large lumps of ice. Then they all hurried back down the valley, leaving the four of us to settle into our Base Camp. Fones and Ans were to make daily ritual of this ice-collecting, continually replenishing the stock whilst we were in the mountains. Some Irian tribes call ice 'white arrow', because of its sharpness, whilst perhaps the Monis associated the white ice with the white fat of their pigs, or with salt, but for whatever reason it held an enduring fascination until it melted.

To us, the Snow Mountains of New Guinea were the most inaccessible mountains in the world – and yet our first impression on arriving in their midst was that they also had the most rubbish. For fifty feet in all directions were strewn mounds of tins, broken glass and old pieces of green canvas. It was like an industrial waste dumping ground. Owing to their scientific character, the Melbourne University expeditions had won the co-operation of the mining authorities, and their camp had been serviced by air-drops and helicopters from Tembagapura. However, the helicopters had not made the last trip to take the expeditions' debris away. The contrast between such carelessness and the scientific discipline of their book, which displayed an intense ecological concern for the area was bewildering. I spent two hours clearing up the mess and putting it into the oil drums. The drums were full of rain water and melted snow, and when I emptied one of them a large drowned rat fell out.

"There are supposed to be marsupial cats and rats the size of sheep around here," said Hilary. "This rat must be a young one."

Fones and Ans were soon settled in, wrapped in many layers of clothing and cocooned in bivouac bags. Hilary and I went on an orientation walk on to the ridge between the Meren Valley and its parallel depression, the Yellow Valley. To the north the snow fields were wreathed in mist and we guessed where they crested before the plunge of the north walls on the other side. We estimated where the New Zealand Pass was, but then its narrow rocky defile appeared to prove us wrong. It was a deep dark slice out of the iced cake of the glaciers.

To the south, pillars of mist filed down the Yellow Valley. Segments of a mountain slid in and out of view. Soon we had pieced together its picture. The Carstensz Pyramid was before us and nothing else mattered.

4

CARSTENSZ

28th – 29th December, 1978

In London in March, 1920, a paper entitled 'The Opening of New Territories in Papua' was read before the Royal Geographical Society. As the speaker, E. W. Pearson-Chinnery, droned on, one member of the audience, a Mr. A. F. R. Wollaston, became increasingly agitated. Wollaston knew as much about the interior of New Guinea as any other European at that time, and he did not agree with Pearson-Chinnery's opinions. Wollaston was one of the last of the great explorers of the Victorian Empire tradition – a scientist, a diarist and a leader, who recorded all the minute details his boundless curiosity and powers of observation could discern. Yet Wollaston was also a prophet and an idealist, with the rare gift of being able to sense the future consequences of exploration, and the damage and the exploitation that would follow. When Pearson-Chinnery finished speaking, Wollaston could contain himself no longer. He stood up and protested, making what was to be his final statement about New Guinea:

Mr. Chinnery objects to inter-tribal warfare. Well, we have spent many years in killing each other, at great expense, to make the world free for democracy . . . he says we must alter – modify – their traditions (institutions, I think is the word) so that they may 'fall into line with the needs of progress'. I hope this modifying of institutions will be very slow. You have in New Guinea the last people who have not yet been contaminated by association with the white races. They have an extraordinarily interesting culture of which we know very little, and we have much to learn from them . . . I believe that the whole of the interior of New Guinea should be kept as a vast ethnological museum, a native reserve where these people can live their own life, and work out their own destiny, whatever it may be. Into that country no traders, no missionaries, no exploiters, not even Government Police themselves should be allowed to go . . . Perhaps it is an impossible dream, but I am looking ahead through two or three more centuries, and the example of the fate of the Tasmanians and the present

54

condition of the aboriginal Australian native ought to be a sufficient warning.

Wollaston had pioneered a way from the Arafura Sea to the South Face of the Carstensz Pyramid in 1913. Ironically his reports were the basis of exploration which eventually culminated in the 1970s in the largest economic undertaking in Irian Jaya – the exploitation of the Ertsberg mine, and the growth of Tembagapura – 'copper town' – just to the south, where two thousand people now live. It had taken Wollaston ninety-two days to cover the last thirty-one miles to the mountain. Now, a few miles to the west of Wollaston's route, a road runs from the coast to service town and mine. This road is the longest in Irian Jaya. It took three years for it to be bridged and tunnelled through the jungle to the mountains, using massive earthmoving equipment, trucks, large helicopters and huge amounts of explosives. The Free Papua Movement and economic demand permitting, the Freeport Mining Scheme will continue for another thirty years, until the ore is exhausted – dramatic proof that Wollaston's dream was, indeed, impossible.

After Wollaston, the interior of Irian defended itself from the outside world until the 1930s when pilots in small amphibious aircraft began to explore and map the main valleys. When Hilary and I were planning our route on the South Face of Carstensz we consulted the first photographs of the area taken by the Dutch Lieutenant, J. F. Wissel, while making reconnaissance flights in an S-38 for Colijn's 1936 expedition. The Dutch failed to climb the Carstensz Pyramid, but did discover the unique copper node at Ertsberg, the largest above-ground outcrop of base metal ore in the world.

On his various reconnaissance flights Wissel reported the presence of a large native population and the people called his plane 'the roaring prow'. No Western explorer has ever discovered a substantial area of habitable land that is not already inhabited.

In the wake of the flyers came the missionaries, setting up a network of missions to the north of the Snow Mountains in the 1950s, and after the missionaries came the mountaineers.

The Carstensz Pyramid had a Gothic splendour. Mist, rain and hail increased its remoteness and inhospitality – and accentuated its size. Hilary and I were never to see it subdued beneath a strong sun and lost beneath the expanse of an open blue sky. Its North Face comprised large, monolithic blue-grey slabs of steeply tilted limestone bedding. We identified the easiest line up the wall, where Philip Temple and the Austrian mountaineer, Heinrich Harrer, had led their team when they made the first ascent of the mountain in 1962. They had followed a ramp that stretched up to the West Ridge, and then made a lengthy traverse along the ridge to the summit.

Between 1971 and 1974 the Carstensz Pyramid was visited by five different expeditions, most of them approaching the mountains from the north-west along the path found by Temple from Ilaga. The original route up the mountain was straightened out with an approach to the West Ridge nearer to the summit. This route was repeated three times, the East Ridge was climbed and the North Face was criss-crossed with four new routes. This face obviously offered some superb climbing, but Hilary and I wanted to tread on new ground.

It had been a copy of a letter from Bruce Carson, to Hermann Huber of a 1974 Munich expedition, that had first drawn our attention to the South Face. Carson, a brilliant young American rock climber, had climbed the Pyramid three times in 1973, but had been killed in the Himalayas in 1975. He had written:

> The best climb yet to be done is the South Face. It would be a major undertaking, however. If you were going to try it, it would be good to climb the easiest northern route first, to have the descent memorised, and to get a look at the hanging glacier and schrunds near the top to the climb. Also, I'm not sure how one can get down to the base of the Face. It might be possible to cross the ridge at the notch between the Pyramid and Wollaston Peak and then descend to the foot of the Face. We didn't get to that notch, so I'm not sure if it would work. If it doesn't work, then it's a very long way around either side – several days. The South Face is definitely a challenging objective.

As Hilary and I looked across the tail of the Carstensz Glacier, we could see the notch which Carson had referred to. We tried to memorise the route to it across scree and glacier, so that we could start our approach to the route in the dark.

Back at Base Camp we scanned the two aerial photographs we had of the Face – Wissel's of 1936 and one taken by Richard Muggleton as part of the Melbourne University project. The 'eternal snow' of the 1936 Dutch book title had shrunk. It was like looking at two different mountains. In 1936 the whole Face had been plastered by a huge, hanging glacier, but in 1972 the glacier had receded, buttresses projected from it and its icefalls looked more complex. It was now seven years since the last photograph had been taken, and we had seen no clues as to the state of the southern side in our view from the north. It was like discussing the dark side of the moon from a couple of satellite photographs.

Since we would only have a week among the mountains we allowed ourselves just that first afternoon's walk to orientate ourselves. There was no time to climb the easiest route up the Pyramid first so as to become familiar with the descent as Carson had suggested, or to do a

SNOW MOUNTAINS OF NEW GUINEA

Bilorai

Ugimba

Kemabu Plateau

Dugundugu North Face

Sunday Peak
(Ngga Pulu)

Meren Glacier

New Zealand Pass

Bakopa Pass

base camp

Meren Valley

Carstensz Glacier

Fairytale Valley

Mine

summit

Carstensz Pyramid

Yellow Valley

Carstensz South Face

- - - - extent of glaciers in 1936

training climb to acquire a feel for the area. We decided to start early the next day for the South Face. Overawed by the aloofness of the mountain and by the seriousness implicit in Carson's letter, we selected our equipment carefully.

Fones and Ans looked puzzled as we sorted out our bivouac equipment and the hardware of crampons, ice hammers, screws, nuts, pegs and karabiners. They coughed a lot during the night, their noise combining with the sniffing of a marauding rat to keep me awake.

At 5.30 a.m. we set out into the mist and darkness. Shapes and distances were confusing and our sketch maps were only a rough guide because since they had been drawn the glaciers had obviously melted. I took out my compass and we stumbled towards an occasional glimpse of whiteness in the night, which we knew to be the Carstensz Glacier.

The toe of the glacier was an ice slope, which tilted back at sixty degrees for three hundred feet. We put on the rope and ice gear. It seemed as if our feet had been cloyed in mud for days. Despite the heavy rucksacks we were carrying, we revelled in the clean, balancing movements of front pointing on crampons. As we climbed into the dawn the soft, silted colours of the Yellow Valley beneath the North Face of Carstensz opened out below us; we could see the freshly-ground browns, yellows and reds left by the retreating glacier. It took us half an hour to cross the notch between Wollaston Peak and the East Ridge of Carstensz, and we hoped that the patches of blue that illuminated our walk heralded a clear morning. But all views have to be snatched in Irian, and cloud was rushing in again as we reached the notch. The Pyramid's East Ridge swept up on our right side. It was easy angled at first, but soon disappeared into a tangle of cloud-swept towers. Looking to the south we saw a hundred feet of scree vanishing into a cauldron of mist. We took long strides downwards, peering apprehensively for hidden cliffs and thrilled with the prospect of untrodden ground. It was a hundred years since exploratory climbs of this type were done in the Western Alps.

We had chanced upon a cliff-free descent, and lost height rapidly. The mist was so thick that the sudden clearings gave the fleeting insights of an erratic lighthouse – we picked out a prominent boulder, memorised the ground between, and as the mist closed in again, we followed the memory until it faded.

We squinted around, looking for the South Face glacier. According to the most recent photographs, we should have been standing on it. We crossed two great ridges that stuck out of the mountainside like the ribs of a skeleton, following a horizontal break in the strata that cut across them. I glanced over my shoulder and saw, for thirty seconds, the Arafura Sea seventy miles away appear in a cloud window. It glimmered beyond the coast and then the hole closed up.

"Hard luck, Hilary, you've just missed it."

But where was the glacier? I reached the second ridge a few feet ahead of Hilary and for a minute I sucked in the only view of the South Face I was to see all day. It looked blank and forbidding, like an alpine north face in the grip of a summer storm. I tried to describe it to Hilary when she arrived: "There's an enormous amphitheatre of sort of tiered shelves and the glacier's really high up, split into two. At least it doesn't look as if we'll be pegging over soggy ice walls. I couldn't see the top though. We'll just have to guess where the middle is and wander up. It looks really loose."

We zigzagged backwards and forwards, climbing over bulges in between the sloping shelves. Small stones were falling constantly around us from out of the mist, and we put our helmets on. We did not dare tie a rope between us, for fear that it would snag around the large poised rocks and disturb them on top of us. Although we were placing our hands and feet carefully, we occasionally nudged large rocks which bounced and thundered into the abyss below.

"Do you think you can manage that bit, Hilary? I'll climb next to you. Just say if you get gripped or need any help."

"Course I don't."

I wondered what would I say to her Mum and Dad if she slipped? If it were Tasker I'd just let him get on with it and think of myself. What a place to bring her for her Christmas holidays. Why were we climbing this tottering heap instead of those clean, solid slabs of the North Face?

The sky was baptising us in the masochistic Irianese art of climbing in the rain – water was pouring down, loosing more and more stones on to us. After two hours of steady climbing we reached the two ice slopes. We followed the thin ribbon of rock between them until it petered out. We put on our crampons and I set off soloing. It was steep, hard, water ice, and sixty feet up I remembered Hilary.

"Hang on and I'll drop a rope."

After another hundred and fifty feet of steep ice we flopped into the shelter of the bergschrund where the ice terminated beneath a ring of rock overhangs. The rain had turned to sleet and we could hear the wind blow from the north across the ridge a few hundred feet above our heads. We were in the Stalls, and wanted to reach the Circle.

It was like climbing in a recently blasted quarry. An unstable pillar of rock dropped down towards us from the lip of the overhang, like an unwrapped packet of yellow biscuits twenty feet high. Flakes of rock broke off beneath my hands and feet, as I edged gingerly up trying to put my feet on the most stable holds. I breathed carefully, concentrating so as to avoid any sudden movement that could endanger my precarious balance. Moving over the top of the overhang was the crux. Instead of a ledge to heave on to, there was a steep slope of half-frozen sand. I hacked into it with my ice hammer and short ice axe and clawed around the lip, stepping high with my feet. The sand moved as I eased my weight on to my boots and kicked furiously up the slope above for fifty feet, as if I were rushing up a down-moving escalator, my blood warming to the excitement of the action. The debris I dislodged cascaded over the overhang above Hilary and blocked the sky from her like a curtain.

If that had been the Circle, now I was in the Gods. When she arrived, Hilary admired the two-foot-wide ledge I was standing on. It ran continuously across the wall, like a pathway carved out of a limestone cave, so that it could be opened to the general public.

"Oh, what a lovely ledge, a good place for a bivouac," she said.

"We might need one, I can't get past this overhang," I muttered. Although it was only mid-day, we had arrived at an impasse that blocked all hope of continuing directly to the ridge. Ten feet above our heads a smooth, ten-foot-wide overhang stretched into the mist in both directions.

We had nearly reached sixteen thousand feet, and were tiring in the thinning air. Our heavy rucksacks had become unwelcome partners inhibiting our movements. I left mine with Hilary, sitting on the ledge, and sidestepped like a crab, into the murk, to make a solitary reconnaissance. The shelf petered out into a shattered rib of rock. I stepped round this into a wide chimney that split the obstacle of the overhang. I wriggled up the chimney until I could see the ridge, shouting: "We're there. We're there!" I returned to Hilary, picked up my sack and we climbed up the chimney together.

The wind across the ridge quickly pierced through our sodden clothes. We lay down and peered cautiously over the edge of the north side. Flurries of hail and sleet blew into our eyes and made us duck. The world beneath was divided from us by hours of mountain. Through scudding cloud we could glimpse patches of the Yellow Valley, two thousand feet below. I felt giddy at seeing the drop, for the thicker mist of the south side had cushioned our previous downwards view.

"Are we on the top then?" asked Hilary.

"I don't know, I think so," I replied. But we were not. Higher towers of rock taunted us on our left, in the west. We peered for a long time along the ridge to the right, trying to extract rock images from the moving cloud, until we were sure there was no point higher than us in that direction. We turned left.

The ridge was as razor sharp as the rock itself, but at least it was stable. Soon the ends of our gloves were torn away. At one awkward step Hilary caught her anorak sleeve and it ripped apart. She cursed the sleeve and rock as if they had plotted the tear, and then cursed the rucksack for pulling her backwards and making her clumsy. She often gave life to inanimate objects, and I told her so.

"Well, I prefer talking to plants, but I can't do that up here," she said, and then confronted me for giving her such a heavy sack to carry.

Our progress along the ridge was halted by a deep gap. I failed to climb down and across it. We had to retrace our steps back along the ridge and down the chimney into the comparative shelter of the South Face. At two o'clock that afternoon we were back on the shelf of the Gods at exactly the same place we had been two hours before. The good progress of the morning had been lost.

The remaining hours of daylight began to tick away in my head like a metronome. This time we traversed left, westward along the shelf. I yelled at Hilary for not trying to climb more quickly, left her again and soloed off on another reconnaissance. I was becoming angry with Hilary, the mountain, the rain and wind and myself. I tried to rationalise and to channel my frustration into energy. I moved faster and faster, alone in a private world of mist and rock. "Why does she always seem to move so slowly when the going gets rough? Why do I shout at her and long for an equal? I'd never do that to any other climbing partner – it's unfair, it's not that serious a situation. But I don't want to spend a night out in this and we must get a move on. What if the summit really was to the east? What if we're going the wrong way up?"

I followed the shelf beneath the gap that had turned us back on the ridge's crest. The ground began to open out and I spotted a line of ramps and gullies leading out of the South Face and on to the ridge. I returned and collected Hilary and my rucksack. We dumped our expensive ice screws in a symbolic attempt to shed some of our loads and set off again.

We regained the ridge beyond the obstacles of major gaps and towers. The rising crest indicated that we were climbing in the right direction. I raced out ropelength after ropelength, towing Hilary behind. Every time she stopped I took a photograph of her, which infuriated her. If she could spare a hand she put it on her hip and shouted into the sleet: "Don't take photographs of me looking like this, my face is all puffy with the altitude," and "Stop bullying me and treating me like a sack of coal – let me climb it properly." She could not hear my replies because her anorak hood was drawn tight against the wind.

A wooden pole lying on the ridge was the first evidence of the summit. We soon found other relics. We opened two rain-drenched tins and found soggy notes from the 1974 Munich climbers and

Carson's party the year before. There were little flags of New Zealand and Indonesia in a polythene bag, and inside a plastic film container were locks of hair. In the mist these were the only signs that we sat on the summit. "Just think, you're the only bird that's been up here, and there's no one higher than us from the Andes to the Himalayas."

"Except in planes," she said. They were brief moments of relaxation. It was 3.00 p.m. and in two and a half hours it would be dark.

I tried to goad her into hurrying. "Come on, Hilary, pull yourself together, an hour's effort will make the difference between a night out up here or not. You don't want to sit up here for twelve hours in the wind and rain, do you?" My tone was deliberately unpleasant.

Our descent of the West Ridge was checked by a forty-foot-deep cleft. It was too steep to climb down on our side. Then Hilary noticed an aluminium nut and nylon sling in a crack – it was a reassuring signpost that we were coming down the normal route up the mountain. We doubled the rope, passed it through the sling and abseiled into the bottom of the cleft.

"I'll go down a bit further and have a look," I said. I threw the rope down again and slid a hundred feet down the wall of the North Face. I stopped and became a gently swaying pendulum, surrounded by moving mist. Screwing up my eyes, I looked into the gloom beneath my feet. Four hundred feet below I saw the reddish blur of a sandy ramp, cutting diagonally downwards across the Face. It was our descent route, but this was not the way to reach it. I hauled my way back up the ropes and rejoined Hilary. We climbed out on to the lower lip of the cleft, and continued down the crest, soon arriving at the point where the top of the ramp met the West Ridge.

The ramp was filled with fine scree. Hilary suddenly started moving more quickly. Eager to lose height, we half ran down, digging our heels in. Within twenty minutes we had dropped nearly a thousand feet. Then the ramp stopped and the rock slabs of the North Face curved away convexly, concealing from us a view of the valley floor. The slabs were scored by shallow channels and water was sheeting down them, turning them into a steep weir.

"Come on, let's go straight down," said Hilary. "It can't be far." Facing inwards, she started soloing down one of the water runnels.

Worried, I clambered after her, thinking that she was becoming over-confident and accident prone. Water was pouring down our sleeves. I feared the rock would be slippery, but it remained rough and clean despite the deluge.

"Let's stop and abseil," I said. "It'll be safer."

Three times we slid down hundred-and-fifty-foot ropelengths until our feet touched gentle ground. We were safe. We would not have to bivouac.

"I never realised you could get so angry," said Hilary.

Within minutes it became totally dark. We realised how wet we were. My head torch failed to work and the darkness was so dense that Hilary's torch was not strong enough to light the way across the boulders for both of us at the same time. I took it, walked twenty feet and shone the light back for Hilary. Stop. Go. Stop. Go. The rain pelted across the beam of the light and the distance to Base Camp stretched beyond our imagination.

"*Tuan!*" Fones and Ans sounded happy to hear the clinking of our hardware as we walked into the camp. That night even the rat did not wake me up.

5

DUGUNDUGU

30th December 1978 – 1st January, 1979

We spread out our equipment with ceremony. It was a great event. We had climbed the Carstensz Pyramid, the sun was shining and we hoped that our equipment and clothes would be dry, for the first time since we had entered the interior of Irian Jaya. It was our first rest day since the tide in our fortunes turned in Jayapura ten days before. We discussed the weather – it seemed to be getting better, and perhaps we might now have alternate good days. However, we spoke too soon, for the sunshine was a brief respite. The early morning wind picked up cloud and rain, and we scuttled about packing everything away again. The gear was still damp for our next adventure.

A wild dog came up the Meren Valley to investigate our arrival, and howled at us. The retreating glaciers of the Snow Mountains had left our camp surrounded by bleak, recently exposed screes and gaunt moraines. It was an inhospitable place, and we wanted to move on.

On New Year's Eve we set out to explore the northern side of the mountains, where the highest cliffs of the range rise out of the tussocky grass of the Kemabu Plateau. Fones and Ans did not want to go with us and preferred to stay at Base Camp. Hilary and I left on our own, carrying enough food for two and a half days, and all our climbing equipment.

To reach the path up to New Zealand Pass, it was necessary to retrace a few hundred yards of our approach route. We walked around a corner and suddenly came face to face with five Indonesians, dressed in yellow industrial jackets and wellington boots. My first reaction was that they were an army patrol sent to arrest us. Our paranoia at encountering officialdom at the mine had not worn off. It was too late to avoid them, so we smiled as if to imply the normality of our being there. They were startled but friendly, and said they were going for a New Year's Eve picnic.

In Wissel's aerial photographs in 1936, New Zealand Pass did not exist, for it was still choked with ice, and the snow cap of the mountains stretched around in an unbroken horseshoe to the Carstensz Pyramid. When Temple found the pass in 1961, however, it had probably been ice-free for about ten years, and was already used by the natives from the north and south on hunting and trading trips. At 14,764 ft. (4,500 m.), it is the highest pass in New Guinea.

It was an impressive canyon, and the prospect of new country lightened our steps as we crossed it. Now without our Moni guides, we could explore the land ourselves. We felt privileged to be there.

At the highest point of the pass, on the path in front of us, was a ring of nine small stones, carefully arranged inside another large ring about two feet in diameter, of eighteen stones. We looked around and saw a human skull on a rock, peering hollowly at us. We had heard that in 1976 twenty-three natives had frozen to death in a storm whilst crossing the pass – perhaps this ritual arrangement was a symbolic remnant or plea for the benevolence of their ghosts.

The wealth and curiosity value of the mine had certainly increased the amount of travel over the mountains during the 1970s. As we descended the northern side of the pass we met three tiny men and two boys, wearing only kotekas and carrying bows and arrows. They were coming up to the pass, having travelled from Beoga, a settlement to the north of the mountains. They greeted us by pulling our fingers, and hastily produced a typed Surat Jalan, which we guessed had been prepared by a missionary. We looked at it, although we could not understand it. We gave them a sweet each and watched, worried for them, as they threaded up into the cold mists that were now building up on the mountains.

There was something lemming-like about this vulnerability to the allure of Western curiosities, that caused people to walk into such a dangerous place, naked and unprepared. It seemed an attraction they could never be inoculated against. When Wollaston was approaching the mountains from the south coast in 1913, he had received daily visits from hill people, come to investigate the strange sights they had heard about. As he neared the mountains, he found many dead huddles of them – forty in total – who had run out of food on the return journey or succumbed to the cold. He was puzzled, because they did not appear emaciated, and concluded that they must have just given up and died.

Below us we could see Lake Larson, named after the American missionary at Ilaga who had been met by the expeditions of the early 70s when they approached the mountains from the airstrip there. Our first priority was to find a boulder to bivouac under, for we had left the tents at Base Camp. We knew that near the lake there was a huge erratic block – the Mapala Boulder – which many expeditions from Ilaga had used as a Base. This was a traditional bivouac, for the Melbourne University had found evidence in the remnants of cowrie shells, fire and bones there that suggested man has traded and hunted wallaby and echidna on the plateau for between three and five thousand years, and eaten and slept under the shelter of the boulder. However, it was at too low an altitude for our purposes, and we contoured eastwards under the vast three-thousand-foot north walls of the three summits of Ngga Pulu. The walls were a dramatic contrast to the rolling snows of their other side, and rose out of the gently undulating Kemabu Plateau with the ninety degree abruptness of sea cliffs. My eyes were increasingly drawn to the crags, searching for possible lines of climbable weakness, and neglecting the discipline of the boulder search.

Hilary found a boulder before I found a possible route. It was an ideal bivouac with a jutting roof that would provide enough shelter to keep the rain out, and a little spring running out from underneath it. There were the tracks of wild dogs nearby, so we placed our food and equipment under heavy stones before going on a reconnaissance.

As we were about to leave, we heard the metallic soaring clatter of a helicopter overhead. Instinctively, we dived back under the rock, ducking like Vietcong evading an airborne gunship. We soon realised how unlikely it was that we were being pursued – the helicopter was probably surveying for the mine, or taking Freeport executives on a New Year's Eve sightseeing trip. Nevertheless, it seemed best to stay out of sight. Twice the helicopter swept backwards and forwards, along the base of the cliffs, then disappeared over New Zealand Pass as suddenly as it had arrived. Its whirring engines echoed for a few moments, and then the sound died away.

Owing to the constantly shifting patchwork of mist, it had taken us until now to become familiar with the topography of the mountains. They were laid out like a rectangle with an open end in the west – the Meren Valley, up which we had come initially with the porters. Base Camp was in the middle. The bottom south line with the Carstensz Pryamid and the north line was interrupted by New Zealand Pass. Glaciers sloped down towards Base Camp from north and east lines, and six miles of vertical cliffs plunged down on their other sides – under which we now stood. The highest of the three summits of Ngga Pulu, Sunday Peak, was on the top corner, where the north and east lines met. It was the North Wall of this that we wanted to climb.

Reinhold Messner compared these North Walls to the Civetta, and they looked as awe-inspiring as any Dolomite cliff. They were broken into several complex towers by steep gullies down which ice from the snow cap occasionally fell. The walls had been climbed previously in only three places, and there were countless other tempting possibilities. But we never saw the complete face in the mist and teeming rain. We sat under our boulder and watched lightning flash down a valley to the east, brewing a huge storm that moved towards and over us. It was like being in the Ark.

"Happy New Year." My attitude clarified, and at ten minutes past midnight I said: "I think this weather's trying to tell us something."

Immediately, Hilary advocated strongly that, instead of the Sunday Peak wall, we should attempt one of the two pillars on the North Face of Dugundugu – the mountain immediately west of New Zealand Pass. "At least we might get up it," she said.

Towards morning the rain slackened and shafts of sombre light broke through the leaden clouds and chased them away towards the west. We left in the half-light, and by the time the sun lit up the backcloth of mountains I had seen enough of Sunday Peak to confirm the decision against an attempt. Dugundugu looked much more tempting. After picking up the cache, we once more sorted out the gear, sifting a different selection for the new objective. This time we did not take bivouac equipment, thus committing ourselves to having to climb the mountain or retreat before nightfall. It was a serious step, and Hilary re-plaited her pigtails in preparation for a hard day.

We gained as much height as possible on the path up to New Zealand Pass, and then traversed across. The North Face of Dugundugu was divided by a great chasm into two pillars, 1,600 ft. high. At the base of this chasm we could see the blue gleam of the ice cap on the other side of the mountain. Dugundugu was the Danis' word for snow mountain – but it was the glacier on the other side of the mountain that gave it the name. The North Face was all rock. The right-hand pillar seemed the more feasible climbing proposition. Its bands of overhangs were split by a long crack which, in the morning sunshine, appeared to be a fabulous line – a clear solution to an improbable buttress. The first two hundred feet looked the most difficult.

We crossed the bed of the chasm and gained a hundred feet of height by unroped scrambling. Hilary anchored herself to a large flake of rock on the edge of the pillar and admired the view. Loops of rope swung down into the abyss. I started climbing, breathing deeply. I had bought some new boots for the expedition, and this was the first steep rock climbing I had done with them. I tested them, balancing on little toeholds. The rock felt familiar. It was, I told myself, just another limestone rock pitch, like carboniferous limestone anywhere – steep, loose, with unexpected pockets and too many holds to choose from, but none of them big enough. I focused all my attention on it, trying to forget that I was in New Guinea and that Hilary was holding the rope. She was soon out of sight.

I launched myself up the rock, swinging out on to the central edge of the pillar. The rock was cut away below me and there was a drop of a thousand feet beneath my boots. Now, with my nose pressed against the rock, the route was not as obvious as it had seemed from below. The crack did not emerge from the gentle overhanging sweep of rock beside me until it broke through a four-foot-wide horizontal roof, thirty feet above my head. I decided to follow a rib of rock to the roof and hand-traversed right to the crack. I tapped in a piton at eye level, clipped the rope in and balanced up.

For fifteen feet, holds curled under the tips of my fingers. Then the rib became smooth. I hung out from one hand and slipped a tiny wire nut into a thin crack, clipped the rope in and started laybacking, feet and hands pushing and pulling, braced against the rib, drawing nearer and nearer to the roof. I knew it was essential to remain calm and to keep on going. All that existed was myself and a few feet of rock.

My arms were tiring and my fingers were beginning to open out. With one hand I quickly hammered a piton in, hoping to grab it before my strength drained completely. But before I could clip into it I started to sway off backwards, in slow motion. I had levered off the top ten feet of the rock rib and was keeling over with it! I screamed as I fell, pushing myself away from the blocks of rock that were falling with me. Rock blurred past, until I swooped on to the end of rope and the downwards plunge stopped. I was hanging clear, slowly yo-yoing up and down on the stretch of the nylon, and spinning at the same time.

"Are you all right?" shouted Hilary.

Although I was now back on the same level, we could not see each other because of the curve of the pillar. "I don't know, I think so. Must have gone about twenty feet. I'll try and swing back in." I grabbed a projecting spike to stop myself spinning, and pulled myself towards it. "Take the rope in, Hilary, I'm just transferring my weight back on to the rock."

As I did so, the two enormous blocks I had stepped on, and the spike I was holding on to, all detached from the mountain and disappeared below me in a thunderous roar. I slipped again, shrieking with surprise. When my weight hit the rope the strain was too much for the nut runner, which snapped out. I fell another twenty feet, jerking Hilary so hard she let the rope slide another ten feet. A few small rocks fell past me, and then there was silence. I was scratched and bruised and my clothes were torn. It was a long climb back up.

I clipped in the rope to the piton of my previous high point and stood up in a sling. It was better to go straight back up on to the climb than to return to Hilary, lick my wounds, rest and risk second thoughts. I traversed on my hands under the roof and pulled myself over it, bracing palms and elbows across the crack. It was 'off-width' – too wide to handjam, too narrow to wriggle inside, easy to get stuck in, and difficult to move up in – and was caked in mud.

"It's like Right Eliminate at Curbar," I yelled, "bloody desperate and no protection." I panted and heaved, wriggled and pulled, inching slowly upwards. After fifteen feet it became wider, and I scraped some finger holds out of the mud, wrenched myself upwards and sprawled on to a ledge, gasping like a landed fish.

Hilary did not waste time and energy by climbing after me. She just fastened on her jumar clamps and came up on the rope, swinging off on the traversing parts and bouncing up and down like a demented puppet. "I hope that was the hardest bit," she said.

"Well, at least we've got going."

Retreat, we decided, would now be difficult, and the roof and overhanging rocks below us gave an extra incentive to struggle on upwards. We had been so absorbed in our acrobatics that we had not noticed it had begun to drizzle. We donned waterproofs.

Above us the main crack opened up into an overhanging chimney, but by traversing a ledge rightwards I found some easier cracks. I swarmed up them, infused with a sense of abandon after the hard climbing below.

"It's about grade four," I yelled. "You'll love it."

She did. "I enjoy that sort of climbing," she said when she reached me.

The climb was starting to flow. The route-finding was deliciously intricate. Overhangs and bulges barred our way but always there was a way to thread around them. The wall leant back in a shallow corner two hundred feet high, like a half-open book on a great tilted lectern. We pranced up it, savouring the freedom of balancing on tiny, solid incut holds. We were feeling in tune with the rock. Clouds slid beneath our feet, opening windows on the valley floor.

The pillar reared up again and narrowed, squeezing us back into the line of the chimney crack. With one boot on either side of the chimney, we bridged up it. Suddenly, the clouds opened. When the deluge began we were trapped in the largest natural water course of the entire pillar. I dodged under an overhang and tied myself to the rock, taking the rope in as Hilary climbed up towards me. This shelter gave me confidence. I was warming to the excitement of the fight.

"Come on, Hilary – with your Geordie mining blood, you should be enjoying this. We've got enough time! We're going to do it!"

She was hit by a shock-wave of water that almost knocked her off the rock, pouring all over her. She blamed me, tossing her sodden, tangled pigtails out of her eyes as she shouted: "Don't take pictures of me. I hate you."

When she started shivering, I felt guilty that I was drier. We continued up the waterfall, and escaped from the chimney as soon as the pillar allowed. In the alternating cycles of rain, sleet and snow, I soon became as drenched as Hilary.

Like most mountain tops of the world, the summit of Dugundugu was elusive. Every time we stopped on a ledge we ensured it was under an overhang out of the rain, and said "The next pitch must get us there. It'll give in soon." But more of the mountain rose up in front of us.

Faced with a smooth slab, fifteen feet high, covered in water, I balanced five rocks on top of each other and teetered on top of them to reach a hold at full stretch. Such tactics would be seen as cheating on British rock, but I was too wet for ethics. I tiptoed up a blank, leaning corner. The climbing was airy and exhilarating and I was lost in it when the air around me lightened, and then blew across my face. My boots crackled on the fractured limestone of the summit. Ten feet away sloped the glacier of the other side of the mountain. Twenty feet away, sky and snow blended together in whiteness.

The wind bit deep into my elation. Hilary seemed an age arriving and I started a shouting match again, which dissolved when her head popped up over the ridge.

"Sorry I yelled, but it did seem to work," I said.

"Which way now? Left?"

"I suppose so."

"I think Dugundugu means slush mountain."

We sank up to our knees as we wallowed down through the snow and haze until we found New Zealand Pass. We dumped our ropes and hardware to pick up the next day and stumbled down for an hour in the relentless rain, hurrying to find the boulder before darkness fell. On the plateau we tripped over tussocks and splashed across small, shallow lakes that in the morning had been doughy, silted flats. The ground dimmed and we stumbled; in the dusk and cloud, all the boulders looked the same. Hilary found it but it was the last thing she did that day.

"You'll have to cook the tea for once," she said.

It had been a savage New Year's Day.

6

AN IMPOSSIBLE DREAM

2nd – 18th January, 1979

When we saw our Base Camp below in the Meren Valley, we halted in alarm.

"Hey, there's a big white thing next to our tents."

Something or someone had arrived at our Base Camp and I felt a sudden wave of resentment. But the new arrivals were not a threat. They were the Frenchmen, Jean Fabre and Bernard Domenech, with whom we'd been in touch back in Europe. Now we compared notes happily on what Bernard described as the administrative steeplechase of Indonesian bureaucracy. Fones and Ans looked on, playing their bamboo mouth harps. All day it rained and rained.

One day remained before the seven knots in the string Hilary and I had given to our porters would all be undone, and they would soon return to collect us. So we invited Jean and Bernard to join us in a relaxed high altitude wander along the summits of Ngga Pulu.

But next morning, Jean decided to go down to the mine to plead for medical aid. He was complaining of a terrible pain in his shoulder and suspected the wet weather was the cause.

"In the South of France," he said, "the cliffs are warm with sun. I am not used to all this water."

Bernard, however, was still enthusiastic to come with us on the snow traverse. We told Fones and Ans that we would be back in five hours and walked towards the toe of the Meren Glacier. The dawn sun soon became watery behind the mist and sleet. We passed occasional cairns that described the dying glacier's one mile retreat over the previous forty years. Without winters to recoup its strength, it was a mystery how the glacier survived at all.

Pitted across the lower slopes of the glacier were many ponds ten feet in diameter of black, sun-absorbing, ice-eating cryolgae. Scientists have not decided how these growths of specialised bacteria originated. Perhaps they were brought by birds from the nearest ice areas, thousands of miles away. But it is certain they combine with the

71

climate to melt away the tiny remnants of the great ice sheet that once spilled over the Kemabu Plateau from the mountains. We rose into perpetual cloud, ploughed through the slushy snow, and became more lost than a couple of professional guides should admit to, and took in all three summits of Ngga Pulu – including the highest, Sunday Peak – almost by accident. At the third summit we found a short note from the Munich men who'd been there in 1974 and a visiting card in a tin tube – 'Alpine International, Reinhold Messner'. After a long descending traverse we emerged into drizzle below the white blanket of cloud. Having gone into the cloud at one side of the range, we had come out of it at the other.

Next morning our porters bounded up towards us like long-lost friends. Everyone except the two Danis from Wanibugi had returned. Our loads were quickly taken off us and distributed.

Suddenly, two of them sprang off into the mists towards the glacier, in the opposite direction to the homeward journey.

"What on earth are they doing now?"

"It'll be raining soon."

"Not more complications!"

Twenty minutes later the two Monis returned, grinning, and carrying under their arms large chunks of ice.

We met Jean Fabre coming up the path. He had avoided any contact with the police at the mine, and instead had approached some sturdy Australians driving bulldozers, who had stared at him, gaping with disbelief as if he had come from the moon. They quickly ushered him through the Ertsberg mine site and down the cable line to Tembagapura, where an American doctor gave him an analgesic and a luxurious bedroom suite for the night. Although he had been kept hidden, Jean had seen much. He was brimming with stories about the town – its two thousand people, cinema, supermarket, cold beers, showers, tennis courts, restaurants, and a loudspeaker playing Tom Jones singing 'The Green Green Grass of Home'. The people below thought him strange to have come to the mountains and had treated him suspiciously, as if he were slightly mad.

After descending to the Carstensz Meadow, we hurried under torrential rain to the makeshift shelter we had used on the way up. The Monis soon lit a fire and showed us some of their loot from the mine and from the journey they had made whilst we were in the mountains – mainly tin cans and boxes. Inside their string bags were precious smaller objects, wrapped with leaves into bundles. They had brought some food for us too – six big tins of fish, some rice and two packets of biscuits. We seized them greedily, for our food supplies were nearly exhausted, and we were perpetually hungry. Now was not the time to indulge in idealistic objections to the existence of the mine. Because it was there we took advantage of it, just as Jean had done in hurrying down to seek medical help.

There were bursts of laughter from the Monis as they gathered around the fire. I longed to understand what stories Fones and Ans were telling the others about the strange antics of the tuans among the Snow Mountains above. The mine must have seemed even more mysterious to them. What did they conclude from the appearance of apparently inexhaustible supplies of metal, cloth and food? For in this slice of the West amid the wilderness, it made better economic sense to replace rather than repair most equipment. As a result, vast quantities of refuse and unwanted materials were simply moved out of the way and abandoned.

Deprived of explanation, the Papuans tended to see only the most superficial aspects of Western techno-culture, and tried to imitate them. We had read of a number of cargo cults that stemmed from the arrival of the copper mine. There was the man who claimed to be a Messiah and convinced a village group to stop the cultivation of crops in the expectation that unceasing riches would be provided if a key could be found to unlock a stone on the mountain. In 1971, helicopter pilots had reported that villages south of the mountains had built large copies of helicopter pads, presumably so as to attract the flying machines to land and lay wealth like golden eggs.

Looking at the Monis around the fire, we felt very protective towards them and apprehensive about their future.

In that long, first day's walk, we covered ground that had taken two days to cross during our approach to the mountains. The rain stayed away until 4.00 p.m. As we traversed the Kemabu Plateau the wedge-shaped tower of the Dugundugu and the dark mass of the Carstensz Pyramid receded behind us, looking like great heads, their dark North Faces shadowed by the sunlight. All their details of chimney, wall and traverse where we had stretched our ropes and our limbs were hidden from us in their distant bulk.

A snow quail whirred away from amongst us and the Monis seized bows and arrows and split up quickly into different directions like a well-deployed rugby team, trying to fend it off and catch it. They ran, crouching, hundreds of yards over the tussocky grass and limestone pavement as the bird flew unconsciously about, apparently unaware that it was being chased. Its every move caused its pursuers vast expenditures of energy. It stopped on a large bush but flew again as Fones raised his bow, and the arrow skittered across the empty branch. Eventually the snow quail cackled away towards inaccessible crags, and the Monis returned to their loads, laughing with the fun of the chase.

Next day we reached Ugimba – civilisation at last. The sweet potato terraces, huts, smiling children and women in a gentle sunlit breeze were ordered and sane after the ferocity of the jungle. I lay down with my head on my rucksack on a deliciously wide stretch of grass and looked with affection at the leisurely pace of old men, toddling babies and rooting pigs. The brand-new rattan bridge was golden in the afternoon sun and the previously muddy waters of the Kemabu River were blue and smooth.

From our map we recognised the track branching off towards Bilorai. I was keen to follow it, so as to avoid losing height. But the porters refused to go into enemy territory, and insisted that we descend towards their village of Titigi, four hours away.

"Damn their stupid war," I said. "I'm shattered. Now we'll never get to Bilorai today."

As the day wore on the shouting and hooting of the Monis died down as they also became tired. However, we knew that we were nearing their home, because their mirrors emerged from their string bags and they put fresh green grass through their noses. One of them even washed his legs.

The outskirts of habitation brought social demands which slowed our pace down further. Every hundred yards there were neighbours to greet and adventures to relate after over two weeks away from home. The tastes of a freshly-picked lime and a constant supply of sugar cane revived our thoughts of different foods. As we waited for the porters to finish their successive visits to different huts, I lay down with my hat over my face, looking at the fine tracery of twigs and leaves through perspiration eyelets.

We were now in mission-land, and different seeds grew from the earth.

"Titigi" announced Fones.

I asked to buy food and, after we had paid two people, word spread that we were hungry. Soon a pile of jungle greens, bananas, sweet-corn, cabbage, onions and beans appeared. Ans cuddled his little boy and his father appeared – an elderly, straight-backed grandfather with a lovely bright smile. The grandfather started to shell beans for us, and soon five other Monis were helping him.

"They're no different from us, are they?" said Hilary.

Without discussion she did the cooking, whilst I sorted out the clothing and equipment we would give away.

"I think we're just a quiet pair, aren't we?" she said.

"Be careful, released prisoners-of-war have died from over-eating." We stuffed ourselves with food.

The next morning we gave each Moni a little pile of gear: shedding the excess baggage reduced our responsibilities and was a gesture of gratitude to our team. Nothing entrusted to their care had been lost. A large, excitable crowd accompanied us up the hill. The lads were whooping with high spirits, singing, shouting and hooting with laughter. We stopped on the edge of no-man's land and paid them their well-earned cash. Although we had given them much more than the negotiated fee, they seemed quiet and disappointed and their lack of enthusiasm upset and puzzled us.

"A few notes must be an anticlimax after all that time. If only we'd got a lot of smaller notes," I said, "they just don't seem to understand money. Perhaps we should have given them more – oh, I don't know – I mean, in the Himalayas you don't spoil porters, you have a responsibility to travellers who come later; it's not fair to cause inflation and encourage them always to expect more every year. I just don't know whether I can apply the lessons I've learned in the Himalayas here; I mean the Monis are so different, perhaps we ought to encourage them to change as much as possible, or they'll be cheated some day." It was a sad note to our goodbye.

We engaged a group of women and children to help us carry our few belongings to Bilorai. They seemed to revel in their impunity as they crossed the frontier, and declined our offers of gifts for their help. One woman carried our purple rucksack on her head, whilst on her back, in a string bag, she carried her baby wrapped inside a bark cradle. The wizened grandmother carried a green polythene bag full of climbing hardware in one hand, swinging it slightly to the rhythm of her gait. Feeling pink, overclothed and overfed, we followed them up the hill beneath the hot sun. We walked past a group of men working on a hut. One of them sang a lead and all the others answered in chorus. It was a song to greet a return.

The change of diet had been too much for Hilary's stomach. She spent a weepy, wobbly day being sick, listening enviously to me bluffing and bartering with the Monis for string bags, stone axes and cutting tools and a penis sheath. I ran an hilarious instructional seminar on how to put a complicated lightweight tent up, with velcro attachments and tension lines. In return they tried to teach me to light a fire by twirling sticks. I enjoyed my last day with the Monis.

On the 10th January, Pilot Tom flew in out of a showery sky. The little plane tossed about as the jungle spread beneath us. Immediately Bilorai receded into the dimension of a vivid dream, I would never return to the Monis and their mountains. Too many forces seemed poised to change and exploit them. It had taken thousands of years for the Moni society to develop in a stable but precarious balance, but it would take only a few years for it to alter totally. The Himalayas will always call me, but these people, this place, seemed too fragile. This would soon be a land of lost content. A solitary, pure-white bird winged from a tall tree, mimicking our flight. We left it behind.

Forever in my memory would be a bird flying.

At Nabire the circle of our Irian Jaya travels was complete. After the garden serenity of Titigi and Bilorai, Nabire was a bustling colonial boom town. We sat on the beach in the long afternoon sunshine, watching boats unloading a ship. Driftwood, whitened by the sun, and sand-scoured by the wind, lay scattered around us. Little grey crabs scurried like shadows on the sand. We heard the distant babble of young voices, like those of children in a far-off school playground. I realised I had never heard a child cry in the highland villages.

"The Papuans don't seem as dignified with clothes on," said Hilary.

"When in Rome . . ." I said. "I suppose they have to learn to wear them when they deal with the outside world."

"Anyway, I hope they always put their *kotekas* on when they go home – they must be more healthy to wear in the jungle than dirty clothes."

"Well, you don't look as if you've stepped out of the pages of Vogue." Our clothes were torn and stained by the jungle. To me she looked like a princess in disguise. Our eyes met.

A thought had crept up on us, unannounced until now. So happy was the reciprocity between us that we had reached a level of understanding that was no ordinary friendship or sympathy. We came out of the highlands on an upper floor, sharing an eternal secret.

Father Tetteroo seemed to know why I had come to see him. Our conversation was broken, as he nipped away every few minutes to check a loaf he was baking in his oven.

"No," he said immediately. "I cannot marry you. It might lead to many complications with the authorities if I were to marry strangers passing through the town, and marriage requires much preparation. You are not Catholics are you?"

"Well, I just thought I would ask," I said.

Whilst trying to recover from the effort of having asked the question, I changed the subject to the Papuans. I had heard of missionaries attempting to eradicate the old beliefs and superstitions by encouraging the natives to make huge bonfires of charms and fetishes. Did this still happen? Father Tetteroo told me a long story.

"I was living in a village and the people, the men, came to me and said 'Father, we are tiring of all our taboo objects, we want to put them in the past. But we have this churn and nobody dares open it. It has never been opened, and nobody knows what is inside it – perhaps it is a crocodile's testicle. We want you to help us and for you to open the churn for us.' So I said: 'Who do you think I am? I am an ordinary man – you are just as capable of opening it as I am.'

" 'But if we open it,' they said 'many calamities will come to us, the rivers will rise and we shall all be sick. Evil spirits will become angry and destroy us.'

"Of course I still refused to have anything to do with it. Eventually a few of them got together and opened it. And what do you think was inside? Crocodile testicles? No, of course not, I will tell you what was there. It was a beautiful, truly beautiful stone axe. And then the people waited and waited – they were very frightened – but the rivers did not rise. And they asked me 'What shall we do with this axe?'

"And I said 'Well, it is a very beautiful thing, you must put it in the church!' And there it stayed until it disappeared when the Japanese came."

In Biak I went to the telephone exchange. The call bounced off the satellite to my parents' home, thousands of miles away, wavering and fading and becoming strong again.

"Hello Dad, sorry to wake you up . . . in Biak . . . it's an island off the coast of New Guinea . . . Sorry, but it was impossible to send any letters from the interior. We had a great time . . . We're on the way home now – just going to spend a few days in Bali and we're flying from Jakarta on Friday."

Centuries of civilisation have not helped the Balinese become robust enough to survive a few years of tourism. Tour operators harangued our every move and treated us like dollar-distributing idiots, we were pestered by Balinese who performed unnecessary services for us and then asked for payment and, when I photographed a field, ten people of all ages asked me for money. It reminded me sadly of how we had been told that even in New Guinea, Papuan natives in their tribal regalia were now demanding a dollar for a photograph. This was yet to reach west to Irian Jaya.

Passengers queued through the security check of Bali's international airport, struggling with bags full of paintings, carvings and batiks and other souvenirs. The girl on duty found the *koteka* I had bargained for in the hills of Irian Jaya.

"I know where you've been," she smiled.

For a moment I felt proud.

7

BACK FROM THE STONE AGE

19th January – 13th March, 1979

On my return, for a while I responded to things spontaneously without defensive or self-conscious screens. Back with the tap water, television and telephones, I could assess the life around me from new contrasts. I was seeing human beings as one of earth's species for the first time.

Hilary flew straight back to her teaching job in Switzerland, and I spent a few days at my house in New Mills in Derbyshire before driving back to Leysin.

In Paris I stayed with friends, Vincent and Marie Renard, who live near the Eiffel Tower. When I walked into the flat, I was surprised to meet Jean Fabre and Bernard Domenech, who had arrived a few hours before from Jakarta. The world seemed small. After Hilary and I had left the mountains they had enjoyed perfect weather and climbed the North Face of the Carstensz Pyramid, and a rock tower near Base Camp. Their porters had not come back to help them move out of the mountains, so they had had no choice but to leave via the copper mine. In such a situation the Freeport authorities could not refuse them entry, but Jean and Bernard were disappointed to have missed their return journey through the highlands.

Back in Leysin it was the ski season. The winter was deliciously cold, clear and sharp. Unlike the soggy sleet and slush of New Guinea, the snow crunched underfoot. In a few weeks' time I would be going to Kangchenjunga, and I went cross-country skiing in training for the mountain. I breathed deeply on the frozen air, and savoured its crackle in my nostrils.

Leysin nowadays exists mainly because of tourism, which supports over eighty per cent of its economy. However, the village's cosmopolitan, tolerant atmosphere was born early this century, when the world's rich sufferers came there to breathe the alpine air and either die or recover in its many T.B. sanatoria. When T.B. became curable, following the introduction of streptomycin in 1950, the economy had to change, and now the many sanatoria with their old lifts, and their wide bed-sized balconies, house hotels, Club Méditerrannée, colleges, schools, clinics and transcendental meditation centres. These old buildings contrast with the new concrete ski hotels and téléphérique buildings that stick out of the ground like artificial teeth. During the winter the village swells with tourists giving the place the self-indulgent air of constant carnival. Nobody seems to wear or use second-hand gear, and everything's brand new.

The departure date for Kangchenjunga was approaching and I had some items of equipment to organise. I went over to Chamonix to arrange boots for the expedition. No trip to Chamonix is complete for a British climber without a visit to the Bar Nationale. Hilary and I walked in late one night, after a moonlit drive between white snow-ploughed walls over the Col de la Forclaz and the Col de Montets. The glass doors of the Bar were steamed with condensation. It was like walking into a pub in North Wales on a Saturday night, just before closing time. There were about thirty British climbers there that I knew, all reeling and drunk. Multiple rounds were being ordered and intermittently glasses crashed to the slippery floor. A snuff-snorting competition was taking place in one corner, and in another some girls were arguing loudly. Behind the bar Maurice served calmly and detachedly. His style had not changed since I had first seen him, some eleven years before. The noise was deafening. I reeled back from the culture shock, took a deep breath – and joined in.

It was a busy weekend in Chamonix, in the middle of the French holidays. Hilary and I went skiing from the Grands Montets, a téléphérique station high on a flank of the Aiguille Verte, nine thousand feet above the Chamonix Valley. The queue was long for the top station, and we waited for an hour in long queues hemmed between railings, like cattle at a market. Whenever a cable car took a load up we all shuffled forward with skis and sticks pointing in the air, with the intensity of a host of Danis holding spears in a ritual dance, preparing for battle.

Joe Tasker was co-ordinating the equipment organisation for Kangchenjunga. Fortunately, when under pressure, he had an ability to focus hard on a job to be done and to seal himself off from all distractions. Having been away from England for so long, I had missed most of the preparations. I returned on the 5th March, and rushed around picking up socks and jackets and breeches, whilst Joe co-ordinated by telephone from his shop in Castleton. Meanwhile, I lectured for six evenings in succession, trying to make some money. We were paying for Kangchenjunga almost entirely out of our own pockets, and it was costing us about £1,750 each.

A week before departure it looked as if we still had a full month of work to do. The day before departure I went to a meeting organised by Dennis Gray, the leader of the Gauri Sankar expedition planned for the following autumn, and it seemed that more was already arranged for Gauri Sankar in six months' time than had been organised for Kangchenjunga in a few hours' time. However, Joe and Doug Scott (who was organising the food) were past masters at last-minute organisation, and Georges Bettembourg, the fourth member, arrived from the States to provide deadline impetus. Eventually, after packing all night, everyone piled into a transit and drove to London Heathrow. I stayed in London for two days after the others had gone, to collect and shop for equipment that had been forgotten or had not arrived in the rush, and to give a lecture to the Alpine Club.

I had decided not to give any big public lectures about New Guinea – it was easier and more palatable to relate dramatics about desperate climbs in the Himalayas. What would the hard-core climbers say about New Guinea? "Pete's snaps of his holiday jaunt with his bird"? "The Noble Savage Show"? "Comparative Religion in South East Asia"? However, I did show the slides to the Alpine Club, the evening before I flew to Nepal. I felt almost schizoid, talking about a past expedition whilst all my thoughts were focusing on the future.

In the front row at the lecture sat an elderly couple, heroes of an earlier mountaineering generation – Professor I. A. Richards and his wife Dorothy Pilley-Richards. Most awesome of his achievements for me, however, was I. A. Richards' critical breakthrough – *The Principles of Literary Criticism*, written in 1924, which I had spent two weeks trying to understand during an Easter vacation whilst I was at university. As I was showing the slides, I could see the white-haired father of modern criticism nodding and then bouncing back, alert, as his wife nudged him vigorously with her elbow. At the end of the lecture, I. A. Richards stood up and spoke with a vitality that denied his eighty-six years:

I remember a story about New Guinea told to me by Winthrop Young which, in turn, had been told to him by Wollaston. When Wollaston was returning from the Snow Mountains, he became parted in the jungle from his companions and his native guides. He soon became completely lost, for not only was the jungle very thick but there was also a dense mist and the ground was steep and muddy. For a long time he fought through the undergrowth, completely disorientated. Then, to his grateful surprise, he saw the back of a figure through the mist. This back was moving quickly, so he hurried after it assuming that he had caught up with one of the porters. And sure enough, after negotiating many slippery obstacles, he eventually found himself among the main group. He turned to thank his guide, but could not identify him.

Months later, after many other adventures, and the long voyage back home, Wollaston returned thankfully to London. To celebrate his arrival, he decided to buy himself a new suit and he went to the tailors. When the suit was ready, he turned around in front of a mirror to admire it. To his surprise, he recognised that the back he had followed in New Guinea was his own.

TWO

KANGCHENJUNGA

8

SPRING

14th March – 4th April, 1979

The great white peaks filed past – Dhaulagiri, Annapurna, Himalchuli; symbolical names that spoke to the soul rather than referred, as in some countries, to historical events or the memories of famous men. Dhaulagiri means 'Mountain of Storms' and Annapurna, 'Giver of Life'. Waters from these high mountains permitted and nourished life. During the long dry season the waters in the lowlands and the foothills dried up, but the great rivers from the snow mountains never ceased to provide the water necessary for irrigation. As well as storing water, the high glaciers carried down finely ground rock to the meltwater streams, and this reached the lowlands as silt and soil. The mountains gave shelter – but also they attracted the winds, clouds and storms that often caused death and devastation. To the people north and south of the Himalayas, the mountains lit up white in the morning, when the lowlands were still in darkness, and in the evenings they turned rose red and were last to part with the sunset. They towered above all other things. Nobody owned them – they belonged to all. Over thousands of years they had been accessible to people of all races and creeds – through prayer. All Indian and Tibetan mythology praised these vast mountains as the home of the greatest gods.

My expedition to the Himalayas the previous year had been to K2, the second highest mountain in the world, in the Karakoram range of Pakistan. Our eight-man team had abandoned the attempt early, after the death of Nick Estcourt in an avalanche. In our retreat we left behind thousands of pounds-worth of equipment, and the expedition left a feeling of futile waste – we had not had the satisfaction of having pushed ourselves fully, only having tasted the route's technical problems, and we had lost a cherished friend. For me the experiences on K2 were a spectre I tried to forget, but which often reared up – and which I hoped Kangchenjunga would purge.

Our present enterprise seemed much more controllable. Nevertheless, I worried about developing some weakness. Using oxygen on Everest hadn't told me if my lungs were big enough for Kangchenjunga without it. For many days before departure I had been absorbing the little subtleties of life, laughing and joking with people, trying, I suppose, to leave them sweet in their attitude towards me. I thought morbid, but realistic thoughts – could this be the last time I should ever speak to them? I tidied my affairs, signed my will, arranged my insurance. I went to see my two little nieces, one tired and irritable with chicken pox, the other just recovering and bouncy. I hoped and believed the iron was still there inside me to help when the going got rough. But it hadn't been called on for a long time. I was recognising again the half-dread, half-thrill of the prospect of Himalayan climbing.

In Kathmandu the expedition organisation had a studied nonchalance. We hired our sirdar, cook and cook boy; equipment and food were bought, assembled and packed. There was the familiar nasal whine of a Hindi song on a transistor. All seemed normal and smooth running. After the uncertainties of Indonesia, the procedures were relaxed and certain.

Doug Scott and I had been trying to gain permission to climb Kangchenjunga since early in 1977. At that time neither Nepal nor India were allowing foreign expeditions to attempt the main summit. My letters to India had received negative replies. Nepal was more ready to open up the peak, though, and Doug's probings there were successful. We gained the first permission to attempt Kangchenjunga from the north west to be granted for nearly fifty years.

Next we had had to find two more team members, and quickly decided on Joe Tasker and Tut Braithwaite. So we had the expedition notepaper printed first and sent them word on it that they had been co-opted – which proved fine as far as Joe was concerned, but unfortunately Tut had to drop out with lung trouble, which rather upset the names on our letter heading. In his place we then invited Georges Bettembourg. Between us, we had been on twenty Himalayan expeditions and I myself had been on two with Doug and two with Joe.

We soon appointed Georges as our physiological trainer. We had met him in the Karakoram in 1978. He and Yannick Seigneur had steamed past our K2 expedition during the walk-in, and had climbed the 26,400 ft. Broad Peak in a round trip of five days. The two of them were back in Islamabad when we had scarcely got a grip on the lower slopes of our mountain. Obviously, the three 'Anglais' had much to learn from Georges. He had us running round the palace walls every morning. It did not seem to matter that none of us had been on an expedition with him before – it helped, for it gave a competitive edge which nudged us into extra effort. He knew what was entailed in climbing big mountains, and seemed bright-eyed, eager, full of energy and bounce, like Tigger in the Winnie the Pooh stories.

We were hoping to make the first ascent of Kangchenjunga by its North Ridge. All the previous expeditions having had any success on the mountain were very large and used traditional siege tactics. Our lightweight, four-man team was only a small hammer to crack a very large nut.

At 28,208 ft. (8,597 m.) Kangchenjunga is the third highest mountain in the world, being approximately eight hundred feet lower than Everest, and forty-five feet lower than K2. Both these two higher mountains had been climbed during recent years without the use of oxygen equipment. On both occasions, however, the successful climbers had been accompanied by large-scale expeditions which had placed stocks of oxygen at the highest camps. We were going to attempt Kangchenjunga without such support, with only two Sherpas to help us carry our equipment between the lower camps.

Ours was a serious enterprise, but it was rarely solemn. We teased each other with quotes from books written by the modern heroes whose achievements we were hoping to emulate:

> In the morning I have a cold shower, run up 1,000 metres on my toes within thirty minutes, and then chew garlic to dilate my vascular walls.
> Every Friday I eat and drink nothing, to train my liver and kidneys to withstand deprivation.
> Every afternoon I ski cross-country for four hours, at altitudes above 3,000 metres.
> My body hardens until I am in total control of it.
> My personal physician advises me on everything I eat, everything I do. He tells me I am a superman.

These quoting sessions with which we taunted each other would then gain pace until the superstar gasped up to the 'death zone' summit amid a blur of nitrogen. We would meekly shrug our shoulders and say "Well, we can only give it a try."

It was always difficult to dissect truth and useful information from the writing of mountaineers for, naturally enough, an author nurtures his own self-image. We counted up how many climbers had been to 28,000 ft. without using oxygen equipment. Many of them were members of the pre-war Everest expeditions who, encouragingly, had all been different ages, shapes and sizes. However, their achievements had occurred a long time ago and it was difficult to relate ourselves to them. Attitudes had changed since those early high-altitude climbers made their masterly understatements. It seemed current practice to inflate achievement. The American jogging craze and the Russian temples of health were both symptomatic of a modern worship of the body, and the public's gullibility to media and advertising pressures continually expounding a belief in 'supermen'. All this was anathema to Joe Tasker's obsessive iconoclastic nature. He did not bow to ego-myths, publicity machines and the human need for heroes, and instinctively he distrusted all dogma about training programmes. Yet during the early days of the walk-in, I was so impressed with Georges and had read so much about training that I could not dismiss it as lightly.

"But I am worried that there is no doctor among you," said Lieutenant Mohan Thapa. He had been assigned to our expedition as liaison officer, to make sure we did not stray out of bounds.

"Don't worry," said Doug, "we'll be taking an oxygen cylinder with us for medical purposes."

However, there was a problem in finding an oxygen cylinder with the right sort of fitting for the mask we had brought with us. Eventually, we met Pertemba, the Sherpa with whom I had reached the summit of Everest in 1975. Pertemba, who was soon to leave Kathmandu with the American-Nepalese expedition to Gauri Sankar, offered to help. "1,500 rupees," he said.

"1,000."

"1,500 – it's a good price."

"If we bring it back unused can we have the money back?"

"1,500 is what I paid for it. Either you want it or not."

He knew that we did, and having travelled widely over the world, Pertemba knew what Westerners could afford, even when they pleaded poverty.

Kangchenjunga lies in one of the most remote corners of the Himalayas, astride the north east corner of Nepal and the western frontier of Sikkim – a country that has recently been annexed by India. We had to travel east and start the eighteen-day approach walk to the mountains right from their foot – the hot malarial plains of the Terai. This strip of level alluvial terrain, only six hundred feet above sea level, situated between the Indian frontier and the foothills, is Nepal's modest share of the Ganges Plain. Our Sherpas took the gear overland in a truck for fifteen hours along the Russian-built west-to-east highway to the largest town of the Terai – Dharan. A day later we flew out via Biratnagar to join them.

At Dharan the British army kindly allowed us to stay in their Gurkha soldiers' recruiting camp. Here I sat down to bring the expedition accounts up to date. The heat was sultry, and a large fan gave little relief. I recognised a familiar face, the narrow eyes and slightly lopsided mouth – our sirdar for the expedition, Ang Phurba. It was three and a half years since I had seen him on Everest and he

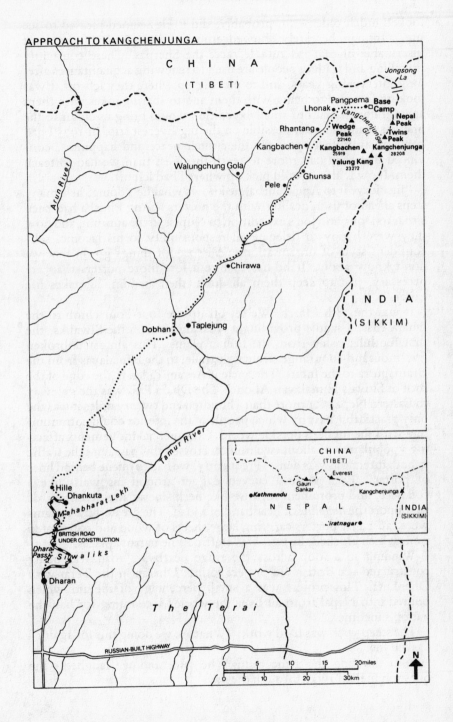

C H I N A
(T I B E T)

Jongsong
La

Pangpema   Base
Lhonak   Camp   Nepal
                                    Peak

Rhantang   Wedge
                        Peak   Twins
                        22140   Peak
Kangbachen   Kangbachen
                        25919   Kangchenjunga
Walungchung Gola   28208
                        Yalung Kang
                        23272
            Pele   Ghunsa

Arun River

Chirawa

I N D I A
(S I K K I M)

Dobhan   Taplejung

Tamur River

Hille   Dhankuta
Mahabharat Lekh
BRITISH ROAD
UNDER CONSTRUCTION
Dhara
Pass   Siwaliks
Dharan

The   Terai

C H I N A
(TIBET)

Everest
Gauri   Kangchenjunga
Sankar
Kathmandu   INDIA
N E P A L   (SIKKIM)
            Biratnagar

RUSSIAN-BUILT HIGHWAY

0   5   10   15   20miles
0   5   10   20   30km

N

looked much older – so, probably, did I. He seemed pleased to see me, although he rarely showed emotion, being one of the most inscrutable of that inscrutable race, the Sherpas. These constantly travelling and trading people are used to renewing acquaintances after long intervening years, and to picking up where they left off. I was looking forward to being with them and to sharing jokes with them again. I hoped that our small expedition would bring us closer to the Sherpas than had been possible on the big Everest trip. In 1975 I had come away with respect for their inner peace and happiness, convinced that they had more to teach the West than we had to teach them. Now I, also, would pick up where I had left off.

"Just leave it to Ang Phurba, he knows what he's doing, he's many steps ahead of us in dealing with the porters." Ang Phurba had been sirdar to Doug and Joe's expedition to Nuptse in the autumn, and now they were happy to delegate all responsibility to his laconic, self-confident style of organisation. "All sorts of things go on that we don't know about. If he has to hire a few more porters than are necessary, just to keep them all quiet, then let him, it makes life easier."

It was the 18th March. We set off up the four-hour climb to the Dhara Pass, a saddle providing a crossing place in the Siwaliks, the first foothills rising from the Indian plains. This almost unbroken five-thousand-foot range stretches parallel to the Himalayas from the Bramaputra to the Indus. The ancient Aryans called it 'the edge of the roof of Shiva's Himalayan Abode'. The Dhara Pass was the gateway to Eastern Nepal; for more than a hundred and twenty miles it was the only practicable pass by which people of the interior could communicate with the modern outside world. Commercial movements affecting a population of about two million crossed this pass, and the traffic in both directions was dense. Frequently, we had to queue behind lines of porters. Each wore a curved dagger around his waist like a codpiece, and prominent tortoise-like neck sinews strained upwards to support the *tumpline* or headband of a load. The greatest traffic jams were caused by porters carrying large sheets of wood and corrugated iron, which blocked the two-way traffic at the narrow places.

Winding in a loop across the ridge nearby, a road was being constructed – a British aid project to link Dharan in the Terai with Dhankuta. This project was a small percentage of the aid which poured into Nepal from all over the world, accounting for half the nation's income.

The steep walk was hard work. "What are we doing this for again?" I asked Joe.

"I'm thinking the same thing," he said, and we laughed – the question melted away through the day.

The only previous time I had walked to a mountain in Nepal had been to Everest during the monsoon. In contrast, the Siwaliks were dry and hot, and so was I.

Georges was holding a ski stick in either hand. "They're really good," he said, "they loosen up your upper body, exercise your arms and take the jolts and strains from your knees. Yannick and I used them all the time last year. You should try them." Joe and I soon copied the technique.

From the Dhara Pass, we could see across a transverse valley the defensive wall of the Mahabharat Lekh. This natural barrier had protected the Nepalese mountain people from the wars and conflicts of the Indian plain. I groaned inwardly to see the climb up to Dhankuta, which was to be our next stop, an important trading place perched high on the ridge.

The route up on to the foothills was punctuated with wayside cafés – small, dingy smoke-stained benches where we sat, sipped sweet milky tea and ate biscuits and fresh oranges. Yellow dogs snapped listlessly, and mangy chickens pecked at spit. Flies like particles of dust danced up and down the sunshafts. The way was dusty and weary, but at least we were climbing out of the heat.

Georges did not hesitate from talking about anything, and tackled topics head on. We discussed the mountains, morality, values, religion, everything. Although he always talked quickly and emphatically, he was not completely at ease speaking English, and his opinions came out abruptly, free of nuance.

"I see God everywhere I look," he said.

Joe quoted Camus mischievously back at him: "If there is a god, then I don't need him."

Joe and I did not give in lightly to Georges' direct honesty. However, I was feeling more gregarious than I had been on previous expeditions, more willing to say what I thought and to exchange opinions. Georges was blunt yet impressionable, and he generated an easy atmosphere. He even managed to break down Joe's defences and squeeze some comments out of his habitual opacity. We were testing each other out in conversation, trying to find common ground and understand and trust each other. Women were the usual early theme – a tenuous mental link to the world we were leaving behind.

In contrast to the huts along the trail, Dhankuta was a spotlessly clean town, with a wide stone-flagged street flanked by whitewashed houses with black-tiled roofs and balconies with window boxes full of flowers. On a rocky promontory above the town stood a giant pipal tree. These trees are sacred to both Hindu and Buddhist, and are usually sited at convenient rest stops. Beneath this one was a *chautara*, a stone bench on which porters could lean their loads. The tree's spreading boughs offered reassuring strong shade in a breeze that blew refreshingly across the ridge. The tree glittered, each leaf shaking separately, in a million different rhythms. The ascent on to the foothills was over, and we fell asleep waiting for the porters.

We gained the ridge we were to follow for the next four days and moods changed. The dry winter was over but the grass was still pale and bleached like straw. It was the most beautiful approach walk I had ever made in the Himalayas, along an open ridge, around shoulders, through rhododendrons full of the promise of the bloom before the monsoon – unlike the ups and downs of the way in to Everest. All along the trail there were hamlets and people. But the terraced fields were dry and dusty, with little agricultural work going on. Four great eagles circled around us – above and below. Spring here is a time when the monsoon is awaited; it's not the same as the complete renewal of nature in Europe. The seasons were confusing me. After a mid-winter south of the Equator, the dream-like powder blue, the crisp coldness of Switzerland in February, and the rain of northern England, there was a freshness and strength in this special hilltop season which gave hope and delight.

We discussed the rights and wrongs of having ladies along during the walk in to a mountain. The porter stages were short, the days were leisurely and I thought that the walking was so gentle and pleasurable that female company would not hinder us. I was going to send carbon copies of my diary to Hilary, Doug was copying his to his wife, Jan.

"How can you be completely honest in a diary which you know someone else is going to read?" taunted Joe.

"I'm not honest," I said. "I lie and show off. Anyway, what's wrong with sharing thoughts?"

"If you were the last person in the world would you write a diary?" asked Doug. "And if we were the last people in the world, would we still go to climb Kangchenjunga?"

When anything of interest happened within or around me I made a mental note to tell Hilary about it. This habit of thinking of things in connection with her enhanced their meaning, and memories jostled with the thought that at those same instants in time she lived, breathed and thought. However, despite the bond of understanding we had found together in New Guinea, I still could not feel I was talking to her; I wrote into the space between. I used my writing as a means of coming to terms with the fact that, though I could not blindly forget, I had to leave much of my past behind.

We walked along the stone flags of the village of Hille, where we met a British agricultural adviser and a German water supply expert, both involved in aid projects. They told us Hille was a prosperous settlement of Bhoti, Tibetan-speakers from Walongchung, which used to be one of the main Nepalese towns controlling trade to and from Tibet, along the Arun Valley before the border closed.

Georges bought a Montreux Jazz Festival tee-shirt.

We walked past comfortable houses. Western music was playing 'Seasons in the Sun' . . . 'Goodbye my friends, it's hard to die . . .'

Georges' head spun round. "Hey, did you catch the words of that song?"

A few minutes later, high above children playing rolypoly on the grass where a graceful cowherdess with gold in her ears sat knitting, we saw mountains. Far to the north, hanging with their outlines faintly revealed like ethereal white clouds above the dark valley haze, much higher in the sky than we had expected, we saw the giants of Makalu and Chamlang and the massive bulk of Kangchenjunga, a complete range in itself: multiple-summited from Jannu to Kabru.

Of the world's first half-dozen peaks, Kangchenjunga is the best displayed. Fifty miles to the east from where we were, the mountain is fully visible from the busy crowded Indian hill town of Darjeeling. Meet anyone who has visited Darjeeling, and his eyes will moisten as he tells you of the sight of Kangchenjunga at dawn – it must be one of the most described and photographed views in the world. But unlike a view of the European Alps, Kangchenjunga from a distance is of a scale that cannot be grasped.

It has been worshipped as a guardian spirit since ancient animistic times by Tibetans and the Lepchas of Sikkim. The Tibetans gave the mountain its name, which is physically descriptive of its five peaks and literally means 'the five repositories or ledges of the great snows'. However, when the great lama Lha-Tsan Ch'enbo introduced Buddhism into Sikkim, he told the people that the mountain was the home of a god of that name, a god who was a defender of Lamaism. Lha-Tsan Ch'enbo gave the name a mythological meaning, and the five repositories became real storehouses of the god's treasures. The peak, which was most conspicuously gilded by the rising sun, became the treasury of gold, the peak which remained in cold grey shade, the silver treasury; and the other peaks were the stores of gems and grains and holy books. When the disciples of Lha-Tsan Ch'enbo came to depict Kangchenjunga in paintings and statues, the idea of treasure led them to represent the god in the style of the god of wealth – red in colour, clad in armour, carrying a banner of victory, and mounted on a white lion.

Kangchenjunga is still regarded as a sacred mountain, and the Maharajahs of Sikkim have always either refused permission or asked for special behaviour whenever European climbers and explorers applied to venture near it. Out of respect for the mountain's sanctity, and upon the request of the Maharajah, the two successful ascents in

1955 and 1977, left the final few feet of summit snow untrodden.

Was the god simply a benign giver of life, a god of wealth, as the name implied? During the 1930 expedition to Kangchenjunga, Frank Smythe detected more than thanksgiving in the attitude of the people towards the mountain. Their main Kangchenjunga dances were held before the harvest, to placate the god, rather than in gratitude afterwards.

> Their prosperity, and even their lives, depend on the good humour of this god, for he is able to blast their crops with his storms, or destroy their villages with his floods and avalanches. There are even dark tales of human sacrifices to this powerful deity, handed down from the remote past.

When Smythe was shown a statue of the god, it had a cruel countenance and sardonic grin. After an avalanche killed one of them, and nearly destroyed them all, he wrote: "Kangchenjunga is something more than unfriendly, it is imbued with a blind unreasoning hatred towards the mountaineer."

As recently as 1977 the lamas of Sikkim accused a large Indian expedition of disturbing the god. A loud explosion was heard from the mountain, followed by heavy landslides and avalanches. It was said that thousands of dead fish were being swept down rivers that sprang from the glacier affected by the explosion and that scores of road construction workers nearby had suddenly fallen sick. Not long after, one of the Indian climbers was killed in a fall during an early stage of the expedition.

I had always thought that a mountain was magnificently indifferent; I had regarded local beliefs as superstitions to be tolerated, and always tried to avoid the temptation of attaching human attributes to a mountain. But this year I began to discover how much your physical experience of a mountain depends on your mental attitude. At times Kangchenjunga seemed to have a mind. If you did not match up, you were quickly rejected. But if you approached with a mixture of confidence, respect and caution, it was usually just possible to come through the worst, and discover a special reward.

From over seventy-five miles away, Kangchenjunga dominated the ridge we were following and gave a new sense of purpose to the walk. A chill sharpness at sunset reminded us of the cold hill that awaited us and before we returned to our tents we quoted to each other suitable passages about the mountain, giggling nervously. I found some awesome thoughts in Jack Tucker's book, *Kangchenjunga*:

> . . . Kangchenjunga is a mountain which does not respond to normal mountaineering techniques. The psychological effects of the ever-present

94

danger from the terrible avalanches which pour down day and night from the mountain, the extreme difficulty and the awful weather, coupled with the very short period when it is possible to climb on Kangchenjunga, make this peak just that much more dangerous and inaccessible. Any expedition which hopes to reach the summit must approach the mountain with something of the philosophy of a fanatic. Every nerve and every fibre must be devoted to one cause – the attainment of the summit . . .

Joe chimed in with the daunting prophecy of Erwin Schneider, an Austrian climber on G. O. Dyhrenfurth's 1930 expedition. "Attempts on this mountain by small parties are doomed to failure from their inception."

"I hope we can do this route fast – perhaps after we've made a reconnaissance," I said.

"We'll just have to try the big breath theory."

"What's that, Doug?"

"Take a big breath of air at the North Col and go for it."

Once inside the tent I sealed out a group of whispering children, the bats, insects and mountain fears of Nepal with a pull of the door's zip. Usually we camped apart – it was important to cherish some privacy, for we would be together for long enough on the mountain. Now I was cushioned from our surroundings, and the dominating mountain ahead. I listened to some music on the cassette player, and lost myself in a book by candlelight, relaxing in an imported, sealed bubble of Western reality. Absorbing books telescoped time. Joe and I tended to read the same books after each other, so that we could discuss them, whilst Georges could never manage more than the first few pages of anything, and Doug had a special collection of books and cassettes that helped his own incessant quest for prophets.

At 6.30 a.m. little Nima, the kitchen boy, brought a cup of tea – a soothing way of bringing in the morning. It was the start of another perfect day on the ridge.

"Do you like our music?" I asked Mohan, our liaison officer.

His English vocabulary was vast, but his pronunciation was barely understandable: "In sweet music is such art, killing care and grief of heart."

"Where's that from, Mohan?"

"Shakespeare, *Henry VIII*, Orpheus' song."

"We haven't got a cassette of that."

After we had wound down from the hectic days that had preceded our departure, we began to wind up for the mountain ahead. Fatigue and stiffness left us and we soon began to feel fit and gloriously alive, happy to know we would be taxed utterly on the climb ahead. The trail seemed like a motorway compared to the paths I had tangled with in New Guinea. Although it was not as crowded as it had been before Hille, a trickle of traders and travellers continued to move steadily by. We walked in the morning and reached the day's camp-site by early afternoon, to laze for a while. Then we played around climbing on boulders – forgotten muscles quickened, and we enjoyed the light-hearted competition. The pace of the expedition was asserting itself.

We camped in a little glade: forty-eight porters, sirdar Ang Phurba, assistant sirdar Nima Tenzing, Kami the cook, Nima Tamang the kitchen boy, Mohan the liaison officer, the four of us. We were glad we did not have a single main sponsor for our expedition, so that our commitment was purely to ourselves and the route.

Four was a good number because there was room for gossip and manoeuvring within the microcosm, but nothing could become too serious because we knew we would soon have to be totally interdependent once on the mountain.

Eighty per cent of our conversation was spent mocking and deflating each other. Joe was best at this, never at a loss for an answer, quick to unmask pretence, a tough teaser, making tight-lipped remarks like gunshots. Sometimes he was a bit too near the mark – he made me wince a few times. We'd been through a lot together, and out of many past altercations a lot of mutual respect and trust seemed to have grown. The comments between us now were just as barbed but neither suspected malice any more. Georges missed many of the jokes, partly because his English wasn't up to it (Doug's Nottingham accent didn't help), but also because I don't think the French – or the Americans for that matter – talk each other down all the time, as a matter of course. We spent a long time one day trying to explain to him what 'taking the piss' means. We trod a fine line in our humour, and it was important for everyone to be tuned in and find the same things funny. Doug sometimes could, sometimes couldn't, or missed a joke on himself, particularly about the 'ego' business and why we were there. He didn't stick with the three of us, but walked alone in a happy haze, scribbling notes in his diary. We all kept diaries:

Today we sped past him and he said "Remember the tortoise and the hare," and I replied that the hare had more time at the end to dream. But now I'm not so sure who is the hare and who is the tortoise! I just can't make out Doug's home-baked psychological musings – or gauge his capacity to move within himself. He's either undergoing a second adolescence or he's in touch with something beyond the range of all the rest of us here. He has a clever knack of self-parody and a ready laugh that makes it difficult to sense his level of seriousness when he drops his heavy lines into a conversation like today's: "with only three trillion heartbeats each at our disposal, we have to focus our energies carefully, on to something worthwhile." And "We're all mobile plants – imagine us turned inside out – we are what we eat." And "The subconscious is very strong on this trip." He loves to float off with words, playing and pondering with them. I'm more inhibited than he is – I think it would be a sort of tense anarchy if all of us allowed our feelings to dominate what we say.

The days on the ridge came to an end and we descended six and a half thousand feet to the Tamur Valley. We could see its blue waters far below, glimmering over boulder and pebbles. On the way down into the heat we stopped for a cup of tea, savouring the breeze that sang through the great trees around us. An ex-Gurkha soldier chatted to us in English, with fond reminiscences of his fifteen years abroad with the British army. His pension was five times as large as the income of a peasant and when he had been on active service the ratio had been twenty-five times larger. Yet his experiences and his money seemed to have had little effect on his present life.

At Dobhan, to celebrate our arrival at a lower and more balmy altitude, we swam in a side river which poured into the Tamur. The broad cheekboned, Chinese-looking Limbus have settled in the Tamur Valley. We walked past their three-storied, balconied houses, marvelling at one of the highest standards of living in Nepal. The high precipitation – both during the summer monsoon and the winter – accounted for this prosperity, enabling the Limbus to grow not only much rice but also winter crops.

Although Europeans did not pass this way very often, our caravan did not raise an upward glance from them. The Western roadshow had not the same curiosity value or attraction here that it had in New Guinea. Ang Phurba warned us not to stop at one particularly surly hamlet – it was, he reported, a haunt of robbers with sharp knives, and Limbus are famous for their knife-fighting prowess.

We decided that the Limbus were pyromaniacs. Day and night, great fires swept through trees and shrubbery around their settlements, clearing a way for the fresh green shoots of spring. The destruction was painful to watch. On the east side of the Tamur, acres of forest had been gutted, but the Sherpas said that this was not spring-cleaning by the Limbus. Out of mischief, the porters of an expedition to Jannu a few years previously had started a fire that had raged until the monsoon put it out. The government had had to pay compensation.

We had been walking for eight days from Dharan when we arrived on the afternoon of the 26th March at Chirawa – a lovely clearing scattered with the blackened stones of old camp fires amid an amphitheatre of great rock boulders fifty feet high. Joe settled down wisely to read *The Seven Pillars of Wisdom*, and we could not entice him on to the boulders by the Tamur River. The bouldering was fun until we arrived at a rock slab fifteen feet high. Georges bounded up this and I struggled up after him. Doug had some difficulty because his ankles, full of metal from his accident whilst descending the Ogre in Pakistan in 1977, wouldn't bend enough. Georges, soon bored, decided to play 'I'm the king of the castle' and gave me a boisterous push off the top of the boulder. I spun round, grabbed for his feet, but he shook me free. I slid down the slab, fingers scratching the rock, and landed awkwardly with my left foot on a tuft of grass. There was a sharp noise like a snapping twig from my ankle.

"Oh no!" shouted Doug and rushed over.

I could not walk any more.

I crawled back up to the clearing and Joe looked up from his book and uttered a few words of sympathy. Mohan's face lost its habitual grin, and the Sherpas shook their heads and tut-tutted. With the strong confidence of a faith-healer, Doug held my swollen foot firmly between his great hands, but I hoped in vain for a miracle cure. It was first-aid by committee, and everyone suggested a different treatment. "Put it in cold water." "Hold it up in the air." "Bathe it in warm salty water."

I tried everything. Georges dashed around performing unnecessary tasks for me, agonising with a guilt that we did not help by our deep amateur probes into his subconscious: "Why did you really do it Georges?"

I lay down in total despair, imagining the noisy insects of the jungle screaming into my ears were trying to eat me up. With my eyes closed, I felt I was just a large, throbbing, decaying foot.

"It sometimes does you good to reach the heights and depths, youth," said Doug.

My grandmother had always said "Horseplay ends in tears!"

For four days three tiny Limbu men took it in turns to carry me towards Ghunsa – the last permanent village on the walk-in. Perched in a conical wicker basket, I felt like an aged and crippled pilgrim being carried towards holy water.

"Well, at least you're being carried up to the mountain, and not down and away from it," said Joe.

It took me two days to summon the courage to face my self-pity and write it down. I could not bear forward-looking thoughts, I only wanted to rest, sleep, forget:

What can I see before me? What can I say? I just can't believe it. It's all so utterly stupid I feel angry. I need these big climbs – I plan my life around them and look what happens! The summit of Kangch seems far away, and I have morbid fears about my Alpine guiding this summer – what if my foot sets itself wrongly? I never realised how much I wanted to climb Kangchenjunga until this injury cast a black shadow of doubt.

We were paying the three shift-working porters who were carrying me a total of two hundred rupees – about £8 – a day. They were earning every note – one slip beneath my twelve and a half stone pre-expedition weight and they could have ruined a knee, ankle or back. A slip could have ruined me too, since at times we were traversing steep slopes many hundreds of feet above the river. I kept rigid, immovable, as they insisted, not wanting to upset the balance, strapped in, with my foot tucked under and fastened with a belt.

The long distance carry was lonely. I missed the lively chatter and repartee of before the accident, and longed for the tea stops when I would catch the others up for a short time. My head became disassociated from the effort of the bodies that carried me, and as we followed the switchbacks of the path I stared stiffly at the disappearing foliage, the river and cliffs.

Nima Tenzing, our assistant sirdar, had appointed himself as my safety-net and moving stirrup. At fifty years old, Nima was a veteran of eighteen expeditions, including seven to Everest, where he had made carries to the highest camp three times and to the South Col six times. He was like the adventure-book Sherpa of the pre-war Everest expeditions, illiterate, unsophisticated, reliable, loyal, with a ready smile and with a constant, almost servile willingness to help and to seek out any job that needed doing. He ambled constantly behind me, safeguarding my tilting over perilous places, his wrinkled brown face grinning encouragement. Nima's everyday work and his religion seemed to blend without distinction between the two. Most of the time he was sunk into a habitual deep prayer that to him was as natural as breathing air.

For me, there was one distraction. We were joined on the trail by a family of Bhoti, who were travelling to their home in Ghunsa – a mother, two small children and a teenage daughter. The mother had a fresh complexion and a kind but mischievous smile. She had, she said, seven other children, and this daughter was soon to be married to a Ghunsa man.

"She'll tell you anything," said Ang Phurba, laughing.

She had realised who was distracting us. Her daughter, Dawa, wore an emerald green coat and had a smile like a sunrise. Dawa enchanted us all.

After three days of being carried, I was beginning to feel less sorry for myself:

One can adjust to anything if one has to. I suppose bad things usually come to an end. I've actually managed to walk a little today, so am feeling a bit more cheerful. Being with Nima is good for me – I'm reluctant to show any signs of suffering in front of the Sherpas. I have to be really careful and am painfully slow, but perhaps there's hope. If will to heal works, then I shall soon be better. I'm focusing all my energies in THE FOOT, massaging, warming, flexing, thinking.

In Nepal, an altimeter can tell you what race of people you are likely to meet. An hour of path separated language, economy, religion and culture. We had crossed the ethnic frontier – the ten-thousand-foot contour between south and north; we had left the strict caste and conformity of the Hindu Limbus and entered a zone of hospitality. At the village of Pele I found the others eating boiled eggs, surrounded by a group of giggling women and children. Their rosy cheeks and robust appearance, their black, sack-like 'chuba' dresses held in place by striped aprons, their chunky Tibetan silver ornaments and necklaces of amber and turquoise beads all woke me from the rocking stupor of my basket-ridden journey. Here, in contrast to the children in Limbu land, the youngsters were laughing, curious, and vivacious. I felt I was looking at one of those old photographs of medieval Tibet taken forty years before by Heinrich Harrer and described in *Seven Years in Tibet*. Pele, the Sherpas told us, was another settlement of Tibetan refugees who had accumulated there over the previous twenty years since the Chinese invasion. There were Nepalese government plans to move them into the foothills, but at the moment they practise transhumance with yaks and grow potatoes, in the same style as the Bhoti, who live mainly in Ghunsa, a few miles higher up the valley.

Nima was now among familiar religious symbols. Carefully, he guided my little party to the left side of stone Mani walls and *chortens*.

"We go round like a watch," he said. It was an old tradition, to walk clockwise, in the same direction as the earth and universe revolves – a tradition which also survives in the Scottish Highlands, in the passing of a decanter, cattle treading out corn and walking around someone to wish them well.

Ghunsa had the air of an outpost suddenly abandoned before the advance of an enemy. Lines of prayer flags flew like tattered, war-torn banners, flapping spiritual longings into the winds – at first sight these flags were all that distinguished the place from a lonely hamlet high up in the Lötschental of Switzerland. The stone-walled houses were roofed with planks weighed down by big rocks. The village stood on meadows which were once the alluvial bottom of a lake, and on either side steep valley sides blocked out the sun.

According to legend, Lha-Tsan Ch'enbo stopped here on his way into Sikkim, and founded a Buddhist monastery. After leaving the village, he had become lost and sheltered in a cave. There, the god of Kangchenjunga visited him in the form of a wild goose and inspired him to fulfil an ancient prophecy by composing a sacred text to guide the worship of the mountain.

When the first European, Sir Joseph Hooker, visited Ghunsa in 1850 it was a prosperous trading community. Further exploration of the district was taken up by the famous 'pundits' – Bengalis, trained by the Survey of India, who collected data from which the earliest maps of the district were compiled. In 1879, Chandra Das, a pundit and headmaster of a Darjeeling school, visited the monastery and reported it as being one of the finest and richest in Sikkim and Eastern Nepal, containing eighty lamas and a dozen nuns. In 1884, another pundit, Rinzing, noted a hundred and fifty well-to-do houses. As traders, used to adapting to different cultures, the inhabitants showed no surprise when William Douglas Freshfield passed through the village on his celebrated circuit of Kangchenjunga in 1899 – and readily accepted his Indian currency. By the time the next Europeans passed through – the 1930 International Expedition to Kangchenjunga – much of the trade had declined. Frank Smyth's rather patronising description of the childlike superstitions of the lamas and their open-mouthed reactions to his gramophone, implied a religious decline also.

Few lamas appeared as we passed the *kani*, and the gilded spire of the *gompa* and some of the monuments were in a state of disrepair. Nima said, "The people here, they give what they can to the monastery, but not so many here now as before."

We stopped at Ghunsa, in order to pay off the porters who had carried our equipment from Dharan and to hire forty locals for the last stage of the walk-in. When the lowland porters had gone, the four of us sat around the fire, sipping a drink of warm, fermenting millet – *tumba* – from wooden jars. We ate our first and last meal of a three-month-old piece of yak – the Sherpas seemed to relish its high smell and strange taste. Slowly, unhurriedly, some of the three hundred inhabitants came to look at us. Ang Phurba was already asking round for porters to carry our gear up to Base Camp. The Bhoti could understand his Sherpa dialect. Both languages are rooted in Tibetan, but have developed as separate dialects because of the lack of east-west contact between the deep valleys of Northern Nepal. I was happy that we were a small expedition – a large one might have uprooted the whole village from their fields. Instead, we were a lucky five-day cash crop bonus – or, more appropriately, a curious flock who paid to be herded up the valley.

The locals were emerging into the spring after a long, biting winter. Many had bad coughs, ear-aches and smoke-reddened eyes. Doug opened up his clinic at 5.00 p.m. He spoke gently through his long hair and wire-framed spectacles, administering to each sufferer after they had explained to him their problems. In the mountaineering world, Doug's toughness, strength and endurance were legendary, and he also had a reputation for volcanic unpredictability and scarcely controlled violence – yet here he had the tenderness of a saint. A crowd of small children stood watching, quiet and subdued, with shy eyes. One, about four, uncomplainingly carried a baby on her back. Meanwhile, I was looking in wonder at countless pairs of healthy feet – everywhere I looked I saw feet jumping, running, twisting, bending, mocking.

"It's a miracle that so many people function so normally," I said.

"No," said Doug, "the miracle is that we ever stop or fall, we're so well-programmed."

During the night it snowed, and in the morning the high mountains slowed down the sun's descent to us. As the sun arrived the day gave way at first to winds, and then to clouds and some rain. We decided to stay for two days, to give my ankle a chance to rest and to acclimatise to our present altitude of twelve thousand feet.

In a traditional porter behaviour-pattern, the locals started exaggerating the dangers and difficulties between Ghunsa and our proposed Base Camp at Pangpema, so that they could claim more pay. An exorbitant price was demanded for the hire of a yak to carry me, so I set off on the 2nd April, two hours ahead of the main party, determined to hobble the rest of the journey without help.

Within the space of two weeks we had passed through almost all the climatic zones of the earth; from the sub-tropical jungle of the Terai to the mountain wastes we were now entering.

The last inhabited settlement, recently occupied for the spring, was Kangbachen – a hamlet of ten houses. The children were wild and grimy and had running noses, but they were well wrapped against the cold and completely unafraid of strangers. It was here that in 1879 the pundit Chandra Das, on his way from Ghunsa to the Chabok La and Tibet, had witnessed a grand offering to Kangchenjunga.

> The firing of guns, athletic feats and exercises with the bow and arrow form the principal parts of the ceremony which is believed to be highly acceptable to the mountain deity. The youth of Gyansar vied with each other in athletic exercise, the favourite amusements of their elders being quoits, back-kicking and the shooting of arrows. I also contributed my share to their religious observances. The scene reminded one of the Olympic Games, and like good Buddhists, I too paid my abeisance to Kangchan, the Buddhist's Olympus.

Chandra Das' colourful account of his journey is permeated with legends about the valley along which we were now walking – the holy waterfall where the eight Indian saints had bathed, the cavern where the key of heaven was concealed, the sacred hot mineral spring and the hollow in the slope consecrated to a mountain nymph.

From Kangbachen we could see the vast glittering flutings of the North Wall of Jannu, and beyond that several magnificent unclimbed twenty to twenty-two thousand foot mountains ('nameless Weiss-horns', as Freshfield called them), flanked our route. I limped along the grass-covered moraine beside the Kangchenjunga Glacier. There was still over twelve miles to go – the glacier owed its length to the heavy precipitation in Eastern Nepal. I was relieved when the porters, spinning the day out, stopped to make a cup of tea at Rhantang. There, the vast panorama of white peaks confirmed why the yak herds regarded it as the special haunt of the spirits of the mountains, a place where 'gods and saints dwell in great numbers'.

We arrived at the next pasture beside the moraine, Lhonak, in the early afternoon. It was exciting to see all the mountains that had hitherto only existed for me in books, to be able to look at Schneider's map and think "Yes, we're really at this point." We could see Wedge Peak, Nepal Peak, Kangbachen and Kangchenjunga itself. To the north were passes and peaks, dry and Tibetan. I wrote:

> The beauty around us has taken me out of myself, and I know it is right for me to be here. After a starry night with a crescent moon, there's a frosty stillness until the morning wind starts blowing uphill. Doug and Georges, in particular, are talking about how happy they are and feel. Today are relaxed into a long discussion about commercialism and personality exploitation in mountaineering. Doug's still upset about the publication of that full page mugshot of him wearing fibre pile gear, which Joe took. How can what he says have any impact if he's used a lot in adverts? How can he say anything political about climbing if he appears to have exploited the sport? It's a problem that certainly worries him.
>
> There weren't many boulders on the ground – mostly we walked across great yellow grass meadows, and my foot managed O.K. Last night Georges and Joe both dreamed that I got to the top, so their psyches must think I'm going to get better. Yet I wish I could see my own role in the climb ahead – am I summit-bound, miracle mending, or just a doomed hobbler and lifelong cripple?

The short day had not tired the girls among the porters at all. Throughout the afternoon they danced and sang in circles – at first high on a rocky eminence beneath fluttering prayer flags – and then down on the meadow. Georges bounced around, doing cartwheels and walked on his knees whilst in a lotus position, much to the hoots and delight of the girls, who played rough and pushed him over. His love of nonsense endeared him to them all. It made my ankle twinge to watch!

In the evening the porters split into two generation groups. For the young it was a social adventure. Their journey was a break from their work in the fields, an excuse to talk and intermingle away from the village. While the young giggled and shouted, the old chatted around their fire, nodding with wisdom and sleep. The Sherpas moved easily between us and the two groups. We were the excuse for the journey, but we were irrelevant.

On the morning of the 4th April the porters stopped.

"Porters, they say this is Pangpema Base Camp," said Ang Phurba.

Once again we fished out Frank Smythe's book *Kangchenjunga Adventure*. We checked the alignment of cliff, glacier and moraine against a picture in the book. Yes, we weren't being dumped short, we were at the 1930 Base Camp. I looked up at the mountain.

"See what I've found," said Doug. "A 1930 tent peg."

9

SERACS

4th – 14th April, 1979

Dear Mr. Boardman,
 I am sending you two photographs of the wall west of the North Ridge
of Kangchenjunga. I have taken them during a flight in 1975. The wall is
very steep ice and rock, but no danger of avalanches. Nearly 1,000 m high.
Be careful with ice avalanches from the N.W. Wall! Pangpema is a very
nice place for Base Camp. With my best wishes,
                                    Yours sincerely,
                                    Erwin Schneider.

We re-read letters, and thumbed again through photographs. The
information in them took on new meaning, with the subject matter in
front of us – the North West Face of Kangchenjunga.

Pangpema was indeed 'a very nice place'. It became our last link
with the outside world, a halfway house of warmth, comfort and
safety, of grass, flowers and running water, to which we could return
and recover after adventures in the upper world of ice and glacier. The
kitchen fire at Pangpema became the pillar of our wandering. Here,
Mohan, the liaison officer, Kami the cook and Nima Tamang the
kitchen boy stayed, in touch with the world down in the valley haze.

The relief that we felt when we arrived at Pangpema, and which we
were to feel many times on returning there from the mountain over
the following weeks, was mirrored in a description by the first
European to go there, William Douglas Freshfield. In 1899, Freshfield
had approached Pangpema from Sikkim, by crossing the 20,156 ft.
Jongsong La – the pass of hidden treasures. The Kangchenjunga
group lies south of the main Himalayan watershed, pointing a
northerly ridge towards it. This ridge separates Sikkim and Nepal,
and the Jongsong Pass cuts across it. Freshfield was accompanied by
the pundit Rinzing, who had been there fifteen years before, crossing
the pass from our present position at Pangpema, into Sikkim, and
suffering an epic descent on the other side – two of his porters had
died from the cold, and he had run out of provisions.

This tragedy clouded Rinzing's memory as he guided Freshfield down from the pass and he declared the party 'lost'. Freshfield was shaken by Rinzing's uncertainty, but persevered, determined to fill in the missing link, the broad blank on the map between known travellers' routes to the north west and north east sides of Kangchenjunga. It seemed that they were descending into a blind valley blocked by cliffs, until a drifting cloud revealed a hidden turn:

> I was suddenly aware of a winged messenger from the outer world coming towards us. A tiny wisp of white vapour floated into sight quite low down between two apparently connected cliffs. We no longer needed to walk by faith.

It had been five days since they had touched vegetation, or walked on horizontal ground, clear of boulders and ice. The descent, happily, shook Rinzing's memory clear. He led the expedition to Pangpema:

> We had returned to a habitable and living world. A sudden cheerfulness seized us . . . A sense of escape, of having come out of their peril, spread itself visibly among the coolies. Their faces brightened, they became more talkative. Our feet no longer hampered by the soft substance of clinging snow, we all stepped out, full of hope.

Eighty years later, Doug, Joe, Georges and I sat on the secure turf of Pangpema, looking up at Kangchenjunga, making occasional detached comments about possibilities and dangers. We were like generals out of gunshot range on a well-protected hilltop, surveying the enemy's positions and discussing the deployment of troops. We discussed some guerrilla tactics, as Georges' binoculars passed between us. We knew not to judge on first impressions and tried to break down the enormity of the mountain into logical, climbable stages. There was an air of unreality, it being understood but not spoken, that if we were the generals we were also the troops. But today, at least, we were safe.

The North West Face of Kangchenjunga might have been designed specifically to repel mountaineers. It is structured in a horseshoe of three tiers of gigantic shelves, separated by cliffs of ice which are the mountain's defences, poised to thunder across any lines of weakness that an eye of faith could imagine. Our eyes wandered up the face, following possibilities, only to be brought to a brutal stop every time by the threat of hanging glaciers. Only the North Ridge looked free from such objective dangers. But how could we reach it without playing Russian roulette with ice cliffs? R. L. Irving and other Alpine Club members had accused Professor G. O. Dyhrenfurth, the leader of the 1930 expedition, of 'having led his men into a death trap'. Yet

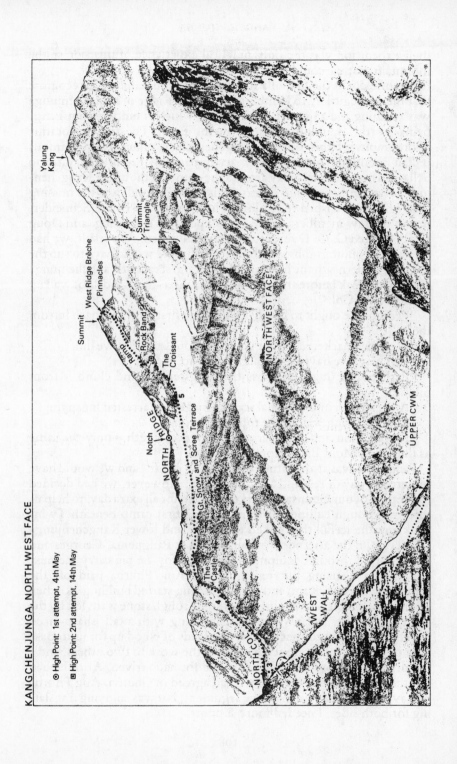

KANGCHENJUNGA, NORTH WEST FACE

⊙ High Point: 1st attempt, 4th May

◼ High Point: 2nd attempt, 14th May

Yalung Kang

Summit Triangle

West Ridge Brèche

Summit

Pinnacles

Ramp

Rock Band

The Croissant

NORTH WEST FACE

Notch

NORTH RIDGE

5

Gt. Snow and Scree Terrace

The Castle

UPPER CWM

3

NORTH COL

WEST WALL

their expedition was the only practical experience of this side of the mountain that we could learn from.

Freshfield was the first of a succession of mountaineers to recognise that the strategic key to climbing the North Ridge of Kangchenjunga was reaching the 23,000 ft. North Col, which is hidden from Pangpema by the double-summited Twins Peak. The first panoramic photographs of this side of Kangchenjunga, taken by the famous Italian mountain photographer accompanying Freshfield, Vittorio Sella, did not show what lay around the corner in the upper Kangchenjunga Glacier, behind the Twins. This 'dead ground' was the missing link which we wished to explore. I had written to Erwin Schneider, one of the few members of the 1930 expedition still living, and Doug had contacted G. O. Dyhrenfurth's son, Norman. As a result, we had a dossier of photographs which showed that we would have to run the gauntlet underneath the hanging glaciers and séracs of Kangchenjunga and Twins Peak before starting to climb a three-thousand-foot wall up to the North Col.

"Perhaps we ought to climb Twins Peak first, and approach it from there."

"We'd be knackered before we started on Kangch if we did."

"Anyway, we haven't got permission for it."

"Perhaps we ought to cross the Jongsong La and climb it from Sikkim."

"And cause an international scandal by getting arrested for spying!"

"It looks a long way to the top from here."

"Eleven-thousand-foot vertical difference, youth – only the same as the top of Mont Blanc from Chamonix."

Pangpema was at an altitude of nearly 17,000 ft., and we would have preferred a day of rest and acclimatisation. However, we had decided to keep six of our Ghunsa porters employed for an extra day, to help us to carry enough equipment to establish a first camp beneath Twins Peak and the icefall that linked the upper and lower Kangchenjunga Glaciers. On the afternoon of our arrival at Pangpema, Georges and Doug sorted through equipment and food for the big carry the next day. Nima Tenzing put tents up and Ang Phurba paid off the remaining porters. Kami and Nima Tamang started building a kitchen shelter by slinging a tarpaulin across some rough stone walls left by the 1930 expedition. Meanwhile, I was arguing with a tall, sharp-faced Tibetan who had brought several yak-loads of wood up for us to Base Camp. He had sub-contracted some of the work to two others, and a hundred kilos more than we had asked for had arrived. Also, he had put the price up from the rate we had agreed in Ghunsa. Ang Phurba was avoiding involvement in the argument, but was enjoying translating for both sides. I needed more support.

"Hey, Joe, you're the hard man with the porters, can you come and help me hassle with this bloke? He needs to be stonewalled. He keeps coming up with a hard-luck story about how ten years ago he was a wealthy man in Tibet, until the Chinese came and took his yaks."

"He looks well-off to me – oh, I know him, he's a real shark. He tried to sell me genuine Dalai Lama hats and boots in Ghunsa."

"Well, we're in the strong position; since he's brought it all here, he's not going to take it back down again, is he?"

"The Sherpas say they can use it all anyway."

"I'd be daft to pay that price, he's just on the make. There'll be inflation here like in the Karakoram if we pay them the first price they ask."

"Just pay him what we arranged in Ghunsa now, let him stew over the problem tonight and open up negotiations in the morning."

In the morning I offered him half price for the surplus and he agreed immediately. The Sherpas and the six porters who had stayed on, thought the whole negotiations were hilarious and I laughed with them, half suspecting that the joke was on me.

We licked envelopes hurriedly, stuffed our letters in a polythene bag and wished our mail runner, Nima Wangdi, a speedy journey. Then we set off towards the mountain. To reach the Kangchenjunga Glacier from Pangpema we had to descend five hundred feet of scree and boulders, then for an hour cross a chaos of unstable moraine before our feet touched the ice of the glacier. The wind brought snow, and soon I was slipping and tripping at the back of the group. Realising that my foot was not ready for big-boulder-hopping, and not wanting to put my recovery back or hold the others up, I returned to Pangpema and went into the kitchen shelter. Its tarpaulin roof was cracking like a pneumatic drill, so I retreated to the sleeping bag inside my tent. I could not relax, and decided in the afternoon to go for a walk and face the bad weather, rather than cower inside from it.

Three and a half hours later I was back, having walked through the blizzard for about fifteen hundred feet up the hillside above the camp, and seen nothing except cloud and scree. Weather like that is never as bad when you go for a walk in it, wind and snow are best confronted. Nevertheless it was so cold it would take us a few days to acclimatise to the change in temperature. The others reached a curve in the glacier which they thought was roughly in a good position for Camp 1, but they were not certain because the visibility was so bad. They had done a phenomenal carry and on their return were consoling about my foot.

"I'm sure it'll be better soon," said Georges.

"These things usually happen for the best," said Joe.

"It was meant to be so we could all wait for you and have to acclimatise," said Doug. The six porters were drinking *rakshi*. 'Stone Cold Sober Again', sang Rod Stewart on the cassette and I lay in my sleeping bag, writing the daily state of mind and foot bulletin:

> I am eaten up at the moment with a restlessness. I have to do something. I can't bring myself to read serious books. It's easier to face one's soul when it's enclosed by a healthy body. I feel terrible thoughts about Georges when I try to walk, and keep asking myself if there was a subconscious, competitive reason why he pushed me. If he has a third party insurance, I could sue him for all the money I'll lose if I can't work properly this summer! I could scream with frustration and anger sometimes, particularly coming down scree slopes, slopes that normally I could slide and leap down. Yet I must reach the top of this mountain.

The storm grew during the evening. I had never known such winds at this altitude in the Himalayas before, they came in terrible gusts. At 4.30 a.m. the wind abated and by dawn the snow cocks in the meadow were chuckling to each other in a temperature of −18°C. We lay in our separate tents spread over the field, talking across to each other, relishing the peace and calm, waiting for the sun to move down to us. It was a rest day, and passed uncluttered until the evening. But I was still in a self-pitying, and uncharitable mood:

> 6.00 p.m. The day is dying and Kangchenjunga has appeared red in sunlight, looking high and vast through a hole in the clouds. I managed a crap today without having to stick one foot out like a Cossack dancer – such is progress. An enormous brown Himalayan griffon vulture flew past this afternoon, mobbed by crows. It was only a few feet away and turned its head to stare at us. It looked unbelievably big, and the fast-swooping crows that were pestering it made it look stiff and ungainly. Perhaps it was intrigued by our rubbish – the Sherpas refuse to burn any of it, since the kitchen fire is of special significance to them and also the folks from Ghunsa said that burning smells cause bad weather. The two Nimas have been down to Lhonak to collect some juniper to burn at their daily altar. I'm all for attracting as much help as they can summon – a large avalanche came off the Twins this afternoon and fell towards the place where the lads think they left the gear yesterday. Why do I respect the Sherpas' beliefs, yet find Doug's musings too superstitious and emotive and react against them? Perhaps I'm just suspicious of mixing cultures too much. I agree with what he says, but his introspection is enough for all of us to take without my joining in.
>
> Georges and Doug have just returned from an excursion to chase after and try to photograph some Himalayan blue sheep. They've also been bouldering this afternoon. Georges is always either hyper-active or sleeping and hypochrondriacal, never in between. He's been bouncing around the Sherpas, discussing with them what makes their wives sing – cooking? washing? chang? Meanwhile, Joe, naturally so lazy when there's nothing

really important to do, has had little Nima rushing backwards and forwards, carrying things to him in his tent. "That's what we pay them for," he says, "it's important to conserve your energy."

I'm sitting in the entrance of my tent playing music, using the last of the daylight to write by. Dusk has cleared the afternoon's clouds, and a growing moon has appeared above our heads. Doug quotes his Chinese Yellow Emperor's Medicine Book as saying that new moons bring strength. He's full of spiritual and nutritional solutions to the climb. He's recently been converted to vegetarianism so, since he organised the food, we have along a lot of different varieties of beans. He's directing cooking operations from his little brown bean book. Tonight it's black-eyed bean stew.

The next day Georges had diarrhoea, and stayed at Base Camp whilst I went up the glacier with Doug and Joe. Walking unladen, I managed to keep up with them – impressed at the distance of the carry they had done two days previously. From the site of the equipment cache we estimated the risks from the encircling séracs. The large avalanche of the day before, from some séracs on Twins Peak, had not reached the equipment, although the run-out slope of fresh debris was only fifty yards away. The only dangers would be from the blasts from avalanches – vacuums and the accelerating air that are generated by a large fall. It was not far-fetched to imagine that everywhere on this north west side of Kangchenjunga was threatened by such blasts. We decided to stay where we were, and put the tents up. Camp 1 was established.

Joe and I had just finished reading *Goodbye to All That*, Robert Graves' autobiography about life in the trenches during the First World War. During all the time we were on the Kangchenjunga Glacier, we were accompanied by the almost constant booming of collapsing séracs, and this book gave us a whole new terminology to play with. 'Cushies' were minor injuries that enabled you to move back from the almost inevitable fatality of the front line. 'Sniper fire' was occasional stonefall. Now, at Camp 1, we tried to distinguish between the splitting and cracking of the glacier beneath us and the different sounds of sérac fire coming from the North Face of Kangchenjunga – the sounds that mattered, that you woke up and tried to run away from, and the sounds that you allowed yourself to sleep through. About every half hour, a sérac fell. It was a fitful night.

"At least when you charge, you're doing something about it, rather than lying here waiting for it to happen," said Joe.

We stayed until the sun lit up our tents. At 9.00 a.m. we walked out into the middle of the glacier to look up at the icefall that guarded the upper Kangchenjunga Glacier, and to estimate the danger of three collections of séracs poised above it.

"All our Derbyshire experience on the East Face of Mam Tor has brought us to expect this," said Joe.

Doug repeatedly encouraged me. "Just come along with us and see how far you can get. It doesn't matter if you decide to turn back."

We wandered through the ice cliffs and crevasses of the lower icefall, building cairns out of the rocks that lay on the surface. Then we reached a bowl of snow, swept into a smooth slope by avalanches from above. It was not a place to linger, and we steadily moved forwards, probing the snow in front of us for crevasses and discovering many. The 1930 expedition had nearly lost one of their porters in such a concealed trap. Although I had needed a pull on the rope to help me over a couple of steps in the icefall, I now broke trail in the snow for an hour, happy to be involved in the action.

Above the slope the glacier surface was slashed by huge crevasses. Joe, then Doug took over and led us through the area, finding a switchback route in the upper curve of the Kangchenjunga Glacier. We had no alternative but to walk along the bottom of one enormous crevasse with high, leaning walls, and we christened it Death Valley. We wanted to find a site for our second camp and also gain enough height to have a clear view of the west wall of the North Col. Our trail behind us looked like that of a drunken man.

"The 1930 camp was further in the middle, wasn't it?"

"The avalanche nearly hit it, Smythe had set off running when he saw it coming down."

"We'd better keep the camp over here, those slopes on the Twins above us look too steep and icy to allow much of a build-up."

We discussed the problem until we all agreed about the siting of the camp. Although we had strong mutual respect for each other's mountaineering judgment and skills, it was important that all of us constantly questioned each other's decisions. We knew that the collective strength and tension of this questioning increased our chances of staying alive. I was overawed by the gloomy history that had haunted the cwm during the forty-nine years since the death of Sherpa Chettan. We were the first people to enter the cwm since then, and the accident weighed freshly on our minds, as if we were ourselves survivors of it.

We had all read various descriptions of the avalanche that nearly wiped out most of the members of the 1930 expedition. They had been trying to reach the North Ridge by climbing the narrowest point of the ice cliff below the first terrace of the North West Face, when a huge portion of the cliff collapsed. Frank Smythe saw it happen from the camp: "Great masses of ice, as large as cathedrals, were toppling to destruction."

Dyhrenfurth was in the thick of it:

A high cracking sound was the first thing I heard. Then I saw that at the very top of the cliff – somewhat to my right – an ice wall perhaps a thousand feet wide began slowly to topple forward. It seemed minutes, though I am sure it only lasted a matter of seconds, before the huge face broke and came crashing down in a gigantic avalanche of ice. The impact of the fragments whirled up a curtain of snow and ice particles which broadened with incredible velocity into a solid, perpendicular wall. I ran towards the left – if running is the right word for moving quickly in deep powder snow at twenty thousand feet, with little hope of escaping. It was a horrible feeling when the blast knocked me over, but as I fell I instinctively shielded my face with my arm. The uproar all around me was frightening. I lay in the snow and awaited death.

Smythe estimated that the debris was several feet thick, covered a square mile of snowfield and weighed one million tons. Miraculously, only one person, Sherpa Chettan, had been killed. The sérac had actually toppled over Erwin Schneider, leaving him unharmed.

During the next few weeks, as we walked below this wall to the face of the North Col, it was to be our constant fear that a similar avalanche might occur and we could not rely on the same accompanying luck if it did.

Doug and I left our loads on the rock around which we had chosen to establish Camp 2. Short gusts of wind scurried across the cwm and we turned to descend. Far across on the other side of the horseshoe of the North West Face rose the aggressive, challenging summit of the 22,140 ft. (6,749 m.) Wedge Peak. It would not be long, I hoped, before we were looking down on it from the North Ridge of Kang-chenjunga.

I was glad to have contributed to the forward momentum of the expedition for the first time. My injury no longer isolated me.

Through the expedition we seemed to pass between us a debilitating baton of sickness and set-backs. Joe and Georges had already suffered from colds and diarrhoea. Now it was my turn. For three days I was ill. I managed to scribble occasional notes in my diary:

I can't remember having felt so sick . . . Joe is rushing around, fixing his overboots, his activity mocking my prone inertness. At dinner I tell the others I won't be able to go back up yet. They're all for sticking together, and not splitting up the team. They'll wait until I'm better . . . The first time I go to the loo in the night is appalling. I can hardly get warm again, and am aching all over with cold. My foot and hands are numb, and I start worrying if I'll pass out from hypothermia. Outside, it snows heavily, and then the moon appears – it's surreal to feel ill in this place. Woke with a splitting head that seems to stretch right round to my back . . . I have a lot of hot water to sip and have now started reading *Sense and Sensibility*; a lovely, civilised change and a contrast to here and now. I still go to the cook tent at meal times, not to eat, but to keep in with all the decisions . . . I at last fit a pair of crampons to my boots – there now, that was a positive step . . . I'm just going to have a go tomorrow. I haven't eaten much for three days, and dread fainting or weakly collapsing on the walk up to Camp 1 – but the foot and body should be well rested. We're all going up to work for a few days till we've stocked Camp 2, and fixed the route up to the North Col. Ang Phurba and Nima Tenzing are going to come and carry loads in support. Then we'll make a quick reconnaissance up the ridge and come back here for a rest and THE MAIL RUNNER. Then we'll climb back up for the summit push. That's the Sports Plan.

The foot was beginning to feel weak rather than broken, and for the first time I carried a load. Crossing the boulder field, I only twinged it once, and Georges and Joe waited for me to chat for a while. The mist swirled in, and we walked past fins and sails of ice to Camp 1.

We were professional old hands, and most of the time assumed that each of us would look after himself. Outward Bound, and other outdoor-education philosophies would have one believe that mountain climbing develops character, courage, resourcefulness and team work. That may be so, but it is also true that mountaineering expeditions can develop selfishness, fanaticism, glory-seeking and cunning. At Camp 1 we played the opening rounds of a half-serious game that was to develop through the expedition – 'High-Altitude Manoeuvring'. The main aims of this game are personal survival, self-image survival, personal success and personal comfort. The first rule is not to be seen playing by the others. If anyone plays too overtly, or extremely, the game – and the expedition – collapse.

The game requires the participation of all the members, and has been played to a greater or lesser extent since expeditioning began. As time distances one from the events the manoeuvring seems less serious and more funny, and one's own involvement seems self-righteous. I filled my diaries with observations of the others' manoeuvring, but few confessions of my own:

Next door Georges and Doug are sharing a tent. Georges hasn't brought any books and can't sit still. Bob Dylan howls out for hour after hour from the cassette player. It's like camping next to a pack of wolves. Doug seems to have got us to cook for the Sherpas. He won't let them cook because they're staying in his tunnel tent, and he's afraid they'll burn it down. So now they're in here, gassing us with a primus stove that refuses to light. Sherpas are always useless with primus stoves. Joe has decided that I'm to cook every evening meal, and he'll do the breakfasts. Now I find I have to cook the Sherpas' tea also . . . Doug seems to have to prove he's strong (we all know he is) by exaggerating the weight he's carrying, and putting the weight the others are carrying down in his estimation. I tried to borrow the cassette deck off him, but he resents Joe's light load and thinks we don't deserve it. But then he apologises. You can't have a maxim 'if I carried it up, only I can use it' . . . I wonder what the Sherpas think of us.

We decided to carry loads up to Camp 2 for two days, and then to climb on above, leaving Ang Phurba and Nima Tenzing to shuttle more equipment up directly from Base Camp. The first day Georges was nudged up to the front, since he had missed the earlier foray on to the Upper Kangchenjunga Glacier. Wind and snow had erased our earlier tracks. He prodded the surface in front of him vigorously with a long bamboo cane, searching for concealed crevasses. It sank in deeply everywhere.

"Good job you're not that thin," said Joe.

As we climbed we improved and marked the route for future ferrying – leaving more cairns and canes, cutting steps in the ice and chopping away the lips of the crevasses we had to cross. Reassuringly, the site of Camp 2 had not been disturbed by avalanches since we were last there.

Back at Camp 1 in the evening Joe and I were lying, wide awake and twitching, listening to avalanches.

"You know on Everest, Camp 2 was hit by the blast of an avalanche which threw a tent in the air with five people in it on top of another one," I said.

"Once hit, twice shy."

"We're right at the end of the run-out for those séracs on Twins Peak. They would pick up a hell of a speed falling two thousand feet."

"Well, there's nothing we can do about it. Anyway, we can identify the shell noises."

I started up at the first thumping of blocks.

"A trial run," said Joe. "It takes two aims for them to line up the target, and then . . ."

"Who's the spotter then? God?"

There was an ominous note in the roar of the second avalanche. I unzipped the tent door, stuck my head out and swore. The sky was filled with falling ice and snow, thundering down towards us with a noise like a jet plane hurtling to destruction.

"Grab the tent and poles, Joe!"

For a few seconds the ice beneath us shuddered and the tent heaved and flapped as we hung on to it. Then the blast faded. I stuck my head out again and saw Georges doing the same. No block had hit us, we had just suffered a dusting and shaking. From the tunnel tent I heard Nima muttering insistent prayers. I wished I could propitiate who or whatever had a finger on the sérac button. The third strike was not as powerful.

"They put too much effort into that second one," said Joe.

"I think we should shift this camp," I said.

Next door, Georges was saying the same. The moon rose and I looked at my watch. 10.00 p.m., Friday 13th.

"We should be O.K. in a couple of hours." We never stayed at Camp 1 again.

The next day we moved up to Camp 2. Nima Tenzing had with him a polythene bag full of holy rice which, whilst chanting prayers, he scattered over potentially dangerous-looking crevasses, slopes and séracs.

"I hope he sticks all that snow together," said Joe.

"I bet there's a Yeti down that crevasse, eating it all up," I said.

When Nima arrived at Camp 2, he took one look at the tier upon tier of séracs and threw the remainder of the rice in a sweeping gesture at the entire North West Face of Kangchenjunga.

THE WALL

15th – 30th April, 1979

We grew self-conscious and fell quiet, afraid to flaunt our smallness beneath the stupendous walls of ice, each of us locked in as much thought as the altitude would allow.

> Are the others as worried as I am? Aren't we being presumptuous? How many times will we have to walk this gauntlet gasping, our legs weaving urgently through the danger-zones? The plod of the light brigade, that's what this is. Once we reach there, we'll be out of danger from the Twins. Once we reach the next point further on, we'll be out of danger from Kangchenjunga. At least the wall to the North Col looks too steep to collect loose snow and ice. It looks steep enough to be safe.

If we could reach the North Col by climbing its West Wall, then we would escape from the sérac-threatened cwm, and above that the North Ridge that curved up from the col to the summit appeared free of objective dangers. We selected a direct route up the wall to the col, tracing a line through its corduroy of rock ribs and snow gullies.

The eyes of 1930 had dismissed the wall as a 'sheer ice-armoured precipice', concluding there was no possible way to the North Ridge except over the ice wall and lower terrace they had attempted. But in 1930, mountaineers did not have our jumars, curved axes and hammers, twelve-point crampons, low stretch nylon ropes and sophisticated rock and ice pitons. Now we looked at the three-thousand-foot wall, knowing that although it was dangerous going to and from its foot, and it would be time-absorbing to climb, at least we had got up similar obstacles in the Alps before. Although obviously very difficult, the wall would be safe and secure, and we would be acclimatising during the effort.

Doug broke the trail into the upper cwm, and we marked our route with canes. It took us two hours to reach a snow bridge across the bergschrund at the foot of the wall, at a point three thousand feet directly below the lowest point of the North Col. There was no logistical framework behind our approach to the mountain, as there had been on the large, systematic South West Face of the Everest expedition in 1975. This time we had just stuffed ropes and hardware into our sacks and set off to have a look. Our expedition had no official leader – which made us an expedition of four leaders. However, decisions had to be made. Despite his insistence on democracy, it was often Doug who, by strength of personality, made the most forceful suggestions during our continual discussions. Joe probably had the hardest time accepting them, but rather than he and Doug butting against each other like two billy-goats, he often kept quiet when the issue was not important enough to risk a confrontation. One has to swallow a lot of feeling, including pride, to unite to climb a mountain. The best way to communicate an idea was to feed it to Georges and persuade him to take it up. Everyone trusted him as being completely open; he could bluntly say what he thought, without inhibitions and no one was offended. The three 'Anglais' knew each other's weaknesses too well. However, we accepted Georges without suspicion.

Someone had to make a suggestion. Nobody wanted to be seen to be pairing off with someone else. Our climbing partners would have to be interchangeable, otherwise competition rather than unity would result.

"How about Joe and Georges climbing together and you come with me?" said Doug.

I was flattered that he had chosen the cripple, for this meant that he would be under the pressure of doing all the leading.

"Tak, tak, tak," exclaimed Georges. It was his favourite French ice-climbing noise, which he followed with his favourite Franco-Americanism "Let's go for eet." He tied on to two of the ropes, pulled his way across the snow bridge and bounded up the slope above.

The bergschrund was at an altitude of twenty thousand feet. We looked along our tracks which shied across the cwm, skirting imagined danger zones, to the dark smudge of Camp 2, on the edge of the smooth white world of the upper cwm, above the confusion of the icefall. The lines of séracs stretched across the North West Face of Kangchenjunga with the poised menace of serried ranks of nuclear warheads. Seventy miles away in the west rose Everest and Makalu.

"We may as well go back to the camp," said Doug. "No point in hanging around here with cold toes."

"Yes, let them get on with it."

Forty-five minutes later we were watching Georges' and Joe's progress through binoculars, with the stove beside us melting snow for a brew of tea; then cloud filled the cwm and it began to snow lightly.

When Georges and Joe returned we eagerly absorbed and discussed the details of their day.

"It's a good hard ice after the first couple of pitches. The rock's very compact – it doesn't like pegs."

"It's an Alpine T.D., like the North Spur of Les Droites."

"It's a long way – I hope we don't run out of rope before we reach the col."

"Who led?"

"Georges. I was load-carrying today. What's for dinner anyway?"

"Bean stew."

"You can't cook beans at this height."

"You can with a pressure cooker."

"I'm losing weight."

"We'll be farting so much we'll be able to climb the mountain by jet propulsion."

"They'll just be taking the Easter Sunday roast out of the oven at home now."

The next day the weather was too bad to move, and we read and talked. The snow, however, did not deter Ang Phurba and Nima Tenzing, who arrived with a load. Nima told us that according to his Tibetan calendar the weather would be bad for three days.

"Look at those crows, they've followed us up."

"Scavengers – they always seem to turn up on every expedition."

"You sure they're not choughs?"

"Probably. Some sort of Corvidae anyway."

On the 17th April Georges kicked his way through the freshly-fallen snow and we filed behind him. Snow slides had buried the equipment left at the foot of the wall, and we burrowed head first for it, our feet kicking in the air. All four of us carried loads up the five ropes that Joe and Georges had fixed and then Doug and I were left to carry on with the climb.

Between 11.00 a.m. and 5.00 p.m., Doug led steadily up steep ice and rock. I climbed up the ropes he fixed, carrying a thousand feet of rope in my sack, my injured foot firmly strapped and braced sideways across the ice, my lungs gasping and my thoughts blurred and wandering with the altitude. The last pitch of the day was a difficult diagonal traverse, halfway up the trail through a rock barrier, and after fighting his way above it Doug was exhausted with the effort and dehydration. He slid down the ropes, and after dumping the load at the high point I followed him.

On the glacier, Doug doubled up with stomach cramps, vomiting from the effort and heat of a day without fluid. We had forgotten to bring water bottles. Beyond him the sun set behind Everest and Makalu. Camp 2 brought refreshment and company. It was becoming our haven, retreat, rest house, our cosy three-tent hamlet. I was encouraged by my foot – it seemed stronger. I was looking forward to a night's sleep, to a rest day whilst Joe and Georges took their turn at the front and to the action the day after that.

The rest day was gloriously hot. Doug stripped to his underpants. We sat in the scorching sunshine, which reflected intensely around the white cwm, turning it into a great oven of ice. The heat made us dozy with glacier lassitude – 'glassy lassy', we called it. Idly, we fiddled with cameras, crampons and headtorches, and looked at the two tiny dots of Joe and Georges, working their way up the shining ice of the wall. We felt comfortably detached in our security and inaction.

There was a load roar and our eyes jerked around till we saw the cause. An avalanche was plunging from some séracs on Twins Peak with the energy of a sudden dam-burst. The spearhead was imbued with a monstrous life, and, on hitting the cwm floor between our camp and the wall, it exploded forwards to cross the glacier in leaps and bounds and then climbed hundreds of feet up the North West Face of Kangchenjunga, having swept the entire breadth of the glacier. We were finely dusted, as the fall-out of snow finally settled.

From their eyrie on the wall, Joe and Georges had a bird's-eye view of the whole incident. Later in the day, when they returned across the lumpy debris of the avalanche, they estimated that it had covered their morning tracks for half a mile, to a depth of ten feet.

It was unnerving to walk back over the debris the next day, despite my rationalisations: "It's taken me about twenty minutes to cross the danger zone. The whole avalanche only lasted about three minutes, which is a tiny, tiny fraction of the time we've been here. And that was probably the most dangerous part of the sérac that fell down, and it'll be safe now."

Doug went first up the fixed ropes, and when he reached a convenient tiny ledge above his rockband, he lit a stove and prepared some orange juice whilst he waited for me. "Here you are, youth, have a sip of this. What do you think of whilst you're jumaring?"

"Oh, I don't know; nothing much really. My thoughts just circle around all sorts of things, it's like dreaming, I can't control them, it's as if they're sorting themselves out."

"Gurdjief would call that sort of thinking a waste of energy – not having direction. Here, will you carry my camera and take some shots of me leading this? I'm going to aim for the end of that ramp. The lads did some steep pitches yesterday."

"The ice looks brittle and Georges said that roof was hard."

"At least we're gaining height; we must be about twenty-two

Kangchenjunga North Ridge, 1979. *Above*, a strong team for a formidable climb: left to right, Doug Scott, Joe Tasker, Georges Bettembourg and Peter Boardman (DS). *Below*, Georges leaving the North Col for the Castle, 1,800 feet above. Strong wind maintained good cramponing snow (PB).

Above, Doug and Georges above the North Col. For the first time we could see Tibet (PB). *Below*, the Summit Pyramid of Kangchenjunga showing the Croissant, Ramp, and brêche beside the pinnacles on the West Ridge (PB).

Pete and Joe at 28,000 feet on Kangchenjunga (DS).

Gauri Sankar West Ridge, 1979. Pete and Guy Neithardt on the Vire Neithardt (JB).

Above, Guy belays the injured John Barry towards Pemba and Fawlty Towers on Gauri Sankar West Ridge (PB). *Below*, K2, 1980. Pete and Dick Renshaw at the fourth camping place on the Shoulder of the Abruzzi Ridge during the second main attempt (JT).

Everest West Ridge, 1980. *Above*, the mountain from the south-west. The level plateau of the Lho La is on the left and the West Ridge cuts diagonally up towards the summit (JT). *Below*, a 3,000-foot avalanche from the Lho La down the 'Burgess couloir' (JT).

Ade Burgess traversing above the amphitheatre towards the Lho La plateau with the slopes up to the West Shoulder on the right (JT).

Above left, Paul Nunn descending the steep wall from Camp 1 (JT). *Above right*, Ade coming up through the ice-coated rocks towards the rock barrier below Camp 2 (JT). *Below*, Camp 2, perched at 22,500 feet, was later destroyed by the wind (PN).

thousand feet. Kangbachen's slowly coming down to our size."

Doug clawed his way on to the smooth ice of the ramp, through the falling snow of the afternoon. A ropelength above his head another rock barrier jutted out. From our binocular studies, we knew it guarded the final slope to the North Col. I was frustrated that my foot would not allow me to help in the lead. However, another big effort, we hoped, would take us there.

We all decided to take a rest day, reach the North Col, go for a one-day reconnaissance up the ridge and then return to Base Camp for a rest, food and further acclimatisation.

I'm feeling better during this rest day than I have done for ages, but as usual, I'm worried about my health – little aches and pains. I know I'm always nervous, but I can't remember if it's usually this much. It's so difficult to compare my fears and performances, past, present and future. One isn't the same when one tackles successive climbs. All the stories, the fears, past experiences and future unknowns, roll in and fall over each other in a mixture of optimism and fear. Looking back, Everest was quite a straightforward affair for me, in that my ambition was very simple and clear headed. Also, I feel older and more vulnerable than I did on the Changabang trip in '76, when there was only Joe and me. Then, being just two generated a barrier of intensity that kept a lot of fears out, and either risks were easier to take then or I was less aware of dangers. Also, the rock was firm granite! Now we're forecasting, health and weather permitting, to reach the top in the first week of May. I hope so.

Ang Phurba and Nima Tenzing arrived with some loads from Base Camp – and some letters. Although they were over a month old, written not long after our departure, we seized our bundles of mail possessively and submerged ourselves in thoughts of home for the rest of the day. I read mine many times and lay down digesting the emotional nourishment, and exchanging snippets of news with the others.

"Why do people always say 'send me a card' – I wish they'd write to me instead. I need it more than they do."

"Look, there's a postcard here from a sixteen-man Czechoslovak expedition trying the West Ridge of Jannu – they've all signed it. They met our mail runner at Ghunsa. Nice of them."

"I wonder if they've got any spare rope."

"Well they've got a doctor – we'll be all right there."

Dawn was icy blue as we shouldered our packs crammed with equipment for the North Col. We manoeuvred for starting positions. "You and Joe had better go last up the ropes in case any stuff comes down – you've got helmets."

One after the other, we went over the bergschrund and up the rope.

As we gasped upwards we were each too involved in a lonely effort to notice the clouds move around us and the snow rest silently on our clothes – symptoms that steadily deteriorated into the violent crisis of a storm.

Thunder rolled through the sky beyond the ten feet of my vision. The others were crouched together, hanging on an ice screw on the ramp. Powder snow streamed over me, building up on my rucksack, pushing me over, exploring ways behind my goggles and into my mouth and nostrils.

"Pete!" Click. "What a photo!"

Four of us balanced on the ice, unpacking and packing our rucksacks, tying our sleeping bags to our waists for the only option – retreat and descent. Powder snow swept over our feet; it was like standing in a thin white flood over a concrete weir. Larger snow slides plunged over rock steps and billowed into the air.

"They're not really that dangerous, they just look dangerous."

"This slope's too steep to allow the build-up for a killer slide."

We danced down the ropes. We were submitting to the mountain's decision, and I realised I was enjoying myself.

In the evening, back at Camp 2, I crouched inside my sleeping bag with the hood pulled over and one arm, with a biro in my hand, extended out of the top like an antenna into the cold to write:

It was a failure-day that felt like a success. It's amazing how fast the weather changes on this mountain. Now it's still snowing lightly – and, worryingly, rather wetly. We hope it's not wet enough for the long slope on Twins next to us to build up all night and knock tomorrow morning's breakfast over. We've decided to go down tomorrow to relax and eat at Base Camp. We need a lot of food – we're not eating enough to sustain these carries to over twenty-two thousand feet. Also, we've lost a lot of weight – must have been breaking down muscles to provide energy during the last few days. We've left most of our gear at the high point – down suits, Karrimats and pee-bottles – I miss them now!

It seemed as if the four of us had been together forever. However, the shift system of alternating the leads on the wall, and the close living at Camp 2, had prevented me from talking much to Georges or Joe for a few days. When we were all together it was impossible to talk about each other. As Joe and I descended through the deep snow to Base Camp we gossiped relaxedly and freely – it was a good safety valve to do so; it improved our perspective on ourselves and our performance and helped the scenery move past.

Back at Base Camp after nine days away, we exchanged genuine warm smiles of greeting. Mohan related the world news. Nima Wangdi had brought oranges, bananas and cabbage with the mail.

Kami and Nima Tamang prepared nirvana snacks of eggs and potatoes. All were tastes from another world.

At first the three rest days that stretched ahead were all that existed.
An outsider, listening to us chatting, happily and excitedly, might
have thought we had reached the summit. Coming down to the
security of Base Camp helped us realise how much under constant
pressure and on edge we had been on the mountain. Beneath the
wind-rattled tarpaulin of the kitchen shelter we reminded ourselves
not to tense with every sound outside. Sudden noises were no threat
here. Georges entertained us, his arms sweeping and eyes glittering
with enthusiasm, with an animated monologue about guiding and
crystal and mineral hunting in the Mont Blanc range. We were away
from the warfare for three days – and three days have a beginning, a
middle and an end. The first night our happiness was total.

It was a long evening, and when I walked across the grass to my tent
I remembered how ill I had been in this place before. Now I could walk
almost properly, and was no longer weak with stomach illness. I had
become more interested in reading, writing, climbing, in everything.
The air was heavy with oxygen, and I slept peacefully. Joe's morning
groan from the next tent, and a cup of tea, brought the new day in.

> Yesterday all was relief to be down here – now the mountain looms back
> into my thoughts. I wonder what lies before us – a lightning push for the
> summit, past a blur of rock and snow? But that won't give time for the
> feeling of 'home' up there, so necessary for confidence.

For three hours we chatted outside my tent in the sunshine – looking
up and across at the storm-plastered mountain, talking out our hopes
and fears, united by the same predicament. None of us knew if we
were physically capable of reaching the summit. Even the two continental super-athletes who had climbed Everest without oxygen
equipment the year before had suffered hallucinations and double
vision. Would our lungs collapse, would our brains swell inside our
skulls and make us faint, would the blood in our legs clot? Would our
hearts palpitate? Would we suffer permanent brain damage and never
think or talk the same again? Once up there, would we be able to make
it back down again?

The distances high on the mountain seemed vast. From Schneider's
map we calculated that the five-thousand-foot altitude difference
between the North Col and the summit was spread over two and a
quarter miles of North Ridge. We flicked through the books and
photographs of the mountain, looking from them, to the mountain
and back.

"Bauer, he's the bloke to learn from. Look what he did with those

Munich men in 1929 and 1931 on the North East Spur. The Alpine Journal said it was the greatest achievement ever: 'a feat unparalleled in the annals . . .' etc.''

"A lot of fanatics, they were. They were still fighting the First World War. He just about says they climbed to avenge the humiliation of the Treaty of Versailles. Listen to what Bauer says here: '. . . stern, warlike disciplined spirit . . . a circle of men who have become one to the death.' ''

"I hope we don't have to be that intense."

"They used snow-holes big enough for eight men and reckoned they could carry loads up to eight thousand metres at half-European-Alps speed."

"They didn't get that high, though."

"I hope we do. Wouldn't it be fantastic if we climbed it and were back down here in ten days' time?"

"A bit improbable, though."

"It's a pity it was a Saturday when we got turned back from the North Col. According to Nima's Tibetan calendar, if the weather is bad on a Saturday it will be bad for a week."

"In Pakistan they say the same thing about Fridays."

"Look, we've still got to reach the North Col and we haven't enough rope to do it."

We had forgotten our geometry lessons. We had brought with us a thousand metres of rope, and Erwin Schneider had told us that the West Wall was nearly a thousand metres high. It had taken us a long time to realise that since the wall was not absolutely vertical, and our route was not completely direct, it was inevitable that we would run out of rope.

"I don't fancy using any of these grotty bits of string around Base Camp."

"What about the Slovaks on Jannu then? They might lend us some."

"That's a good four-day round trip to their Base Camp."

"Ang Phurba might nip across if we ask him nicely."

Ang Phurba agreed to trot down to Ghunsa and up to the Base Camp of the Slovak Jannu expedition, to try and borrow some. We sent a humble begging letter – and a fruit cake as a peace offering. He returned two days later, carrying four hundred feet of rope and a tin of vodka, and justifiably demanding a day's rest.

On the K2 expedition I had sent a lot of postcards inscribed 'Only 9,000 ft. to go!' Four days later we had abandoned the climb. Now we had no newspaper contact demanding a supply of regular pot-warming reports to remind a public about our adventure. I decided only to write to Hilary and my parents until I had something positive to report.

Our sleep became deeper, with fewer remembered dreams, until it was time to return to the mountain.

We returned to Camp 2 in the brilliance of the morning. We were fitter, with clearer thoughts and hearty appetites. It seemed as if we had never left. In the afternoon the mist came down and we lay in our tents, shouting out our pulse rates at thirty-second intervals:

"37."

"41."

"47."

"47!"

"You two aren't very fit."

"I'm reading pornography."

"I've got a hangover from the vodka."

At 4.30 in the morning our defences were low against the grim realities of the day. Georges had been complaining of stomach cramps during the walk up. He was still not feeling well and had not slept. Joe had a headache and was sleepless also. I felt frustrated and impatient. "Well, if you weren't sleeping you should have taken a sleeping pill like me," I said.

"You're not as alert if you take drugs," said Doug.

"Are you all going to stop every time someone has a bad night?" I said.

"You've no sympathy when someone else is ill," snapped Joe.

We decided to postpone the move another day. I lamented the lost time in my diary:

I've never been on such a frustrating stop-go expedition. We've already had more rest days than Joe and I had on the entire Changabang trip. It's misty and very still outside, and we're back exactly where we were a week ago. I want to get up there and to get to grips with the problem, one way or another, because time, strength, supplies and good weather all slip away. Georges oscillates in his Latin way, like a yo-yo. Joe calls him a butterfly. Now it's his liver or gall bladder. I dish out pills and eventually he decides on a course of Septrin. Suddenly Tigger is back bouncing optimistically about, which irritates throbbing-head Joe more, and is a bit tactless.

On the 28th April Doug, Georges, Joe, Ang Phurba and Nima Tenzing and I set off in a line up the fixed ropes on the wall, intending to establish a camp on the North Col. Doug and Georges moved up quickly with light loads, and by late morning Georges was fighting up an overhanging chimney that split the rocks below the final snow slope. Meanwhile, the Sherpas were having difficulty jumaring the tension traverse and vertical step of the halfway rock barrier that Doug had first led. Nima had to give up and go down; Joe and I divided his load between us. Then Ang Phurba became stuck for an hour. By

1.00 p.m. I was two thirds of the way up the wall and four hundred feet below Doug and Georges, who were now hauling their sacks up the chimney.

Suddenly Joe shouted and I looked up at a sky scattered with falling rocks. I dodged sideways but as the rocks exploded around me my left forearm was smashed just above the wrist. I felt as if I had been hit by a bullet. Overcome with fright, pain and rage, I wanted to fire back and shrieked with the thought I was crippled. In a state of shock, I eased off my two gloves and saw a depressing swelling and gash. Blood dripped on to the snow. Joe came down and filled with sympathy when he saw the mangled damage. He had managed to duck under an overhang. One of the rocks had missed Ang Phurba's head by a few inches. Joe related a detailed story of how he had once broken four bones in his wrist when he tumbled off Three Pebble Slab at Froggatt, and how his wrist had looked exactly like mine.

"I couldn't feel a thing for ten minutes. Then the pain came."

"This doesn't seem to be my trip, I wonder what I've done wrong," I said.

"You must have sinned," said Joe. "Perhaps it was going to New Guinea with a bird."

"It's almost as if the rocks were pushed on purpose," I said. "They couldn't have been aimed better."

"It was carelessness."

"The clumsy idiots could have killed all three of us. When you get up there, tell whoever knocked the rocks off, from me, tell them, tell them . . ." I turned in anger and abseiled, one-handed, down the ropes. I crunched so furiously into the ice that one of my crampons came off. As I strapped it back on I took deep breaths and told myself to calm down. It started to snow. At the bottom of the ropes I met Nima Tenzing, waiting for Ang Phurba to return. When he saw my wrist, he shook his head and said it was better to have a broken wrist than a broken head. I walked to Camp 2 alone and doctored myself.

During the night I woke, imagining arterial contusions and poisoning, and changed the dressings on my wrist. I spent the following day lying in the tunnel tent, reading and writing, plucking at the tangle of the present.

Dawn: Nima, next door, is muttering 'Om Mani Padme Hum' over the roar of the stove. Ang Phurba wakes up to the brew. He was very tired last night and seems so this morning too. He has a sore throat, and stiff limbs from all the hard ice of yesterday – "harder than the South West Face of Everest," he said.

The western sky is unusually dark, with a thin light on Wedge Peak . . . Now it's thundering and snowing heavily, straight down with no wind. The noise of falling séracs pinches awake my 'irrational' fear of avalanches.

The others only reached the col in darkness and a snowstorm last night. They still had quite a way to go when I last saw them. I wonder (with half concern, because they're quite capable of looking after themselves) how they're faring today – whether they'll come down or sit it out. If the camp's good they'll stick it out I expect. I wish in a way Joe had come back down with me yesterday – it's far more fun to chat to someone, though I feel quite cheerful. I made a lot of noise when I was hit – like a child – and feel embarrassed about it now. I've been 'in the wars' this trip, as Gran would say. 'It's all in the lap of the gods,' to quote Doug. Perhaps I'm cracking up, but I do wonder about superstitions, fate patterns. I'm amazed – perhaps a bit shocked – at my own determination to get up this climb. It seems to go on and on, and I long to get it over with. We've only had five days' climbing in the last two weeks. Day after day passes, and a breakthrough must come.

Mid-day: The Sherpas knock snow off their tent. It's linked by a guyline to mine, and makes a startling booming noise, which wakes me up. These Kangch storms do seem short-lived. I fell asleep whilst this morning's storm was raging and now I wake to calm. Even the choughs are back. I've re-dressed the cut on my wrist again, and it feels slightly better – or perhaps it's because the air is warmer . . . I saw figures on the col a while ago, through the binoculars. I wish I was there with them, looking over into Sikkim, I hope they don't plan to go for the summit before I get up there tomorrow.

5.15. Thunder returned in long rolls and sharp cracks. This place wears on my nerves. It's snowing for the fourth time today, piling deep on the glacier. To think we had a month's perfect weather on Everest in '75! Half an hour ago I exchanged waves with a figure on the col – at least I could tell through the binoculars that he was waving, though I doubt if he could see me. I've sorted our loads for tomorrow.

Dusk: It's stopped snowing and some stars and a misty crescent moon are shining, but lightning still flashes over Kangchenjunga.

It snowed all the next day. Followed by Ang Phurba and Nima Tenzing, I went back up the familiar ropes and over the landmarks of three thousand feet of mixed ice and rock, pulling with one hand, determined not to turn back this time. Powder avalanches poured over us, and one of them concealed a rock, which hit Nima Tenzing and injured his back. Nima insisted that we continue, and that he was capable of going back down alone. He tied off his load to a piton and descended.

I heard voices in the mist above. Doug and Georges were coming down to pick up some equipment that they had left below the final slope. They had not guessed we would come back up in such bad weather, and had been clearing loose rocks.

The wall was littered with abandoned stuff-sacks and gear left in the forays and about-turns of the previous two weeks. Georges' chimney was desperately strenuous, but the last slope fell back to forty-five degrees. The Slovak rope was strung down it, and I clipped in. I counted my steps from one to twenty-five, and then rested my head on my ice axe and gasped for breath. I was determined not to let Ang Phurba catch me up, to keep him out of sight in the mist. The rope was tied to a large boulder. I stood on top of the rock and the wind met my face. The wall was below me. I hope I don't have to come up there again, I thought.

II

ORDEAL BY STORM

30th April – 5th May, 1979

I followed the tracks into Sikkim. For thirty feet across the broad swathe of its saddle, the col was blasted by the westerly wind. Then the snow became deep and powdery, the light warmed my face, and the wind died as suddenly as it had lived. The sun burnt through the clouds, catching a teeming sky full of swaying points of light like the spray from some distant waterfall. Although there was no view that afternoon, the change of angle and the prospect of company were enough recompense after the loneliness of the long distance jumar.

"Hey up, youth, come inside – there's some hot orange ready for you."

I sipped the drink gratefully – I had become dehydrated through hours of gasping up the ropes. "I'd better not finish it all – Ang Phurba's coming up soon with a load."

Two tunnel tents were dug into a trench in the slope, sixty feet down on the other side of the col. They looked well settled, like two larvae who had wriggled there to hibernate.

"You'd better move in with Georges," said Doug. "We're all organised in here."

"I'm glad you didn't go without me," I said.

"The weather's been too bad to think of it. How's your wrist?" asked Joe. He had a headache and explained that he had been out-manoeuvred the night they reached the col. "I was the last to arrive and was greeted by 'Where are you going to sleep?' We only got one tent up and I had a bad night all scrunched up at the back of it. I've had a headache ever since. Yes, I've tried everything – Fortral, Panadol,

Codeine, sleeping pills – the lot. Nothing'll shift it. Doug found this place. Good eh?" Then Joe closed his eyes and replied only in monosyllables.

Ang Phurba arrived and looked at the camp site with a nod of approval "You go from here to the summit?" he asked. He then unpacked his load, drank, and went back down the wall to Camp 2, leaving the four of us alone on the North Col.

The tents were linked together by a sleeve entrance. We took it in turns to cook, carefully handing food and drinks between us like astronauts passing precious materials between lunar modules in space.

"It's lovely and relaxed here after all those noises at Camp 2," I said.

There was a sharp cracking from inside the slope. "It's O.K., does that all the time," said Georges. "You see we're camped on a sérac. I think we're slowly moving down into Sikkim, but we'll be O.K. for the short time we're here. It's a good reason to climb quickly." At least it was a change to worry about toppling over rather than being hit from above by rocks and avalanches.

Daylight left us to the sound of our own breathing and the creaking of the slope. "Things are looking up," I wrote in my diary. "It's great to be here."

The sun arrived early, for we had moved from the west to the east side of the mountain. The condensation on the inside of the tents crackled off in sheets.

"It's really good outside," said Doug.

Excitedly, I followed him out to photograph the morning. The dawn wind across the col splashed my face with cold. To the west the upper cwm of the Kangchenjunga Glacier, with the tiny dot of Camp 2, was still in darkness. Wedge Peak had lost its thrusting aggression and sank below us into the earth. Seventy miles away the Kangshung Face of Everest glowed with yellow light. To the east, towards the rising sun, I could see the white glaciers, brown moraines, low cloud and a blur of peaks in Sikkim; stretching down directly behind us was the many-fluted east side of the North Col, attempted to within a few hundred feet of our camp by Reggie Cooke in 1937. Also rising out of Sikkim was the North East Spur of Kangchenjunga, which joined the North Ridge high above our heads at 25,390 ft. This long spur was crested by many suspended towers of ice – obstacles which three expeditions had struggled across – the Germans in 1929 and 1931, and the successful Indian expedition in 1977.

Joe rarely articulated his suffering – he just lay in his own quiet gloom. No one suggested that we postpone the attempt until he recovered and, without a word of complaint, he announced he was going down because his headache was still severe.

"He's the only true hard man amongst us," said Doug.

After Joe had gone the snakes and ladders pattern of our attempts was continuing. Most of the steep, difficult climbing was, we hoped, behind us. We were now poised to discover if, as Freshfield and Dyhrenfurth had foretold, the North Col was the technical key to the riddle of the North Ridge. The three of us remaining changed our clothing for higher altitudes. We had already replaced our conventional double boots of leather and fur with special, space-age ski boots of plastic and foam. These were lighter and warmer, though too cumbersome for steep climbing. Plastic boots had been used in Himalayan climbing since 1975, enabling small teams to go high without oxygen equipment and return unscathed by frostbite. However, the revolutionary importance of these boots had received little publicity, and we, like most climbers, had been cautious and conservative about such a radical change of equipment. Now we were convinced. We took off our fibre pile suits and put on looser-fitting, one-piece down suits topped by windsuits; and then packed our sacks with hardware. After a couple of oatmeal biscuits and a drink of tea each, we were ready for our first steps on to the North Ridge and for the upper part of the mountain.

"You be the guide today, Georges, you're the snow and ice man. I'm too tired from yesterday," I said.

Doug agreed, and Georges was raring to go. Georges came from the guiding tradition of Argentière – his father was a guide, and his grandfather on his mother's side was the famous guide Georges Charlet, brother of the even more celebrated Armand Charlet. These men were reputed infallible gods of their profession, whose mountaineering judgments were accepted without question by lesser mortals in the French Alps. When Georges was surging with confidence, as on that morning, shouting "Let's go for eet," we smiled "Charlet a dit," and followed willingly.

Georges kicked up the ridge, like an eager dog on a lead. His climbing style was alive, light and energetic, and contrasted with Doug's strong, solid, purposeful movements. Fortunately, the strong wind maintained good cramponing snow, and our progress was rapid, despite the altitude. We steered well clear of the large drooping cornices that overhung Sikkim, and threaded our way around rock pinnacles. Occasional patches of hard, rippled ice mirrored the white light of the sky.

"How about stopping for something to eat, Georges?" He took a lot of persuading, so Doug and I sat down on a convenient knoll and opened a tin of kippers. When the rope brought Georges to a stop, he realised he had no alternative but to pause with us.

We were just in the lee of the ridge, so could enjoy the view. "We're nearly as high as the main Twins Peak," I said. "It looks really straightforward from the North Col, only a couple of hours."

"In the wrong direction," said Georges.

"There's Siniolchu," said Doug, "and that must be Chomolhari way over there in the distance. The pre-war trips all walked past that, then all the way across the Tibetan Plateau to Everest." With an expansive sweep of his arm, he described the great arc of the route around us.

To the north we could see for the first time the gentle lines of the purple, snow-streaked drumlin-shaped hills of Tibet – a distant, deserted world of austere calm compared to the young, assertive Himalayan giants nearby. Perhaps, as Freshfield had fancied when he saw Tibet from the Jongsong La, those unknown, unnamed hills were within the horizon of Lhasa itself, and the imagination could leap, using them as stepping stones, to the golden terraces of Potala, the palace of the Dalai Lama.

Above us, the North Ridge steepened into a rock buttress six hundred feet high: to our left this stretched around above dangerous-looking slopes of deep powder snow to the North East Spur. To our right the buttress increased in size to become the wall between the second and third terraces of the North West Face of Kangchenjunga. The Germans had seen the snowy side of this feature, and called it 'der Zuckerhut' – the sugar loaf. Its avalanche-prone slopes had turned them back in 1931 at a height of 25,260 ft. From the angle of our viewpoint, the buttress looked more like that of a heavily defended castle – so we changed its original name. We hoped that from where we were we would be able to climb the Castle by what appeared to be the weakest point in its defences, a steep arrowhead of snow that split the buttress, capped by a hundred-foot rock step. To reach the foot of the couloir we traversed diagonally away from the crest of the ridge and out of the wind to a small depression underneath the buttress. There we left our loads of food and equipment, estimating our height as 24,400 ft. We had climbed eighteen hundred feet from the North Col – a good morning's work and exciting progress after the days of struggle for every inch on the wall below the North Col.

Georges led us all down at a cracking pace. I envied his total confidence but, now we were unladen, Doug and I could just keep up with him. Our speed became urgent as the wind increased into a blizzard and snow hurtled across the ridge and into Sikkim. It was impossible to see further than a few feet, and we followed our crampon marks of the morning, determined not to stray on to a cornice. We reached the tents of the North Col camp – Camp 3 – by two in the afternoon, after descending from the Castle in under an hour.

Lying back in camp, we discussed tactics all afternoon, trying to identify the different weather patterns of this higher altitude. At dusk I wrote:

> The wind is whipping over the North Col, and the mountain above is ever-changing in the turbulence. No matter how brilliant the morning is, the weather has always deteriorated by mid-day. Throughout the whole trip, we've not yet had a 'summit day' of all sun and no wind. Weather permitting, we may 'go for eet' tomorrow, and dig in beneath the Castle. On the upper part, above the Castle, the weather will be critical. If it's calm I think we have a good chance. We've sorted out gear and food which, including the stuff we've left up there, should be enough for a four or five day round trip. I think I was dehydrated last night. It's a losing struggle to try and get six pints of fluid a day and anywhere near the minimum three thousand calories inside us.

In the morning, whilst Doug and Georges were packing up one of the tents to take with us, I went down the West Wall for a short distance and drew up some of the Slovak rope for us to fix through the Castle. At 8.00 a.m. we all set off up the North Ridge. My turn to lead was long overdue, so I went first. Sometimes the wind was so fierce we had to stop as it gusted. At the toe of the Castle, a lot of snow had drifted around the corner into the shelter of Sikkim, and it took a long time to break trail for the last two hundred yards to our proposed site for Camp 4.

The snow slope that split the Castle curved around beneath the buttress in a wind scoop, and it was through the ridge so formed that we started digging. It was 10.30 a.m. when we began to carve holes, fifteen feet apart, on opposite sides of the ridge. Doug and I were both convinced of the need for a snow cave at this height to use as a stable base for forays higher up, and Georges soon agreed as he became involved in the digging, calling it the Mont Blanc Tunnel.

"You'd never work this hard for anyone else," said Doug, shovelling soft snow rhythmically into Sikkim.

"I always liked den-building as a kid," I said.

By one in the afternoon, we had met in the middle and shaken hands. "Where's the champagne?" yelled Georges. An hour later we had enlarged the hole into a magnificent grotto. We slid inside and closed out the view through the entrance with large blocks of snow.

In the excitement of the digging we had forgotten to put our windsuits on top of our down suits, and by the time we were inside the cave we were wet with snow and perspiration. It took a long time to warm up. We were tired. The altitude made us feel heavy and all movement was an effort. Doug was positioned at the back of the cave, and when he lit the stove it went out because of the lack of oxygen. He was reading *Journey to Ixtalan* by Carlos Castenada, underlining parts in red and clutching it like a Fundamentalist with his Bible.

"Preparing for the journey, youth," he said.

I suspected the other two were being lazy and that I was being out-manoeuvred – they probably felt the same. Georges seemed to be ordering me about, lying in the middle and telling me to seal the draught, and then demanding brews at 10.00 p.m. and 3.00 a.m. Then Doug suggested that we had one at 5.00 a.m. Although I knew how important it was for us to take plenty of fluids, I was convinced I'd spent all the night melting ice over the stove. Starting with a few handfuls of snow, each pan of water took an hour to prepare.

In the morning, when we broke out through the entrance, we could see the dome of 23,460 ft., Nepal Peak, soloed by Erwin Schneider in 1930 from its other side. The weather looked encouragingly settled.

It was easier to prepare ourselves in the cave for the day's climbing than it had been in the cramped tents lower down. We were sealed and protected in a constant temperature and tomblike silence from the weather outside. Here there was no frozen condensation to knock into our sleeping bags, or a groundsheet to spike with our crampons. We wriggled out into the daylight fully armoured to 'do battle with the elephants', as someone said.

"How about you leading, Doug?" I suggested, trying out his mock gruff but effective way of giving suggestions. Georges and I followed him from the hole and along the little ridge until it merged into the snow slope. We moved together, holding the ropes in coils between us.

I was very worried about the state of the snow and I sensed that Georges was too. Doug was too far in front for me to make out his thoughts. I hacked into the slope, searching for changes in resistance. Large cup crystals of depth hoar lay beneath the surface – ice crust like ball-bearings of instability. After Georges and I had crept apprehensively upwards for two hundred feet, we shouted up to Doug to belay. A film clicked through my mind, showing us all sloughing off into Sikkim. Just standing on the slope, waiting, I felt helplessly committed with the other two. I started hating the predicament, and then hating climbing, utterly and in general, and wishing myself out of it.

A hundred and eighty feet below the top of the Castle Doug belayed to an ice screw, to which Georges and I added a deadman snow anchor. Neither placement could be trusted. Above us, the icy slope steepened to sixty degrees. Doug plodded up until, ten feet below the fifty-foot rock step that crowned the slope, he placed another ice screw and shouted down, reassuring us that it was secure. Immediately I began to relax, and joined him to hold his rope whilst he steadily bridged his way up a groove in the rock. The ring of a rock piton, and a tape sling dropped over a spike, were welcome news that Doug was lacing us back on to the mountain, and signalled the end of my nervousness. After an hour the soles of his boots disappeared on to the top of the Castle. I clambered up to join him, relishing the feel of the warm, rough rock.

"Well done, Doug, I'm glad you led that." Georges followed close on my heels.

"I don't feel quite myself."

"Neither do I."

"I don't understand it, we should be O.K. We've only come about six hundred feet."

"Still, we're at twenty-five thousand feet now."

I screwed up my eyes, trying to ward off the dizziness. The concentration of the climbing below had protected us from the altitude. We staggered towards a large rock, where we left a cache of equipment. Then we walked two hundred feet across easy angled ice and rocks until the great snow and scree terrace was before us and we could glimpse the summit triangle through the wind and cloud that buffeted us.

"It doesn't look too far."

We slid back down, fixing ropes to within a hundred feet of the snow cave. Now we only had two climbing ropes left. The descent took only half an hour, and we were back in the cave at one in the afternoon. When we had first come to this place, it had seemed the wildest, most desolate, most remote spot in the world. Now, within a few hours, it became home. Later it would mean life itself to us.

"I don't like that wind up there, it's worrying."

"Those towering clouds seem to boil up from Sikkim during the morning until they knock their heads against the westerlies. Then all the turbulence starts."

The ridge above our heads was the battle zone.

Although I wasn't hungry, I forced food down. We were eating very little, yet we were burning many calories during the day. I felt very sleepy and spent a comfortable afternoon and night resisting Georges' pressure to do the cooking, and thinking of the summit. At last we were going to try for it.

The morning of the 4th May started late with a stupid, wordless confrontation, after we'd stated our positions. Doug had already said "I've cooked every bloody meal on this trip."

I'd replied, "You had to because you always chose the place with the most room."

Now I wasn't going to light the stove after my lengthy session two nights previously. Georges felt self-righteously that he'd cooked the

135

day before. I waited until Doug told Georges to light the stove. I felt very silly. It was 7.30 by the time we were ready to leave, and a long day stretched before us. We set out for the summit.

By 9.10 we were on top of the Castle. We picked up the equipment we had left the day before and hobbled awkwardly in our ski boots and crampons across the loose stones. At first I was amazed at our progress – that we could actually walk at such an altitude. Features I remembered from binoculars and photographs glided towards me as I panted past, a detached, living figure on those images. I could see the blue tarpaulin of Pangpema Base Camp, far below, and occasionally could glimpse Camp 2 beneath my feet. We traversed beneath the lines of crags of Point 25,390 ft., where the North East Spur joined the North Ridge.

"Those crags look like Stanage from here," shouted Doug.

Then we walked into the path of the westerlies.

The winds were gusting across the Great Snow and Scree Terrace at sixty to seventy miles per hour. The rope between us flapped wildly in the air and caught around our ankles and ski sticks and snagged on boulders and ice crustations. Our hoods and balaclavas whipped across our faces. Frequently we slumped kneeling to the ground, bracing ourselves against sudden, furious volleys of splintering ice and snow. The blowing, stinging cloud began to imprison our vision to the rock and ice at our feet – we could have imagined ourselves wintering on an Arctic plateau, were it not for our bizarre, bulky, muffling ice-clad oversuits and our lungs tolling 25,700 ft. We were aiming for the Croissant – a large crescent-shaped buttress at the foot of the steep two-thousand-foot summit triangle. The easiest way to the summit seemed to the right of it; but that lay directly in the path of the wind. We stopped and tried to discuss. We knew that our only chance of surviving the night would be somehow to escape from the wind. The snow was so hard-packed that our axes, saws and shovels could never have built shelter before we succumbed to the cold. Our experience of Camps 3 and 4 had told us the Sikkim side of the ridge was sheltered. Doug took over the lead and we aimed for a distant notch on the North Ridge, at 26,000 ft., where we hoped to cross into the calm of the other side.

The notch hovered beyond our grasp through the cloud for a long time. Doug was first over. Blinded by spindrift, we almost flew over it – the winds were now blowing continuously at eighty to ninety miles per hour. As I crossed the ridge, I felt my back stabbed by thousands of needles, as if my whole body was disintegrating. The spindrift blinded my goggles. I screamed into the blast "I can't see. Are you safe? Can I come down?"

"Pull yourself down with your ice axe," shouted Doug.

On the other side we knelt, dazed, trying to collect our thoughts. Below us the forty-five degree slope curved away into whiteness. Here there was no wind although it was roaring through the notch above our heads. Doug had also suffered agonising shocks of static.

"I didn't know whether to mention it," he said. "I thought I was falling apart."

It was 3.00 p.m. We spent three hours weakly hacking at the ice, until we had excavated a small ledge that was just big enough to take our tunnel tent. Doug did most of the digging and Georges erected the tent. The altitude was debilitating – I felt as if my body was tied down with lead weights. Once inside, we considered the possibilities for the morning. We would attempt to go up. If we tried to rest for a day at twenty-six thousand feet, we would probably weaken and lose the chance of climbing the remaining twelve hundred feet to the summit. We fell asleep for a short while and woke with headaches. The stove kept on going out but Doug steadfastly prepared some soup and then a hot water bottle for Georges, who was suffering from the cold. We took a sleeping pill and two aspirins each and relaxed, listening to the wind beating the night above the ridge. We fell asleep to beautiful warm dreams.

I was awakened suddenly by snapping fabric and a world in uproar. "The wind's changed."

I looked at my watch. 1.30 a.m. The tent was shaking and pushing against us. I felt enveloped in comfort and willed it to stop, so that I could travel away again into sleep. But soon we were all wide awake. We turned our torches on. The tent was flapping and crackling wildly, throwing frost everywhere – and our lives depended on it. Where had this wind come from? Why? Why? Slowly, the danger sank in. At 2.30 a.m. the centre hoop snapped and we knew we would have to start fighting for our lives. We held on to the hoop in turns as our fingers numbed, trying to stop its jagged ends from ripping the fabric, taking it in turns to throw on our boots and crampons, fumbling with straps. We shouted curt instructions to each other, cold and disciplined, devoid of emotion, going through the motions of survival – detached and playing to the audience of our minds.

"Georges, hold this for a minute!"

Only our eyes showed caged terror, sharing the thought that this was probably the end. My mind was racing. Not much chance of getting out of this. Family, loved ones, friends; if I do get out I'll have terrible frostbite. We haven't even climbed the mountain. If there is a God, then please, please stop this wind. Why should he? Am I strong enough for this? Is this the time? Concentrate on yourself, we must all do that. No time to pray.

Short lulls of a few seconds gave false hopes. Doug looked out. "The anchors are pulled. We're being blown off the ledge, the whole tent's moved two feet, we'll have to get out fast!" He squirmed outside and held on.

We were within a second of rolling down and down into the stormy darkness. The wind was at hurricane force, tearing strips of fabric off the tent.

"Don't leave the gear, don't abandon."

Georges and I furiously packed the sleeping bags and wriggled out of the tent. We collapsed it, ripped it open with a knife and pulled the remaining equipment out, and the wind snatched the tent away. Dawn was now struggling out of the streaming cloud, rocks the size of dinner plates whipped up from the ridge, were swinging through the turbulence like meteorites. I could not even kneel on the ledge without being knocked over. Georges, then Doug, disappeared up the slope above, pulling the mad tangle of ropes, trying to claw their way to the notch. They made it on their third attempt, and my rope went tight. A dark shape hurtled past. "God, no, somebody's fallen." It was Georges' sack.

I struggled after them, pulled by the ropes, hauling myself through the notch with my ice axe. It was like trying to crawl into a jet engine at full throttle.

We reeled and stumbled across the Great Snow and Scree Terrace in a dream, resisting our bodies' cries to lie down, sleep. There was so much ice on our faces we could barely see. Now was the time we could give up, let go the end of our strength and sink to the earth. If only there was time to sleep. Voices filled my head: "Must get down." "Must get down." "Hurry." "Hurry." "Now is the time mistakes are made."

But we had been so near to certain death, our fear was dulled. The day before little windslabs of snow had worried us. Now, we took no care, crunching them beneath our feet.

We reached the snow cave at 8.00 a.m. The entrance was buried and Doug shovelled it out. We drank some hot orange juice and tried to thaw out our feet and hands. I swallowed Vaso-dilating pills.

We reached the North Col at 10.20 a.m. and ate some freeze-dried apricots and melted another drink. Georges was becoming snow-blind, and was complaining of dark vision. We dosed him with eye-drops. Our injuries were coming to life and now we could assess them for the first time. Doug had sustained frostbite on the upper joints of four fingers whilst he had held on to the tent in the wind. I had frostbite on a big toe and on my nose. We had been lucky.

We decided to leave our high-altitude equipment and clothing on the North Col and try to reach Base Camp the same day. The ice on the wall had hardened. We scurried down the ropes and ploughed across the glacier from the foot of the wall to Camp 2. Behind us the wind and cloud of the storm swept across the sky with such speed that Kangchenjunga appeared to rotate in the opposite direction. I realised my ankle and wrist were no longer troubling me.

12

BEFORE DAWN

5th – 14th May, 1979

"I thought – 'Why am I down here rather than up there – dying with you lot?'" Joe was waiting for us at Camp 2, with Ang Phurba. Hot drinks were simmering and he was very glad to see us, talking excitedly: "The wind was like an express train down here. We thought the whole camp was blowing away – Ang Phurba and I had to hang on to the tents for most of the night. We couldn't sleep. That's why we didn't do a carry up to the col this morning. I knew if you hadn't found shelter last night you'd never have survived."

"Where's Nima?"

"He's down at Base Camp. We had to take him down with his back injury. I don't know how serious it is. He could walk O.K. though. It's probably just badly bruised. Ang Phurba and I came back up yesterday."

"How's your headache?"

"Seems fine now. I was really depressed when I came down from the North Col – I felt about an inch high when I arrived here. Looks as if I've got a second chance now. Since my head cleared I've been trying to enthuse Ang Phurba into going for the trip, but he's non-committal – you know what he's like, super cool. He's brilliant crossing the moraines and coming up the glacier though – he knows the way like the back of his hand. I just put my feet where he does, and it seems a different walk. He's deceptively fast. We came up in three and a half hours yesterday, all the way from Base Camp. Just try following him down now."

Crevasses had moved, snow had melted, and the route had changed. The intense vigilance of the descent fell away like scales and I took photographs of the sunset, seeing beauty with a power I had not known earlier during the expedition, and feeling gloriously receptive to everything around me. Joe and Ang Phurba drew ahead through the moraines.

"Get the spuds on," I shouted. I jumped from boulder to boulder, invigorated by the thought of Base Camp and strengthened by the rush of oxygen. I arrived in the twilight, sweating.

The momentum of our experience kept us talking fast. We sat in the warm firelight of the kitchen shelter. "I was really scared," said Georges.

"I've never known a wind like that," said Doug.

I wanted to forget the ordeal for a while, and changed the subject. "You should see the inside of the snow cave, Joe, it's revolting. Everyone's gobbed on to the ceiling – the colour changed depending on which fruit juice we'd been drinking. And it got noisy too. You know what Georges' throat gargle sounds like. Give us a gargle, Georges."

We ate our first meal for two days. It was our Base Camp favourite – egg and potatoes. Doug sipped some whisky to dilate his fingers and passed the bottle round. Kami promised a cake for the next day. Mohan told us the U.K. Election results. "If we'd got to the top, we could say we'd staged the climb as a protest," said someone.

The thicker air lay around us like the slow support of warm water. For a few hours, delicious warmth and rest and the smell of wood-smoke, vegetation and damp earth, anaesthetised thoughts, suppressed doubt and banished problems. Our minds were stilled and wide open. I spent the day reading, to draw me out of myself. My wrist was still swollen, one big toe was numb and black under the nail, but my ankle was O.K.! By the late afternoon, I was ready to start writing:

The quality of our survival is good. All these are surface scars around an inner calm. Memories of the battle anchor me here in perfect equilibrium against the alternating swell of mountain above and the valley and home below. I, the fortunate man alive today, still have much in common with the man who fought the storm. I am so happy to relax, feeling confident that I can climb the mountain, having survived such a night at twenty-six thousand feet. I now know to what extent our equipment can protect us and what distances we can cover up there. I now know I don't have to be a superman. It was a rich experience – I've learned a lot, and feel a strength flow from it. Perhaps I needed, almost enjoyed it, for this feeling. I have to admit honestly, that I would not have missed it. Out of one of the worst experiences of my life, I've learned again how precious life is – we've a new measure for our lives. The mountain has to make us work, has to be uncertain. Through the effort and the weeks the mountain is seeping into us. Through this communion, I am sure, we shall eventually discover the key, and I am beginning to feel ready for it.

Next day the mail runner, Nima Wangdi, was due.

"Jan writes a bit every day," said Doug.

"So does Hilary."

"That sounds like a duty to me," said Joe.

I almost dreaded letters, and I think Doug did too, in case something had happened, in case they were not happy letters, in case something in them disturbed us from climbing Kangchenjunga. We could hear the wind on the mountain, a faint, far-off murmur which emphasised our shelter. A night's rest revived my aches and pains:

> 6.10. 7th May. I can hear the cackling of the snow cocks and the distant thuds in the kitchen, as morning tea is prepared. There are six inches of snow on the ground, and the sun is shining on Kangchenjunga from the east. The wind doesn't look as bad up there today. The sun will reach here soon, and I look forward to it, because I've woken up feeling tired, chilled and a bit ill. I wonder if that's a wheeze in my lungs. I'm taking deep breaths, willing a full recovery. Perhaps the mail will bounce me back again.
>
> 10.30 a.m. The sun is beating down and I'm back in the tent after breakfast, listening to music and sheltering my blistered face which looks as if it needs a skin graft. Doug, Georges and I all agree we feel worse today than yesterday. After a brief lull, all the effort and exhaustion of the last few days have at last caught up with us. We're no longer keyed up and excited by the storm, and all our injuries seem to matter more and they hurt more. A cold burn from my watch on my wrist, and ear-ache have just emerged. Also, I've a sore hip from lying on my side without fat cushioning – my buttocks have been burnt up in energy! Joe seems naturally a bit worried if his headache will return and how he's going to perform higher up, having missed the storm and not having been to eight thousand metres like us. Doug said, "Yesterday I felt like going back up – today I feel like going home." He says his fingers are only good enough for one more go, and that it's the quality of the struggle that counts. Now he's been on a lot of trips, and is getting older, reaching the summit does not matter as much as it used to.

I did not want a retreat, not like the violent urge to go away, fly home and forget, that I had felt after the disappointment and tragedy on K2 the previous year. I wanted to recapture the glorious sense of well-being and satisfaction that I had experienced after successful climbs on other expeditions.

I glanced through Charles Evans' book *The Untrodden Peak* – the story of the successful 1955 expedition. I found George Band's photograph, looking down on the Great Snow and Scree Terrace from the summit, two thousand feet above. I projected out little figures on it, slowly moving upwards. I wrote:

> Never in our climbing careers again, I'm sure, will we be in such a position on such a good new route. Doug has been asking his 'I Ching' for a forecast, but the answers are, as usual, ambiguous but interesting.

At the meal time Georges suggested to Doug and me that we exchanged our diaries, to see what we had written about the storm. We declined. My diary was my confessional and, whilst the mountain was still in our lives, such raw descriptions were unsharable and may have caused arguments. Seen through the blurred memories of three anoxic brains, the truth would have presented three different faces. I wrote:

> After such a crisis, we all inevitably write that which helps our own self-esteem. For example, Doug probably thinks he saved all our lives by hanging on to the tent – and, true enough, I suppose he did. But we have to believe in ourselves, as well, to survive. Also, we were each so much alone in what we had to face in that storm, so whatever story we tell afterwards can only be our own.

The weather was settling:

> Tantalisingly, it's a calm night with a brilliant growing moon and cloudless starry sky. If man's strength really does grow with a full moon, our timing might be right yet. No mail runner came today. I didn't realise how much I was expecting him until he didn't turn up.

The next day, the 8th May, was the last of our planned three days' rest at Base Camp, before going back up on to the mountain. After breakfast Doug said: "If the mail doesn't come today, I think we should wait until it does. If anything happens to us up there, they'd like it if we'd read their letters."

"You morbid bugger," I said.

"You've got to be ready for it, youth. It's easy to die, and it only affects them."

"Well, let's just hope he turns up. We've got to get a move on."

It was a beautiful morning and the usual two split levels of cloud – the still shapes in the cwm, and the wind plume along the North Ridge above the North Col – had both disappeared. After the storm, we had descended the eleven thousand feet from the notch to Base Camp in a day, but it would be a long, paced effort of four days, camp by camp, to return.

"It's perfect weather, from here to the summit."

"Just a few gentle zephyrs to waft around your face and keep you alert," said Joe. "I wish it'd been like that three days ago."

"I wish we were up there now."

"It's impossible to predict what it'll be like in a few days' time."

"When it's really bad, it seems to take a week to re-form, to re-settle."

"I don't think there's a pattern."

"This is the first 'summit day' we've seen up there."

"It could be the calm spell, starting early."

"Did you bring the description of where the Indians went up the last bit, Doug?"

"No, it didn't give a lot of details anyway, and we don't want to lose the sense of discovery, do we? I remember they said it would be 'nearly impossible' without oxygen."

"The BBC said that their air-dropping of supplies up to sixteen thousand feet 'wasn't quite cricket'."

"I wouldn't object to a high-altitude helicopter whisking us back up there now."

"I'm dreading going back up those fixed ropes."

"It's much more fun above the wall, isn't it!"

The two successful expeditions to climb Kangchenjunga before had placed their summit teams on the top at the end of May: in 1955 Brown and Band had reached the top on 25th May, and Streather and Hardie the following day. In 1977 Prem Chand and Nima Dorje Sherpa had reached the top on the 31st May. We had read Charles Evans' reasoning behind the timing of the 1955 expedition:

> Towards mid-May there's a regular change in the pattern of the weather in the mountains of Eastern Nepal: the north westerly winds prevalent in the first half of the year slacken, and there is a short and variable, but fairly dependable spell of fine, still weather before the onset of the south west monsoon at the beginning of June, the monsoon that brings not only heavy snowfalls on the higher slopes, but warmth, which rots the deep snow through and makes it dangerous.

So far, the weather had not shown any predictable patterns, and we suspected that this was an over-simplification.

The settled weather mocked our impatience and after noon we grew tense as we waited for the post.

"Joe, have you still got *The Seven Pillars of Wisdom*?"

"No, Ang Phurba's reading it."

Ang Phurba often spent a long time inside his tent, reading, and I went over and disturbed him. "Ang Phurba, have you finished *The Seven Pillars of Wisdom*?"

"Yes."

"Did you enjoy it?"

"Yes."

"What was it about?"

"Arabs."

I couldn't concentrate enough to read more than the first few pages.

We gathered in the kitchen tent as shadows lengthened. "He must arrive today, it's fifteen days since he left."

Nima Tenzing, his back injury now recovered, stood on a nearby hilltop, his sharp eyes scanning the horizon. We listened to the BBC World Service – a quiz game, news and a music request programme. It was almost dark when Nima announced he could see Nima Wangdi coming. Our earlier accusations of 'the laziest man in Nepal' changed within fifteen minutes to friendly greetings for the man we most wanted to see in the world. We snatched the letters greedily. I felt awesomely excited, as if I were about to open exam results. A quick scan by the light of the pressure lamp – there was nothing amiss in my private world; but they were a month old. I hardly noticed the meal, and went to my tent to read the letters for an hour and a half. Joe put some suitable music on the cassette player – 'The Tracks of my Tears', 'Help me make it through the night' – until Georges complained about the noise. It was a restless, dream-filled night.

We left Base Camp in the cool of the next morning, and arrived at Camp 2 at 9.00 a.m. We wrote our reply letters there, to be sent down with Nima Tenzing and Ang Phurba two days later. The glacier had moved and melted during the three days we had been away, and we had to re-pitch the tents. We heated up some potatoes and rice, pre-cooked at Base Camp, and ate and slept well, feeling relaxed and confident.

At 4.30 a.m. on the 10th May, Camp 2 was stirring. There was a strange, calm sky, overcast with wisps of clouds, not cold at all. If it were the Alps these would not be good signs. But here – who could tell?

Ang Phurba was to accompany us to the North Col, carrying a load which included a bottle of oxygen, for emergencies.

When we arrived at the bergschrund at the foot of the wall's fixed ropes, we discovered that the Sherpas had accidentally left two jumars at Base Camp. So we had eight to distribute between five people. Since Doug had frost-nipped fingers, and Ang Phurba was carrying the heaviest load, they both needed two each. After a short argument, Joe, Georges and I drew matches for the remaining four. Georges won. We climbed the ropes through the morning and into the early afternoon.

Camp 3 – North Col. Dusk. I'm lying at the front of the tunnel tent brewing up. Fortunately Doug slid one of his jumars down the rope to Joe, to help him climb the steep chimney pitch, and Joe slid it to me after he'd finished with it. That made a big difference to last time, when I only had one jumar and a fresh wrist injury as well. Joe cut his finger quite badly on that pitch, and left the rock covered in blood. He's patched up O.K. now, though. The early morning mist cleared, and it was hot work. It took us all about six hours to reach here, and Ang Phurba went straight back down almost immediately. We all arrived very thirsty. We've only one pan here – we left the other at Camp 4 – so it's a hassle, melting enough snow to rehydrate. We brought Georges' little tunnel tent, to replace the one that disappeared into Sikkim during the storm, and cut a new platform for it. Georges is in it with me. He's asleep and making sighing and grunting noises. A fine spray of snow falls constantly on the camp from the wind over the North Col. This tent is not as sheltered as the other, and occasional gusts of spindrift remind me of last week's epic. The plan is to go up to the Camp 4 snow cave tomorrow. Because of the wind, there doesn't seem much possibility of shelter above that, so we've accepted Georges' suggestion to leave tomorrow midnight and make a single night/day four thousand foot push to the summit. "To follow through the night the moving moon" – was it Byron who said that? I reckon we've got enough supplies for ten days if necessary (including some bread from Base Camp). Like last time, we've all agreed – we don't want to come up that wall again! As for the mountain above, who knows? I'm sure we're capable of climbing it, but one bad weather setback could do us in so much we'd have to go all the way down (groan) again. What was Gide's paradoxical truth – that man's happiness lies not in freedom but in the acceptance of a duty? Well, we're all doing this as a sort of duty now, but I feel more disciplined than happy about it. I'm longing for civilisation, pints of Robbies mild in The Swan, the lads, Leysin, everything.

At four-thirty the next morning I made the first brew, Doug took over and made a second, and we were soon ready. Doug and Joe climbed on to the ridge first, and Georges and I followed. The sky was a deep blue and the intense wind plucked at our faces which were still tender from the storm. Our legs were tired from the previous days' pull and push up to the North Col, and it took us all morning to reach the snow cave of Camp 4.

4.00 p.m. 11th May. That wind is awful. It whizzes from all directions and during a gust you have to brace yourself this way, and then that way, gasping with the altitude. I let my clothing protect me, my body fight it, and my mind wander. Confused strings of thoughts whilst climbing and resting at this altitude are not unpleasant – the mind fastens illogically on event, place, person. I'm looking forward to safer living and pleasures down below. We're all lying in the snow-hole now. It has shrunk since we were last here, and we're packed together like sardines. We had to do quite a lot of enlarging to get the four of us in. Above our heads are the hachured hacking lines of the first excavation. I stare at them in front of my face – it's like being imprisoned in a disused mine. Georges has just done a sustained cooking session and wants us all to know about it! It's a problem to keep toes warm in here. We've discussed leaving at midnight for the big push, but none of us feels confident because of the wind and our fatigue. So we'll take a rest/wait day here – we've got enough food and it's Joe's birthday tomorrow. He'd forgotten till Doug reminded him! Although it's a deep-freeze, it's better than camping. This climb is keeping us guessing right till the end. It's calm outside the snow-hole, but it's impossible to know what the wind is doing on the ridge above us without going there. Did we imagine that good day, three days ago, when we looked up from Base Camp? All the others are snoozing here in the fridge.

The next day we did not move. I kept looking at my watch, waiting for the time to pass.

3.10 p.m. 12th May. A day in the void, and birthdays mean nothing up here. We've had plenty of time to worry about the weather, legs and lungs. We woke with headaches, which cleared when we enlarged the entrance to the snow-hole. We staggered out for some sunbathing this morning – it seemed a perfect, calm day. Below us were the peaks and clouds of Sikkim. We aired our gear until fear of dropping things and spindrift drove us back in. Once more we've no idea what the weather is doing, it seems to change every half hour. I don't know if we'll have the strength to make another attempt. It's all a great unknown. I wonder if other climbs have such uncertainty – I can't remember. It would be good if we could see the summit, to psyche up, but it's out of sight. I hope it's the best plan to miss a night's sleep, to try for four thousand feet in one go. We'll see. I think wistfully of the lovely snoozes we had on Everest, using oxygen cylinders. It's like in a submarine, 'On the Beach' in here. It's very cramped, and I feel irritable. But in my mind I see times ahead – not having done it, having done it.

Between seven-thirty and one-thirty that night we took turns to crawl out of the tunnel entrance to the cave, and to scan the sky for signs of settling weather. The light of the moon was blocked by scurrying clouds of powder snow. Eventually we decided to stay for another day, and tried to sleep.

As the second day progressed, the idea of staying there much longer began to be more painful than the prospect of another summit attempt in bad weather. Somehow the plan to leave at midnight was brought back more and more.

2.35 p.m. 13th May. I didn't want to climb Kangch on the 13th anyway! But as the weather turned out this morning, we'd have been O.K. going. It's all rather soul-destroying and we're even more irritable than yesterday. Joe is managing, with Doug, to avoid any cooking. Joe seems worried about up top – less self-assured than usual. Or perhaps he's just being quiet. No one's saying much. The ceiling is slowly coming down and we're lying on the border of sleep, often crossing it. I don't think we have the will to stay here another day, getting on each other's nerves. This unease outweighs our fear of another storm. We'll just have to take pot luck. Not long now and we'll know.

We crammed a freeze-dried meal inside us and filled two bottles with water to take inside our down suits, protected from freezing. At 5.30 p.m., against all our better judgment, we decided to go.

"The weather couldn't be more inauspicious," said Doug.

There were three levels of cloud below us, beside us and above, and a strong wind was blowing mad maypoles of spindrift along the surface of the snow slope that split the Castle. At dusk, the lower clouds of valley and sky began to fuse slowly into a continual greyness. The rope had become iced up and, flung by the wind, had snagged across the ice wall seventy feet above the snow cave. Joe, Doug and I stamped our feet in the entrance to the cave, looking at the soles of Georges' cramponed boots as he traversed airily across the wall to free it. It was a bold burst of energy. "I think it's the start of one of those days," he said, when we grouped together at the top of the Castle. It was 8.00 p.m. and dark clouds were gathering around our heads. The moon appeared briefly, but soon hid behind flurries of snow and refused to reappear. We had miscalculated, for it was now sliding along a course behind the mountain. We switched on our headtorches. I put on a white surgeon's mask, to stop the blowing ice chips from encrusting my face, and to warm the air I breathed.

"The wind's not as strong as last time," I shouted.

"We should make it if it doesn't get any worse," said Doug.

Our headtorches flickering, we trudged on, wobbling awkwardly over the broken ground. Every few minutes we leant into the wind on our ski sticks, gasping for breath. As we crossed the screes my left crampon came off three times. Doug, to whom I was tied, waited patiently as my clumsily mitted hands fiddled with the straps. The other two disappeared into the darkness.

We found them sheltering behind a large boulder, heating a pan of orange juice. I almost said "Where are the others?" During that night voyage across the Great Snow and Scree Terrace, we all felt that our team was bigger than it was, that we were a large group.

"The weather's cleared on worse nights than this," I said.

"Let's go for eet," said Georges.

Our thick protective clothing was working well, distancing us from our situation. Doug produced a crampon spanner. "See if you can fix it, youth. Get it right." After much adjustment I changed the pattern of the lacing and the crampon was secured. We trudged on.

The dark shape of the Croissant appeared occasionally through patches of mist, lit by stars, but the summit triangle was covered by constant cloud, and the moon was lost behind the ridge. Our head-torches cut a swathe into the moving whiteness. The weather seemed to be deteriorating, but to what extent we judged differently. The darkness, altitude and weather combined to blur the distinction between our minds and the mountain. We were wandering in a mind-landscape, like sleepwalkers.

On a mountain, four is never an easy number for discussion, and decisions are difficult at midnight, at 26,000 ft. in the teeth of the wind. Was the weather worsening? Should we stop here and try to bivouac? We could not agree and confusion resulted. Georges was streaming forward, unaware that doubt was seeping into the ranks behind. Doug started digging into a snow bank, and Joe joined in. I said I thought the snow was too hard and wind-packed, and that it would take too long. To persuade Joe I shouted "I've got more experience snow-holing."

"Well, you go and find a better place then."

I went over to Doug. "Will you untie from the rope? I'm going to try higher up."

Joe untied from Georges as I moved away. I exchanged some shouts with Doug, feeling embittered about the disagreement with Joe. They soon disappeared behind me as I followed the dim shape of Georges into the storm, towing the empty rope.

The slope steepened beneath my axe and boots. I kicked upwards, twelve paces at a time, unable to match Georges' speed, trying to glimpse his light through the sweeping mist. Georges had reached the rocks of the Croissant, and was following their edge. He stopped at the first sign of a hole. I caught up with him. We chopped an entrance and slid inside the bergschrund, out of the wind.

The yellow light and narrow space brought us sharply back to the present.

"I knew someone was following me but I didn't realise it was you," he said. He lit the stove and sheltered it with his gloved hands from the cold draught that flowed beneath the surface between the ice and rock. I started to enlarge the hole, using my feet and axe, trying to keep warm and make the sense of a home out of the chaos of the night. It was 12.45 a.m.

The summit filled Georges' head. "We must not stop here. It is bad to stop at this altitude. We must go now, make or break, for the summit. There will not be another time."

I was pulled along in the wake of his enthusiasm. It seemed easier and more positive to agree to move than to insist on staying. Georges had the momentum and I took the opportunity to hang on to it.

However, it was reassuring to know that we had found a sheltered burrow to retreat to.

Georges wriggled out of the hole and I followed him into the night. We hugged the edge of the rocks. My mind clung to a few simple thoughts, 'This is it', 'After this I can go home', 'The Summit'. I couldn't remember the topography, except that we were to aim vaguely for two gullies that would lead on to a long diagonal snow ramp that reached up to the pinnacles of the West Ridge, nearly two thousand feet above the Croissant. I left my ski stick in the steepening slope and pulled my axe from my holster before Georges did, lacking his confidence on the wind-packed snow.

Georges started traversing rightwards. "We're on the Ramp," he shouted. The sky cleared for a few seconds, and we saw the Pinnacles in the deceitful grey light of the moon. "Twenty minutes away," shouted Georges. They had looked near, but not, I thought, as near as that. Georges thought we had climbed one of the gullies. I did not think we had.

Rocks barred our upward progress. "It's the wrong way, Georges – at least it is for tonight."

I led two ropelengths to the right. The slab of snow I was climbing on felt hollow and unstable and my headtorch revealed a maze of slabs of rock and snow. I was lost. "Always trust your own judgment, Pete," I repeated to myself. I screamed into the wind "Georges, we're far too low. We should go back to the cave and wait for the others and for daylight!"

Georges joined me. "We mustn't lose the height. We've gained three or four hundred metres, we're so near," he said.

"Let's wait for dawn then," I said. "It's about an hour away."

It was a cold hour. We kicked out a little ledge and stamped and shook our chilling feet and clapped our numbing hands, hoping that visibility would improve and that the weather would change with the dawn. As the sky lightened, the cloud that blew around us thickened. A voice started singing in my head that this was folly. I hoped Georges was hearing the same.

"Let's go down," he said.

"What, down to the Croissant bergschrund?"

"No, down!" Then he changed his mind. "We'll wait in the bergschrund until the sun comes."

We plunged down through the storm, surprised at our speed, for the angles of night had eased with the light of dawn.

Back inside the bergschrund we tried to melt some snow. The fuel was fading so we changed cylinders. The stove seal leaked with the intense cold, so we threw the cylinder away and chewed nuts. Georges shook my hand, saying "It's been enough for me, to have been a few hundred feet from the summit." He went outside. I dug and chopped the hole, building a springboard for a future try.

Georges shouted in to me. "The others are coming. Come outside."

"How far are they away?"

"About twenty minutes below us, coming up."

"I'll stay inside and work on this ceiling."

I heard Georges saying "We've just been a few hundred feet from the summit." Doug's voice sounded cold and angry. I shouted up arguments from the hole, but the snow muffled my words. Doug lowered himself in, unhappy that the team had split up and reacting from hours of concern about us.

"When we saw only Georges just now, we thought you'd been rolled away by the wind. This is a team effort. We must always stick together on this trip, all four of us, and not go sneaking off for the top."

I explained how I understood the confusions of the night.

"It was a good effort anyway," said Doug.

Joe and Georges joined us. Attempting to be objective, we discussed whether the bergschrund was a better shelter than the one Joe and Doug had carved out during the night. At least it was higher up. Outside, visibility was no better, and the decision was down.

We dumped some equipment and the ropes, our faces caked with ice, and tottered back across the Great Scree Terrace in the windy dawn. I was the last one to leave the bergschrund, but had such a strong feeling that others were behind me that I stopped and looked around.

A lot of snow had fallen during the night. We returned to the Camp 4 snow cave a lot tireder and weaker, and having been not much higher than when we had left.

13

SOFTLY TO THE UNTRODDEN SUMMIT

14th – 16th May, 1979

Like monstrous red, dead worms, we lay in our sleeping bags, trying
to rest in the snow cave – exhausted, set-faced and rarely speaking,
our tongues like leather and our minds floating. Our strength was
ebbing away. Outside the snow hissed and sifted. It took a long time
to extricate my pen and diary, and hunch myself up to try to write
some sense into the situation. It was my last entry:

3.00 p.m. 14th May. I'm not feeling very coherent – in fact I'm totally
spaced out after our night wandering around in the blizzard. We could not
have chosen a worse night for our 'lightning' attempt. The weather on this
mountain is bloody awful and I want to come home. But I also want to
climb Kangch. The problem is, how much energy one expends in a night
like last night – we're much tireder now than after the tent strike storm.
Every time we have less bounce, less resilience, less energy. But so near yet
so far . . . Everyone is exhausted, grim, and monosyllabic. I know we are
deteriorating, but cannot tell how much our judgment is becoming
impaired. Georges says he's had enough and is going to Base Camp
tomorrow. 'Fewer mouths to feed' is one of my less sympathetic reactions.
We are too high for pity. We'll probably go down to the North Col and
pick up some food, and then the day after tomorrow go back up to the
Croissant where we have found a bergschrund (it needs enlarging). Then
we'll make the next (third) summit attempt on the 17th. If only it had been
good weather last night. Now we'll probably be quite satisfied if we reach
the Pinnacles on the West Ridge (the point where the '55 expedition
reached the ridge from the other side). The top of Kangch is open to
discussion. I seem to go O.K. at high altitude, but cough like everyone else
when I get back . . . It's quite a calm day now outside the cave after being
cloudy and blustery. We always seem to hit this weather wrong.

I spent the afternoon tending the stove – I thought if I did a long
cooking stint I could rest self-righteously for a while, and escape from
the long tension-ridden hassles about whose turn it was next. I

prepared tea, beef soup, shrimp creole, and then melted some water to fill a bottle. I felt irritated every time someone asked "What time is it?" for my watch was in my pocket. To reach the stove I had to lean across Georges, which hurt my bad wrist.

Our conversations flared and dwindled and the little jokes amongst us had died. I wondered how determined the others were – it was impossible to assess objectively. Joe was focusing himself entirely on recovery, never offering to cook or brew-up, just lying down, cocooned, sleeping and resting, accepting all offerings. He said little, except that he wanted two days' rest. I hoped he was not weakening, because I trusted his judgment implicitly, and felt there could be something invincible about our combination.

Doug was at the back of the cave, nursing his frost-nipped fingers, saying more than anyone. He was tiring mentally with the constant re-covering of ground between camps, which he found boring and negative. Most of all, his family worries obsessed him, and he longed to be home with his wife and three children by his birthday on the 29th. I could not assess this worry, its stature was beyond me. He was on the verge of giving up the climb, and said he certainly would not have more than one more go, although he agreed it would be a pity to leave, when so near, for want of 'a ha'penny-worth of salt'. I admired the way he was trying to persuade Georges to stick with us – I hadn't the energy to argue.

All that appeared of Georges was a noise and a nose stretching from the circular hole that was the tightly-drawn hood of his sleeping bag. He seemed isolated and withdrawn, as if he were missing communication with men of his own language. The freeze-dried meals nauseated him, and he refused all food. He was going down, and mentioned parallels with routes in the Mont Blanc range that one completes without actually continuing to a summit. He was satisfied, and I respected the firmness of his decision. Perhaps he knew himself better than we did, and had the courage to act on that self-knowledge.

I did not want to leave the mountain until we had climbed it. The summit was still my obsession. Our two attempts at 26,000 ft. in blizzards had given me confidence. I felt our weather problems were because we were still too early in the season, and that we should use the food we had left at the North Col in anticipation of the ten days' settled weather before the monsoon that Charles Evans' book had predicted would arrive.

The next day dawned so blue and calm that at first I resented it. The storm had spent its energies and the sky promised stability. Doug announced that he had received a revelation during the night, as clear as if it had been written. He knew he must have a go for the summit, and that he must not go down. Joe and I said nothing. Doug proposed forcefully that we left that morning. I bit back the comment "What would happen if we all had to obey our own different dreams?" – for I knew he was right. The discovery of a third Gaz cylinder clinched the decision, for it meant that we did not have to return to the North Col to re-stock. I agreed to go, regretting having spent so much energy cooking, the previous day.

Doug made a final plea to Georges; "Do you feel like sharing our adventure?" he asked. "Do you want to have another try with us?"

"I agree with the concept, using the weather, but I haven't the juice," said Georges. He hurriedly packed his equipment and set off down, quickly disappearing beneath the convex curve of the North Ridge.

Some of our equipment was still icy from the previous attempt, so we started to prepare on the little ledge outside the snow-hole, in the sunshine. Spindrift soon drove us back inside. We packed slowly, at the same pace as our minds were adjusting to the idea of another upwards move. At 8.30 a.m. we were ready, and relieved to see the tiny dot of Georges reappear on the North Col. The sky remained free of clouds.

It was Joe's turn to break trail through the Castle, but he was still reluctant to leave. After kicking six steps at a time up to the foot of the fixed rope, he stopped and shouted that he was going too slowly and needed a day's rest. Doug went up to encourage him, and then took over the lead. I waited for them to gain more height, before starting, so that we would spread our weight over the dubious slope. I hoped that we weren't taking on too much after so little rest from the all-night effort.

When Doug reached the Castle he stuck his head over the top and shouted "There's hardly any wind."

Joe and I joined him, and it was true. Now, after all the hesitations, doubts, errors and setbacks, there was, suddenly, a discovery. The air was unbelievably calm – so calm we talked in half whispers, as if not wanting to disturb a sleeping storm. It was as if the earth had now decided to help us.

"Highest cairned footpath in the world, youth, twenty-five to twenty-six thousand feet," said Doug. He was full of energy and built a string of cairns a hundred yards apart across the Great Snow and Scree Terrace. If stories about high-altitude brain damage were true, we might need them when we descended, as emphatic signposts of deliverance to hallucinating minds.

Occasional clouds towered up from below and blew across the terrace, but we sensed it was just an afternoon bluster, and the sky remained blue above us. We were soloing, for we had left our two ropes above, at the bergschrund the day before. Now we were unencumbered and free of the tangled procedures they imposed.

Doug was first to reach the cave at 2.30 p.m. and I, then Joe, arrived at half-hour intervals after him. We each chose a corner inside the bergschrund to work at with spade, saw and ice axe. There was no waste disposal problem, because the gap between ice and rock plunged deep into the mountain. I tried to order the progression of my sawing and slicing, but my oxygen-starved mind was distracted by instructions from imaginary Irishmen and Welshmen. After two hours we had cleared enough space for the three of us to curl down and rest; I managed to book the middle, and Joe was manoeuvred to below the entrance. Using karabiners as clothes pegs, we hung a sheet of aluminium foil from a rope to reduce the draught.

I crawled outside. The mountain was shaking its head clear of the sea of afternoon clouds. Particles of ice were dancing down the snow runnels of the summit triangle, glimmering in the fading light of the disappearing sun. We had nothing to fear from the weather. However, two thousand feet of unknown snow above us could hold unpleasant surprises. I cut some blocks of snow and, as I dropped back inside, I slid them across the entrance of the hole – like the hatch of a submarine.

"Freeze-dried turkey, I'm afraid, Doug." He overcame his vegetarianism, for there was no alternative on the menu.

We had arranged a code with Georges, that on his return to Pangpema he would listen to the evening weather forecast and light signal bonfires if the forecast was good; one if it was encouraging, two if it was very good. But once we were inside, we did not want to lose heat, get snow on our clothes or disturb the manhole. We took sleeping pills and lay inert, conserving heat, like tramps sheltering in a wintry city.

Doug suffered from his fingers during the night, and asked for painkillers. Warmly nestled between the other two, I slept well and woke feeling calm. We drank tea and fruit juice and ate a cupful of cereal, then packed our equipment – cameras and films, a small deadman, two ice screws, two rock pitons and a hundred and fifty feet of rope. We would travel light, and not take emergency equipment, but trust to speed to take us to the summit and back that day. Through gaps between the blocks of the entrance, I could see blue sky. I was the first to worm my way out and announce a perfect day. "If we can't do it today, we're dummies." I yelled down excitedly into the muffled world of the hole, an escaped prisoner announcing sunshine to the inmates of a cold, dark dungeon.

I led off at 8.00 a.m. The sunshine touched the slope only thirty feet away, and we moved into it; climbing further to the right than the Croissant – along the line which Georges and I had followed fifty-four hours before. This time, however, the terrain where we had been lost in the vicious night storm seemed to flow past us as we climbed. I managed twenty paces at a time, and the vast area of rocks that barred access to the Ramp grew near surprisingly quickly.

Although we had studied the area through binoculars from Pang-pema, I could not remember the topography in such detail as Joe and Doug. When I reached the hollow snow slab that had unnerved me two nights before, I was too far to the left, so Doug took over and led for a hundred feet up the right-hand of two gullies that split the rocks. Then Joe traversed a snow shelf to the left-hand one, which he climbed in two tricky rock pitches. "My Rock Band," he grinned.

Because his plastic ski-boots did not fit, Doug was wearing conventional leather and fur boots, and his feet were troubled by the cold. "Can you do the leading?" he said. "I'm expending a lot of energy with each step, trying to keep my toes warm."

Above us, a triangle of snow narrowed into a neck between some rocks, and I led through this to the start of the Ramp.

"Will you stop a few minutes whilst I warm my feet up?" asked Doug.

I needed no persuading to take a rest. Twelve hundred feet above us, looking deceptively near, the Pinnacles on the West Ridge dominated the unbroken thirty-three degree sweep of the Ramp. The way was clear. Our confidence was increasing with the height. Our brains were not exploding, the blood in our legs was not clotting, our hearts and lungs were not palpitating – we just needed to take a few more rests than usual. We were in a good mood.

Joe took over the lead and climbed strongly and steadily through loose and slabby snow. I went to the back and as we moved together we kept the rope stretched between us, in case part of the slope sheered away beneath our feet. My thoughts fell into step behind the others, and I was too involved to worry about the time we were taking. 'At least these tracks will show us the way down, unless they become covered by spindrift. We won't be having another go – we shouldn't need to. We should definitely reach the Pinnacles now. Just keep concentrating. Will I faint if I close my eyes? When will the hallucinations start? I want to climb higher than the Pinnacles. I want to reach the top, to feel inside that I've climbed Kangch.'

Joe reached a curled hollow on a small snow arête, and we stopped there for fifteen minutes whilst Doug took off his boots to warm his feet. Joe unzipped his down suit and held the cold feet against his stomach.

"You're going well, Joe," I said.

"I'm pleased to hear that," he answered, "I thought I was going really slow."

I looked around to assess our position. We were about five hundred feet below the brêche next to the Pinnacles on the West Ridge. We were now higher than all surrounding summits, except Yalung Kang, the West Summit of Kangchenjunga. The slow descent of the summit of 25,919 ft. Kangbachen was a vague and distant measure to our progress. The rocks of the Croissant disappeared beneath the steep ground under our feet. The top of the North East Spur looped like a broad white caterpillar on to the North Ridge. The terraced séracs of the North West Face now supported our height, and the séracs of Twins Peak, so feared from below, looked tiny. The soft hills of Tibet were warm red and sunny. The architecture of the Himalayas, which had seemed chaotic and hostile down on the glaciers, now appeared simple and bold. The summit triangle of Kangchenjunga reigned over the vast silence of a world in order. We were now climbing its throne, and all our efforts of the past weeks lay below us, forgotten.

It was my turn. Whilst I had been following Joe, it had been easiest to relinquish my fears about the snow to his decisions. Now I worried about the hollow noise of the wind slab beneath my boots. At first I kicked my feet into it, but this used too much energy and took too much time. I spread my weight on to my feet and hands and scuttled across like a crab to safer snow, pulling the others, unsuspecting, in a sudden burst of activity. A long broken rib of black tourmaline ran down from the brêche, a line of security above an ocean of changing snow. The involvement of my hands and the integration of moves that the rock demanded, drew my mind away from abstract thoughts. I brushed snow from holds and eased my weight from foot to foot, and drew levitation from the joy of the movement. I was in the shadow, and sunlight streaming from the ridge drew me upwards, gasping with excitement and straining against the invisible reins of thin air.

Roofless pillars of fading and re-forming cloud and low dazzling sunlight greeted me. Light moving air touched my face and drew my eyes to the south. This was the point on the West Ridge which Joe Brown and George Band had reached twenty-four years before, and until now no one had been there since that expedition. Through a hole in the cloud below me, I could see the Great Shelf of the Southern Yalung Face, from where Band and Brown had climbed. It looked flat, white and near. If we had known that side of the mountain, we could have considered going down that way, but such knowledge had to be earned.

I was grateful to be alone for a few moments on the other side of the mountain. It was as if my insides, that had been hard, now thawed, and I felt released from the tension of the Ramp. The calm of the afternoon, the warm sun and the rough golden gneiss of the ridge seemed to tell me that I had been there before. The blue shapes were disturbingly familiar and were shimmering and richly humming, like a memory. I clutched the ridge and steadied myself, and then picked up some rocks, gripping them tightly in my hands.

The Ramp had taken six hours to climb. It was 3.30 p.m. and the sun was falling. I took in the rope as Joe climbed up to join me. The southern view appeared in his mirror sunglasses, and lit up a smile. He took in Doug's rope.

Brown and Band had followed the West Ridge. Just below the summit, Joe Brown had climbed a crack in a sheer wall, after turning up his oxygen supply to six litres a minute. However, the day after, Streather and Hardie had avoided this struggle by a traverse on the southern side. This we hoped to find. At twenty-eight thousand feet, the slightest unnecessary effort would take a heavy toll on our resources of strength.

"We've got a chance," I said.

"What time d'you think we ought to turn back?" asked Joe.

"5.15," I said. "That'll give us an hour before sunset."

Doug arrived. "Hang on, hang on," he said. "Just wait ten minutes whilst I take some photos, and then I'll take over for a while."

We did not know exactly where, or how far away the summit was. Doug, then Joe, then I climbed across little ribs and gullies in the South Face. We were filled with wonder and excitement. Below us, the Great Shelf appeared and disappeared through drifting clouds; Jannu, buttressed and strong soared up to the west, beside the descending sun. To the south east, in Sikkim, great anvil-shaped clouds boiled up.

Doug stopped twice to confirm that we wanted to continue. Then he climbed behind the skyline and reappeared suddenly on top of a large block of rock. "The top's ten feet away," he shouted.

I stuck up a thumb, Fantastic! – and followed the rope as quickly as my lungs would allow. It was 5.15 p.m., and there was not a breath of wind.

We straightened up and looked around, our smiles expanding from deep inside us. We stumbled about, taking photographs, shaking our heads, inarticulate, heady with success. 'I should be thinking great things,' I thought. But none came. For a few moments I could hardly speak. For long seconds I felt overwhelmed by the happiness of pure carefree and uninterpreted emptiness, separated from the knowledge that we had yet to descend.

"I've so forgotten myself as to shake hands," said Doug.

"I'll wait till we get down," replied Joe. "No chorus in my head."

We had been on summits before. We had dreamed of them, for their lure endures for ever and there is no escape, for summits match dreams. But this one we did not touch. The top was ten feet away.

It took three attempts for the delayed trigger-released mechanism on Doug's camera to work. Our frozen smiles came easily.

"The South Summit looks near."

"That flat-topped mountain must be Kabru. Isn't Jannu a long way below us?"

"I can't believe it."

"Don't touch the top, Doug, we want to get down again – mustn't upset whatever lives there."

"I'm trying to climb round the summit – it's too corniced anyway."

"It's a quarter to six."

"Come on Doug, stop taking photographs, we're not actors, it's time to start off down."

"You'll be glad of the copies, Joe."

"Me? I'm only a shopkeeper!"

As we turned to leave, a large black alpine chough with ragged wings flew from nowhere, flitted above our heads and disappeared. 'One a birth, two a death.' This solitary witness seemed a good omen. We left the summit untrodden, hoping that it would always remain so.

The sky, rock and ice were steeped in red around us. We moved quickly, trying to lose as much height as possible before darkness. We had been allowed to sneak up but would we be allowed to sneak down? I felt strongly that we had to cheat someone, something, for the descent, for our lives. I thought 'Everything I've ever learnt must now help me down. If I relax my discipline slightly, I shall trip and fall.'

Flickering storm clouds were dancing towards us from Everest and Makalu. The sunset then reappeared behind them. We raced against the storm and darkness. Now, thicker air combined with our urgency to draw us downwards, and our speed briefly reassured us. I waited at the brêche whilst Doug, then Joe, descended the tourmaline rib. The shadows of the Western Ridge and Summit reached down the summit triangle to the Croissant. The flanks of the North Ridge and the Twins glowed in the setting sun. The upwards moves of the rock rib were still fresh in my mind, and I reversed them, clinically. We had reached the Ramp. A large black cloud was sweeping across the sky towards us, its skirt torn with orange-grey light.

We lost our earlier tracks in the darkness and spindrift. Doug tumbled over a step in the snow and fell ten feet before skidding to a stop. We put our headtorches on, and I went first since, unlike Doug and Joe, I did not wear glasses or contact lenses. Lightning flashed and spread around us, too brief to be a guide. Little nicks in the snow showed me the way, and I kicked into the crust and slab that I had feared earlier. In the dark valley below, at Pangpema, a lone fire winked at us like a chink of light from fires within the earth. They had seen our headtorches! They knew we had done it! They were with us! I felt strong.

At 9.00 p.m. we found the entrance to the bergschrund cave. Doug slid in to light the stove, and Joe and I chatted for a while, as excited as the safely-landed passengers of a wounded aircraft.

14

DOWN WIND

16th May – 2nd June, 1979

We sipped tea inside the shelter, sealed in for the night, oblivious to the hovering storm outside. Sleeping pills could not dispel the intense cold, and we twitched restlessly through the night. Occasionally Doug groaned, as spasms of pain shot through his body from his frost-damaged fingers. Joe cared for him, feeding him analgesics, whilst I pulled the drawcord of my cowled sleeping bag tight. The cold seeped in through all our protective layers. Our minds clung to the ballast of one thought: we had done it!

In the morning our movements were sluggish.

"5 – The Great Snow and Scree Terrace; 4 – The Castle; 3 – The Ridge, 2 – The Wall; 1 – The Glacier and Séracs," Joe listed the obstacles we had to descend to Camp 2, to safety.

"Life's simple up here – not much to pack," said Doug.

We stuffed our sleeping bags into our sacks, fumbled with boots and crampons and tottered out into the cold dawn. We were weak with dehydration and cold, and for many days had eaten little. It was tempting to allow gravity to guide our steps, for our bodies responded feebly to the signals of our minds. In the harsh world of high altitude, a climber must obey his inner conscious voice, for the simple instructions of that voice are his only defence: "Kick into that slope to break through the windcrust, change the axe over to the other hand, clench those fingers and warm them up, wipe the snow from your glasses, don't trip on that rock with your crampon points, keep going, it's not far now."

Descending unroped, we drifted apart, but re-grouped many times to sit out the waves of dizziness that swept over us. It was the worst time.

Doug swung down the ropes that hung down the Castle and

reached the snow-hole first. He shovelled out the buried entrance. The ceiling had collapsed to within three feet of the cave floor, but there was enough space for the three of us to lie down beside the stove and melt some snow. We rolled the drink around our mouths before swallowing it – it had the recuperative effect of a miracle-cure.

"Three to go," said Joe.

The wind had paused only for our summit day. Now it had returned. Its freezing violence pushed our bodies, lashed us with our rucksack straps, and plucked at our woollen hats and down hoods. Coils were whipped from our hands, and the rope seemed imbued with a mad life of its own. Yet this wind came from a blue sky that stretched from us to Everest, and implied no threat. It was a relief to reach the North Col and step from the wind-blasted crust into the deep powder of the sheltered Sikkim side. Here we could talk without shouting.

We drank again, and rooted through the camp-site for food, gathering together our strength and concentration for the three thousand foot descent of the wall. There was too much equipment to carry down, for heavy loads would make our movements even more cumbersome, and increase the risk. Yet we were loath to abandon it; so we tied it all up in bundles and threw it down the wall.

After two and a half hours on the North Col, we could not afford to rest any longer, for it was mid-afternoon, and there were still two obstacles to descend before nightfall. We set off on the tense repetitive ritual of clipping and unclipping our friction devices, sliding down, ropelength after ropelength.

The wall was melting. The high afternoon temperature heralded the approaching monsoon, but we had been living in freezing air for many days, and the change of temperature caught us by surprise. The wall was falling down around us and crisp snow had turned to watery ice. Great black rocks, loosened by the heat, keeled over and crashed down at the slightest touch of rope or crampon. Water ran freely down the rope and, whenever we could shelter beneath overhangs from falling rocks, we slaked our thirst. Doug, descending first, ripped an anchor from the soggy ice and snow, to be held by the rope above. We tiptoed down, our eyes bright and swivelling with watchful concentration.

Some of the equipment we had thrown down had burst from its containing sacks, and we could see a few tattered remnants hanging irretrievably on the wall. The rest was scattered over a wide area on the glacier. We had arranged for Ang Phurba and Nima Tenzing to come and help us. Two tiny dots had left the tent of Camp 2 when we had started down the wall. However, they were moving painfully slowly, and when we reached the bottom of the ropes they still had a long way to come.

Joe put out his hand. "You know me, Pete, I've waited till we're down," he said. He had studiously withheld the gesture since the summit. Even now it came too soon. We quickly discovered why the Sherpas were approaching so slowly.

Normally, half an hour sufficed for us to reach Camp 2. This time half an hour saw us floundering in waist-deep, wet snow, only a few hundred yards from the bottom of the wall. We took off our sacks and crawled, dragging them beside us to distribute the weight. Lightning flared in the west, and large snowflakes fell from the darkening sky, hiding the menace of the séracs that flanked us.

"Best Success-Juice, Sahib?" Nima Tenzing was carrying a kettleful. It was a happy encounter. He and Ang Phurba pressed on to retrieve the gear we had left piled at the foot of the wall. Night fell and we lost their tracks.

The pattern of crevasses had changed. Doug and I yelled abuse at each other. "Watch that rope, Pete, you're supposed to be a professional guide."

"Shut up, you middle-aged hippie."

"You're just a middle-class achiever."

"Working-class hero."

Fun was not far away, for we could smell safety. The solitary tent of Camp 2 loomed up, blanketed with snow, and the two Sherpas arrived back simultaneously. They fed us hot sweet tea and a large meal, as we snuggled in the back of the tent, rapturously warm and relaxed, and comforted by the purr of the primus stoves. There was no longer any need for sullen manoeuvrings around the stove. Cooking had been an aversion we shared. But to be cooked for was heaven. We were cosseted like sick children, and had to take no more decisions. Ang Phurba was more chatty than we had known him before.

"Better to have walkie-talkies on mountains like Kangchenjunga," he said. "Big problem us knowing what you do."

In his calm, offhand manner he delivered the latest Himalayan news, gleaned from the transistor radio at Base Camp. Gauri Sankar had been climbed by an American-Nepalese expedition, and Ang Phu, one of the most talented of Sherpa mountaineers, and our companion on Everest in 1975, had been killed. We were too tired to absorb the meaning of the news, and it only brushed the surface of our minds before we fell asleep. Outside the tent, the snow stopped falling and a new moon rose for the third time since we had arrived below Kangchenjunga.

We left early, to beat the snow-softening sun, and tantalised by the prospect of a Base Camp breakfast. Doug forged on ahead, and Joe and I chatted inconsequentially. Occasionally we stumbled, learning to walk again on boulders and level ground. The rush of oxygen brought on by our loss of height anaesthetised the weariness of our wasted limbs.

I was apprehensive about Georges' reaction to our success. I need not have worried. He bounded down the moraine to us, carrying fruit juice, and hugged us exuberantly in fond Gallic embraces. He never mentioned any disappointment of his own, and we were never to suggest it. My apprehension was foolish, and my heart warmed to him with affection and respect.

He chattered excitedly: "How was it? We could see you nearly all day, except when you went behind the ridge to the top. I took many photos through the zoom. The others were really involved, and kept on looking. It was really exciting. Did you see my fires? You missed them the first night? The weather forecast was bad, but I thought what the hell, and lit two, to encourage you! Hey, and there's some girls here. Dawa and her friend. They came up with wood and eggs. They're really cute, it's like they've come from another planet."

Dawa was there, with her lovely smile, and I hardly dared look at her. A griffon vulture wheeled in as if in a salute above our heads. Mohan and little Nima Tamang greeted us, proudly grinning. Kami had baked a chocolate cake and we quickly drained the bottle of whisky. The meadow of Pangpema was greener than it had been on our previous return. It was as fragrant to our senses as it had been to Freshfield on his arrival there from the Jongsong La, eighty years before. It seemed so long ago since we had seen fresh grass growing in the spring.

After breakfast the following morning, I climbed the hillside behind Base Camp. The dawn light was still low and soft, and the ground was sprinkled with snow. I hoped that the uphill effort would clarify my mind. As I climbed, I disturbed a group of twenty bharal, or Himalayan blue sheep. For half an hour I followed them quickly up the hillside, staying within fifty feet of them, admiring their deft, goat-like movements over the steep ground. The sun arrived and lit their shapes, and they bounded away, to disappear behind a distant spur.

I had climbed nearly two thousand feet and stopped to sit on a boulder before my mind was blunted with fatigue. My stomach was gurgling, unused to the rush of food since our return. I pondered the inevitable questions that accompany a mountaineering success. Had the mystical experience of reaching the West Ridge been no more than the result of a combination of lack of oxygen, food and water, and perhaps an excess of negative ions in the air? "That hill, cragged and steep where truth stands." Mountains do not reveal truth, I decided, but they encourage something to grow inside – something I was not yet able to explain fully. Our adventure had ended, and I tried to sense the birth of a new direction. Wordsworth loved mountains, but wandered most of his life beneath the fifteen-hundred-foot contour. He had not needed experience of such violent stimulants, such risk, to shock him into moods of awareness. It seemed silly that the summit was so important, and a near-miss so different. Had I become over-reliant on these extremes, as Marie the painter had hinted in Paris so many months before?

I was feeling ecstatic, yet did not hope to sustain this ecstasy through my life. I wanted to measure my life through contrasts, and to do that I had to return to 'the other life'. On the mountain, too much inter-personal exploration would have weakened the united front we had tried to hold together for the climb. Antagonisms had never been allowed to become open, and had always been defused at an early stage. However, back in the other life at least people had other preoccupations; it was possible to relax and allow relationships to develop more subtly, without being under constant pressure. That was where the other side of the balance – the true interest of human-ity – lay.

Pride, self-esteem and ambition are seldom analysed by the moun-taineer, but we all admitted that we were looking forward to a few heady days on our return – to be patted on the back by our mates in the pub, with a pint in hand, no more. The disaster on K2 had left me lost for a year, but now, for a while, my ego was re-asserted. I was happy to have emerged unscathed, with only a black toenail and a few numb finger ends. I had gained confidence and learnt much. I thought of future projects in a new light and was dazzled by the possibilities. My fear of high altitudes had been exorcised. Six weeks of effort and acclimatisation had helped us find a key to the summit. Our three forays above twenty-six thousand feet had acclimatised us specifically for great heights.

The morning light had flattened across Kangchenjunga, and I returned to the camp. The night's snow had melted. We had a day to pack before twenty porters arrived from Ghunsa. Georges left, in-tending to visit the Slovak camp beneath Jannu the next day, to thank them for the rope. With him went Mohan, skipping like a spring lamb and humming with happiness, released from his long Base Camp vigil.

Doug had already filled several large kitbags, marked KHUMBU. He and Georges had permission to attempt three Nepalese peaks in the autumn – Kussum Kangguru, Nuptse and Everest – and Ang Phurba was to take the equipment with him to his village near these moun-tains, before the monsoon stopped flights. Doug's thoughts had transferred quickly to his next project, as if Kangchenjunga had already been absorbed into his vast Himalayan experience. After my dreamy morning walk I was shocked by his speed, and argued with him, demanding some tents for my autumn expedition to Gauri Sankar.

On the morning of the 20th May we walked away from Base Camp. It seemed as if the spell of Kangchenjunga had held us from leaving the mountain for a lifetime. As we waded across the river plain at Lhonak, our thin bare legs made us look like storks. By early afternoon we had reached the edge of the forest above Ghunsa. Our first steps beneath green trees stirred in us a sense of total peace.

"I still can't believe we've climbed that mountain," said Joe.

We lay down on the grass amid yellow flowers. The milky river below us filled the air with sound and a light wind brushed the treetops, faintly sighing. We closed our eyes, relishing the warm oxygen-enriched air and the scent of the flowers. After many weeks in a barren world of snow and rock, we were in a garden, beautiful and haunting as though pre-visited. We slept deeply until mid-afternoon, and woke refreshed. That sleep was Kangchenjunga's parting gift.

We had left a lot of muscle on the mountain, and our thighs and joints ached as we jolted down through the forest.

Below Ghunsa it was Peer Gynt country, with gloomy mist clinging down the steep, wooded hillsides, and the fire a cosy focal point. Oxygenated elation had worn off, and I was glad of the rest day the porters demanded. Doug was making fun of Joe's iconoclastic nature.

"He's going to love talking about this trip when we get back. I can just see him now in the Moon, hands outsplayed in an earnest blue-eyed expression: 'Well there we were at twenty-eight thousand feet, just three ordinary johns like us. Anyone could have done it. It all felt really normal.' "

When school finished for the afternoon the usual crowds gathered round, and some excitable youths started a water battle around us with old plastic syringes. One of them, escaping from his pursuer, tripped up over the fire and knocked our dinner flying. Kami lost his temper and laid into the culprit with his foot, which started a wild rumpus. It was the first time I had seen a Sherpa lose his temper and go out of control. Usually they erred the other way, and were too polite to say what they thought. Doug looked over his glasses at Kami and admonished his Buddhist conscience severely. The dinner was put on to simmer again, while we enjoyed salivating and watching Kami and little Nima co-ordinate the meal. Nima, our kitchen boy, was one of two young Tamang brothers whom Ang Phurba had adopted in his house in Khumjung. Joe was perceptive about hierarchies and often teased Ang Phurba that he, a member of the Sherpa super-race, exploited Nima like a slave – and Ang Phurba laughed, for he, also, had just read some short stories by James Lester about black slaves in America.

I asked Ang Phurba how he would spend the money he earned during the expedition and he replied immediately "Yaks." Material comfort, or moving to Kathmandu where he could exploit the tourist and expedition trade more effectively didn't interest him. More important was the prestige that a large herd of yaks brings among the Sherpas. Yaks are a time-honoured investment, and it was good to know that the old ways have not yet completely changed. No men of Ang Phurba's village have yet sold their houses and permanently moved to Kathmandu, despite the fact that most of the households contain at least one member sometimes engaged in work connected with mountaineering and tourism, and some of the younger men spend as much as eight or nine months of the year away.

Now we were thinking a lot about returning to our friends and families, but the Sherpas didn't seem worried at all. Long absences are commonplace to them, and they know that news is not expected of them until they turn up unexpectedly to announce their own return. Only Kami talked about going home, because he had to help his father organise a festival in Namche Bazar.

At the bridge at Dobhan, the magical halfway crossing of our return, children were splashing in the river. We stood aside on the narrow trail to let through hundreds of people coming towards us. We watched, fascinated, as lissome young girls in saris of brilliant reds and blues, and large families of three – perhaps four – generations, all dressed in their finery, walked past. They were going to a wedding and stared back at us blankly. Hindus do not understand foreign tourists. No doubt, to them we were just paisa-wallahs, who had so much money they could travel – not to visit relatives or to attend a wedding, but just to see new things, without knowing anything and leaving their work and family to wander like cows.

When we reached the high ridge, we looked back towards the mountain, but it was hidden by the approaching monsoon. Georges paused to have his future told by a Brahmin soothsayer from a village among the terraced fields far below. Laughing with embarrassment, Mohan translated the questions and answers. Only one answer was correct: "Did I get to the top of Kangchenjunga?" asked Georges.

The soothsayer said nothing, but raised his hand to the sky and pointed at the tip of the index finger.

We left the Sherpas and the porters a day behind, and pressed on to Hille and Dhankuta. During one long, thirty-mile day we walked continuously, without breaking step. It seemed as if we were 'lung-gom' mystics, following one of the legendary energy meridians of the Himalayas which Doug had described to us during the walk-in.

At Biratnagar airport we weighed ourselves out from the mountain with the concern of boxers after a fight. I had lost nearly two stone.

As we flew to Kathmandu over the gathering monsoon clouds. I pointed the zoom lens of my camera back at the massive bulk of Kangchenjunga, and across at the black prow of an impregnable-looking mountain – Gauri Sankar, 'The Eiger of the Himalayas'. I would return before the summer monsoon was over.

Four days later we were among the rolling green hills of Derbyshire.

15

SUMMER

2nd June – 18th September, 1979

Climbers have a phrase for their need to compensate for all the weeks of deprivation – retraining in the pub. My return from Kangchenjunga coincided happily with the annual Mynydd Climbing Club 'Carnival Crawl'. This event comprised a circular tour of all the eighteen pubs in the district of New Mills, the evening before the town's Carnival Day. The only rules are that you down a drink in each. About twenty members assembled for the occasion, and Hilary and Steve, an American friend, arrived after an eighteen-hour drive from Switzerland, just in time for the start. The crawl begins by crossing the moors above the town, to take in the peripheral 'country' pubs. It was my first exercise since the walk-out from Kangchenjunga. The drinking was spiced with a few games of darts and pool, and I played whatever Blondie records were stocked in the various juke boxes on the way. Debbie Harrie had been our cult figure on Kangchenjunga. Hilary, not having been on such a crawl before, was discovering corners of New Mills she had never dreamed existed. We had not seen each other for a long time, and started as surface-shy strangers, warily circling. However, it did not take long to relax.

Steve started off by not knowing anybody; by halfway he knew all of our group, and by the time he reached the demanding rapid succession of six pubs in Market Street, he was striking up long and involved conversations about Vietnam and the world in general with strangers nobody knew.

"What beautiful people!" he kept on exclaiming, and went to the fish and chip shop to order mushy peas.

It took a couple of days to recover from the evening.

The Kangchenjunga team met one last time, at Joe's shop at Hope, in Derbyshire, to sort out our photographs together. No doubt, in the history of expeditions, ours had been relatively happy, but during that afternoon we achieved a fleeting unity that had been rare during the climb. Talking among ourselves, and with Georges' American wife, Norma, Joe and I realised how much Georges had been suffering from a lack of communication during the climb. Although Georges' English was excellent, he had missed many of the subtleties of humour, discussion and disagreement among the three English – subtleties on well-understood levels, evolved on many expeditions together. Also, I began to understand how Joe and I had often presented a strong complicity on many issues – an unspoken understanding that was a product of our long weeks together on Changabang, and which was invisible to us, but apparently impenetrable to those outside.

We realised that we had not got a usable expedition photograph of the four of us together. We walked past trees, trembling and bowing under the touch of a June breeze, out on to a green meadow. There, we played dandelion clocks whilst Norma clicked away with a couple of cameras. Two landmarks dominate the Hope Valley – a very tall factory chimney near Castleton, and the dark bulk of Mam Tor, the shivering mountain, a summit encircled by the ditchlines, visible from afar, of an old Bronze Age settlement. For photographic background, we chose Mam Tor.

The afterglow from Kangchenjunga was disturbed by the shadow of Gauri Sankar stretching out across the summer. In mid-September I would be going back to Nepal on the Gauri Sankar expedition. I had committed myself to this nearly two years before, whilst I was working for the British Mountaineering Council in Manchester. A letter had arrived announcing that the Nepalese authorities were opening the mountain to expeditions. A day later Dennis Gray, the General Secretary of the B.M.C., came into the office and saw the note.

"I might get a trip together to have a go at that," he said.

"Hard luck, I've already sent a telegram," I said.

It had seemed wise to join forces. A few days after my return from Kangchenjunga I met Dennis Gray and the other two members, Tim Leach and John Barry, to discuss our expedition. It was still not clear which route the American-Nepalese expedition had climbed that spring (the news which Ang Phurba had announced during our descent from Kangchenjunga). However, it did not matter, for there were many challenging new routes to do on the mountain. We reaffirmed our intention of going, and agreed to write off for more information and photographs.

Fortunately, the other three members of the expedition seemed prepared to do most of the work. Tim Leach, an architectural student, had the largest job, in organising the equipment. The wheels were in motion, and as yet I was only partially turning with them. I had difficulty in appearing enthusiastic about the whole new project, for Kangchenjunga had left me exhausted and sated at the same time. I was drained of the physical and mental energy for any more prolonged effort and worried that by going to Gauri Sankar I might be pushing things too far. It was the first time I had committed myself to a double-Himalayan-season-year. Yet I felt I could not back out, and trusted that feeling. I had three months' grace for rejuvenation, and appreciated the summer with the intensity of a soldier home on leave. Not that I could afford to be idle. Earning some money again was an urgent priority, so I returned to Leysin where Hilary had got a temporary job at a local hospital. My foot and wrist were still weak and so she introduced me to a Canadian physiotherapist who had worked for the Canadian Olympic team, and whose eyes glittered when I told her my problems.

"It's ages since I've worked on an athlete," she drooled.

After two weeks with her I pronounced myself cured.

Returning to Switzerland offered a change in socialising styles. The bar regulars at the Club Vagabond, where the International School of Mountaineering is based are mainly Anglo-Saxons, or what the few English there call patronisingly 'colonials' – Australians, New Zealanders, South Africans, Canadians and Americans. Before he was killed, my predecessor as Director of the climbing school, Dougal Haston, wrote a novel, *Calculated Risk*, based on Leysin, which abounds with descriptions of the Vagabond's 'beautiful people' – all in their mid-twenties and good-looking, cosmopolitan, promiscuous and boozy; without the cry of a child, the quaver of an old-age pensioner or the stern voice of work and responsibility within earshot. The real situation is not quite so playful. Nevertheless, the happy social atmosphere, the wide variety of people, good music and cheap beer make the bar a more relaxed haven than the rather austere Swiss bistros.

While I was away on Kangchenjunga I had been appointed President of the Association of British Mountain Guides, so on my return found myself in the thick of the impassioned ongoing argument about the conditions of Britain becoming a full member of the International Union of Mountain Guides. This had been accepted in principle two years before, but the prejudice against us was strong.

"In my village a child touches and begins to understand snow as soon as he can walk, he has a feel for mountains from an early age – but all your guides were born in cities."

"The English? But they *hire* guides. They can't become guides themselves!"

Beneath all these objections was an undercurrent of tribal and trading protectionism – a suspicion that, once the gates were opened, barbaric hordes of unkempt British, out for loot, would stream in from the north and steal all the clients.

I attended the summer meeting of the International Union which coincided with the annual fête of all the guides in the Swiss canton of Valais, at Bettemeralp, a village high above Brig in the Rhône Valley. On the Sunday morning the guides attended an open air mass, and the priest blessed the banners of all the different sections. The music of the long alpenhorns, the grey uniforms of the guides and the white robes of the priest, the sunlit mountains and meadow, all combined to give a special harmony. The ritual and commitment reminded me of Sherpas being blessed by a lama before going on an expedition.

British mountain guides in the Alps have a valuable friend in Madame Joan Pralong, the post-mistress at Arolla. She is, by origin, a Geordie who married a Swiss eighteen years ago. Although not an active climber herself, she has a passion for mountains and mountaineering, and believes in the dictum 'Mountains may divide peoples, but they unite mountaineers.' She saw immediately the problems of misunderstandings between the British and Alpine guides, and masterminded a number of casually relaxed meetings between British and Swiss mountaineers. It was at these get-togethers that I first met André Georges from La Sage, the great nephew of Joseph Georges, the famous alpine guide and companion of I. A. Richards and Dorothy Pilley, and Denis Bertholet from Verbier. Denis had been a member of the first expedition to attempt Gauri Sankar in 1954, and he lent me a number of invaluable photographs of the mountain.

In early July I suddenly became leader of our expedition. I received a letter from Dennis Gray, explaining that he was having to drop out owing to financial and work pressures. It was a sad loss, for Dennis had led an expedition to the mountain in 1964 that had nearly reached the summit, and for many years Gauri Sankar had been a personal ambition. Now with only two months to go, I had to find his replacement. Fortunately, a local Swiss guide of about my age from Leysin offered to come along. Guy Neithardt frequented the Club Vagabond, had climbed with Dougal Haston and worked for the climbing school. He spoke English with a northern accent – learnt, he said, 'in bars' – was tolerant of the idiosyncracies of British mountaineers and appreciated their sense of humour.

Like most Swiss, Guy had a strong loyalty to his village and I had learnt much from him about what it meant to be a 'Leysenoud'. His joining us meant that, apart from a small expedition John Barry had been on to India, I was the only member of the team with any Himalayan experience. This, I hoped, would be a good thing, because we could approach the mountain without too many preconceptions, and it would be a refreshing change for me to climb with talented alpine technicians.

A letter from Al Read, the joint leader of the American-Nepalese spring expedition to Gauri Sankar, enthused me further:

> I can imagine how you feel about our success on Gauri Sankar. We were very fortunate to have made it! It is an incredible mountain and certainly another route by you will be a very worthwhile endeavour.

Al went on to describe how his expedition had climbed the West Face direct to the North Summit. This meant that the South Summit and the West Ridge up to it, which had been the route his expedition had originally contemplated, was still unclimbed. Al listed its difficulties, but thought it 'might be worth a go'.

When I was fourteen, I had travelled to Manchester to hear my first mountaineering lecture entitled 'Gauri Sankar, the Eiger of the Himalayas'. Don Whillans had described how their 1964 expedition was plagued by Tibetan bandits and how the Japanese in 1959 had been robbed down to their underpants. The incomprehensibly vast size of the mountain and the complex topography of the area around it had fascinated me. They had toiled for weeks through dense leech-infested jungle and across the lower spurs of the mountain's ridges, before only just failing to climb the North Face.

Vivid recollections of that lecture began to link hands with a recurring memory – of being on the summit ridge of Kangchenjunga. Once a mountaineer has climbed so high, for the rest of his life he dreams of returning. I no longer needed to indulge, rest, sleep and forget. Mentally I was ready for the mountains again. But when I went rock climbing in one of the Leysin quarries, I was shocked at my weakness and consequent lack of confidence. Simple problems I had solved many times previously were scary. The first time I took two clients from the climbing school up the Tour d'Aï, one of the spectacular limestone towers high above Leysin, I made a mistake that was due to carelessness rather than weakness, however. I took my boots off at the foot of the South West Face to change from shorts into breeches. One of my boots toppled forwards and bounced six hundred feet down the scree, towards Leysin. It was a long hop to retrieve it, but it would have bounced even further if it had dropped in the Himalayas.

Each week I left Leysin with one or two clients to climb in different areas. I was surprised to find that north, east and south, within two or three hours' drive, it was possible to escape the crowds. Here there was a 'Hello' contour, below which the crowds of passers-by averted their eyes, but above which mountaineers and walkers were few, and greeted each other cheerfully. I was filling out my mental picture of the characters of different mountains, their ridges, faces and hidden cwms. We never covered the same ground twice. I was fitting together the jigsaw of their valleys and passes, delighting in 'connected knowledge'. The maps of Switzerland became alive, and I was building a structure of memories and associations that helped me feel more and more at home.

On a succession of climbs, your senses are continually sharpened by moving quickly between two different worlds; the tension and isolation of the climb, and the gregarious comfort of safety, friends and beer in the huts and valleys. The emotions of departure and return, which are separated by long stretches of time on an expedition, are – in the Alps – compressed within a single day.

Towards the end of my alpine summer the peace of mind I had regained in the mountains was shattered by a phone call from my mother in England, to tell me that an exploratory operation on my father had discovered a tumour on his pancreas.

Travellers always take it for granted that nothing will change at home while they are away. Home is the reassuring place where there is always love and shelter, without obligations – always trusted to be stable, so terrifying when it changes. First came shock and despair, and then I clung to disbelief. My father was only fifty-nine. There was a tradition of longevity in the family, all my grandparents had lived well into their eighties, and one Gran was still a lively eighty-seven. Surely the disease would not be fatal?

A few days later Hilary and I drove to my parents' home in Bramhall on the Cheshire Plain. We visited my father in hospital, and he seemed cheerful, smiling bravely and trusting of the medical care he was receiving. Afterwards with my mother, we subjected the utterances of physicians and surgeons to intense analysis, at times basing future hopes and fears on nuances of expression. I had always distrusted miracles, but now my father's life was hedged, I believed in them.

One of the most advanced cancer treatment clinics in the world, the Christie, is in Manchester, and my father was to start fortnightly treatment there with the latest American drugs. He came home from hospital. He was restless. I spoke to him as he paced around the room, as if being relentlessly stalked.

"I suppose you know from your climbing what it's like to be gripped?" he said.

I tried to comfort him, but realised I didn't know, and had never learnt. He never expressed darker thoughts than that. I could only try to imagine how his illness erected a barrier between him and the healthy world.

The organisation for Gauri Sankar now became a remote point of reference for me; an emptiness. My responsibilities divided me, and I went mechanically through the motions of preparation. If I went to Gauri Sankar, I determined to climb the mountain quickly and safely, and come back home again as soon as possible.

Hilary had to fly back to her job in Leysin, in time for the start of the autumn term at the American School. During a few afternoons I went rock-climbing on gritstone crags of the Peak District – Baldstones, Gardoms and Stanage. Gritstone is an old comforter. The crowds are one of its charms, for they soon break up as you recognise the groups amongst them. Easy friendships are renewed and made – local friends, and friends from Leeds, Sheffield, Birmingham and London. And gritstone routes never change – the same holds and moves and problems are always there, to be quickly remembered. On the gritstone edges there are no tempests to transform the landscape, no slopes to avalanche nor splintering rocks to fall. My university climbing club at Nottingham used to hold competitions around pub tables – someone started to read the description of one of Stanage's four hundred, fifty-foot-high routes, and you scored if you were the first to recognise it. Some climbers got the right answer after the first three or four words.

The American climber, Yvon Chouinard, once remarked that 'all climbers are a product of their first few climbs' and it is true that a person who learns his climbing on small but difficult crags may take up big-wall climbing or become an alpinist, or an expedition mountaineer, but his first love will always be free climbing on the crags. I have never lost a yearning to revisit gritstone. Stretching, reaching, pulling, pushing, it is the best exercise in the world.

I climbed into the evenings. The wind softly combed the moors, and clouds paced slowly, alternating light and colour from bright sunlight to black storm – until the sun finally set in a red blaze. By late August, the green in the valleys below was tired, but the rock was always warm.

I returned to Switzerland for the first week of September, to finish writing some articles and to drive a carload of equipment and food for Guy to take to Kathmandu – he was flying a few days later than the other three of us, since he was finishing his final course to qualify as a guide. At the Swiss frontier, the customs demanded that I empty the car and carry all the stuff across to a building to be weighed. I lost my temper and told the customs men they could keep it and eat it. They reassured me that the money would be repaid if the food and gear left the country, but they would not let me in until I had paid about £100 duty. When I arrived in Leysin, I parked the car outside my apartment and received a parking ticket. I moved the car, and someone inside another chalet threatened to call the police because I was using their parking space. The next day I was summoned to the police station for a different reason.

Whilst I had been away, a false and misleading article about my climbing school had appeared in a Valais newspaper, saying I was certifying Swiss and foreign guides. I had, in fact, just run an alpine training course for one British guide; it would have been illegal for me to certify anyone. However, two Swiss climbing school directors had canvassed a wide protest, and triggered off the remorseless wheels of bureaucratic inquiry. The legitimacy of my work permit and my right to run a climbing school was being questioned. I felt threatened and mildly paranoid after these brushes with authority, which jarred with the settled peace I had found in Leysin – where the friends I had made and my love for the surrounding mountains justified my feeling at home.

The political problems of my work in Switzerland were not helped by dogs back in England snapping at the tail of the Gauri Sankar expedition. Ken Wilson, former editor of *Mountain Magazine* and self-appointed guardian of the moral conscience of British mountaineering and its politics has a fiery, outspoken manner which regularly entertains all those not under attack. As a member of the Mount Everest Foundation Management Committee, which was supporting the trip, he had criticised our expedition as being too weak for the difficulties of the mountain. When John Barry, the director of Plas-y-Brenin Mountain Centre, joined the team, Ken had spoken as a member of Plas-y-Brenin Management Committee, and said that the centre could not afford John's absence in the Himalayas. When Dennis Gray dropped out, and I invited Guy Neithardt, Ken reverted to his Everest Foundation role and criticised its subsidy of foreigners.

Now John Barry was coming under heavy pressure from a number of sides not to go with us and fifteen days before we were due to leave, he sent me a telegram resigning from the expedition. It took a day on the telephone to England, canvassing support and playing on John's conscience until he decided to stick to his guns and come with us.

During the final week before our departure, I received a prize at a reception in London for my book *The Shining Mountain*. My father was determined not to miss the occasion, despite his illness, and with my mother he arrived on the train from Manchester. I felt sadly proud of him. Hilary also flew over for the day. Our relationship had had many tense moments during the summer, for I had had little time to share with her, little time for the pauses, the constant exchanges of thought that are essential if love is to progress. It was hard, being apart, for we changed apart. I was condemning her to another long and worrying wait, constantly checking the postbox. She had strength, and said goodbye without crying or smiling.

During the final days I lived two lives. My house in New Mills was filled with chaos as John and Tim arrived with food and equipment to be packed. The telephone rang incessantly. Then I would leave the Gauri Sankar expedition in New Mills and visit my mother and father, talk with them, and relax. I reassured myself that they were both loved members of a community, surrounded by the warmth of friends and I knew that my brother would be travelling regularly from his home in London to see them.

When Tim, John and I flew from Heathrow, I trusted faintly that things would sort themselves out and that the expedition would make sense once we saw the mountain and arrived at its foot. But I was filled with aching guilt. I knew that I had not been honest with myself, that I had avoided three questions: 'Will he die?' 'Will he die whilst I am away?' 'Should I go?'

I was haunted by the sight of my parents at their front door, waving goodbye, after I had spent the afternoon in the garden, picking apples.

THREE

GAURI SANKAR

16

FIRST TIME

19th September – 8th October, 1979

Gauri Sankar has deep religious significance for both Hindus and Buddhists. Sankar (the North Summit) is the Hindu god Shiva, married to the goddess Gauri (the South Summit). The Buddhist Rolwaling Sherpas living south of the mountain can only see the South Summit and call it Jomo Tseringma. Throughout Buddhist Lamaism, to as far away as Sikkim, Tseringma is considered the most holy mountain of the Sherpas.

In 1971 a small group of Norwegians visited the village of Beding in the Rolwaling Valley below the mountain and suggested to the inhabitants that they should petition the authorities in Kathmandu for their peak to be protected from 'conquests' and big expeditions. The gesture, they felt, of leaving the upper few feet of a mountain such as Kangchenjunga untrodden, was not enough. *Mountain Magazine* printed a photograph of a Rolwaling villager signing the petition with his thumbprint. Better than any words this picture spoke that the protest was heartfelt, a significant gesture from such a normally tolerant people.

The Norwegians were among the founders of an increasingly influential school of thought in the seventies called *Friluftsliv*, which called for a less competitive attitude to climbing and a more environmentally sensitive approach to the mountains. They drew parallels between what had happened in the Alps over the last hundred and thirty years and what they could already see happening in parts of Nepal over thirty years.

The inviolate summits of Gauri Sankar were an ideal symbol of the principles and beliefs that the Norwegians wished to protect, because they were not only important in the religion of the surrounding peoples, they were also a world-famous challenge to mountaineers. Gauri and Sankar were two of the last unclimbed seven-thousand metre summits in the Himalayas. The spectacular profile of the mountain was prominent from the plains south of the Himalayan chain, and all photographs of it showed razor-sharp ridges, loose vertical rock faces and avalanche-swept gullies. Hence, the mountain was well-known among the world's mountaineers as a 'last unsolved problem' of high-altitude climbing, and more than forty expeditions had applied for permission to climb it. A number of illegal attempts had been made, including one of Japanese origin, which was stopped by Nepalese authorities in the autumn of 1973.

There was a great deal of hesitation before Gauri Sankar was once more added to the 'permitted' list along with forty-seven other peaks, late in 1977. For some time it had been uncertain whether the mountain was in Nepal. The 1960 Nepal-Tibet/China agreement generally followed the watershed. However, a map published in 1968 and researched by Erwin Schneider, showed the North Summit firmly in Tibet. It was only early in 1979 that the Chinese conceded this northerly loop of high-altitude territory including both summits to Nepal, whilst retaining all the northern and eastern ridges and approaches firmly in Tibet.

The government of Nepal stipulated that at least two Nepalese be members of the expedition to make the first ascent, one of whom was to be included in the summit team.

Al Read's position in Kathmandu, as President of Mountain Travel Nepal, enabled him to submit the first successful application under the new regulations. Owing to Gauri Sankar's significance, he composed the expedition of five Nepalese Sherpas and five Americans. As co-leader, he selected my Everest companion, Pertemba Sherpa. In the spring of 1979, the expedition duly climbed the mountain, and an American and a Sherpa left the higher, Northern, Summit decisively trodden.

Once the North Summit had been climbed, the joint conditions ceased to apply. However, we wanted to include a Sherpa in our autumn attempt, so that the spirit of the co-operative effort with the Nepalese could be maintained. A Sherpa could help us to climb the mountain in a manner as sensitive and respectful as possible to its religious significance. Our lightweight expedition, we hoped, would leave little mark on the mountain.

At the Sherpa Co-operative building in Kathmandu, Tim, John and I met members of a Norwegian expedition, among whom was Nils Faarland, one of the original exponents of *Friluftsliv*. He was tall, a brown crew-cut accentuating a slightly mournful expression, carefully dressed in breeches, a fawn anorak and silk scarf, which contrasted with our tee-shirts and denim shorts.

Nils asked that we did not tread the top of the South Summit, beyond the point at which we could reasonably say we had climbed the mountain. The Norwegians were going to attempt another holy mountain – Numbur. He confessed they had only discovered its special status when the preparations for the expedition were long under way. Didn't he feel guilty about attempting a sacred summit, we asked?

Nils spoke English slowly and carefully, as if dictating a statement: "Yes, I do, I wish I had known. But it gives us a good incentive to carry out this expedition in the best possible way, in an alternative style. We have only natural fibre equipment – we have no nylon clothing, and very little steel or aluminium. We want to get away from the techno-culture, and use equipment that is the least harmful to nature and at the same time durable and suitable to our purpose. The gap between man and nature is getting wider, and we want a re-union."

"Haven't you got nylon ropes?"

"Yes; we had hoped to bring silk ropes, but it was not possible. Maybe for the future."

"Have you had much stuff specially made?"

"No, we have bought it all from the shops at retail prices. In this way we can stay out of 'the circus'. It is wrong for manufacturers to keep on generating new models, just to keep their sales competitive, and to use expeditions to the Himalayas to promote their products."

"Must have cost you a bloody fortune!"

"Fortunately, our leader, Arne Naess, works in shipping and he deals in money. So we can forget about money and concentrate on more important things. I have talked with many lamas about what we should do. They say that, to respect a special sacred mountain, we should not attack the mountain aggressively, but we should get the monasteries near the mountain to bless the expedition and should bring ourselves closer to and live with the mountain with good thoughts and an open mind, and think of our tents as transportable *gompas*."

"How do they decide which mountains are sacred, then?"

"That's a big question. Better to say that once all nature – rivers, seas, forests – was sacred, but now only some mountains remain unpolluted. Usually, special sacred mountains are covered with permanent ice and snow, and have double peaks. But more important than shape, you recognise a sacred mountain by the feelings it evokes – strength, fear or joy."

"Nobody in Kathmandu's mentioned to us yet that Gauri Sankar's sacred."

"It depends very much how strongly man is attached to his original culture. Many Hindus and Sherpas, in particular those who have had long contact with people from our culture through technical assistance

projects and tourist feeding, have been so affected by Western attitudes – which are cut off from nature – that they deny the existence of
sacred mountains altogether."

Nils continued to talk, emphatically. When we parted we caught a
taxi.

"I prefer to walk, and not to use such machines," said Nils.

"I wonder if he walked here from Norway," said John, after we had
left.

"I bet he goes to the dentist when he's got a toothache," I said.

"Imagine what he'd be like if he got his teeth into one of the real,
no-holds-barred personality sellers like Messner."

"Bloody nutcase."

"It must be costing them a bloody fortune, staying in single rooms
at the Yak and Yeti."

This was an opulent Hilton-style hotel; we were staying at the
Himalayan View. It was the cheapest place we could find with a
shower.

"What a name for a hotel," said John, "you can see bugger-all."

We continued to discuss Nils, sniggering uncomfortably.

"He's wide open to piss-take."

But he had impressed us.

"You've got to hand it to the lad," said John. "He certainly believes
what he says."

Our capacity for spiritual self-questioning was exhausted, we
wanted to discuss the more prosaic details of our expedition, and also
we were in need of light entertainment.

"Council of War," recommended John.

"Decisioning to be made over a beer," I announced.

"Right oh, Skip."

We went to the rooftop restaurant of the Yellow Pagoda and,
sipping Nepalese beer, watched the sun set over the city.

"These Nepalese birds are gorgeous," commented John. "Only
five feet high, but four foot six inches of that is SMILE."

We stepped into the metal cage of the hotel's lift. I was apprehensive. "I bet this is a relic from the Rana Dynasty, a real museum piece,"
I said. I went on to explain the theoretical action to take if a wire snaps
and a lift were to lose control. "You jump up and down, and so you
have a fifty-fifty chance of being in the air when it hits the ground – if
you're in the air, you only fall a few feet."

Intrigued by this suggestion, John started leaping up and down as
the lift started moving. It madly bounced about like a puppet on the
string.

"Stop it John, you only do that in an emergency!"

One hundred feet above the ground the lift shuddered to a stop. Our heads were level with one of the floors, peeping through the grill.

"Now look what you've done – you've probably jerked the wire off the cog," I said.

We started shouting for help. Scores of pairs of legs appeared from nowhere, jabbering excitedly in Nepali and milling around in front of our noses. Fear in my eyes, I bridged across the walls of the cage, holding myself in the air and anticipating the downwards plummet. Tim seemed puzzled by my nervousness; John was amused by it and laughed from the back of his throat. An hour later a mechanic arrived, solved the mysteries of the jamming and winched us to safety. We descended by the stairs.

"You were really scared," said Tim.

I felt ashamed, as if I had failed the test of some adolescent ritual.

We spent our first few days in Kathmandu on a seemingly endless administration circuit – British Embassy, visas, trekking permits, insurance, sorting equipment and communications. Our preparations were simplified by delegation. Our Sherpa sirdar and fifth member of the team was Pemba Lama, who had been on the 1975 Everest trip, as well as seven other Himalayan expeditions. Pemba's help made shopping simple; we planned with him what food and equipment we needed, gave him some money and he disappeared into the bazaar and bought it.

As our foreman, Pemba was entrusted with the recruiting of the Sherpa cook and cook boy to accompany us. However, I did not like the cook – he seemed shifty. I trusted my first impressions, for you can often read a Sherpa's character on his face. So I complained.

"This is the most important job of the expedition, Pemba."

It transpired that Pemba's choice had been pressured, either by family or outside interests. All was resolved the next day, when Pemba introduced us to our new cook, Dawa.

"What happened to the last one, Pemba?"

"Unfortunately he is sick and cannot come," was the grinning reply.

Pemba was tall and well built, and the expanse of his wide smile was broken by a gold-capped tooth, a relic from a motorbike accident. Sherpas generally climb for money, and not enjoyment, but Mike Cheney had told us that Pemba was different, that he was an ambitious mountaineer, and Mike asked us if we would, if possible, allow Pemba to accompany us to the summit. Pemba was keen to live up to this reputation, and he was fully aware that the prestige of being an accomplished mountaineer was helping him in his career. Pemba's family was a lowland clan of Sherpas, from Solu, contrasting with the Khumbu Sherpas, such as Ang Phurba and Nima Tenzing, who lived at higher altitudes. Like many of the modern generation of Sherpas,

Pemba retained his house in his home valley, but rented rooms in the heart of Kathmandu – where he invited us to meet his wife and eat lunch. We threaded our way through a warren of alleys and court-yards, into a corridor and up some twisting stairs. In a corner were a Buddhist altar and butter lamps, and a sophisticated cassette player with many tapes of Western music.

Like all Sherpas, Pemba was an astute, intuitive and cheerful fleecer of expedition finance. 'Joining money', 'deposits', 'advances'; he tried to bargain for them all. Nils had touched our consciences, and we paid for holy rice, coloured prayer flags and a contribution towards a Kathmandu monastery, where a lama had blessed our expedition. Then our liaison officer, a Hindu sub-inspector in the Kathmandu police force, joined in the demands for equipment and advances. His name was Sankar Pradan – the same as the mountain we were going to attempt. Throughout these negotiations, Mike Cheney played an intermediary role. His position was invidious – as an employee of the Sherpa Co-operative, he had to represent the interests of the Sherpas and see that we employed as many of them as possible; and as an Englishman, Mike had to be careful he did not abuse our trust in him. Small and thin, with a large hooked nose and baggy military shorts, Mike was an ex-Darjeeling tea planter. He had never worked in England. He was one of that perennial group of Englishmen and women who are born with a hunger and nostalgia that can only be set at rest in the East. Nepal had absorbed him completely.

Sankar was demanding that we give him a tent.

"Don't pull rank on me, mate," said John.

"John used to be a captain," I explained.

Sankar told us that though his pay as a lieutenant in the Kathmandu police force was only twenty-one rupees a day – about seventy pence – which was the same as we would be paying our porters during the approach march, he was not begging. It was in the regulations. We sought the arbitration of the Ministry of Tourism at our expedition briefing. Yes, we would have to buy a tent for him.

At the Ministry of Tourism, we met Arne Naess, 'the man who deals in money', the leader of the Norwegian Numbur expedition. A dynamic, wiry, forty-two year old, based in London, Arne seemed more in tune with the British climbing mentality – and humour – than Nils. His expedition's two thousand nine hundred kilos of baggage was stuck in Delhi, and he was about to fly back to sort it out.

Our expedition was poised to depart. We booked a bus, and piled all our equipment into it, followed by fresh vegetables, our Sherpa team, and numerous other, unidentifiable hangers-on, out for the free ride to Barahbise where we planned to recruit our porters. We appeared to have more cassettes (forty-two) than any item of climbing equipment, including pitons and karabiners.

"What a sight!" exclaimed John, "all held together with string, straps, hope and a lot of luck."

Sankar arrived, garlanded with flowers of farewell by his wife and relations. The friends of Dawa, the cook, had been plying him with chang all morning, and he was drunk and panicking about lost equipment. This endeared him to John, who recognised the symptoms.

"Only time Sherpa can't help himself is when drunk," said Pemba.

All was ready.

However, Guy had not arrived. He had been due the previous day, the 24th September, but had not arrived then or on this morning's flight from Delhi. Tim offered to go to Barahbise and back with Pemba, and we asked the Sherpas to hold the porters there until our arrival.

"If I'd been Tim's age I'd have gone," said John as the bus clattered away, "but I don't fancy twelve hours on a bus in this heat." He turned to Sankar "Belay the last pipe, Lieutenant."

Embarrassed by the change of plan after all the formalities of farewell, Sankar reluctantly went home.

Kathmandu days drifted into each other . . . time, precious time. John was appointed chief Guy-collector, and armed with a brief description of Guy and primed with some basic French, taxied to the airport twice a day in the hope that Guy would arrive.

I had first met John during a mountain guide's test on Ben Nevis in February 1977. Unlike other soldiers I had met in the mountains, he had determinedly and quickly proved that he was a keen and able amateur climber. Nevertheless, he was proud of his soldiering background. We had long arguments about the moral value of physical courage. I placed courage on the lowest rung of virtues. I argued that, anyway, the grey areas of daily city life offered more challenges to courage than the glamorous and black and white problems of mountains or the battlefield, and that courage was often just a euphemism for a mixture of anger, pride, stubbornness and physical strength. Although John had since left the Royal Marines to become director of Plas-y-Brenin, he had not lost his strong commitment to idealistic warrior virtues – the readiness to sacrifice oneself in the service of a common cause, disciplined submissions to rank order of the group, a veto on showing fear in the face of danger and, above all, a very strong bond of friendship and trust between men.

John loved to make me cringe with his military parlance. "Right oh Skip," he said, whenever I suggested anything, and when I asked his opinion, he replied: "What do I think? I don't," or "Awaiting orders, Skip. I need to be briefed."

Much to his disappointment, the only orders he received from me were a few mutters. It was a humorous change from the taboo on recognising leadership roles on Kangchenjunga. We discussed endlessly the nuances of difference between 'friendship' and 'solidarity'. John – and Tim – were horrified at my stories of the high-altitude manoeuvring on Kangchenjunga and other expeditions. I realised I had been on too many expeditions with the same people. This time I had to start from the beginning.

As we wandered around, John and I chattered so much that Tim could not get a word in. I had been the same age when I went to the Hindu Kush in 1972, and remembered vividly my shock on seeing an Asian slum for the first time. I projected these memories of my earlier self on to him. But Tim kept his own counsel. He seemed not to be quite on our humour wavelength – or was he above it?

Guy was not on the morning flight of the 27th September. We all went to the airport in the afternoon. The Norwegians were there. All their baggage had arrived, and the customs were charging them £4,000 duty.

"Why didn't you under-value it all?" I asked.

They were sadly resigned to this 'contribution to the king'. Again, Guy did not arrive. In our conversations he was assuming the role of Arch-demon, and the others were beginning to question my choice of the team. We decided on an emergency plan to replace a minimum of the ropes and tents he was bringing by a quick shopping spree, and to leave without him the following mid-day.

"Flexibility – one of the principles of war," said John.

As we left the airport, just as we were getting into a taxi to return to the town, we saw Gauri Sankar for the first time. One hundred and thirty miles away, the mountain glowed in the setting sun. "Absolutely fantastic!" Our spirits soared.

I understood why Gauri Sankar was thought for so long to be the highest mountain in the world, and why it was confused with Everest, which is out of sight, far to the east. For us, its magnificence was a summons. For me, that sight of Gauri Sankar was a turning point, it gave me confidence.

The following morning John telephoned from the airport. "Guy's arrived. Yes, we've flannelled all the gear through, and for nothing. Bullshit beats brains every time. He's had a trip of Homeric proportions that makes our journey out seem a journey to paradise. Fire in Bombay airport, delays, diversions, the whole works. I've never been so pleased to see someone I've never met in my whole life – this is the seventh time I've been here. He's shattered – but he speaks perfect English!"

The team was together at last. Guy's feet had hardly touched the ground before he was loaded into the Sherpa Co-operative Land Rover, along with Tim, John, Pemba, Sankar and myself. We drove north for three hours, along the road built from Kathmandu to the Tibetan frontier after the signing, in April 1960, of the Treaty of Peace and Friendship between Nepal and China.

Barahbise was the last outpost of beer country. We savoured the last drops. Two middle-aged American ladies were there, heavy with make-up and jewellery, sipping Coca-Cola.

"Quite a change, Barahbise from New York," quipped John cheerfully. They had been to the Tibetan border in a taxi, and were only staying in Nepal a few days before leaving for Bali.

The forty porters were about to desert, having waited for four days, but we only smiled when their foreman, the Nykay, came to complain. All past problems were irrelevant. The Nykay was a Sherpa from the Rolwaling Valley, and wore a flat Chinese cap with the sinister air of a Far Eastern guerrilla. Our tents were pitched, the porters' loads were ready, and Dawa brought us a mug of tea. He had the cook tent organised like a well-drilled section – John's ultimate accolade.

In the morning Pemba tied pieces of purple string around our necks. "From lama, Kathmandu. His blessing – don't move it," he explained. Pemba's father was a lama at Junbesi monastery and this gave authority to his instructions. The day was hot and steep, and our sweat ran freely with the dye, staining our tee-shirts an alarming blood colour.

"I've never been with such a funny-shaped team of lads," I said.

"The big, the tall, the short and the thin," said John.

"John's big and short, Guy's tall and thin, Tim's thin and short, and I'm normal," I said.

We argued as we walked.

John and Guy tried to carry porters' loads. As they staggered about, eyes bulging and necks juddering with the strain, a small boy aged about nine walked past beneath a similarly enormous load.

"That can't be doing him any good."

"I think we should ask the Nykay to pay him off."

Then four barefoot girls walked past carrying loads. "I don't know how they do it," said John. "Seeing them would make women's libbers shut-up."

Guy was still dazed by his journey. "I have no idea where I am," he said. "It's as if I've parachuted somewhere in Asia." We showed him our position on the map.

Pemba and Sankar started a 'these porters and the people of this place are robbers' scare, and we split up among our caravan to keep a watchful eye on our belongings.

"Don't group together, lads, if they throw a grenade it'll get all of us," barked John.

We climbed three thousand feet from rice terraces, through jungle to rhododendrons and, on the 30th September, we crested a ridge, in a cool mist, and celebrated with glasses of *rakshi* or millet spirit, renowned for its taste of vinegar and dirty dish cloth.

I had been slotted into the role of the expedition's hypochondriac. Much to John's merriment, I fastidiously avoided all wriggling fauna, and the contamination of dubious food and water. In reply, I teased him for his absentmindedness and clumsiness. He had burnt a hole in a tent with a candle, lost his watch, and forgotten to bring from North Wales the soups, binoculars, two tents and detailed notes about the walk-in.

"No wonder you married someone who could look after you!" I taunted. Conversations with John had the cut, thrust and parry of a sword fight as we tried to penetrate the armour of each other's pretences. One morning the barracking went too far and became physical.

I was toiling up a steep muddy slope behind John. He came across a snake, sleeping on the path, and quickly flicked it at me with his umbrella. The snake wrapped around my leg and I danced about until I had shaken it clear. I was furious, and hit John as hard as I could with my ski stick.

"There're poisonous pit vipers around here."

"It wasn't poisonous, I could tell from the shape of its mouth," said Guy.

"My last trip was nearly ruined by thoughtlessness like that," I yelled. "How, how . . ." I searched my mind for the epithet . . . "how childish, how unprofessional."

The others all snorted with laughter as I stalked off, sulking for over an hour. I did not play the fussy hypochondriac again, and John did not throw any more snakes.

For nearly a whole day we walked along a rough road linking the Kathmandu-Tibet road in the west with the village of Jiri in the east. The road had been begun two years previously, as a Swiss Aid project, and was now half-finished. We marvelled at thousands and thousands of terraces – vivid monsoon greens etched over the foothills below, their ripples accentuated by pale, slanting sunlight. Rice was evidently thriving up to the six-thousand-foot contour – rice that had been planted in June, before the monsoon. Tall, chalet-like houses dotted the slopes, contrasting sharply with the poverty we had witnessed during the previous days. But what was the cost of this apparent prosperity?

These hill sides below – and above us, implied the most serious and dramatic erosion problem in the world. Nepal's midlands were once covered with forests, but in the last twenty-five years over half of the land has been cleared to provide fuel and more space to grow food for the rapidly-expanding population. Meanwhile, in the Bay of Bengal, an island of forty thousand square miles of silt is building up from the washed-away soil of Nepal. In his deeply-concerned book, *Stones of Silence*, George Schaller noted with despair:

> The biggest export of Nepal is soil, some sixty billion tons being carried by its rivers down into India each year. Nepal will soon be derelict unless it protects its watersheds. Once man has destroyed what the mountains have offered, the forest and the soil, there is no reprieve.

We left the road at the town of Charikot. Youths in Western clothes tried to persuade us to photograph the local dwarf, and their sniggering contrasted with the fresh-faced cheekiness of the children who left their sloping football pitch to practise their English, surrounding us at the evening's camp-site at Dolokha: "How are you?" "Where are you going?" "We are very hungry, you give us rupees." I had camped there in 1975, on my way to Everest, and recalled the same conversations then.

Village life was nearing the climax of the ten-day most important national festival of Nepal – called, among many other names, the Durja Puja, or Dassera. High wooden swings with fibre ropes were the main holiday attraction. We had passed many of them beside the trail, and watched young men, including our porters, propelled skywards energetically and competitively, hooting with laughter. Whenever there was an opportunity, we also had a go. The swings were so popular that watching children rarely had a chance to ride!

That evening the sounds of drums and trumpets, cymbals and gongs, floated up the hillside. Sankar explained the Hindu significance of the festival, which celebrates the rescue of the goddess Durga from the clutches of the nine-headed demon buffalo Mahisasoor. On the tenth day, after nine days of praying, the God Rama kills the demon, and good triumphs over evil.

"I, also, have seen the Hindu movies in Kathmandu," laughed Pemba.

I could not decide if his laughter was from embarrassment at our interest; from thinking that Westerners and his generation of Sherpas should know better than to listen to such old-fashioned superstitions; or from a belief that religion doesn't necessarily have to be serious.

"I hear that Gauri Sankar is a very sacred mountain," I mentioned to Sankar.

He looked up sharply. "Who told you that?" he asked.

191

The following morning we stepped along the cobbled street of Dolokha, sheltering beneath our brightly-coloured golfing umbrellas.

"This is the day of the year all people wash and change their clothes," said Sankar. He himself was, as usual, dressed immaculately with neatly combed and parted hair. Through doorways we saw women scrubbing and sweeping. Naked children splashed around and kneaded their clothes in water troughs. Everyone had flower petals and coloured rice on their foreheads. The unhurried, purposeful activity carried on as we walked throughout the village. We could have been invisible. We followed Sankar to the temple. Mist swept around us, and the buildings dripped with moisture. We passed brightly painted lion statues.

"This temple is for the god of courage – he rides on the lions," said Sankar.

"We'll need some of that," said John.

An old man with long hair was sitting cross-legged on a small enclosed platform of smooth, red, hardened mud, tinkling two hand-bells, chanting prayers and staring, in a trance. Sankar offered to daub me with rice, but instinctively I refused. Guy wrote in his diary:

We leave this place. Everything is strange. Pete confides in us with an open smile, but he is not at peace. Nobody feels at ease. Have yesterday evening's stories of divinities affected us? At Pete's request, everyone inspects whether the good-luck string is still around his neck. Ouf! So one doesn't risk the anger of the gods. One can take that how one wants, but still the atmosphere was odd. I can't stop thinking that a group of people, all in a religious trance, emit something. Are these vibes communicated to us, or is it just our imaginations that are working too hard?

We dropped swiftly three thousand knee-jarring feet to the Bhote Kosi – 'the river that rises in Tibet', which we were to follow. Within the space of two hours the change in country was startling. We watched with delight a troop of monkeys swinging through the trees. John wished his little boy, Bounce, could see them. We camped that night at Pikhutu in a meadow of sand and grass beside the river.

A couple came in at dusk from a village an hour away up the hillside, carrying a baby with terrible boiling-water burns over his head, neck and chest, at least thirty per cent of his body. We asked when this happened – four days ago. His pulse was fast, breathing difficult and he had taken no food or drink since the accident. He was only just alive. John ripped some cloth from his sleeping bag liner to cover the child, who opened his eyes briefly in the torchlight. We gave them two hundred rupees and urged them to go to the hospital – though we knew it was three days' walk away. How could they have done nothing for four days? They thought everything would be closed for the festival. We stared incredulous at their helplessness and seeming lack of concern. Why had none of the locals moved a finger to help? Perhaps they did not realise the seriousness of the child's condition. Or did they just accept death more readily than we? The parents walked off into the night with their son. None of us had the heart to talk. We turned aside, each to his own tent and his own thoughts.

Our eyes, blinkered by days of mist, opened wide next morning to see Gauri Sankar astride the gap at the end of the valley. A cloud smoked between its two summits. The West Ridge, our chosen route, curved across the view, a giant 'S' shape, tipped forward on its side. The mountain's features, picked out by the morning sunlight, slotted into our minds that were already imprinted by our well-thumbed file of photographs. 'A climber's nightmare'; 'Deeply notched, as if bitten by a disgruntled giant' . . . I fought off other people's descriptions of the mountain. Perhaps I would only be able to understand its form from this distance. A climber approaches each mountain virtually blind, and has to learn to see as if for the first time. I looked at it through half-closed eyes, struggling to perceive the symbolical power of the double peaks. A pair of horns. The goddess's lap where the eye comes naturally to rest like the lap of horned Isis, upon which the pharaohs sat; the nurturing, fertile, birth-giving mountain.

The sight of the mountain triggered off an hour's animated discussion about the route, and about the importance of acclimatisation. Pemba was very talkative compared to Ang Phurba. He chipped in with 'tourist herding' stories, including some lewd gossip about the unashamed washing habits of French girls on treks. His descriptions, delivered with ribald humour, were so vivid that we peered around every river bend, expecting to see nubile Parisiennes, merrily splashing each other.

Although he was less excitable and his English was slower, Guy did not usually miss as much of the conversation as Georges had done on Kangchenjunga. But when the three 'Anglais' drifted into the inevitably recurring topic of rock climbs in Britain we did not think how much it excluded and irritated Guy.

The rock climbing discussions also highlighted our different attitudes. Since I had begun going on a succession of expeditions, I felt I was losing touch with hard technical climbing and its animated move-by-move analysis. I was aghast when Tim said that routes like Right Wall and Citadel were 'all right'. We used to tease him about his descriptive vocabulary and the way he divided the quality of life into five tiers: 'superb', 'magic', 'all right', 'rubbish' and 'crap'. The eight years' difference between us was a climbing generation, and to me Tim seemed very youthful in his black and white judgments. But there is a lot of no-nonsense Yorkshireman about him and no one could do the routes he has done, like soloing the North Faces of the Grand Charmoz, Les Droites and the Super Couloir, without having his own strengths and self-confidence. At least he was coming out of his early silence and learning to answer and abuse us back, and he asked me many questions about 'going professional'. To him life seemed clear – one climb after another.

It was a relief to have turned north, away from the crowded foothills and the busy east-west route. On the 4th October John looked up from the map. "Base Camp's fifteen miles and ten thousand feet up. We're in for some scrambling, lads!"

During the previous few days an occasional leech had fastened on to us. The porters called them *tsuga* – a menacing noise, like an emphatic sucker. Now, the jungle was swarming with the enemy. Hundreds of them dropped from trees, latched on to us as we brushed against leaves, and caught hold of our shoes. Unseen, and unfelt, they humped about, through lace-holes, underneath socks, up our legs and, on reaching the warmest, juiciest places, injected anaesthetic, anti-coagulant, and sucked our blood. Every few minutes we stopped to fight them off. The leech-deterrent textbooks recommend flames or salt. Usually we just gargled screams and flicked them off. The record number repulsed on one foot was over twenty. The leeches recognised John as a fitting opponent in their plunder, and his feet became sieves of pouring blood. At lunchtime we fled to a boulder in the river, from where we could see them approaching without cover, waving their terminal suckers like scanning radar. Guy never had a chance to smoke his Gauloises. As soon as he lit one it was passed between us, a burning brand of leech destruction.

As we gained height, we climbed out of enemy territory. Hanging on the opposite wall of the Bhote Kosi, we saw the opening of the Rolwaling Valley – 'The furrow made by a plough' – and the home of the Rongsherwa Khambas, who celebrated the sanctity of Tseringma. The first expeditions to attempt Gauri Sankar – the Franco-Swiss under Raymond Lambert in 1954, the British led by Alf Gregory in 1955, and the Japanese in 1959 – all approached the mountain up this valley. Beyond it, to the east, there was a route over a high pass, the 18,745 ft. Teshi Lapcha, to the Sherpa town of Namche Bazar in the Khumbu district below Everest. A traditional route of trade and migration between Rolwaling and Khumbu, in recent years it has also been frequently crossed by groups of tourist trekkers.

We were climbing into a hanging valley, even more abrupt than the Rolwaling. Beside the steep track, the Bhote Kosi plunged over falls and rumbled through boulder-choked pools. Then the ground flattened. We had reached Lamobagar – the open ground.

The first building was the whitewashed police station, next to another one marked 'Customs'. The authorities were waiting for us. Our trekking permits were seriously inspected and a message that we had arrived was sent in Morse to Kathmandu.

We had a tea party, Nepalese style, on two lines of chairs facing each other. One of the policemen stood aside, loosely holding a rifle.

"Lee Enfield 303," identified John, snapping a film into his camera as if he were loading one. "They were used in the First World War – really accurate."

We asked the questions. No, few Westerners had ever been there – apart from the Americans in the spring. Yes, there was still some trade with Tibet, mainly for salt, butter and tea; but now the old traditions of deals between individuals were not legally allowed, and the people did not like negotiating with impersonal Chinese officials in the Tibetan villages. No, eight thousand feet was too low for yaks, but the villagers kept goats, cows and shaggy cow-yak mongrels. Yes, of course there were many Sherpas, Rongsherwa Khambas, and Tibetan refugees in Lamobagar, over half of the two-hundred-and-fifty population – they lived on the other side of the river plain half a mile away around a *gompa*. It looked a hard life. With a mixture of awe and superiority, like officers of the American cavalry surveying an Indian reservation, the police pointed at distant clusters of grey stone houses.

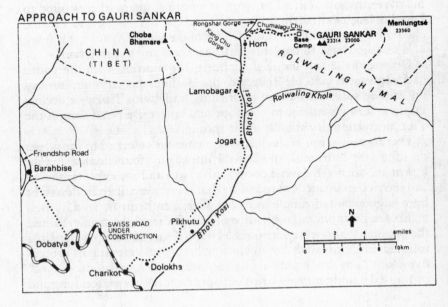

We camped in no-man's land, halfway between the Hindus and the Buddhists. Tim and Guy paid off the Barahbise porters and Pemba and Nykay started to negotiate for a new set from the village. At dusk John and I set off to investigate the sound of a drum. We walked into a small courtyard in front of the *gompa*.

About twenty girls in Tibetan dress were jumping around, laughing and giggling. If it had started as a dance, it had deteriorated into a rough game of 'hop and knockdown'. A bearded lama in his midthirties jumped up and guided us into the front room of the *gompa*, where about fifteen men were dishing out chang from an enormous tub. I think they had been drinking it all day, and they were determined to induce us into the same grinning state.

"Great, an ale up," said John. "Enough to convert me to Buddhism."

We squatted down and they plied us with chang, continually filling our bowls up as we sipped – such is the custom. By the time Guy and Tim arrived we were mellowed and lightly happy. Next to me was an old Tibetan, wrinkled and dishevelled, with long pigtails and a few whiskers. He was most intrigued by my hairy legs. On my other side was a sad youth with big teeth. He spoke a few words of English and seemed to want to travel with us, to escape, for us to open a door for him to the outside world. But he did not even have the will to join us as a porter. He turned out to be the village loafer, and an 'asker' – demanding an umbrella, film and cigarettes.

Guy conversed with a mother and daughter, much to everyone's hilarity – the girl wanted to work as a porter, the mother wanted to know if Guy was married. Guy referred the first request to Pemba, and politely declined any implications of the second.

We dashed back to the tents in the darkness and pouring rain.

Despite the chang-induced euphoria, the meeting with the youth had depressed me. He reflected the decline the community had undergone since the days of flourishing trade with Tibet – a decline that was a raw contrast to the hope and enterprise I had seen in the Tibetan community at Hille in the spring.

There was no sign of the festivities when we returned to the *gompa* the following morning. Another of Lamobagar's four lamas, a smiling little man, opened the inner doors with a large and ancient spring lock, and showed us inside. On top of an altar there were three Buddhas, lit by a huge enclosed candle in a container. Pemba prostrated himself before the Buddhas and took some of the wick from the candle. Round the painted walls were pigeonholes full of sacred books. The lama touched our heads with one in blessing before unwrapping its protective cloth. The book was about six inches thick and loose-leaved, composed of long narrow strips of paper each about two feet long and six inches wide, printed in Tibetan letter-press. Pemba could not read Tibetan, but his Sherpa vernacular was sufficient to communicate our questions. The lama did not know how old the books were, but they were there in his grandfather's time. Each little strip of fabric hanging from a book indicated that someone had read it all.

The lama recommended prudence in what we were going to do and told us our Base Camp must be a holy place, and we must not kill animals there.

The village houses were scattered among huge boulders. Another lama approached us, shuffling. I wondered whether they were prayers he was muttering, or memories of better times that no one cared to listen to. He was of a different sect, and on Pemba's advice we gave him money too. Prayer flags, invoking the benevolence of mountain gods, were strewn above a bridge, and they fluttered with the swing of the wires as we crossed. Although they were faded and torn, the flags still worked, said the Sherpas. The sunshine crept down the vegetated hillside, and on to an old man who was trembling with the early-morning cold. He was supporting himself with a hand on the shoulder of a small boy. They both watched silently as we turned up the Rongshar Gorge. Many Sherpas believe that it was through this gorge that their ancestors migrated into Nepal five hundred years ago, after travelling one thousand two hundred and fifty miles from the Khams Region of Eastern Tibet. According to legend, they were shown their new home in a dream. We were now walking towards the land of their spiritual and ethnic origin.

The river was older than the mountains. It maintained its channel from the highest plateau in the world as the Himalayas began to rise during the Eocene, fifty million years ago. The great canyon of the Rongshar still deepens as the mountains continue to lift.

The footpath was rarely frequented, but still survived the encroaching vegetation, threading muddily and improbably across the precipices above the shadowed gorge. We met a father and son, returning with the trade of Chinese plastic shoes and Tibetan butter from the north. I envied the comradeship that must have grown between them, over the days and nights of their lonely journey.

The path dipped steeply to the river. To the north east, another gorge joined the Rongshar – the Kang Chu. This torrent drained a finger of land that projected into Tibet – land that was only ceded to Nepal in the 1961 bargaining. In this valley lies the village of Lapche (La – Rimpoche 'precious hill') the hallowed birthplace of Jetsun Mila Repa, a wandering lama poet and saint who lived in the eleventh century, and taught by parables and song. Mila Repa was one of the Bodhisatvas, a reincarnation of Buddha, who lived under rocks and in caves, where the faithful still go to see his footprints. It is said that he converted Tseringma, the goddess of long life, to Buddhism.

The early Everest expeditions approached the mountain from the north, as for them Nepal was the forbidden land. Both the 1921 and the 1924 Everest expeditions descended the Rongshar Gorge as far as the Nepal frontier. A. F. R. Wollaston, who relinquished his New Guinea ambitions for the lure of Himalayan exploration, reported in 1921 that the locals were "a friendly and good-tempered people, much given to religion." Thirty years later, in 1951, another Everest reconnaissance party had descended the gorge. Eric Shipton and Mike Ward had become lost whilst exploring the northern side of the watershed. Then one of their Sherpas said he could recognise the northerly opening of the Rongshar as he used the route when smuggling horses. "At once the geography of the region became clear," said Shipton. The group had no permission to be in Tibet, so they travelled at night to avoid detection. Even so, they were chased back into Nepal by Tibetans waving swords.

According to Erwin Schneider's 1968 map, the border followed one of the Rongshar's tributaries, the Chumalagu Chu. We stopped at the confluence, before climbing up this valley towards Gauri Sankar. It was here, at 7,200 ft., that Dennis Gray's 1964 expedition was abandoned by its porters. They were forced to establish their Base Camp in this area – probably the lowest base camp ever used by a Himalayan expedition.

The peaceful atmosphere of the Rongshar had changed since Wollaston's remarks. Dennis and his team had to call in twelve Nepalese soldiers to protect the camp, when it was threatened by armed Tibetan bandits – robbers who, according to Don Whillans, "are not too particular about their choice of victims. National reputations, climbing clubs, permits, mean nothing to those lads; if you've got something, they want it!" We asked the Nykay about robbers, and he reassured us that the last problems had been five years before – the Nepalese and the Chinese authorities now had a firm grip on the area. He related gleefully the story of the 1959 attack on the other side of the mountain, and pranced about miming Japanese climbers and Sherpas brandishing ice axes and fencing with Tibetans on horseback.

Gray and Whillans and their small team had spent weeks hacking through the undergrowth of the Chumalagu Chu, and ferrying loads towards the mountain. "It was," said Dennis, "some of the thickest jungle in the world." They had marked their route with red paint – some of which was still visible. As we started to duck through the jungle, these marks – combined with the traces of the American-Nepalese expedition of the spring and the knowledge of our porters, most of whom had carried for that expedition – helped our routefinding.

"We're on the Tibetan side of the river," I said to Sankar, pointing at the map.

"If we're in Tibet, then we must go back," he said.

"I think the map's wrong then."

The porters shouted, hooted and whistled as they ducked through the steep mossy undergrowth on the sides of the colossal gorge. Everyone slipped and slid on the greasy black soil of the bamboo thickets. Bamboo is a solid plant, and a secure, if sharp, handhold. There were some dangerous sections across the muddy cliffs above the river, and we split up and anchored ourselves, helping the porters across as they struggled with their thirty-kilo loads. They thanked us with their eyes. The roaring of the water was so loud that we could not speak without yelling.

At dusk we crowded beneath the kitchen tarpaulin suspended from tree branches to wait for the meal, preferring the communal warmth of the fire to the isolation of our tents.

"I wonder why Ang Rinzi prefers to bring the food around to us?"

"I don't think it's a religious reason – it's because they don't want us to see what variety of food they are cooking, or how many people we're feeding."

"What's sizzling in that pressure cooker? I bet we don't get any."

"Must be feeding about fourteen people."

"We'll make a stand for some of *their* chili and potatoes tonight."

The Sherpas cushioned us. On my earlier expeditions we did all the cooking and hiring and firing of porters. Now we were overseers with only a vague idea of what was going on. Were we, as Jung says, living in bottles of Western air, protected from our travels by objectivity, causality and all the other intellectual apparatus? Pemba and Sankar had tried to use the porters' flints but without success – they were townies like us.

Upon popular request, John told us some of his favourite stories: 'The Two Hundred Thousand Ton Punch', 'The Man Who Went Out to Buy a Packet of Cigarettes and Ended Up in Peru', 'The Punch-up at the Courmayeur Disco', and 'The Day I Ambushed a Pig'.

"You've got to be an Irishman to talk like that," I said. "You won't be able to bullshit your way up this route you know."

"It doesn't matter if these stories aren't true," said Guy, "it is the way they ought to have been."

"All my stories are true," said John. "Just wait till I get back from this trip; I'll have a few more!" John had the gift of making everyone laugh.

Stars scattered across the sky, above a frail mesh of interlacing twigs, and we peered at their white brightness through the interstices of the plaiting. John expressed simple wonder at them all. Guy countered with a reel of boggling facts and figures, describing the size of the universe.

"That's the cosmology lesson over for tonight," he said.

"Isn't John naïvely endearing?" I said patronisingly. Endearing – we finished the evening trying to explain the word to Guy.

Throughout the approach march we had been worried that the regular afternoon rainfall would be falling as thick snow on the upper reaches of the route. At dawn we peered worriedly at the snow-covered distant mountainside above the jungle, hoping that the covering was light, and would melt with the early-morning sun. We knew that the barefooted porters would never carry through snow, and were rushing them up towards Base Camp before any long period of bad weather with major storms blew in. We crossed the river with some logs and ropes, and continued the ascent through gnarled and stunted trees swathed in bearded lichens which made the air glow green. The sphagnum covered the stones with a thick carpet and we had to kick in up to our ankles. But the jungle cleared with altitude and we were able to make camp on a small open bluff amid the rhododendrons. When the clouds opened a brief window the view 5,000 feet down into the Rongshar Gorge was breathtaking.

"Un pays de loups!" said Guy.

We no longer had to stoop through rhododendron shrubbery. We walked upon open slopes of stunted juniper. Then steep alpine meadows reared up into broken rocks. The mist came down; and the route zigzagged intricately up cliffs. We were now at home, in mountain country. We talked mountaineering politics. Only our deepening breathing told us we were reaching sixteen thousand feet.

"Base Camp," announced Pemba, after consulting one of the Lamobagar porters. We hurried about, muffled figures erecting tents. The falling snow surrounded us with a white, moving void. There was nothing to see.

17

KNIGHT MOVES

9th – 26th October, 1979

I awoke with a start, to a thunderous booming. Pemba was knocking and shaking the snow from my tent and daylight filtered through the fabric as he cleared it.

"The Americans also had bad weather," he said in a matter-of-fact tone. "The first few times a mountain has bad weather. Then, after many people have come, the god goes away and the weather is good."

Outside, the cold light of dawn revealed mist and whiteness. The snow continued to fall. Pemba and the other Sherpas began to prepare a ritual, with a meaning sunk deep in time.

The pattern of the earliest rituals has always been for man to make an offering and, by giving, to achieve a receptive and aware state so as to become part of the interplay between himself, the earth and sky and the gods. When Buddhism came to Tibet in the seventh century, it was absorbed by the resident animist faith of many gods – the B'on religion. Today, the Sherpa religion, Tibetan Lamaism, is a thick mixture of the old animism, manifesting itself in mysticism, magic and demonolatry, overlaid by a layer of Buddhism.

The earliest myth of the founding of Tibetan civilisation, concerns the building of the Samyang monastery, the first Buddhist monastery in Tibet. The people, so the tale goes, worked very hard every day building the monastery, but every night evil demons came and destroyed their work. The people were making no progress at all, so they asked the Guru Rimpoche what to do. The Guru said it was no wonder they were having trouble, they weren't making the gods happy, only spending a lot of money. When he taught them how to perform an offering ritual, the gods helped the people build the monastery, not only keeping away the demons, but also carrying the heavy things and working while the people slept, so that the building was completed in a very short time.

The ceremony held at Base Camp on the 10th October, before we set foot on Gauri Sankar, followed the basic pattern of a Tibetan Buddhist ritual. Pemba had arranged a garland of little flags on a string between two poles and an altar was built just outside the kitchen shelter, consisting of a flat rock surrounded by four vertical stones with a little butter on the point of each. We all sheltered from the snow beneath umbrellas while herbs were thrown on a plate of burning embers on the altar. Behind it was a large tray of offerings – some rice, chocolate, nuts, a cup of milk, bits of cheese, a can of beer and a bottle of whisky. The Sherpas sang, throwing rice and spirit in the air as further gestures of invitation and welcome. This wining and dining of the gods was to make them more friendly and obliging towards us and to encourage them to struggle against the malevolent demons of the area.

Two porters stayed to keep us supplied with wood. One of them, Pemba Sherpa, was a lama and read the appropriate Tibetan text for Tseringma, throwing fistfuls of rice in the fire. He also soaked a juniper sprig in milk and whisky and sprayed the fire with it. The ceremony lasted half an hour. Towards the end he put a small piece of juniper in the palms of our hands with a taste of whisky which we had to lick up. Finally Sankar, our liaison officer, raised the Nepalese flag and led an unsure rendering of the Nepalese national anthem. Although a Hindu, he had taken part without self-consciousness.

At the end of the ceremony the mist suddenly tore apart and a ray of sunlight poured through a rent in the cloud. The rainbow colours of the prayer flags shimmered in the diagonal light and the rocky promontory of our Base Camp became a glowing island amid boiling cloud.

The weather was so bad, and the fleeting clearing was so dramatic, it did seem that we'd angered, and then momentarily pleased someone. Emotionally, the ceremony was valuable.

The shafts of sunshine encouraged us upwards. After the ceremony was over we started up the snout of the glacier, to make a reconnaissance. According to Schneider's map and Al Read's information, Gauri Sankar was separated from Base Camp by a ridge a thousand feet above us. The Americans had approached their West Face route by abseiling down the other side from a notch on the ridge.

However, we had taken a risk, climbing eight thousand eight hundred feet out of the Rongshar Gorge in three days to Base Camp at sixteen thousand feet; our rapid approach had been against all the acclimatisation rules of 'taking it easy'. The spring expedition had taken six days over the same distance. Now we determined to spend at least a week acclimatising to our new height. Guy was enjoying every minute now he was 'above the height of Mont Blanc'. He was still fresh from his three-week Swiss guide's course and was climbing steadily, whilst a residue of acclimatisation had stayed with me from Kangchenjunga. When John had come to the Himalayas before, a headache had grounded him at Base Camp for a week, but this time he found the rapid gain of altitude over the previous days tiring but not debilitating.

Like seasickness, altitude sickness strikes unpredictably. As we kicked up the heavy snow Tim was moving slowly, vomiting occasionally, but forcing himself upward.

We crossed a slender snow bridge above a deep crevasse. The mist had closed in soon after we left Base Camp, as if Tseringma's appeasement had only brought a brief respite. Now wind blew thick snow around us. The snow levelled out and dark rocks signposted a ridge. The altimeter read 17,000 ft. Wind met our faces from a new direction and static electricity buzzed in the air. But where was the notch? Rocks and snow tilted in confusing directions and opinions differed. We huddled around the map and compass, and split up to make fifty-foot forays in the gathering blizzard. No clues made sense.

"We'll have to wait for a good day," I said.

"Acclimatisation training," said John.

We plunged back down our line of tracks to Base Camp. The light was fading, and the tents were smothered in snow. The one hundred and fifty multi-coloured prayer flags stretched high above the ice-hewn rock and rubble were unaffected, a garland of greeting and protection. The prospect of the climb's uncertainty was awesome and we still had not even seen the mountain.

We were in the middle of a two-day storm. If the snow had fallen earlier, we would have been stranded far below Base Camp. That night snow piled deep around us, only to melt in the warm morning air. John was flooded out of his tent. "I'm going to call this Camp Niagara," he announced.

I spent the day reading and sleeping. Beneath the shelter of the kitchen tarpaulin, John and Guy sorted fifteen days' food to take on to the mountain. Occasionally someone hurried between tents, well wrapped and bundled up beneath the falling snow. The sounds of the kitchen, and conversations, were muffled by the heavy stillness. The two wood porters huddled all day around the fire. Tim did not emerge.

At sunset the clouds began to move in horizontal plumes in the valley below us. Jagged peaks were etched beneath the Milky Way, beyond the black depths of the Rongshar Gorge. Our tents were poised on the edge of space. We stooped into them and lit candles to keep out the cold night.

"Pete, get your camera." Dawn brought a rush of excitement. We could not see the mountain we had come to climb, but we could see its angular shape. The two summits of Gauri Sankar announced themselves as two vast, beaming shadows silhouetted across miles of morning air.

"God, it looks enormous."

"And steep."

After a quick breakfast, we shouldered our first loads, to establish our cache at the foot of the West Ridge. The sun came rolling on to us as we broke trail up the glacier, breathing purpose into our cold climbs. Its dazzling splendour bared the bones of the mountain and provided the missing clues to our earlier confusion. The ridge was bifurcated, and we had to cross a spur and traverse to the Notch. At last the mountain stood before us, and we lay down our sacks and straightened up to look at it. Pemba scrambled confidently to the summit of a nearby rock pinnacle for a better view.

When the first Sherpa peoples passed Gauri Sankar on their journey from Eastern Tibet, the mountain was already alive in their imaginations. When they saw the mountain itself the old worship of the goddess that they brought with them was intensified.

> The goddess Tseringma has a beautiful, well-shaped white body, the colour of which is reflected in the mountain snow. She has a light, slender face like the moon, three eyes and shining snakelike blue-black hair that has been arranged high and is decorated by a ruby. In her ears hang beautiful earrings and in her hands she holds a vase of eternal youth and a prayer wheel, with jewellery that is more precious than those belonging to any human being or god. She wears a thin, soft, tight clothing, and sits straight on a lion of very light colour. *

In the present century, even the taciturn Lancastrian, Don Whillans, was to remark, as he turned back from Gauri Sankar: "It's a lady."

We were daring to touch the untouchable. The mountain did not fall back in cloud-swept terraces of vast distance like Kangchenjunga, it curved across our vision with a massive strong presence, stretching around to touch us at one of the tips of its horseshoe. Huge tentacles of ice dripped down from the summit snow caps.

We pointed and swept knowledgeably with our hands, asserting ourselves despite our insignificance, as climbers are wont to do when nervous.

"This must be the point which Clough and Whillans reached in '64, before they went back down and traversed round at a lower level to the North West Ridge."

"The American route looks steep."

"Yes, but we're seeing it head on, and they said it was a lot more feasible than our ridge."

* From an original Tibetan Lamaist text, quoted by F. W. Funke in his *Religiöses Leben Der Sherpa*, 1969.

"A bloody good effort."

"Lambert walked around the mountain in '54, and said it was impossible everywhere above eighteen thousand feet."

"Well, that's been proved wrong since."

"Our ridge looks a long way round."

"It's knife-edged for a long way."

We cut the West Ridge up into pieces, for our hearts were not yet big enough to absorb its scale. The expansive, overwhelming vision of the mountain threatened to flood us with exhilaration and awe – feelings that were easiest to control by treating our presumption as a job of work to be done. First we would descend three hundred feet from the Notch on to the Tseringma Glacier that flowed out of the arms of the horseshoe into Tibet, and would follow the glacier beneath this low arm of the West Ridge to place an advance camp almost at the same height as us, from where the ridge rose steeply for two thousand five hundred feet towards an ice-cream cone of a summit – Point 19,800 ft. After this sharp cone the ridge looped horizontally for about a kilometre, rose again into another horizontal section and finally buttressed a rock wall beneath the plateau of the South Summit. According to Schneider's map, the route was over four kilometres long from the start of the difficulties. And then, if we had the energy, there was the traverse to the North Summit.

"It's simple," announced John, "just get on the ridge and keep on it to the top. Tim can do the rock steps, Guy the elegant ice arêtes, you can do the plods, Pete, and I'll do the bits in between. It's in the bag. All we've got to do now is climb it."

We tied a couple of ropes together and slid on to the glacier to begin the long traverse. Fresh snow lay deep, and airlocks boomed a protest at our disturbing steps. "Trespassers will be avalanched" thundered the shaking surface. We glanced at Guy for reassurance.

"The angle is slight, it won't go," he said.

The sight of the mountain above our heads gave us the excuse to stop, gasping with the altitude, and gaze.

We marked our tracks with prayer flags on bamboo poles, and cached our loads on regaining the ridge at a gentle dome of snow. Clouds moved around us and it was snowing as we returned to Base Camp. The day's purpose had been accomplished, and we were relaxed and happy. We had started.

These beasts of burden days melted into each other. Three times we repeated the pattern of the first day, carrying loads up to the Notch, down the abseil and then across the Tseringma Glacier to dump food, fuel, tents, ropes and equipment on an ever-increasing pile. The afternoon snows and night winds brushed over the surface, illumin-ated by distant lightning, stippling our tracks until the glaciers became

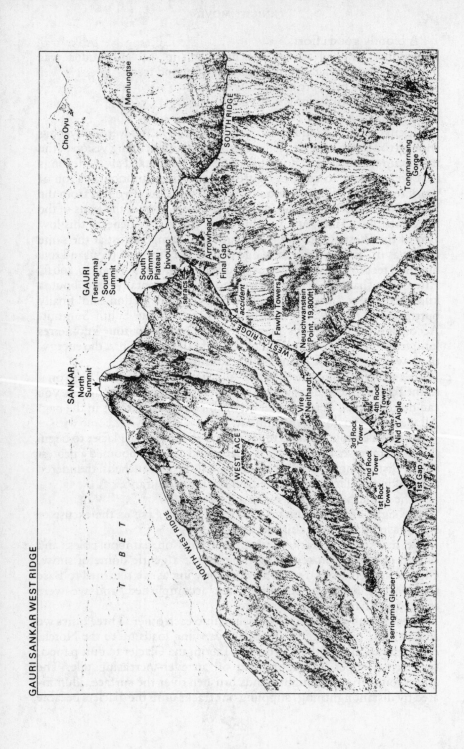

GAURI SANKAR WEST RIDGE

innumerable virgin ripples of snow. In the morning we broke trail again.

On the second day Guy stayed at Base Camp, nursing a cold before it became any worse. John was always in a lively, argumentative mood at breakfast time. That day the topic started with Apartheid, Rhodesia and Colonialism. Then it degenerated into a vivid description of the night's bowel movements.

"You're just trying to shock me."

"That's not shock, it's prudery."

John was suffering from diarrhoea, and I reached the cache of equipment at the foot of the West Ridge before him. I went back down to help him with his load, but he insisted on refusing the gesture, despite my taunting him as a *Boy's Own* hero.

We all had different styles of determination. No one seemed to play the high-altitude manoeuvring game on this expedition – and with only one player the game collapses. On other expeditions I had not encountered the self-sacrificial quality that John had, and was encouraged when occasionally his offguard comments hinted that he was weakening.

"Must say, my strong ethical feelings about using porters or Sherpas evaporate a bit every day when I carry one of these loads," he said.

Our team needed a leader; this I discovered when the others agreed to my tactics, and did what I suggested. However, this was a new role for me.

I was uncertain what to do about Tim. He still had not come with us since the reconnaissance in the blizzard, rarely emerged from his tent and was eating little. Yet whenever we asked him how he was, he always replied chirpily "Much better, I'll be with you tomorrow."

Sankar had felt very ill when we had first arrived, and we had decided to take him down to Lamobagar, when he suddenly recovered. We assumed that Tim was just taking a little longer.

The clouds boiled up from the jungles of Nepal at about eleven in the morning, and hampered our attempts to reconnoitre the ridge. The first difficulties of the ridge were four rock towers, stacked on top of each other – or so we thought. On the third day Guy and I emptied our loads and went for a scramble to discover a four-hundred-foot-deep gash between us and the first tower. We returned on the fourth day with John and wandered around down snow slopes and rocks, failing to resolve the best way down into the gash. Nevertheless, we decided that the next day, the 16th October, we would leave Base Camp for the last time and make a final carry to our load dump, and there establish an Advance Camp.

We had spent a lot of time discussing Tim's condition. Now we had to do something. On his brief appearances he had been looking ghastly, only nibbling, saying nothing, head in hands and we had resolved to take him down when we returned from our final carry. At dinner time, John went to see him. He returned with serious news.

"He doesn't know what time of day it is, whether it's light or dark, or even that we've been up the hill today."

We decided to give him some of the emergency bottle of oxygen we had brought with us. But we could not find it. The bottle had not been seen since Kathmandu, where it must have been stolen.

Snowfall prohibited movement in the darkness. Through the night John checked to make sure that Tim was not slipping into unconsciousness. Immediately at first light, the following morning John and Pemba Sherpa, the wood porter, set off to help Tim down. Pemba Lama, Dawa, and I started after them as soon as we had packed tents and food, and Guy had prepared a first-aid kit for me to take down, and gone over how to inject Lasix intravenously. He remained at Base Camp with Ang Rinzi and Sankar.

As I descended I was hoping, 'He's been so stubborn, if only his stubbornness can pull him through now.' More oxygen, loss of altitude, was the only cure for cerebral oedema. The self-reproach that accompanies tragedy was creeping in, 'If only I had insisted he went down before.'

Tim was lying inert in his blue fibre pile suit, beside a stream. John was standing over him, in the sunlight. I stopped on the slope above, my heart sinking with futility. John read the question in my eyes, and stuck his thumb up.

"He's just resting," he whispered. "He's incredibly weak, but I think he's going to be all right. It'll be a slow business – he's been vomiting and falling down a lot. He can hardly walk, but refuses to let me carry him – understandably."

After eight hours, we were all nearly four thousand feet lower down, at the Rhododendron Camp. Tim was resting in his tent, and was starting to smile at John's cheerful banter. John and I relaxed beside the fire, our conversation released by the slackening of tension. We had had a fright. As the sparks flew upwards into the evening air, topics came and went inside our heads, and we talked as idly as two housewives over a fence.

The next morning John and Pemba set off back up to Base Camp, to start on the route with Guy. Before he left, John spoke to Tim gently, like a father. That afternoon I wrote in my diary:

We got Tim down just in time. Now he's talking more, and starting to feel disappointed. He's waking up to what happened to him. He took a lot of persuading this morning, and firm words. It's even harder to take dis-

208

appointment at that age, you just don't see round a predicament. He's eaten something at last, though, and is reading *The Ginger Man*, so he must be perking up – haven't noticed him read before. He doesn't want to write his career off as a high-altitude climber and wants to go back up again. Yet he's so weak he hasn't moved from his tent all day.

"When I put as much effort into something as I have into this trip, I don't give up," he said.

Warm, reassuring letters arrived with Jetha, the mail runner, the following day. Tim was recovering quickly. On the morning of the 19th October, I set off upwards from the Rhododendron Camp. I exacted a promise from Tim not to move anywhere for at least four days, and left him in the care of Dawa, the two wood porters and Sankar, who had come down to help. I walked up the four thousand one hundred feet to Base Camp in under three hours, feeling fit and perfectly acclimatised.

Ang Rinzi, the kitchen boy, was alone at the camp, and pleased to have some company. He handed me a letter:

To: P.D.B.

From: J.B.

You will need to bring: a) cup
                               b) spoon
                               c) soup bowl/plate
                               d) mattresses as req'd
                               e) inner tent
                               f) water bottle
                               g) JB's foam and Guy's bidet
                               h) vibrator
                               i) cans of beer
                               j) kitchen sink

I think we have everything else – a mighty big think that. The Vango tent was hugely unpopular with them what had to carry it! You could be lucky to get a night in it. Hope all was well below. See you. John.

John, Pemba and Guy had left Base Camp the previous morning. I could see the remnants on the ground of the farewell ceremony – the burnt juniper, the holy rice scattered towards the mountain. I packed my sack, preparing to follow them. Ang Rinzi pointed at the numerous cat tracks in the snow – he didn't want to be left alone with lynxes. I reassured him that Pemba Sherpa was to come up and stay the following day. Base Camp was a bleak place.

I set off, keen to find out what was happening on the mountain. The silence was only broken by my breathing and the crunching of my boots on the snow. Crossing the Notch was the final transition to a life of ice and rock, dominated by the West Ridge.

They did not hear my arrival above the roar of the stove, until I zipped open the tent door. "Ay up lads. Where's the brew then?"

"Come into the galley, mate."

I crouched inside. "Seven letters for you Guy – looks like five are from Helen. You beat me by three, and John, I'm sorry, there are not any for you."

"I think I forgot to tell Kath we were having a mail runner," he said.

"You're not in the jungle now, you know." The letters were the last voices from home before the mountain.

John and Guy had split up and found two ways to the icy col at the bottom of the gash. Next day we would start up the first tower. The weather was settled, and high above, the West Ridge wrapped around us, filling a two-hundred-degree sweep across the night sky.

Pemba was on breakfast duty. The day started before the sun arrived, with the stove lighting – the taps of the pump followed by a soft purring. As snow melted in the pan, Pemba chanted prayers. The smell of burning incense stick drifted to the rest of us in our sleeping bags – a reminder of the mountain waiting outside.

It was a day full of contradictions, false starts, misleading clues and wrong turns. John and Guy went first, and Pemba and I followed carrying rope and equipment. Several traverses, diagonal ascents, gullies, rock steps and rope throwings later we were all on top of the first tower, having reached it by different ways and having left the snow slopes criss-crossed with tracks.

"Looks as if a rabbit warren's come out to play," I taunted the day's leaders. Pemba and I dumped our loads beneath the second tower and returned to Advance Camp to put a brew on. Guy continued directly up the wall of the second tower:

> It rises up and I have to take off my crampons. I climb steep almost holdless snow-covered rock for a long way, feeling clumsy in my big double boots, and get a good handjam, which allows me to put in a piton with the other hand. But what's the point in continuing? There must be an easier way. It would be desperate to carry loads up here. I abseil a hundred feet back to John. It is late, and night has fallen when we reach the Advance Camp, shattered.

Dinner was ready when they arrived, a cheerful meal in the snug social unit of the Vango tent, Swiss, Irish, English and Sherpa freely insulting each other.

Guy described how next day five ropelengths circumnavigated the problem.

John is in front today and climbs 'comme un chef' – after a long traverse on the north side of the ridge, he goes straight up in the direction of the summit of this enormous second tower, up three hundred and fifty feet of rockslabs covered in powder snow. A short storm blows in, and the hail bounces down the slope and over us. John reaches the top and shouts with excitement: "It's unbelievably exposed up here." As we return in the blizzard, we misunderstand each other and accidentally let go of a rope, which disappears down the slope. We rejoin Pete, who is sheltering from the storm in a rocky niche, waiting for us. John just runs down the ropes. Then there are long 'easy' bits where it's necessary to concentrate very carefully. I tell myself that, after all, 'Je suis guide', and there is no need to fall. I arrive last at the col in the gash and think 'They could have waited.' I lose my temper. Oh blow these bloody English, I'll get along all right by myself. The storm has passed, and the sunset is extraordinary. In fact, they are both waiting for me on the other side of the col. Good. We return together. It's my turn to be porter tomorrow.

That evening, I wrote my own verdict on the day in my diary:

This ridge is a *long way*. Point 19,800 ft., the ice-cream cone, still looks days away. It's becoming clear that there's a lot of hard work and time ahead of us on this climb. To be gone through day by day. Our movement is positive, upward, and we must sustain it.

John wrote:

Some difficult climbing and always this enormous ridge ahead. We hardly seem to make any progress even after an exhausting day's work. Great fun coming down the fixed ropes at night. Fantastic views – all very exciting, but the main feeling is one of effort. Don't like to be defeatist, but I think it is perhaps more than four men can chew. Suspect Pete feels the same. Still keep plodding on.

The summit of the second tower was perfectly flat. "Good place for a camp-site," I said.

"A mite short on space, and long on exposure," said John.

As we started to climb the third tower, we looked back to see that the second tower leaned drunkenly to the south, with a gravity-defying tilt.

"Like the Leaning Tower of Pisa," said John. "If we camp there, it'll boast the world's most precipitous lavatory.

The south side of the ridge was sun-toasted and ice-free – a pleasant change from the cold shadow and powder snow up which we had come.

"Watch that rock John!"

Two hundred feet of scrambling up piles of loose blocks balanced at forty-five degrees on the sunny side took us to the top of the third tower.

We stood on the rocky, airy crest of the ridge beneath the fourth rock tower. "You don't mind if I have a go at leading, John?"

"You sure you can manage?" he grinned.

I tiptoed across the friable wafer rock of the south side of the tower, trying to distribute my weight, tapping my feet on to the largest holds, and touching finely balanced rocks until they tumbled into the void. The afternoon sun roasted my back. I hung on a piton and belayed. This was what I really enjoyed. Not humping loads of food and fuel and letting my mind wander – but pure, exploratory climbing, so demanding as to absorb concentration completely, mind controlling body, shrinking the world to the rock in front of my face, pinning my thoughts to here and now.

"You'll have to lead through John – you should be able to handle it, the rock looks more solid above me."

"Just leave the technical stuff to me, Skip."

John launched himself over a bulge and climbed quickly up a shallow groove in the wall.

"Watch out!" I ducked as the shadow of a large rock fell past me.

"Should be better now. Fantastic climbing," John did not pause until he reached the top of the tower, a hundred feet higher up. He sailed back into view, sliding down the rope to land beside me. We were both pleased.

"The ridge seems to fall back a bit up there," he said.

"Didn't you put any runners in?"

"Hadn't got any." We waved to Guy, tall and perfectly balanced on the top of the third tower.

We grouped together on the second tower. "There's no way I'm going to sleep in a tent on here," said Guy. "It's not a camp-site, it's a . . . 'nid d'aigle'." And so it became – not Camp 1, but 'The Eagle's Nest'.

Guy had also had an enjoyable day. "It's so different, being alone," he said, "and in the middle of the Himalayas! I'd have felt I had wings if it hadn't been for the heavy sack – oh, and that rope we dropped yesterday, it'd got snagged and I soloed down to get it. I tied on to it and climbed back up. Really strange – I felt as if I was being belayed by an invisible second."

Pemba had been down to Base Camp to pick up some paraffin and nylon tape. He returned with disquieting news. Pemba Sherpa, the wood porter, had not come up from the Rhododendron Camp as arranged to keep Ang Rinzi company. Yet the tents were still visible far below at the Rhododendron Camp. Perhaps something had happened? And Ang Rinzi was becoming very anxious, alone with increasingly bold snow cats.

A rest day announced itself before anyone articulated the idea. Nobody wanted to get up, and we snuggled into our sleeping bags until it was too late to go on to the mountain. I felt that deliciously guilty sense of a reprieve, like when you hear rain on the roof of an alpine hut in the early morning and you know you don't have to get up. Then the sun came.

"Sun Sun Sun here it comes."

The Vango tent was our community centre. Over breakfast we flicked through the photograph file endlessly analysing, discussing and digesting the problem. We were trying to learn, to divine the mountain by trial, error and experience, so that we could climb it, safely, surely, sanely. Our minds wandered over the possibilities. We had made mistakes, would make more, but there was a saying 'The shortest way between two places is three sides of a square.'

"I'm glad I haven't my reputation to think of," said John. "What euphemism are you going to think up to call our tactics, Pete? 'Modified' alpine? 'Capsule-style'? You will notice, Guy, that these useful expressions, democratically selected by our leader, embrace a wide range of ethical weaknesses in an ever-degenerating spiral towards traditional Himalayan strategies." John blathered on, his barracking undermined by his complicity in the enterprise.

We counted the gear – seventeen ropes, thirty karabiners, twenty-five rock pegs, fifteen ice screws, four deadman snow anchors, three lightweight tents.

"O.K. John, you're good at arithmetic, how are we going to fix two and a half thousand feet of rope along a ridge that's over two miles long?"

It was, in Royal Marine parlance, a 'make-and-mend' day. We clowned around, modelling food and equipment for suppliers who had asked for photographs of their products in action. On the mountain we would have other things to think about. We picked randomly, like free-range hens, at little tasks. We aired our sleeping bags and clothing in the sunshine, sewed and repaired, cut nylon into slings and sharpened crampons. As we were learning about the mountain, so our equipment began to feel part of ourselves. At high altitude there are few clues in the survival game, and it is important not to miss them. Only in rare moments could we allow ourselves to love the mountain. Love requires a relaxed flow of communication, and we would have to be too wary for that.

I could not accept that our footsteps, as the Sherpas seemed to believe, would pollute the mountain. "Tseringma, we are one of the earth's species, so why can we not tread here? . . ." I stopped the prayer, laughing at myself. What was I talking about? It was, after all, only a mountain!

"A brilliant idea, this rest day," said Guy. An intimate, reassuring ritual, it had the mental therapy of a spring clean. We stoked up with food and drink and crawled back into our sleeping bags to dream of the view from the summit. The 'weekend' was over.

During the night the world below returned to gnaw at me. I awoke composing endless letters about mountain training disputes, the climbing school, my parents and Tim. Pemba had left during the rest day to pick up some more freeze-dried food and to keep Ang Rinzi company at Base Camp. In the early morning, he returned – with Ang Rinzi! Pemba broke the news – Tim and the rest of the expedition had packed up and left the Rhododendron Camp. Pemba had not seen any sign of them. Perhaps Tim had suddenly deteriorated and had to go down. Ang Rinzi would not stay with the snow cats any longer, and so he had brought him up. Had he made the right decision, he asked?

We discussed the problem for over an hour and, as we talked, another dilemma was emerging. John voiced his concern about his job – it was now becoming obvious that the climb would take much longer than we had thought, and that he would not be back in time for a crucial management committee meeting on the 13th November. The fact that he had not received any news, and his wife was pregnant, was also beginning to trouble him.

I was angry. "Look John, we've all got our own worries. Why did you leave it till now before remembering your responsibilities and stopping us all in our tracks. Don't have a black Irish mood and throw this guilt trip on us now. Ten days, fourteen days, what's the difference? Expeditions are like marriage, you have to stick with them, for better or for worse! We're spending far too much time bothering about things that have nothing to do with climbing the mountain – the Tim problem, your problem, they're all just energy drains, and we need all the energy we've got to get up the hill."

Eventually we evolved a master plan – next day Pemba would escort Ang Rinzi down the mountain until they discovered Tim's fate, and then arrange an extra mail run to carry an apologetic telegram from John.

We returned to the mountain with relief, as if fleeing from the moral problems of another planet, a different reality. Guy and I moved up to the Nid d'Aigle, and John drew satisfaction from carrying an enormous load in support and helping us scrape off a patch of snow on which to pitch the tent. "I really enjoy hard work," he said before going back down, "but fancy coming thousands of miles to dig a hole."

A child spends hours absorbed in play, building dens and dugouts in trees and mud. The climber constructs his new home high on the mountain, and quickly settles in. Below our perch on the fantastic parapet of the Nid d'Aigle, the sun threw strangely clipped shadows across the southern face, and Guy and I smiled like children. He cooked spaghetti bolognese and we talked about Dougal, the hero of his youth, about Everest, about our ridge. We almost forgot where we were.

The next day was perfect. Above the fourth and last rock tower the ridge leant back. Guy seemed designed for ridge climbing. With the seemingly careless poise of a gymnast, he balanced up rocky arêtes, uniform coils of white rope in one hand, the other balanced nonchalantly on rugosities. His studied grace and precision matched the photographic poses in French books on mountaineering technique.

"Let's see how far we can get."

We were travelling light. We climbed pitch after pitch, elated with the altitude and the sun's warmth. The new springboard of the Nid d'Aigle had released intense energy from within us and we felt that we could climb upward forever. But the declining sun reminded us to return to shelter. We had climbed a thousand feet of new ground.

We soloed downwards. Far below us, on the white glacier, a pageant of tiny black specks moved backwards and forwards, enacting a mysterious drama to us. Now two orange tents glowed on the Nid d'Aigle. John was ensconced there, and when we arrived he unfolded the plot.

"I was just about to leave Advance Camp this morning when guess who hoved into sight but Tim, bent double under an enormous sack and eyes set fast on the summit. He seemed right as rain, if a bit pale about the gills. He carried a light load with me up to here – he's really improved, moving slowly, but otherwise O.K. Says he'll do another carry – he's staying at Advance Camp. Seems really impressed with the mountain – it's the first time he's seen it. Pemba and Ang Rinzi have gone back to Base Camp. Oh and Guy, you know that down suit you gave to Pemba? He hasn't got it with him – he flogged it in Kathmandu." We crammed into one of the tents and cooked and chatted into the evening.

"Your turn as rope boy tomorrow Pete?"

"Yes, Captain."

Guy and John climbed through the morning to the previous day's high point whilst I fixed ropes and anchor points on the way. When I caught up with them, John was hanging on to steep ice, fifty feet above Guy, his whole weight balanced on the front points of his crampons, and his enormous calf muscles bulging out of his gaiters.

"Dancer's legs these, mate. Just point me at this hill. No problem.

Great ice." A large chunk fell away as John brandished his axe, and hit Guy in the mouth. Blood dripped from the wound on to the snow. We crouched into the slope, wary of further missiles.

Two hundred feet above, a granite overhang jutted out into the sky. For us it was an important landmark, the day's 'project'. Many days before, Guy had seen this from the glacier, and espied a tiny ribbon of snow that cut across it. Now he claimed ownership of this ledge, and we christened it the 'Vire Neithardt'. Pitons sang into the firm rock and we followed John as he edged across.

"What can you see around the corner, John?"

"Fantastic, it's snow, it's the ice-cream cone. Just a snowplod to the point from here, have a look yourself."

The sun had come through the cloud, the wind had dropped and the rock was golden. The vastness of Tibet to the north was in darkness. We plunged back down into the shimmering mist. Imperceptibly, by degrees, the climb had come alive.

18

BORDERLINE

27th October – 4th November, 1979

A jagged, milk-white crystal guarded nearly two miles of the Ridge. It floated in the air, tethered insubstantially to rocky buttresses, a fragile spire of arrested harmony. Thin shadowy lines and narrow flutings glowed for an instant, then faded. The shifting light helped us to glimpse a hint of its variety but not even the thickest cloud or the darkest night could disguise its shape.

At last we were climbing pure ice and snow. I crouched beneath the roof of the final overhang, watching showers of ice cascade improbably from far out above my head, falling clear through the air for hundreds of feet. The roof blocked news of John's progress, and the only measure was an occasional pull for more rope. Then the rope tugged for me to follow.

John was astride the ridge, gripping it between his knees as if holding the mane of a great bucking white horse.

"Haven't got a belay. I've hacked a bit off the cornice and feel fairly secure," he announced.

John seemed unperturbed, whereas the exposure unnerved me. The new airy situation demanded mental adjustment. The giddy drop screamed into my head 'Don't fall.' Was this classic hubris? Were we over-reaching ourselves? We were black flies, crawling on to a white paper origami – except that we had no suckers on our hands and feet, just a few inches of driven steel suspended us above the void.

"You're in a morbid mood today," said John. "You seem obsessed with thoughts of death."

"Just a mild attack of jitters," I confessed. "The snow seems a bit sloppy and loose, and I don't like the look of those cornices." I climbed above him, carving steps and smashing the cornice down into the depths of the North Face of the ridge. I uncovered a small rock from beneath the snow, and spent half an hour tapping a wobbly piton into an icy crack. We had no ropes left to fix. "It'll be the big pull up tomorrow," I said.

John stormed into the lead again. There was no protection. "Exciting stuff this," he yelled.

The only marks of his passing were a few crampon scrapes on the surface. I followed him, chopping steps.

"You may as well lead to the top," I said. "I'll consolidate a pathway."

We could look across at the next section of the West Ridge. It looped a long way down the other side of Point 19,800 ft. to a heavily-corniced horizontal section half-a-mile long.

After four hundred feet we stopped, for we could go no higher. "I'll just lick the tip of the ice-cream," said John. He pushed his head through the summit and looked around. "Amazing place, incredible drop on all sides – but it's a hell of a long way! What do you think?"

My mind choked at the sight of the endless sweep of the ridge – it was too long to absorb. We were both depressed.

"Was Changabang like this?" he asked.

The Changabang climb had been just as exposed, and just as much hard work, but every rop⸱⸱⸱ ⸱⸱⸱ had gained height and there had not been this constant danger of cornices and poor belays.

"Going down and then horizontal all that way is going to sap us," I said.

"Guy dismissed it as one hour – maybe two – step-cutting," grinned John. "I wonder what he'll say when he sees it – Nom de Dieu!"

"Hacking out a camp-site'll have to come first."

"It's gripping enough standing here."

It had been a long day wound with tension and a taste of things to come.

We met Guy on the way down. He was coolly starting up the arête towards us, carrying a heavy load. His poise looked characteristically nonchalant. "What a sensation! All alone above a sea of cloud!" He greeted us smiling with enthusiasm, carved a slot and left his load and descended with us. During the long abseil, the rope John was sliding down pulled out the piton it was secured to. He managed to jump on to a ledge and keep his balance.

The hazards and decisions of the day time were simple – black and white, compared to the problems that surged back during the hours of night on the Nid d'Aigle. It helped me to turn on my torch and write them down:

We initially planned just to leave fixed rope on the difficult bits, but now it's becoming clear that a full scale 'capsule' leapfrogging technique running the rope out between camps is the only way we've got a chance of doing the route. Now we're going to have to pull up all the ropes below the Nid d'Aigle – and after tomorrow, all the way below Point 19,800 ft. So I have to decide what to do about Pemba and Tim. If all that mattered was to reach the top, then it would be obvious to ask them to go back to Base Camp. Why?

a) Pemba has just come back up here after two days' holiday at Base Camp – a strained thigh he says. (Why do Sherpas always come up with childlike excuses? After all, he just wanted to chat with his mates.) He seems impetuous, and more at home with a jumar than an ice axe. We can only trust him to carry loads.

b) Our progress is determined by how fast the lead pair can put out ropes over new ground. So far, one man carrying loads has been able to support this progress – and it doesn't look likely that we'll go any faster higher up. It's possible that, with five of us, there will be some redundancy – one or two passengers.

c) Our food and fuel supply is already sparse, and with two extra mouths along our time will run out more quickly.

d) All these are minor issues compared to Tim's health and ability to acclimatise. Tim cannot have recovered completely, so quickly, after having been so weak. And we are now going so much higher. If he turns ill again, high on the ridge, trying to get him down could kill us all. Of course, the summit isn't the most important thing – our survival is. We cannot justify sending Pemba down now. Guy doesn't think I'm hard enough to make Tim understand, and he's probably right. Tim wouldn't be the same problem if he wasn't so blindly determined. Whatever I say probably won't make much difference to what he does anyway. I'll dash down in the morning to see him. But this isn't war, we're not an army requiring orders – the mountain is still unknown. So perhaps it's best that we're all on it together, wanting to climb it together.

In the morning, Guy and John prepared to go up to establish a camp on Point 19,800 ft., with Pemba in support. A pan of water was knocked over, delaying breakfast, and then Guy burnt his down suit on the stove. He started to mend it laboriously with little pieces of Elastoplast, cursing.

"If it was physically possible on this camp-site," said John, "you'd say that Guy had got out of bed on the wrong side this morning."

I wanted to descend to Advance Camp before Tim moved, so I left them packing.

It was many days since I had touched this ground. Our first probings there had been exploratory, exhausting and uncertain. Now I felt confident, having lately balanced above dizzier heights than these. I was down in an hour.

Tim was sitting in the entrance of the Advance Camp tent, heating up a drink. The inside spoke of ordered independence. Next to him was a load, neatly packed, to carry up to the Nid d'Aigle. Behind him, his sleeping bag and equipment were carefully folded, as if prepared for a kit inspection at Scout Camp. I had intended to tell him how thoughtless he'd been, not sending Pemba Sherpa up; how we'd spent more time talking about him than the climb, and how worried we were that he'd be ill again when we were up on the ridge. But on seeing him, all these intentions died, and it was obvious there was only one solution – he should come with us.

"Glad I got down here before you set off. Can you pack up your personal stuff and I'll help you carry up any food that's left. I'm going to pull the ropes up. Any tea?"

Tim was visibly relieved. "Magic," he said.

It took all afternoon to pull up the ropes. As we climbed, it started to snow. We were taking away all the lower rungs to use them higher up the ladder. The physical gesture of commitment was made, and now the concomitant isolation and self-reliance could enter alternately to exhilarate and agitate us. Our momentum would be spurred.

Or so I hoped. Tim and I reached the Nid d'Aigle as Pemba arrived from above, singing cheerfully to himself. "John and Guy coming down," he announced.

"What!"

Yes, there they were, swinging down the ropes in the twilight. The sports plan was disrupted. After their late start, Pemba had become stuck for an hour whilst jumaring up the fourth tower. They had divided his load between them, but had arrived on the summit of the point too late to dig a camp-site. Nevertheless, they had uncovered some better anchors on the ridge.

John, Tim and I crammed into one tent. It had been eleven days since we had been together. There was much mocking and laughter. I did not realise how Tim's joining us upset the social balance of the team, as Guy recounted:

I feel very uneasy. The three British sleep together, and I am installed with Pemba. Nevertheless I go to eat with them, but I feel a complete stranger to all their discussions. To them I am the Swiss guide, to be laughed at. Well, they'll see. I hate being a stranger, put on the side. A very bad calculation on Pete's part. I feel alone against the three of them. It would be good for them to find themselves alone sometimes.

At dawn I tried to stir some action, for once a sergeant major in a dozy barracks. "Come on Pemba, get a brew on. Come on John, can't you see the whole trip's sliding. We've probably got, I reckon, a one-in-three chance of reaching the South Summit. We've got to make more progress."

"Snow cat came here last night," said Pemba, pointing at tiny tracks in the snow around the tents.

"How'd it get up here?"

"Must have come up the south side."

"If it can climb like that we ought to put a rope around it and get it to lead the rest of the route."

That night John described the day in his diary:

Big move to Camp on Point 19,800 ft. Guy and I are to occupy so we can only carry our own kit and two ropes each. Has snowed a bit during the night so no tracks and slippery rocks. The other three follow with heavy loads to stock the camp. Arrive at the Point early afternoon, very hot and fairly tired. Pete arrives shortly after, then Tim, then Pemba. Pemba goes back down straight away. We set about hacking a camp-site on this knife point. The map'll have to give it a lower height after we've finished with it! Pete and Tim descend at about 4.00 p.m. Guy and I carry on digging and chopping in snow and ice until 5.30 when just before dark we try the tent for size – it fits! Tie it down with ropes and axes. Sort out gear on the edge of nowhere and go in tent where somehow we forget there is a six thousand-foot drop immediately outside the door. Calling the camp 'Neuschwanstein' after mad King Ludwig's Bavarian cloud castle. Guy says he keeps on hearing Wagner's 'Lohengrin'. Plenty of food but no tea. You wouldn't believe this camp-site. Gear hanging everywhere. All has to be tied on. I'm on the outside! Will try to push the route along the ridge tomorrow.

Back at the Nid d'Aigle the same night any satisfaction I might have felt with our logical progress received a jolt when Tim staggered me with the assumption we should be going alpine-style beyond Point 19,800 ft. It hurt my pride to have to justify more pedestrian tactics and my defensiveness is evident in my diary entry about Tim:

This feeling that the younger and ambitious, particularly Yorkshire-bred climbing generation are so prickly and opaque, must slot me as an older, done-it-all-not-much-to-learn-now-set-in-my-ways greybeard! When I went to the Hindu Kush in '72, we pushed ourselves so hard we found our limits and only just got away with it. Perhaps Tim would have been best going on a trip with his younger mates, having a few epics, making a few mistakes, surviving and learning his own level that way. The youthful plunge and a measured pace don't seem compatible.

The early morning sun lassoed the turret of Neuschwanstein, nearly two thousand feet above us, picking out the orange of John and Guy's shelter on the tip. We envied them for the warmth of the sunshine. Pemba, Tim and I packed up our camp, our fingers stiff with cold. One of the tent poles slipped out of Pemba's hands, to stop on a ledge a hundred and fifty feet down the South Face. Although he had just vomited up the kippers he had eaten for breakfast, Tim climbed down unroped to reclaim it, following the tracks of the snow cat.

John and Guy were inside their tent when we arrived with our loads. It was one-thirty in the afternoon. "What's up John?" I asked.

Guy was sitting silently in the back of the tent, and I could not see him. John was their spokesman. His face was gloomy with disappointment, and he shook his head as he broke the news. "Thrown a wobbler, I'm afraid. It's unjustifiable Pete. Guy and I have had a long talk about it. We did a couple of ropelengths. The whole ridge is unstable – I could feel it vibrate when Guy cut a step a ropelength away. There's no security – the nearest rocks are hundreds of feet away. We only had that eight-mil non-stretch rope to climb on too. There are immense double, triple cornices, all just about to fall over. I nearly came down to stop you wasting the effort coming up."

"Well, we're all here now. We've shifted all the food and gear up, we may as well stay the night," I said, and did not comment further. This was not the time for a back-seat driver to voice opinions.

We cut a platform for a second tent, and Tim, Pemba and I installed ourselves. That night, huddled in the corner, I wrote:

> The first night in a new camp is always the worst and has to be well sleeping-pilled, to forget these monster drops on all three sides. It's an amazing place. We have to resign ourselves to the creaks, thumps and groans from the ice. A fast return home now is deliciously appealing, but we must have another look. Tomorrow will prove if they are right. I wish I'd been here to encourage them, but I've wanted the back-up to run smoothly, hence all the hard work but safe support jobs I've given myself during the last two days. Tim is now loving the excitement of our position, and to him retreat is not a word. His ambition appears cold and hard, and should give us impetus. But everyone must agree about the next step. I want success, or justified return.

Guy did not sleep much that night. He was first to break the silence of the morning. "I have been thinking for many hours, like before a big route in the Alps," he said. "I am not going to give up two months' work just like that. This is no place for those who are homesick. This bit of ridge is mine, my problem, and I am going for it."

John was stunned by Guy's change of heart, but quickly recovered: "Guy, I'll never mention your German family origins again, you're a Frog, through and through."

After breakfast I descended to the fourth tower to recover the first six ropes. I looked around, imprinting the ground on my mind, and anticipating any problems that might arise during descent. Between each ropelength as I came up I left orange nylon slings around the rockmarkers for our return.

As I climbed back up the ice ridge towards the camp, I saw, across hundreds of feet of space, the tiny figure of Guy moving cautiously along the back of the gigantic cream roll of snow. Between us and below us was the shadowed world of the north side. And today, certainly, he would reach the security of a clump of rocks on the ridge – the Red Tower.

The whole team was back together on Neuschwanstein by four in the afternoon.

"We should have stayed out longer," said Guy, "but I persuaded the others to come back. I thought it would take a long time but Tim had made a motorway of steps behind us and it only took half an hour." He was excited at the day's progress. "Sometimes my mouth was dry with fear. At one point John said to lasso the cornice – it was shaped like a mushroom and it worked! Amazing. We've put a big sling around it, it's a good runner. In another place, where the ridge was too thin to climb on, I descended down and up again on the south side; very delicate. Fantastic climbing!" In his diary he wrote: "The team is back together again, morale has increased, and I think we should crack it. My vengeance is complete, upon myself and the others."

The two tents on Neuschwanstein were pitched almost on top of each other, five feet apart.

"God, you're timid," mocked John as I twisted more ice screws into the mountain, to tie myself on to that night. He and Guy, in the upper tent were doing all the cooking for the five of us. The dome-shaped tents were much more roomy than the claustrophobic tunnel tents we had used on Kangchenjunga; nevertheless, it was a cosy squeeze for three people. Tim, Pemba and I lay in our tent, waiting to be fed, and listening to the conversation above us.

"Look Guy, you're not in Switzerland now. Why can't you have double standards of hygiene like the rest of us? Clean cutlery, pristine pots, cordon bleu cooking just don't make sense up here. You've used most of the expedition's toilet paper to wipe your Karrimat."

"Pass me a spoon, John."

"Here you are mate."

"Hey, clean it first, it's got a lump of yesterday's soup on it."

"I'll chew it off."

"You, you, you're an animal!"

"Snarl."

The days had slid into November. Soon the winter winds would arrive to threaten our fragile hold on the ridge. We had not much time.

Tim was by far the best technical climber of the team, to be deployed as a last secret weapon. On the 1st November, I held the rope as he took the lead. However, he was not yet attuned to cornice-climbing, and spent three hours traversing steep and difficult ice beneath the ridge, changing his mind, and returning again. Meanwhile Guy, on a load-carrying day, arrived from the back, uncoiled a rope of his own, tied on and soloed along the top of the ridge above us. This helpful gesture had an unspoken but implicit message: 'I told you so.' Then John breezed into view, having spent an enjoyable morning pulling up five ropes from below the other side of Neuschwanstein.

"It's great being on your own for a time, isn't it?" he said. "I looked across and couldn't see you, so I assumed you were galloping along and would need some more rope – so I brought some. Didn't realise you hadn't actually moved anywhere yet."

Logistically, the expedition had piled right up behind the front. Needled, I led across a large cornice, my anger having overcome my fear. Guy advised me where to place a deadman anchor. The rope became tangled. I misunderstood him, suspected a patronising tone, and cursed him loudly. Guy said nothing, left his load and sped back along the ropes towards Neuschwanstein. We never discussed the incident. Only John followed me.

At last the ridge had stopped going down, and was starting to loop gently upwards in long, horizontal sections interspersed with short steps. I took the lead again, demolishing the cornice with two-handed blows of my ice axe, and carving a path along the top of the ridge.

"It's all right when you get used to it," I yelled. "I don't know what all the fuss is about, my granny could walk along here; it's no worse than the Midi-Plan traverse."

John arrived and we hung from an ice screw. "It's not quite how I remember the Midi-Plan," he said. "I mean, on the Midi-Plan hundreds of people have already tested the cornice for you. Still, I get the idea now – Piolet Bludgeon – no technique, no art, just brute force and ignorance."

It was growing late, but experience had taught us not to succumb to the temptation of an early return to camp. We capitalised on the afternoon's momentum. John smashed his way a ropelength forward. I joined him, and we both sat astride the ridge, chatting happily. Honour was restored.

The sun hung low in the sky, a great star whose light was caught by thousands of tiny icy particles suspended in the air around us. The arm of the West Ridge pointed back to the sun, and we followed it. Beyond, a tiny figure was silhouetted on the tip of Neuschwanstein.

This ridge was a cutting edge between light and shade. A mighty barrier, it divided winds and snowstorms, cultures and countries. Also, it was our only delicate support between earth and sky. A full moon illuminated the final ropelengths of our return to the tents.

Early the next morning, Tim shot off along the ropes whilst everyone else was dozily preparing their equipment and loads for the day. His sense of urgency was infectious.

"If you wait here any longer, Guy," John taunted, "it'll be three in the afternoon and time to come back." The gibe worked, for Guy soon left in hot pursuit of Tim:

> A strong wind blows from the North, and it is bitterly cold. But when I am below the crest on the south side, it is quite warm. I join Tim at the end of the ropes, and he lets me lead the first pitch. The cornices are enormous and lean from side to side. I crawl along until I can put in an ice screw as a belay. We alternate the leads. "Stick to the ridge," I advise Tim. A lot of chopping is necessary. It is hard work and our progress is slow. All of a sudden I am faced with a series of three towers of ice and snow. I tell myself that this time . . . however, nothing collapses.

For three hours John and I sat on the rocks of the sunny side of the Red Tower, exchanging thoughts. We watched Tim and Guy, gazed at the mountain and scanned the great distances for signs of changing weather.

"I hope they find a camp-site somewhere around that rock tower. Trouble is, it'll be no higher than the last one, I mean, look across at the American route. Heightwise, we've hardly got anywhere, we're just traversing around the headwall of the valley – doing the Tsering-ma Horseshoe! We're really going to have to be careful on the descent, whatever happens, I don't fancy teetering down here all dizzy and dehydrated."

"Do you think we're being too cautious? Perhaps we should go for it."

"No, not on this route, not with this team. We're getting tired enough as it is; I mean, we're out on a limb and really committed already."

"You mean you don't trust us?"

"Or myself. I just don't want to take that much risk. There are too many unknowns. I've got this nagging feeling that we're constantly overstepping ourselves. And you've got to admit, it's been erratic displays of pride, anger, competitiveness, and ambition that have got us all this far."

"You hypocrite! You could say that about any climb."

John was our sounding board. Always charitable in his opinions, he had the ability to put the most delicate of problems into the most tolerant words with a disarming humility. The armed forces had taught him to accept the foibles of others when there was no other choice, and to recognise and rise above the problems of close living. He never complained or excused himself, and seldom asked for help.

He was ashamed to mention difficulties, and believed that our little team was sacred, whatever its weaknesses. John was the least selfish of us all.

Pemba arrived after a morning's snow-melting at the camp, and the three of us moved on together. Meanwhile, Guy and Tim had reached the larger rock tower that marked the end of the horizontal section and the start of a steep fifteen-hundred-foot step in the ridge.

> The sixty-foot-high rock tower blocks our way. After some discussion, Tim leads halfway up it and belays to a rock spike. The security of solid granite at last. There is a lovely, simple key to the problem – a beautiful little rock ledge down on the south side of the tower (in fact we now see it is a group of towers) which leads to a col on their far side, at the point where the ridge stands upwards again. The others arrive and we dump loads. If we do a lot of cutting, we shall be able to put a camp here; twenty thousand feet – only two hundred feet gained in many days. It is dark when we arrive back at Neuschwanstein.

The next day, 3rd November, John and I returned to the fifteen-hundred-foot step. John was exuberant. "This is the sort of climbing I really like," he said.

We had no equipment left for a leader to protect himself. This meant that if the leader fell at the top of a hundred-and-fifty-foot ropelength, he would fall three hundred feet. However, John was irrepressible, seemingly unconcerned. His spirit was unleashed upwards and he soared after it. I just paid out the rope, grinning encouragement at his comments.

"Look at that front-pointing," he said, lurching over an ice bulge, "the grace of a thousand startled gazelles."

"Hardest bit of climbing so far," he gasped, panting for breath above an overhang. "Quite hairy, this," he yelled, teetering across a cornice higher up. We quickly climbed ropelength after ropelength, until there was no more. "Terrific," he concluded. "All that sideways scuttling on the horizontal was getting me down."

Brimful of joy, we swooped back down the ropes. It seemed that in two days the scales had been tipped in our favour.

Whilst we had been climbing, Guy, Pemba and Tim had spent four hours excavating a magnificent platform on the ridge that was just big enough for two tents. The cornice was carefully left intact, so as to protect the tents from the northerly and westerly winds. This shield, and the proximity of rock, helped us quickly feel at home there. Although the new camp-site was in an equally improbable position, it lacked the frighteningly dramatic vulnerability of Neuschwanstein. John christened it 'Fawlty Towers', after the BBC TV comedy. Tim and Guy then returned all the way back along the ridge to spend the night at Neuschwanstein, to be in a position to pull in the ropes and rejoin us at Fawlty Towers the next day.

Pemba was a connoisseur of fixed-rope ridges. He often compared our behaviour, our route and our equipment to those of Japanese expeditions he had been on. "On ridge like this," he said, "Japanese put in many many snow pickets and make hand-rail. Your ropes aren't safe. Japanese have many more members. On Ama Dablam climb, we were seven climbers and seven Sherpas." However, he was impressed at our care and effort in making our tent platforms. "The Japanese they have very rough camps. They just dig in snow not ice and then tie round with ropes."

Pemba rarely mentioned the religious significance of Gauri Sankar, but quietly he undertook a rearguard action of appeasement, to offset the possible damage of an insensitive climb. Daily, he sang, chanted prayers and lit incense, and did not hear our mutterings of "What a cheap stink." His supply of holy rice was nearly finished, and he did not know that John had left at Base Camp the polythene bagful he had given to him. He taught us not to turn our plastic cups upside down. "It is the same with porters' baskets – they must always be open to the sky."

When John burnt one of the sides of his cup against the stove, Pemba told him "Now you will have bad luck!" Our rationally trained minds found it difficult to accept the explanation, and Pemba always smiled with embarrassment. Some of his superstitions seemed as divorced from their long-forgotten meanings as our own Western ones about horseshoes and spilling salt. Just as they had done on Kangchenjunga, two black yellow-billed choughs followed us up the mountain, swooping around us in the cross-currents and turbulence around the ridge, rarely settling.

"They're probably the same two," said John.

Pemba did not eat much of the evening meal – fortunately for him. It was a bad night. The few teabags that were left were with Guy and Tim, on Neuschwanstein. We melted throat lozenges, then chocolate, with snow to make drinks. Then we made a mistake – we did not mix enough water into the mashed potato powder. We woke in the middle of the night, our mouths parched and stomachs swollen with dehydration. We melted snow for three hours, restlessly trying to calm the internal torture.

Morning clouds dispersed and the morning wind died. The night's frost melted as the sun touched the tent, and lay as ice on the groundsheet. Pemba left to pick up ropes from Tim and Guy as they moved along the ridge towards us, and John and I waited, to relay the ropes up the mountain. After the rough night, we were glad of the chance to melt and drink some more water.

The rest gave a chance to shed scales. It was warm. I looked at my bare feet for the first time in many days. I peeled my silk suit off, and dead skin fell around like a snowstorm. I ran my hands over my shoulders and my ribs, rediscovering my body. Where had all the muscle gone? I was more like a bedridden hospital patient than a mountaineer. I twisted and turned the little mirror to encompass my face and saw matted hair, blotched, purple scars, scabs and weary lines. I was underneath that, somewhere.

We counted our possessions. At a stretch, we had four to five days' food left. We had no ballast to throw out. Like Robinson Crusoe, we knew that commonplace, insignificant things suddenly become precious when they are all that you have between yourself and thirst, hunger and cold. Seldom would life be simpler, but such simplicity cost no less than everything.

We looked around. Below us, the South Face of the West Ridge plunged in a three thousand foot sweep of ice to the Tongmarnang Gorge, a tributary of the high Rolwaling Valley. Far to the south west we could see the soft pencil lines of the Siwaliks. To the west the lines of three rivers cut their swathes through the Himalayas from their headwaters in the north – the old trading routes of the Trisuli, Sun Kosi and Tamba Kosi, all known locally by the name of Bhote Kosi. Beyond and between them stood proud mountains – the distant hulk of Himalchuli, the Langtang Peaks and, nearest of all, the aggressive spire of Choba Bhamare. Most arresting was the dominating height of a double-summited peak to the north west. This peak, the only mountain above eight thousand metres to lie completely inside Tibet, was called Shisha Pangma. The Sanskrit name was Gosainthan, meaning 'the place of the saint'.

The first European to explore the area around Shisha Pangma was Heinrich Harrer, who was to make the first ascent of the Carstensz Pyramid in New Guinea nearly twenty years later. At the outbreak of the Second World War, he and a climbing companion, Peter Aufschnaiter, were interned by the British at Dehra Dun, in India. In 1943 they escaped into Tibet.

From the upper waters of the Rongshar Gorge, where it threaded between the mountains of the Lapche Kang and the north side of Gauri Sankar, the other New Guinea explorer, A. F. R. Wollaston had, in 1921, taken the famous first photograph of Gauri Sankar, showing a mountain perfect in outline and proportion. Wollaston remarked on the contrast of this area with the barren Tibetan Plateau. Here, he found soft, fragrant air, and flowers and trees in profusion, and called it 'The Valley of Roses'. In June, 1924, after the traumatic loss of Mallory and Irvine, Colonel Norton led his expedition's retreat from the monsoon on Everest to recuperate here for ten days. Gauri Sankar was revealed slowly to them, through a rent in a curtain of cloud, until they saw fifteen thousand feet of it, from top to bottom. The sight made them giddy, and they acclaimed the vision 'a dream mountain'.

Norton rested his team at a Tibetan village called Tropdo, at the base of the northern side of Gauri Sankar. Like the 1921 expedition, they went hungry for meat. Norton complained in his diary that there were no chickens to be eaten, for the locals believed that if animals were killed in the sacred precincts of the mountain, misfortune would befall the village. I wondered if this was the same village that John and I could see – its cultivated fields splashed a different shade on the slopes, and its buildings just visible to the naked eye. Don Whillans, when he contoured on to the northern, Tibetan side of the mountain in 1964, had said he could actually see people there, walking about. According to our porters, a Chinese bus now went to within a day's walk of that village. John and I weren't the first, or the last, climbers to attempt Gauri Sankar and think wouldn't life be simpler if it could be approached from the north. However, Tibet remained to us the mysterious land – its secrets could not be revealed. Whether we could respond to it or not, Tibet focused spiritual energies on the sacred mountain in a particularly conscious way.

At mid-day, Pemba had not returned with any ropes, so we decided it was too late to move. If we were to leave now, it would be mid-afternoon by the time we reached our previous day's high point. There was no point in tiring ourselves for such limited progress.

"We haven't stopped for eleven days," I said.

"It is Sunday, after all," said John.

Meanwhile, on Neuschwanstein, Tim and Guy had also had a bad night:

> Tim cooks. What a horrible catastrophe: he succeeds in putting two packets of Knorr soup in half a litre of water, pours in two tins of meat and then stirs it a little – absolutely revolting. Then, during the night, he vomits *in* the tent – over his sleeping bag, boots, groundsheet, me, everywhere. And the smell.
>
> In the morning, after cleaning what we can, we leave to take in the ropes along the horizontal arête. The method which I have devised is simple. The first goes along the fixed rope to the anchor and then belays the other who follows whilst coiling the rope at the same time. I am very angry with Tim who will not do what I want (!) Then later I apologise for having shouted at him. All is sorted out. Eventually Pemba arrives to help carry some rope.

When Pemba returned to Fawlty Towers, he told John and me that Tim had been ill. A few minutes later Tim arrived swathed in ropes – angered at our inactivity and accusing us of being lazy, of not coming to help. The sudden onslaught bit deeply and quickly. I didn't ven try to explain why we had not moved, but was overwhelmed with a rage that I could not control. I longed to reply calmly, but could not. I was amazed at my over-reaction. Feelings had been building up, and Tim had triggered something in my unconscious.

Tim gave his sleeping bag to Pemba to air, and left to help Guy. I started to rationalise my anger to John, and then stopped. In our other lives, at lesser altitudes, a confrontation can help strike through complexities to clarify and reduce a problem to a hard solution. But the stakes were too high to take that risk again. The mountain had amplified our words, and they could not be revoked. I relied on John to soothe our wounds.

There was a gust of wind and a slithering sound. We watched aghast as the knot attaching Tim's sleeping bag slipped through and the bag slipped into the abyss of the South Face.

Pemba offered to go down and fetch it, but was understandably relieved when we did not insist.

Guy arrived. "It was full of vomit anyway," he said. Like Tim, he was upset that we had not come to help them.

This time, however, I had my answer ready. "Well why don't you have a rest day tomorrow?" I suggested.

When Tim arrived, he accepted his loss without comment. We all donated extra clothing to keep him warm, and he slept between John and myself. It was all we could do.

John relieved the tension. "Well, it's probably keeping some surprised peasant down there cosy," he said, looking into Nepal.

During the night a loud curse and clatter awoke us. John had stretched his arm out through the air vent so as to empty a pee-bottle, but had been unable to get his hand and the pee-bottle back in, so he had dropped it.

"It was a monkey's-hand-in-a-bottle-situation," he explained. "There was nothing I could do about it but let go."

19

CLIFFS OF FALL

5th November, 1979

The sunlight moved on to the mountain like the hand of a great clock – a constant reminder with long fingers that pointed at our mood. Today it was a reminder not to nestle down into the seductive cosiness of our sleeping bags until the day warmed up, but to light the stove and to stir ourselves out into the daunting cold.

"It'll be worth it, it'll soon be over, today's our big day, a big push is in the air."

John and I left the tents, racing the steady creep of the sunlight along the ridge. We thought the end was in sight, and our optimism was born again. Scepticism dissolved and fell away like the wisps of morning mist in the valleys below.

"I feel great," said John. "Ready for the charge, Sir."

John was prepared to tear upwards without protection, and revelled in the risk and daring of hanging tenuously in high places above the void. John's confidence and ability were irrepressible – if he climbed into danger there were surely untapped reserves to help him climb back. A day following him was fun.

A dead heat. We arrived at the top of the ropes at the same time as the sun. Pemba was following us, carrying a rucksack full of ropes. It was 10 a.m.

Like occasional monstrous waves escaping from a far-off storm, expanding their pent up energy unexpectedly across a calm lapping sea, the winds of approaching winter were beginning to whip across the West Ridge of Gauri Sankar. I looped a sling of nylon tape around a small rock spike, fastened myself to it. There was no ledge to stand on and the sling supported my weight as I leant out to watch John's progress. Our tiny figures were silhouetted far away on the West Face of the mountain. I paid the ropes out – an eleven millimetre climbing rope and an eight millimetre terylene non-stretch rope for fixing – as John gripped the ice ridge above me. After he had climbed a hundred

231

and fifty feet, the eleven millimetre rope ran out and he called for me to release it and to continue to belay him with the eight millimetre. Then he went out of sight on the north side of the ridge.

I did not see him fall. The wind carried the tune of pitons sinking into rock – and then, nothing. He made no sound of warning or alarm. Suddenly, the climbing rope he was trailing snaked wildly into the sky and disappeared, and the fixed rope scythed down the ridge towards me.

'He's fallen. The rope'll never hold.' I braced myself and then the shock came, jerking me upwards. The rope tore through my gloved hands and I let it slide as it whipped and snagged on the ridge. Accelerating thoughts slowed down time: 'He's pulling me off the anchor, the rope'll snap, I'll go too.' And then the force stopped. The rope had cut deep into the ridge forty feet above me. The rope was loose. 'He's gone.' I pulled it, hard, and it resisted. It had become caught – or John was on the end, unconscious, horribly injured, dead.

"John! John!" The wind snatched my shouts away, and there was no answer. A coldness inside suppressed my welling feelings of dread. I tied the rope off to the one beneath, uncoiled another one and, belaying myself, climbed out into the shadow of the North Face. I saw him.

His diary reveals what had happened.

First new pitch of the day – feeling strong and happy – no man has ever been here before. The wind is strong but crampons and axes bite hard on the arête. Ropes tangle beneath Pete and I am preparing to wait while he sorts them out when a hideous shriek sounds above, followed by an incredible blast of wind that nearly plucks me off the arête. I cling on tight on either side – it only lasts a few seconds. I consider going back down to Pete to try to find a less exposed alternative but decide to carry on. See rock belay above, but can't reach it on the climbing rope, so tell Pete to untie and hold me on fixed rope only – he extends it by knotting it to the end of the one below. Reach belay, put in pegs and am just about to tie on when another hellish shriek and blast of wind unbalances me. It is a good stance so I do not worry over-much until I find myself out in space. A frantic grab at the rock does no good, and down the North Face I go – tumbling over and over, hitting rocks and snow and falling forever in slow motion. I am dead, I am sure of it. Soon the rope will snap. There's thousands of feet to the ground and I hope that I am knocked unconscious before I get there. I think of Kath and little Joseph. Puzzled. No Panic. No Fear. Thoughts clear and rational. No effort under the sun can help. Really blown it this time.

Then I stop. The rope has held. I am alive and little J. has a dad. I seem to have broken my left wrist and twisted my left knee, but I am alive. I behave irrationally, shouting "I will not die, I will not die." I grab my jumar and start climbing like a madman up the fixed rope which has held me by snagging on the arête. I have fallen about two hundred feet. I shout to Pete whom I cannot see that I am O.K. – more or less. At last he sticks his head round to see me below him. He throws a rope across and I swing to him. I am a wild sight, having lost my hat and bleeding from the head. He is wonderfully calm as I reach him and he holds me as I burst into tears at the relief of being alive.

I looked into his eyes, trying to gauge the extent of his concussion. Had the blood come from his ear or nose? Was he sure, in his shocked state, there were no other injuries? John was apologising, insistently. He said he could abseil, and started down, protected by a top rope. He reached a knot in the rope and fingered it, confused. I realised that someone would have to abseil with him and, after a flurry of knots, followed him on another rope, yelling to Pemba: "Leave your sack, John's hurt. Go down and tell the other two to come up." The turbulence had carried the noise of our shouts down the mountain. I could see Tim and Guy struggling to put their boots on and packing for the emergency. By the time they reached us we had descended two ropelengths.

Tim and Guy were cool and reassuring.

"Well Guy, this is what Swiss Guides' Courses train you for," I said.

We knew we could help John to the camp. Soon the ridge was criss-crossed with ropes, descendeurs, karabiners, slings and willing pairs of hands. For the first time on the expedition we worked smoothly and efficiently together, united as a team. After three hours of descent John was lying down in the security of a tent.

"I'll never forget the noise that wind made," he said, shaking his head. "It was the scream of an animal."

"This'll make a good end to the story," said Tim.

20

FINAL CHOICE

5th – 8th November, 1979

"I feel as if I've just gone fifteen rounds with Rocky Marciano," said John. His head was clearing, he said, but his speech was slurred and his face was cut and puffy. His knee was badly swollen, his wrist crooked and his hand unusable. His wind suit was torn and scraped.

"Even Marciano couldn't have done that much damage," I said. "You look as if you've been through a combine harvester. How come you didn't shout when you fell off? You didn't make a sound. I'm sure I'd have screamed my head off."

"My Dad once told me that if you're going to die, to die quietly," he said.

Guy bandaged him and we all watched carefully for signs of head injury. Crammed together in one tent through the rest of the afternoon and early evening, there was no privacy for the patient, as he lay back listening to the objective discussion of his doctors over his body, occasionally interjecting a comment.

Could we tie all the ropes together and descend the North Face? The ridge was too insecure, too risky to descend. He would have to rest at least two days, for the concussion and shock to resolve themselves. "I don't want to be the reason you give up," he said. "I'm heartbroken I won't be able to continue the climb, but you're right, I've a lot to be thankful for; I'm alive."

We wanted to succeed. No one wanted to abandon the route. But we were a family – or, at worst, a marriage of convenience. Survival and success went together, never the last without the other. Guy

234

mooted an idea. Pemba could stay at the camp with John, and he and Tim and I could go along the ridge for a day or two, and have a look at the final difficulties. On one thing we were all agreed. There would be no splitting up for the descent, we would stick together.

I could not sleep. A bright moon filled the tent with flat light and a cold wind shook the walls. Although he had taken painkillers, John twisted and turned, unable to drift into a sleep that would relieve him of his wrist's nagging ache. Tim, without his sleeping bag, was struggling to keep his feet warm. Neither of them complained. The day had been, as John said, 'a seminal experience'. It had shocked us into focusing together, all other squabbles transcended and forgotten.

On the morning of the 6th November we ate the last breakfast – two fistfuls of muesli each. That is, all of us except John:

> I don't eat since I can hardly justify it, lying on my butt all day. Pete and Guy are off early at 6.30 a.m., followed by Tim with ropes at 9.00 a.m. Pemba is left behind to look after me! Wrist hurts like hell, but leg not too bad – walkable at least. Watch with increasing envy the progress of Pete and Guy along ridge. We have to be quick – there's only about three or four days of food left, and that's skimping.

The loneliest moments for a climber are felt during a long lead without protection. I inched my way up the pitch which John had fallen down the previous day, my eyes darting circumspectly around, suspecting lurking treachery. But there were no vicious blasts, no hideous shrieks, for today the mountain was tranquil. I saw John's rucksack, stashed carefully on a rock shelf by him before he fixed the anchor. I clipped into the two pitons.

Above me was a leaning rock tower, capped by a jauntily tilted, pointed cone of snow. I traversed beneath it, my crampons and picks biting into hard ice as I moved between jutting rocks. These rocks were just big enough to stand on, and served as harbours of security where I could breathe deeply and recover. I laughed at myself. I had styled myself an anchor man and escort, not chief risk taker on this expedition, but now there was too much risk and too few people, so the risk had to be shared. And now it was my turn to lead, I was enjoying myself. Voices filled my head of old friends, veteran Alpine Club members, male and female, that I had met over the previous year. I told them what was happening. They understood and we appreciated the setting together. My mind detached itself and soared upwards, beaming back images of our tenuous hold on the mountain. My nose brushed against the rock tower. I scraped away snow and ice with the adze of my ice axe until I uncovered a crack. A piton rang home. I belayed Guy and looked up at the snow cone. "And now for the Archbishop's Hat."

I always laughed at Guy for his 'ski instructor's smile'. Whatever the situation, it was always impossible to distinguish a grimace from a grin. But when I looked down on his smile as he held my rope, remarks that were on the tip of my tongue wavered in a rush of transmitted kinetic energy. As far as I was concerned, it was a smile of encouragement.

I kicked up the airy crest of snow. The ropes looped down through space to Guy, with the purposeful sweep of a suspension bridge. Their graceful arc added to my confusion. Rope, cornices and slopes all tilted crazily away from one another. So how was I supported here? I hacked away four footsteps in front of me at a time before moving up. The steep angle confined the swings of my axe. Like a skier learning the improbable discipline of leaning out, I stood out in balance as much as I dared, keeping my weight over my feet. One little mistake . . . if I should fall off here? I concentrated.

"Can you send up a deadman, Guy?"

I planted the device firmly in the ridge and clipped in the rope. Now only two were left. We would need this one higher up, Guy would have to take it out when he followed – but my mind insisted on it now.

We had reached the top of the fifteen-hundred-foot step in the ridge. The chaos of undulating whipped cream cakes and hidden steps blocked our upwards plans, and each ropelength was a revelation, alternately cheering, and then disheartening. We all led dangerous sections of the ridge, and longed for more equipment to make the climbing safer.

Tim arrived. "I don't trust these deadmen," he said. He and Guy took it in turns to hold my ropes. A huge unfurled sail of snow shadowed the northern side and I hung below it for an hour, cutting deep into the ridge, looking for rocks and cracks. I had only two large angle pitons, and I placed one sideways in an icy crack, tapping it gently so it did not split. It seemed to grip for an inch of its length. Tim and Guy joined me and clipped in. There were no footholds to relax on to. We balanced sideways along the inside edges of our crampons.

The clear line drawings in books on mountaineering techniques portray the safe traversing of corniced ridges as a simple matter. The climber assesses the width of the cornice, and estimates where its potential fracture line would be were it to collapse, and then walks beneath this fracture line. However, the West Ridge was not so clear-cut, because usually the snow overhung on both sides. We were balanced at a point between an icicle-skirted overhang on the south side, and the enormous cornice leaning over the north side. There was no alternative but to follow the tell-tale crack lines where the two opposing forces were beginning to part company.

Vivid, nightmare pictures of terrible precision rose in my mind, of the thunderous collapse of towers of snow in earthquake proportions. Occasionally, a step collapsed and a hole appeared, enabling me to see through to Tibet on the other side. It was a journey surrounded by creaks and whispers. Slowly, the rock shelf on the other side drew nearer. There were more yards to cross than years in my life. At the end, I clutched the solid rock mooring with fervour – not elation. It was three in the afternoon.

I relinquished the lead to Tim, after peering over the next obstacle. More serried ranks of towers and cornices rose into view. The spectacle rubbed salt into my scarred nerves. This ridge was endless. I was drained of mental energy.

"I'm too tired to do it," I said, and turned, to leave the next problem to the other two.

I retraced our steps. The soft evening light and my fatigue dulled my mind to the risk and exposure. I resigned myself to a complete, unquestioning trust in the ropes we had strung below us. It seemed that the mist would soften any fall.

Back at the camp, John, Pemba and I watched the tiny red figures of Tim and Guy returning across the snow turrets, which were now golden in the sunset. Even at this distance, it was possible to identify an individual from his shape and the way he moved.

My reports were pessimistic, but the other two had seen more ground. "Tim forged across two appalling pitches," said Guy when they returned, adding – ever-optimistically – "I think another day's climbing should put us in reach of the top."

"The fixed rope had got caught under the icicles on that last pitch you led," said Tim. "We had to solo it and a step collapsed on me."

We tried to assess our progress from the photographs we had brought of the ridge. Doubts ebbed and flowed about the route, until the conversation turned to another obsession we shared – food. We had been spinning out our meagre supplies for a long time and were constantly hungry. We wriggled and groaned in masochistic ecstasy as we tantalised each other with imaginary menus.

"Be careful when you get in the tent, Guy. Don't knock anything over, Pemba's got turkey, roast potatoes, sprouts and gravy on simmer."

"Followed by fresh air and snowballs and nowt warmed up."

On the 7th November, breakfast was a piece of chocolate and two cups of tea each. When we had finished there were only three teabags left. Tim and Guy were first to leave for the front line. There were only a few ropes to carry in support; I decided to wait at the camp until late morning, before following them – logistically it would be a waste of effort, but I wanted to be there.

John was feeling much better, and was beginning to contemplate joining us for the final push.

"I hope that if my hand is less painful I can jumar to end of fixed ropes and then plod easy snow slopes to summit. Not sure whether this is realistic – hand is useless and getting down from here could be an epic in itself. Still, I can give it a try and come back here if it doesn't work."

Pemba was still on ward duty, keeping an eye on John, and singing to himself. It was evident from the way he was quick to suggest a retreat for more supplies, and by the way he looked towards Base Camp, that Pemba longed for the opportunity to chat for a few hours with his friends in his own language. This morning he spotted three figures near the Notch. They had come to look for us. We signalled by flashing a spade in the sunlight, but there was no reply. We had been away many days, and I wanted to tell them "Don't worry, we're all right, we'll soon be back." Pemba continued to gaze for a long time after the figures had gone.

We could only guess how near we were to the summit – or whether it was possible at all. However, I roughed out a telex message, announcing our success:

Base Camp 10th November. Expedition successful and all safe and well. First ascent of Tseringma, 7,010 m. Southern Summit of Gauri Sankar made by Boardman, Leach, Neithardt and Pemba Lama at 1500 hours on 8th November after prolonged struggle up very difficult West Ridge. Send love to all and longing for home. Will inform further on arrival Kathmandu approx. 18th November.

There was no way the message could be sent, it did not commit us, but it was a reassuring if rash projection into the future. I doubted that I would have the energy and confidence to write it when we returned. I signed off my diary: 'To be continued when recovered!'

Tim had been reluctant to give up the idea of following a line he had spotted beneath the ridge, traversing across the South Face. Most of his alpine climbing had been up steep north faces, and ridge climbing was new to him. Today, however, he understood what was needed. His perseverance brought a fresh momentum to the climb, and helped shed all thoughts that we should abandon it. By the time I reached the end of the ropes, he had crossed more of the ridge than I had dared to hope possible. Tracks threaded below, above and between leaning snow towers and enormous, madly waving cornices. The wind plucked the ropes as they hung through the air between the towers. Guy was pleased when I joined him.

"I thought you weren't coming," he said. "Tim's climbing like there's no tomorrow. He's done some crazy leads. Incredible. A bit back there he said 'Bloody hell, Guy, you'll never believe how happy I am.' He had stood on a cornice, then stepped off it and hit it with his axe. The whole thing collapsed and fell down the North Side."

Guy's voice was tired and droopy. He had missed his rest day. "I'm going down after the next pitch," he said. "I have no strength left in my legs."

Tim had just traversed a cornice on its south side, but had now noticed a safer way following a band of rocks beneath the overhanging snow on the north side. Guy tiptoed across this to join him. The holds were tiny and the climbing delicate. The ridge was beginning to declare its attachment to the West Face of the mountain. The impending sweep of this leaning rock wall gave a new dimension to the abyss. Occasionally, ice flaked off from the séracs on the edge of the plateau of the South Summit, to plunge down it without hitting anything for two thousand feet.

All day I had been assessing the feasibility of John coming up the climb. We all agreed now that he would not be able to do it with one usable hand. I was relieved that Guy would return first and break the news – it was two-thirty in the afternoon when he went down.

When at rest, Tim was trembling with the vast expenditure of nervous energy that the ridge demanded. Once in the lead, however, he climbed coolly. The cornice was now too narrow and fragile, so he climbed steadily and calmly across the sixty-five degree wall on the South Side. Occasional ice bulges forced him to hug the mountain, so as to keep his balance over his crampons. I belayed him astride the ridge with my left foot in the sunshine of Tibet, and my right foot in a Nepalese snowstorm. The weather was sharply divided by a wall of turbulence that stretched hundreds of feet above me. The scene had a haunting unreality, as if I were witnessing a vision of schizophrenia.

Tim appeared and disappeared through flurries of snow. After I had paid out a hundred and twenty feet of rope, I heard the ring of a piton and a shout: "Come on, Pete, there's no stance but the peg seems O.K."

There was no room to change over belays, so I led through, hand traversing around some rocks towards the end of the cornice. I tapped in our last piton and peered around the corner.

It was a depressing sight. There was a gap thirty-feet-wide and fifty-feet-deep in the ridge, with a little col at the bottom of it. An overhanging rock wall between my airy perch and the col barred progress. I had come the wrong way. We would have to cross the cornice. I flailed at the piton with my hammer but it refused to budge. "I'll have to leave this till tomorrow," I said. Time pressed us to return down the line to the camp. The next day we would return for the summit.

That evening John was quiet and monosyllabic with disappointment. It was awkward to discuss the route tactfully in front of him. We studied photographs showing how the ridge joined the West Face. There would be some difficult climbing, but it was not easy to calculate how much. However, there was not much packing to do. After some disagreement, we decided not to take sleeping bags but to take a stove and pan. We would try to be up and back within a day – if necessary completing the climb in moonlight. Tim and I would leave first, followed after two hours by Pemba and Guy.

As long as we felt our intimate way up the mountain, accidents could be averted. Yet, within, fear built up unashamedly. When controlled, fear can bring strength. But unleashed fear made us cling to the mountain in a tight panic. In some ancient cultures 'to clutch the mountain' was a euphemism for 'to die'.

When I reached the big cornice that I had led across two days before, the fixed rope was once again snagged around icicles. Tim had evidently been unable to release it, for he was now moving amid the snow towers higher up, having soloed across the pitch. I tried flicking it around, then pulling it – without success. 'He could have waited,' I thought. 'We might have sorted something out together; now I'll have to solo it.'

I made two moves up the ice and stopped. An internal warning bell was ringing urgently in my head. It was as important a statement as had ever been made to me and I knew it had to be obeyed. The sun was stifling me in my down suit, and I felt hot and clumsy. The memory of the cornice was etched too deeply. I was hanging on too hard. I could not control the dread inside me sufficiently to force myself upwards; I could not summon a hard, brittle shell of will to protect me from the mountain, and it threatened to overwhelm me. Death was too near for me to resign myself to the risk. It was an absolute necessity that I should survive and return. He had been prepared to solo it, but I was not. To hell with my pride and the waste of time. I yelled up to Tim for him to come down and help. A distant curse, and the figure descended. The older gunfighter had backed out of the final shoot-out. He said nothing and I did not explain.

At the end of the ropes Tim retrieved the piton I had placed the previous day, and climbed over the crest. He slipped around and beneath the cornice on the north side, turning the frozen wave by the same route a surfer would have used on its fluid, rolling counterparts in the Pacific. The rope bit a deep notch through the eaves of the cornice, and I lowered him into the gap.

The ridge now rose up in a four-hundred-foot arrowhead of ice and rock that leant against the wall beneath the South Summit's ice cliffs. Tim started working his way methodically up the lower and steepest section. His crampons and picks splintered the friable ice, and chunks clattered down into the abyss, leaving thousands of smaller particles suspended around his rope through the air.

Pemba joined me at the gap. "Best to take cornices on the left side, like chortens, for good luck," I said.

He grinned. He was impressed with the ridge and the distance from the camp. It was the most difficult climb he had ever done, he said. Then he pointed at the South Summit. Five eagles were circling around it, their wings golden brown in the sunshine. I tried to take a picture, but the film in the camera was finished. I fumbled to insert another. But the eagles were gone.

Guy slid into the gap. We all looked up the dangling rope at the soles of Tim's cramponed boots, a hundred feet above our heads. Tim was fixing a belay.

"You could count the number of pitches with runners on this route on the fingers of one hand," I said. "Will you follow him Guy?"

We followed Tim up the rope. Pemba was ever eager to gain height and he hung close on my heels, unnerving me, as if he were trying to read over my shoulder. The blade of the Arrowhead leant back to fifty-five-degree snow that dripped in great icicles over a thirty-foot overhang below our feet. This rock overhang blocked our view downwards of the main South Face of the South Summit. There was nothing between us and the glacier five thousand feet below. For a while our talk was bold.

"Not long to top, Sir, what do you think?" said Pemba.

"There's no way I'm going to spend the night on the plateau," said Tim.

After three unprotected pitches, Tim was tired and Guy took over the lead. There were no more concealed gaps, and for the first time the way was clear. A hundred-and-fifty-foot knife-edge of snow stopped abruptly in the rock and ice wall of the South Summit Plateau. The western flying buttress of Gauri Sankar sank into the mountain without trace.

"I'm not stopping here," shouted Guy when he reached the meeting point. "I've put an ice screw in but it's no good. Can you tie another rope on?"

A narrow diagonal ramp of rock thinly coated in ice leant back above him at sixty-five degrees. As soon as he stepped leftwards off the ridge, Guy was balanced above the West Face, the top five hundred feet of which cut away in an overhanging wall beneath him.

Guy's long body stalked sideways across the wall with the patient stealth of a hunting spider. He devised a cunning protection by threading thin nylon slings through linked bubbles in the ice. No one uttered the thought that he should hurry, for we all knew it was a long and difficult lead. Talk of the summit died, for the day was ending. We had only one rope left. I tried to memorise the ground above him, as he moved up a groove and attached himself and the rope to a rock spike. High on the left was a gap in the sérac wall. Two huge, grotesque horns of ice signposted a gateway to the plateau.

I tied off the rope to the ice threads as I followed him. If one of them should break, I would swing, perhaps irretrievably, like a pendulum into the darkening abyss. The thought obstructed a job to be done, and I chased it from my mind. I was heady with altitude and the exposure, and the risk was not painful. The irregularities of the earth below were lost beneath a gently undulating swell of fluffy grey-blue clouds. The last rays of sun picked out the thin white line of rope looping above the last crest of the ridge and the little red figure of Tim, clinging to the ice. I hid my emotion behind the detached eye of my camera. Firelight glowed across rock and ice, and then faded. Soon the cold would arrive.

"Looks like it's my turn," I said to Guy. He nodded, smiling. The effort was to be shared.

I kicked my crampons into the frozen snow, climbing as quickly as possible in the twilight. I was soon panting in the thin air. Ribs of snow concealed dead ground; the ice horns were farther away than I had thought. Night was rushing in, filling me with the fresh energy and balance of urgency. The front points of my crampons skittered. I had reached the ice of the sérac wall; it was brittle and, as I turned in an ice screw, large dinner-plates flaked off. Eventually one sank in and I tied off the rope for the others to follow.

Like a blind man learning Braille, I felt my way across the ice, feeling the surface for a more forgiving texture. I smashed with my ice picks and ice tinkled away down the slope and into the darkness. It took three or four blows to clear the debris and implant the serrated edges enough for confidence. In the blackness gravity lost meaning, and angles were indecipherable. There were no guidelines for balance. Two ice-screw running belays helped me relax. I squeezed around a bulge of ice and saw the outline of the col between the two horns against the night sky. "It's not far now!" I shouted.

Four on one rope move slowly, and it was a long, cold wait, hanging from an ice screw in the darkness. When Guy arrived he belayed Pemba. We imagined the possibility of the sérac wall toppling over and down the South Face and made facetious comments.

"It would be a long ride," said Guy.

"Might make our descent easier if it falls over whilst we're above it," I said.

I took advantage of the security of the anchor and extricated my head torch from my rucksack. The light flooded the ice around us, but beyond it cut a feeble stroke until it was lost in the night. As soon as some slack rope became available, I raced eighty feet to the col, scrambling over the lip on my knees.

"Hey, lads. I'm there!"

21

TSERINGMA

8th – 9th November, 1979

It was a strange, new, horizontal world, a world of white spaciousness, of level snow crusts and wind-curved slabs and distant cliffs, all
expressionless in the flat light of the now rising moon. I walked away
from the edge, towing the rope behind me, staggering drunkenly
through the snow crust and breathing deeply with relief. It was 9.00
p.m. The night was clear. Far away to the south west, beyond dark
ridges, were the flickering lights of a town. But here, in the fringe of
the plateau, there was not a glimpse of rock or living thing.

The wind cut into us, and we were tired. We would have to stay
here for the night. If only we had brought our sleeping bags! We were
standing on a shelf two-hundred-feet-long and a hundred-feet-wide
just beneath the edge of the plateau. We wandered around beneath a
small ice cliff, looking for a sheltered hollow, but the wind eddied
relentlessly around every corner. We started to dig in, but the snow
was hard and progress difficult. The altitude turned our movements
into slow motion in the flat moonlight. Fortunately, where it was level
it was possible to quarry with our axes large flakes of snow two inches
thick to use for walls. As soon as the niche was big enough to fit him,
Pemba slotted in and hunched around the stove to melt some snow.
We had no food, and warm water was the only sustenance we could
hope for. At this altitude, in this cold, without nourishment, we
would soon weaken.

Tim wriggled into the trench, his head near Pemba's feet. Meanwhile, Guy had discovered a narrow crack in the ice wall thirty feet
away, and was excavating a tiny personal hole.

"I thought we were going to dig a big hole and all cram in to keep
each other warm!" I protested. I started lengthening Tim's and
Pemba's trench for myself. Soon Tim had turned it into a semi-
detached. Self-sufficiency had capped the day and that night we could
not be together. We hunched down in our separate, coffin-shaped

244

prisons. Although Pemba, Tim and I were lying head to toe, we could have been miles apart. We were no team now – each of us was imprisoned with his own discomfort, his own thoughts and his own will to survive.

My socks were wet with condensation from my foam inner boots, and I had no spare pair. My feet were soon cold, and I reached down to warm them, whilst trying not to knock down the protective wall of snow behind which I was wedged. The cold spread through my body until my muscles were bound up in a senseless ache. I forced myself to shiver. Outside, spindrift scurried along the shelf, opening up crannies and sifting around me in an icy blast. By three in the morning I knew that I should not stay there.

I retrieved the stove and pan from beside Pemba and built a windbreak of snow around it. Once lit, the flame sputtered ineffectually – but I could not wait. I stumped around, trying to warm up my feet.

Guy appeared. "I haven't dared fall asleep too deeply," he said. "I've been enlarging my hole and dozing a bit."

"Any room for me? My trench is bloody useless."

Guy had excavated a narrow cave. I squeezed in after him with the stove, my back blocking the entrance. We sipped the little water that had melted, and my feet began to tingle with life again, next to the warmth of his limbs. Our heads nodded drowsily until dawn.

"Well, Monsieur Guide, you go first, I'll go at the back – I'm only here as escort anyway." We roused Pemba and Tim from their trenches, and handed them the pan of water.

We all tied on to the rope, and were ready – eager to move out of the freezing shadow of the mountain's threshold, and into the sun.

There were no shadows on the plateau. It opened out into a great, white, unfolded hand offering its snows to sun and wind. No man had touched this vast whiteness since the mountain was born and now, after a long and dangerous journey, we had reached it. Tseringma – the musical name for the white goddess circled in my mind. Pemba had reported some lamas as saying she had already fled to Southern Nepal. Or was she still the mountain? And were we fit to tread here?

The wind gusted across the plateau, plucking up thousands of ice particles in its path, scouring our faces. We held up our gloved hands in front of our eyes and faces as shields against the painful blast. The sun could not chase away the numbing cold. The snow surface was wind-crusted in a slabby pavement that occasionally collapsed under our weight. The angle permitted us to walk, crouching against the wind. Guy selected a cautious, dogleg line of ascent to the summit. It was a weary, trance-like effort with frequent pauses in a long line.

Four of us on the rope caused a chain reaction – whenever one slumped, hands on knees, to gasp for breath, the rope jerked and everyone was quick to snatch the chance of doing the same.

I smelt the fragrance of juniper in the wind. No, it was not an offering from Pemba – but now he was throwing rice into the air. Noises and buzzings filled my sleepless head. The ascetic fasts until his body chemistry produces visions. Hunger, thirst and exhaustion, cold and altitude have strange effects. But sciences and physiology were not all. Only a bold and senseless man would approach a sacred summit with a sneer at superstition.

The mountain was still a deep, serene, purposeful unknown and our last steps were awed and hesitating. The ridge that bounded the edge of the plateau arched upwards and then curved down, without a dramatic declaration of its highest point. We were sated by days of constant tension on ice towers and cornices, and the safety of this gentle summit was a relief. We could stand without fear. We arrived on the ridge a few feet below the top, smiling. We had agreed not to touch the highest snows a long time before. Pemba attached a small Nepalese flag to his ice axe. For want of many words, we shook hands, our defences down.

"Thanks Pete, better than staying in Leysin," said Guy. For a few seconds, his voice was thick with emotion and tears were in his eyes. 'Je suis à 7,000 metres, sur un sommet inviolé!"

The perfect, clear view was a tangible prize that we had won. Peaks rose to greet us on the summit, rotating sentinels in a vast and cloudless panorama. For many days Tseringma had screened this sight from us. The Northern Summit of Gauri Sankar, seen from the side, loomed up as a leaning spire. It was beyond our power to reach it and return. Cho Oyo, Gyachung Kang, Menlungtse, Everest, Lhotse, Makalu were all higher than us, but Menlungtse was the nearest and the loveliest vision of all. A mighty white obelisk of snow and pale pink granite, whose shape matched that of the Matterhorn from the east, Menlungtse harbours the yeti in the wild valleys of its feet, still unclimbed, isolated in the middle of its glacier-filled basin, and guarded by the Tibetan frontier.

The cold dark blue of the sky over the mountains spoke of winter, but to the south west the sky was pale and warm. We stayed on the ridge for fifteen minutes before the wind drove us down.

Surely Tseringma would not let us get away with this? I looked down, from snow to brown rocks, to green forests, to cultivation, to unseen distance. Now we had to descend without an accident. Our line down and across the plateau was straighter than that of the ascent, for now the wind was behind us and we were more confident of the snow conditions. We reached the bivouac site at ten-fifteen, just as the sun was touching the rucksacks we had left there over three and a half hours before.

The ice pitches of the previous night were unrecognisable. The angle had slackened, but the edge of the drop was a near-reality, rather than a dark thought. I went down first, and Tim climbed down at the back with the unprotected task of recovering a rope.

We steeled ourselves against the dizziness of hunger and fatigue. For four and a half hours we descended the ridge, grimly holding on to the idea of safety at the camp, and through this discipline, transcending time, space, fear and suffering. We strung out along the ropes like beads on a broken necklace. The previous day we had pulled up some of the ropes above the camp, and now we gathered together to safeguard each other down the final section.

John congratulated us. He had some soup ready.

"It's the best soup I've had in my life," said Guy.

John had been on the verge of losing hope – we had been out of sight for so long, and the night had been so cold and windy. He had decided that something must have gone wrong. In despair he had written a note to say he was soloing down to try and find help. Then he had seen us, and counted us, coming down.

We had been away two days, and some unknown event was locked up in the heart of that slice of time.

"There was only one thing wrong, John."

"What was that, mate?"

"You weren't there with us."

He could not reply.

22

AUTUMN . . . TO EARTH WITH LOVE

10th – 20th November, 1979

The ordeal was beginning. We had pulled up the ladder and had left it above us. We had not the time or energy to recover it, and to lower it again. A mile of ground lay below, between us and safety, and there was no fixed rope to guide us down. However, the 10th November was clear. Some of our earlier tracks remained. The storms of approaching winter had stayed away. Our bodies cried out for safety, food and rest. We were worn out cars running on 'empty'.

John recorded:

> I don't want to see another ridge like this in my life. We set off at 9.00 a.m. after oversleeping and eating a freeze-dried meal for breakfast (first for a long time, and the last). A long way to descend – we will need all the daylight. Pete and Guy and I move on one rope, with Tim and Pemba behind. I soon realise we are in for an epic. We totter back along the knife-edges of the ridge – if one had slipped he would have taken the other two. Had to concentrate as never before and I kept having waves of nausea. I nearly faint every time my hand touches anything and my knee keeps collapsing on me. Agony for me – I have never been in such pain.

Our lives depended on no one slipping. Guy and I kept on glancing at John, pulling in and letting out coils of rope as we moved; calculating if we could thrust in an emergency ice-axe belay, or if we could jump to the other side of the ridge – should he fall. We acted with unspoken suspicion, as if we were policemen chained to an epileptic on the steep roof of a skyscraper.

"It will be safer if we rope up more closely," said Guy.

"But then all our weight will come on to the cornice at once," I said. "We must spread apart."

Occasionally I slumped to my knees and rested my head upon my ice axe, summoning all my powers of concentration, trying to recover some strength. When we were halfway along the ridge I felt dizzy, and asked Guy to take over in front. There was little room for John and Guy to manoeuvre past.

"Don't you worry," said John. "I won't do anything stupid, I want to give little Joseph a cuddle again."

We strove towards those we had left behind. It was a universal impulse.

We reached Neuschwanstein at mid-day. Guy and Tim had left a half tin of butter, half a pot of marmalade and a small carton of peanut butter. Within a few minutes, we had eaten the lot – neat. The food revived us a little, and we continued the descent.

We had three ropes between five of us, and there were long waits at the anchors. As the afternoon drew on, our initially optimistic sights for the day's end reduced from Base Camp to Advance Camp, and then to the Nid d'Aigle. I went down first, to find the slings I had left in place ten days before. Guy had the nerve-wracking task of climbing down last. The steep ice below the Vire Neithardt was too difficult to climb down, so we lowered two ropes for an abseil. As I slid down, I was preoccupied with finding the next anchor. Without realising, I went past it. I felt the end of the ropes run through my hands. Instinctively, I clenched my grip. The rope ends were within three inches of slipping through the friction device, and I was within a second of falling three thousand feet to the glacier. My mind shrugged off the near miss – nothing had happened. I spotted the nylon sling of the anchor a few feet above me, peeping out of fresh snow, and climbed back up the rope to it.

It grew dark when we were three hundred feet above the fourth rock tower. The wind increased with the night, chilling us until we ached with cold. Myself, Tim, Pemba and John descended a ropelength, down a rock slab.

"I'm going to abseil," shouted Guy. "It's too dangerous to climb down in the dark."

I became angry. "You'll waste too much time," I yelled. I put my rucksack on a ledge and climbed back towards him. "It's easy," I said. Then I felt ashamed. Guy had been taking risks for all of us for many hours. When I joined him he sensed that I had understood his point of view.

"I can't concentrate any more," he said.

"O.K., I've come to relieve you."

As I climbed down, I knocked my ice hammer from its holster. It bounced down into the darkness, clattering and sparking against rocks. The others had descended another ropelength. The wind snatched our shouts, playing with them in its eddies.

"Can I come? Are you ready? Are you all tied off?"

Pemba seemed nearest. "No, O.K." he shouted.

"What? No, or O.K.?"

Shivering with cold and impatience I detached the rope and started down, shouting "Abseil down a double rope." The messages were confused by the wind, and the others had missed an anchor, and only had one rope with them. This they had doubled, dropped over the fourth tower and Tim was abseiling down it.

"But it won't be long enough, Tim. Stop!"

Tim halted on a small ledge, a few feet before he abseiled off the end of the rope. We lowered another one down to him, and he continued to the foot of the tower.

"Pemba, you go first with Tim and start putting the tents up at the camp."

John was next to disappear down the ropes. A few seconds later there was a terrible scream – and then a long silence filled with the dread of our imaginations.

"Oh God – he's fallen, Guy."

Then he replied to our shouts. He had pendulumed, smashing his wrist and yelling with pain.

The darkness was total – the moon was behind the mountain and our headtorch batteries had all died. We crawled the last three hundred feet to the camp on our hands and knees. The rope became snagged, and Guy had to untie and solo along the ridge. "I've just aged two years in twenty minutes," he said when he arrived. It was 9.15 p.m.

Inside the tents, we warmed our frozen feet and sipped water. "He who sleeps, dines," someone said as we closed our eyes.

The next morning, safety was tantalisingly near. We were tempted to abandon caution and to move quickly. However, the mistakes of the previous evening reminded us to descend in a slow, safe routine. At the col in the first gap that had so confused our earlier forages, we were still undecided as to which was the best way to Advance Camp. Pemba soloed over the ridge, to start melting water at the camp. We chose the bottom, longer and easier way.

Ski sticks marked the top of the snow slope, where we had left them two and a half weeks before. Beside them were flags on two marker poles, still wafting prayers to Tseringma for our safety. We had little strength left, and this last slope stretched before us, an agonising eternity. Guy reached the flags first, and detached one of them, to keep it with him.

John arrived at the Vango tent of Advance Camp before I did. He dumped his rucksack and came down the slope towards me, offering to carry mine.

"Do you mean it?" I asked.

"No," he said.

We walked the last few yards to the tent together. Pemba had left Advance Camp before we arrived – yearning for the company of his friends of Base Camp. However, he had left some water and an open can of beer. 'Heldenbrau – fit for heroes' – it was solid with ice, and we held it over the stove until it started fizzing. We lay in the tent for four hours, drinking tea and devouring baked beans and Spam. By late afternoon, we had regained enough strength to continue.

The snow was soft and collapsed under our weight, dragging at our feet. The three-hundred-foot plod up to the Notch was, by common assent, the last piece of climbing we wanted to do for a while. Behind us, the massive backcloth of Gauri Sankar glowed in the sunset. Tim was first over the Notch, and descended to Base Camp alone. I shouted to him, but he only paused, hearing just the noise, not the words.

"He could have waited," I said. "After all that time up there it would have been good to go down together."

"I just don't understand him," said John. "When I was his age this sunset would have moved me to tears."

"Oh laissez-faire," said Guy. "It will come, in time."

As we moved over the ridge, the snow yielded beneath the gravity of our downwards steps, no longer hindering us. We strolled down the glacier, breathing deeply and looking around. Now Gauri Sankar was hidden, a remembered presence behind our backs. Our impassive observer for many weeks, the great spire of Choba Bhamare stood black against the dark sky. And then the slope curved away below us, and we saw the tents and prayer flags, copper in the last light, as if burning with inner flames. We paused. These were last moments, tinged with regret – never to be forgotten or taken away. The evening's shadows grew dark and cool.

The Base Camp team came to the toe of the glacier, to greet us wreathed in smiles. John's right hand at least could join in the flurry of shaking.

"Ang Rinzi, me old codger – a face of a thousand stories! Fantastic, a brew. I'll never forget your cups of tea, Ang Rinzi. Good evening Lieutenant; Dawa, you old drunkard. How about a nosh, been munching painkillers for days – distinctly lacking in calories. Pemba Sherpa, say some prayers of thanks for us; Jetha, you winged messenger – where's the letters?"

We were enveloped in warmth and affection. It was an overwhelming evening, a hectic relocation into a world of food, people, and safety, and the first opening of the door to the life we had left behind. Over the previous days our stomachs had shrunk and we were soon bloated with food and cups of tea. Nevertheless, it felt as if we had more to eat and drink that night than during the whole of the previous week. We had climbed the mountain in a single attempt, and there had been no chance of recovery in between tries, as there had been on Kangchenjunga. We had become worn out gradually. Food, initially planned for four people for fifteen to eighteen days, had eventually been stretched to feed five people for twenty-three days.

Harbouring private thoughts, we hunched around a guttering candle, quickly scanning our letters for news – good or bad. A telex message in a sealed envelope made my heart jump – no, it was all right, it was a greeting from a friend. At first view, my news was reassuring – but of the time-lapse since the letters were last sent I knew nothing. Early in the morning Jetha would leave with news of our success, and Pemba Sherpa would descend to recruit porters from Lamobagar.

"I must write a report now to the Ministry," said Sankar. "What are the heights of your camps and the dates you reached them? How high is the South Summit?"

The Scheider map had disappeared in the darkness and confusion, so we guessed the answers. It was 1.00 a.m. when I finished writing letters, and much later when my thoughts stopped spinning.

Sleep had carried me elsewhere when at dawn a gust of wind shook the tent, touching my feet like moving ground. I woke with a start, thinking the camp-site was collapsing and we were being blown off the ridge – and then relaxed. The tense, rigorous safety code of high camps, of belays, tie-offs, insulation and measured movements could be forgotten. No, that was not a cornice creaking – Ang Rinzi was making tea, cups of tea unlimited! It was marvellous to be waited on and to get up late. My swollen lips and my eyelids were stuck together. Numb toes – the bivouac; scratched hands – the night-time ice pitch; my body reminded me where I had been. Smelly body, lank hair, piles, dirty clothing, the dank taste of unwashed teeth, all re-emerged after a long exile in the sterility and singlemindedness of high altitude. Body and mind were different up there.

"This is the best Monday morning of my life," said Guy.

Porridge for breakfast, jam and chapattis for lunch, noodles and sauces for supper, hunks of cheese, fruit cake – the food slid down and we remembered the sensation of taste.

"We must have been really dehydrated up there," I said. "I've drunk about twelve pints of tea since we came down, but I've only peed three or four times.

"Where's the wumpum?" asked John.

"Dawa says it's evaporated."

"Sure, probably in his breath."

Pemba was humming with happiness. He and Dawa finished the cigarettes and made little wooden pipes to smoke Guy's tobacco. He washed John's hair for him, and cleaned his boots. "Now your shoe is smiling too," he said when he had finished.

We had returned to music, and the cassette player was turned on all day. The breeze wafted snatches of music and song around the camp, filling our heads with associated thoughts of home and drawing us into ourselves. We were vulnerable.

Alone in my tent, I read and re-read the letters, slowly.

The struggle on the mountain, although it had affected me profoundly, was self-indulgent and superficial compared to my father's illness, and its effect on him. He had written to me from hospital:

> I suppose everyone reacts differently to a sudden onslaught of illness. I have become sharply aware of the stupidity of previous preoccupations with petty and trivial aspects of life. I am trying to relax and put myself completely into God's hands, as he works through the skill of the people who are looking after me here, and who are praying for me in the most wonderful and loving way.

I wrote in my diary, carefully:

> Human beings can adjust to almost any conditions. Or from a distance, they can appear to have quickly adjusted. The threat or realisation of death guides the mind away from minor concerns to the clarity of religion, strengthening what has always been there.

The recuperative pause was short-lived. The sudden squalls, restrained by the stability of the late summer, at last broke completely free. During the night the wind changed to a hollow, monotone, roaring ceaselessly with the confidence of a newly designed express train. In the early hours Ang Rinzi abandoned the cooking shelter as it collapsed. The Nepalese flag was torn away, never to be seen again.

"That was the Base Camp Closing Ceremony," said Sankar.

The porters trickled in and out of Base Camp with their loads after mid-day on the 15th November. Below the rocks we walked on to the cushioning grass, our eyes watering after long exposure to the throb of sunlight on snow. Had it, I wondered, been a year's exposure, and this the only true return?

The noise of the wind that we had left, plucking the mountain high above us, stayed in our heads for many hours, emphasising the contrasting peace and patience of the forest. Slowly, the forest grew in our senses. We stopped for the night, stretching luxuriantly beside a warm fire, smelling the vegetation and the woodsmoke and watching the light flicker on dark, still clumps.

The night's coating of ice on the ground soon melted in the warm morning air. On the mountain we had wound ourselves up beyond minor aches and pains, but now that we were below the itch contour, the jolting of the descent re-aroused them to their restless work. Slipping and sliding from tree to tree, our weak, sticklike frames tottered down, to a polyphony of insects.

The ancient route of trade along the Rongshar was, after the jungle and untracked mountain, like the broad swathe of a Sunday afternoon path through an English wood.

We arrived at Lamobagar at the same time as the fresh early light spread across the flat level ground of the village. Children and old people glanced at us briefly.

Sankar strayed behind us, to change and groom himself in the bushes before the arrival at the police post. His high spirits mirrored those of Mohan after Kangchenjunga.

"You look a bit less glossy than when we were at the last party here, John."

"You don't look exactly unwrinkled yourself, mate."

We drank rakshi, relieved to hear that the news of our success had been radioed out five days before. We changed our porters to the lightly-clad Tamangs of the lower hills.

Baskets of oranges coming up the trail were signposts to the fertile south. We rolled the fruit around our mouths. A Tibetan girl accompanied us on the trail. For her, the long trek from the bleak plateau of her homeland to this abundance was a journey to paradise.

In the evening we sipped bowls of fizzy, fruity chang, and ate yams – the first sweet potatoes I had tasted since New Guinea. We soon chewed up a tough old chicken. However, John wished it had not developed its muscles by running to us from Kathmandu first. The joke was too much for Dawa, who was already wobbly with chang and he tripped over the fire. Ang Rinzi fielded him, explaining loyally, "Too much oxygen for Dawa down here, Captain."

The sun never became hot in those golden autumn days. In the morning it moved up in a slant and in the afternoon it declined, always low in the sky, reaching us only for a while, even as the valley widened. The river was lower and the leeches had shrivelled away into hiding. A white shrouded corpse was carried down to the water, for the ritual cleaning before cremation. Goats and buffalo passed us on the trail. An occasional light breeze filled the air with flying leaves. Fields whispered drily. Everywhere people were at work, goitred women and little children, harvesting the winter's grain with sickles and storing it high on platforms in trees and on poles.

Next day Jetha rushed along the path towards us with mail from Kathmandu. It was good to hear his squeaky, funny voice – to shake him by the hand. He had been so reliable on this trip when communications had mattered so much. We sat in a sunlit spot beside harvested fields, and read our letters – my last one was Hilary's, posted on the 9th November, our summit day. She had spent spring and autumn, the two most beautiful seasons, alone, and described them to me.

One minute at a time, the days grew shorter. We camped at Pikhutu, a beautiful site remembered for a warm swim, and a dying, scalded baby in a primitive world. But the baby had not died, said the people of the hamlet. The family had passed through the village on their way back to their home. We had just missed them. Their departure and return had coincided with ours, to the very day. The baby was healed.

We had come the full circle. Our thoughts warmed to the baby. For the cost of eight pounds we had saved his life. We glowed with self-righteousness, for here was palpable evidence that our expedition was justified. But beneath that glow was awe and humility. It was the baby that had done the surviving – he had found the capacity to cling to life through a long, rough journey, and to struggle back to health from the edge of death.

The following day we climbed out of the valley, leaving the river, a thread of blue below us, stretching into the foothills. At the village Charikot, the syncopated rhythm of drums throbbed in the evening air.

"Is it another festival, Pemba?"

"No, Sir, the bank is having a party. Oh yes – and one thing, the people here, they say, we are not Gauri Sankar expedition, we are too small, we are trekking group." Climbers and Sherpas all chuckled at the joke.

Gauri Sankar hovered, burnished by the sunset, above the grey twilight struts of its foundations. A cloud drifted between its two summits.

23

WINTER

20th – 30th November, 1979

The aeroplane banked towards the west. In the space of a single eyespan, I saw them, from Dhaulagiri to Kangchenjunga – the snows of the Himalayas, the silvery line that dances on the edge of the world. Six times in seven years I had arrived, climbed in this range and departed. Now the geography was becoming clear, my knowledge becoming connected and I was seeing the relation of these mountains to each other. During those seven years, my eyes had seen east and west, from the stepping-stones of summits, for fifteen hundred miles. With each new view, the pattern had grown inside me. Now the framework was there, and I would spend a lifetime filling in the gaps. These mountains would always be part of my life.

There was a Buddhist saying: 'Fashion your life from a chain of deeds, like a garland is fashioned from a chain of flowers.' And here was a chain of sunlit mountains above a sea of cloud.

We folded up the white scarves, and ate the oranges that the Sherpas had given to us as parting good-luck gifts at the airport. The expedition was under control. We had paid the wages and debts, the journey home was organised, thank-you postcards sent, the expedition report written, and I had even had a haircut. The surface of my mind could become calm, and something far deeper could rise up. I brooded quietly, away from the others.

Will he die? Will he die whilst I am away? Should I go? I now knew the answer to the first question. Beneath my seat was a sheaf of letters. Before they had known I was safe and returning, brave letters from my mother and Hilary had been open to an optimistic interpretation, they had told me to get on with climbing the mountain, not to worry. On the mountain I had tried to bury uncomfortable, distracting truths.

Then, in Kathmandu, I had opened a recent letter from Hilary, telling me to stay in England on my return, to help my mother shoulder the fearful responsibility of caring for someone so ill, after she had been alone so long. My mother was worried that I would not be prepared to see the deterioration in my father's condition. The realisation that he would die became suddenly conscious. I re-read early letters, seeing clearly what was guarded, how much they had hidden from me, and how much I had chosen to ignore.

In England, it rained for four days. The trees had long since let go their leaves to the winter. Each evening my mother and I drove through the wet, lamplit streets to the hospital in Manchester.

His face was thin and pointed and his teeth bared in craving for life, yet he was quiet and detached, as if halfway to the quietness that awaited him. He smiled often, reassuringly. Only his eyes were sad, but there was no fear of death in them, only a sadness at seeing his future no longer projected in a world with us – a world he knew he would miss. Fear was a terrible journey, but with sorrow he had at least arrived. We talked of little things, his car, the weather. I looked into his eyes, happy to have survived, to be there. Many things went unsaid, except in our eyes. I tried to think like the mountain, like the earth, and they helped me to balance and stand, fortifying me with their peace. I was supported by the steady weight of the whole journey behind me. The night before he died I showed him a colour poster of Kangchenjunga. "That's lovely, beautiful," he said.

Some words are worn down by time to their simplest sense; 'At one with the world.' 'In loving memory.' My mother, brother and I soon found out that though the loss was personal, it was not private. Our emotions were shared, and my mother had not been and would not be alone. My father had known this when he wrote in his last letter: "It really has been wonderful to receive such a sustained love and concern . . . this love is what will endure and be everlasting."

I flew to Switzerland for the weekend, to see Hilary and to collect my things for a stay in England. There was fog at Geneva and the take-off was delayed. I had time to think, to come to terms with my father's death. Why him? Why us? I needed to have known him better. Grief would persist, an old wound that would never heal, that would always re-open. But then, why not him? Everyone, at some time, would have to endure the finality of pain and suffering – starting with those around you, and then with those nearest you, and ending with yourself. At first, my father's death had seemed so special, uniquely affecting my family and those around. Yet bereavement and death were common experiences which everyone must go through. Life could not be trusted unless peace was made with death; until life's impermanence and imperfection was accepted, and that acceptance allowed to heal.

The aeroplane took off, climbing steadily through a barrier of turbulent cloud.

I, a mountaineer, in the Dionysian fervour of my high youth, intoxicated with my talents, had climbed mountain after mountain, pushing the limits of my skill, vanquishing death in a series of false victories. However, although I had seen death before, I now saw it as a personal fact, for the first time. I realised there was no sense in rushing. There was no hurry. There was no mathematical progression in always climbing harder routes and higher summits. There was no need to try to fight death off, by shrinking from the fact and acting as if it did not exist, did not affect me. I had learnt about motion, but now had much to learn about stillness. I would find a trusting pace that suited my life and the mountains. I was calm.

The pilot had a sense of humour: "Ladies and Gentlemen, as I have explained to you before, there are problems in Geneva owing to ground fog. I have now heard from the control there, that we cannot land. We have been diverted to Zurich. I apologise for this. Arrangements are being made to carry you onwards from there to your destinations. However, we have a consolation in that the Alps are above the cloud. Now our journey is a little longer, you will see more of them."

I was already looking out of the window. Mont Blanc, the Grandes Jorasses, the Dru, the Aiguille de Tour and, yes, the distant Matterhorn, were tranquil in the winter sunshine. I loved them, but not with the trembling shock of first love – that could only recur in echoes and finer shades. But I knew them better. I respected them deeply, understood them a little, and loved them more tenderly. It was the last day of November.

EVEREST THE CRUEL WAY

Joe Tasker

Contents

Acknowledgements

This is a personal account of the British Everest Winter expedition. There are as many different facets to the story as there were people on the expedition. However, in putting together this account, I received substantial contributions from Brian Hall, Allen Jewhurst, Paul Nunn, John Porter, Pete Thexton and Mike Shrimpton. I am indebted to Christopher Falkus of Eyre Methuen and George Greenfield of John Farquharson for their enthusiasm and Ann Mansbridge for her painstaking editorial work and rigorous discipline which kept me to a tight schedule. To my colleagues who made it possible to complete the book in the time available, and to Jill Hield who typed the manuscript with most helpful speed and efficiency, I owe a particular debt of gratitude.

Bass Ltd, New Era Laboratories, the 3Ms, the Mount Everest Foundation and the British Mountaineering Council all provided financial support and many companies, particularly Mountain Equipment and Berghaus, provided material support, all of which made the expedition possible in the first place. To these, and to the team above all, I owe thanks for the experience about which the book is written.

CHAPTER ONE

A Step Further

Everest has a magic which cannot be explained away. To the general public it is perhaps the only mountain which it is even partly comprehensible to want to climb. To a mountaineer, involvement with Everest can become obsessional. Our attempt to climb the mountain by its most difficult route, at the worst time of the year and without oxygen was the furthest point yet reached in the long history of Everest and in the story of a climber's need to explore the limits of what is possible.

After a chequered history of mistaken assertions regarding height and misnomers, the mountain we now know as Mount Everest or Sagarmatha became recognized in 1849 as the highest mountain in the world with a definitive height of 29,028 feet. It was seventy-two years after this that the first expedition to Everest was mounted. It took another thirty-two years before the summit was reached.

The first ascent in 1953 by Ed Hillary and Tenzing Norgay, as part of the team led by John Hunt, was a turning-point in world mountaineering. Whatever controversy was to arise subsequently regarding the use of oxygen and size of expedition, the mountain which had defied all attempts for three decades was finally climbed and new vistas of what was possible in mountaineering were opened up.

It was ten years before the next major step forward on Everest took place. The American expedition under the leadership of Norman Dyhrenfurth succeeded in climbing the mountain by two routes. The South Col route was ascended in a conventional manner but Tom Hornbein and Willi Unsoeld made the audacious first ascent of the West Ridge from the Western Cwm and, abandoning their camps on the West Ridge, went over the top to descend the South-East Ridge in what is still regarded as one of the most committed and impressive achievements on the mountain. This ascent marked a switch away from a simple repetition of the established South Col route and a focusing of attention on more difficult and uncertain ways of reaching the top.

Each generation has to find and test its own limits; this is the only way of maintaining the vigour and intrinsic interest of the sport. The next problem on Everest to preoccupy mountaineers was the ascent of the difficult South-West Face. Only after many attempts by large and very strong expeditions was this problem finally solved in 1975 by Chris Bonington's team. This expedition aroused, in its turn, much controversy beforehand for the futility of the exercise and the cost involved. Success silenced the critics and in retrospect it can be seen that not only did the expedition promote general public interest in mountaineering in this country, with positive benefits for many climbers, but it also liberated the climbing world from preoccupation with this one problem and gave credence to the pursuit of other improbable goals.

Thereafter the pace of exploration on the mountain increased. In 1978 Reinhold Messner, Peter Habeler and Hans Engel repeated the original route on the mountain but without the use of supplementary oxygen. They descended without any obvious, lasting ill-effects, and thus definitively demonstrated the feasibility of climbing any mountain in the world without oxygen. Mountaineers could now concentrate on finding the most demanding way of climbing a mountain rather than on how to transport great weights of oxygen equipment up to a certain point in order to guarantee success. At its most satisfying, mountaineering does not need the certainty of success, it needs a worthwhile objective reached against all the odds. The ascent of Everest without oxygen gave new life to the sport.

In 1979/80 the Poles, with their usual knack for choosing a formidable and punishing objective, were the first to mount an expedition to climb Everest in winter. After a long siege, they succeeded in climbing the original route, basing their tactics on their experiences on Lhotse in the winter of 1974/75. During that attempt they had experienced such savage weather conditions, cold, wind and snow, that they had felt that without life-giving oxygen support they would not even have been able to breathe. Officially their ascent of Everest is not recognized as a winter ascent by the Nepalese government as they actually reached the summit after the formal end of the season which, in Nepal, is held to be from the beginning of December to the end of January.

This is a very short season considering how much longer the climbing takes in winter due to the demoralizing effect of the intense cold and, in the context of the Polish expedition, calendar dates count for little in classifying what is and what is not winter. There is no doubt that for the major part of their expedition the Poles were on the mountain in very 'wintry' weather.

1980 saw the stunning achievement of Reinhold Messner in climbing Everest on his own, without oxygen. Far from being exhausted, Everest was continuing to be the setting for revolutionary advances in mountaineering.

It does not take research to find something which is the 'next great problem' to tackle. We benefit from and profit by the achievements of others; it is as if a particular exploit passes into the experience of mountaineers as a whole and everyone's horizons are widened so that we see what is the next logical step to take. For the small team of us who formed ourselves together during 1979 and 1980, it seemed the most obvious thing in the world that we should now look to an ascent of Everest during winter, by its most difficult route and without oxygen. To any one of the many people who were to ask 'Why?' in the months preceding our departure, the only reply possible was: 'Because it is hard and because it is uncertain.'

We never achieve mastery over the mountains; the mountains are never conquered; they will always remain and sometimes they will take away our friends if not ourselves. The climbing game is a folly, taken more or less seriously, an indulgence in an activity which is of no demonstrable benefit to anyone. It used to be that mountaineers sought to give credence to their wish to climb mountains by concealing their aims behind a shield of scientific research. But no more. It is now accepted, though not understood, that people are going to climb for its own sake.

The reasons people climb are diverse, ranging from a simple satisfaction at physical exercise to a single-minded need to find ever harder and more punishing problems to solve. The central theme is one of testing the self to a greater or lesser extent at whatever level of the game we choose to play it. In the sense that it is unnecessary to play this game at all, climbing is a useless activity; in the context of discovering oneself, testing the limits of one's ability, exploring the boundaries of fear, determination and endurance, climbing is a means of self-fulfilment and a source of great satisfaction. The other delights of climbing as a way of life, the enjoyment of an outdoor environment, the simplicity of expedition life, the pleasure at being physically completely fit, are all bonuses beside this central theme.

For Reinhold Messner, the urge to test his own personal frontiers drove him to climb the 26,660-foot-high Nanga Parbat on his own. The same quest was to inspire the small group of eight of us to make plans to attempt Everest in the cruellest conditions imaginable, in winter.

CHAPTER TWO

The Idea and the Team

The thought of climbing Everest in winter had never entered my head. I had once finished an article on trends in mountaineering by mentioning the untapped potential of the Himalayas in winter, but my mind was occupied with other projects. In early 1979, with Pete Boardman and Doug Scott, I had climbed the third highest mountain in the world, Kangchenjunga, 28,208 feet, by a new route and for the first time without the use of oxygen equipment. Subsequently my thoughts were taken up with the return to K2, 28,253 feet, the world's second highest mountain. In 1978 a team of eight of us had attempted to climb the difficult West Ridge, but we had retreated and abandoned the climb when our companion, Nick Estcourt, was swept to his death from 22,000 feet in an avalanche. In spite of the traumatic memories this mountain held for us, there remained the compulsion to climb it and a team of four of us planned a new attempt for 1980.

My days were filled, when back in Britain between expeditions, with a crazy mixture of ceaseless telephone calls, occupation with running a climbing equipment shop and endless preparations for the next expedition. Into my shop, the Magic Mountain, one day in the autumn of 1979 came Chris Bonington and Brian Hall, ostensibly shopping for gear of which Chris, after two-and-a-half decades of climbing, still does not seem to have enough. With Chris out of earshot, Brian quietly asked if I was doing anything during the winter of 1981/82 and, if not, would I be interested in going to Everest with a small group of people, which he and

Alan Rouse were organizing, to climb the West Ridge.

Inevitably Chris Bonington's name is associated with Mount Everest, but he is representative of an older generation, with a more traditional approach to expeditions, having a formal leadership and hierarchical structure of command and organization. By waiting until he was out of range of hearing, Brian was letting me know that he did not want Chris to know anything about the project. It was a non-verbal communication of the intention to form an expedition more along the lines of the successful expeditions we ourselves had grown accustomed to, lightweight in logistics, small-scale in terms of numbers and democratic in organization.

Usually I have been involved with the planning of an expedition right from the start, or had a reasonable idea of the possibility of being invited. This invitation, however, came completely without warning. I had a moment in which to give a reply – Brian was getting a lift to the Lake District with Chris, who was in a hurry. I had a sensation of giddiness as the beauty of the idea, the breathtaking audacity of such a suggestion, hit me and at the same time a rapid vision of all the impossibilities – work involvements, lack of money, lack of time, personal relationships – the traditional dilemma of the climber, the conflict between his career, social life, love life, security and the fulfilment which comes from the all-absorbing commitment to some heady project. I gave Brian a quick 'yes' and agreed to speak with him later. A few days later I received from Chamonix a letter from Alan Rouse with details of their plans and a typed list, with my name and address already on it, of the eight members of the expedition. My consent had been taken for granted; asking was simply a formality!

The winter of 1981/82 seemed suitably far off, almost two-and-a-half years away, and I could comfortably shelve the idea until nearer the time. In the last eighteen months I had been away on three expeditions – nine months in total, hardly leaving myself time to unpack from one trip before re-packing for the next. My shop was being run on a chaotic basis, the days just not being long enough for all that there was to do, and I relied heavily upon the invaluable work of the shop's manager, Alf. There had already been one casualty in my private life as a result of my absence abroad, when I came back from the second expedition in six months, with a six-week period at home between the two trips, to find that my girlfriend had decided she had had enough of associating with someone whom she only saw every few months.

I was returning to K2 in the spring of 1980 and after that I planned to spend some time at home to concentrate on work and generally getting my affairs into some sort of order. A longish spell at home seemed very desirable, with even the possibility of finding the leisure to do some rock climbing which expeditions preclude. At the end of that spell was the enthralling prospect of Everest in winter, which I had not focused on clearly but which in the back of my mind I knew was the next logical step for me.

Some months after I was first invited we learnt that the winter period of 1981/82 was not available to us, making our options 1980/81 or some date five years hence. Suddenly the leisured approach to Everest vanished – a hard decision had to be made. The later date was hardly worth considering, for by then the route may well have been climbed, taking away some of the unknown element. The 1980/81 date, less than twelve months away, was a little too close and we would be hard pressed to raise the money and organize the equipment for then. For my part I was already committed to an expedition to K2 which, all being well, I would only be back from three months before going away again. Life was going a little too fast. It seemed clear that 1980/81 was the only sensible choice and, faced with a decision, I realized that it was all-important for me to go on the Everest winter expedition because it promised to be extremely hard, and improbable, the finest challenge in the sport that I could conceive of. It was so obviously the next logical step forward in mountaineering, to climb in the Himalayas in winter, that I felt the idea had been part of my consciousness for years. Come what may, I decided to go.

The team was to be made up of a small group of friends, most of whom had climbed together for a number of years. The birth of the original, daring idea was due to Alan Rouse and Brian Hall, who had taken part in a bold, lightweight ascent of the 25,300-foot Jannu in eastern Nepal. Both Alan and Brian had climbed all over the world with first ascents and impressive repeats to their credit, particularly in South America where they had spent many months. They had used their worldwide experience to start a guiding service which had the whole world as its territory.

Alan, in the early 1970s, had been representative of a volatile new generation of rock climbers. Whilst still in his early teens, endowed with a fine natural ability which was belied by his studious air of abstraction, he was instrumental in setting a new trend in climbing with the boldness of some of his ascents. Unusually for someone who excelled in one facet of the sport, he began to transfer his attention to the bigger mountains, disclosing a drive and imagination beneath the deliberately cultivated exterior of a person dedicated to enjoyment and anarchy. He seemed a complex character, able to engage in the most serious of discussions and gain the respect of people from all walks of life, yet sometimes finding himself inexplicably involved in the most outrageous of escapades. Whatever he embarked upon, he wanted to go to the limit with it. He had studied mathematics at Cambridge and one sometimes got the impression that he tolerated, good naturedly, conversations on any subject but that his mind was flying along at a rapid pace and that he could assimilate concepts and spit out answers with the speed of a computer. Attacking Everest in winter was an astonishing idea but it was typical of Alan's cheek that he should have come up with it.

For a number of years, Brian and Alan had been close friends, Brian providing a sound, organizational sense to counterbalance Alan's prolific ideas. There was a contradiction in Brian in that he had acquired a reputation for outlandish, wild behaviour but when he turned his attention to organizing such a thing as an expedition, he displayed unsuspected responsibility and a forceful persuasiveness which ensured that his side of a job was always completed.

Alan and Brian had climbed in South America with the Burgess twins, Aldrian and Alan, two of the climbing world's most colourful characters. Identical twins, tall, broad and blond, of Viking descent, seeming to have inherited their forebears' predilection for rape and pillage, they are known as strong and resourceful mountaineers, specializing in survival. Alan Rouse used to say of them that they were the best people he had ever met as companions on a mountain. They were an automatic choice.

Paul Nunn is a prominent figure in mountaineering, not least for his infectious laugh which accompanies each tale from his vast repertoire of anecdotes and tall stories. Paul has been an established figure in climbing since many of us could remember. There is a restless energy about Paul which sends him off every year to some part of the world on a filming, if not a climbing, assignment, and the same restlessness, the same determination not to miss anything that might happen, keeps him up till all hours of the night to be the last one to leave a pub or party. He has an endless capacity for conversing on any topic imaginable and a wry scepticism about life in general. Paul, without being overweight, is a solid bulk. His massive hands wrapped round a mug of beer seem to demonstrate a strength of personality as well as of physique. His experience over many years covers most of Europe, the Pamirs, the Caucasus, the Karakorum and the Indian Himalayas. As a lecturer in Economic History, he has a respectability that many of us lacked, and Alan asked him along on account of his solid background as a mountaineer as well as his potential for raising sponsorship from local firms to whom he was well known.

Pete Thexton was asked to come as the doctor, but his unpublicized record of achievement in the Himalayan regions of Kulu and Garwhal hinted at a quiet determination and hidden strength. Physically Pete appeared small, but he was stocky and strong. He is one of those people who change in appearance each time one looks at them, leaving the impression that they have been totally underestimated. He was least known of all the team to any of the members but on paper, at least, if there was going to be anyone as doctor, Pete was as well qualified as any doctor we knew to appreciate the medical problems of high altitude and also take part in the expedition as a full climbing member. To an ambitious climber, though, the added burden of ministering to the sick was a potentially frustrating responsibility.

John Porter, half-American, half-English, lives in an out-of-the-way town on the west side of the Lake District. One of the mystery men of the climbing scene, appearing periodically to go off on an expedition, usually with Polish climbers, and achieving a high reputation for his persistence and ability, he had climbed in the Hindu Kush, in India, and South America.

If Alan Rouse was of a scientific temperament, John was of an artistic one, with all that that entails of vague dreaminess, and the ability to reproduce the apt quotation. He always has a puzzled air and the resigned acceptance of a person who does not capitalize on his opportunities because he is too preoccupied with more abstract thoughts to be concerned with the practicalities of life.

I had not climbed with any of the members of the team, except for a rock route in North Wales once with Brian, but I lived close to most of them and saw them frequently on social occasions. I can only presume from this that in selecting a team, Alan and Brian felt that I would be able to integrate successfully with everyone else.

Expeditions can be so arduous, the members living in such close proximity to each other, that it is vital to have a group of people who are able to get on with each other and work together. It is not essential that the team be made up of close friends; friendship and the ability to work together do not necessarily coincide. The bond which is formed by members of an expedition who have worked and struggled together goes beyond friendship, it is more akin to the relationship with a brother whom one knows intimately and accepts for all his faults as well as his good points and virtues.

I was interested at the prospect of forging the strong bonds of new friendship with seven people whom I knew and liked, and whose achievements I admired, but cautious too at the potential for discord that was contained in an enterprise which would throw us all together, for a long spell, under the most trying conditions.

1980 was a hectic year. We were faced with the problem of amassing the equipment and money for the winter expedition a full twelve months sooner than we had expected. Had it been another pre- or post-monsoon expedition it would not have been so much of a problem. The winter in the Himalayas, however, was a largely unexplored period for climbing and, from what little information we could gather, conditions would be much more unforgiving than at any other time of year. Our preparations would have to be rigorous and our equipment, as far as we could ensure, faultless.

The history of winter climbing in the Himalayas is very brief. The arrival of winter was generally felt to mark the end of the climbing season, as with the British attempt on the South-West Face of Everest in 1972. After nearly two months of continual effort, by the middle of November the lead climbers were moving to establish their top camp close to the rock band. On reaching the site for Camp 6, it was impossible to pitch a tent in the prevailing wind and climbing on the Rock Band above was also out of the question. Dougal Haston looked round the corner of the buttress onto what had been regarded as an escape route, an easier option of reaching the summit, to find that in such wind there were no easy options. Without his oxygen mask he felt that he would not have been able to breathe.

They had gone to their limit and, although success had eluded them, they had the inner satisfaction of knowing that it was through no weakness on their part that they had not made it. This was the start of winter, and as John Hunt was to say of the expedition later, 'No one who has experienced the appalling conditions prevailing at high altitude in the Himalayan winter can doubt that Bonington's team stopped in their tracks at the ultimate limit of human achievement imposed for the time being, by natural forces.'

In winter the 'jet-stream', the high winds which blow at anything up to 130 knots, usually at altitudes of around 35,000 feet, drop to lower altitudes, taking in the upper reaches of the Himalayan peaks. Little is known about wind behaviour on the mountains in winter but the widest-held belief was that above 25,000 feet a mountain was taking the full force of the jet-stream, and severe disturbance due to turbulence would be felt below that.

It was into this jet-stream that Haston, Scott, MacInnes and Burke climbed on that November day in 1972, and against which they realized it was impossible to make any progress. Meanwhile, emphasizing the contrasts of winter, Jimmy Roberts was sitting on the hillside of Kalipatar at 19,000 feet, watching the lead climbers through binoculars. Comfortable under a hot sun in a clear sky, he could not understand the reasons for the retreat.

He could only see the tiny figures moving up or down; he could not tell that the temperature was perhaps −30 °C to −40 °C, nor that the wind was gusting at 100 mph. The coming winter was a deceptive time of extremes.

Polish climbers, somehow setting their own standards outside the mainstream of the climbing world, were the ones who applied themselves directly to the problems of climbing in winter in the Himalayas. The performance of Polish climbers has long given cause for astonishment. They seem to have an aptitude for choosing bold, dangerous climbs which are often completed under duress and against great hardship. It seems fitting that it was the Poles who were the first to step into this punishing arena with their winter ascent of Noshaq, a 24,580-foot-high peak in the Hindu Kush, during January/February 1973.

They were well prepared in some ways, and learnt much during the expedition. They experimented with ointments as protection against the cold; they described the winds as being of hurricane force and temperatures ranging between −25 °C to −50 °C at night. With tents ruined by the winds and themselves worn out with fighting against them, they had given up hope of reaching the summit when they were blessed with a spell of fine, calm weather and reached the summit on the night of 13 February.

Some members suffered from frostbite but the expedition was an outstanding success. Already, on the way home from that achievement, they started planning their next winter expedition for 1974/75, only this time to Lhotse, 27,923 feet high, the fourth highest peak in the world.

There they met the same harrowing conditions as on Noshaq. Three members had to return to Kathmandu due to illness and their inability to recover in the hostile climate of Base Camp. The rest fought a two-month-long battle against the wind and cold, finally being driven back only a few hundred feet below the summit by the unheralded arrival of a vicious storm. Without oxygen masks, like Dougal Haston, they felt that they would not have been able to breathe in the wind-driven snow. Their permit for the mountain expired on 31 December and, although they had come prepared for a long siege lasting until March, they had to withdraw or risk a total ban on their climbing in Nepal for a number of years.

From these few sources of information on winter mountaineering we were able to cull only an overall impression of an extremely bleak and hostile environment where daily existence was totally concerned with survival, leaving little chance of relaxation. Success seemed improbable, and if achieved it would only be through extraordinary hardship and persistence.

For me, once the dream had taken possession there was no other way; for friends and climbing colleagues, from the security of their own, more sane, future plans, the West Ridge of Everest in winter was a gruelling fantasy for which they expressed pity rather than admiration.

Early in 1980 we heard that the same team of Polish climbers had succeeded in climbing the South Col route up Everest on 17 February. They had applied the knowledge gained on the two previous expeditions to Noshaq and Lhotse, taken oxygen to assist them against the dreadful cold and winds, and through persistence against the most severe storms, finally reached the top.

The South Col route is the way the mountain was originally climbed and the way it has been climbed most often since. Sometimes it is disparagingly called 'The Yak Route', indicating its lack of technical difficulty and illustrating the stories of some expeditions only reaching the summit because the members are pushed or pulled up the route by their Sherpas, in much the same manner as the Sherpas treat their Yaks, the local beasts of burden. However, in winter there is no easy way up Everest, or indeed up any mountain.

Once again the Poles were caught in the skeins of bureaucracy in that the permission to climb Everest only came through to them in December, so they were half-way through the winter before they reached Base Camp. The official definition of the winter season by the Nepalese Ministry of Tourism is from 1 December to 31 January. This left the Poles little time to complete their ascent. An extension was allowed to 15 February, and a further extension requested. A couple of extra days were allowed but not the full length of time desired. It was a fitting reward for their determination that the Poles reached the summit on the last day that they were allowed to climb upwards.

Due to the arbitrary definition of the 'winter season' there was some doubt cast upon their claim to have climbed Everest in winter, as the date on which the summit was reached officially fell outside the dates defining winter. Consequently, in official terms Everest was still unclimbed in winter.

Mountaineers have long grown accustomed to the rules governing expeditions to the Himalayas but it comes as a surprise to many people that to be allowed to attempt to climb a peak in any of the Himalayan countries one has to 'book' it, and pay a fee ranging from £50 to £60 for modest peaks of around 20,000 feet to approximately £1,000 for the giants of Everest or K2. This is only the first step towards the mountain. One has to agree to abide by all the rules governing behaviour during the expedition, whether it be not photographing strategic bridges or only climbing between the fixed dates of the season allotted.

To citizens of a country which has not been invaded for a thousand years, such sensitivity over border security is incomprehensible. To people who are accustomed to wandering over their own hills and those of neighbouring countries at will, charging a fee to climb a mountain seems ludicrous. The Himalayas, however, mark a natural frontier which spans some of the most sensitive borders in the world. Periodically, in times of confrontation, whole mountain areas are put out of bounds, and only gradually, as international relations ease, are foreigners allowed back into the mountain regions, and only then when hedged about by regulations and accompanied by a government-appointed officer.

We would, of course, think nothing of it if we heard the fee charged for booking Wembley Stadium. It might be objected that this took some building and the fee is therefore justified, but we also have natural resources which we are prepared to pay for, whether it be underground caverns or stretches of wasteland and a ticket collector charging you for parking your car. The Himalayan countries are all poor countries who use the demand for one of their own natural resources as a means of raising revenue.

The prospect of making the first overall winter ascent of Everest was very appealing but there was no doubt in any of our minds that the Poles had done what they set out to do – they had climbed Everest at the worst time of the year, whatever arbitrary definition of season might be attached to it. For us there were enough unknowns about our own projected ascent not to feel that the Poles in any way exhausted our interest in the mountain. The West Ridge is the most difficult route yet achieved on the mountain. It had been climbed in its entirety only once before, by a large Yugoslavian expedition, and we planned to climb it in winter and without oxygen, testing further the limits of the possible.

Our expectations of finding a suitable sponsor for the expedition were disappointed. We needed £15,000 in cash, a minute amount in comparison with most other expeditions to Everest, for which the cost more normally amounts to tens of thousands of pounds. The low cost of our expedition was due both to our reliance solely on our own efforts on the mountain, and to our intention to climb without supplementary oxygen equipment. The cost of oxygen equipment and the logistics involved in transporting it up the mountain add enormously to an expedition's budget. We would have Sherpas at Base Camp, a small group comprising Sirdar, cook, cook boy and mail runner. The Sirdar coordinates hiring and organization of porters. The cook and cook boy relieve the expedition members of the more mundane tasks in order that they can concentrate on the climbing. Although the cost of hiring and equipping this Base Camp staff, along with equipping and paying our Liaison Officer, can add as much as one third to the budget of a small expedition, this cost is small in comparison to that of kitting out a team of Sherpas to act as load-carriers on the mountain.

Everest in winter did not fail to excite everyone's imagination, but in a period of extreme economic decline few firms felt that they could justify supporting a sporting venture when they were operating on a short working week or laying off many of their workers.

Alan was occupied with the task of raising money, spending much of his time on the telephone or meeting possible sponsors. Our hopes were raised and dashed time after time.

In the midst of all the preparations, I left for the expedition to K2 with two members from the 1978 attempt, Pete Boardman and Doug Scott, and Dick Renshaw, partner for much of my early climbing activities. In a way I could not concentrate fully on Everest until K2, 'the savage mountain', was safely finished with. It was an expedition lasting three-and-a-half months, at the end of which I emerged emaciated and exhausted after a prolonged assault which culminated in three of us, a few hours away from the summit, being buried in the middle of the night in an avalanche. It was as near to death and resurrection as I have been. When the horror of burial and suffocation was over, we spent three days slipping closer and closer to exhaustion as we fought for survival during the descent from the mountain.

I felt as if I had been to the brink of the abyss and looked over the edge; I felt purged by the experience. Rather than being deterred by the ordeal, I realized more clearly than ever before that climbing mountains was what I wanted to do. The reasons are not easy to define; the closest I can come to explaining them is that it makes me the person I am; going to the absolute limit of one's capabilities in anything is always satisfying.

My interest in Everest was not diminished, I had simply kept it dormant whilst I concentrated on K2. During the return from Pakistan my attention gradually centred fully on what was to come. Pete taunted me with comments on my folly at planning to leave again so soon, less than three months after our return. He had been on two expeditions the previous year and found it almost too demanding on his time and energy. This year he was planning a trek in the Himalayas. It was going to seem strange going on an expedition without Pete. We had hardly known each other before our two-man expedition to Changabang in 1976 when we had spent forty days completely alone together. Miraculously, our mutual assessment of each other's capabilities had proved accurate, and when we came out of our wilderness after the forty days we had not only realized a fantastic dream but had found a bond of friendship which, without words, could enable either one of us to anticipate the other's thoughts and reactions. It was to be the basis for further mountain ventures together.

Pete was disappointed that he had not been asked to come with us for the winter expedition. He had already been to the top of Everest once in 1975 with the South-West Face expedition, and he said that he did not really want to go again, but he would have liked to have been asked.

For my part, in the absence of someone on our team that I knew well, I hoped that I would have the experience and maturity to accommodate to all the different personalities in situations of stress, without any of the abrasiveness which is sometimes inevitable in the process of getting to know a person's inner self.

Alan asked me to be co-leader in the U.K. with a view to raising sponsorship. Unlike the more traditional styles of expedition with a strict, authoritarian leadership structure, the expeditions we had all been involved with were organized on a much more democratic basis. If there was a leader, it was as if by rota. From the point of view of obtaining permission from the Nepalese government it was necessary to have the name of one person as leader; for contacting sponsors it is essential to have a leader or co-leader as spokesman. Amongst ourselves we each regarded the task of every member as equally important. For my part, I was very relieved to be free of the burden of organizing the equipment, a job which requires a great deal of paperwork and time – time being my most scarce resource. In my role as fund-raiser I set out to investigate the possibilities of making a film of the expedition and also to contact the main media outlets to arrange news coverage.

Exploring the prospects of making a film offered a new, interesting departure. Allen Jewhurst is a close friend and a director of Chameleon Films, which specializes in making independent adventure films. After some casting around to get the feel of the idea, I asked him to go ahead with arrangements to bring a film crew with us. The initial hope of raising money in advance, by selling the rights to a television company, came to nothing, but if a successful film was made we stood a chance of recovering some of our money afterwards.

I had known Allen for a number of years and greatly enjoyed his company. He had had a flirtatious relationship with the climbing scene since 1976 when he and his partner, Chris Lister produced the film of the ascent of the Trango Tower. As a friend I was glad for him to come with us, but as a business man with his own company I had never quite understood him. He seemed to have some involvement with most aspects of the TV world, and if it was not him personally it was 'one o' me companies', as he was fond of saying in his broad London accent. The offices of Chameleon Films in Leeds seemed to be plush and elegant beyond the visible means of the company. Since I only ever visited his offices after dark, I was never sure if the whole operation was not somehow reminiscent of the film 'The Sting' in which the façade of a betting office is erected to defraud someone (albeit a crook himself), and that if I returned in daylight I would not find the premises under a totally different guise. In fact, the Chameleon offices are still very much there and the company has a reputation as a serious programme maker.

Allen was full of enthusiasm for the idea of making a film and he enlisted the services of Mike Shrimpton as cameraman and Graham Robinson for sound. Mike had done some rock climbing and had travelled to most places in the world on TV assignments. On meeting him I was impressed at his thoroughness and ready grasp and appreciation of points at issue. Graham was very quiet, had no experience at all of climbing, and a look of panic would cross his face when anyone asked him if he was really going to Everest.

From past experience I knew that the presence of amiable out-siders to the climbing team can help to prevent the pressures and tensions of expedition life from getting out of proportion, but it was a major worry that something might happen to one of the film crew, who inevitably would not have much experience of the mountains they would have to live in, in bitter conditions, for the best part of three months. It was worry for their own sakes and for the sake of the expedition as a whole which affected me, for if any one of them did have an accident it would seriously affect the morale of the rest of us. On the 1972 South-West Face expedition, Tony Tighe, who was there simply to lend a hand round Base Camp, was killed during the final days of the expedition when a serac in the ice-fall collapsed on top of him. During the Polish winter attempt on Lhotse, Stanislaw Latallo, one of their film crew, died from exposure and exhaustion. There is danger all the time, and it is more likely to strike if one's attention is focused on something other than the conditions on the mountains.

Given these reservations, everyone on the team was keen to cooperate in obtaining the material to make the best possible film. Having 'outsiders' along, especially ones who are recording your every move and word, can be a cause of conflict in itself and an incentive to reticence. We hoped, however, that by being closely involved in the filming ourselves it would be 'our' film, the film crew would be an integral part of the team, and we would thus have the opportunity of making the best, most accurate and intimate film on mountaineering that had ever been made.

John Porter was occupied amassing the food we were going to take with us in what little time he had free whilst organizing the Kendal Mountaineering Film Festival. Pete Thexton was left to his own devices selecting and collecting all the medical equipment, pills and medicines he thought we would need. Paul Nunn was away on the Royal Geographical Society Karakorum Project for a while and on his return he lent a hand with negotiations over the film contract and provided a central gathering point for all the equipment, food and medicine in his house in Sheffield, where his patient wife watched her home being overtaken by the creeping monstrosity of the expedition. The Burgess twins, Al and Ade, who had been absent in Canada during most of the preparations, were sentenced to drive around collecting and packing all the outstanding pieces of equipment which had not already arrived.

As the date of departure drew nearer, so the number of calls from the press, television and radio increased. Whenever I had to speak to them I found myself repeating, as if rehearsed, the same things; my mouth seemed to produce the words while my brain was preoccupied with a dozen other things. Talking about a climb before I had actually done it was something I had never felt easy about. There was an element of shyness due to the doubts I had about my own competence or ability to succeed on any particular climb. I preferred the attempt to be my own private affair, or something shared with my climbing partner, but in going to the Himalayas it becomes necessary to announce beforehand one's intentions in order to obtain permission from the government in question and also to raise the necessary finance. It was an uncomfortable feeling on the first expedition I was involved with to have to tell people a full year beforehand what our intentions were.

Everest still excites the public's imagination more than any other mountain and there is a fascination with the dangerous aspects of attempting to climb it. Without having set foot on the mountain, the climber setting out for Everest can be the focus of the dangerously seductive attention of the media. He is a modern-day gladiator whose fascination is that he is stepping into an arena from which he knows there is a chance that he might not return. This knowledge may be something that he would rather cope with privately but the arena which draws him, and the particular arena of Everest which was drawing us, is a public one and we had to accept the consequences.

After an interview in which I had been open and sincere, but which was one of many interviews in which I had been open and sincere, I would feel empty and a little drained. The words and conversation had not penetrated to my inner being, I had given a 'performance', thus protecting the real self inside. It made me uneasy to participate in exciting the interest of the public climb which involved all eight of us pushing ourselves to the limit and courting death for a sustained period of time. I would have preferred to be reticent about the whole enterprise but, without being rude, this was not possible, and at least cooperation would mean that the media would have the facts right.

Alan had suggested that half of the team went out at the beginning of November with all the equipment and food. They would sort out the formalities, clear customs and start walking with all the baggage and porters. The rest of us would fly out two weeks later, taking a flight from Kathmandu on a small plane to Lukla, an airstrip part-way along the route of approach to Everest. The whole approach march can take up to eighteen days from leaving the road. Flying to Lukla would cut about ten days off the journey. Alan had felt that those of us who had been away once already that year probably needed a bit more time in Britain. As usual, things arise to fill the space available, and although the feeling, after all the equipment and food had gone with the first four on 3 November, was something like the calm after a storm, there were many loose ends to tie up.

I was relieved to be spared the full length of the walk-in. Usually it is a time for relaxing; most of the problems of organization have been solved, life becomes a very simple one of walking, resting and a gradual focusing of the concentration on the mountain ahead. The formalities in Kathmandu, however, and all the petty tasks of buying local food, equipping the cooks and Sherpas of the Base Camp staff, are very demanding, and I felt that the four of us who were going later had been given the softer option.

Somehow, though, I regretted not leaving with the first four. They would be involved with the expedition right from the start, they would be getting to know each other and growing together, a vital part in forming the strong bonds which would be essential for us in working together on the mountain.

As a complete surprise came a phone call from No. 10 Downing Street – an invitation to lunch with the Prime Minister and her guests, the King and Queen of Nepal. I treated the call as a joke, thinking that some friends must be pulling my leg. I rang the number I had been given and sure enough the call was answered with 'Hello, Prime Minister's office'.

I was due to fly to Nepal the day before the lunch date, but after consulting the other members it was clear that nothing would be lost by my flying out two days later. I was intrigued to pass through that well-known doorway.

Paul Nunn, Brian Hall and John Porter took the plane on Tuesday 18 November. I spent the remaining time in London making final arrangements with the *Observer*, to which we would be sending back news reports, and similarly with ITN. I had discussions with a publisher who was interested in the story of the expedition and from Pentax I picked up an enormous 6×7 cm camera which they were loaning to us for the expedition.

On the Wednesday I was running down Whitehall, late for the luncheon appointment, and hurried through the security checks outside No. 10 Downing Street and in through the door. It was as if I had stepped into Dr Who's time-ship, the 'Tardis'; outside it is a small, old-fashioned police box, inside it is enormous, exceeding, in some scientific fantasy, all proportions of the external shell. We are familiar with the little door of No. 10, with the policeman outside, resembling the entrance to a small terraced house. Inside, staircases lead up and down, passageways branch off in all directions; there are innumerable doors, antechambers, spacious gathering places and a large dining hall. I shook hands with Mrs Thatcher, who appeared and spoke exactly as on television. The King and Queen of Nepal seemed tolerant of the ritual introductions, a formality which they were having to repeat throughout their stay in Britain. With relief I recognized a familiar face, John Denson, the British Ambassador to Nepal, who had welcomed us back from our success on Kangchenjunga with a champagne toast at his embassy residence. The meal was conducted at a brisk pace, the whole procedure obviously orchestrated by a master of ceremonies to fit in with the Prime Minister's busy schedule. Politely but firmly the meal was brought to an end and there was an irresistible momentum to leave. I stepped out onto the street, saying goodbye to the Densons and promising to visit them in Kathmandu, and rushed off to complete the thousand remaining things I had to do before leaving.

CHAPTER THREE

Going to the Widow Maker

Three months after returning from the expedition to K2 I was at Heathrow airport again, ready for another departure. One of my sisters, Carmel, her fiancé, Andy, and my girlfriend, Maria, were there. It was a strange parting. I was frantically re-packing, trying to avoid excess baggage charges; there was a delay whilst some ticket confusion was cleared up in the queue in front of me, and when it was my turn the flight had closed and there was a chance I might not get on. I rushed from one desk to another guided by idiotic, mistaken directions. My single-minded pre-occupation with expeditions over the past months had been distressing to Maria, who felt very much incidental to my climbing plans. Now at the last moment there was no time to talk. I was at last checked in and we ran up the escalator before the final turn round for the goodbye, having hardly conversed for the hour we had been at the airport. Maria had a suddenly tearful and drained face – so much was left unsaid before I turned to go through the hole of an entrance as if to execution.

I do not feel lonely on an expedition, and I do not feel a dread of separation. An expedition is all-absorbing and fulfilling in itself. I have known more loneliness in a city than on a remote mountain where I have been absolutely alone for a week, with not even the sight of another person. On a mountain I have an identity, a purpose and a place within the lives of other people. If there are times when one is physically alone it is not through any personal rejection, but because a vital role is being performed.

It was a relief to settle into my seat on the plane knowing that I was at last rejoining the mainstream of the expedition. For the last two weeks I had felt uncomfortably separated from the members of the expedition who had gone on ahead. There were innumerable things which kept occurring to me which I had not sorted out before leaving, many letters I would have to write from Kathmandu, but already the discord due to diverse, competing demands was beginning to fade away. By the time we reached Base Camp the whole pace of life would have slowed down and life itself become very simple.

On the flight from Delhi to Kathmandu I had a view of the snowy mountains we had come to climb. They seemed more snowy than in summer, but it was not white everywhere; at least we would not be on snow all through the approach march too.

I joined Paul, Brian and John in Kathmandu, that amiable city, which was a staging post for us in our transposition from one culture to another. We flew on to Lukla, from where we walked for two days, in easy stages, to Namche Bazaar, where we hoped to meet the rest of the team.

The woods through which we walked were still mellow with the colours of autumn, in the shade there were patches of frost and at night the air was distinctly chill. From a clearing in the woods on the way up to Namche Bazaar we caught our first glimpse of Everest peeping menacingly above the crest of the Nuptse ridge. A huge plume of cloud streamed from the top, a chilling indicator of the power of the winds we were coming to face. Like a vision, the sight disappeared as we continued upwards through the trees, to be glimpsed again only briefly before we were much closer to the mountain; but the memory remained to haunt our imaginations as a warning of what was ahead.

We seemed to have been thrown into a way of life for which we were ill-prepared. Our progress from Britain, by way of aeroplanes which finally deposited us in the heart of the mountains, had been too rapid to allow time to adjust. I had a great sense of culture shock, feeling a little numbed mentally. At night it was very cold and all our warm clothing was still with the advance party who were some days delayed. We stayed in a travellers' rest house in Namche Bazaar awaiting the arrival of the rest of the team.

Namche Bazaar is one of the main villages of the Sherpas, members of the tribe of Tibetan origin who, turning from trade to agriculture, have become world famous for their mountaineering feats, for their endurance and reliability. This village clings to a hillside and is a centre for commerce, whereas the other villages above and further up the valley are located in places where agriculture is more feasible. The whole area has been adopted by New Zealanders who, taking their example from Ed Hillary, have organized the area on a national park basis, introducing measures designed to conserve wood and prevent soil erosion. Their efforts are met by a mixed response from the local inhabitants, but there is no doubt that they have been effective in bringing education and medical care to the area.

I went to visit Ang Phurba, who had been Sirdar or chief Sherpa on our expedition to climb the north side of Kangchenjunga in 1979. He was a laconic but totally reliable and resourceful complement to our team. On a visit to Britain at the end of 1979 his first quest was to find a broad-brimmed cowboy hat such as he had seen me wearing on the expedition. He was at home with his wife and three children, relaxing during the winter months. Expeditions for him were over until the spring, the work in the fields was all finished and he could pleasantly pass the time with that philosophical calm of people in the east.

Like most of his fellow Sherpas, Ang Phurba is a keen and able worker on an expedition, but does not have an interest in climbing for its own sake. With a record of expeditions which many of us would envy, he regards his climbing activities simply as work for which he gets paid. The attitude of the Sherpas to the visits of foreigners was summed up by a conversation which was translated for us in which it was made clear that we were regarded as reincarnated beings. In our former lives we were believed to have been so bad that we had been sent back into these mountains as a punishment. Had we behaved ourselves formerly we would have found ourselves in a much more comfortable setting! Ang Phurba and I drank chang, the Sherpa rice beer, and chatted about mutual friends. The centre-piece of the room was a wood fire, and lining the walls were huge copper bowls used to store water during the winter months when outside all is frozen.

Ang Phurba's home was unconventional in having a chimney above the open fire. For some reason the idea of chimneys does not seem to have made an impact on the Sherpas. Intelligent and resourceful as they are, the Sherpas seem to adapt to cold and discomfort rather than taking measures against it. It is not unusual to see a fire stoked up high with a cluster of bodies around it and windows and doors wide open to let some of the smoke which fills the room escape. It was not clear whether the common belief was that the smoke preserved the wood inside the houses (which were indeed blackened and festooned with sooty fronds) or whether it was to keep heat from escaping along with smoke up a hole. For whatever reason, Sherpas, and especially the women, spend their lives crouched, with smarting eyes, over smokey fires, and often have irreparably damaged eyesight by the time they are in their thirties.

The nearby hospital in the village of Kunde is staffed by voluntary doctors from New Zealand and is supplied largely with copious medicines from the many expeditions which pass by. It was built as part of the welfare scheme, started by Ed Hillary, providing hospitals and schools throughout the Sherpa villages. This hospital is a model of airiness, insulation and efficient heating. For some reason the Sherpas do not take example from this; they continued to huddle, snivel-nosed, through the winter months in their dark and draughty, smoke-blackened rooms.

The hospital was to be our link with the outside world. Twice a week the New Zealand doctors send out their mail on a tiny Pilatus Porter aeroplane. The plane lands on an airstrip resembling a football field tilted at a considerable angle, poised above a deep valley. The flight into and out of this airstrip is spectacular and exhilarating. It was built to service the Japanese Everest View Hotel, a luxury hotel built in a position on a hill from where one can just see the summit cone of Everest. Everyone who stays at the hotel flies in, but the sudden jump up from the 5,000-foot altitude of Kathmandu to nearly 11,000 feet is often too much. It is not unknown for death to occur after such a rapid transition. Many of the visitors have to be met off the aeroplanes and supported all the way to the hotel where they collapse within reach of an oxygen bottle, with which every room is equipped, and stay there till their departure.

From Base Camp we would be sending back once a week our mail runner who would deliver his mail bag to the hospital. There it would be put on the plane from which it would be collected on arrival in Kathmandu by our expedition agent, who would then stamp and supervise the posting of mail, despatch of news film and cabling of newspaper reports. A long chain of communication, but we could sometimes have mail back in Britain within a week of sending it from Base Camp.

On 27 November Alan and Pete arrived with thirty of the porters they had hired to carry our 150 loads. By this time we had been waiting anxiously for several days, but the reasons for the delay were now explained. The Japanese expedition which would be attempting the normal route on Everest, effectively on the opposite side of the mountain, had hired eight hundred porters. This virtually cleared out the villages of available manpower, since much of the local workforce was already taken up with a new road-construction project. What villagers were available to carry for us were only prepared to go a certain distance, being unwilling to cross the mountain ridges separating their known, home valley from the next valley along the way. This entailed a constant paying-off and rehiring which in the end caused the porter caravan to be divided up into smaller, more manageable groups. Alan and Pete had come on ahead with the first group to let us know what was happening.

We moved up from Namche Bazaar to the more secluded village of Khumjung where we hired a house in which to stay, store all our baggage and find some privacy from the constant questions of the trekkers who frequent Namche Bazaar. There were few trekkers about; those that were about were well wrapped up, shocked by the cold and full of questions about our expedition. There was no two-way conversation; they seemed so overawed by the thought of climbing Everest that they did not offer anything of themselves; they were probing, searching for our motivation, our experiences, our fears. It was embarrassing and irritating to be such a focus of attention, and it became a habit with us to retreat into the isolated world bestowed by the stereophonic headphones of the little cassette players we had. This blocked out all outside sound so that, in the most selfish way, one could be oblivious of any conversation going on.

We learnt from Alan and Pete some of the tales of the walk in; the Burgess twins, nicknamed, for their propensity for carrying heavy loads, after two well-known rucksack manufacturers, Berghaus and Karrimor, racing along in competition with each other up and down hill. The porters loved them and mimicked their muscle-bound walk, striding along, arms akimbo, pretending to carry a cassette player which one or other of the twins seemed to have eternally glued to his hand, playing Blondie or some punk rock alternative at full volume.

We discussed tactics on the mountain, whether it would be best to climb as two groups of four or some other variation. Brian evolved a theory concerning the wind direction, and deduced that we could be assisted by the wind as it would be coming from behind, and that it would be so strong that more oxygen than normal would be blown up from below. Alan seemed to think that the colder air of winter would be denser, thus containing more oxygen and effectively lowering the height of the mountain in air-density terms.

The delay we were experiencing, although allowing those of us who had not walked in a chance to acclimatize, was worrying and we were all relieved at the arrival on 30 November of the infamous Burgess twins and the film crew of Allen, Mike and Graham.

Although clearly on unfamiliar territory, the approach walk of the last two weeks had enabled the film crew to accustom themselves to the primitive mode of existence which they were to share for the next couple of months. Their professional conditioning to keep on filming whatever the circumstances had helped them to adjust quickly to the strange environment and their methodical organization had been invaluable in assisting with the marshalling of over one hundred unruly porters. The actual filming arrangements for the mountain had not yet been finalized. Mike was keen to go as far as he could but, since his climbing experience was limited, we were reluctant to make any commitments about whether we would be willing to have him working on the mountain at all in case it meant assigning someone to look after his safety. There was a definite pecking order in that the film was clearly regarded as secondary in importance to climbing the mountain and consequently the opinions of the film crew tended to be regarded with less weight. On the whole I did not envy them their work, which would inevitably entail their spending much time inactive at Base Camp. Even if Mike was to come part way up, the main filming on the mountain was expected to be done by the climbers.

Officially we were allowed to set foot on the mountain from 1 December, and days lost early in an expedition are hard to make up later. I found myself regarding this reunion of the whole team as the real start of the expedition. Previously we had all been scattered with no chance of interaction, but once together we could begin to share ideas and form a close-knit team which would be effective on the mountain.

We were five days from Base Camp, and we left Khumjung before our Sirdar, Dawa, arrived with the remaining thirty loads. He, being well known in the region, had been left to bring up the rear.

The trail led steadily upwards, habitation and vegetation grew more sparse and the little comforts of life which had been gradually diminishing were pared almost right away as we drew closer to the mountain.

I walked along one day with Ade Burgess, discussing how it had been for us on Kangchenjunga and K2, what it was like to be so high without oxygen support equipment on those mountains. Undeniably it had been arduous but it had not been another dimension of experience, it was more of the same excruciatingly hard work. On Kangchenjunga three of us had spent a night in a snow cave at 26,000 feet, climbing the next day the 2,000 feet to the summit and descending, in the night, to the same snow cave. It had not been a fight against an unwilling spirit; inside I knew I wanted to continue, but like an old man whose mind is still active when his strength is failing, the question was whether my body could perform all the necessary movements to reach the summit before dark. Every half-dozen steps upwards left us panting, gasping in lungfuls of increasingly rarefied air. We had reached the summit one hour before dark, without hallucinations, without distorted perception or dizziness. The only indication that our brains were affected by the altitude was that we did press on to the summit, in the face of a rising storm, knowing that we would inevitably get benighted.

Next day I walked along with Al Burgess, only identifiable from his brother by the stubbly beard which gave him a mischievous appearance. We talked again of high altitude, K2 and Kangchenjunga. Al and Ade are quite different in temperament, outlook and even in some ways in their appearance, but these differences are only noticeable as one gets to know them both better. Even then, after not seeing them for a while, it is easy to mistake one for the other. In talking to one or other of them I usually felt a certain air of uncanniness, as if each one knew already what had been discussed with the other. As I talked again of K2 and Kangchenjunga, I could not help feeling that Al already knew what I was going to say, and that he had possibly only forgotten that I had already said these things the day before.

There is such a sense of togetherness in their awareness of each other, their intimate knowledge of each other, that the twins give off the impression of strength that any union of separate parts gives. The girlfriend of one of them said that it is disconcerting to have a close relationship as no woman will ever be as close to either of them as they are to each other.

In the few days of preparations in Kathmandu, Al had met a girl who had become quite fond of him. She was planning to come up to meet him after we had finished on the mountain. We were planning to get Ade to grow a beard and impersonate his twin brother, with us in collusion calling him Al, to see how long it would take her, if at all, to spot the trick.

We left the village of Pheriche, climbing steeply up a narrow valley, enclosed by snowy mountains. At a col we passed a row of cairns, which stand, ominous as tombstones, to the memory of the Frenchman and five Sherpas who were swept away by an avalanche in their attempt to climb the West Ridge of Everest in 1974.

Lobuje is the last inhabited place on the way up to Everest. It consists of a few Yak herders' dwellings which are now occupied on a more consistent basis, catering for the trekkers who make it this far. A saying which has come into use is, 'See Lobuje and die', a dictum arising from the dangers inherent in this trek. Lobuje is at approximately 14,000 feet and to the unwary or unfit the possibility of a fatal attack of high-altitude sickness is very real. A small hospital has been built by the Japanese at Pheriche, the last village on the trail, specifically to care for the visitors who become sick.

Each day now we were only walking for a few hours. It would have been possible, but unwise, to do more. The height gain between each stage was considerable and at this altitude it is the going up high too quickly which causes high-altitude sickness. In 1978 I had visited this area on the way to Nuptse, the third peak of the Everest massif, when one member of our team became critically ill at Lobuje. We carried him down to Pheriche 1,500 feet lower where he was cared for by a Sherpani girl. He recovered and subsequently married the girl. The story is legendary in this area, the fairytale fantasy of a rich stranger carrying off his true love having been given credence by this event.

Unlike the mountain folk of India and Pakistan, Sherpa society is delightfully open and relaxed. It was possible to laugh and joke with the womenfolk, something unheard of in Pakistan. A tea house at Lobuje was run by a Sherpa girl, fluent in English and French. We spent an evening sitting, with eyes smarting from woodsmoke, drinking chang and playfully flirting with the Sherpa girl and her friends. Everyone does much manual labour in this hill society, carrying heavy loads and tilling the fields. Even the women are very strong and any attempt at going further than their rules of decorum permitted was firmly rebuffed. They were fascinated by our two blond clones, the Burgess twins. Blond hair is unknown among the Sherpas, and this together with the twins' incredible size in comparison with the diminutive Nepalese people and their similarity of appearance made an obvious focus for the giggling attentions of the easy going Sherpanis.

The girl running the tea house knew Samji, the girl who had married my expedition companion.

'Samji my friend. You want to marry Sherpani like her?'

'In England we have "one night marriage", what about that?'

'One night no good, all night very good,' and she would relapse into ribald convulsions of laughter with her friends.

Gorak Shep was the last camping place before Base Camp. We pitched our tents on the sandy bed of some long since disappeared lake. From the hill behind it is possible to see Everest and we took it in turns to wander up for the view. I waited till late in the afternoon to catch the sunset on the mountain and sat for a freezing hour, growing progressively more numb in the chill breeze, recording the exquisite change of colours – from pink to deep orange – on Everest and the hills around. There did not seem to be much wind this day, but now the mountain looked huge and I was numbed with cold on a lowly hillock watching the sun slip away from the summit 12,000 feet higher.

We had a bleak, windswept evening meal, raked by sand from the dried-up lake bed, with the food congealing on the plates before there was time to finish eating.

We reached Base Camp on 6 December, end of one mode of existence and start of another. The winter snows had not lingered. Our tents had to be pitched on the icy desert of the lower Khumbu glacier. Rocks churned up by the imperceptibly moving river of ice littered the surface. We spent a whole day hacking platforms from the ice and pitching tents with rocks to which we tied the guylines. It was worth the effort to make each tent site comfortable as we expected to be there for many weeks.

To the north the camp was overlooked by the steep walls leading up to the Lho La Col, the lowest point on the West Ridge, and the complex slopes leading up to the West Shoulder, 6,000 feet above us. In 1978 I had seen an avalanche break away from the walls of ice guarding the Lho La, sweeping down in seconds and covering our camp, over a mile distant, with fine snow. Anything in its path would have been obliterated. I had thought then that any attempt to gain the Lho La was suicidal, but the Yugoslavs had found a cunning, though difficult, route up the rock buttresses to the left, avoiding most of the danger. We intended to follow this safer line.

CHAPTER FOUR

Attacking the Ramparts

The weather was fine and clear but definitely chilly, even on the sunniest day. It was hard to relax for long, for the cold penetrated right to the core. Paul, Pete and Alan were sick with dysentery or some related illness. We had thought to escape such illness in the sterile atmosphere of winter but the watering place for our last camp at Gorak Shep had been a stagnant pool and we suspected this to be the cause of the trouble. Only during the daylight hours between 8.30 a.m. and 4.30 p.m., if the sun was out, was there any semblance of warmth; those who were ill had little encouragement for recovery from our chill surroundings. Paul steadfastly refused Pete's panacea for dysentery-related illness, the much feared Flagyl, the effect of which was sometimes more debilitating than the illness for the three days of the dosage. Paul, having gathered on his travels much experience of strange illnesses, preferred to try to cure himself in his own way. Almost all of us were afflicted with colds, snuffles and coughs.

Alan was preoccupied with the tedious task of paying off our porters, calculating the expedition's expenditure and ensuring that we had enough cash available in Nepalese rupees for all our expenses until returning to Kathmandu.

John, having shelved his responsibility as food organizer during the confusion of the approach walk, now got down to the task of locating and making available the rations and the delicacies designed to make Base Camp life enjoyable.

Brian continued his never-ending work of sorting out and

distributing the equipment which he had worked so hard to design and amass specifically for this expedition. Everything had to be accounted for; if there was anything lost or forgotten there was little chance of replacing it before the end of the expedition.

Al and Ade Burgess and I were privileged to be free to make the first exploratory steps towards finding a safe route up the 2,000 feet of rock to the Lho La.

It was only meant as a reconnaissance, we wanted to find the point at which we left the glacier, so we went only in light clothes and light footwear. We hugged the edge of the glacier, hopping along the piles of unstable boulders, thrust to one side by the movement of the glacier. We risked breaking an ankle or worse if a boulder should roll over, but by skirting the edge we were keeping safely away from the fall line of the seracs, the walls of ice tilting forward from the Lho La, the debris from which lay scattered in a vast swathe across the glacier.

I was a little breathless, unaccustomed as yet to the altitude of 18,000 feet. I did not want to show my breathlessness to the twins, who are always fit as a result of their constant training sessions all the year round. Implicitly I was weighing up my partners, and felt that I was being evaluated too in terms of performance and ability. There was an unspoken bravado and tongue-in-cheek banter which seemed to acknowledge the folly of our chosen pursuit. I revelled in the company of these two brothers, feeling in no way excluded from the rapport which they had with each other.

The sun warmed the rock and, unhampered by rucksacks or heavy, warm clothing, we found ourselves scampering further and further up the gradually steepening hillside.

We had heard that this approach to the Lho La was threatened, if not by ice avalanches, then by rock avalanches. Doug Scott and Georges Bettembourg had made a foray up these slopes in 1979 and came back with awestricken tales of the lethal rockfall which showered down out of the walls above. There was indeed much evidence of newly fallen rock and no trace at all that any-one had been here before, causing us to doubt if we were heading in the right direction.

There were several buttresses of rock separated by wide gullies full of loose stones and unstable blocks. We rushed across the gullies, fearing to be caught in them by fresh falls of rock, seeking the safety of the buttresses which stood out from the slope clear of the danger. Ade climbed up the side of one buttress thinking he had seen the obvious way up; Al and I tried another way. Once through an area of broken blocks and round a corner, we found we were on a logical progression of ledges, steps and ribs. Ade, having reached an impasse, stayed below, sheltering under a bulge of rock lest we dislodge any stones whilst climbing above him. Underfoot there was much loose rock and we realized that for safety any of us coming up here would have to stay close together. Like this, any rock dislodged could be either stopped or avoided more easily. If we were separated by long distances, anything dislodged would have a chance to gain lethal momentum and possibly strike the unwary without warning.

There was still no indication that the line we were taking would lead to the plateau of the Lho La. We were gaining height steadily, Base Camp was a tiny cluster of tents in the distance from which the echo of a voice sometimes reached us, and the hidden valley of the Western Cwm was gradually revealing itself. We were getting close to the huge walls of ice which guard access to the plateau, but in safety, to one side, we were able to look on with respect at the tortured ice formations frozen in the act of toppling over. This wall of ice, hundreds of feet high, was the end of a great bed of ice sitting on top of the rock of Everest's West Ridge. The rock is at a gentle gradient and the layer of ice is in gradual movement, slowly and inexorably sliding to the precipice beside which we were climbing. As it reaches the edge, great chunks, weighing thousands of tons, break off and crash down, scouring the gully below, and rising in a billowing cloud of ice debris which obliterates all in its path. Such avalanches are one of the nightmares of Himalayan climbing. I felt a reverential awe in gazing upon the birth-place of such colossal forces.

Al and I chased each other up the rock buttress, which after a jumble of loose shale, broken blocks and razor-sharp flakes had changed as we got higher to firm granite on which it was a pleasure to climb.

'It's like following a goat,' Al shouted up to me as I disappeared from his sight and found we could continue even further. I did not feel as fit as a goat but could move rapidly for short lengths of time before becoming breathless. I knew that if we did too much we would exhaust ourselves and probably spend the next day recovering from headaches. It was so exciting, however, this journey of discovery, that it was impossible to resist going just that little bit further.

A steep, difficult-looking corner blocked the way, but above it the angle of the rock eased back. Al gingerly edged his way up, spreading his legs wide and balancing his toes on small rugosities in the rock. In Britain it would have been the sort of climbing we could do without thinking; here on Everest we could not help but be influenced by the situation, climbing unroped at 19,000 feet, with the debris of danger lying all around. This instilled more caution than the difficulties justified. Al found some good hand-holds, pulled himself onto easier ground and I followed.

A ramp led upwards to a level shoulder on the crest of the buttress and a couple of rusty tin cans. It was an encouragement that we were going the right way. A nasty looking gully of loose rock and snow separated us from some grey slabs and at the top of the wall above us we could see a line of weakness, a groove or corner, which seemed to end after about 300 feet on the Lho La plateau. It was far enough for the day. A slight breeze cooled away the warmth of the sun; without lingering further we turned to descend.

On the way down we built cairns from small rocks to mark the way for the next time we came up. Down below Ade was waiting, chilled to the bone in his light clothing. Al and I had been warm enough, moving all the time. Ade had been crouched in the shadow of the bulge of rock for an hour, as we, heedless of time, had gone much further than intended. United once more, we stumbled and slid down the slope of unstable boulders to the glacier.

From above we had noted the way back to camp across the ice. Although this way would mean crossing the avalanche debris from the ice walls of the Lho La, we estimated that we ran a greater risk of serious injury by carrying on along the boulder field. Many of the boulders were precariously balanced one on top of the other and big enough to crush a foot or break a leg if dislodged. It took ten minutes to rush across the hard packed avalanche cone to where we guessed ourselves to be out of danger, all the while spying crevasses into which to jump and shelter should an avalanche come sweeping along.

We brought the good news of our progress back to a camp busy with activity. Brian, sleeves rolled up, pad in hand, was surrounded by boxes from which were spilling out ropes, stoves, tents and umpteen other items of equipment which he was ticking off against a list and trying to organize into readily identifiable heaps. John, dressed in strange green padded pyjamas, strutted about with a continually worried air from one pile of food to another. He broke away periodically to try to explain, with an expression of resigned patience, to Wan Chup, our cook, what each sort of food was for and how to cook it.

There seemed to be many things missing or mislaid, and the thrill I had felt at our day of discovery disappeared as we became caught up in the mundane tasks of Base Camp organization. After searching repeatedly through kitbags and boxes there were still many things unaccounted for. We questioned ourselves first, our own disorganization, but too many vital pieces of clothing and equipment, jacket, trousers, ice axe, were missing from different loads for it to be a coincidence. Inevitably suspicions arose about the honesty of our Sherpa staff.

In order to be free to concentrate on the climbing, and also to look after Ram Singh, our Liaison Officer, we were hiring a cook, Wan Chup, who, according to the Nepalese laws of stratification, had to have a cook boy, Mingma. We were also employing another Mingma, who was to be our mail runner. To look after this group and to organize porters or yaks and any transactions with the local community we had to have a Sirdar, or head Sherpa. This was the role of Dawa, whom we had left to bring up the rear with the remaining loads.

We were completely in the hands of these, our Base Camp staff, in that we could not keep a check on all our equipment all of the time. Fortunately the Nepalese generally and the Sherpas in particular have a high reputation for honesty. On the expedition to Kangchenjunga we had handed over the money to Ang Phurba, our Sirdar, and he had hired and fired the porters as necessary, presenting us with a detailed, if crudely written, set of accounts from time to time. We therefore struggled against admitting to ourselves the possibility that this time our Base Camp staff might be dishonest.

Dawa, who was reputed to be a very capable and experienced Sherpa, arrived with the remaining loads. He resembled, with his tanned complexion, reflective sunglasses, gleaming smile and elegant clothes, a continental ski-instructor rather than a rugged man of the hills. His English was perfect. None of the missing equipment was to be found in the loads he had brought. On the contrary, more that should have been in those loads was missing.

Alan had already had a confrontation with Dawa at the very beginning when he had obviously postponed the start of the walk-in for a day on the pretext of there being a hold-up with the porters. Alan had discovered that the real reason was that Dawa had wanted to spend an extra day in the company of an American girl whom he had met whilst leading a trek.

It was odious for us, amidst the raw beauty of the mountains, to have to deal with problems of corruption which we had thought to have left behind. The Sirdar is responsible for the safe transport of the loads of the expedition by which he is employed. There is quite a degree of latitude in this, especially at the end of an expedition when much of the equipment is sold off cheaply or abandoned, but too much of our equipment was missing to let the matter drop.

Dawa refused to accept responsibility for any losses and insisted that everything had arrived. There was an atmosphere of discontent at Base Camp. Much energy seemed to be used up in arguments with the most sullen and uncooperative group of Sherpas I had known. The food we were eating had deteriorated from the wonderful dishes the cook was known to be capable of. There were plenty of tins of food we had brought out from Britain, but these never appeared, and our meals were a tedious affair of rice and dahl (spiced lentils). John was furious when he walked into the kitchen tent to find Dawa consuming a full tin of ham himself. His explanation was that he was testing it to see whether it was suitable for himself and the rest of the Base Camp staff. At our insistence on having more than rice and dahl ourselves, the tinned food subsequently appeared on the table – the tin having been heated to thaw out the contents and placed unopened on the table with a tin opener. The cook excused himself by saying that he did not know how to handle tinned foods.

It transpired that it was this same Dawa who had sown the seeds of doubt about whether Messner and Habeler had really climbed Everest without oxygen in 1978 and had gone on subsequently to accuse Messner of having stolen treasures from Nepalese monasteries some years previously. We were all uneasy about the situation; Alan felt very much the responsibility of making a decision on this. It was not a step he wanted to take lightly. If he were to dismiss Dawa it would be a serious blow to his career as a Sherpa and so far we had heard nothing but good reports on his capabilities.

Alan decided to let things stand for the moment but Base Camp was not a place I felt comfortable in with all this discord.

Undoubtedly we had been disappointed to learn that a Japanese expedition was to attempt to climb the mountain at the same time as us. Their objective was to be on the opposite side of the mountain, climbing by the South Col route, the way by which the mountain has been climbed many times before. We knew little about their expedition until we reached Base Camp, having heard that it was an attempt at a solo ascent by Naomi Uemura. At thirty-nine, Uemura is the most famous of Japanese mountaineers and amongst other things had completed a solo crossing of the North Pole. At first it had hardly impinged on us that anyone else would be on the mountain. We imagined that Uemura's solo ascent would involve him and possibly a couple of Sherpas as Base Camp staff. Everest seemed big enough to accommodate him as well as us. It was a complete surprise on arrival, therefore, to find that there were dozens of Japanese climbers, journalists and television people occupied with this much-vaunted 'solo' ascent. They also had an even larger number of Sherpas equipped to work on the mountain.

We would rather have had the mountain to ourselves but as

it was we would only come into contact with the Japanese at Base Camp. Their route would take them off at right-angles to the direction we were going. They would have to climb up the tumbling chaos of the Khumbu ice-fall into the snowy valley of the Western Cwm. There they had to traverse beneath the South-West Face of the mountain to reach the opposite side to where we would be climbing. From our precarious vantage points on the way up to the Lho La, we could sometimes see the minute dots of the Japanese or their Sherpas picking their way through the maze of crevasses and toppling blocks in the ice-fall, as they went round to the south side of the mountain. Paradoxically, though their route is the easiest way up, gaining it entails crossing the most dangerous and accident-fraught area of the mountain.

Accepting that the Japanese were our neighbours, camped only a few hundred yards away, Alan went over to pay a courtesy call. He came back with an invitation for all of us to go across in the evening for a meal. It promised to be a welcome change from rice and dahl.

The Japanese tents were in a slight hollow, not completely visible from our camping place. From above a swelling in the surface of the glacier could be seen the many pinnacles of their orange tents. It looked to be an enormous camp. Towards evening, well insulated for a short journey, we trooped across in the direction of their lights.

On closer acquaintance the many pinnacles appeared to be clustered closely together; my perception could not resolve what I was seeing. A large tent flap opened, spilling electric light out onto the ice, and we stumbled inside after each other, blinded by the unexpected brightness. We were inside a huge marquee. The pinnacles were not closely grouped tents after all, but one enormous tent with many points, the like of which I had never seen before. Outside an electric generator throbbed away and a string of glowing bulbs ran the whole length of this grandiose construction. The chimney of a wood-burning stove disappeared upwards to be lost in the voluminous folds of the tent's inner lining, and a long, low narrow table ran the length of the room with armchairs made from bamboo cane on either side of it.

Sometimes I have the sensation that I am no longer contributing to events, but am being controlled by them as they happen. I could not quite grasp what was happening – Everest, winter, cold and discomfort and suddenly we were in a cocoon of luxury, surrounded by smiling faces, flashing and whirring cameras and microphones, warm and comfortable. Some small plastic bottles were produced from a box and Naomi Uemura, grinning broadly, said: 'This is Saki. We bring to celebrate our summit climb. But now we celebrate you coming.'

We all drank and sat and grinned. More details of this un-believable tent registered in my mind. I did not like to stare – I felt as if I was in someone's private rooms. Along each wall was a row of curtained alcoves perhaps six feet long by four feet wide. These were the sleeping places for the Japanese members, with a thin partition of nylon as a concession to privacy. At the furthest end of the tent was a bank of electrical consoles. 'Is that a hi-fi system?' one of our team asked hopefully.

'No, it is a facsimile machine for weather reports from Delhi.'

The cost of transporting all of this equipment must have been enormous, and only the name of Naomi Uemura had made it possible. The whole expedition was sponsored by a Japanese television company and newspaper.

I was interested to meet Uemura. The chubby-faced, boyish looks gave no suggestion of the man's acknowledged hardiness, nor of the determination which had driven him during the many months of his solo Arctic crossing.

'How is Don Whillan? Is he still climbing?' Uemura had spent a long time with Don on Everest's South-West Face in 1971.

He seemed at ease, with a youthful enjoyment of drinking and joking. It was not the hardship he must have put up with in his Arctic crossing but the deadly boredom of months of solitude which I found amazing.

'Are you married? What does your wife think of you spending so much time away?'

'My wife is very happy for me.'

The Japanese were interested in our ages. Uemura felt, at thirty-nine, that he was coming to the end of his active years.

His expedition was also partly a scientific project, with three scientists taking bore samples from the glacier and sending them back to Kathmandu. Two doctors, a journalist and a film crew completed the team. Uemura had spent some weeks in the region during the winter of 1979/80 and had realized then the importance of having a comfortable Base Camp. For this reason he had returned to Japan where he had two purpose-built tents made to withstand the wind and cold.

Further down the table other members of our team were having different conversations. There were a number of other Japanese climbers on the expedition, one of whom said: 'I have contract to go to 200 metres from summit. After that only Mr Uemura goes alone.'

Someone was talking to the Sirdar of the Japanese Sherpas: 'The British expedition will reach top of mountain before Japanese, because Japanese use Sherpas who want money and so make expedition last longer.'

We had stumbled into the tent blinded by the light, now we stumbled out, drunk from the unaccustomed quantities of alcohol, thanking our hosts profusely. Course after course of strange delicacies had appeared before us, most of which I found myself picking at and discreetly leaving to one side. I noticed most of our team doing the same. Our digestive systems had still scarcely adjusted to the altitude and the food we were more familiar with; to have forced down exotic morsels, with to us a bizarre taste, would have invited disaster. I hoped that we had not caused mortal offence in terms of the Japanese code of conduct, but there was no way to tell from their excessive demonstrations of politeness and goodwill.

Back at our own camp we separated each to his own tent. The Japanese set-up was certainly a contrast. As I slid, fully dressed, into my sleeping bag, I looked at a thermometer: −11 °C!

On Tuesday 9 December John joined Al and Ade Burgess and myself in going back up towards the Lho La. There were still many jobs to do round Base Camp and four was quite enough at one time to be working on the route. It also gave those who had been struck down with dysentery a chance to regain their strength.

More familiar this time with the way, we lost no time in reaching the high point of the previous day. Al, moving powerfully on ahead, skirted below a wall of rock and traversed back above it. John and I were below as he crossed a slope of loose stones, sending showers of them down onto us. I was out of line of fire, but John was caught in the open, cursing loudly as the stones bounced off his helmet. Al stopped moving as we shouted abuse at him and stayed motionless and looking apologetically sheepish until we had caught him up. We did not let ourselves get separated again.

We had brought a rucksack each full of rope to fix in place on the more difficult ground. We would have to go up and down many times before we were finished with the mountain, so to save time and ensure safety we had brought rope to leave as a handline where it was necessary, once we had climbed a section. On the biggest mountains it is hardly possible to climb continuously upwards day after day. A period of acclimatization is essential. We did not have a fully predetermined plan about how to climb the mountain, but we were finding that the best method was to fix rope on the difficult ground. Sometimes we only climbed a few hundred feet a day, but with rope once fixed in place, ascent was much more rapid. To have placed a camp after only a few hundred feet would have been futile and would have necessitated carrying enormous weights of tentage, food and equipment. By linking together the efforts of each day to place a camp only after a major section was completed, we gave ourselves a chance of acclimatizing in the process and made a more economical use of our resources.

An area of grey, granite slabs stretched up out of the evil-looking gully at which we had stopped the day before. I stayed back filming the other three as they scurried across the broken, rocky bed of the gully to a promontory on the far side. Being in the bottom of the gully held the sensation of being in the bottom of a rubbish chute, a focal point for anything thrown from above. The gully was an alien place. We felt much more at ease on the smooth, grey slabs above.

These were not difficult, but it would save time, when carrying a heavy load, to have a rope in place, and if it should snow heavily there were many other places where we would have to consider fixing ropes.

It had been another clear, fine day when we had left. Rapidly it had changed; the ambient air temperature was always well below freezing point, and it was only the heat of the sun which gave the impression that a day was warm. Once the sun was masked by cloud, or a wind started, the bitterness of winter made itself felt. By the time we had reached the grey slabs we were cold. For once the Burgess twins, usually so careful, were caught unawares, and as soon as they had used up the rope out of their sacks they rushed off down to avoid the danger of exposure.

John and I, better clothed, were able to continue. John felt guiltily responsible for the weather. The Sherpas had caught him burning some rubbish at Base Camp that morning and had given him a ticking off. They had said it was bad to burn rubbish as it brought bad weather. John surveyed the results of his handi-work with a resigned air. None of us is really superstitious but on a mountain, when living at a high pitch of nervous tension, one can be susceptible to anything that is said or held with conviction. On Kangchenjunga we had not walked the last ten feet to the summit as the people of Sikkim believe this would desecrate the home place of the gods they believe live there and cause them to send floods and earthquakes in revenge. We did not see any gods and of course did not hold these beliefs, but an ominous storm was homing in on the mountain and a huge black bird hung over the summit watching us. No word had passed, but none of us thought to trespass further.

John has a slight, stooping build, belying a tough resilience. As I got to know him I realized that his quietness was reflective. He was what I would consider to be an intellectual, nurturing his knowledge and reproducing it at the most apt moments. He has an apologetic manner which conceals the strengths which moti-vate him and which earned him the respect of the Poles with whom he had taken to climbing after a visit to Poland as part of an official exchange group of mountaineers.

As he descended a precarious ramp into yet another horrifying gully I was glad that he did not seem perturbed at the prospect before us. This gully was steeper, encircled at the top by a basin of convoluted ice. How steep it was was hard to judge, and secretly, with the cowardliness of innermost thoughts, I hoped that John would have enough rope to get the measure of the difficulties before I took over.

He climbed along the edge of the gully, up onto the ice as far as he could go. I joined him and he led off again, this time forced into the bed of the gully, a runnel with dirty smears on the ice where rocks had struck on their way down. More loose blocks were balanced one on top of another and John eased his way past them, his legs spread wide across the narrowed funnel of rock which reared up out of the top rim of the ice. He went out of sight, the rope still moving slowly upwards, then came the sound of the hammering of pitons into rock and a shout for me to come.

It was my turn to go first, I had to cross the gully and climb up the opposite wall of ice to the overhanging groove of rock which appeared to end on the crest of the ridge and on the Lho La plateau. The ice still looked steep, even from close to, and I felt nervous.

A thirty-foot-high step of rock blocked the way to the ice; it required some delicate moves, awkward in the huge, clumsy boots I was wearing. I felt the surge of nervous excitement as I moved tentatively upwards on small footholds to where I could place a piton and achieve some security. The ice was steep but it was pockmarked with weather-worn holes into which I could step, and a few projecting rocks frozen into place provided the infrequent handhold. As usual the encounter was not as frightening as the anticipation. I reached the bottom of the rock wall running into the overhanging groove and secured the rope.

Above I could see signs of the Yugoslav expedition – the tattered remnants of a wire ladder and frayed ropes. The 300-foot groove above obviously presented considerable difficulties, It was late in the afternoon, we had used up all our rope and I turned to descend.

The following day Paul, Brian and Pete, carrying heavy loads of rope, went up to make a cache of equipment ready for the major assault on the groove and the anticipated breakthrough onto the Lho La. They were now recovered from the illness, having only lingering coughs and sore throats which the cold, dry air continued to irritate. Alan had been hit worst by the dysentery and was fighting hard to shake off the sickness which was sapping his strength. He busied himself round Base Camp with calculations of the expedition's finances, food and fuel-consumption and general estimations of our progress. The sickness seemed to be going right through the camp; Ade was next taken ill.

Five of us went up next; Al and John fastened themselves into the overhanging groove preparing for a long siege. Brian and Pete laboured up with more loads, signalling their movements with periodic bursts of noisy coughing. I lodged myself onto a ledge on the opposite side of the gully with a movie camera and watched Al's distant, matchstick moves up the yellow rock.

The remains of the wire ladder hung temptingly down the groove, but the wire was frayed and the rungs bent and twisted either from rockfall or winds. I could see Al testing it and hesitatingly groping his way upwards on the rock with grunts and pauses for breath, preferring to climb the rock which he could rely on than trust to an abandoned wire hawser. His muffled exchanges with John belaying him carried across the gully; it was clear that he was having a struggle.

Some rock broke away from under one of his feet and ricocheted across the gully to just below where I was sitting. John looked over to me. Neither of us said anything; there was nothing to say.

The groove and the wall up which Al was finding the way was exceptionally difficult climbing for the altitude. It looked as if it might be technically the most interesting climbing on the route. We would not be able to cope with anything as difficult as this higher up the mountain, as the ever more rarefied air would not sustain the strenuous efforts required. I was partly envious and partly relieved that someone else was leading this section. I would have liked the satisfaction of solving this particularly difficult problem first, but there were other essential roles to play; I was filming the ascent for ITN; Brian and Pete were carrying loads in support, possibly the most tedious and unrecognized contribution to any expedition. Given that with honour I could sit back, I did feel a guilty self-indulgence at watching someone else struggling to force a way up the rock and fix rope in place for everyone else to follow.

The gully was deep and caught the heat of the sun. The wind did not penetrate but could be heard whistling over the top of the ridge, a few hundred feet above. The heat of the sun loosened some rocks; with increasing frequency stones began to fall past my eyrie. Had the stones been falling when I had arrived there I would not have stayed but I had been there half an hour before the first fell and had come to feel at home. It was slow progress up the groove; I did not want to miss filming the last moments as Al exited onto the ridge, and I sat for three hours, pressing myself hard against the rock behind me to avoid the stones which by the end were falling every ten minutes. Once Al knocked down a massive block which shattered on impact and sprayed all around me. John looked helplessly on.

Al reached a ledge at half height and John climbed up the rope to join him, using jumar clamps which slide up the rope but not down again, taking most of the difficulty out of the ascent. The second half of the wall went more quickly and a jubilant Al shouted down that he had reached a platform, but not the Lho La plateau we had hoped for.

I was as relieved as he was; I could quit the perch in the firing range and ferry my load up to the top of the ropes Al had fixed in place. It was indeed an impressive performance by Al, as I realized on reaching the groove. The first twenty feet was over-hanging and, even with the ropes in place, very strenuous. It took me an hour to climb the wall and join John and Al. Pete and Brian appeared in the gully below and I warned them to stay clear on account of the falling stones.

Enough had been achieved for the day. Short of energy and time we returned to Base Camp.

Psychologically it was very good to have overcome such a major obstacle, though disappointing to find that further difficult ground barred the way to the plateau. If the whole route con-tinued as hard and slow as this section it boded ill for our chances.

We sat in our dining tent discussing tactics and experiences. The tent was shabby and cold by comparison with the Japanese pavilion. We had one small paraffin stove on the table to give a semblance of heat, but it was necessary to wear padded clothing even inside. Huddled together round the yellow light of a par-affin lamp we resembled the scenes I had seen in photographs of Shackleton's men in their winter hut. This was the norm for our existence now – spells of hard work interspersed with periods of inactivity occupied in formless discussion of strategy and often drifting into another exchange of yarns from the past.

Al, still buzzing with the thrill of the hard climbing he had done, told us one tale in which he outlined a patent technique from his teaching days for keeping his class, in a rather rough school, quiet: 'I used to play loud music on the hi-fi I'd fitted up in the class – Jimmy Hendrix or Frank Zappa – have it on really loud so they couldn't hear themselves talk, so they had to work and anyway they were used to the constant noise at home of the TV so it was better for them to work with noise.' All this was recounted with a constant flexing of the shoulders and a devilish grin on his face.

More loads were carried up next day but harrowing winds drove everyone back down without further progress being made. In the middle of the night I was half aware of the noise of the wind and of people's voices and footsteps. In the morning our camp was a shambles. Three tents were collapsed, their poles broken, and others were badly awry. An enormous plume of cloud spewed horizontally north from the summit of Nuptse.

The previous day one of the visiting party of Japanese, admiring our down suits, oxtail soup and route up to the Lho La, had pointed at a motionless wind generator, which had not so far produced any electricity – 'I hope it never works.' It was now spinning furiously.

The whole day was taken up with patching tents, reinforcing tent poles and building crude walls, from the rocks littering the ice, as wind-breaks round the tents.

Dawa and the rest of the Base Camp staff stood, watching our exertions, without the slightest offer of help. Feelings against Dawa had become even more antipathetic since Alan, in going through the accounts, had discovered that Dawa had spent three times as much bringing the loads he was in charge of to Base Camp than Alan himself had. Seven thousand rupees more than expected had been spent. Dawa explained this away by saying he had had to pay more for porters as they were unwilling to carry in winter and one porter had fallen and broken his leg, for which he had had to pay for hospitalization. It was a plausible, but un-satisfactory explanation.

The arrival of our mail runner the next day brought a welcome bundle of mail, but also a letter from our expedition agent in Kathmandu, through whom we had hired our Sherpas. Alan had written to him about earlier difficulties with Dawa, and in his reply our agent said that if we did have difficulties we should go ahead and dismiss him. An enclosed copy of a letter direct to Dawa from the agent emphasized his displeasure at the reported conduct, and mentioned this as casting further bad light on his behaviour after the incident with the Numbur expedition the previous year, an occasion when much valuable equipment from a Norwegian expedition had mysteriously disappeared.

On being questioned, Dawa launched into a diatribe against the affluent members of expeditions who come and employ Sherpas who do not want to work for them but who want the money and have no alternative.

There was mention in the letter from the agent of Dawa's expressed intention to leave us, as soon as we reached Base Camp, to go to America with the girl who had caused him to delay the start of the approach march. There were too many damning coincidences and too much suspicion on our part for us to let the matter go any further. After much agonized soul-searching, Alan went to speak to our Liaison Officer and explain to him that we wanted to dismiss Dawa.

Mr Singh, the Liaison Officer, was the representative of the government of Nepal and it was through him that any complaint and request for action had to be formally made. He was a small, shy man who rarely entered into conversation unless spoken to and spent much of his time performing a self-imposed routine of exercises and singing Hindu songs. However, when confronted with the unpleasant task of executing the wishes of the team, he did not demur. He readily grasped the issues involved and concurred with the conclusions reached. Dawa was summoned and formally dismissed.

It was a sad episode which seemed totally at odds with the spirit of the expedition, but with Dawa's departure, though brought about with pain, came welcome relief, much as the removal of an aching tooth.

Alan was deeply affected by the incident and the events leading up to it. He had been one of the most explicit exponents of the concept of our expedition as leaderless. I had spent some time with him prior to our departure, making frequent journeys to London during which we discussed the rationale behind the expedition. He firmly believed that all of us were sufficiently experienced not to need a leader in the traditional sense of having an overall director of affairs. In fact he felt such a system would be counter-productive in that it could easily engender antagonism amongst a group of highly individualistic human beings. However, he accepted the title of 'leader' as being necessary in dealing with sponsors and the media in Britain, who found it impossible to cope with the concept of a 'leaderless expedition', and with the Nepalese government, who insist on having someone nominated as leader.

It thus fell to Alan to express the decision of the group and no matter what his philosophy of democracy was, the very fact of being spokesman seemed to cause him to be more deeply affected by the responsibility of having to express a group decision than his own part in that decision warranted.

Alan's training as a mathematician led him to delight in intricate discussions involving logic and hypothetical musings which went over most of our heads. He has something of the sophist in him, taking the opposite side in an argument for the sake of prolonging a debate, and he did this in the discussions over Dawa in order to ensure that we erred on the side of mercy rather than acted too quickly and unjustly, until it became clear that a source of continuous discord would not be removed until Dawa was dismissed.

Even democratically appointed leadership brings the loneliness of decision-making, but a cheering indicator that this decision had been the right one came as soon as Dawa left. The rest of the Base Camp staff, who had been a sullen and uncooperative group after the arrival of the Sirdar, were transformed immediately he left. They could be heard singing and chatting as we had not noticed them doing for a few days, and there was a new attitude of cooperation and willingness to help.

CHAPTER FIVE

The Lho La

For two days the weather had remained calm and clear. Expecting the worst, we tended to be suspicious of our good fortune, believing that we had not seen the real face of winter yet, for otherwise, apart from the short days and bitter nights, this would be an ideal season for climbing compared with the unstable spells before and after the monsoon. As it was, lower peaks, not so much affected by the jet-stream winds and requiring shorter time for their ascent, could well be climbed in these clear December days.

Alan was feeling physically much better as well as psychologically relieved that the incident with Dawa was now over, and he went up with the Burgess twins and John Porter. In spite of it being his first time out from Base Camp, Alan was able to reach the top of the overhanging groove and spent all day with John tediously hauling loads up from below. It was too exhausting to climb the ropes now in place and the wire ladder which had been repaired with a full sack on one's back. Climbing the corner consumed time and energy, so whilst the twins found the way and fixed rope along the ridge above the corner, Alan and John formed a stock pile of equipment.

The rest of the ridge was unexpectedly hard. Behind the yellow wall of rock, up which ropes had been painstakingly fastened, was a vast amphitheatre 200 feet wide separating the top of the wall from the Lho La plateau. It plunged in 2,000 feet of avalanche-scoured rock and ice to the glacier. Blocks of ice stood, like rows of houses, waiting their turn, and the loss of equilibrium as the mother bed of ice advanced, to plunge and shatter into a million pieces to form another immense avalanche. If hell were a cold place its entrance would resemble this.

To reach the Lho La the twins had to climb in a rising arc along the ridge of rock which encircled the top of the amphitheatre. Much of the way was easy, with short steps of vicious difficulty, overcome with much exertion and panting. The very atmosphere of the place was enough to inspire nervousness, but the rock itself had also become massively loose. The final hundred feet horizontally rightwards to gain the snow was on blocks adhering, without visible support, to the wall behind. 'The traverse of the eggshells' became its name. On reaching the snow, out of rope and ready to descend, Al was disappointed to find still no sign of a place in which to pitch a tent or dig a cave.

At Base Camp Paul, Brian and myself made ready to go up the next day with every intention of establishing a tent or snow cave, in order to stay on the mountain. The film team had been strangely inactive for a while; I began to wonder if they were being affected by the altitude and slipping into a routine which made it seem as if there was not enough time to do everything, but proved a tendency to put off doing anything until another occasion. Many expedition films fail to succeed entirely on account of this – just surviving on a daily basis at Base Camp can be quite exhausting enough. Allen, director of the film, however, had gone up to the start of the fixed ropes in the company of the lead party, to weigh up camera positions. Unfamiliar with the route, he had sat and waited till Paul, who was making a short carry with a load to the start of the fixed ropes, arrived and descended with him.

It was dusk when John, looking worn and weary, burst into the dining tent where the rest of us were settling into our places for the evening. A growing anxiety at the late return of everyone from the hill was immediately relieved. John sank down onto a box for a seat and questions about the day's climbing started. John has a way of not answering questions immediately nor in the way expected.

'The others aren't going to get here before dark, I don't think they've got torches and they are short of a pair of crampons.'

Everyone looked at him; they were not the words expected in answer to the questions. My mind ran over a check-list of essentials and their whereabouts – ice axe, crampons, torch, spare torch, mitts, boots. Brian next to me seemed to be doing the same. John took the silence for reluctance to stir out into the cold night: 'Look, those guys have been working hard all day and are struggling down in the dark. Are you going to sit here on your arses? They need torches to get across the glacier. I'd go back but I'm knackered.'

It was a startling outburst. John, fully dressed for the cold outside, still with his crampons on, did not realize that anyone going out into the night would have to get ready. It might take ten minutes, it might take two hours to locate and return with the other three, but to venture out unprepared invited disaster. Bare hands would be numb in minutes.

Brian and I scratched around in the dark inside and outside our tents, trying to remember where things were, and, prepared as best we could, hurried urgently over uneven ground towards the slopes up the Lho La. The night was still but there was no sound carried on the air; tragedy in the mountains can occur from the most innocuous situation, and flutterings of unease tightened my stomach. Where the ice was no longer roughened by rubble we stopped and strapped crampons to our boots to allow us to walk more easily on the undulating, glistening surface. We followed the pools of light cast by our torches along the marks on the ice made by the earlier passage of our feet and then, unheralded, the chattering voices of swaying figures rose up from out of a hollow to meet us. There was laughter and ribald curses from the trio making me feel foolish for the anxiety I had felt for them.

They were tired and indeed had no torch; Alan and Al were sharing a pair of crampons – one boot each securely bound with a row of metal spikes to give purchase on the ice, the other, rubber-soled, slipping and unbalancing their gait, making a mockery of any pretensions to be experienced mountaineers.

There was a warm comradeship in our meeting.

'Thanks for coming to meet us, lads,' said Ade, 'it's really been hard work getting across in the dark.'

We returned together to camp, seeing the dining tent now as a cosy haven by comparison with the outside world.

I awoke with the disturbing memory of a dream in which I was hanging by the neck and a vision of failure on the route. There were no grounds for these unsettling dreams except that I had gone to sleep with a familiar feeling of apprehension before embarking on the next stage of the climb, the next step into the unknown.

Movement and a sense of fitness banished such chimeras in the bright light of day. I reached the top of the fixed ropes by 1.30 p.m., weighed down by a sack which held, though containing only the essentials for a stay of two or three nights, 40 lbs of food and gear. Paul and Brian, similarly laden, were also toiling up the ropes to stay.

We planned to start digging a snow cave and, if this was not big enough to sleep in by evening, to erect a tent for the night. We had little hope of a tent lasting very long in the winds of the Lho La, but hoped to dispense with it after one night. There was nowhere in sight that seemed suitable to start digging a cave. Hard, icy snow swept upwards at too precarious an angle for siting a cave. Rationalizing the situation, I knew that we would not do any digging at all this day, there was still some gear to be picked up from the cache at the top of the corner and there was not even a place where we could put up a tent.

Dumping my sack, I scrambled upwards on easier ground, kicking the edge of my boot into the snow and holding onto the rock against which it abutted. It was a foolish but delightful romp, liberated from the weight of my sack and the constriction of being fastened into a rope. I would not be allowed even one slip, not one error of judgement, but I had the strength and confidence of fitness, reaching up and testing each handhold before pulling up on it; kicking a boot into the snow and trying my weight on that foot before committing myself to it completely. The enthusiasm was rewarded; a broad ledge, ten feet wide, opened up to my left. It was littered with rocks, easily wide enough for a tent and the rocks could be made into a wall as a wind-break. Reassured at this alternative to a frantic attempt at excavating a snow cave as a shelter for the night, I turned to descend and propose the change of plan to Paul and Brian.

I had not looked down as I climbed upwards free of the ropes. As I turned now and saw the ice runnel up which I had come, ending abruptly at the edge of the precipice of the amphitheatre, I felt sick and nervous at the insecurity of my position. I descended the 200 feet back to the lifeline of the ropes with my stomach knotted in apprehension, clutching more tightly than was warranted to every hold, inescapably aware of the folly of my situation.

Paul had reached the end of the ropes when I arrived back. He agreed that it would be most sensible to pitch a tent immediately than risk having no shelter ready by nightfall.

'Did you pick the tent up? I couldn't find it!'

'No, I looked in one of the sacks half way up the corner, it wasn't in there.'

'Damn, I wonder if Brian's got it.'

'What's it like up to the ledge?'

'O.K., but be careful. You'll be safer with crampons on.'

I slid down the ropes strung along the rim of the amphitheatre and regained the top of the corner with a pleasurable ease which made ridiculous the effort needed to climb upwards on the same ground. I could hear Brian long before I could see him, as his coughs, which I could only imagine to be painful, echoed up the corner.

There was no tent with the gear at the top of the corner and Brian did not have it either. I slid down the ropes of the corner, imagining an ignominious retreat if there was no tent to be found and dreading the long haul back up the ropes if there was.

The tent was concealed in a sack which Paul had not examined; I shouldered the sack and started back up.

The preliminary plan of digging a snow cave for the night had been absurdly ambitious; we had barely time to erect the tent, build a protective wall of rocks and gather snow to melt for the evening meal before the sun slipped from the sky and the rapid night took over.

Brian was weary from the journey up. He sank into the dark interior of the tent, thrusting out a grateful hand for mugs of liquid and plates of food as they were prepared. Sometimes his pained face would appear in the light of the stove as he strained forward, shaken by another spasm of coughing.

Heavy-boned and big-framed, Brian gave me, as I grew to know him, the impression that he was always pushing himself hard. If it was recounting lurid stories, Brian strove to produce the most startling; if it was outrageous behaviour, Brian would outgross anyone. On the mountain I could see him driving himself on against the affliction of his crippling cough long after I would have let myself turn back. Brian was continually forcing himself along the road of excess in his search for the palace of wisdom. I imagined his throat to be raw and bleeding.

Again the night was suspiciously calm. I was numb when I crawled back from the edge of the platform from where I had been futilely attempting to make a radio call to Base Camp thousands of feet below, but only the lightest breeze rocked the tent. Our platform was awesomely poised on the very brink of a precipice, but somehow tucked away from the wind streaming across the Lho La plateau. We spent a restless night, the three of us pressed close together, suffocated with the tent door closed and chilled with it open. Next day I had a headache and the three of us were slow to make a start.

To find a more level area of snow in which we could dig a cave without risk of slipping down a steep slope as soon as one stepped outside, we headed for the plateau of the Lho La itself. A basin of firm snow, split by a number of crevasses, gave way to easier angled slopes which descended to level ground. I was ready to go and Paul suggested I lead off, fixing rope onto aluminium stakes driven into the snow until I was no longer above the gulf of the amphitheatre. There was no advantage to the climbing in having a rope there, but we would have to cross and recross this slope many times, and it would be so much safer with a hand rail in place. Without the rope to hold onto, a gust of wind could overbalance someone and throw him down the slope into the amphitheatre.

I was nervous of starting off, the slope of snow looked steep, but it was an optical illusion, the yawning abyss a hundred feet below influencing my view of the situation. When I was clear of the abyss, I drove a final stake into the snow and shouted to Paul and Brian to follow.

The snow slope I was on eased down for three hundred feet into a level plateau; this in turn swept northwards and down, losing itself in a jagged maze of ice pinnacles; remote, mysterious Tibet lay brown in the distance. Across the plateau rose the icy escarpment of the West Ridge, 3,500 feet of snow, rock and ice to the rounded dome of the shoulder. Lurking elusively, a thrilling sight behind the Western Shoulder, was the summit – so far away. A banner of cloud streamed off it, the symbol of winter, barren and windy. That was our objective but, as usual, I found myself shelving any thought of what was to come and concentrated on the task of the moment.

Brian had spent the summer in the Karakoram at the other end of the Himalayas taking part in the ski descent of Baltoro Kangri. He was enthusiastic about a snow cave they had dug there which, according to the description, sounded like a palace. Paul and I, professing less experience in such matters, looked to Brian for suggestions as to the best place and method of construction.

There was a science to it; an optimum angle of slope; a method of achieving the correct lengths of entry into the slope before starting to form a chamber. It was hard work, there was no science about that. We were at 20,000 feet and the maximum spell of digging that any of us could do was ten to fifteen minutes. We took it in turns.

John and Ade arrived in the course of the day while Brian and Paul were digging and I was having a rest. 'You're foreman are you?' Ade joked when he came, watching shovels full of snow being ejected from the hole.

They brought news of Pete injecting the cook boy with an anti-nausea drug; the sickness seemed to be circulating right round the camp. Alan was ill again and Al had gone down with the same thing. Usually on an expedition all germs seem to disappear. It is so cold that they are killed off or rendered inactive. This time, however, in spite of the cold, we seemed to be afflicted by a particularly virulent strain, and once the sickness took hold, recovery was very much harder.

John and Ade did not stay long. They dumped the loads

which they had brought up and hurried down. By 4 p.m. we had dug out a small cave, big enough for one person. The snow was hard, ideal for climbing, taking only the front points of the crampons to give a secure foothold, but tiresome for digging. The early stages were the worst as the entrance had to be a narrow tunnel to keep out as much wind as possible, which meant that only one of us could work, sometimes on knees sometimes lying on one's back, labouring away under showers of ice splinters. It did not look much for a day's work but there was room now for two people kneeling upright to dig all the time, and next day we expected progress to be much quicker with a habitable snow cave by the time we finished.

Somehow I was manoeuvred into being cook again, a laborious task with much of the time being taken up just melting snow to get the liquid to make a meal or a drink. From start to finish, in order to obtain the necessary bodily intake of fluid, cooking a meal can take three or more hours. I kept dozing off whilst waiting for the snow to melt and the water to boil. The boiling point of water at high altitude is much lower than at sea level. Due to the decreased air pressure, the water vaporizes at a lower temperature, but the heat is not there to cook the food. Most things take two or three times as long to cook as at sea level.

'Does one of you two want to have a go?'

'You seem better acclimatized than us – we need the rest!'

I realized how Dick Renshaw must have felt on K2 when Pete and I had languished in our sleeping bags whilst he, uninfluenced by any mood of lethargy, used to be up first thing in a morning preparing breakfast to get us moving. There is some mechanism of passive resistance on expeditions which conspires to instil a reluctance to make more effort than absolutely necessary, so that making a cup of tea can come to seem like a monstrous task. Yet more than on any other expedition the dehydration effect of altitude and cold was making it essential to drink more than the accepted minimum of eight pints a day and to force oneself to eat whether one felt like it or not. Without the liquid, altitude sickness and headaches occur much more readily, and without the food we would be weak and much more susceptible to the cold.

After another fitful night we worked on the snow cave until the middle of the afternoon. We were weary now and my fatigued muscles seemed to be contributing little to the enlargement of the cave. Al arrived and I followed him down to Base Camp, having dismantled the tent lest it should be blown away by the wind. Paul and Brian followed later. There was the warm ache of tiredness in my legs as I crossed the glacier back to camp and the thicker air of Base Camp made me drowsy. Alan, worn out by his debilitating sickness, looked jaded and depressed.

We now had a base for action on the West Ridge itself. The ascent up to the Lho La had been technically much more difficult than we had expected, and more difficult than anything else we hoped to find higher up. It felt to me like a preparation, an essential and unavoidable part of the climb, but nonetheless only a preparation, and that it was from the Lho La that I would begin to feel that real progress was being made. For the three of us who had been up there it was time for a rest but I envied the discoveries that those who were going up next would make as they explored new ground.

CHAPTER SIX

Progress and Punishment

The mail runner arrived while we were on the mountain. With the welcome letters was the surprise of a newspaper, the *Observer*, three weeks late but a prized arrival all the same, complete with colour supplement. We were sending back news reports to the *Observer* and they had agreed to mail to us a copy each week during the expedition. I spent a whole day leisurely soaking up every bit of world news, cinema critiques, book reviews and even business news. It mattered little that it was all three weeks out of date.

Our shy little Liaison Officer, glued to his radio for much of the day, sometimes volunteered a snippet of news, or the Japanese passed on something they had picked up on their radio. It was thus we came to learn of, and be shocked unaccountably by, John Lennon's death. There was a strange sense of *déjà vu* in this two-stage arrival of news. One associates newspapers with almost the same instantaneous transmission of news as the radio or television. For us the time-lag between the two was so great that the news from the radio had passed into the subconscious long before the paper arrived, so that I read the *Observer* with an uncanny and mistaken sensation of prescience.

There was no organized manner in which we went up on the mountain. In keeping with the democratic ideals of the expedition it was held that everyone was capable enough and experienced enough to make decisions themselves on the mountain; everyone was mature enough to work to his maximum and consequently there was no need for any direction of effort. Thus there was no order in which anyone went up to carry loads or occupy the snow cave or push the route further. Not everyone was in agreement over this. The Burgess twins were vociferous in their condemnation of what they called 'random attack'; John believed that everyone should do a certain number of trips just carrying loads up to the Lho La before moving up. Alan was adamant that everyone was working to his limit and that no more could be expected: 'There may be an uneven distribution of what is being done at the moment, but by the end of the trip it will all have balanced out.' Nevertheless, there was feeling in some quarters that more organization and coordination would not be a bad thing.

The Burgess twins, John and Pete moved up to occupy and enlarge the snow cave. Two of them stayed in the tent for a night until a second adjoining cave was dug, making ample space for all eight of us. They made the mistake of leaving the tent up on a windy night and on the next day, going to ferry some gear across from it to the caves, found it collapsed. The 'unbreakable' fibreglass poles had been eroded away by the action of the wind shaking the tent incessantly throughout a night and rubbing the poles against a rock used to hold the tent down. Inside the snow cave only the sound of the wind penetrated as a distant drone and it was possible to forget its power and persistence.

At Base Camp, intermittently resting and carrying loads up to the Lho La, I was hard put to decide on the best way of utilizing a rest day. The hours of sun were so short and life outside those hours was a misery. The meal times were the focal points of the day, starting with the rattling of pans and kettles in the early morning, signifying the preparation of 'bed tea', the most welcome tradition established by the great pioneers of Himalayan mountaineering. Before the day can start, the ritual of tea being brought round and thrust with a grinning 'Morning, sahib, tea' into the tent has to take place. One feels its absence with an irritation similar to that when the milkman has somehow failed to deliver and a cheerless breakfast with black coffee and no cereal starts the day. It is as if it is a God-given right and impossible to stir from the sleeping bag without it. But once the tea arrives and the whole, hot pint swallowed, it is not many minutes before there is a series of scufflings and pulling of cords and zips as everyone is forced to rush outside to relieve a full bladder. The worst situation occurs when the bio-rhythms are not properly regulated or a pre-dawn sortie into a chill world is brought on by the Pavlovian rattle of kettles and cups from the cook tent.

The dining tent was the centre of the camp, the place where we socialized, discussed, bragged, argued and ate. I felt isolated in my own tent, but unable to concentrate in the dining tent if I wanted to read and there were conversations going on.

One discussion revolved around tactics on the mountain. Alan was all in favour of using snow caves all the way. He and Brian had been part of a team that had climbed the North Face of Nuptse in 1979 and had been impressed with the use of snow caves there. I believed that he was underestimating the difficulty involved in digging snow caves at altitude and said that we would need a cave for at least six people on the West Shoulder at about 23,000 feet and four people at 25,000 feet. I calculated this on the basis of having a rotation of people on the mountain both for digging the caves in the first place and going to the summit at the end. Unless there was accommodation for at least four people at 25,000 feet there would be a gap of several days between one pair going for the top and the next pair.

The twins descended from the Lho La and a discussion turned towards the summit. Faced with the overwhelming reality of Everest in winter, all fanciful ideas bandied around in England had disappeared and now Al voiced his opinion: 'I think that it's going to need all our efforts to get two people to the top. There's no way we are all going to get there. Two of us getting up will be good enough for me.'

The style of expedition we had all evolved relied not upon a meticulous, computer-planned strategy but more upon experience and the ability to judge, on the spot, how best to utilize our resources. We had no selected summit pair; we all had an equal chance of making an attempt to reach the top. Who it would actually be would depend upon how well anyone was performing at that time. The ideal would be for everyone to make it but the 'wastage rate' on mountains is high and this never happens. We decided on the number and location of camps or snow caves as we went along, aiming to have, at the end, the facility for at least two people to occupy the final camp at 27,000 feet, in striking distance of the summit. In the next camp down, in our case at 25,000 feet, there would have to be room for the returning summit pair and those moving up to take their place. The next camp down again, needing less effort to establish, could be larger than required to hold the rest of the team, in order to accommodate also anyone returning from above. The camps lower down needed to be large enough to facilitate the establishment of the higher camps, and once this had taken place they would become simply transit points on the way up the mountain.

The work done so far and that which remained to do was staggering. It did not do to think of the mountain – Everest, the biggest mountain in the world – it was best to think only of the next little bit, at most to consider the general direction to the next possible camp site, but in detail only the few feet immediately ahead. My mind quailed if it tried to comprehend the whole, but it could cope with bits at a time.

From the snow caves on the Lho La – Stalingrad as we called them (in memory of the bitter winter campaign of the Second World War around that city) – the occupants had attacked the slopes up to the West Shoulder. The twins and John Porter crossed the hostile moonscape of the Lho La and John described reaching the bergschrund, the crevasse which forms where easier angled ice rears up into the steeper wall of a mountain:

Over night the wind had dropped to a gentle gale blowing up from Tibet. We had been late leaving the cave and the shadow cast by the West Shoulder had already receded half the distance across the Lho La between the cave and the start of the slopes. When we reached the bergschrund, Ade, jangling with the snow stakes and ice screws hanging from his waist, volunteered to lead.

The crevasse separating us by ten feet from the vertical wall of ice opposite was tenuously bridged by a jumble of perched, interlocking ice blocks from some earlier avalanche. Ade made a frightening hop-scotch over these blocks and picked away at the steep, brittle ice with his axe and hammer, trying to lodge them securely. Al filmed his brother's struggles; time passed slowly and the cold penetrated our down suits.

There was fifteen feet of vertical ice before the angle eased back. Ade tottered upwards, suspended above the pale blue depths of the crevasse by the picks of his ice axe and hammer and the crampon points protruding from the front of his boots. His movements were slow but deliberate and, just as the sunlight streamed round the ridge onto us, he was over the worst and securing himself on the easier ground above.

Al and I, in turn, swung up the rope now fastened in place. The slope stretching upwards was not difficult, firm snow enabling a steady ascent. Much more of a problem was making a secure anchor for the rope which we were fixing in place and leaving to provide a rapid way of descent and re-ascent for the future. We led out each rope length in turns, at the end of which it was necessary to dig a deep trench to find firmer snow into which to drive the three-foot-long aluminium stakes. The rope was fastened to a stake and the other two would come up carrying rucksacks filled with more rope.

The slope was at an aggravating angle, too steep to allow one to relax into automatic movements, and yet not quite steep enough to bring out the full concentration needed on more difficult ground. We were disappointed to realize we had only climbed about 600 feet in all before it was time to return to the snow cave.

At Base we received the news with satisfaction. Radio contact had finally been established by the simple expedient of synchronizing our watches, so that both parties were attempting to make contact at the same time! Crackling over the air came Ade's voice. It had been difficult, and particularly cold, crossing the bergschrund and the wall of ice behind. He asked for comments on the line to follow. A thousand feet above the point they had reached, a barrier of overhanging, ice-smattered rock spanned the face. It was difficult from their position on the face to decide on the most suitable place to aim for. Too far to the right would bring them into the fall-line of the ice cliffs which projected threateningly above the barrier. I had considered the problem earlier and suggested making for a groove through the barrier into which a tongue of ice penetrated. Usually, where there is ice or snow, the angle of slope is easier. Vertical rock often sloughs it off.

During a warmer season we might have considered doing without the ropes on some sections, and even considered climbing the mountain in 'alpine style', starting at the bottom and continuing to the top in one journey, rather than fixing ropes in place and descending each night to an established camping place. Neither way is easy. Climbing alpine style means carrying everything one needs for survival on one's back; food, cooking equipment, tent or snow shovel. Too heavy a sack and the chances of reaching the summit are much reduced, for a load of 30 lbs is crippling above 20,000 feet. For us, climbing in winter, we had to have much more warm clothing, food and fuel than in summer and the difficulties of our chosen route were much greater than the routes normally followed on the mountain. Progress would be unconscionably slow and the consequences of being caught out by night and storm would be quick and lethal. Fixing ropes in place gave us a quick descent to a secure camp or cave and a means of more rapid ascent to the high point from where further progress could be made.

Whichever way a big mountain is climbed it is rarely enjoyable; the comparison is really between the tedium of climbing and descending known ground several times, making steady upward progress with only the leading pair receiving the real thrill of discovery and contest with difficulty, and the excruciating punishment of attempting to push on upwards each day without the body having a chance to adjust itself to the altitude. In time the composition of the blood alters, more oxygen can be absorbed, the heart does not need to work so hard, adaptation to cold takes place and one's ability to cope with the abnormal conditions of altitude and low temperatures is increased. Trying to rush upwards before this adaptation occurs can be fatal. The slow, measured ascent, fixing ropes and descending each night to sleep lower than the height reached puts the body to much less risk.

The twins and John made sorties from the cave onto the icy slopes to climb and fasten more ropes to stakes driven into the ice, or to pitons driven into rocks which protruded in places. A rope is 150 feet long, a useful, manageable length. Five rope lengths fixed in place represented a day's work. Stretched out flat on the ground, five rope lengths represents barely 250 yards, which would take a matter of minutes to pass over. The next day, John started leading on the wind-swept ice of the West Ridge:

> We mounted confidently up the ropes we had fixed, and continued upwards with more ropes towards the rock barrier above. The barrier appeared deceptively close but we were 1,000 feet above the bergschrund before we reached the first slabs of rock leading up to the jutting overhangs. We were faced with a confusing sweep of blank granite up which there seemed to be no way to climb. I led across leftwards, with less optimism, to what looked to be a more feasible line up some ice runnels which cut through the rock towards a narrowing in the overhangs above.
>
> At one point we were unexpectedly immersed in a hissing spindrift avalanche – nothing serious, just a massive bombardment of ice crystals. Ade was thirty feet down to my right, the sun directly behind him, and he came miraculously aglow as the ice particles bounced into the bright light. A red and blue halo formed around his down suit and sack.
>
> I was dissatisfied with the slowness of our progress, but looking across the Lho La to the distant, dark speck which was the snow cave, I realized the scale of the slopes we were on. I knew that Brian and Pete were waiting in the cave and I anticipated their scepticism about the meagreness of our efforts; we had fixed rope for only 400 feet this time. They would appreciate the problems themselves when they took over next day.

The twins and John descended to Base Camp leaving Pete and Brian to solve the problem of the rock barrier.

Paul, Alan, Brian and I had carried on ferrying loads up to the Lho La. There was no point in our moving up yet, and there was no more useful function we could serve than to stock up the Lho La camp, Camp 1, so that when it should be necessary for everyone to stay up there would be plenty of food, fuel and rope.

Brian and Alan decided to go up to stay, to replace two of the others after a couple of days. Alan was struggling against the disability of his racking cough and bouts of nausea, determined not to be left behind on account of any sickness. But on the day they were to stay up, Brian, leading the way up the slabs into the top gully, dislodged a rock which bounded down gashing Alan's hand. Shocked and deterred, hardly able to use his hand, Alan resignedly returned to Base Camp.

I was spending a fair amount of time in Paul's company during these days. Without any decisions, it turned out that we were involved with similar tasks and found ourselves toiling up together several times with that rueful comradeship of the 'badly done by'. We were not badly done by, but we self-indulgently allowed ourselves to imagine that we were being Sherpas for the others. There was a solidity about Paul, a reassuring air of common sense sometimes betrayed by a manic laugh which reaffirmed his stated views on the oddity of life. Most of the times I had met Paul before the expedition had been in a pub or at parties where he would be discoursing at length, with slurred speech, on complex subjects which I failed to understand at the time and did not remember afterwards. Overall it left me with the impression that he was particularly intelligent but I could not follow what he talked about.

There was no real pairing off of anyone, but the film team, media oriented, was looking for patterns, and seeing Paul and I together on more than one day seized the opportunity to take some film of us climbing the lower slopes. Having gained some confidence about moving about on the easier ground, and familiarity with the route in the lower part of the rock buttress before the ropes started, the film crew were in the habit of venturing up themselves to find vantage points for their cameras. The debate on their role had not been concluded. There was still some uneasiness amongst the climbers about leaving the film crew alone on the mountain, and it was as difficult for us to judge how hard it was for them to cope with ground we covered as a matter of routine as it is for someone who can drive to imagine the difficulties someone sees who cannot drive. Much later, Allen Jewhurst described an incident which fully justified our fears:

A lot of thoughts go through one's mind in fifteen seconds. Our cameraman, Mike Shrimpton, was sliding down a slope with a drop of 1,500 feet below him. We had decided to reconnoitre the route up to the Lho La and find good camera positions. It was also a reasonably safe area to see how well Graham, our sound recordist, could cope with the climbing. I had climbed the route with Peter three days earlier. After three hours we found ourselves in a disconcerting situation. At 19,000 feet we had drifted off the route and were lost. We told Graham to stay put on a rib of rock on the left of a gully. Mike was to search out to the right and I to the left. After a few minutes I recognized the route to my left, over a rise. As I turned to call Mike, I saw him sliding down the gully. A loose rock had given way and he was falling towards Graham. Mike was a goner, I was sure, and what of Graham? If left alive with Mike dead, how would he react? Graham had never climbed in his life before and here he was at 19,000 feet with his friend falling to his death.

Graham watched astounded. Mike stretched out his arms, clawing as he fell, his fingers caught on a lip of rock and he came to a halt against Graham. With precise calmness, Mike politely told Graham to move a foot to the right. He took over Graham's perch and fifteen minutes later we were back on route with two decisions made: not to get lost again and not to tell the climbers.

Base Camp was a world away from life on the mountain; the difference was as great as that between life in Britain and life at Base Camp. For the first 1,500 feet on the ice slopes the climbers were out of sight. I had inherited the duty of making the radio calls and my conception of those on the mountain was influenced by the tiny, crackling voices which came over the radio. Without realizing it, I associated the little voices with the minute figures last glimpsed through a telephoto lens, climbing slowly up to the Lho La, and half imagined my friends on the mountain to have

become matchstick men. It was a foolish flight of fancy brought
on by the enormity of our objective.

The twins and John arrived down with more details of their
progress above the Lho La and information on the line which
Brian and Pete were intending to try through the rock barrier.
They were awed by the effort required for the distance they had
covered, by the relentless cold, even though the sky might be
clear, and by the work which remained.

The film crew had an enormous lens mounted on one of their
cameras and someone was forever peering through it to see if
there was any sign of Brian and Pete. An excited shout went up
when they were spotted; invisible to the naked eye they appeared
as real people through the powerful lens, though it was only
possible to distinguish them from each other by the colour of
their clothing. I felt as if I was peeping in on a private, personal
conflict. The two matchstick figures were close together. The red
one, Brian, was above the other; from his questing movements I
could see he was having difficulty. A telescoped view can be deceptive, making some things look easier, some harder; by all
indications this was a crucial section with which they were
struggling, and Brian described how it was:

I felt cold and quite remote from mankind. Base Camp, the
tiny coloured dots on the glacier far below, was a different
world. Standing here, hour after hour it seemed, as Pete led
across steep ice and into the rock band, I had time to reflect on
our isolation and remoteness. Already the 'norm' had become
Base Camp life, a 'norm' far removed from a life surrounded
by the conveniences and comforts of our civilization.

Pete was having problems, finding himself being forced leftwards as one icy groove after another resisted his attempts to
climb it. I was impatient with Pete's slow progress, feeling the
urge to have a go myself and having to refrain from making
what I thought would be helpful suggestions. As time passed,
I became bored with the depressing scene of cloud dropping
lower and lower over Pumori and Gyachung Kang, and the
view down the Rongbuk glacier to the barren hills of Tibet.
A twenty-six-mile marathon could be run in less time, I

reflected, than it had taken us to climb up the 1,500 feet to this point.

Paradoxically, this was just the opportunity I had been waiting for. I had been ill for the first few weeks of the trip with a bronchial complaint aggravated by the dry, cold air. Plagued by an incessant cough, my role until today had been one of supporting and load-carrying for the fitter members. Illness and constant load-carrying were not what my pre-expedition dreams were made from. Visions of surmounting difficult ice gullies, smooth slabs of rock and steep snow slopes, dreams of leading the way for rope length after rope length, had all been shattered; shattered by sickness and drudgery. Some of the team were fulfilling their dreams. I had not been, and I was questioning my own ability to cope with such a difficult route and such harsh conditions.

This time on the mountain I had started well, reaching Camp 1 quicker than I had ever done, and was enthusiastic at the prospect of breaking through the rock band. Now it was getting late, an earlier headache and grogginess had passed off but the wind was gaining in strength and the cloud was thickening. Impatience at the late hour conflicted with impatience to be leading myself. I was excited to realize that when it was my turn I should break through this impasse to the easier ground above.

With Pete finally established on a poor ledge but firmly fastened to pitons driven into rock, I followed eagerly. Where Pete had had to climb carefully, axes planted in ice, crampon points grating on rock, I, safeguarded by the rope, tried to hurry and generate some warmth. My lungs almost burst; I became light-headed and dizzy through trying to force myself without sufficient oxygen. I arrived at the ledge in a tangle of ropes. My mind was as active as a garden snail, my hands without feeling from the cold, and it was a long time before the ropes were untangled.

When I started up the ice gully from the ledge, the dizziness returned; I climbed more slowly. From the top of the gully, I saw the solution to the problem of surmounting the final overhangs. An undercut ledge ran leftwards to a bottomless corner of rock. This ran up to the barrier of rock which over-hung this area at the narrowest point. If I could get through the overhang here, we would be on easier ground and a major obstacle would have been conquered.

Leaving the groove I was in to gain the ledge felt extremely precarious and the 'high' of leading was soon shattered by terror as my arms rapidly tired and the prospect of hurtling backwards down the groove loomed large. I gained the ledge with my last strength, but the strain of the previous few minutes had unnerved me so much that what I had regarded as a large platform now seemed barely wide enough to catch the points of my crampons. I could not rest, but clung on for dear life. 'Watch the rope, Pete,' I shouted down. 'I'll try to get a peg in.' The peg went all too easily into a crack in the rock, seeming to prise the rock away with it, but it gave me confidence and I edged leftwards to the corner.

The corner was clogged with snow but I could rest; my terror was forgotten and I was beginning to enjoy the day. Down below it was Pete now who looked bored, fidgeting and stamping his feet impatiently. For him, I knew, time would be passing slowly. For me, time did not exist; the climbing engrossed me completely.

I cleared the snow from the corner, discovering plenty of holds, and reached the overhang quickly. After a rest, a heave upwards and a swing leftwards landed me on the easy ground above.

There was a sense of fulfilment, a sense of achievement, but now that I was over the difficulty time did matter; night was near, wind-blown snow obscured the view down to the Lho La and the urgency of the situation made itself felt. I waited till Pete had arrived up the rope and dumped his load and we hurried off down.

Abseil followed abseil till we reached the easier slopes as darkness fell. The way back to the cave of Camp 1 was vague in the mist and dark. Several times we were blown off course by the wind and it was with relief that we chanced upon the debris of our food packages and the gentle rise up to the cave.

It was 22 December. Alan, Paul and I planned to go up the next day to take over from Brian and Pete, whom we expected to be tired after breaking through the rock barrier. I awoke on 23 December to steady snowfall and low cloud. The radio call to Pete and Brian told us that conditions were too bad to climb at the time; if the weather cleared they would do some more, if not they would enlarge the cave further and dig a snow-hole toilet, to make living conditions more bearable at Camp 1, before coming down to Base Camp. We decided not to go up ourselves until the weather cleared and I felt a guilty thrill that we might after all be at Base Camp to celebrate Christmas, and receive the next batch of mail which was due at any time. If the weather did clear there was no question but that we would go up, whatever the sentimental attraction of celebrating Christmas, as fine days were too precious and irretrievable to pass up.

The snowfall did not let up all day; heavy, persistent flakes brought a hushed whiteness to the camp. Brian and Pete shoved their way through the drapes of the dining tent entrance towards evening, covered in snow and still wearing crampons. Brian was gasping hard as if he had just survived an Arctic epic; Pete, controlled, strode across the tent and with measured slowness unfastened his crampons and sat down.

This was the first real encounter that any of us had had with the mountain in severe conditions and Brian's description of their descent from the snow cave gave a disconcerting impression of the forces with which we were contending.

The storm of the previous evening had worsened during the night. We guessed that no one would come up from Base Camp in such weather and Pete and I resolved to descend as quickly as possible. We did not know what it would be like to be caught in a winter storm on the mountain, and the possibility of being stranded for days seemed very real.

I left first and had difficulty standing upright against the wind as soon as I was out of the cave. The rope ran up the slope from the mouth of the cave for 200 feet to a snow stake. From there it went horizontally for another 300 feet to the first rocks from where the descent proper began. I clipped onto the rope with a clamp which I could slide along, but which would lock onto the rope when I wanted it to. This section of slope seemed to be catching the wind at its strongest. Facing into the wind, I could not breathe, and I tried to make progress backwards. I could not keep my footing as the wind just blew me over. I went down on my knees, my head held low, and crawled up the slope. Constantly I was lifted from the ground, only to be stopped from being blown away by the rope which was taut in the wind and singing under the tension.

The best method of movement was to rush and then rest. Fast movement is not easy at altitude, but movement was essential. I rested in a ball, face buried in arms, then rushed upwards for ten feet before collapsing, panting, in a crouch once more.

It was even more difficult where the ropes ran horizontally across the slope. Here I had to revert to moving backwards. The slope had steepened sufficiently to prevent me crouching in a ball and I could not face into the wind, nor could I move backwards at a rush. The force of the wind had reached a new peak and I seemed to be spending more time in mid air, like a kite, than on the surface of the snow. Even facing away from the wind it was difficult to breathe. A vacuum was formed on the side of my body in the lee of the wind, and I was panting furiously to overcome this unexpected suffocation. With my mouth thus gaping, ice started to form inside; the cold air I was sucking into my lungs was making them ache; my whole body was cold.

Panic started to take hold of me and I tried to reason that it was not too late to turn back. I felt dizzy and lethargic as the wind pushed me first one way, then the other and I became completely disorientated. I knew my body heat was being whipped away every second. It seemed a silly place to die, just a few rope lengths away from the safety of the cave.

My fear increased when I heard my own voice saying: 'Come on, move!' and the words came out as nothing more than a drunken slur.

I recognized that I had reached the point where the ropes crossed a six-foot-wide crevasse mostly concealed by snow –

normally a place to avoid, but now it appeared as a friend. Still attached to the rope, I launched myself into its depths and an eerie calm set in. I was still panting and disorientated but the panic had been taken out of the moment. I had time to recover and consider whether to return to the ice cave or battle on to the rocks.

Half an hour later I poked my head out into the wind, which hit me like a wall of liquid. I went for the rocks, fighting every step with my body angled at 45° into the wind. I do not remember the final hundred feet along the rope, only the sense of relief as I collapsed in the lee of the rocks.

Pete arrived after a similar struggle and my spontaneous outbursts of terror and amazement were lost in the wind; but he did not need any descriptions from me.

Lower down, we came into snowfall, the once familiar route now disguised beneath a thickening blanket. Once easy ground was a nightmare of uncertainty; the ropes, sometimes buried deep in the snow, were swollen to three times their thickness with coatings of ice. We slipped and slid downwards for six hours, finally stumbling into Base Camp just in time for Christmas.

Brian had some criticisms about the route up to the West Shoulder. He felt that there had been a tendency by the twins and John to take the most obvious line, leaving Pete and himself to sort out the difficulties when the going became too hard. 'Let's think about it more carefully in future,' he said.

Opinions did differ, but the main obstacle was now overcome and it seemed good that this should have been achieved in time for Christmas and that we should all be down together to celebrate.

CHAPTER SEVEN

Christmas

The abnormal darkness for the time of the morning and, above my eyes, the sagging slopes of the tent from which there came the intermittent rustle of sliding snow, told me that the camp was still enveloped in the storm we had woken to the previous day. There would be no movement upwards today either, and aware now that we would all be seeing Christmas in together I was secretly relieved. It was not good to lose a single precious day of work on the mountain but now there was no option I could relax. The significance of Christmas now permeated my consciousness and I noted in my diary: 'An unreal situation – and at the same time so normal. All the residue of Christmases past, conviviality, warmth, presents, lights, friends, girlfriends, family – and here we are, here I am, waking to snowfall and grey, heavy weather at Base Camp. The bright spot being that we are all here and the mail runner should be back today, though weather was so bad yesterday that no plane would have come in, so it will be just mail from last week.'

All day was spent in lazy preparation for a Christmas feast. We had decided to have our party, American style, on the evening of Christmas Eve, since we were all together but, if the weather improved, three of us would be leaving to go up. Suddenly I realized how much it meant to me to celebrate Christmas and how eager I was for the mail runner to arrive.

John had miraculously preserved a small supply of drink – brandy, sherry and whisky – for this occasion and some decorations and ornamental lights appeared. The dining tent took on a festive atmosphere as John, alternating between cook tent and dining tent, his face glowing more and more brightly, supervised events in the kitchen and helped himself to the chef's traditional tots of alcohol.

Five of the Japanese came over at our invitation to join our celebrations. Uemura, storm bound at Camp 2, sent us Christmas greetings, and our Sherpa staff caught the spirit of our enthusiasm. Wan Chup, for once, worked willingly under John's painstaking directions.

As darkness fell on a camp blanketed in snow, trays of delicacies were ferried across into the dining tent; dressed crab, smoked oysters, pâté and more sherry. The constant roar of the wind from the Lho La was drowned by the cacophany of sound from our largest cassette deck which was thrust into the bottom of an empty, drumlike container to enhance the volume.

After a while the Japanese beamed their thanks, made their excuses with inscrutable politeness and left.

The main meal, chicken, stuffing, reconstituted powdered potato and dried vegetables, arrived and more whisky was found. John had kept his *pièce de résistance* a close secret and he produced it with a flourish, flaming Christmas pud and brandy sauce. I felt bloated and content. The one flaw in the day had been the failure of the mail runner to arrive, perhaps on account of the snow.

By eight o'clock we were all laid out, drowsy and warm with the repletion of good food and drink. Stories were swapped and more banter passed around. Most of us were wearing our thick, red, down suits, making the tent seem like a gathering-place for Father Christmases. Ade, his nose a red glow, grinned mischievously and went off into a fantasy about job prospects: 'That must be a good number – being Father Christmas with all those girls that come to sit on your knee.' He and his brother now looked more alike than ever, since Ade had grown a rough beard and we relished the prospect of seeing again Al's girlfriend from Kathmandu, who had written to say she would meet us on the way back.

Only Paul and Alan remained talking. Sometimes one got the

impression that Alan missed the complex, intellectual discussions of his Cambridge days. Often he led the way in ribald humour, but underlying this was the suspicion of a keen intelligence which was yearning to be tested. Now Paul and Alan were locked in a discussion which centred round something about logarithmic equations inside a cube tending towards a point. Paul gave every appearance of holding his own, but to me it was totally incomprehensible and I gathered from the quizzical frown on Allen Jewhurst's face as he went off to bed that he was baffled too. I left as well and sank into a drunken sleep. Vague thoughts about the route, prompted by a starry sky, were lost in an alcoholic haze.

Perversely, the next day, Christmas Day, started fine and Paul, Alan and I made ready to go up to the Lho La. Just another work day for us and I envied those who remained their extra day of relaxation and celebration. It was 11 a.m. before we were ready to leave and the weather had changed. Clouds were blowing up from the south and streamers of snow were trailing off the ridge of Nuptse. There was every excuse to change plans and stay at Base but I was uncertain whether I was being influenced by common sense or the effects of the alcohol still lingering in my body. I left before delaying further and weakening. Paul and Alan, feeling no better, followed.

The well-known way up to the start of the ropes was transformed. Deep snow concealed all the familiar ledges and footholds, my hands became numb and gloves wet from the constant groping in the snow for holds. I dislodged a huge rock which lay buried and hidden, and blamed my impatience for getting ahead of the other two. I waited a long while but grew cold in the strengthening winds. I hurried on to warm up and started up the ropes of the overhanging groove without seeing Paul and Alan. From the half-way ledge I heard shouts and dimly through the swirling cloud made out a figure far below. It was difficult to hear against the noise of the wind, but it was Paul and I understood from him that he was turning back to Base Camp.

I reconsidered what I was doing. In less than an hour I would be at the snow cave; it would take longer to get back to Base Camp. I continued. The alcohol was probably still poisoning my system because the roar of the wind across the plateau above my head was like that heard inside a railway tunnel. Snow was falling thickly and it was no longer the fine day I had started out on. We had all been lulled into a false estimation of the winter here by the relatively fine days we had experienced. I was in-adequately clad, and urgently forced myself upwards before the cold penetrated to my bones. At the end of the rocks and start of the snow up and across to the cave I strapped on crampons, buffeted all the while by the wind. I could not keep my footing and pulled myself along on the slopes I had first crossed ten days ago, doubting then the necessity for fixing ropes. I reached the caves and escaped into the calmer recesses of the first one, feeling bruised, battered and exhausted. There was no sign of Alan behind me.

Pete and Brian had blocked the entrance with rucksacks but spindrift had forced its way in through every little crevice. Everything inside the cave, sleeping bags, clothes, food, was covered in a fine layer of snow. Someone's down suit was lying there so I slipped into it; mine was still over at the tent site and I did not want to venture back there. It took half an hour to clean the cave of snow, and after gathering a rucksack full of snow from outside I settled into a sleeping bag with a book.

At 6 p.m. I learnt on the radio that Alan had turned back too. Paul and Alan had both found they were going so slowly after the previous day's excesses that they were very cold and feared lest they should not reach the cave before dark. They had taken the safest course and retreated. Ade was on the radio and he told me the mail runner had arrived. This completed my sense of isolation and loneliness.

'Is there any for me?' I asked hesitantly.

'Yes, I won't be able to bring any gear up tomorrow, my sack will be full of all your bloody letters. I haven't got any, I'm gonna open some of yours.'

After a few more ribald comments Ade signed off and I crawled back into the cave, to a rather dull and empty Christmas evening on my own. I could sense a nostalgia in one part of me which I did not want to take hold; I blocked it off, not thinking about who I might have letters from, forcing my thoughts into reading a rather predictable terrorist novel and made a meal, which was unenjoyable without someone to share it, last as long as possible.

The night on my own was a strange one. I blocked the cave entrance with rucksacks against the windblown snow which was billowing in. I had a suspicion that if I relaxed from a detached, unfeeling frame of mind, the bizarre nature of my situation – being alone at 20,000 feet on Everest, a mountain haunted by the ghosts of climbers dead on its slopes – might become disturbing. The cave was in sight of the spot where Mallory and Irvine had disappeared in 1924, and where their bodies may well still lie. I preferred to consider myself as being unaffected by superstition and I pushed out of my mind the sense of total loneliness which hovered on the fringes of my consciousness without the company of others to alleviate it. If I let such thoughts form and inner fears take hold, I felt they could possess and unbalance me. Sleep, once I had finished eating, came mercifully quickly and I was able to linger in an unthinking doze next morning until it was light, time to move and I could look forward to the arrival of more people and my post.

Four people arrived in the middle of the afternoon of Boxing Day – the twins, Paul and Alan – as I was finishing replacing some ropes which had become badly worn by the action of the wind rubbing them against the rock. I finished the work and joined them at the caves. I asked Ade for my mail. He looked startled and suddenly alarmed: 'I think our kid's got your letters.' He had not and I was filled with a welling resentment at their thoughtlessness. I was tempted to burst out with an attack on them for their lack of consideration but Ade looked so crest-fallen and was so full of self-criticism that I suppressed my annoy-ance. The twins are usually so thoughtful and considerate of others and they would censure themselves more heavily than I ever could, as they knew how highly prized letters are on a mountain. The fault really lay with us all, in that we had not established a system by which messages and letters were auto-matically passed upwards, rather than left to the initiative of individuals.

In the morning the wind streamed strong and steady across the plateau between the caves and the slopes up to the Western

Shoulder. Paul and I were to go up and complete the route through the rock barrier. Al and Ade would carry loads in support, and Alan, feeling fully recovered now, was going to make some necessary alterations to the caves.

It took half an hour, staggering in the wind, to cross the Lho La plateau. As I reached the opposite side the slope swept increasingly steeply upwards to end at a gap in the ice, the bergschrund, ten feet wide, where the angle changed abruptly and a vertical wall of ice reared up on the other side. The crevasse was unfathomably deep and it was twenty feet up the vertical wall to where the angle eased off, but a rope was in place now, stretching across the gap, up the wall, and on up the slopes above. I clipped my ascendeur device onto the rope, slid it along and swung alarmingly across the bergschrund and up the wall to the slopes above.

The wind was coming from my right, the south. The hood of my down suit projected forward round my face like blinkers on a horse. Vision was severely restricted and the wind bounced off the snow and onto my face, icicles forming from my condensed breath on beard and moustache. A long repetition of movements upward was punctuated with frequent halts to regain my breath. I was panting hard, and I found I was having to face continually to the left to avoid the discomfort of icy blasts of wind against cheeks and nose.

I was impressed with the distance up to the rock barrier; the time taken, the gruelling slog up 1,500 feet of ropes, two and a half hours from the caves to a cluster of pitons, karabiners* and spare rope left by Brian and Pete at their high point. The difficulty of climbing the rock barrier was disguised for me now the ropes were in place, but I could see why it had taken a whole day for them to climb 300 feet and marvelled at the achievement. A slight anxiety and excitement gripped my stomach in anticipation of what we would have to face ourselves.

The ropes ended at a ledge on which I crouched against the wind, peering down at the others on the slope below. Time passed; I seemed to be sitting right in the path of the wind. I

* Snap links which, when attached to a piton or other anchor, are used for running the rope through.

hunched myself up to present as small a target as possible; the cold ate into my bones.

It seemed like hours before Paul arrived; I was numb and useless. Paul too was chilled; his feet wooden and without feeling. Should we go on or not? I did not know if I would be steady enough to lead out on new ground. The wind had been too strong to move on without someone to safeguard me with a rope. Paul vacillated, but he too wondered about the wisdom of continuing in the state we were in.

I gave it a try. Movement restored some warmth and I was able to climb upwards on a runnel of ice partially sheltered from the wind. The exposed ledge I had left was probably the worst possible place to hang around. When I had the rope anchored to a steel spike, an 'ice screw', driven into the solid bank of ice up which I had climbed, Paul joined me. He had not been able to regain any warmth and Ade, close behind, volunteered to take his place.

The rock barrier far exceeded in difficulty anything we could see ahead. It was not easy ground by any means but there seemed no reason for us to reach an impasse here as we had done before.

I climbed up a band of brittle ice, my crampon points fracturing and splintering the surface before finding purchase. A wind-formed ramp of snow led more easily to a slab of shattered rock into a crack in which I drove a piton. A little higher and I had reached the end of the rope. I led out another 150 feet, legs straddling a shallow depression in the rock and crampons, awkward and insecure, scratching and sparking on the granite. Ade came up, tying off the rope at each anchor point I had placed and casting an appraising eye over my work. He was the only one amongst us with an officially approved guide's certificate and the lingering effects of his training still permeated his thinking.

I pressed him to lead for a while. It is much more exciting and satisfying to be out in front rather than humping a heavy load in support, though both are of equal importance. Ade unselfishly was not insisting on having a turn in front as he had done a good deal of the leading lower down. He did take over, though, and traversed diagonally rightwards up a sloping ledge of broken rocks, on and up over some black, insubstantial rock coated in ice. He made careful, measured progress for another 300 feet before the time was all eaten up and we had to descend.

Before we did, I clambered up a rib of rock for another forty feet to a vantage point from which to spy out the upper slopes. Ade followed and we were pleased to see that few obstacles comparable to the rock barrier lay in the way for the next 2,000 feet.

We had overstayed our time limits. The sun sank behind the distant hills as we abseiled back down, casting rosy tints on the glistening ice through the rock barrier. It was dark before we wearily entered the snow caves.

Brian, Pete and John had come up earlier ferrying loads. I was surprised to find that John had not stayed, for we needed him to pair off with Al the next day so that the rest of us could have an easier day, taking our time, carrying loads in support. It seemed that there had been some dispute about movements. John had intended to stay up but Brian had insisted that there were enough people on the Lho La already, and John should stay below. There were five people at the Lho La but the work above was very demanding. The cold drained the energy and fatigue came on much more quickly than I had experienced before. The wind had a wearying effect, so it was better to keep a rotation going to replace people and distribute the work as much as possible. To have enough usable time in the day to break new ground and fix ropes we had to be up early and move fast up the already established route. Everyone else was too tired or due to descend, and I reluctantly faced the prospect of another's day exhausting work as now I would have to partner Al.

As Ade explained, the situation probably arose out of a discussion at Base Camp on Christmas Day. The subject had been raised about work distribution. In the absence of dictation from above, this was the democratic process at work. The twins and John were strongly of the opinion that some people were working much harder than others, whereas Pete and Brian were just as convinced that everyone had done about the same. Alan was convinced that everyone was working to his own personal limit, which was all that could be expected or was possible. Since no one wanted to establish a formal rota, clashes of opinion were inevitable.

Al and I did not do so much the next day. I was tired and left the cave late. It was not such easy ground as first thought and I found Al to be super-cautious, and from his comments gathered that he found my methods and standards to be on the careless side. Climbing back up to the previous day's high point, I was hard-pressed to keep up with his purposeful, steady pace. He abided by the Diemburger theory which maintains that slow, no matter how slow, but constant movement is the best way to achieve progress at altitude. I could not stand the tedium of constant movement and when Al glanced back to see how I was doing I shouted up to him that I preferred 'interval training', actually preferring the intervals to the training.

We ran out nearly 500 feet of rope and Paul and Alan toiled up as we finished for the day with heavy loads of rope and a tent. It was dark again before we regained the cave after a wild sunset.

At last my mail had arrived. There was a card for Christmas from Maria showing a chorus line of eight buxom girls from the 'thirties, and the back of the card was smothered with the lipstick-imprinted shapes of different lips. Alan was disgusted that I could not tell which were Maria's. There was also a letter from my mother saying she was having a Mass said at Christmas for our safe return. This made a remarkable impression on everyone.

John was now here to stay, Brian and Pete were due to come up the next day, so Alan, Paul, Al and I descended. It was hard to sustain the energy to do anything effective for more than a couple of days without a rest and decent food. There was plenty of food in the caves but cooking a meal was a three-hour task and there was a tendency to miss out on eating and succumb to the ever-present feeling of lassitude induced by the altitude.

It was a stormy morning; the wind drove flurries of snow into the caves; John and Ade kept poking their heads out and trying to decide whether or not to go onto the route. John wanted to go to find out what it was like to climb in really bad conditions. Ade, more cautious, did not want to waste a day battling upwards only to be driven back and find themselves too tired to utilize the next day should it be fine.

I met Brian and Pete, coughs still troubling them, as I went down. The roar of the wind became more faint as I got lower and I felt with surprise the sun's warmth when it peeped through the clouds. The mountain was still wrapped in a swathe of cloud, still ravaged by the winds, a microcosm of turbulent weather all to itself.

In four nights I had become conditioned to accepting a furtive existence amidst constant wind and cold. Base Camp was luxury by comparison. I revelled in the warmth of a sun which cast splendid light on the pinnacles and blocks of ice which reared up out of the glacier. A footpath had been trodden through the new snow which was painfully bright.

The mail runner had already left but I busied myself with writing cards and letters, an occupation made unpleasant by the cracks and sores in my fingers. The constant cold and necessity to handle rough objects lacerates the fingers and the cuts often turn septic. It was painful even to hold a pen. Graham, the sound man from the film crew, had slight frostbite in one of his fingers.

Of the three film-crew members, Graham was the least certain about making this film. He was the quietest member of our whole group, often spending hours at a time without saying a word, soaking up with amazement the many tales of adventure and lawlessness which dominated conversations. After one series of stories from which one could only deduce that the streets inhabited by the Burgess twins were pregnant with violence, Graham did interject a wry comment of 'Yes, I can't walk down a street in Harrogate without thinking someone's going to jump me from a doorway.'

On another occasion Al, after reading a book about a con-man who drugged and murdered his victims, was questioning Pete about whether there was an antidote one could take if one felt a strange drowsiness creeping over one and suspected poison. Al clearly saw such knowledge as relevant to his own life-style. Graham parodied him with a bubbling smile: 'Is there anything you can take, Pete, if you feel the point of a knife in your back? Anything to stop that taking effect?'

Graham had gone up onto the lower slopes with Allen and Mike to do some filming and sound recording. For the climbers, being filmed made little difference except that it took longer to get from one place to another as we were often asked to repeat a section so that it could be filmed from a different angle. The film crew were static for most of the time and even when the sun was out the actual air temperature was still well below zero. Only movement kept one warm. One day Graham's feet and hands were numb without him realizing it. Once numb, they can freeze solid without one knowing. It is only while one feels the cold that one knows there is still blood circulating and sensation still there.

Without knowledge of all these details Graham was not aware of anything except that he was more clumsy at handling things and it was only on returning to Base Camp, where his hands and feet thawed out and pain came with the returning sensation as the blood tried to revive the dying tissue, that he realized his toes were 'frost-nipped', that is in the first stages of frostbite, and he spent many hours standing up, stamping his feet up and down to induce warmth and clasping his hands in his armpits. Graham found he could hardly eat any of the food, just the smell of it revolting him. This was a feature of living at altitude and is not uncommon. He seemed to shrink visibly before our eyes and having weighed himself on some scales at the Japanese camp found that he had lost two stones in weight.

During these days a visitor arrived, an Australian who had braved the rigours of winter to come up to Base Camp, relying upon us to feed and shelter him. It is part of the agreeable spirit of the mountains that such hospitality should be shown, but I did feel he took too much for granted and found that I resented the intrusion into our very private world as much as if I walked into my house to find a complete stranger making himself at home and asking questions about my private affairs. I realized that I had come to terms completely with our life in the mountains and felt like an animal in a zoo when anyone came to stare and probe with questions.

He did, however, bring disturbing news. He had been at Lobuje and seen our mail runner offering for money to the Sherpani who ran the tea house, packets of biscuits and bags of coffee which could only have come from our food store. This further evidence of dishonesty amongst our staff revived anger which is more virulent for being aroused by the behaviour of someone to whom one has shown particular friendship. It seemed to emphasize the distance, which exists in those inscrutable beings behind the flashing smiles, between them and us. The mail runner's job is particularly important and dependent on honesty, and once more we had to approach Mr Singh and ask that someone be dismissed.

Our shy Liaison Officer was being asked to perform some unpleasant duties. We were still no closer to him than at the start of the expedition. He had his own routine for the day and only ate with us because we insisted on it, though after a while we realized he preferred the extremely hot and highly spiced food of the Sherpas. He only spoke when spoken to and he answered my provocative attempts at getting him to open up more with the patient air of a teacher handling a troublesome schoolboy.

'Wales is part of Great Britain like Nepal is part of India,' I said in a deliberately outrageous answer to one of his questions.

'Mr Joe, you are always teasing me,' he replied. 'Nepal is not part of India. It is independent country.'

Alan hooted with laughter at this and congratulated Mr Singh on having got my measure.

Later on a murmur of anticipation went through the camp as the mail runner was spotted. Being British and reserved, and the twins, our strongarm men, being away on the hill, we felt some embarrassment about how to handle the situation. Mr Singh, a changed man as he took on his role of policeman, called the mail runner over to his tent.

There is usually an implicit welcome and congratulation to the mail runner on his arrival, and the contrast this time was wounding. None of us could understand the exchanges which took place, but we gathered that the mail runner had brought back some of the biscuits and coffee he had been seen trying to sell, saying that he had taken them in mistake for some other food the cook had instructed him to have for his journey. The Liaison Officer did not accept this, for he believed that the mail runner had been warned by some yak herders who had brought wood and food up to the Japanese camp and called in to ours before going down.

An argument erupted, the Liaison Officer leapt to his feet and lashed out at the mail runner who took off down the glacier. The rest of us, film team included, stood there open-mouthed and helpless at this scene. After a long while the Liaison Officer, extremely agile in pursuit, brought down the mail runner and proceeded to rain blows on him. A very subdued Sherpa was led back to camp and sat abjectly in front of the tent where Mr Singh sat in judgement. Tears flowed down the cheeks of the mail runner as the sentence of dismissal was pronounced and the retraction of all the much valued clothing and equipment was made.

Another unpleasant incident which took the pleasure out of the arrival of the mail.

Base Camp no longer seemed a place to relax. The visitor who had brought news of the mail runner's dishonesty had gone but returned with a group of trekkers he had met lower down and persuaded to come up to enjoy the hospitality of our expedition. It was an added burden to our cook staff and when the visitors were asking questions and making suggestions about the climb I felt that they were making an unwarranted intrusion into a very personal, intimate matter. Most of them were ill-equipped to deal with the savage conditions of Base Camp life and had to borrow clothes and tents to survive. I was unashamedly glad to see them go.

On the mountain we followed progress via the radio and telephoto lens. The matchstick figures were on the vast snow slope leading to a ridge of rock at the top of which we hoped to find a sheltered camp site.

On New Year's Day Alan, Paul and I set off back to the Lho La. We did some filming on the way up but I did not feel too good. Whether it was ennui at finding myself going over the same ground for the ninth time, slight sickness or the subconscious wish not to miss out on another celebration day I could not ascertain. After talking with Paul I dumped my load and hurried down to catch up with Mike and Allen who were making their way back to camp. They were surprised to see me and shamefacedly I explained to them that it just was not going well for me that day, so we returned together. I felt as if I had given myself a holiday. On passing through the Japanese camp we were summoned inside for some of their celebratory New Year drink and tasty morsels of yak meat cooked in tiny slivers over their wood stove.

The Base Camp was empty except for the film crew and myself. The cook and one cook boy had gone down to Namche Bazaar to organize the transportation of some essentials of which we had run short. Only one of the Sherpa boys remained and he produced an excellent evening meal. There was a peace and tranquillity that had been missing for the last few days, and the four of us made a small enough group for warm, meaningful chatter until late into the night.

Graham informed us that the Japanese had reported finding Yeti footprints in the Western Cwm, where they had their Camps 1 and 2. They had filmed them and sent the film back to Japan. We were highly sceptical.

I felt much better on 2 January and went up on my own, gathering extra items on the way and labouring up with a particularly heavy sack as a self-imposed punishment for the weakness of the previous day.

CHAPTER EIGHT

Grim Nights

The site for Camp 2 had been reached. Twenty-eight rope lengths, over 4,000 feet of rope fixed in place, stretched up from the plateau of the Lho La to a twisting rib of rock a thousand feet below the crest of the West Shoulder. That distance was quite far enough between camps, any further would have produced a diminishing return in that so much effort was being expended in just reaching the top of the ropes that if the camp was located any higher, a day's rest might have become necessary to regain strength after reaching Camp 2.

Pete and Ade had run out the final rope lengths, but there had been some conflict over the roles of those active on the hill, as I learnt on reaching Camp 1. Ade and John had climbed together one day and intended to do so on the next day. Brian and Pete were carrying loads in support. Pete was annoyed at the assumption that he would play a supporting role on two days running, and he protested strongly that he was not only a doctor but also a climber and that there was no point in his being on the mountain if he was not to have his share of the more interesting business of leading.

John and Ade had been working on the assumption that it was better for those who were fittest to do the work which demanded most effort and since Pete had been a long way behind them whilst they were leading it seemed most efficient to continue in the lead themselves.

John has a preference for avoiding confrontation, for withdrawing from an argument to preserve the peace even though he is not convinced of the other view. When Pete maintained that he was climbing as well and as fast as anyone, John stood down and let Pete partner Ade next day.

This disagreement typified the difficulties of a democratically organized expedition; we all had differing views and opinions. Ade did not like to see decisions being made out of, as he saw, a sense of personal pique and he bluntly told Pete that he did not expect to be kept waiting. If Pete was as fit as anyone, he should reach the high point at the same time as Ade himself.

Pete was the least known to anyone on the trip. He had an individualist streak in him, preferring to walk on his own and to go off for solitary excursions. So far I had not been impressed with his performance; in comparison to the twins, in spite of the charts he kept of everyone's movements, he had done considerably less. It came as a disturbing surprise to hear of his forceful demands when the twins were characterized by a selfless application to whatever task arose.

On the day they set off together, Ade arrived at the top of the ropes long before Pete and, since it was relatively easy ground, laid in place another 300 feet of rope before Pete arrived. They completed together another 600 feet of climbing before finding a place suitable for a camp.

John and Ade descended to Base Camp as I came up. Al and Paul had gone up to pitch a tent at Camp 2 and Ade suggested that Alan and I did the same. After a comfortable night at Camp 1, in the now familiar caves, Alan and I set off for Camp 2. Brian and Pete were going to carry a load up and then descend to Base Camp for a rest while we continued with the route.

I like to be either at the back of a group or well ahead. When every step is an effort it is difficult to match one's pace to another person's and if I am in front I tend to assume that those behind could move faster but for my holding them up. If at the back I can make my own pace. On this occasion I got well ahead, counting off each rope as I left it. Twenty-eight rope lengths seemed endless, but the first fourteen were the worst – 4,000 feet of slow, upward trudging, facing away from the wind. I expected to arrive in mid-afternoon at Camp 2. The weather was not fine. Clouds covered the sky, streaming rapidly from the crest of the West Shoulder. The wind sometimes threw me off balance and I looked forward to settling into a tent when I reached the camp site.

Paul and Al were surprised when I arrived, being convinced that the weather was too foul for anyone to think of coming up. Consequently there was no platform dug ready for a second tent. I took it for thoughtlessness and told them so. They had had a bad night in the coffin-like confines of the box tent. Paul and Al were both big and broad-shouldered; in the tent they were too squashed against each other to rest properly. There was only one door which opened directly onto the outside and to cook they had the choice of keeping the door zipped closed and suffocating from the fumes from the stove or leaving it open and being covered in snow from the icy blasts of the wind.

Even if the weather had been better, both Al and Paul were suffering too much from lack of sleep and the constant buffeting they had felt from the wind through the tent walls. The only virtue of the tent was that it had very thick poles and seemed proof against the wind.

I set to with some annoyance to dig a platform out of the slope directly above the box tent. Paul cursed me and explained, with common-sense arguments, that I was knocking down great chunks of snow and ice which were building up behind his tent and forcing it off its platform. I was frantic at the thought of being caught by nightfall without a well-erected tent, long icicles hung from my moustache and beard and my hands were numb. Clouds concealed even the cheering brightness of the sun and snow stung my face.

Paul came up to help me erect the tent, one I had used in ferocious weather on K2 and had every confidence in. Now I could not manage it at all. The savage wind kept grabbing at the tent; I tried and failed many times to locate the poles in the necessary places. Paul held on but I was the only one who had used these tents, had sung their praises and now could not expect more than minimal help as the method of erecting it was too complicated to be passed on when every shouted word was snatched away by the wind. I bent one of the aluminium tubes into place to form an arc from which the tent would hang. The pole snapped. I felt a fool for advocating the use of this tent. The weather on K2 had been terrible, but the quality of the cold on Everest was much more severe. My useless hands fumbled with other poles as I tried various ways of botching up my blunder. Paul watched with mute, helpless interest. With the poles finally in place I suspended the light inner tent from the arcs formed and turned to pulling the orange outer tent over the framework. It is the outer tent which gives the structure strength. When properly in place the arcs hold the outer skin in tension and a stable dome is formed. The last manoeuvre of pulling the outer tent over the end of the pole is hardest and in my struggles, with the tent lifting in the air, another pole snapped. I was furious but allowed my fury to rage without stopping my movements for a moment. Brian appeared, dropped his load, and grabbed the tent too.

It was not a perfect job, but when we had finished the tent was upright and, for the moment, withstanding the wind. We drove stakes into the snow to anchor the tent and buried the edges with blocks of ice and more snow. I dived inside, Paul scuttled off to his own tent and Brian hurried back down to Camp 1. These slopes were no place to linger needlessly, and tears were already forming in my eyes at the pain of frozen fingers returning to life.

Alan arrived late in the afternoon and settled into the tent with me. The icy platform beneath the ground sheet was uneven, and near the edge it was insubstantial. The useable floor space of an already tiny tent was much reduced. We both shuffled into sleeping bags and, pressed close against each other, tried to impose some sort of order onto the chaos of food and gear strewn inside the tent. If it was not done before dark we would have no hope of locating anything we needed.

An icy layer began to form on the inside surface of the tent fabric as the condensation from our breathing came into contact with the cold material and froze. It was 5 p.m. and almost dark before we were reclining in uncomfortable readiness to prepare the evening meal. Suddenly we heard the slow, rhythmic crunch of footsteps outside and the sound of Pete coughing; he had just arrived.

'Pete, it will be dark soon, what are you doing up here?'

He had set off with a load, as we knew, but, instead of descending in time to regain Camp 1 before dark, had continued. There was no sleeping bag for him and no room. He had on his down suit, the normal clothing up here, but it was so cold that a sleeping bag as well was necessary to survive the night.

'Oh, I'll be all right.'

He seemed unconcerned and passed by to visit Al and Paul at the other tent. I was amazed when he did not leave for another half hour. There were ropes all the way down to the level plateau of the Lho La but in the dark it is so easy to make a fatal mistake.

'Have you got a torch?'

'Yeah, I'll be all right,' he repeated and crunched off. Alan looked at me with incomprehension and shook his head.

The tent we were in differed from the box tent occupied by Al and Paul in that there was an inner tent and outer shell. The outer shell came right down to floor level and had a flap on which we had placed blocks of ice and snow. We could thus open the doors on the inner tent without the wind blowing in. This enabled us to collect snow to melt and allowed us to ventilate the tent whilst cooking.

Hoar-frost formed a thickening layer on every surface; a dangling piece of nylon cord grew to three times its usual size with the accumulation of ice crystals on it. Outside the wind swept ceaselessly across the ice slope into which we had cut a slot for the tent.

Each gust which shook the tent sent down showers of ice, and undermined any confidence in it surviving the night. One of us had to be attentive to the stove the whole time to prevent it overturning and soaking clothes and food. It was a wretched, squalid scene.

I was too uncomfortable to sleep easily and the noise from the wind banging at the tent kept me in a state of nervous anticipation. The box tent was twenty feet below but communication was impossible. Alan has the enviable ability of relaxing and sleeping in the most painful circumstances, an accomplishment which he attributes to his drunken youth at Cambridge when he frequently spent the night where he fell. I needed a sleeping pill to block out the discomfort and anxiety.

The whole of the next day was spent enlarging the tent platform and building a protective wall of snow blocks as a wind break. There was no let up in the ferocious buffeting of the wind and stinging snow flurries; no opportunity for consultation; each person did what he thought best. Al felt ill after two successive nights of disturbed sleep and insufficient food. He shuffled off down.

Our purpose in being at Camp 2 was to continue upwards but until we had a comfortable camp we could do little and against this wind there was no hope of progress. All efforts were focused on merely surviving the savage, inescapable cold. The tents seemed like flies against the massive wind which battered the mountain. I was incapable of undressing sufficiently to relieve myself, the cold was so severe.

In the midst of another wretched night I awoke in terror feeling snow on my face and in the bewilderment between nightmare and wakefulness shook Alan and asked if he was alright. It was the recurring nightmare which had troubled me ever since the avalanche high on K2. The sensation I had experienced on waking to find snow pouring remorselessly down and crushing me under a black, soundless blanket before losing consciousness, had left a lasting mark on my psyche.

Alan reassured me that nothing had changed. The tent was still shaking in the wind and a torch, shone inside, showed the constant showers of hoar-frost which fell from a layer a quarter-inch thick which covered the walls and roof.

Alan had a rough night which left him listless and weary next day. He descended to Camp 1 to escape for a while from the horror of life at Camp 2. Paul came by a little later. He too felt dreadful after a third night spent in the path of the winds. Even though the wind did not penetrate the tents, the noise wore on the nerves and there was the ever-present anxiety that the fabric of the tent would tear or the poles would break. Inside the tents the air temperature varied between $-30\,^{\circ}\text{C}$ and $-40\,^{\circ}\text{C}$. A stove did not seem to make any difference, we had to wear gloves the whole time, and rather than raise the temperature a stove only increased the depth of hoar-frost which formed inside the tent.

I shared a drink I had ready with Paul, who described the discomfort of the box tent before descending to the secure caves of Camp 1, and I was left alone.

Alone again on this hostile mountain. I wrote in my diary, which had become little more than a series of notes to mark the passage of time: 'On most mountains there is some respite; once on the Lho La there is a constant battering of the psyche and body by the wind and cold. It really is grim waking up here to a tent coated with rime.'

A weak sun made a pale appearance through the clouds but the rime never left the tent all day. I wondered what I could do. Camp 2 was at 22,500 feet; I considered going on my own to survey the ground above or dropping back to bring up some rope and equipment which had accumulated at various points on the way. Being left alone took the urgency out of doing anything, and since each time I opened the tent door a swirling cloud of snow blew in, I let the day slip away completely without stirring outside.

There was no radio at Camp 2 and no means of guessing the movements of anyone else. The cold and altitude had a numbing effect on my sensitivity as well as my flesh. I did not stir from my sleeping bag all day, welcoming the extra space now that Alan had gone, and drifted periodically in and out of sleep, like someone in a hospital bed. No one else arrived that day and as dark came on I prepared a solitary meal which I ate as a duty.

I took two sleeping pills to wipe out my stark surroundings but was woken at 10 p.m. by the crash of wind against the tent. I lay for the rest of the night listening and worrying whether the tent would hold. Morning was welcome for the arrival of light but the wind did not lessen; I was too fatigued to make any progress outside, and reluctant to undergo the chore of stowing all the gear strewn inside the tent and face the unpleasantness of descending to Camp 1.

I can no longer remember the experience of being alone; I find it hard to comprehend that I spent three days without stirring above the tent at Camp 2. Like the gum anaesthetized by the dentist's needle, insensitive but not dead, I performed the minimum necessary to survive but languished in comatose inactivity whenever possible. Three days and no possibility, no thought of upward movement. I did not miss the company of others but noticed the passage of time in which I had not said a word. Sometimes I did think aloud but cut off any philosophical musings which probed the sense of what I was doing.

By early afternoon, having glimpsed the mental lassitude which can induce the physical paralysis leading to death, I had resolved to escape downwards. I packed gear into rucksacks which I placed outside into a maelstrom of snow, found the lifeline of rope, and headed down. My legs, unaccustomed after my confinement to exercise, collapsed under me as I slid down the ropes and my hands fumbled weakly at each knot. When I reached the level plateau of the Lho La, standing freely for the first time in days, I dropped one of my ascendeurs which slid down a slight incline for fifty feet. I was too tired to go after it. Stumbling and falling, I made my way back against the wind to the snow caves.

Innumerable accidents occur when people become separated or isolated on a mountain. In the prevailing wild weather, Paul and Alan were anxious lest I should try to fight my way down alone or remain trapped for days if no one else could get up.

'It's all right leaving someone on his own if you want an exciting story to take back,' said Alan, 'but not if you want to climb a mountain safely.'

I relaxed into the security of the cave as Alan prepared endless drinks and food, which he passed over to Paul and me. We had done no more than spend a few days at 22,500 feet but we felt as if we had survived a traumatic ordeal and could luxuriate in the relative comfort of this cave of Camp 1. The temperature inside was only $-10\,°C$.

Later in the afternoon John arrived and the sight of the three of us languishing in sleeping bags brought on a torrent of recrimination from him. He was highly critical of the lack of progress above Camp 2, and censorious of the amount of food we were consuming whilst lying inactive at Camp 1.

With the slow deliberation of the self-righteous I explained to him the conditions we had experienced, and gradually it sank into

John that the sunny days he had been enjoying at Base Camp bore
no relation to the brutal life on the mountain. Contrite and apologetic, John agreed that he was 'sounding off a bit' without sufficient awareness of our situation.

Ade was also meant to be coming up with Mike, the cameraman; John had last seen them doing some filming in the overhanging groove. Mike had done some rock climbing in Britain
but even though we had ropes in place all the way to the cave
now we preferred that one of us should be with him on the
mountain as much as possible. The amount of camera equipment
which was accumulating at the Lho La was alarming; it clearly
showed the differences of emphasis between the climbers and the
film crew. I felt strongly that not a single day should be lost in
climbing the mountain through attention to the film.

By dark the fierce winds still ripped across the slopes outside
and there was no sign of Ade and Mike. The never distant unease
surfaced. I left the warmth of my sleeping bag, fastened on my
harness and crawled out into the night. I could not stand in the
wind. I clipped some ascendeurs to the anchored rope and pulled
myself up the incline. After 100 feet the ropes crossed the slope
horizontally but still I could not stand. I crawled on all fours, my
harness fastened to the rope by the ascendeur which allowed me
to pull myself forward without sliding back. I could not see in
the dark, I could not look up into the wind without my face
being stung with snow and numbing instantly. It was only 300
feet to the rocks at the far side and three times I was picked up
and thrown up the slope by the force of the wind. I felt idiotic
and presumptuous against such power. I descended to the top rim
of the amphitheatre and peered into the dark; no sight, no sound
above the wind. I shouted uselessly and turned back.

At the far side of the traverse across the slope a shadowy figure,
cowled and ominous, stood waiting. It was Paul, his back to the
wind, waiting to make sure I was safe. No word passed, we
descended to the cave and in the calm inside I told them I had
found nothing.

A radio call at 6 p.m. to Base Camp revealed that they had not
arrived back. We arranged a re-call at 7 p.m. and with relief heard
that Ade and Mike had appeared ten minutes earlier. I always

have a slight sense of foolishness as if I have been over-reacting in such situations, but to wait until one is sure that something has gone wrong is to invite tragedy.

We spent a restless night; the roof of the cave seemed to lift with the force of the wind, ear drums popped with the sudden pressure changes as the wind hammered at the entrance, the thump of the blasts kept everyone's nerves on edge.

Morning brought no change. We concocted a meal from freeze-dried scrambled egg mixed with chunks of tinned ham. It tasted almost like real food.

By 1 p.m. we were too tired and dispirited to stay up any longer. The weather showed no signs of improvement and I radioed down our decision.

Once at the top of the corner I slid down away from the constant roar which had been with me for days; it was like a climatic deconditioning process. A thousand feet lower and a parting in the clouds let sunlight filter through and warm my body. I began to relax and the tension of the last few days ebbed away; these walls of rock which had taken all our efforts were now reassuring and pleasant to pass over. I realized that I had not relieved myself for three days and a sudden overwhelming urge forced me to rip open my harness, down suit and underclothes to release three days of constipation just in time.

CHAPTER NINE

'In the mountains one forgets to count the days'

There was a poor bag of mail waiting for us. Alan fretted at the continued lack of letters from his girlfriend. I tried to reassure or commiserate with him since I had not had a letter from Maria for three weeks, nor from my mother, who writes dutifully every Sunday. My attempt at reassurance had the opposite effect. Alan just thought I was more inhuman and unfeeling than him. On expeditions I had come to make a deliberate point of not letting emotional events affect me. I feel the lack of letters deeply but to worry about what might or might not be happening in another way of life is to conjure up a punishing fantasy world which can disturb one's thoughts and influence one's decisions. For many years whilst I trained to be a Catholic priest I lived in a dream world, planning for the holidays when I could really live, escaping mentally from the strait-jacket of a rigid time-table, strict rules and enforced behaviour. Having left that regime, I had an antipathy towards any tendency to live in fantasy worlds, preferring to think only about what I knew I could do and not to live in hope only to be disappointed or to find that the reality did not live up to my dreams.

On an expedition I exercised a possibly harmful capacity for viewing situations and events from my other life in a detached, anaesthetized manner. Of late, expeditions had gone on for a long time and on returning to England I found it took me quite a while before I regained the habit of feeling and emotion. This was very difficult for anyone close to me.

The heavy snows we were experiencing were affecting flights to Syangboche, from where our mail was collected. This was one reason for the small offering brought by the mail runner.

A party of eight Italians had arrived and made a Base Camp near ours. They were intending to climb Lhotse, the fourth highest mountain in the world, by the route which had defeated the Poles in 1974/75. They were a jolly bunch, a little disconcerted by the rigours of winter and concerned that their clothing was not adequate. They brought a comment from Reinhold Messner, who had climbed Everest twice without oxygen, and who is regarded as something of a god in Italy. He considered it impossible to climb the mountain in winter without oxygen.

I believed that he would have produced a different opinion if he had set his mind to attempting just that. Part of the reason for our being on Everest in winter was to find out what was possible.

It was true that some discouragement prevailed in our camp. The long spells of fine weather from December were gone, and any forecast picked up on Radio Nepal only spoke of winds of 100 knots, sometimes 120 knots, precipitation and cloud. The forecasts were of little help. In contrast to other seasons, the weather seemed to change radically in a very short space of time and without warning. The Japanese expedition was also having difficulty contending with the unpredictable arrival of sudden snow storms.

Life was comparatively easy physically at Base Camp and mentally relaxing for me with the knowledge that for the moment I was due a rest. A book I was reading, written in the style of Hemingway, about the Caribbean, sub-aqua escapades and cocktails on hotel verandas at sunset contrasted dreamily with our spartan existence. I missed a radio call one morning because I had left the set outside my sleeping bag and the batteries were cold. Normally I slept with the radio close to my body to keep it operable. My camera too had to be kept in my sleeping bag and I often dropped off to sleep in the escapist cocoon of sound on the headphones of a Sony 'Stowaway', a tiny cassette deck, which was also pushed down into the warmth.

From Base Camp I could see through the powerful telephoto lens that the tents at Camp 2 were still in place, but on the radio we learnt that no one had yet moved up there. A whole day had been spent assisting Mike with his loads of film equipment up to the Lho La and more gear had still to be collected from where it had been dumped. This was just what we had been wary of, having to spend valuable time shepherding one of the film crew up or down the mountain. There was a clear conflict of interests between the demands of the film and the needs of the climb. Lost days were irreplaceable and although we could not reasonably leave any of the film crew to move about on their own on any difficult sections this had to be the last time that efforts to climb the mountain were distracted by the film. I felt an infuriating annoyance at what seemed to be such an obvious mistake in priorities.

Al and I planned to go back up the next day, 10 January. Paul and Alan were afflicted by a return of the dysentery which had lingered round our camp and needed a little more rest.

Life at Base Camp had settled into a routine. There were no more problems with the staff except that the food did not have the same variety or taste as it had had during the approach march. The cook was battling against adverse circumstances in trying to produce palatable food on the temperamental stoves. Even the custard which was produced was uncooked or burnt. We summoned Mingma, the cook boy, to complain, as custard is the easiest thing in the world to make. He did not seem well suited to have his efforts rejected. With bad grace he took back the custard, taking a flying kick at some broken stoves which lay outside.

Al kept us entertained with another story of bewildered involvement in violence from an occasion when he and his brother, on a rare visit home, had taken their mother out for a meal. On leaving the restaurant to drive home they found that someone had broken into the car and was sitting in the driver's seat ready to drive off. As he described it I could visualize the two of them moving into action as in a scene from a gangster movie.

'I was a bit worried about what to do,' said Al.

'Why? Were you frightened?'

'No, it's just that you never know what your mother is going to think, do you? We just roughed him up a little bit.'

On the return to Camp 1 for once I was moving faster than Al, but I suspected that he had a heavier load than me. To gain the slopes leading up to where we had ropes in place we had to cross beneath the threatening walls of ice hanging below the Lho La. It only took fifteen to twenty minutes to pass over the exposed area and there were two schools of thought about the best line to take. In 1978 I had seen a monumental avalanche from the Lho La. All seemed quiet in winter but I chose to take an indirect line which entailed an uncomfortable scramble for a long way up the unstable rocks skirting the glacier. The Burgess twins, exponents of fitness and speed, took a line for as far as possible up a gully directly in the fall line from the ice walls. They maintained that they could run to one side out of the way of anything falling. We came to call their way the 'Burgess couloir'. I told them that I would rather take ten minutes longer to get up the mountain than present the slightest opportunity of being caught in an avalanche. The other members of the team oscillated between the two schools of thought.

It was not unusual for me to part amicably from other people and wend a separate way up to where we picked up crash helmets and harnesses to start the more difficult climbing.

Mike Shrimpton was in residence at the caves filming our approach and clearly awed by his surroundings. Ade and John, Pete and Brian had gone on up to Camp 2 that day.

For the rest of the afternoon we lay inside the cave in sleeping bags, discussing the route, the film and climbing in general. Mike questioned us on our ideas for a title for the film. 'How about "Everest – Another Pawn in the Game"?' He was trying to locate the significance of trying to climb Everest by even harder, ever different routes, and our reasons for doing it. I did not think it was a very compelling title, nor that it did justice to the continual development of mountaineering and exploring of the frontiers of the possible.

Al and I promised to rendezvous with Mike next day in the afternoon when the light was good as we descended from carrying loads up to Camp 2. We intended to reclimb the rock barrier so that Mike could film it. Mike had begun to appreciate some of the problems we had raised when he was proposing the film equipment he would like on the mountain. He had the biggest movie camera I had ever seen outside of picture books as it was and he was still not satisfied with the tripod I had carried up with great effort.

Mike was a real professional. As the expedition had gone on I had acquired an increasing respect for his energy and thoroughness in tackling his job. The television industry is hamstrung by union regulations and conditions and sometimes I wondered how Mike came to terms with the subconscious demands this background made on him. There was no conceivable way in money terms that anyone could be compensated for putting up with the conditions on Everest in winter. We had had problems in the first place owing to union rules that stated we should take along an electrician whose job is to set up and plug in the lighting. The fact that there was no electric power source on Everest carried no weight and the thousands of extra pounds which a surplus film crew member would entail resulted in our making the film as an independent enterprise.

Mike was on Everest because he wanted to be there, and the breadth of his experience as cameraman on 'Whicker's World', Arthur C. Clarke's 'Mysterious World' and many other assignments which had taken him to most countries in the world gave him a maturity and broad-minded vision which was an asset to the team as a whole.

The next day we were planning would be a demanding and exhausting one but if successful would mean that a major part of Mike's filming programme on the mountain was completed. Thereafter smaller cameras handled by the climbers were to be used. We talked late into the night before snuggling down into sleep.

We were woken in the middle of the night by the unnerving thump of the wind driving, in powerful gusts, into the snow cave entrance; the increase in pressure made our ear drums pop, and thereafter I was awake for the rest of the night, vaguely aware of the restlessness of Al and Mike, lying listening to the frightening roar of the wind outside. The thump of the wind and subsequent pressure waves were as I imagined it to be in a bunker under mortar attack. We were quite secure, in my mind I knew, but the four others had gone up and were occupying the fragile tents of Camp 2. I could not imagine the tents surviving such winds. Anxiously we awaited the radio call at 7 a.m.

I crouched in the entrance of the cave, buffeted by a wind which seemed to have concrete solidity, holding onto an axe driven into the ice as I called up Camp 2 on the radio. No reply. Every half hour I opened up the radio, hoping for some sign that the four at Camp 2 were alive. At 8.30 the radio crackled in reply. Ade was saying something about a tent being destroyed in the wind then the message came to a strangled end. Uneasily I conveyed the news to Al and Mike and periodically we crawled along the tunnel entrance to peer at the slopes of ice, glimpsed through swirling cloud, waiting for a sight of figures descending and the relief that this would bring.

At 10 a.m. I saw a figure through a telephoto lens moving hurriedly downwards. Ade arrived, instantly reassuring us that no accident had happened, and John followed some time later. All were safe but the collapse of the tent had thrown John and Ade on the mercy of the wind. John's hands had frozen solid and, near fainting with pain from the cold, he had pushed himself into the cramped confines of the still standing box tent where Brian and Pete had a pan of tea heating. John thrust his hands into the hot liquid and gradually the circulation returned.

Ade reckoned that the box tent would stand against the wind but Brian and Pete were finding life quite miserable inside. Every gust of wind showered them with the ice which lined the tent. He did not know whether they planned to stay up at Camp 2.

Disconsolate and bewildered, we retired to our sleeping bags and lay all day listening to the howling wind outside, feeling the thud of impact when it drove into the entrance.

Brian and Pete appeared out of the swirling mist towards late afternoon and occupied the other cave with John. Morale was at a low ebb and progress against such savage, elemental fury seemed impossible.

Ade explained that the wind had somehow got underneath the tent, lifted it up and snapped the poles. Fortunately this had happened at 6 a.m., just before dawn. The chaos of such an event in the full dark of night was too frightening to contemplate.

Ade was tired; we fed him drinks and food, and he dozed on and off. In the course of the afternoon we discussed our chances on the mountain. Ade was of the opinion that we had no hope of making any significant progress from the tents. Even if they withstood the wind it was not possible to rest well enough to do a day's work. Spending a night in the tent took all one's energy. He suggested a snow cave as the only possible solution.

Time seemed to be running out on us. Camp 2 had first been reached eleven days before and since then all eight of us had spent some time in the tents without moving any further up the mountain. I suggested siting a cave 1,000 feet higher where the slopes eased off before the final crest of the shoulder. I had come round to accepting a point of view I had been against earlier because of the effort involved. Al and I agreed to go up, put up with the discomfort of the box tent, and work regardless of the weakening effects of the altitude and discomfort until there was some semblance of a cave for the next party to occupy. We would have to descend after this as, even if all went well, we expected to be exhausted after such a sustained bout of work, but it presented the only chance of establishing a secure foothold high on the mountain. With a cave higher than the tent site we hoped to avoid placing another camp before 25,000 feet, thus cutting down on some of the time and effort. It seemed a logical proposal.

The two caves of Camp 1 were connected by a window hole, but because of the draught which streamed through we kept the hole blocked with a rucksack and spare clothes. Thus without thinking we had come to a conclusion without involving John, Brian and Pete. Next morning, as Ade left to go down for a rest, since now there was only room for two people at Camp 2, and he wanted to be ready to take over once the cave was dug, he poked his head into the other cave and found complete disagreement with the proposal. It seemed so logical a solution to an impasse we had now battled against for almost a fortnight that I had assumed it was in everyone's minds.

All three in the cave next door felt it was too risky to place all our hopes on finding a place suitable for digging a cave on ground no one had yet reached. Their proposal was to dig a cave at the site of Camp 2. Arguments in favour of both points of view were pushed back and forth. Nothing was lost, the bitter weather precluded any movement for a time anyway. A compromise was reached. Al and I would continue with our plan but the other three would also come up and start to dig a cave near the tents as a fall back position should the first plan prove over-ambitious. They could not stay up at Camp 2, but would dig for as long as possible before returning to Camp 1.

Next day I woke early and looked out of the cave at dawn. The sky was clear and the wind less strong. A bank of cloud low in the sky to the south seemed far enough away to present no immediate threat. We breakfasted, fastened on crampons and harness and prepared to go. The bank of cloud now filled the sky completely to the south, the front edge already catching the West Shoulder, and Nuptse's summit poured forth its own stream. Al and I looked at each other undecided and annoyed. I felt as if the mountain, like an anonymous, perverse bureaucracy, was treating us without feeling.

From the confines of their cave, Brian said he thought we should go up and Pete echoed his opinion. Their tunnelled view revealed only blue skies. Even on seeing the advancing cloud Pete was forthright in his insistence that we should go up: 'It doesn't matter if you go up and the weather turns bad. If you get worn out again at Camp 2 there are plenty of other people to replace you.'

Even had I agreed with his philosophy I resented being pushed like this into an action I was uncertain of. Al and I wandered down away from the cave, down the upper slopes of the Rongbuk glacier into China. We wanted to wait an hour to see if the weather improved and also to gain a view of the summit which, from the caves of Camp 1, was hidden by the Western Shoulder. The slopes formed a gentle descent for half a mile before breaking up into crevasses and becoming a convoluted mass of ice towers and pinnacles where the glacier changed direction.

Across the glacier basin from where we stood we could clearly see the North Ridge, scene of many of the early attempts to climb Everest, and lost somewhere in the ice-coated immensity of the upper slopes of the mountain were the bodies of Mallory and Irvine. I felt very much the novice gazing on history. From the

head of the basin rose a fine line of snow bisecting the rock of
the North Face. Somewhere in that region Sherpa Ang Phu had
died when he slipped whilst descending during the Yugoslav
expedition to the West Ridge in 1979.

Above our Camp 2 on the West Ridge we could see that the
slopes eased back and a thousand feet above the camp there was
a hollow in the snow which gave hope of a possible site for a
cave.

We returned to the caves of Camp 1 to find Brian retching
outside. In the relentless cold of the winter he had no hope of
recovering if he stayed on the mountain. He and John descended
to Base Camp.

That evening on the radio Ade called us up and let us know
that one member of the Japanese team had been killed when he
slipped from the ice slopes below their Camp 3 on the other side
of the mountain. I did not know the man in question; he was as
anonymous as any fatality mentioned in a news bulletin. I felt
no sense of loss as at the death of a friend, but a sickening sense
of the futility of this whole enterprise of climbing, the inherent
folly of the pursuit, pervaded my thoughts. We settled down to
sleep that night talking about our roles as pawns in a game of
our own choosing.

Al, Pete and I left next day in similar weather to that which
had made us uncertain about starting the day before. The wind
streamed steadily across the plateau and the slopes up to Camp 2.
I was surprised to recognize in the crisp surface of the snow the
marks of my crampons from the last time I had been up. My
crampons were completely different from anyone else's, having a
distinctive rectangular shape. In spite of all the snow which had
fallen, the constant action of the wind had swept the slopes clear,
preserving the imprint. At any other season more snow may fall,
but the temperature is higher, the snow contains more moisture
and adheres more readily to a surface, and above all the wind is
neither so fierce nor so constant. I was ahead of the other two
and saw one figure turn back from the start of the ropes. At
Camp 2 I spent some time clearing the tent of snow, making it
ready for a late return. If our plan was to work we would be
climbing till nightfall and would want to just tumble into our

sleeping bags on our return. Much snow had infiltrated the tent during the events surrounding the stormy evacuation of a couple of days ago. Twenty feet above the box tent lay the sad wreckage of the tent I had spent three nights in some long time ago. The platform we had laboured so hard to dig was still there, partly covered in drifted snow, through which poked tent material, abandoned rucksacks and broken tent poles.

Suddenly Pete came into view, rising over the shoulder of rock above the tents and dropping down. I had assumed it to be Al who was coming up. Pete explained that the wind had chilled Al to the point where he was worried he was getting frostbite. The prospect of five hours pulling upwards on ropes in the same wind caused him to turn back and descend to Base Camp. It was more than just feeling chilly. By this time we had been at Base Camp or above for five weeks and the punishing effect of living in such extreme cold was taking its toll. Sometimes it was too difficult to force down the unappetizing food on the mountain and even at Base Camp the meals seemed to be less and less palatable. Without a big daily intake of food it was impossible to keep warm.

Al's absence was a blow. I regarded the twins as the strongest and fittest of us all, so for Al to go down was psychologically very discomforting. Pete and I made ready to climb, neither of us really knowing each other, and with that detailed politeness which characterizes the interaction of strangers, we agreed upon a way of tackling the wind-scoured slopes above.

The uncertain weather of early morning had changed unnoticed into an afternoon of blue skies, sun and only light wind. I led off. The climbing was not difficult but troubled by slabs of loose snow adhering uncertainly to the underlying firmer surface. I skirted round these slabs, fearing lest they give way and the accumulated might of a vast area should transform the insubstantial patches into an overwhelming, deadly wave. I led for 300 feet, stopping frequently to rest and, when Pete took over, relaxed in the enjoyment of a rare, fine day. For the first time I was actually enjoying being on the mountain; the view north into the brown, mysterious land of Tibet, the receding rows of hills to north and south, their contours etched more beautifully by the sinking sun, all filled me with a suppressed sense of privilege and exaltation. Unfortunately it was an enjoyment I could not share, for Pete was far above me. Much of climbing on a big mountain is solitary, many hours are passed in the sole company of one's own shadow, other people separated by distance or weather from communication.

I wanted the afternoon to go on and on. I wished that everyone else could share the experience, for this if anything would revive the flagging spirit of the expedition.

When Pete had fixed 300 feet of rope in place I took another turn and took a false line up a runnel of snow beside an area of glassy ice. Pete corrected the error by traversing beneath the ice, and we lost some time in sorting out the ropes. He disappeared round a ridge of snow, and when the rope stopped moving I followed.

Nothing prepared me for what I saw when I came round the ridge. My attention was on the rope and on my crampons trying to find purchase on an icy passage. The slope had eased back completely now and I was almost walking. Looking up I was halted by the towering sight of the summit pyramid of Everest, looming up so close, reddening in the setting sun which threw into relief all the cracks and wrinkles of this ageless mountain. I looked and looked as the colours changed, the red deepened, and dark shadow crept inexorably upward finally to wipe all colour away. Pete shared his thoughts with a brief: 'Great isn't it?' and we made ready to return to Camp 2 well pleased with the day.

The unexpected sight made such an impression on me that I slid down the ropes, bubbling with eagerness to radio down the news of our progress. I tried a call at 5.30 p.m. before reaching the Camp but had no success and my numb, clumsy hands, cramped by the post-sunset chill, made me fear to use the radio lest I dropped it. It was a mere half hour back to the tent compared with the whole afternoon we had spent climbing upwards.

When we did make contact at the pre-arranged fall-back time of 6 p.m. I transmitted the satisfaction both of us felt at breaking through the impasse we had reached at Camp 2 and our enthusiasm inspired by the sight we had seen. Ade, at Base Camp, was surprised. They had had a cold, windy day below and had expected us to fare worse. He promised to come up next day with Paul and Alan.

The satisfaction at the day's work and the conviction that we would be able to get a snow cave above helped us face the prospect of a grim night in the coffin of a tent which remained standing at Camp 2. The box tent was only just big enough for two of us. No movement could be made without the cooperation of the other person. Pete drew himself up into a corner of the tent to make room for me to cook. I had explained to him the great disinclination I feel to wake up on a morning and that if it suited him I would cook all the evening meal if he would cook the breakfast. Since there was only room for one person to cook at a time this made a logical division of work. For the next three hours I melted snow, made a stew, made drinks and passed them over.

'I'm glad you like plenty to drink,' said Pete. 'I was with Brian and he preferred to go to sleep rather than eat and drink.' Pete was acquiring a reputation for being a big eater, maintaining a capacity to funnel food down endlessly. On an expedition it is an admirable accomplishment as normally everyone loses weight due to the loss of appetite, with the consequent diminishment of strength and stamina. In spite of the value of being able to continue eating, Pete's ability to do so did arouse a sense of annoyance and envy. It was irrational, but part of the inevitable dynamics of a living situation where comfort is at a minimum and sensitivity close to the surface.

It was so uncomfortable in the tent that there was little hope of dropping off to sleep. We each took a sedative and dozed fitfully. I was half aware of Pete being restless and muffled groans escaped from him each time he moved. At midnight I did not feel as if I had slept at all and when I spoke to Pete he said he could not sleep either because of some pains in his side. We took a sleeping pill each and I took two headache tablets. It was a heavy dosage and I woke at dawn dazed and groggy. Pete, unaccountably, was wide awake. He prepared breakfast and I trailed unenthusiastically after him to the top of the ropes, our high point of the previous day.

There was no need to fix rope on the ground we had reached

as it was only gently sloping, and the weather had remained un-characteristically calm for a second day. We did run out some rope, however, until we arrived at a bank of snow in which we intended to dig a snow cave. Without the guide-line of a rope it could be impossible to find the cave in a blizzard or hold on against a wind.

My head had cleared of its earlier muzziness. Pete, smaller than me but more stocky, disguised in a similar spaceman's garb of quilted red suit, plodded up steadily. He had a purposeful pace; I projected onto him the assumption that he was unaffected by the debility which I felt. Even walking close together little was said, I was panting hard and any comment I made sounded as if I attached great weight to it after much deliberation; in reality I was pausing to catch my breath between each word.

We started digging into a bank of snow, steeper than the slope we had climbed, intending to burrow horizontally into the hill-side in a narrow tunnel before making a larger cavern. The site was some incalculable distance below the crest of the West Shoulder. Pete thought it to be only a short distance; I thought it would take at least an hour to climb. I am not sure if it is an effect of altitude or simply lack of objects by which to estimate scale, but gauging distance is a difficult and often disappointing exercise on a mountain.

Ten minutes of digging was enough to tire us, so we took it in turns. The snow was perfect for excavation. Unlike the Eskimos, who have dozens of words for snow, our language is limited. If there was a word to describe the ideal snow for a snow cave, it would have applied to the snow we were digging, firm without being icy. I took a turn, kneeling in the deepening shaft we now had running into the hillside, the white snow of the surface turning blue in the inner recesses of the shaft with the diffusion of light through it. I noticed a black mark at the end of the tunnel which by this time was six feet deep. Suspecting a rock, which would render our efforts futile, I struck at it and the snow around gave way to reveal a dark hole. At first I recoiled in shock, but when nothing more happened I crawled forward and stared down into a gaping crevasse, totally enclosed with a roof of ice and festooned inside with fantastic formations of crystalline ice and blocks of snow, a winter wonderland. Some huge blocks spanned the crevasse, forming a shelf; to the left the hole dropped away into bottomless blackness. I withdrew in awe and motioned Pete to look in.

Crevasses have connotations of terror for a mountaineer and my first instinct was to start afresh elsewhere. Pete was similarly nonplussed. If it was sensible to use the crevasse as a shelter it would save us two days of excavation, but if it was unstable we could wake up to a slow death from suffocation or a plunge into a newly opened chasm.

We decided to enter the crevasse and examine from inside its potential. We kept the rope fastened to our waists and tied to some stakes driven firmly into the snow outside, a lifeline to safety. I dropped inside onto the shelf, feeling as if I was entering forbidden territory, with the nervousness of a burglar on his first job. We took up separate stances and flailed away with ice axes at the ice formations hanging from the roof. The roof was only a couple of feet thick in parts and a blue, suffused light penetrating the snow illuminated the interior. We used the snow knocked down from the ceiling to level the floor, and as we grew more at home in this icy fairyland I crawled to the furthest end in one direction where the cave funnelled down to a cone, and the bright light showed that the roof was thinnest. I knocked down with a sense of regret the weird, fantastical formations, widening the cave. Pete worked on making a new entrance as the hole we had dropped in through was eight feet above the floor. After a couple of hours, completely at ease in this pit now, we had enlarged the cave sufficiently for three people to sleep inside, with plenty more space that could be easily cleared. We were well pleased with our work; in a matter of hours we had ready a cave which we had thought would take days to prepare, and in two days we had broken through the psychological barrier which had surrounded Camp 2.

When we came to leave we had difficulty escaping. Pete, tunnelling away to make a new entrance, had been doing so directly below the hole by which we had entered. There was fifteen feet of snow to dig through and he had only partially completed it. Thus there was a gaping cavity and nothing on which to stand to reach the upper hole. I struggled and berated Pete before managing to claw my way out. Pete similarly struggled, much to my satisfaction.

We had let ourselves have an easier day than the one before, now that we had achieved our objective. We reached the tent at Camp 2 comfortably before dark and transmitted the happy news of our fortunate discovery. Pete and I intended to ferry all our gear up from Camp 2 to the snow cave, Camp 3, next day, before going down for a rest.

The radio call brought bad news. Wan Chup, the cook, was critically ill and Pete was asked to consider going down in his capacity as doctor. He had the symptoms described to him over the radio, vomiting: delirium and excretion of blood. Pete guessed at a perforated ulcer. The doctor from the Italian camp had come over, but if there was no improvement Pete resigned himself to descending next morning.

It had always been a *bête noire* of Pete's, that just such a conflict would arise between his responsibility as a doctor and his wishes as a climber. There was no way round it, Wan Chup did seem seriously ill, and although Pete was the first to acknowledge that doctors cannot wave magic wands, if Wan Chup died the whole expedition would be stigmatized for its irresponsibility if it was known that the doctor was out of reach on the mountain.

Pete's face wore a look of glumness for the rest of the evening. I agreed that his first responsibility was to descend, but I regretted to see him go. This had been the first time I had had anything to do with him on the expedition and I had come to realize that the anonymous person who kept in the background, who had not seemed to be going as strongly as some, was in fact driven by a purposeful determination. Perhaps he had been overshadowed by the extrovert garrulousness of some of us or was simply pacing himself until he had found his own level. Whatever the explanation, I was now impressed at the new person I had seen emerge in the last couple of days. There was every reason for all of us to be mystified by Pete. He seemed genuinely to enjoy being on his own, often walking for hours at a time far from the company of anyone. Before we reached Base Camp he sometimes went off on a sortie by himself, soaking up new sights without needing to share the experience. On the mountain we had grown accustomed to his eccentric tendency to set off late and often arrive so late that we came to call him the Midnight Cowboy.

I felt a fraud beside him. Suddenly on returning to the tent I was overcome with fatigue but, obliged by the pact of my own instigation regarding the cooking of meals, I had to prepare the food. I spent the next three hours melting snow and making drinks and meals. These I passed to a reclining Pete who seemed unaffected by the exertions of the last two days and ate hungrily everything I gave him. After heating the water for the main meal, I realized that I could not face eating it, so I handed a huge panful of lasagne to Pete. I had the useless satisfaction of seeing him for the first time unable to finish a meal.

Another squashed and restless night passed, worse than the last, listening to Pete's groans, to the wind outside and finally capitulating to the recurring temptation to take a sedative in the search for sleep.

Pete gave me a brew of tea before leaving in the morning. An earlier than usual radio call told him of the anxious vigil kept beside Wan Chup's feverish bed by the members down below. Reluctantly he left and I dropped off to sleep, now that I was no longer constricted in the tent. I woke at midday with a clear head and hurried to ready myself before Ade arrived and caught me still in bed.

It was 1 p.m. when he reached the tent on his way to the cave above. I had a warm drink ready for him but he still mocked my idleness. He continued on to the cave and I followed, glad at the thought that I would be spending no more nights in that tent. As I toiled, heavy laden, up the same slopes for the third day running, the snow turned pink with the setting sun. Far below, a red matchstick man appeared by the tent of Camp 2. It was Paul on his way up, but it would be dark before he reached the cave.

Paul had stopped off at Camp 2 and added even more weight to his monstrous, heavy load. His familiar hearty laugh had something of a chagrined resignation to it now. Ade gave out news of the air of discouragement which was hanging over Base Camp. It was the middle of January and the feeling was that the attempt to climb the West Ridge was turning into a war of attrition which was taking a heavy toll. There had been discussion about fixing a date in early February for the porters to arrive and for us to leave Base Camp if we were not in striking distance of the summit.

This was demoralizing news, especially so in contrast to the euphoria of the progress of the last few days. If only everyone could have a couple of perfect days on the mountain such as Pete and I had experienced, attitudes would change and morale would be restored.

The cave at Camp 3 was spacious, and consequently much colder than Camp 1. A constant draught streamed up, seemingly from the bowels of the mountain, through the black hole at the far end of the cave. Paul, for all his fatigue, could not eat much as he had developed an aversion to the freeze-dried food we had and which was the mainstay of our diet. It was an unpleasant night, the three of us, huddled together, unembarrassed, to share our bodily warmth.

At night we slept totally enclosed in our sleeping bags, still wearing every bit of clothing except boots. The hood of the sleeping bags could be drawn closed round the head, leaving only a small hole for ventilation. We woke each morning to an icy layer surrounding the hole, formed as breath condensed and froze to the outer surface of the bag.

By luck the cave at Camp 3 was in the lee of the West Ridge, sometimes gaining protection from the wind. On the morning after our first night in the cave, Paul volunteered to spend the day improving the accommodation and digging the new entrance. Pete's excavations were still unfinished and entry to or exit from the cave still necessitated negotiating an eight-foot drop. Paul's task was to burrow through fifteen feet of snow outwards from the floor level of the cave and to block in the first entrance.

I felt that Ade and I had the more desirable option; we set off to reach the West Shoulder, to investigate the route along the crest of the ridge to Camp 4. Words do not emanate of themselves the slowness of movement, the lassitude at such heights; memory cheats and passes over the blank spaces between events; half an hour to put on boots and then strap on crampons sounds ridiculous but is normal. Life on this mountain was a slow-motion actuality.

We were ready to leave, hovering on the outside of the cave; the momentary hesitation before breaking new ground, the slight reluctance to go first. Ade pulled out his bar of chocolate-coated mint cake: 'Should give me energy,' he said. 'I need it.' It sounded a good idea, though I was not a follower of the Burgess devotion to diet control and energy foods. I ate a few squares and Ade swallowed all his. 'You've not eaten a whole bar, have you?' I was incredulous at his capacity to consume so much of the same sickly sweetmeat at one go. 'I need it to get up there,' he laughed, intrigued by my astonishment, and he strode off powerfully upwards as if to make his point.

The snow was firm and the crampons held securely. Crack lines crossed the surface and we came upon an area of larger crevasses. At any other season these would have been worrying illustrations of the lethal mobility of the slope, but one of the few advantages of winter was proving to be that movement of the snow, as well as of humans, was, if not stopped completely, considerably slowed down. We were reasonably sure that there was no danger of avalanche.

Sparkling streamers of snow came whirling over the West Shoulder as we neared the crest and climbed into the wind. Ade was a distance ahead and, unwilling to capitulate to his credence in diet-determining performance, I busied myself taking photographs of his silhouette against the rising sun, thus disguising my slower pace.

We carried ropes and snow stakes, but were not using the ropes for the moment. Though icy, the angle of the slope was easy. A slip could mean a fatal, uncontrollable slide for 5,000 feet but this was our medium; this was the everyday routine of a mountaineer as familiar or dangerous as driving a car. The growing wind, tugging at my body, heightened my concentration; in my hand was an ice axe, a third support, held ready to drive into the ice to arrest any fall. The silhouette above disappeared over the crest of the ridge. I could not hurry to catch up; I could only continue at the same steady pace, frequently halting, and enjoying the sight of Pumori, which towers above Base Camp, dropping away below.

Ade was sitting on a lone rock protruding from a rounded

plateau of wind-hardened snow, bending now against the force of the wind. There was probably a smile on his face but ice masked his mouth and goggles concealed his eyes. Behind him a huge panorama unfolded – the walls of Everest. Lhotse and Nuptse formed an arc round the plunging basin of the Western Cwm, one of the hallowed, forbidden places of the earth. The Cwm is the valley leading to these mountains, the entrance to which is guarded by the formidable Khumbu ice-fall. We were surrounded now by mountains, snowy ranks receding into the distance on every side. A few years ago I would have found the sight appalling, so many mountains to climb, so much suffering to reach their summits, so much effort needed and so many doubts about my own ability and resolve. Now I had come to know that I would not stop climbing; this mountain scene was exhilarating rather than oppressive, full of endless opportunity. Sometimes I feel as if mountains have become an addiction, the pleasure gone, the compulsion to partake remaining. Rarely blessed with the enjoyment of the moment, I had come to realize the satisfaction of going to the limit, physically and mentally, of dipping into danger and exhaustion, of returning full of enthusiasm for life and appreciation for every part of existence.

My feet trudged on over the humps of the plateau. Ade said he was feeling the altitude but I pressed him to go further. The plateau narrowed to a ridge, the ridge reared up, a knife-edge of snow running into the summit pyramid which now looked close. To our right the slope fell away steeply, 3,000 feet to the bottom of the Cwm. I was tired too. Only the desire to reach the Shoulder and see a new panorama, after weeks on the slopes below, had driven me up. Ever-cautious, Ade was wary of going too far along the ridge. The wind was gusting strongly; if it gained more strength it could easily pick us up and throw us over the ridge or drop us into the Western Cwm. We agreed on a point to reach before turning back, but we had been looking at different points, and when the ridge steepened to an angle where it would have been foolish to continue without ropes, Ade suggested that we had come far enough for the day.

We had reached 24,000 feet. The remainder of the ridge looked more difficult but providing the wind was not too strong we should be able to reach a site for Camp 4. It would have to be another cave, gruelling as its excavation might be, at 25,000 feet. Beyond that a ramp of snow cut diagonally leftwards into the North Face to a narrow gully slicing the vast yellow rock area of Everest's summit pyramid. That was the last major obstacle. We fastened our sacks of gear to a stake driven into the snow and turned back, well pleased.

We descended to Camp 3, pilgrims returning from some holy shrine. The distance we had covered was vast and descending required total concentration, but we were back with Paul before the afternoon was far gone.

The new entrance was ready, the old one sealed with blocks of snow, but light came through this thinner layer and through chinks between the blocks. The cave inside was illuminated as by the patterned windows of a clerestory.

Alan flopped into the cave unannounced at the end of the afternoon. We had not established satisfactory radio communication yet from Camp 3 so we were uncertain about the movements of anyone else on the mountain. Alan let us know that John was due to arrive at the Lho La that afternoon and should be on his way to Camp 3 the next day.

Paul had hardly eaten since he had arrived. A drink and some soup was all that he could manage. He was apologetic, seeing this inadequacy as detrimental to his own strength and therefore the strength of the team. It was a little more uncomfortable with four of us; there was plenty of room, we were utilizing perhaps only one-third of the cave, but only this third was widened and levelled for use. At the far end was the bottomless pit which we would never fill but which provided us with the luxury of an indoor toilet.

Alan had the worst position, at the edge of the levelled area, using rucksacks to increase his sleeping space. Paul and Ade in the middle were warmest, sheltered from the draught by warm bodies on every side.

I was ready to go down next day, in need of a rest and making way for replacements. Paul felt he should descend as well, being too weak from lack of food to be capable of going further. Ade was listless after three days' continuous movement upwards. He intended to rest for a day before going up again. Only Alan was keen to do something positive; if nothing else he would descend to the now redundant Camp 2 and ferry up the remaining gear.

Alan crawled out through the tunnel and came back with the disheartening news that it was blowing a gale outside and snowing. He disappeared again after a while and when he did not return we presumed him to have gone to Camp 2. Paul made ready to go down, voicing his misgivings and expressing his anxiety that he might be obliged to return to Britain if the expedition was to go on much longer. He had given an optimistic forecast of his return as being the middle of January. It was already 18 January and if we went on longer it would be the middle of February before we got back. Paul was a college lecturer and had a more rigid time-table than most of us.

Rather than leave Ade without the certainty of a partner, I decided to stay on another night. We passed the day eating and drinking as often as the motivation allowed. Night came without the return of Alan or the arrival of John. Spindrift had been blowing into the cave and we sealed off the entrance with rucksacks.

Although we could receive some radio transmissions, we were not in line of sight with Base Camp and our messages were not getting through. It takes a stronger signal to transmit than to receive and after several tries Ade gave up, though even from inside the cave we could sometimes hear the calls from Base. Al's flat voice came weakly over the air: 'Base to Lho La and Camp 2 or 3 do you read me?' repeated over and over.

'In case you are listening . . .' the words trailed on lost in the crackle of interference.

'Just listen to our kid's voice,' complained Ade in disgust. 'If he put some expression into it we might be able to pick something up. He's just droning away.'

There was an uneasy feeling about the way things were going. I was not really much use at the moment. I had been on the mountain for ten days and knew I needed a rest if I was going to contribute anything more. The question was growing whether Everest really was too difficult in winter. Certainly the cold was more insupportable, sleep was difficult and headaches were more frequent than usual. Even inside a down suit and a sleeping bag feet were nearly always chilled. On eating a meal, warmth could be felt percolating down to the toes as combustion of the food took place. As a topic of conversation this often replaced the weather in its popularity.

The Burgesses have the disadvantage of being unable to sleep on their sides. Alan put forward the explanation as being the width of their shoulders, no pillows being high enough to support their heads. Whatever the reason, Ade was forced to lie on his back, facing upwards to a ceiling, a couple of feet above him, which was festooned with 'long, gangly, white fronds', as he described them. Each time he coughed, a shower of these fronds descended, dislodged by the slightest movement of air. The cave was anyway filled with the fine particles of snow driven in by the wind through any crevice. A torch beam would lance through the air, catching the floating particles in its light like a beam from the lamp of a bus in a London fog. In one wall of the cave was an unsuspected crack to the outside through which fine snow was pouring. It was the worst night yet in a cave.

Powder snow covered everything when we woke. A dim light filtered into the cave; there was no sound of the wind. There was no increase in warmth with the morning, the thermometer showing a steady $-20\,°C$. I put some lumps of snow into a pan and lay back waiting for it to melt.

Two hours later I prepared to go down to Camp 2 to clear it of any remaining gear. Ade needed to rest further. I pulled aside the rucksacks blocking the exit. A small shaft remained of our tunnel; the rest was filled for fifteen feet with snow. At the far end of the shaft sunlight caught the snow. The storm was over but we were snowed in.

When I dug the tunnel clear and popped through to the outside it was still blustery, but there were clearings in the sky, and the force of the storm was spent. A new, crisp whiteness coated the mountainside and the ropes leading down were buried.

I ferried up more sleeping bags and food from Camp 2, and brought the ruined tent to use as a curtain on our tunnel. Gradually we were improving our living quarters.

No one else arrived that day and with little remaining reserves of strength after eleven days on the mountain I resolved to descend next day. Ade too was tired and he came down. Deep banks of snow covered the slopes, and our steps dislodged these, precipitating small avalanches. It was better that we should do this than wait for a dangerous accumulation to form and an overwhelming avalanche to sweep down of its own volition. The wind was constant but not too strong. I was stumbling, but it was from fatigue rather than the wind.

Near the bottom a lone figure was coming upwards. It was John, distinguishable by the colour of his clothes. He was covered in snow from pulling clear the ropes and caked blood from some unmentioned mishap was mingled with the ice on his face when we met him. With the lack of radio communication we had come to an awkward imbalance of movement on the mountain. John, on his own, would be able to achieve little at Camp 3 and I did not envy him his lone vigil up there till someone from below should join him.

John had been at Camp 1 on the night of the most recent storm and he had a woeful tale of waking to find that he too was snowed in. Desperate to relieve himself, he had done so into a plastic bag and disposed of it some hours later when he had finally dug himself free.

Troubled with doubts about the present situation on the mountain, we left John to continue upwards and ourselves trailed on to Base Camp.

Enthusiasm at the progress we had to report was tempered by the general gloom about our chances of success. There had been more sickness in the camp. At our instigation Brian, Pete and Al went up, in spite of ominous weather signs, to the Lho La and we entered a period of intense discussion at Base Camp about tactics and our prospects.

By afternoon it was snowing steadily. We were anticipating the arrival of the mail runner but had doubts about the likelihood of his bringing any mail. Two Sherpas, however, arrived first, one of them, Nima Norbu, being our new Sirdar to replace Dawa.

He brought unwelcome news of knee-deep snow down at Syangboche and the unlikelihood of flights into the airstrip for many days.

Base Camp was no longer a comfortable place. Since before Christmas we had had few spells of fine weather. The tents sagged under the weight of snow and even if a day started clear, clouds usually enveloped the sky before it was out and the camp was little more than a bleak, chill wasteland. I began to prefer the idea of being back on the mountain – at least there I expected to be uncomfortable, to have to struggle to survive. I felt cheated here and annoyed when I found that at every moment of the day I was conscious of being cold.

A scrapyard of blackened, useless stoves lay outside the cook tent. One by one our stoves, paraffin and petrol alike, had packed up under the extremes of winter, fourteen stoves in all. Alan and Brian had gone on a borrowing mission to the Japanese camp and returned with two enormous paraffin stoves which we hoped would last us for the rest of the expedition.

The Japanese equally were stalled by the conditions on the mountain. As well as being shaken by the death of one of their members, several others of the climbers and five Sherpas were frostbitten. Some of the Japanese displayed on their cheeks and noses the tell-tale purple weals of once-frozen flesh; one of the Sherpas was going to need part of his foot amputating and another some fingers. A train of yaks had been summoned to carry them down to the airstrip, and hospital.

On 20 January three Japanese had left their Base Camp to go back up for one final attempt. The Italians, who were attempting Lhotse, had not made much progress beyond the trail which they shared with the Japanese to the foot of their mountain. From the start they had seemed lost in face of their objective, with clothing and tentage hardly different from what they would use in the Alps. They too were running out of steam.

The only way to obtain a semblance of warmth was to sit in a tent, when the sun was out, with the doors zipped closed to exclude the breeze. The heat of the sun on the tent walls raised the temperature inside to a luxurious degree and, though I preferred the more sociable atmosphere of the dining tent to the solitude of my own, the rare opportunity of restoring circulation was too good to miss.

I lay there one day enjoying the solar heating and the glowing feel of warmth returning to my feet, thinking over events. At 7 a.m. I had listened in to Ade making the radio call to the Lho La. The sky had been unsettled but held the promise of clearing. His brother was exhausted after breaking trail for several hours up to the Lho La. The walls and slabs of rock were much changed from when we had first climbed them. Snow a foot deep concealed footholds and left the hands numb from groping through it to find purchase. The journey to Camp 1 took twice as long. Brian had had a bad night and did not feel like moving. Ade exhorted his brother to persuade Pete to go on up to Camp 3 where John, from whom we had heard nothing since passing him on the way up, was still alone.

By 9 a.m. the sky at Base Camp was really overcast and on a second, prearranged radio call, Ade was told that the weather on the Lho La was atrocious but Pete had left nevertheless to relieve the beleaguered John. It was good news – at least there was some activity.

From the experience of reaching the West Shoulder I was convinced that given good weather we could climb this mountain. The Shoulder is at a height of approximately 24,000 feet and it had felt similarly bad to 24,000 feet on any other mountain at other times of the year. The main difference was the force of the wind, the deadly cold and the rapidity with which the weather could change. 'If only the weather would hold,' I wrote in my diary. 'I won't mind the suffering involved; I do not think that the cold plus lack of oxygen plus dry air will be what will stop us.'

This sort of expedition was not something I had wanted to become addicted to and subconsciously the conviction had formed that if we should get up Everest this time I would not come again to the Himalayas in winter. I wrote further: 'I suppose I have always connected mountaineering at its limit with arduous, almost unbelievable hardship, for our generation this is it – the Himalayas in winter, when a few short hours of warmth are all one can expect, if lucky.'

A commotion outside heralded the arrival of Mingma, our

cook boy, who was now acting as mail runner. In spite of the lack of flights he had some mail to offer, residue from a previous flight or brought by some other mysterious route, we could not fathom. Disappointingly, there was no newspaper. We were all together in the dining tent, Graham rocking back and forth on his feet trying to encourage the circulation, the brief sun of mid-day now concealed behind grey clouds.

Ade and I had been insistent, on coming back to Base Camp from Camp 3, that there should be people on the mountain at each of the camps all the time, and that if the weather was bad they should stick it out ready to push the route further or move up to relieve those at the front. These ideas came out of our own experience of waiting for support and seeing John going up on his own with no back-up. But the continuing hostile weather, and now the news that Pete was forcing himself to go up to Camp 3 in a storm, was taken as a rebuttal of this suggestion. Alan advocated waiting until the weather did clear and then having everyone move onto the mountain together with the potential of thus doing eight man-days of work instead of two with the rotation system.

We had reached 23 January. Our permission for Everest was due to expire on the 31st of the month. Alan had used the Japanese radio connection with Kathmandu to ask for an extension of our permit. We were granted an extra two weeks.

Food and fuel were running short and our diet had become very monotonous. The question of arranging a date for departure arose once again. Still enthusing from the positive progress I had been involved in, I argued against any suggestion of fixing a date for departure: 'If we state that we will leave by a certain date, we will have already decided on the outcome of the expedition. Psychologically we will have given up. We should not be thinking of how efficiently we can leave, but of continuing, if there is a chance of getting up the mountain, even after our permit has run out.'

Alan pointed out that such an action would inevitably alienate the government of Nepal, since in the past they had reacted strongly against anyone breaking their rules.

'Climbing is all about breaking rules. It's in the nature of the game. Would the North Face of the Eiger ever have been climbed if the climbers of the day had abided by the laws laid down forbidding any attempt on it? We should think of extending the permission again, sending down for more food and fuel, not letting their lack dictate our movements.'

As official leader, Alan was in an invidious position. Any one of the rest of us could do as he wished, break any number of laws, but the responsibility lay with the leader and the sanction most often enforced is to ban the leader from Nepal for a number of years. For a keen climber this was anathema, especially if the punishment was enforced for an action of someone other than himself.

Basically there was agreement that at some stage we would have to make a decision about leaving; we could not stay forever. Alan and Brian, as the two who shouldered most of the burden of organization, wanted to have considered the practicalities and time-scales involved in departing from the mountain. It was agreed that a certain amount of good weather was necessary for success and that by the end of the month we would have a clear idea of the likely outcome. Allen Jewhurst volunteered to stay behind as long as need be in Kathmandu to clear up any formalities and forward the gear if this would set minds at rest regarding delays in getting home.

The discussion cleared the air. There was a renewed sense of commitment to stick it out to the end. Photographs, maps and books were pored over and passed round to glean every bit of information and encouragement. The contours of the summit pyramid were compared on the map with those of other known areas of the mountain and the final chapters of the book by Hornbein and Unsoeld on their ascent of Everest, triumphing at the eleventh hour against all the odds, were taken as an example.

Conversation drifted down from the intense level of the afternoon and by evening, after an unsuccessful radio call at 6 p.m., we were given to musing on more light-hearted subjects. The abominable snowman entered the conversation and its existence on Everest, as reported by the Japanese, given as a reason for the lack of communication from those at Camp 1 on the Lho La. Alan developed on this theme and went off into a wild fantasy about Pete and his ferocious appetite, sketching out a scenario of the climbers who vanish one by one from the Lho La with only Pete surviving, growing fatter and fatter, to be last seen making off down the Rongbuk glacier. Ade summed up the erosion of our senses after so long in the mountains as he tried to make out a list of basic equipment needed for his next expedition. When, after an hour of pondering, he had only three items on his list, he looked up with a puzzled expression and said: 'It's hard to think, after a few weeks here, isn't it?'

CHAPTER TEN

Attrition and the Turning Point

24 January dawned snowy and dull. Depression seemed to hang above and below. However, radio communications were at last effective. Pete had taken up with him some wire with which he had rigged up an extension aerial and the same had been done at the Lho La. Communications could now be conducted from the comfort of the sleeping bags inside the caves.

There was no progress above Camp 3. John had been hit by a return of amoebic dysentery and was trying to nurture his strength to descend. Brian and Al lower down at Camp 1 had attempted to go on up to Camp 3 but had had to retreat after being battered and tossed about by the winds.

Paul and Alan were ready to go up onto the mountain but whilst no progress was possible for anyone up there they stayed at Base Camp where the energy drain was less. Paul had misgivings about voicing the need for his return home, not wanting to undermine the momentum of the trip. He stated briefly and clearly why he would have to leave, intending by so doing to put his case and then let it be forgotten. He was going up one more time, knowing that there was no possibility of his reaching the summit in the time left, but meaning to put every effort into helping the expedition for as long as he could.

Maurizio, the lone Italian at their Base Camp, frequently visited us in his search for company. He was not a climber but had come with the expedition to act as interpreter. The rest of his friends were at Camp 2 in the Western Cwm, his only contact with them for many days being by radio. True to style, the Italian cuisine was enlivened with blocks of parmesan cheese, hunks of ham and other long-forgotten delicacies. By one means or another Brian, a ruthless negotiator, had managed to strike an extraordinary bargain by which we obtained a selection of these in exchange for some of the freeze-dried food for the mountain, of which we had an abundance and for which most of us by now had acquired a hearty aversion. For a time the much-loathed 'noodle stew', to which we had been reduced, was kept at bay.

The Japanese encampment had an air of gloom too. We were always welcome and for a change of scene one or two people would pay them a visit from time to time. The visits had recently grown more frequent in an endeavour to obtain a more accurate assessment of the weather. They had their 'facsimile' machine which reproduced a weather map transmitted from Delhi and received a weather report by radio from Kathmandu from a member of their team who had returned there to sort out formalities after the death of one of their team.

The map and reports bore little relation to the mountains by which we were surrounded. Such convoluted terrain creates its own weather and all we could look for from the broadcast information was a general trend. On 24 January the Japanese informed us that the information they had received was that it was impossible to make any predictions for the next week. The weather map was a mass of tightly packed lines covering the whole Indian sub-continent.

The members of their own team were stuck at Camp 2. They had tried to make progress to Camp 3 and up to the South Col but had been forced back by wind and poor visibility. Now their food was running very low. They could not descend to Base Camp because the route through the ice-fall had been destroyed with the collapse of several walls of ice, ruining the bridges across crevasses which they had so laboriously built. A repair party from below would have to go up first to replace the ladders.

There was a set of bathroom scales at the Japanese camp and we weighed ourselves. Alan and Graham had lost two stones each in weight. They were both gaunt, lean figures compared to their normal appearance. All of us believed we had lost weight but found there was little or no variation from our normal weights. Ade found he had put on weight, a discovery which made him feel much better.

A hurricane roared all night over the Lho La. I lay in the comfort and security of my tent at Base Camp listening uneasily, aware of the demoralizing effect such a wind would have on Al and Brian in the cave of Camp 1. The 'mortar bomb simulation' would be pounding all night. Later in the day an apologetic Al and Brian arrived back, justifying their departure from Camp 1 by commenting on the debilitating effect, physically and mentally, of lying for day after day in the ice cave, waiting for the weather to improve. They felt themselves losing strength all the while and had decided to come down.

The wind did not touch us at Base Camp but just after sunset a roar which was not the wind had brought us rushing from the dining tent to see, vague and formless in the twilight, a billowing cloud of avalanche debris pouring out of the 'Burgess couloir'. One of the ice cliffs at the edge of the Lho La had collapsed. A grey, seething wall of snow advanced imperceptibly, menacingly towards the camp. Out-lying streamers flung a dusting of powder snow over us and our tents, but the main mass passed by, its force largely spent in its journey of over a mile. Ade had a wry grin on his face when we had settled back into the tent.

After dark a very wasted and weary-looking John pushed his way into the dining tent. He spoke of the horror of life at Camp 3 during the storms, of the cold and the snow which forced itself in through every tiny crevice and the subsequent maelstrom of whirling snow inside. He had become very weak from dysentery and had had no option but to descend, sorry himself not to have gone further and leaving behind a disappointed Pete who was equally unable to make any progress on his own. John's experience at Camp 3 had been quite an ordeal, culminating, as he describes it himself, in a disturbed night and harrowing descent:

The night in the cave was one long groan. The cold penetrated deep into my bones. Sleep was impossible. The moment I dozed off, my breathing became fitful and irregular. I would open my eyes, gasping for air in the frozen, roaring blackness. At first I felt unutterably fatigued.

By 11 a.m. I knew I had to descend. The diarrhoea had returned, and through coughing so much I had developed a severe pain in my chest. I was worried that pneumonia might set in.

Outside, the weather was bad but no worse than on the days I had hauled loads up from Camp 2. Pete, keen to go on, was disappointed at my decision to go down, but he knew I had no choice. I fell over frequently as I tried to make ready to descend.

Getting down the ropes was a nightmare. The wind blew me over unexpectedly from first one direction and then the other. I was attached to the rope at all times, but once I heard an unmistakable 'click', just as I was about to launch off down the rock barrier, as the karabiner which fastened my harness to the rope came unclipped. Without emotion I re-secured it and continued.

I was only half way down when my diarrhoea overcame me, adding to my suffering. I could not stop. When I reached the Lho La the wind was too strong for me to walk. I crawled the half mile back to the caves, still being blown over by the wind and bouncing along like a ball. My cherished hope was that someone would be waiting for me at Camp 1 with a hot mug of tea ready, but the caves were empty. I dug the snow from the entrance before crawling in and beginning the ignominious task of cleaning myself up.

I still felt extremely ill and decided to continue the descent, lest I should be unable to do so next day if I stayed.

Only when I reached the rocks at the start of the descent did I become aware of the time. I had no strength to hurry, but forced myself down in a slow, dazed routine, checking and re-checking before I made a move. I reached the glacier at dusk.

'Not long now,' I reassured myself, relaxing slightly as I switched on my head torch. But where I had expected to find a familiar trail there was only soft, deep snow and avalanche debris. Soon it was completely dark and the light from my torch began to fail. Unfamiliar ice towers appeared all round and I sank through the soft snow at every second step, expecting each time to find the blackness of a crevasse rushing up towards me. I was lost, and the only solution was to retrace my steps and find somewhere to spend the night out.

Adrenalin kept me going and I had almost regained the edge of the glacier when I caught sight in the distance of the light of someone moving about at Base Camp. Relief penetrated my exhaustion and I trudged in the direction of the light. New snow obscured all tracks, but I knew the way now. I wondered if I would recover strength to go up again. There was the noise of chatter from the dining tent, I entered and the bright light and warmth hit me like the memory of a lost world.

John could stomach no food and retired to his tent early.

It was sickening to wake to a fine day on 26 January. This was the first fine day for some time and there would be no progress still. Alan and Paul left to re-occupy Camp 1.

Late in the afternoon we caught sight of Paul through the telephoto lens nearing the top of the steep corner. He and Alan had been delayed by the deep snow which still covered the route and when there was no reply to the radio call at 6 p.m. it was an indication that they would probably be too tired next day to go on up to Camp 3. Towards evening the clouds blew up swiftly from the south.

The plan was for Ade and myself to go up the next day, hoping to occupy Camp 1 as Paul and Alan went on up to Camp 3, and for us to wait there until we could move up to replace them after they had pushed the route further and retired for a rest. Pete was also up at Camp 3, but he would be in need of a rest after being stranded there for several days through some bad storms. The basic business of survival in such cold and at such altitudes is a trying ordeal.

John was the other person who had a formal job to return to by a certain date. However, he dismissed such anxieties as he felt and resigned himself to the prospect of finding he had no job left on his return. He wanted to stay till the end.

As Ade and I left next morning to go back onto the mountain

I called by John's tent to see how he was.

'Much better thanks Joe, I should be able to get back up there the day after tomorrow.'

Relieved at John's recovery, Ade and I set off, Ade at his usual steady rhythm with me panting behind. He even tempted me up the quicker route of the 'Burgess couloir', reasoning that any loose stuff would have been dislodged by the cataclysmic avalanche of two days ago.

As we reached the steep walls of the corner, Pete came into view, sliding swiftly down the ropes. Pete always seemed to be carrying a sack with something in it. Most of us tried to conserve energy and in descent carry nothing at all. For whatever reason, possibly to make sure that he always had extra clothing to hand, Pete's sack usually looked full.

He was reluctant to be going down, he said, but he had broken a rib. There had been no accident but he had never shaken off the hacking cough by which he had been troubled for weeks now. During a prolonged bout of coughing one of his ribs had cracked.

'Does that mean you are out of it now for the rest of the trip?'

'Oh no, it's happened before and it got better. In another few days I should be okay!'

It was news to me that he had broken a rib earlier but now I realized the reason for his groans at night when he had shared the tent at Camp 2 and marvelled at his taciturnity.

'See you soon then,' and I continued to Camp 1.

When we arrived at the cave, Alan was in residence. Paul had left early in the day for Camp 3 and could be seen as a tiny speck of red on the way up to the West Shoulder. The cave was as familiar as home. Supplies were a little more sparse and the ceiling above the cooking area was blackened with the soot from an accident with a stove. Otherwise nothing had changed.

Alan busied himself melting snow and passing us drinks. He was still racked with frequent coughs and periodically, as if by auto-suggestion, I found that I too was succumbing to a bout. Once started, there was no escape. The cold, dry air compounded the irritation in the throat and the victim's body would be shaken by the hacking cough until randomly flung free of its spell. The nights at Base Camp as well as on the mountain were often punctuated by staccato bursts of noise disturbing the sleep of the sufferer and all those around.

On the radio we heard that the Japanese had called a halt to their expedition and had started evacuating the mountain. In the little time that they had left they had no hope of the weather improving sufficiently to enable them to reach the summit. The Italians too were doubtful of their chances and with the Japanese withdrawing, the way up the ice-fall would be more difficult to maintain. Inevitably these items of news turned us to discussion of our own situation. If we did not make some very definite progress on this attempt, we too would have little hope of climbing the mountain. Alan reckoned that we needed ten days of good weather if we were to stand a chance.

One improvement at Camp 1 had been the construction by Pete of a toilet. Previously we had used the bare hillside, digging a small hole as the need arose. Since the Lho La was rarely free from wind, 'going to the toilet' at any time, but especially at night, was a most undesirable ordeal. Our clothing was designed to allow the performance of the necessary functions, by means of long zips, without having to undress completely. Nevertheless, a substantial area of the back and buttocks was still exposed. The operation was usually completed with the greatest of haste and one scuttled back to the sheltering cave feeling decidedly vulnerable and helpless against the demands of nature which could come at any time of day or night. I had got into the habit on expeditions of trying to establish a discipline in my bodily rhythms of only going to the toilet once a day, and that once in the morning. That way the whole business was completed along with all the other morning duties, otherwise it might mean disentangling oneself from harnesses and ropes and performing in even more precarious and unpleasant situations.

Even at the Lho La camp the problem was that whichever way one faced, the wind would always find the weak spot and even reaching a suitable place was a tricky manoeuvre with the risk of slipping or being blown down the slope outside the cave. We wore all of our clothes all the time, except boots, and the sensible thing to do was to dress completely in crampons, mitts and ice axe, but this conflicted with the tendency to want to rush outside, get the job over with quickly, and get back inside to the warmth of a sleeping bag once more.

So Pete, in a labour of love, had worked on his own for some hours digging a trench into the hillside and erecting a wall with blocks of snow on three sides of the trench. It was crude but effective and although the narrow track to the toilet became icy with use, most of the danger was taken out of this necessary function and Pete had the satisfaction of having built a toilet with the most splendid view in the world down into Tibet, over-looked by the summit of Everest and flanked by the walls of Nuptse.

Long after dark, lingering over the evening meal which was enlivened by some bacon from the exchange with the Italians, there was an unfamiliar rustling outside and Paul startled us when he burst in out of the night. He looked haggard and morose. He had climbed two-thirds of the way up to Camp 3 before coming to a standstill. For him the expedition had gone on too long, he had no reserves of energy, and pains in his back due to an attack of hepatitis a few months earlier had begun to grow unbearable. It was almost night when he had turned back and he had realized by the slow progress he had made that he would be able to achieve little from Camp 3 anyway.

In the morning Paul was still in pain and he regretfully explained his decision to continue on down to Base Camp. For him the expedition was over. He expected to be gone before we got down again and we made our goodbyes.

'Give everyone a ring when you get back home, tell them we won't be long, will you?'

Without Paul we were missing a solid, reliable workhorse. Throughout he had been willing to fit in and perform some of the least exciting but essential roles. I was sorry to see him go.

Alan left first, crossing the Lho La towards the ropes. Ade and I tested each other's sacks, gauging the weight of food and gear we were taking up to Camp 3. Thirty-five to forty pounds, they didn't feel heavy outside the cave but half way to the bottom of the ropes they felt burdensome. We caught Alan up at the berg-schrund where he was waiting to take some photographs. I loitered long enough to let Ade go in front – he seemed to have more energy than me – then I swung up the ropes after him and started the long, tedious haul to Camp 3, counting off each 150-foot length of rope as I passed the anchor point: one gone, thirty-five more ropes to go. Alan followed, always keeping at least one full rope length behind so that the weight of both of us was never on one anchor.

Ade soon outdistanced me, though Alan was going at the same pace. The three of us journeyed up hour after hour, separated by only a few hundred feet, without a word. The wind was strong enough to make us keep our hoods up, though the sky was clear. When I came through the trying stretches of the rock barrier, Ade was nowhere in sight. He had disappeared behind a rib of rock and from the top of it I could see jets of steam outlined by the sun which had not reached me yet revealing his location.

I never caught him up. Try as I might, my pace seemed slow, my sack a dead weight. When I reached the vicinity of the abandoned Camp 2, there were ten more rope lengths to go – almost there, only another hour and a half. Below, Alan had dropped back; he would be late.

The shadows were long down the Rongbuk glacier and the sun was setting before I arrived at Camp 3. I plunged inside down the long curving tunnel and grabbed the movie camera, an ancient Bolex. Outside, I filmed the boiling mass of clouds, spewing from the summit and catching the orange tints of the sinking sun. I was awkward from the cold. The metal clung to my fingers as I risked using the camera without gloves and the warmth was sucked out of them by the cold casing. I made a clumsy mess of changing the film and tumbled back into the cave unsatisfied with my efforts but helpless from the pain of the cold in my hands.

It had taken me seven hours to reach Camp 3. Ade had done it in only five. Long after dark there was still no sign of Alan. The position of the cave precluded any sighting and only a descent of several hundred feet or a traverse across some precarious ice slopes would allow a view down to where he was last seen.

At 6 p.m. on the radio call Alan's voice came through from Camp 1. He too had ground to a halt well below Camp 3 and fearing benightment had descended while he still had strength and daylight left. We were relieved that he was safe but alarmed at the progressive weakening of the forces on the mountain. Alone again in this inhospitable ice chamber, Ade and I manoeuvred and shuffled like dogs in a new bed until we were ensconced in sleeping bags with food and stoves to hand and a pile of ice chunks ready for melting.

The hours of darkness in the Himalayas are long. In winter they were even more so, but sleep was harder to find. I was wary of taking any sleeping pills after the bad experiences the last time I was up. Consequently I passed a fitful night, my sleep disturbed for unknown reasons. Perhaps it was the cold draught through the cave, a particle of ice falling from the ceiling onto my face or contact with the ice-coated exterior of my sleeping bag as I turned over. Sometimes I was aware by his movements and altered breathing that Ade was awake too. I pestered him for the time. I had a watch, but to illuminate the face I had to press a button on the side. My fingers were too numb from the cold to do this.

Dawn's flat light filtered in through the walls of snow. The insulating mats on which we were sleeping were covered in a fine layer of snow which had settled from the air in the night. Ade made moves to light the small gas stove and start the day. I confessed to him that I felt nauseous and headachey. The prospect of doing anything was not appealing but to decide to make no move upwards today would mean further demoralization.

I got up to relieve myself and look outside. Beyond the crude curtain we now had over the entrance, the tunnel was lined with several inches of fresh snow. I crawled up it and poked my head out into a gale. Cloud was low and more snow was falling. I felt a guilty relief at the thought that we could justifiably have a day of rest. It would be too dangerous to attempt to go up onto the West Shoulder. At 8 a.m. we radioed down the situation. It was similarly wild at the Lho La, but Al and Brian were setting off from Base Camp to reach Camp 1.

Ade ministered to me all day making drinks and food. I was apologetic about my disability: 'I'm sorry I'm leaving you to do all the work.'

'That's okay, you did it for me last time.'

It was −21 °C inside the cave; the only advantage it had over the cave lower down was that here we had an inside toilet.

In civilization one can hardly imagine passing a whole day and night lying next to a person with whom one is not emotionally involved. Little conversation passed between us, what little was to be said had already been reiterated many times in the weeks past. Making another cup of tea was an event as important as a dinner party, and took about as long to prepare. Gradually, through the administration of several pain killers and the intake of much liquid, my headache disappeared.

Even from Base Camp it was possible to misjudge the mountain. I sometimes used to wonder what could possibly stop us from putting one foot in front of the other, in making at least some progress. Lying in the cave was full of frustrations; we were drawn to satisfy our curiosity about the rest of the route, keen to advance a stage further. We could have gone outside, could have gone so far but without even discussing it we both knew the futility of such a gesture. A gesture as much demanded from within ourselves to ensure that we were not taking the soft option as from anything else.

I had spent a lot of time now with Ade and enjoyed the generous comradeliness of his company. He and his brother were quite different, I could see more clearly now, but different in a close way as if aspects of the same personality. This closeness seemed so strong that I was subconsciously surprised that they could perform independently of each other and made no obvious effort to make sure that they were teamed up. Ade was the more 'serious' of the two, often looking askance at the antics of his brother, who had a reputation for inadvertently wrecking things. Somehow a trenching tool had broken in his hands when digging a tent site at Camp 2; somehow the aerial on the master set of the radios had snapped when he was using it; somehow the syringe Pete had asked him to open in the tense moments round Wan Chup's sick bed had disintegrated in his hands. Al surfaced from each escapade with a self-mocking grin. One got the impression that Ade sometimes wanted to disown him.

Our food was a little better than it had been due to the discovery amongst the foods we had exchanged with the Italians of some easily cooked meals which tasted almost real. Tea and coffee had come to taste very acidic and the drink of preference was now one made from mineral salts and designed to help athletes. Whatever its benefits in that respect it made a refreshing change from tea and helped us consume the essential quantities of liquid.

The second night was as bad as the first. This time we both took a sleeping pill which Ade produced from his own little select pack of medicines. He assured me that they did not leave a nasty hangover like the others. We had too long to sleep though, and the effect of the pills wore off in the middle of the night leaving us back playing the waiting game to see if we could move at dawn.

Both of us felt queasy by morning. We were unsure why. There was plenty of air in the cave and we had both been to such altitudes many times before. It is not unusual to have headaches the first time one reaches a certain height during an expedition, but after several weeks one can expect to be completely acclimatized. We could only assume that it was caused by constantly breathing extremely cold air and having a cold draught passing over our faces.

Ade made the breakfast but I was on my knees retching for a while before I felt well enough to take anything. The day was clear but still windy. If we were to make any progress at all on the mountain we would have to resign ourselves to climbing, if it was possible, in the wind. We radioed down our intention of taking some gear up onto the West Shoulder to assess conditions.

We took some coils of rope and digging tools each, intending to make a dump of gear along the ridge, thus easing the next day's work when we expected to go right through to the site for Camp 4. Since our loads were not too heavy we took a movie camera each, Ade the big, heavy Bolex and I the smaller, cartridge-loading Autoload. Mike was not to come any higher than the Lho La and now, in the absence of the professional, we felt less inhibited about our untutored efforts and also more responsibility to take film.

The Autoload was easy to handle. There were few controls and the cartridges were readily slotted in, even with mittened hands. A cartridge only lasted for sixty seconds though, hardly enough time to get into the rhythm of filming. Ade was off in front again and I tried to capture the ecstatic view of him silhouetted against the sun with streamers of wind-driven snow snaking down over the glistening ice and past his feet. There was no way of checking our results until we arrived back in Britain – it was a matter of shoot it and see.

Sixty seconds seemed a long time at altitude until I checked the film counter. The film had snapped with the cold. Without much regret, having tried to do my duty, I put the camera away. Anyway, as I reached the rounded plateau and climbed into the wind I was occupied more and more with trying to keep my balance against the fierce gusts.

Ade was sitting on the same lone piece of black rock we had come across on our first visit here. He had the weighty Bolex pressed to his eye recording my erratic gait. For hand-held filming it is best not to breathe while the finger is actually on the trigger to avoid camera shake. Any effort to hold one's breath at altitude for more than a few seconds brought on a rapid, panicky gulping for air. The oxygen was already scarce enough without cutting it off completely. As I reached him, Ade pulled the camera away from his face. A white streak of frost-burn lined his nose where the cold metal of the camera case had frozen into place. Ade did not know it had happened till I shouted above the noise of the wind to take care. His whole face was numb and he would not feel any pain from the frost-burn until it warmed up. More of a perfectionist than me, he had taken his goggles off to see more clearly through the view-finder.

We soaked in the splendid panorama for a while. Communication was hardly possible. The wind was far stronger than the first time we had come up to this point and to go further would be risky. This was a risk we felt we would have to take if we were going to get any further. Roped together would be the only way to advance, giving ourselves a chance of safeguarding each other against any slip. Sometimes I looked at the rest of the route as if it were just a short step, sometimes it seemed infinite. The only way to treat it was a little bit at a time.

We turned to go back, dumping the gear beside the rock, the

incongruous spade, proof even against Al's latent destructiveness, was thrust into the snow to mark the spot. We believed we could make headway against the wind and would return next day, with luck with reinforcements, and make our way right along the ridge.

Back at Camp 3 we were puzzled to find no sign of any new arrivals. By dark still no one had arrived and the clear skies had gone, replaced by turbulent, snow-filled clouds.

We expected an explanation on the radio call but nothing came through from Camp 1. From Base Camp we heard the alarming news that John had not recovered from his sickness and had left for home with Paul. Pete was on the radio and he explained that he had found John to have a chest infection as well as dysentery. John was unable to eat and had decided to leave for lower altitudes rather than grow progressively weaker trying to fight the illness in the inhospitable Base Camp.

A quarter of the strength of the team had thus vanished. Logically there were many reasons for Paul and John to have left but it was a savage blow and seemed to mock our attempts at getting any further. There was no blame to attach to their decision to leave, Pete himself had been adamant on the radio that John stood no chance of recovering, but with the arrogance of the fit I did feel a wordless frustration and fought hard within myself to maintain optimism. Their departure, however, compounded by the failure of anyone to arrive, aroused grave disquiet in our minds. For a couple of hours after dark Ade and I chewed over what was going on and whether up at Camp 3 we were as isolated and out on a limb as we felt. If no one was able to reach Camp 3, what prospect did we stand on our own? Certainly we could probably reach the site for Camp 4 and start digging a cave, but apart from the strain of working unsupported at such an altitude for several days we would soon run out of food and have to descend.

We resolved to do some straight talking next morning on the radio. If no one was coming up, we were not sure that the risk involved in going further along the West Ridge was worth taking. This night too passed with fitful sleep but this time it was for other reasons than the unpleasant physical conditions by which we were surrounded.

CHAPTER ELEVEN

Straight Talking

Al came on the radio for the morning call. Ade spoke to him. It was the best possible pairing for a dialogue. Intimate as they were, with no means of subterfuge, these two could be more blunt and more open than most people ever could be to their closest friends.

Ade made the first call: 'Camp 3 to Lho La, come in please.'

Al replied 'Lola,' as he used to pronounce it, 'to Camp 3, hearing you loud and clear. How do you hear me? Over.'

'Loud and clear. What is going on? Why has no one come up? Do people intend to come up? Over.'

'It was too windy yesterday and no one here feeling good. It is too windy again today to cross Lola.'

'Look, we went up to the West Shoulder yesterday to see what it was like. It was windy but we should be able to get further. If we can go up there in the wind you should be able to get up here.'

'Well, I don't feel well at all and Brian and Alan here have doubts about their effectiveness even if they can reach Camp 3.'

The exchange between these two was punctuated by pauses waiting for the 'Over', to mark the termination of one side of a message and signify readiness to receive the reply. Only one party could speak at a time as the transmit button cut out reception of sound. The normal tendency to interject comments into a conversation as it went along was thus thwarted and in an exchange as crucial as this there was a lot of frustration in waiting the turn to speak.

Ade said: 'If no one comes up to Camp 3 they won't ever get acclimatized to the altitude. It's best to come up and have a day's rest here if necessary instead of waiting at the Lho La to feel fit. That's 3,000 feet lower. Is anyone going to come or not?'

'The feeling here is that you are being over-optimistic about the chances of getting further.'

'Look, we went up there yesterday specifically to find out and we reckon it is worth trying to push on even in the wind if we are roped up.'

'Brian suggests that you and Joe go along to establish Camp 4 if you think it possible and if it is, people can then come up to give a hand.'

'We need help now. We need at least the moral support of knowing that we aren't sticking our necks out going along that ridge, which won't be easy, only to find we've done it for nothing.'

'If you and Joe are doubtful about your ability to get along there, and you're going better than any of us, what chance has anyone else got.'

'Look it's black and white. We can't do everything on our own. If no one comes up there is no point in us going on.'

'Don't try to put the onus on us. If you want to give it a go getting to Camp 4 then do so.'

The artificially clipped manner of the dialogue also lent bluntness to the comments. With anyone else making this exchange there would have been the risk of arousing hostility by such sharp retorts. However, the anger which I knew Ade felt and which he was trying to express to his brother was curtailed by the formalities of radio talk. Ade swore for me to hear as his brother's monotone replies came out of the radio. There was a clear polarization between the two camps and we seemed to be talking in circles.

Brian described the same radio interchange from the viewpoint of Camp 1:

'The three of us, Alan, Al and myself, lay side by side in the ice cave, surrounded by a jumble of clothing and gear. Alan was huddled up, his down-suited body protruding from his sleeping bag, a morose expression on his face. Al had the walkie-talkie in his hands.

I broke into the exchange which Al was having with his brother: 'What the hell do they mean – need our support? What are we sat in this ice box for if it's not support? Let me talk to them, Al!'

'No, I just want to finish talking to Ade. They must realize that there is no way we can get to the top now.'

I agreed with him: 'Yes, can't they see that with Paul and John on their way home, Pete with a broken rib, you with a bad chest, me and Alan totally demoralized, we just haven't got enough people left to make an attempt on the summit?'

Suddenly Alan burst out angrily: 'Fuck 'em! Give me the radio! Lho La to Camp 3, do you receive me? Over.'

'Ade from Camp 3. We receive you strength one. Please repeat. Over.'

Alan twiddled with knobs and the aerial before shouting into the radio and receiving Ade's reply. 'Receiving you strength four. If nobody will come up to help us we cannot continue alone. We need your support. If you can't come up, we will come down. Over.'

Aside from the radio, Alan responded with more impatience: 'What the hell are they talking about? We've been sat here for seven days out of the last ten. We've had three good days in the last month when we could climb along the West Ridge. We need eight continuous days of good weather to get to the top. I'm bored with lying here day after day, feeling cold, ill and hungry.'

'Lho La to Camp 3, Alan here!' he shouted into the radio, pausing between each word so that the message was emphatic. 'If ... the ... weather ... gets ... better ... will ... come ... up. ... No ... point ... otherwise. ... Just ... get ... tired ... at ... Camp ... 3. ... You ... are ... only ... two strong ... enough ... to ... push ... above ... Camp ... 3 .... Over.'

'Camp 3 to Lho La. Sorry, reception bad. Please repeat. Over.'

'If ... weather ... gets ... better ... will ... come ... up. ... Over.'

With that, Alan's voice finally cracked and he croaked in a whisper: 'Oh Christ, somebody else try to get some sense out of them,' and he finished with a fit of coughing and retching.

Suddenly Pete broke in: 'Hello Camp 3 and Camp 1, Pete speaking from Base, can I add a few comments? Over.'

'Hearing you loud and clear. Over.'

Pete: 'There seems to be a crucial discussion going on. I know I have got a broken rib but if I can have a say in it my vote is for pressing on. I'm not saying we can do it now at this late stage but I think we should stick it out for another few days. Things might just work out for us. What do you say to that?'

I took the radio from Ade.

'Hello, Joe speaking. Those are my feelings too. Time is short but we might as well use it. We do need some support, though.'

Pete: 'Could you and Ade just stay up another few days and do what you can?'

'We could certainly stay up another few days but after that we will be out of food. We need at least a commitment from others that they are coming up. I don't fancy sticking my neck out not knowing what is going on.'

'Can't you give a demonstration of what is still possible by going along to Camp 4? That might change the whole attitude.'

'We gave a bloody demonstration yesterday. What do you think this is, a circus? I don't think it's time for demonstrations. Everyone at Camp 1 seems to disagree that there's any chance left of us getting up the mountain in the weather we are stuck with now. If they can't get up now, what is the likelihood of them coming up in three days' time? We aren't putting the onus on them of calling a halt – the onus *is* on them. We are getting nowhere with this conversation. No one is saying what they really mean. Before coming to any hasty decision, let's think about it. Let's have another radio call at eleven to give everyone time to think things over.'

We switched off. Ade and I relapsed into a glum silence. We both knew each other's minds. We wanted to go on even though we knew there remained little chance. The most rewarding achievements only come from succeeding against the greatest odds. On the other hand we had more than the weather to contend with. Ade and I had been lucky in escaping most of the ills which had bedevilled the expedition and when one is fit it is hard to comprehend how great problems can be, both mental and physical, for someone who is sick. There had been a lot of debilitating sickness and Everest in winter was showing no mercy to the sick. Brian had just recovered from yet another attack of dysentery. Alan, a skeleton of his former self, could hardly be understood over the radio, his voice was so hoarse, and now Al too had developed a chest infection. There was no doubt that sickness makes everything seem so much more difficult and even were it possible for anyone to drive himself on the result could be fatal.

Ade was convinced that there would be no change of opinion. It was indeed a vain hope. The date was 31 January. We had been on the mountain for nearly two months. The constant cold, bitter, brutal winds and snow storms had steadily eroded our strength and resources. Perhaps Everest was too big an objective to tackle so early in this new phase of Himalayan exploration; the problems were far different and less obvious than in other seasons. I did feel in one part of my mind that there would be some relief in giving up this interminable struggle; the mental and physical strain of sustaining such effort over two months is extreme and no matter what the disappointment at not reaching the top there would be the pleasure of having survived, the satisfaction of knowing that we had battled with Everest at the worst time of the year and had not lost anyone or had any serious accidents.

While waiting for 11 a.m. and the decision either way, we made another drink and started sorting out which gear we would take down and which we would abandon.

Outside only the eyes of an optimist could see the weather as being reasonable, and for the past month, apart from two days, we had known only storm and wind. There was no indication that we could expect any better in the next few days.

At 11 a.m. we opened up radio communication again.

'Hello Camp 1 and Base are you listening? What is the position now? Are there any new thoughts on the situation? Over.'

Pete came on the radio and there was a dialogue between him and Camp 1. Brian gave his view of it:

Pete's voice was enthusiastic, I could tell, even over the little radio.

'Pete to Camp 1 and 3. I think that whilst we still have time left and people on the mountain we should keep trying at least for another week. Perhaps we'll get a spell of good weather. Can't anyone from Camp 1 get up to Camp 3? Over.'

I resented Pete sitting at Base Camp and trying to tell us what to do.

'Thanks, Pete, but winds are too strong today. Could not get up the ropes, but see no point in going up anyway if there is going to be just more bad weather.'

Alan sat up from a bout of coughing and, echoing my own and Al's sentiments, said into the radio: 'Get lost, Pete, you're just complicating things.'

Pete obviously did not hear this at Base Camp and Al commented after some thought: 'I suppose Pete's got just as much right to his opinion as everyone else.'

'Yes,' I said, 'it's just that discussing the potential end of a trip which you've worked on for the past six months, over a radio with poor reception, does not lend itself to friendly conversation.'

Joe's voice cut across the radio with icy tones: 'If you don't come up from Camp 1 in support we might as well come down. Over.'

At Camp 3 we heard Al reply:

'If you want to stay up we are prepared to back you but there doesn't seem much point.'

'Is anyone coming up?'

'No one is really fit enough to.'

The refusal to come to the point and the oral fencing round the real issue continued.

Ade groaned. He left the radio on 'receive' and we heard Pete come in again from Base Camp and conduct a long dialogue with Camp 1 on the same lines as the earlier discussion. To me, Ade said: 'Nothing has changed. We might as well face it. They're never going to come up. By support we're talking about different things. I think they mean they'l l be praying for us. They can't help being ill, but wait till I see our kid. I think this winter game has been too much for everyone.'

There was a look of resignation on his face and he started to stuff gear into a rucksack for descent. I lay back, listening to the discussion flying back and forth between Camp 1 and Base Camp. Pete was putting up a spirited argument for maintaining the impetus. The response from Camp 1 was that he was misjudging the situation on the mountain and that he himself was not of much use anyway with a broken rib. The discussion went on and on. Half an hour passed and Ade was ready to leave. The attitudes of everyone concerned were exactly the same as they had been at the start.

'There isn't going to be any change,' said Ade, 'I'm going to set off down. Might as well try and get to Base Camp in one go. See you later.' He pushed his sack up the tunnel and disappeared.

There was no reference on the radio to us at Camp 3 expecting a reply and I too busied myself retrieving valuable pieces of camera gear and sleeping bags. When I was ready to leave I waited a while longer, listening to the still raging discourses which seemed to have gone in circles for a full three-quarters of an hour. Still no change, and I scrambled up the tunnel for the last time, turning my thoughts to the consolations which remained – no more grim nights in that hole, the gradual return to civiliza- tion and comfort.

My rucksack was exceedingly heavy. Both Ade and I were taking down the maximum possible knowing that now there was no need to conserve energy and that it was unlikely that anyone else would be coming up to retrieve gear. As I swung down the ropes on the steepening slopes back to the Lho La, I had to fight the wind which was throwing me off balance and I asked myself how realistic I had been in declaring that it would have been possible to make further progress in such weather. Did I really think we stood any chance now of getting up the mountain or did I simply not want to lose face by capitulating to a more rational assessment of our situation? I did not know the answer myself. The way down to the level plateau of the

Lho La seemed interminable. I could see Ade, a distant figure far below, and a tiny speck which left Camp 1 on its way down. I sank to my knees to rest at every anchor point, longing to be out of the wearying wind.

The level plateau of the Lho La was only a change, not a relief. The furious wind knocked me back and forth and I paused frequently, waiting for a lull before staggering on a few steps. The final slight rise up to the cave of Camp 1 took forever. I felt self-conscious under the scrutiny of Alan who was waiting at the cave entrance with a drink ready.

Al had already gone down. Alan and Brian were staying at Camp 1 to pack everything up and clear as much gear as possible off the mountain. Ade left as soon as I arrived and I hastened after him in order to reach Base Camp before night-fall.

I had to dump my sack half-way down. My legs kept giving way beneath me and once clear of the roped areas I knew I could easily retrieve the sack the next day. The sun had set and only a glimmer of light remained when I reached camp, walking into a barrage of questions, and confronted by a camera and microphone from the film crew wanting instant reactions to the decision to call off the expedition.

Ade was involved in an angry dispute with his brother. 'Bloody support,' I heard him say. 'You couldn't carry a shopping basket to a supermarket, let alone a sack of gear up this hill.' Al looked crestfallen and apologetic. Harder words could fly between these two than between any of the rest of us, and Ade was clearing his system of all the resentment that had built up over the last few days before the task of winding up the expedition should take precedence and form us into a working team again.

CHAPTER TWELVE

The Wind Up

A mail bag had gone missing – a multitude of letters and cards, ninety minutes of film, $300 in travellers' cheques. Our postal system had finally shown a flaw. We had sent the mail bag in question at the beginning of January and it had taken a month for it to be reported to us that it had not arrived in Kathmandu. None of us kept track of to whom we had written or when; that mail was irretrievable. Mike Shrimpton, professional to the last, had a note of every roll of film he had sent off, and dutifully he set off back up to the Lho La to retake as much of the missing footage as he could. There was much coming and going at this time retrieving gear from the mountain and Mike went up with Brian and Pete. Pete showed an unsuspected propensity for conservation even going back up to Camp 3 once to rescue what bits Ade and I had been unable to carry down. Some things were too bulky but rather than abandon them Pete made a couple of large bundles and trundled them down the 3,000-foot slope to the Lho La, rescuing the remains much later when he himself arrived.

The Japanese and Italians were also in the process of dismantling their Base Camps. Hordes of porters and Sherpas arrived, invading our solitude and picking like looters at every unattended piece of equipment or box of food. They had long grown accustomed to expeditions winding up and abandoning much valuable gear so that they have come to take it that they have a right to anything left around. These were Sherpas in a different light from what we had seen before and the camp had the feel of a beleaguered garrison as we cleared up, burning rubbish and packing our belongings ready for departure.

Mr Singh became ill and did not appear from his tent for three days. The only sound emanating from that direction was indistinguishable between singing and groaning. Graham, camped beside him, reported hearing the same sounds throughout the night and believed the strain of nearly three months in the mountains was beginning to unbalance our shy Liaison Officer.

Finally we left, the familiar smell of juniper wood smoke from the Italian camp trailing after us for a long time. The chaos of packing, loading yaks, arguing over rates and weights, all compressed into a straggling line of ponderous animals as we made our way downwards into deeper snow where the wind had not blown with such force.

In only a short time Everest slipped behind the wall of Nuptse and our self-imposed exile was over. I had a feeling of freedom, of walking unencumbered by any constraints; alive again with no dangers ahead to face up to; alive with dreams still intact, with a goal to aim for. This had been a punishing experience. We had kept in control, we were all returning without loss of life or limb in the party, but in two months we had grown to accept as normal the most harrowing living conditions we had known and had tried to climb the highest mountain in the world by its most difficult route. The Japanese, with a different style of expedition on a different route, had been turned back from a similar height on the same mountain. Some of our party thought that Everest, in winter, without oxygen and especially by the West Ridge, was impossible. The time needed to be spent on the mountain had left us weak and unable to combat illnesses. The winds had been relentless and it was often physically impossible to move in them. There was no doubt that we had every justification in retreating before we found ourselves fighting for our lives with no physical or material resources left. But the objective remained. Perhaps we needed this expedition to learn what was necessary for success. Few people dare to say that any problem in mountaineering now is impossible to solve; failure only enhances the prestige of the objective. After dropping somewhat in esteem in recent years due to the numerous ascents of the mountain, Everest was now restored to its pre-eminent position. Winter mountaineering in the Himalayas opens a new chapter in the sport with the ascent of Everest as its greatest prize.

We made our way over several days to Lukla, the air strip from which we were to fly out. The lower valleys, with trees laden with snow, had a more familiar look of winter than the Base Camp we had left where the barren wastes change little with the arrival of more snow.

We met a Sherpa, 'Long' Tensing, who had been with the Burgess twins on an earlier expedition: 'Success?'

'No.'

'Members all O.K.?'

'Yes.'

'On Everest that is success!'

In Kathmandu the pace of life changed. Months away from modern communications and we were like savages undergoing culture shock. The first night back and we found ourselves at a party in an embassy house. They were all the 'beautiful people' of Kathmandu but we were ill at ease. Lost in the mêlée of noise and strangers, we clung together for reassurance, unable to make conversation or relate to what was happening.

We were eating in a restaurant once when a shaven-headed girl, dressed in the purple robes of the Buddhist faith, walked up to our table. She looked from one Burgess twin to the other.

'Which one?' she said, and Al, his gaping mouth demonstrating his bewilderment, recognized the girl he had met on the way in.

The twins stayed behind to forward all our baggage and the rest of us, gradually separating off from the close-knit group we had become, boarded the plane for home. I was not prepared for it. A million strings were drawing me back but those strings came from another side of a wall and did not have any meaning until I should be amongst them again. As we approached London I felt a sense of nervousness as if I had become estranged from life at home and that back in the mountains we had left some unfinished business.

Conclusion

Was it worth it? Was it worth the effort, the cost, the pain? Should we have listened to all those on the one hand who said that our chances of climbing the mountain in winter were minimal or those on the other hand who said that the concept of a 'winter season' was a perversion contrived to extract excitement from the ascent of a mountain which had already been climbed?

We thought it was worth it, and already the competition for further attempts is fierce. Now that the winter season is officially accepted, the mountain is 'booked' by one route or another for the next four years. Another Japanese expedition is planning to climb the South Col route for 1981/82. An Italian expedition in 1982/83 hopes to attempt the West Ridge. In 1983/84 a French expedition is on the West Ridge and another Japanese expedition will attempt the South Col route. In 1984/85 a different Italian expedition plans to try the West Ridge.

We knew that the odds were against us, we knew that conditions would be extreme, but it is in the nature of the sport that if there is any chance at all it is worth a try. We had some grounds for optimism. Over the last few years improvements in clothing and footwear have been immense, giving us cause to believe we would be reasonably safe against the cold if we took care. The experience of the members of the expedition was vast and the familiarity of everyone with the practice of lightweight, highly mobile ascents encouraged our expectations of being able to cope with the ascent of the enormously long West Ridge. The route itself, because everything was frozen into stillness, was relatively safe from stonefall and avalanche danger. There were, of course, the problems of the wind, the ever-present wind, but in retrospect the West Ridge route may, in the upper part, where it enters the narrow Hornbein couloir through the summit pyramid, be sheltered from the main brunt of the wind. Movement may thus be easier and it may be conceivable to use a tent without risk of it being demolished.

In the end we were defeated by sickness, which severely depleted our physical resources; by the extremes of cold and the weather generally which could change, it seemed, in minutes; by the enormity of the undertaking which, at the end, left us overextended. By contrast with the spring, when it is possible to sit out warming in the sun, even at 26,000 feet, there was never any relief from the cold. As time went on we began to have doubts about the ability of any group to stay on the mountain for a sustained period of time without experiencing a rapid deterioration.

At this moment, attempting to climb Everest in winter and without oxygen by whatever route seems dangerously close to the limits of what is possible for man, leaving little or no margin for error. Going high entails overcoming severe problems at any time of the year and the experience has been likened, even when fully acclimatized, to that of someone who suffers a chronic lung disease. Actions and thoughts are markedly affected for the duration of the stay at altitude and the description of observing a person's movements on a mountain as being those of a 'sick man walking in a dream' holds true in varying degrees all the way from Base Camp to the summit.

Given that adaptation to altitude is influenced by cold and wind as well as the rarefied air, the area we were exploring in trying to climb Everest in winter was fraught with more problems of acclimatization than we could anticipate.

Sir Edmund Hillary had used the Silver Hut Scientific and Mountaineering Expedition in 1960/61 to investigate his theories of acclimatization. Through the winter he and his team had exercised and undertook research at and around 19,000 feet and in the spring went on to attempt Makalu, at 27,790 feet the fifth highest mountain in the world. Three of the party reached 27,400 feet before high-altitude sickness struck. The rest of the story was one of a painfully fought retreat, as the party staved off the almost inevitable tragedy, and sickness and frostbite seemed to be picking them off one by one.

The expedition has become a legend of bravery and self-sacrifice when by all accounts it should have been a model of methodical preparation and an assault by the most superbly acclimatized group ever to attempt a high mountain. As Hillary said, they came 'within a whisker of disaster'.

The actual turning-point of the expedition was caused through an accident, but as Hillary concluded himself, in his book *High Adventure*, the team was already severely weakened by the very programme of training it had set itself.

> I had always expected Makalu to be the final testing ground of my acclimatization theories and believed that the long periods my men had spent at 19,000 feet and above would make them so adjusted to living in rare atmospheres that Makalu would not be too formidable an objective for them even without the use of oxygen. And then perhaps Everest without oxygen might be the next step? But now I realize that my theories were a little too optimistic and these long periods at high altitudes were possibly our undoing. Despite the superficial adjustments made to 19,000 feet and the excellent physical and mental work done at this height, there is much evidence to indicate that resistance to disease was greatly reduced. Also it was almost impossible to gain sufficient daily exercise at 19,000 feet, so the party lacked the hard physical condition to enable them to be battered by the bitter winds above 24,000 feet and yet come back for more. Only Harrison and Ortenburger, the two newcomers to the team, showed the expected reserves of strength, and they had not been subjected to the slow and insidious sapping of weight and vitality experienced by the rest of the party over the previous six months.

Our stay at Base Camp was not as extended as that of the subjects of the Silver Hut experiments but the effects were the same. Other studies have shown that it probably takes years rather than weeks before a person can become fully acclimatized, with the same work capacity as at sea level. Undoubtedly the winter conditions did weaken our team as a whole, making us easy prey to any illnesses which arose for whatever reason or were imported by visitors to Base Camp. Endurance and resistance to cold were much impaired as the weeks went on and the risks of being caught without physical reserves high up were great. Our living conditions contrasted sharply with those of the Japanese but our performance differed little and overall we suffered less from frostbite. Certainly our superior clothing may have helped us in this but the savage extremities of climate both parties had to endure probably blanked out any advantages they gained from a more comfortable Base Camp or we gained from more effective dress.

To achieve success under anything but the most unpredictable conjunctions of good fortune and fine weather, the problem of residence on the mountain must be overcome. Our experience of life at altitude in winter was of conditions worse than we would wish to consider as an acceptable or feasible basis from which to work. It was not a question of volition; if, under circumstances when normally one would expect to be well acclimatized, the norm is to wake with headaches and nausea, only the greatest perseverance will drive a person on and that perseverance will be ill-advised. Dr Charles Houston, in an excellent work on high-altitude physiology, comments on the effects of cold air on the face as producing high-altitude pulmonary oedema. This was precisely what we were finding. With the low oxygen intake during sleep combined with extreme cold we were hardly in fit shape the next day to be effective.

Hillary also comments on the attempt to climb high without additional oxygen support, a support which certainly obviates many of the problems associated with altitude and cold. After an initial enthusiasm when he was looking forward to the eventual ascent of Everest without supplementary oxygen, he seems to change his opinion as a result of the traumatic experience of his team on Makalu: 'None of us have any doubts that the summit of Makalu can be reached without oxygen, but my feelings have undergone a considerable change in this matter. I doubt if the risks involved in working at this height without oxygen make the effort worthwhile.'

Oxygen does help combat the cold. I often thought enviously during the trip of descriptions I had heard from the members of the South-West Face expedition of the sensation of warmth percolating through to tingling toes and finger ends as they strapped on their oxygen masks for sleeping. Moving oxygen cylinders up a mountain, however, does multiply enormously the problems of an expedition. There is much debate on the 'ethics' of using additional oxygen to 'bring a mountain down to a lower level', but the debate seems slightly irrelevant if using oxygen equipment brings along other problems to replace those it solves.

Drawing from our experience on Everest during winter, we found we were agreeably surprised that deep snow was not the problem we expected it to be. Conditions were consequently safer in that we did not risk being wiped out by an almighty avalanche of snow on the slopes we were climbing. This may not always be the case, as the Italian expedition to Makalu, which reached approximately 24,000 feet, had to abandon all of its equipment at Base Camp because the snow was too deep to evacuate it.

Of course the lack of problems with snow was due to the very much increased problem of wind. This was far more savage and persistent than we could have imagined and virtually ruled out the possibility of using tents on the mountain. Tents proved to be undesirable anyway due to the cramped conditions, the constant showers of ice falling from the rime-coated ceiling and walls, and the noise from the wind. The air temperature was colder in a tent than in a cave too. Caves were the best answer and, although they did require much effort to dig, in the context of the overall effort of climbing the mountain it was well worth while. The solution to sleeping arrangements may be to erect a tent inside a snow cave, thus providing a possible cocoon of warmth to try to offset the effect of being surrounded by extremely cold air. A small paraffin heater might even be worth considering at the lower camps.

The Base Camp needs to be luxurious. For even a shorter campaign the erosion of physical and mental resources through putting up with spartan conditions is detrimental to an expedition. Constructing some form of hut may be the answer. A current expedition which is spending three years circumnavigating the earth via both poles is using a cardboard hut for the crossing of the Antarctic. This cardboard is almost as strong as wood, being of a multiple-ply construction, but much lighter. It can be pre-formed to be readily erected, thus providing a solid, insulated shelter from the worst weather. The Antarctic leg of the circum-navigation is now completed and the hut was successfully used as a base at the South Pole over Christmas. A hut such as this, lightweight but solid, with heaters inside, would have been most welcome with us in our Base Camp.

Base Camp should be positively comfortable, and the sleeping arrangement of the Japanese communal tent is one solution, even though it may be contrary to the inclinations of the more insular British. Without a comfortable base, no one stands much chance of shaking off illness, which for us was a major adverse factor.

Most expeditions have some story about their food and attitudes to it vary from the *haute cuisine* of some French expeditions to the blunt assertion of Tilman, the famous eccentric and explorer, that he did not mind as long as there was some. For winter a good diet is vital. Food is usually the least expensive part of an expedition's budget and to maintain the well-being of the party throughout it is essential that the food should not only be nourishing but also desirable. Our sound-man, Graham, gave great cause for concern towards the end of the expedition as day after day he could only face eating biscuits. He was a gaunt, shrunken skeleton of the stocky fellow who had left Britain.

There are other, smaller details about winter in the Himalayas, such as the necessity to have fully mechanical cameras. Automatic, battery-operated cameras and shutters just did not function for more than a few minutes in the cold. Rapid-attaching crampons save valuable tens of minutes and clothing must be of the best. There are many such details but of overall importance is the strategy of ascent in winter. The only winter success of 1980/81 was the Japanese ascent of Baruntse at 23,687 feet during December.

December seems an ideal time for ascents of peaks of modest altitude. There can be spells of relatively fine, if cold, weather.

Snow conditions can be excellent. The Japanese on Baruntse were in the area long before the magical date of 1 December, training and preparing. They were able to waste no time in acclimatization during the official winter season itself and reached the top before the onset of the unstable weather which we experienced. For higher peaks, which inevitably may take longer for all the reasons associated with winter itself as well as altitude, it would be worth tackling a smaller peak at the end of the post-monsoon season. A smaller peak should be less affected by the jet-stream and less exhausting on personnel but enable acclimatization to take place without eating into the limited time of the winter season itself. It seems that an ideal situation would be to descend to warmer climes, maybe even to Kathmandu itself to rest and restock in its excellent eating places, before returning fully fit, acclimatized and well nourished to the main objective.

We come back to the question of whether it is worth it at all. The cost for our expedition was not high. The whole expedition of eight climbers and three film crew cost £18,000, including flights, porter hire, food and equipment which had to be purchased. The whole enterprise was made possible by the financial support of some companies and material support from others. Ours may well be the least expensive serious expedition to climb Mount Everest and the total budget was minimal in comparison with many other sports ventures. (Cunningham and MacInnes in 1953 did intend to climb Everest by having one 'sheepload' of food and equipment, the sheep being part of the food, and relying upon looting the Swiss camps of the 1952 expedition.) The risks involved are at the heart of the sport; without risk there would not be the same intrinsic interest. One does not court risk for its own sake, but calculates the risk involved in doing something worthwhile. Reaching the summit of Everest or any mountain is seen to be worthwhile for a complexity of reasons – psychological, physical, material. For whatever reasons, one wants the view from the top.

Given the right combination of motivation, fitness and weather conditions, I think it is possible to climb the most difficult routes on the highest mountains in winter.

The winter season in the Himalayas has opened a new era in

mountaineering. There is no need to 'create new goals'; there exists range after range of untapped reserves of elusive, difficult objectives. Irresistibly one is drawn back. If not to Everest, to other summits. The pain is forgotten and the dream remains.

Appendices

Without formulating a vast appendix, a few notes are given here on the particular medical and filming problems presented by winter in the Himalayas. Pete Thexton has written about the medical problems and Mike Shrimpton has written about the special demands made on the film equipment.

Medicine on the Mountain

PETE THEXTON

I put together a larger, more comprehensive medical kit for this trip than I had been accustomed to for other expeditions. The anticipated long exposure to extreme cold and wind gave a high probability of some members of the expedition suffering serious cold injury. It is feasible to reach some sort of hospital in two to three days of hard walking, but it was reassuring to be as independent as possible of any hospital.

At Base Camp, illness proved to be a major recurrent problem. Surprisingly, dysentery was the major complaint. The whole Base Camp area is a filthy place, due to the many expeditions which have camped in roughly the same spot. This may have been the source for some of the illness and it certainly did not help in trying to preserve hygienic conditions. Our staff had frequent contact with the staff of the two other expeditions nearby and with Sherpas coming up from the valley with more supplies. Infection may have been transmitted through these contacts and it was more difficult to eradicate than it would have been if our camp had been in total isolation.

On the mountain itself we had no serious cases of altitude sickness although headaches, nausea and inability to sleep were common problems. Owing to the nature of the route and the weather conditions, implementation of the most effective remedy for serious altitude sickness, rapid descent to a much lower level, would have been highly problematical. The most common and chronic complaints were coughs and sore throats due to the continual exposure to the very cold, very dry air. There was no easy cure for these. Large quantities of unpleasant-tasting lozenges were consumed but the cause remained and the coughs and sore throats persisted, leading to at least two cases of chest infection and two broken ribs. There was some cold injury – cracked finger-ends, numb toes and cracked lips – but the most serious case of near-frostbite was averted by the speedy employment of a pan of hot tea and someone's armpits. The highly developed and effective clothing combined with the long experience of all the team members in recognizing and rapidly treating problems was the main reason for the avoidance of severe cold injury.

There was some problem connected with the storage of medicine in that any liquids such as plasma or contact lens solution were permanently frozen. Where necessary the liquid had to be kept in a warm place either on the body or inside an occupied sleeping bag if it was to be required at short notice. The cold was an advantage in some cases such as the plasma, used for blood volume replacement, which remains stable when frozen.

Illness had a very definite effect on the climbing and on the outcome of the expedition. Most members were out of action at one time or another. The dysentery did respond quickly to treatment but cases were frequent and debilitating. The coughs and chest infections were more long-term.

Prolonged existence in an extremely cold environment was the root cause of our medical problems. This and the inadequate intake of food due to the diminishing supplies of palatable items and a general decline in appetite all combined to lower the resistance of everyone at a time when it needed to be at its greatest.

Movie Making

MIKE SHRIMPTON

In general every assumption that one normally makes about any piece of film equipment has to be questioned in preparing to film in temperatures well below zero. I hardly believed it possible to amass and make ready all the equipment necessary in the two weeks available. In 1975 the BBC film unit had taken six months to do the same job. The opportunity of filming on Everest seemed unique and instead of looking at the impossibility of the whole task I tackled each job one by one.

The key was finding Samuelson's Film Services, who supplied almost all of the equipment. Being able to tackle the problems of preparing each piece of equipment under one roof simplified the task greatly. The cameras needed 'winterizing', which involves a complete strip down of all the mechanical parts, removal of all greases and oils and replacement with non-freezing, thin oils, or no lubricant at all. The job was not a problem but the time required to do it was. Samuelson's could treat all of their cameras, but the main sync-sound camera I was planning to use, the Aaton 7, had its own problem. It is of a modern generation of cameras designed for almost totally silent running. The tolerances between the bearing surfaces are very tight and the bearing materials have different shrinkage rates, so that in extreme temperatures ($-25\,^{\circ}$C) the moving parts seize up.

The solution to this problem lay in fixing minute heating elements adjacent to the critical points and wiring back through an external switch to the camera battery for power. Had time been available, the same could usefully have been done to the drive mechanisms of at least one magazine, and a thermal jacket developed to encase both camera and magazine.

As back-up and for use in Base Camp, I included Arriflex BL and ST cameras. For the climbers to use on the mountain, I obtained some clockwork cameras, in particular a Bolex and some Bell and Howell 200T autoloads. The pocket-size autoload, using snap-in fifty-foot film cassettes and fitted with a twin lens turret, is still the only 16 mm-film camera suitable for the highest altitudes. Being clockwork, these cameras are more reliable, even if they produce a less perfect result, than a camera which requires an electric power source high on the mountain.

How to power the cameras was only second in importance to the cameras themselves. Batteries are inefficient in low temperatures and driving cold equipment puts a much greater strain on the resources of the battery. Extremely cold batteries will not accept a full charge and there would be an extra power demand from the heating elements. Transportation of heavy items such as batteries and generating the power to recharge them were major problems in themselves.

Several four-amp-hour nickel cadmium battery belts, having sufficient capacity to meet the heavy current demand, and able to be worn for insulation's sake under clothing, were the main-stay of the power requirements. Where weight was a prime consideration, I had a supply of very compact Aaton 1.2-amp-hour, 'onboard' batteries. These also could be used remotely from beneath clothing. At Base Camp we constructed an insulated box for protecting batteries, in the process of being charged, from the cold. An in-line ammeter cable to place between camera and battery to measure the camera's current-consumption and, correspondingly, a battery test meter indicating battery condition under load helped to avoid being 'stalled', when least desired, by a flat battery.

I selected a variety of lenses to cope with the diverse situations we would meet. A 10–150 mm Angenieux zoom lens was good for everyday use, backed up by a 12–240 mm lens to go from the wide and general to the close and particular, thereby giving an impression of scale. A fluid zoom control gave smooth opera-tion in arduous circumstances. As prime lenses I had a 9 mm T 1.3 high speed Zeiss lens for tent and ice cave interiors and a Canon 800 mm telescopic lens gave good pictures of action on the mountain.

Even after winterizing these lenses it was imperative to ensure that no condensation was allowed to form as this would freeze between the control rings and make lens adjustment impossible. Without winterization, under test, we found that the moving parts became stiff and eventually seized up completely.

To avoid condensation on metal equipment being brought inside it was necessary to place it in a polythene bag whilst still outside. Once inside it was only safe to remove the bag when the condensation had stopped forming on its outside. Condensation used to form even in the ice cave and freeze immediately.

For tripods I took a Ronford F15 with a fluid head and, where weight was a critical factor, I had a Saatcher and Wolfe fluid-head tripod made from carbon fibre. Neither of these required special treatments, but a geared head would have been useful for the Canon 800 mm lens.

The actual film used was Kodak Eastmancolour 7247. This is consistent and has such good exposure latitude characteristics that it could cope with the extremes of contrast. Modern celluloid bases used in film manufacture are very flexible and show only a slight increase in their proneness to snap as temperatures drop to $-30\,°C$. At $-40\,°C$ film becomes very brittle and, should it snag during exposure, it shatters into thousands of very sharp pieces. Newly loaded film freezes to metal surfaces inside a camera due to its moisture content. We only experienced shattering of film once, but several times film did snap inside cameras.

The film sound equipment by contrast was much less of a problem. Nagra SNs were the bases of the recording equipment and worked faultlessly throughout the trip. The problems arose with the microphones. The batteries in the Micron radio mikes were rendered useless by the cold. ECM 50 mikes plugged directly into a Nagra SN solved the problem of live recording, but these had to be fitted with extra large foam windshields to combat excessive wind noise. However, the plastic-coated cable on the ECM 50 tended to crack in the cold, causing microphone failure. Other cables with neoprene insulation remained pliable in all temperatures.

Two courses of action would have resulted in better footage on the expedition. One would have been a preliminary evaluation trip to the Alps which would have helped the film crew to familiarize themselves with rope techniques and movement on snow, ice and rock. This would have increased the ability of the film crew and given the climbers confidence in leaving them to look after themselves. It would also have helped establish the rapport earlier between the two parties which was essential to the making of a successful film. Finally, in retrospect, I think it would have been better for us to have become acclimatized ahead of the climbers on the expedition. This would have helped us film the early stages of the expedition unhampered by the problems of altitude, and also to keep at the front of the action for as long as possible.